MILITARY NECESSITY

What does it mean to say that international humanitarian law (IHL) strikes a realistic and meaningful balance between military necessity and humanity, and that the law therefore 'accounts for' military necessity? To what consequences does the law 'accounting for' military necessity give rise? Through real-life examples and careful analysis, this book challenges received wisdom on the subject by devising a new theory that not only reaffirms *Kriegsräson*'s fallacy but also explains why IHL has no reason to restrict or prohibit unnecessary military conduct on that ground alone. Additionally, the theory hypothesises greater normative significance for humanitarian and chivalrous imperatives when they conflict with IHL rules. By combining international law, jurisprudence, military history, strategic studies and moral philosophy, this book reveals how rational fighting relates to ethical fighting, how IHL incorporates contrasting values that shape its rules, and how law and theory adapt themselves to war's evolutions.

NOBUO HAYASHI is Visiting Lecturer at the United Nations Interregional Crime and Justice Research Institute. He has two decades of experience researching, publishing and teaching, including practice at court where he authored submissions, advised prosecutors and delivered expert presentations at academic and diplomatic conferences. Dr Hayashi specialises in the law of armed conflict, international criminal law and public international law. His most significant works cover military necessity, threat of force, and the law and ethics of nuclear weapons.

MILITARY NECESSITY

The Art, Morality and Law of War

NOBUO HAYASHI
United Nations Interregional Crime and Justice Research Institute

CAMBRIDGE
UNIVERSITY PRESS

CAMBRIDGE
UNIVERSITY PRESS

University Printing House, Cambridge CB2 8BS, United Kingdom

One Liberty Plaza, 20th Floor, New York, NY 10006, USA

477 Williamstown Road, Port Melbourne, VIC 3207, Australia

314–321, 3rd Floor, Plot 3, Splendor Forum, Jasola District Centre, New Delhi – 110025, India

79 Anson Road, #06–04/06, Singapore 079906

Cambridge University Press is part of the University of Cambridge.

It furthers the University's mission by disseminating knowledge in the pursuit of education, learning, and research at the highest international levels of excellence.

www.cambridge.org
Information on this title: www.cambridge.org/9781108484718
DOI: 10.1017/9781108689359

First published 2020

Printed in the United Kingdom by TJ International Ltd. Padstow Cornwall

A catalogue record for this publication is available from the British Library.

Library of Congress Cataloging-in-Publication Data
Names: Hayashi, Nobuo, author.
Title: Military necessity : the art, morality, and law of war / Nobuo Hayashi.
Description: 1. | New York : Cambridge University Press, 2020. | Includes bibliographical references and index.
Identifiers: LCCN 2019038895 (print) | LCCN 2019038896 (ebook) | ISBN 9781108484718 (hardback) | ISBN 9781108723497 (paperback) | ISBN 9781108689359 (epub)
Subjects: LCSH: Intervention (International law) | War (International law) | Humanitarian intervention–Moral and ethical aspects. | International law and human rights.
Classification: LCC KZ6369 .H39 2020 (print) | LCC KZ6369 (ebook) | DDC 341.6/3–dc23
LC record available at https://lccn.loc.gov/2019038895
LC ebook record available at https://lccn.loc.gov/2019038896

ISBN 978-1-108-48471-8 Hardback

To Klára V

CONTENTS

ACKNOWLEDGEMENTS

In early 1999, the very first sparks of curiosity ignited in my head while aboard a no-frills flight from Geneva to London. Over the following two decades, what began as little more than a jumble of intuitions scribbled on the margins of an *Economist* magazine has somehow transformed itself into journal articles, book chapters, a doctoral dissertation and finally a monograph.

I gratefully acknowledge the four anonymous reviewers appointed by Cambridge University Press for their encouragement and constructive feedback on my book project proposal. Tom Randall and his team have been unfailingly helpful throughout the publication process. I am indebted to the Norwegian Centre for Human Rights, University of Oslo Law Faculty, for hosting a good part of this project and for giving me access to its facilities and resources. Thank you, Professor Carsten Stahn, for guiding me through the process of thesis preparation, and Professors Helen Duffy, Terry Gill, Larissa van den Herik, Robert Heinsch and Jann Kleffner, for approving the final dissertation.

I also take this opportunity to express my more personal gratitude to the staff at Kaffebrenneriet on 15 Olaf Ryes plass and at W.B. Samson Grünerløkka opposite Birkelunden Park, both located just outside of central Oslo. They always kept my coffee cups full and tolerated my frequent – and no doubt unprofitable – overstays. The same goes for friends and colleagues from Norway, the Netherlands, Switzerland and elsewhere who stood by me through some of the hardest days of my adult life.

This book would not have materialised without the support I had received from my family in Japan and Hungary. Above all, I thank Klára, my most loving and patient wife; Daniel, our gentle and affectionate son; and Klára, his adoring baby sister.

TREATIES AND ASSOCIATED INSTRUMENTS

TABLE OF CASES

Permanent Court of International Justice/International Court of Justice Cases

Interstate Arbitration Cases

International Military Tribunal Cases

Post-Word War II Cases

Miscellaneous National Cases

European Human Rights Commission/European Court of Human Rights Cases

International Criminal Tribunal for the Former Yugoslavia Cases

International Tribunal for Rwanda Cases

International Residual Mechanism for Criminal Tribunals Cases

Special Court for Sierra Leone Cases

Extraordinary Chambers in the Courts of Cambodia Cases

International Criminal Court Cases

ABBREVIATIONS

ABiH	Army of Bosnia and Herzegovina
API	Additional Protocol I
COIN	Counterinsurgency
C-o-S	Chief of Staff
EBO	Effects-based operations
ECCC	Extraordinary Chambers in the Courts of Cambodia
ECtHR	European Court of Human Rights
EMP	Electromagnetic pulse
EoC	Elements of Crimes
FARC	Fuerzas Armadas Revolucionarias de Colombia
HCJ	High Court of Justice
HVO	Croatian Defence Council
ICC	International Criminal Court
ICCPR	International Covenant on Civil and Political Rights
ICJ	International Court of Justice
ICL	International criminal law
ICRC	International Committee of the Red Cross
ICTR	International Criminal Tribunal for Rwanda
ICTY	International Criminal Tribunal for the Former Yugoslavia
IDF	Israel Defence Forces
IHL	International humanitarian law
IHRL	International human rights law
ILC	International Law Commission
IMT	International Military Tribunal
IS	Islamic State
JNA	Yugoslav People's Army
LOAC	Law of armed conflict
LOIAC	Law of international armed conflict
MICT	International Residual Mechanism for Criminal Tribunals
NATO	North Atlantic Treaty Organization
PCIJ	Permanent Court of International Justice
POW	Prisoner of war

SCSL	Special Court for Sierra Leone
SS	Schutzstaffel
TO	Territorial defence
UK	United Kingdom
UKHL	House of Lords of the United Kingdom
UKSC	Supreme Court of the United Kingdom
UN	United Nations
UNESCO	United Nation Educational, Scientific and Cultural Organization
UNTS	United Nations Treaty Series
US	United States

PART I

Introduction

1

Introduction

It is often said that international humanitarian law (IHL)[1] is developed with a view to striking a realistic and meaningful balance between military necessity and humanity, and that the law therefore 'accounts for' military necessity. What it really means to say so, however, remains obscure. This obscurity has given rise to different opinions.

Kriegsräson,[2] as well as its more recent variations, holds that the military necessity of a given act 'rights' or 'repairs' its unlawfulness that positive IHL rules may otherwise establish. Although the law

[1] In principle, this book uses the expressions 'international humanitarian law' and 'IHL' throughout. For our purposes, the discipline's other monikers, such as the 'law of armed conflict', the 'laws and customs of war' and the like, should be considered essentially synonymous.

[2] This doctrine is named after the German maxim '*Kriegsräson geht vor Kriegsmanier*' ('Necessities of war override rules of war'). In essence, *Kriegsräson* asserts that military necessity permits any belligerent conduct conducive to success and overrides unqualified rules of positive IHL that obligate contrary action. Isabel V Hull, '"Military Necessity" and the Laws of War in Imperial Germany' in Stathis N Kalyvas, Ian Shapiro and Tarek Masoud (eds), *Order, Conflict, and Violence* (Cambridge: Cambridge University Press, 2008) 352, pp. 359–74; Coleman Phillipson, *International Law and the Great War* (London: T. Fisher Unwin, 1915), pp. 133–38; James Wilford Garner, *International Law and the World War*, 2 vols. (London: Longmans, Green and Co., 1920), vol. I, pp. 278–82; ibid, vol. II, pp. 195–98; NCH Dunbar, 'The Significance of Military Necessity in the Law of War' (1955) 67 *Juridical Review* 201, at 203–04, 207–08; William V O'Brien, 'The Meaning of "Military Necessity" in International Law' (1957) 1 *World Polity* 109, at 119–37; Geoffrey Best, *Humanity in Warfare: The Modern History of the International Law of Armed Conflicts* (New York: Columbia University Press, 1983), pp. 172–79; Mika Nishimura Hayashi, 'The Martens Clause and Military Necessity' in Howard M Hensel (ed), *The Legitimate Use of Military Force: The Just War Tradition and the Customary Law of Armed Conflict* (Hampshire, Burlington: Ashgate, 2008) 135, pp. 137–38; Gary D Solis, *The Law of Armed Conflict: International Humanitarian Law in War* (Cambridge: Cambridge University Press, 2010), pp. 265–68; Etienne Henry, *Le Principe de nécessité militaire: Histoire et actualité d'une norme fondamentale du droit international humanitaire* (Paris: Pedone, 2016), pp. 286–354.

accounts for military necessity, its rules cannot be construed so that the belligerent[3] is denied the option to do what it needs to succeed. On this view, where an IHL rule is formulated without military necessity exceptions, it merely indicates that the rule's framers[4] deemed its prescriptions generally consistent with considerations of military necessity. Whenever the rule collides with the actual military necessity of an act, the latter trumps the former. Consequently, positive IHL admits military necessity pleas even in defence of conduct that deviates from its unqualified rules. *Kriegsräson* found support in Germany during the late nineteenth century. It remained influential among German military and international lawyers until the end of World War II. Since its rejection at post-war trials,[5] *Kriegsräson* has been thoroughly discredited.[6]

[3] In this book, the term 'belligerent' refers not only to a party to an armed conflict but also to a combatant member of its armed forces.

[4] The expression 'framers' refers primarily to states that validly posit IHL rules by forming custom and concluding treaties. On the role allegedly played by judges at international criminal tribunals in 'supplanting' the pre-eminence that states have traditionally enjoyed in this regard, see Michael N. Schmitt, 'Military Necessity and Humanity in International Humanitarian Law: Preserving the Delicate Balance' (2010) 50 *Virginia Journal of International Law* 795, at 816.

[5] *In re Rauter*, in 16 *Annual Digest and Reports of Public International Law Cases* [1955] 526, p. 543; *In re Burghoff* in 16 *Annual Digest and Reports of Public International Law Cases* [1955] 551, pp. 554–57; *United States of America v Wilhelm von List et al., Judgment, Trials of War Criminals Before the Nuremberg Military Tribunals Under Control Council Law No. 10*, 15 vols. (Washington, DC: United States Government Printing Office, 1950), vol. XI, 1230 (hereinafter *Hostage*), pp. 1255–56, 1272–73, 1296; *In re von Lewinski (called Manstein)* in 16 *Annual Digest and Reports of Public International Law Cases* [1955] 509, pp. 512–13; *United States of America v Alfred Felix Alwyn Krupp von Bohlem und Halbach et al., Judgment, Trials of War Criminals before the Nuremberg Military Tribunals under Control Council Law No. 10*, 15 vols. (Washington, DC: United States Government Printing Office, 1950), vol. IX, 1327 (hereinafter *Krupp*), p. 1340; *United States of America v Wilhelm von Leeb et al., Judgment, Trials of War Criminals before the Nuremberg Military Tribunals under Control Council Law No. 10*, 15 vols. (Washington, DC: United States Government Printing Office, 1951), vol. XI, 462 (hereinafter *High Command*), p. 541.

[6] Office of the Judge Advocate General, Canadian Forces, *Law of Armed Conflict at the Operational and Tactical Levels* (2000), p. 2-1; UK Ministry of Defence, *The Joint Service Manual of the Law of Armed Conflict* (2004), p. 23; Georg Schwarzenberger, *International Law as Applied by International Courts and Tribunals: The Law of Armed Conflict*, 4 vols. (London: Stevenson and Sons, 1968), vol. II, p. 136; Christopher Greenwood, 'Historical Development and Legal Basis' in Dieter Fleck (ed), *The Handbook of International Humanitarian Law*, 2nd edn (Oxford: Oxford University Press, 2008) 1, pp. 38; Solis, *Law of Armed Conflict*, pp. 265–68.

1.1 Towards a New Theory of Military Necessity

Most modern theories take *Kriegsräson*'s fallacy as a common point of departure.[7] They agree that IHL accounts for military necessity, and that this entails the inadmissibility of military necessity pleas *vis-à-vis* the law's unqualified prescriptions.

One widely held view takes the matter further. Not only does IHL refuse to let the military necessity of an act remedy its unlawfulness. More importantly, the law also affirmatively 'wrongs' or 'vitiates' an otherwise IHL-compliant act should it prove militarily unnecessary. The fact that the law accounts for military necessity does not leave the belligerent at liberty to do what is, after all, lacking in military necessity. Where positive IHL rules authorise action, it only means that whatever they authorise is generally considered militarily necessary. In the event of a collision between an act being militarily unnecessary, on the one hand, and it being lawful according to positive IHL rules, on the other, the former defeats the latter. A militarily unnecessary act breaches IHL, all things considered, whether it is consistent with the law's positive rules or not.

This view is predicated on two central assertions. To begin with, military necessity creates directives, especially of a restrictive or prohibitive character. Implicit in this construal is the notion that it is illegitimate to perform militarily unnecessary acts. In other words, 'that which *can* be done without *must* be done without'. Furthermore, the restrictive or prohibitive property of military necessity remains intact through the process of IHL norm-creation. This property now operates as an independent, free-floating layer of normative restraint over and above positive IHL rules.

Another view also shapes today's military necessity discourse. According to that view's proponents, military necessity may not be pleaded anew with a view to defending conduct in breach of unqualified IHL rules. Nor, for that matter, may humanity be invoked as a justification for such conduct either. The underlying idea here is that military necessity and humanity are inevitably in conflict with each other. Every IHL rule embodies their compromise struck during its creation. Where the rule is unqualified, neither pleas are admissible.

[7] This is also true of some influential pronouncements on the matter – such as, for example, the 1863 Lieber Code – that were just ahead of, or contemporaneous with, *Kriegsräson*'s emergence in Germany. Articles 14–16, Instructions for the Government of Armies of the United States in the Field, 24 April 1863 (hereinafter Lieber Code); Hull, '"Military Necessity" and the Laws of War'.

In order for this theory to work, the following propositions need to be true. First, what is militarily necessary is always inhumane, whereas what is humane is always militarily unnecessary. Second, both military necessity and humanity are considerations that generate imperatives. In other words, the framers of IHL rules have reason to obligate militarily necessary acts and forbid militarily unnecessary acts. Similarly, IHL framers have reason to obligate humane acts and forbid inhumane acts. Third, both military necessity and humanity are involved in the process through which every IHL rule is created.

These contemporary theories all treat military necessity as a reason for belligerent conduct's normative regulation in one way or the other. For the most part, however, they appear to be somewhat casual suppositions – rather than the products of vigorous reflections – or, in any event, obstinate dogmas from which their adherents are often unwilling to depart. One may question whether a given act's military non-necessity really makes it appropriate for prohibition, or whether an act's military necessity really makes it obligatory, under IHL. Military necessity's normative characteristics, including how it interacts with other notions such as humanity, have yet to be properly investigated.

Modern theories also conflate the three distinct contexts in which military necessity appears.[8] In a material context, it is important to ask whether behaving in a particular way on a specific occasion constitutes a military necessity or non-necessity in view of its stated military purpose. At issue in the context of IHL norm-creation is what the law's framers should do about a given kind of conduct, once it has been agreed that the kind of conduct in question is militarily necessary or unnecessary in the sense just described. There are two key questions in the juridical context of positive IHL. First, should an act in breach of unqualified IHL rules nevertheless be deemed lawful if it was militarily necessary? Second, should an act lacking in military necessity be deemed unlawful even if it otherwise complied with the letter of the law?

No existing theory systematically probes military necessity's normative properties or accounts for its various contexts. This book develops and defends such a theory.

[8] Gabriella Blum, 'The Laws of War and the "Lesser Evil"' (2010) 35 *Yale Journal of International Law* 1; Diane A Desierto, *Necessity and National Emergency Clauses: Sovereignty in Modern Treaty Interpretation* (Leiden and Boston: Martinus Nijhoff Publishers, 2012), pp. 333–47 (criticising Blum).

1.2 Structure

We will consider two principal questions. First, what does it mean to say that IHL accounts for military necessity? Answering this question involves, among other things, clarifying what military necessity means. Admittedly, military necessity can mean different things to different people. It seems nevertheless instructive to begin by specifying whose understanding of the notion matters, and for what reason. Second, to what normative consequences does IHL accounting for military necessity give rise?

This book is organised as follows. There are eleven chapters in total. The book's nine substantive chapters, excluding this introductory chapter and a concluding chapter at the end, are grouped into three parts (Parts II, III and IV). Each part deals, respectively, with: (a) military necessity as fitness of the means taken vis-à-vis the ends sought in war-fighting; (b) military necessity as a set of reason-giving considerations behind how the framers of IHL create its rules; and (c) military necessity as it appears in positive provisions of IHL and international criminal law (ICL).

Chapters 2 and 3 (Part II) briefly discuss military necessity in its material context. This, it may be said, is the context most familiar to planners and commanders tasked with tactical, operational and strategic decisions, as well as military historians assessing their efficacy.

In Chapter 2, I endeavour to illustrate what it means for a given belligerent act to be militarily necessary or militarily unnecessary in its most elementary, practical sense.[9] This chapter will offer answers to questions such as when an act is amenable to military necessity assessment; how similarly competent assessors may reasonably disagree about an act's military necessity; whether an act must cause the fulfilment of its objective in order to be considered militarily necessary; what factors help assess whether an act constitutes a military necessity or a non-necessity; and whether military necessity assessments of specific acts can be meaningfully generalised.

Chapter 3 addresses itself to three major objections against the idea that we can consider military necessity in its material sense.[10] First, by assessing an act's material necessity or non-necessity, one may already be passing judgment on its quality as something desirable or undesirable,

[9] For an earlier version of Chapter 2, see Nobuo Hayashi, 'Contextualizing Military Necessity' (2013) 27 *Emory International Law Review* 189, at 195–211.

[10] For an earlier version of Chapter 3, see ibid, at 211–22.

what a competent soldier should or should not do. In other words, it is possible that necessity assessments are by definition normative assessments. Second, pursuing military necessities and avoiding non-necessities may mark not only a belligerent's competence *qua* member of an occupational group, but also a person's competence *qua* moral agent. To put it differently, the very point of fighting competently may well be a normative one. Third, it is arguable that soldiers should refuse to deem unethical acts militarily necessary, all things considered. Consequently, only ethically competent fighting should count as truly vocationally competent fighting.

This part shows that, in its material sense, military necessity reflects a two-fold truism. It is in each belligerent's self-interest to do what is necessary, and to avoid what is unnecessary. Together, Chapters 2 and 3 prepare the conceptual foundation on which to build Part III's examination of normative military necessity, which shifts our perspective from that of military practitioners and historians concerned with whether an act is militarily necessary, to that of law-givers concerned with how a kind of action should be regulated *once* it is deemed consistent or inconsistent with military necessity.

Part III (Chapters 4–7) reflects on military necessity in its normative context. This is also the context in which I endeavour to elucidate what it means to say that IHL accounts for military necessity. Here, the military necessity or non-necessity of a belligerent act provides the framers of IHL rules with reason to decide whether it should be obligated, permitted, restricted or prohibited.

Chapter 4 considers whether military necessity helps modify the legitimacy of a given type of belligerent act.[11] In so doing, it engages several key questions regarding the relationship between the act's military necessity or non-necessity, on the one hand, and the evil or non-evil it may be deemed to entail, on the other.[12] One may ask, for example, whether an act deemed to be lacking in military necessity becomes illegitimate *for that reason alone*. We look into the possibility that, while

[11] For an earlier version of Chapter 4, see ibid, at 223–54.

[12] Recall here that the preamble of Hague Convention IV (1907) expresses the drafters' 'desire to diminish the evils of war, as far as military requirements permit'. Preamble, Convention (IV) Respecting the Laws and Customs of War on Land, 18 October 1907, in force 26 January 1910 (hereinafter Hague Convention IV [1907]). War-related evils may include, inter alia, death; injury and attack on the bodily, mental or moral integrity of persons; property destruction and damage, adverse change of ownership or control; and detrimental change in social institutions or procedures.

the legitimacy of an evil act does depend to some extent on its status as a military necessity, the legitimacy of an un-evil act does not.

Chapter 5 summarises a major theory on the contemporary significance of military necessity.[13] We will call this theory the 'inevitable conflict thesis'. Its primary concern is to ensure that IHL framers resolve the irreconcilable demands of military necessity and humanity, devise a workable compromise between them, and prevent the belligerent from being bound by conflicting IHL rules. The theory's proponents find it important to preclude military necessity pleas vis-à-vis unqualified prohibitions. We will witness how they treat military necessity as inevitably in conflict with humanity. It becomes necessary for them to establish that both military necessity and humanity demand some acts and condemn the others. They endeavour to show how, with respect to any given belligerent act, the framers allow humanity to trump military necessity, allow military necessity to trump humanity, or find some middle ground between them, and posit an IHL rule accordingly. This, according to the theory's adherents, is what accounting for military necessity and humanity really means. They insist that the entire *corpus juris* of positive IHL embodies this compromise and that neither military necessity nor humanity pleas are consequently admissible vis-à-vis unqualified rules.

In Chapter 6, we question this theory on two grounds.[14] First, is what is militarily necessary always inhumane, and is what is humane always militarily unnecessary? Is it not true that some belligerent acts are both humane and consistent with military necessity – or both inhumane and lacking in military necessity, as the case may be? Second, do military necessity and humanity always generate imperatives? Is it really of any concern to IHL framers that the belligerent perform militarily necessary acts and avoid militarily unnecessary ones? Would it not be more likely that military necessity considerations are normatively indifferent? Could the same not be said of at least some humanitarian considerations?

Chapter 7 reappraises the inevitable conflict thesis's two further grounds.[15] Does what military necessity indifferently permits or tolerates always conflict with considerations of humanity? Where humanity demands what military necessity permits, or where humanity condemns what military necessity merely tolerates, would the belligerent not satisfy

[13] For an earlier version of Chapter 5, see Nobuo Hayashi, 'Military Necessity as Normative Indifference' (2013) 44 *Georgetown Journal of International Law* 675, at 688–703.

[14] For an earlier version of Chapter 6, see ibid, at 703–26.

[15] For an earlier version of Chapter 7, see ibid, at 726–49.

them both by acting as directed by humanity? The question, then, is how the framers of IHL rules approach behaviour that jointly satisfies military necessity and humanity – more specifically, when the framers elect to obligate such behaviour without qualification, and what explains situations where they decline or fail to do so.

Chapter 7 also considers acts that humanity condemns yet military necessity permits, and those that humanity demands yet military necessity merely tolerates. Despite their appearance to the contrary, we have reason to wonder whether these acts are still capable of joint satisfaction. Our objective here is to discover how IHL framers capture such possibilities in the rules they posit. Chapters 6 and 7 give us what may be termed the 'joint satisfaction thesis', in contradistinction to the inevitable conflict thesis introduced earlier.

Part III shows how military necessity functions as a set of normatively indifferent considerations in IHL norm-creation. For IHL framers to posit an unqualified rule is for them to exclude all contrary liberties that belligerents would otherwise wish to pursue on account of military necessity. Elsewhere, the framers permit such liberties exceptionally, indeterminately, principally or unrestrictedly. The combination of these eventualities is what it means to say that the law accounts for military necessity.

Chapters 8–10 (Part IV) bring us to military necessity in its juridical context. Here, we consider three normative consequences to which IHL accounting for military necessity gives rise. First, juridical military necessity may manifest itself through exclusion. Second, it may take the form of an exceptional clause. Third, it may appear as a negative element of crimes. These consequences primarily affect belligerents claiming or disputing compliance with the law's applicable rules, as well as those called upon to determine if a given act constituted an IHL violation or a punishable offence under ICL.

Chapter 8 deals with exclusion.[16] At issue is whether normatively indifferent considerations such as military necessity may be invoked in defence of acts inconsistent with unqualified IHL rules. It might be asked whether the inevitable conflict thesis is correct in asserting that all positive IHL rules, including those that are unqualified, involve military necessity and humanity in their norm-creation. If it were shown that not all positive IHL rules do so, would the thesis's adherents not be compelled to acknowledge that military necessity or humanity might be

[16] For an earlier version of Chapter 8, see ibid, at 749–78; N Hayashi, 'Contextualizing Military Necessity', at 262–79.

invoked in defence of conduct at variance with at least some unqualified rules? We query whether the very adoption of an unqualified IHL rule excludes all pleas purporting to justify contrary behaviour that military necessity or humanity indifferently permits or tolerates.

Our discussion on juridical military necessity's exclusionary effects also raises questions about what kind of normative consequences *non*-indifferent considerations could generate. In Chapter 8, I hypothesise situations in which acting as demanded by humanity may become lawful despite the law's unqualified obligation to the contrary. Conversely, it may be asked whether an act's compliance with the letter of positive IHL can be vitiated if humanity condemns that act.

Chapter 9 delves into juridical military necessity as an exception.[17] We begin by considering what military necessity clauses signify and how they modify the content of the primary rules to which they are attached. This helps us distinguish juridical military necessity from the state of necessity, a circumstance precluding the wrongfulness of an act under the international law of state responsibility.

Chapter 9 also examines what requirements military necessity clauses impose. For what kind of purposes must the act at issue be taken in order to be eligible? Does it matter whether the course of action taken compares favourably to some alternative course or courses of action and, if so, in what way? Is proportionality a requirement? How should we approach matters of available information, contemporaneous knowledge and hindsight? A key question here is whether and, if so, how the requirements of juridical military necessity differ from those factors used to assess material military necessity.

Chapter 10 looks into juridical military necessity as a negative element of war crimes and crimes against humanity.[18] This chapter seeks to clarify the mechanics through which the absence of military necessity appears as an element of some offences. We consider its definitional, procedural and evidentiary ramifications, as well as its relationship to necessity as a criminal law defence.

Chapter 10 also reviews in detail how the International Criminal Tribunal for the Former Yugoslavia (ICTY) and the International Residual Mechanism for Criminal Tribunals (MICT) have dealt with

[17] For an earlier version of Chapter 9, see Nobuo Hayashi, 'Requirements of Military Necessity in International Humanitarian Law and International Criminal Law' (2010) *Boston University International Law Journal* 39, at 49–101.

[18] For an earlier version of Chapter 10, see ibid, at 101–38.

the matter. What does the case law of these entities on property destruction and population displacement reveal? Is it in line with the requirements of military necessity clauses discussed in Chapter 9? To what extent can the military necessity of property destruction be meaningfully assessed by reference to the notion of military objectives? On what basis do judges find forcible displacements militarily necessary or unnecessary? Similar questions are asked of the nascent jurisprudence of the International Criminal Court (ICC).

1.3 Theoretical Underpinnings

This book may be thought of as a '*grundnorm*' study of IHL. It is not strictly so in the Kelsenian sense of the term,[19] but in a more colloquial sense that military necessity and humanity are often seen as the two pillars upon which the entire IHL regime rests.

This is a 'basic norm' book, insofar as it focuses primarily on elucidating the meanings and normative functions of military necessity in IHL. Consequently, this book prioritises depth over breadth in the selection of its discussions. That it does so is also apparent from the fact that its nine substantive chapters are essentially a chain of practical, logical, normative and juridical reasoning. Of paramount interest is the careful and comprehensive treatment of major conceptual arguments and supporting authorities that underlie representative instances.

Through his 1958 article 'Positivism and the Separation of Law and Morals',[20] followed by his seminal *The Concept of Law*[21] three years later, H. L. A. Hart developed his theory on soft positivism – also known as inclusive positivism – and defended its tenets against formalism, rule-scepticism and natural law.[22] He did so chiefly by identifying three main

[19] That is, as a 'transcendental-logical presupposition' that objectively validates a positive legal order. Hans Kelsen, *General Theory of Law and State*, Anders Wedberg (trans.) (Cambridge, MA: Harvard University Press, 1949), pp. 115–17, 395–96; Hans Kelsen, *Pure Theory of Law*, Max Knight (trans.) (Berkeley and Los Angeles: University of California Press, 1967), pp. 201–05; Joseph Raz, 'Kelsen's Theory of the Basic Norm' in Stanley L Paulson and Bonnie Litschewski Paulson (eds), *Normativity and Norms: Critical Perspectives on Kelsenian Themes* (Oxford: Oxford University Press,1998) 47; Tony Honoré, 'The Basic Norm of a Society' in Paulson and Paulson (eds), *Normativity and Norms* 89.

[20] HLA Hart, 'Positivism and the Separation of Law and Morals' (1958) 71 *Harvard Law Review* 593.

[21] HLA Hart, *The Concept of Law* (Oxford: Clarendon Press, 1961).

[22] As well as Ronald M. Dworkin's interpretive theory of law, if one counts Hart's 'Postscript' at the end of *The Concept of Law*'s, second edition (HLA Hart, *The Concept of Law*, 2nd edn [Oxford: Clarendon Press, 1994]).

flaws in the command theory of legal positivism that John Austin had championed,[23] and then proposing three corresponding remedies for them.[24]

This book draws inspirations from Hartian jurisprudence in more ways than one. First, it follows Hart's argumentative techniques. Put simply, Austin's classic positivism is to Hart's inclusive positivism what the inevitable conflict thesis is to the joint satisfaction thesis. The idea that military necessity and humanity inevitably conflict with each other entails six major assertions, namely:

1. What is militarily necessary is always inhumane, and what is humane is always militarily unnecessary;
2. Both military necessity and humanitarian considerations generate imperatives;
3. Compliance with military necessity imperatives precludes compliance with humanitarian imperatives;
4. Accounting for military necessity and humanity is about pre-empting their conflicting considerations leading to the adoption of conflicting IHL rules;
5. Every positive IHL rule embodies a compromise between irreconcilable demands of military necessity and humanity;
6. Neither military necessity nor humanity pleas are admissible vis-à-vis unqualified IHL rules.

This book exposes flaws in each of these assertions. It is also from their revisions that the joint satisfaction thesis, with military necessity's normative indifference as its centrepiece, emerges. On this view,

1. Some belligerent acts may be both militarily necessary and humane, or both militarily unnecessary and inhumane;
2. All military necessity considerations are normatively indifferent, as are some humanitarian considerations;
3. The belligerent always has the option to act in a manner that simultaneously satisfies both sets of considerations;

[23] These flaws are, respectively, the uncertainty of substantive legal rules, their static character and the inefficiency of the social pressure through which they are maintained. Hart, *Concept of Law* (2nd edn), pp. 91–94.

[24] These remedies consist of three types of secondary rules, i.e., a 'rule of recognition' (to rectify the primary rules' uncertainty), 'rules of change' (to rectify the primary rules' static character), and 'rules of adjudication' (to rectify the inefficient social pressure used to maintain the regime of primary rules). Ibid, pp. 94–98.

4. Accounting for military necessity and humanity is about failing, declining or electing to obligate jointly satisfactory behaviour and, if electing to do so, about obligating such behaviour unqualifiedly, principally, indeterminately or exceptionally;
5. Not every positive IHL rule embodies the military necessity-humanity interplay;
6. Unqualified IHL rules exclude military necessity pleas, but it is not clear whether they also exclude pleas emanating from humanitarian imperatives.

Hart also deployed elements of inclusive positivism in his critique of other jurisprudential theories. Similarly, the joint satisfaction thesis helps explain why IHL has no reason to restrict or prohibit a militarily unnecessary act *for its lack of military necessity alone.* Where commentators advocate an IHL ban on a particular act ostensibly on account of the act's lack of military necessity, they often invoke what is, in substance, humanity's contrary demand. Military non-necessity merely exposes the act's inhumanity bare.

Second, I identify myself broadly as an inclusive legal positivist of a conceptual[25] and descriptive[26] cast. It is not an integral part of the joint satisfaction thesis that a norm's inconsistency with humanitarian considerations prevents it from becoming a valid IHL rule. Rather, the thesis acknowledges instances where the law's framers leave the belligerent at liberty to do what humanity condemns and to refrain from doing what

25 WJ Waluchow, 'The Many Faces of Legal Positivism' (1998) 48 *University of Toronto Law Journal* 387, 394–95 (emphasis in original): 'It is conceptually possible, but not necessary, that determinations of law can be a function of moral considerations . . . According to Inclusive Positivism, our concept of law, as revealed (partly) in a conceptual analysis of our linguistic and legal practices, includes morality as a possible, though by no means necessary, basis for determinations of law. According to modern versions of Inclusive Positivism, it is the accepted rule of recognition that determines which, if any, moral considerations figure in determinations of law. So *whether* morality counts in determinations of law is not itself a matter of morality. Rather, it depends on which criteria of validity exist as a matter of accepted social practice within a legal system's rule of recognition. But there is nothing to prevent these criteria from being moral in nature.'

26 Ibid, 396 (footnote omitted; emphasis in original): 'As a matter of observable fact, there are systems of law in which determinations of law are a function of moral considerations . . . Inclusive Positivism, in both its conceptual and descriptive forms, is supported by the existence of [legal systems in which determinations of law sometimes depend on moral factors]. It is perhaps worth noting that even if it were true that there were no such systems, this would not invalidate or falsify the conceptual version of Inclusive Positivism. As Jules Coleman observes, this version is vindicated so long as we can conceive of at least one *possible* world in which such a system exists.'

humanity demands. At the same time, the idea of joint satisfaction also entails the possibility that an otherwise valid IHL rule effectively becomes inapplicable wherever compliance with it contravenes humanitarian imperatives. Although no more than a hypothesis at this point, a regime of IHL whose rule of recognition includes conformity with humanitarian imperatives is not inconceivable. The same may even be said of a rule of recognition requiring conformity with chivalrous imperatives.

Third, the joint satisfaction thesis seeks to describe how the actual process of IHL norm-creation, as well as its actual legal consequences, can be most accurately understood. In this sense, the theory's primary strength lies in its explanatory power. The idea of joint satisfaction itself does not instruct IHL framers to promote any given normative outcome. In other words, joint satisfaction is not a substantive thesis about what belligerent behaviour IHL should obligate or prohibit. Rather, it is a theory that studies IHL from what Hart called an 'external point of view'[27] – or, to be more precise, from 'a point of view' as Joseph Raz puts it.[28]

[27] Hart, *Concept of Law* (2nd edn), pp. 88–91, 242, 255–56, 291.

[28] Joseph Raz, *The Authority of Law*, 2nd edn (Oxford: Clarendon Press, 2009), pp. 153–57. Legal statements are made from 'a point of view' when, for example, a practising lawyer advises his or her client, a legal scholar expresses his or her professional assessment, or a Catholic specialist in Rabbinical law offers his or her Jewish friend expert counsel. See also Joseph Raz, *Practical Reason and Norms* (Oxford: Oxford University Press, 1999), pp. 170–77.

PART II

Military Necessity in Its Material Context

2

Fitness of Means and Vocational Competence

Within a strictly material context, military necessity can be seen as an *a*moral notion that separates competent fighting from incompetent fighting. To say that 'doing this or that is militarily necessary to such and such a degree' is to signify that the conduct in question conduces towards the materialisation of a given military end to such and such a degree.[1] Conversely, to say that 'doing this or that is militarily *un*necessary to such and such a degree' is to signify that the act does not so conduce to such and such a degree.

Understood thus, military necessity in its material sense embodies a two-fold truism. First, it is in the self-interest of each belligerent to do what is militarily necessary and to avoid what is unnecessary. Second, it is against each belligerent's self-interest to forgo necessities of war or to encumber itself with non-necessities of war. Pursuing necessities and avoiding non-necessities form a morally neutral component of the belligerent's vocational competence – that is, 'to get the job done'.

Material military necessity, then, is a function of the end sought (Y), the means taken or considered (X) and the circumstances prevailing or anticipated at the time (Z). First, the belligerent desires Y. Second, it identifies a range of realistically available courses of action (X_1, X_2, X_3, . . . X_n), each having reasonable chances of generating Y. Third, it chooses and pursues one option (X_1) that is superior to the other options (X_2, X_3, . . . X_n) in view of Z. The more conducive X_1 is towards Y's materialisation and the more suitable it is in view of the circumstances, the more of a military necessity X_1 is than X_2, X_3, and the like.[2]

1 Pietro Verri, *Dictionary of the International Law of Armed Conflict* (Geneva: International Committee of the Red Cross, 1992), p. 75 (emphasis omitted): 'In its wider sense, necessity means doing what is necessary to achieve war aims.'

2 It may also happen that, under the circumstances prevailing at the time, all of the realistically available options have such limited chances of success or are so inefficient resource-wise as to leave the outcome's abandonment as the only rational course of action.

2.1 Ends, Means and Circumstances

An ancient Benedictine abbey stands atop Monte Cassino in southern Italy. During World War II, Adolf Hitler ordered the hill to be incorporated into the defensive complex of the Gustav Line against the Allied advance from the south.[3] Monte Cassino was situated at the mouth of the Liri Valley with a commanding view of all of the valley's approaches.[4] The valley provided the most direct gateway to Rome.[5] An entry into it became urgent for the Allied forces in view of the protracted battle at the Anzio beachhead, another strategic point for the purposes of weakening the Gustav Line.[6] The task of opening a Liri Valley entrance fell to the forces under the command of Lieutenant General Sir Bernard Freyberg.[7]

In January 1944, Allied commanders were instructed to make every effort to avoid damage to the abbey.[8] This, however, was subject to a proviso added by the headquarters of General Sir Harold R. L. G. Alexander to the effect that '[c]onsideration for the safety of such areas will not be allowed to interfere with military necessity'.[9] On 9 February, Lieutenant General Mark W. Clark authorised Freyberg 'to fire against the monastery if in Freyberg's judgment military necessity dictated this action'.[10] Major General F. S. Tuker, Freyberg's subordinate charged with weakening the Gustav Line at the Liri Valley, determined that the abbey had to be destroyed.[11] When requesting an aerial bombardment, Freyberg stated that Tuker 'who is making the attack feels that it is an essential target and I thoroughly agree with him'.[12]

Clark was of the opinion that the abbey's destruction was unwarranted.[13] He believed 'that no military necessity existed, that a bombardment would endanger the lives of civilian refugees in the building, and

[3] Martin Blumenson, *The Mediterranean Theater of Operations: Salerno to Cassino* (Washington, DC: Center of Military History, United States Army, 1969), pp. 155, 311.
[4] Ibid, p. 403.
[5] Ibid, p. 226.
[6] Ibid, pp. 353, 385–96, 401.
[7] Ibid, pp. 401–02. Freyberg was in command of the provisional New Zealand Corps with the 2nd New Zealand and 4th Indian Divisions under its control at the time. Ibid.
[8] Ibid, pp. 398.
[9] Ibid, pp. 398–99 (footnote omitted). Alexander was the commander of the 15th Army Group at the time. Ibid, p. 34.
[10] Ibid, p. 403 (footnote omitted). Clark was the commander of the US 5th Army at the time. Ibid, p. 28.
[11] Ibid, p. 403 (footnote omitted).
[12] Ibid, p. 404.
[13] Ibid.

that bombardment would probably fail to destroy the abbey and would be more than likely to enhance its value as a fortification'.[14] Major General Alfred M. Gruenther, Clark's Chief of Staff, was told that Alexander had faith in Freyberg's judgment and that '[i]f there is any reasonable probability that the building is used for military purposes . . . its destruction is warranted'.[15] Gruenther also informed Freyberg of Clark's view on the matter. One account of Freyberg's reply states:

> General Freyberg said he had gone into the matter thoroughly with [Tuker], who was quite convinced that bombing the monastery was necessary. Freyberg added that he thought it was not 'sound to give an order to capture Monastery Hill and at the same time deny the commander the right to remove an important obstacle to the success of this mission'. A higher commander who refused to authorize the bombing, Freyberg warned, would have to take the responsibility if the attack failed. Gruenther said that Clark was ready to authorize the bombing if Freyberg considered it a military necessity. According to Gruenther's record, General Freyberg then said that 'it was his considered opinion that it is a military necessity'.[16]

An aerial bombardment was scheduled on 13 February and, after a delay, initiated two days later.[17] 'Almost 600 tons of high explosive virtually demolished the monastery.'[18] The abbey's destruction did not bring about the hill's capture, however.[19] As Clark had foreseen,

> the bombardment of the abbey had failed to break the Gustav Line at its critical point. Not only the major bombing on 15 February, but the relatively heavy bombings on successive days, which had further reduced the monastery, failed to dislodge the stubborn and skillful troops in well-nigh perfect defensive positions. The ground and air commands in the theater were profoundly disappointed. Had the ground forces been unable to take advantage of the bombardment? Or were the bombers incapable of eradicating tactical positions and therefore useless for direct support of ground attack? No one seemed to know . . . In the final analysis, no one had been altogether certain what the bombardment was supposed to accomplish except to flatten the abbey. The escalation of the air effort from a relatively modest attack to an overwhelming strike had achieved nothing beyond destruction, indignation, sorrow, and regret.[20]

[14] Ibid, pp. 405–06.
[15] Ibid, p. 405.
[16] Ibid, p. 406.
[17] Ibid, pp. 406–07, 409.
[18] Ibid, p. 411.
[19] Ibid, p. 417.
[20] Ibid.

It took the Allied forces another three months to break through the Gustav Line on the Liri Valley (15 May)[21] and to capture Monte Cassino and its abbey (18 May).[22]

Whether the attack on the abbey did or did not constitute military necessity was hotly debated.[23] It is reasonable to assume that Freyberg and Tuker were professionally competent soldiers, and that they found in good faith that the abbey's destruction was militarily necessary. It is reasonable to assume, however, that Clark and others were similarly competent soldiers who came to different conclusions, also in good faith.[24] Opinions of other persons associated with the Allied action were divided as well. For instance, Major General Fred L. Walker noted:

> This was a valuable historical monument, which should have been preserved. The Germans were not using it and I can see no advantage in destroying it. No tactical advantage will result since the Germans can make as much use of the rubble for observation posts and gun positions as of the building itself. Whether the Germans used the building for an observation post or for emplacements makes little difference since the mountain top on which the building stands can serve the same purpose.[25]

According to Martin Blumenson, United States (US) President Theodor D. Roosevelt told the Vatican that 'he had issued instructions to prevent the destruction of historic monuments except in cases of military necessity. The bombardment, he said, had been unfortunate but necessary'.[26]

Suspected use of the abbey by the Germans for military purposes exacerbated the situation. The German forces undertook to ensure respect for the abbey, although their commander, Henrich von Vietinghoff, acknowledged that the monastery had 'good observation posts' and 'good positions of concealment'.[27] Initially, some Allied commanders received intelligence to the effect that the Germans used the abbey.[28] Others disagreed, however, and later confirmed that the information was not accurate.[29]

[21] Ernst F Fisher, Jr, *The Mediterranean Theater of Operations: Cassino to the Alps* (Washington, DC: Center of Military History, United States Army, 1977), p. 77.

[22] Ibid, p. 78.

[23] Blumenson, *Salerno to Cassino*, pp. 405–06.

[24] There were other sceptics too, such as Major General Geoffrey Keyes, Major General Charles W Ryder and Colonel Mark M Boatner. Ibid, pp. 405, 407.

[25] Ibid, pp. 413 (footnote omitted).

[26] Ibid, pp. 415–16.

[27] Ibid, p. 400.

[28] Ibid, p. 408.

[29] Ibid, pp. 413–14.

For Freyberg, the abbey's destruction ($X_{DestroyAbbey}$) was simply a means by which to capture Monastery Hill ($Y_{CaptureHill}$). The surrounding circumstances included the abbey's structure, the hill's topography, weather conditions, weapons and communications equipment available, and so on ($Z_{CassinoFebruary1944}$).[30] In the event, the particularly thick outer walls of the abbey had 'resisted the blasts and although breaches appeared none of them reached the ground level'.[31] This, combined with unintegrated employment of airpower, 'did nothing to lighten the task of the infantry, which was unable to take advantage of the confusion and destruction by staging a correlated attack'.[32]

All else being equal, one course of action (X_1) can be more or less militarily necessary than another course of action (X_2) by virtue of their relative conduciveness towards a given purpose (Y). In view of Monte Cassino's capture as the Allied objective ($Y_{CaptureHill}$), destroying the abbey ($X_{DestroyAbbey}$) before advancing the infantry was arguably more militarily necessary than advancing the infantry ($X_{AdvanceInfantry}$) without first destroying the abbey would have been, under the circumstances prevailing at the time ($Z_{CassinoFebruary1944}$).

Alternatively, all else being equal, a given course of action (X) can be more or less militarily necessary towards one purpose (Y_1) than towards another purpose (Y_2). For instance, under the prevailing circumstances ($Z_{CassinoFebruary1944}$), destroying the abbey ($X_{DestroyAbbey}$) was arguably more militarily necessary for capturing the hill ($Y_{CaptureHill}$) than it would have been for drawing the German strength away from Anzio ($Y_{WeakenAnzio}$). In Nigel de Lee's words:

> The Higher Command seemed to be losing sight of the object of operations ... the object was not necessarily to attack and capture the Monte Cassino features. The object was to menace the enemy's position on the Gustav line as to induce him to withdraw from the Anzio front sufficient forces to preclude his exerting any sort of decisive pressure there ... There were two quite reasonable operations in that region that could be undertaken which would threaten the safety of the Monte Cassino feature sufficiently to draw Axis reinforcements.[33]

[30] Blumenson, *Salerno to Cassino*, pp. 402–03, 408.

[31] Nigel de Lee, 'Moral Ambiguities in the Bombing of Monte Cassino' (2005) 4 *Journal of Military Ethics* 129, at 135 (quoting GR Stevens, *Fourth Indian Division* [Toronto: McLaren and Son, 1950], p. 286).

[32] Ibid.

[33] De Lee, 'Moral Ambiguities', at 133 (quoting a letter from Sir Francis Tuker, Lieutenant General in the British Army, to Major General Henry 'Taffy' Davies [26 May 1965]). See

In the further alternative, all else being equal, a given course of action (*X*) can be more or less militarily necessary in relation to a given purpose (*Y*) in one set of circumstances (Z_1) than in another set of circumstances (Z_2). Destroying the abbey ($X_{DestroyAbbey}$) was arguably more militarily necessary for capturing the hill ($Y_{CaptureHill}$), given the abbey's topographic dominance over the hill ($Z_{CassinoFebruary1944}$) than, say, if it had not had such dominance ($Z_{CassinoFebruary1944ButNoTopographicDominance}$). Winston Churchill described the abbey's topography as follows: 'The height on which the monastery stood surveyed the junction of the rivers Rapido and Liri and was the pivot of the whole German defense. It had already proved itself a formidable, strongly defended obstacle. Its steep sides, swept by fire, were crowned by the famous building.'[34] One commentator argues that the material military necessity for the abbey's destruction was circumstantially undermined by the difficulties associated with coordinating aerial bombardment, artillery bombardment and infantry attack:

> What Tuker describes here is a complicated attack that requires the co-ordination of three different branches of the service and where timing is crucial. But war is characterized by what von Clausewitz called friction. In war, things have a strong tendency not to go the way they were planned. In other words, the probability that the precisely co-ordinated campaign Tuker asked for could have been delivered under the circumstances was extremely low.[35]

The Monte Cassino experience shows that the material military necessity or non-necessity of given belligerent conduct is relational, evaluative

also Reuben E Brigety II, 'Moral Ambiguities in the Bombing of Monte Cassino' (2005) 4 *Journal of Military Ethics* 139, at 140: '[O]ne might morally fault the Allied commanders not for their professional incompetence in the conduct of the assault, but for their lack of strategic imagination in assigning such grave military significance to capturing Cassino and the Abbey. Given that General Clark was advised by General Tuker that the only possibility for success was to launch sustained and devastating air strikes on the target, which would have caused more damage than General Clark initially indicated would be acceptable to him, the Allies might have (and arguably should have) re-evaluated if there was another way to achieve their broad operational and strategic objectives in the Italian campaign without taking Cassino.'

34 Winston S Churchill, *The Second World War: Closing the Ring*, 6 vols. (Boston: Houghton Mifflin Company, 1951), vol. V, p. 499. Alexander provided similar descriptions of topographic details of the hill as well as the difficulties confronting the Allies to Churchill. Ibid, pp. 508–09.

35 Uwe Steinhoff, 'Moral Ambiguities in the Bombing of Monte Cassino' (2005) 4 *Journal of Military Ethics* 142, at 142.

and situation-specific. It is relational, because the degree to which such conduct is militarily necessary changes depending on the availability of alternative courses of action, military ends and circumstances. It is evaluative because, with enough facts, the proposition 'destroying the Benedictine abbey atop Monte Cassino on 15 February 1944 constituted a military necessity for the Allies' is susceptible to reasonable assessment – although the determination may differ from assessor to assessor. It is situation-specific, because the military necessity assessment of particular action cannot be seen meaningfully outside of its factual setting. Accordingly, a generalised proposition postulated a priori in a manner that holds true for all, always and everywhere – such as 'destroying a building sitting atop a strategically important hill constitutes a military necessity' – is insusceptible to reasonable assessment.

2.2 No Need to Show But-for Causation

Establishing material military necessity does not entail *sine qua non* ('but-for') causation. Generally, upholding the but-for causation between one event at a given moment (E_t) and another event at a subsequent moment (E_{t+1}) amounts to asserting the truth of two propositions. They are, respectively, that both E_t and E_{t+1} in fact occur, and that E_{t+1} would not have occurred had it not been for E_t. The military necessity or otherwise of the conduct occurring ($E_t = X$) is capable of comprehension even where the purpose sought by it ($E_{t+1} = Y$) does not, in fact, materialise. Nor, even where E_{t+1} materialises, does military necessity require that E_t's occurrence be E_{t+1}'s *conditio sine qua non.*

2.2.1 No Causation Required

Acting in accordance with military necessity does not imply overcoming what Carl von Clausewitz called war's 'friction'.[36] Friction may well deny

[36] Carl von Clausewitz, *On War*, Michael Howard and Peter Paret (eds. trans.) (Princeton: Princeton University Press, 1976), pp. 119–21. Barry D Watts offers the following taxonomy of Clausewitzian friction: danger's impact on the ability to think clearly and act effectively in war; the effects on thought and action of combat's demands for exertion; uncertainties and imperfections in the information on which action in war is unavoidably based; friction in the narrow sense of the internal resistance to effective action stemming from the interactions between the many men and machines making up one's own forces; the play of chance, of good luck and bad, whose consequences combatants can never fully foresee; physical and political limits to the use of military force; unpredictability

the military purpose's materialisation, despite the very best and otherwise effective courses of action being pursued.

Operation Market Garden is a case in point. According to one authoritative account, 'Operation MARKET-GARDEN accomplished much of what it had been designed to accomplish. Nevertheless, by the merciless logic of war, MARKET-GARDEN was a failure. The Allies had trained their sights on far-reaching objectives. These they had not attained'.[37] The unattained objectives included securing a bridgehead beyond the Neder Rijn, effectively turning the north flank of the West Wall, cutting off Germany's 15th Army, and positioning the 21st Army Group for a drive around the north flank of the Ruhr.[38] The account continues:

> Though MARKET-GARDEN failed in its more far-reaching ramifications, to condemn the entire plan as a mistake is to show no appreciation for imagination and daring in military planning and is to ignore the climate of Allied intelligence reports that existed at the time. While reasons advanced for the failure range from adverse weather (Field Marshal Montgomery) and delay of the British ground column south of Eindhoven (General Brereton) to faulty intelligence (the Germans), few criticisms have been leveled at the plan itself. In light of Allied limitations in transport, supplies, and troops for supporting the thrust, in light of General Eisenhower's commitment to a broad-front policy, and in light of the true conditions of the German army in the West, perhaps the only real fault of the plan was overambition.[39]

With the possible exception of faulty intelligence, the reasons offered above are typical indicators of an operation's Clausewitzian friction.[40]

stemming from interaction with the enemy; and disconnects between ends and means in war. Barry D Watts, *Clausewitzian Friction and Future War* (Washington, DC: National Defence University, 1996), pp. 30, 32.

37 Charles B MacDonald, *The European Theater of Operations: The Siegfried Line Campaign* (Washington, DC: Center of Military History, United States Army, 1963), p. 198.

38 Ibid (also explaining that '[t]he hope of attaining these objectives had prompted the ambition and daring that went into Operation MARKET-GARDEN. Not to have realized them could mean only that the operation had failed').

39 Ibid, p. 199. See also Winston S Churchill, *The Second World War: Triumph and Tragedy*, 6 vols. (Boston: Houghton Mifflin Company, 1953), vol. VI, pp. 198–200 (describing how weather and dangerous river conditions contributed to the Allies' difficulties in Operation Market Garden).

40 Of course, not all commentators look upon Operation Market Garden's failure so charitably – to put it mildly – by describing its difficulties and shortcomings as instances of Clausewitzian friction. Norman Dixon, *On the Psychology of Military Incompetence* (London: Jonathan Cape, 1976), pp. 145–48, esp. 148 (citation omitted): 'For the student of military disasters, the attack on Arnhem ranks with Kut and the Bay of Pigs fiasco.

Moreover, many of the measures taken during the ultimately unsuccessful Operation Market Garden were militarily necessary for the operation. By way of example, one might note the assault on the Arnhem highway bridge by Lieutenant Colonel J. D. Frost and his battalion,[41] as well as their subsequent effort to maintain their foothold on that bridge.[42] By all accounts, securing the Arnhem highway bridge under the circumstances prevailing at the time was one of the operation's most crucial components.[43] The actions of Frost and his men were eminently relevant to the objectives' materialisation. They reached the bridge and held their position amid intense enemy action, mounting casualties and increasingly untenable conditions.[44]

Admittedly, the objectives' non-materialisation may – and, sometimes, does – indicate the military non-necessity of the measures taken in their pursuit. Consider the fall of Singapore in 1942, for example. In a rather dramatic fashion, the British objective of defending Singapore from Japanese forces advancing through the Malay Peninsula failed to materialise. This failure has been attributed to a series of measures, some inadequate (e.g., the stationing of only severely limited and largely obsolete ships and aircraft) and others affirmatively detrimental (e.g., relentless self-deception and under-preparation), that were taken by British and Australian commanders.[45] It does not follow, however, that an objective's failure always entails the measure's lack of military necessity, or that a measure constitutes a military necessity only where its objective materialises.

2.2.2 No But-for Required

Nor does military necessity involve *conditio sine qua non*. Causal elements of *conditio sine qua non* are by their very nature indemonstrable. What is often treated as a causal *sine qua non* is really the description of a singular event rather than the statement of a purported causal law

Through inappropriate risk-taking, underestimation of the enemy, the neglect of unpalatable information and a failure of technology, military decisions by able brains, at high levels of command, brought down misery and chaos.'

41 MacDonald, *Siegfried Line Campaign*, p. 171.

42 Ibid, pp. 171–72, 179, 185–86.

43 Churchill, *Triumph and Tragedy*, pp. 196–97.

44 Ibid, p. 198.

45 For further discussion, see Timothy Hall, *The Fall of Singapore* (North Ryde: Methuen Australia, 1983), and our treatment of military non-necessities below.

governing similar combinations of events.[46] There may be other elements of *conditio sine qua non* that are demonstrable, but they are either mere analytic connections or incidental connections.[47]

Moreover, having made allowances for Clausewitzian friction,[48] each belligerent is always faced with a *choice* among a range of courses of action in view of its objective. This or that particular range may be a *sine qua non* with respect to this or that particular objective. Once the range is defined, however, the particular course of action chosen from that range is never truly a *sine qua non*. It is rather a matter of choosing that one course of action which is the *best*, all things considered. What makes the particular choice the best is a function of various criteria, such as the one that stands the greatest chances of accomplishing the objective, or the one that is the most resource-efficient, or the one that is the most politically acceptable among co-belligerents.

For instance, there is nothing *sine qua non* about the Allied forces landing on the beaches of Normandy for the purposes of invading north-west Europe. Landing at Normandy was a military necessity, but *not* because the Allied invasion of north-west Europe would have otherwise been unsuccessful. This one cannot know. It cannot be ruled out that landing at some other location might have also led to a successful Allied invasion of north-west Europe.[49] Landing at Normandy was a military necessity because its beaches were the *best* among other candidate locations, all things considered.

There may be one element – namely, the genius of the military leader – that comes closest to being truly irreplaceable. In all likelihood, Emir Faisal's forces would not have taken Aqaba but for Lieutenant T. E. Lawrence.[50]

46 Donald Davidson, *Essays on Actions and Events*, 2nd edn (Oxford: Oxford University Press, 2001), pp. 15–17, 149–62, esp. p. 16 (emphasis in original): 'What emerges, in the *ex post facto* atmosphere of explanation and justification, as *the* reason frequently was, to the agent at the time of action, one consideration among many, *a* reason.'

47 HLA Hart and Tony Honoré, *Causation in the Law*, 2nd edn (Oxford: Clarendon Press, 1985), p. 115: 'If a man is knocked down and injured by a vehicle the fact that he is a man, human, and has a body, is something which is logically entailed by the description of the event with which we start and whose cause we may seek.' See also ibid, p. 116 (explaining that the act of shooting a gun successfully requires 'the fact that the cartridge was charged with explosive').

48 Von Clausewitz, *On War*, pp. 119–21.

49 Here, the possible *sine qua non* range of courses of action would have been to carry out a landing somewhere. Without such a landing, it is quite difficult to imagine how the Allies would have successfully invaded north-west Europe.

50 TE Lawrence, *Seven Pillars of Wisdom* (London: Jonathan Cape, 1935), pp. 167–68.

Nevertheless, the mere fact that military genius may practically constitute a *conditio sine qua non* for some of the objectives it achieves, does not mean that one can intelligibly speak of military necessity only where such genius is at play.

2.3 Military Non-necessities

Wars can be poorly fought in various ways. Wastefulness, excessiveness, inappositeness, futility, purposelessness and the like are improvable military non-necessities that are not solely the products of irreducible friction. They would typically emanate from ill-advised, unrealistic or otherwise inadequately defined military goals, from ill-chosen means, or from their poor execution under the prevailing circumstances. De Lee suggests that the military necessity of attacking the Monte Cassino abbey diminished materially, if also morally, because it was conducted unprofessionally.[51] In reality, uneconomical wars are often the combined result of these acts and goals.[52]

As noted earlier, material military necessity is a relational and evaluative notion. The degree to which X_1 constitutes a military necessity for Y is relative to the degree to which some X_2 constitutes a non-necessity for Y. There are two manners in which material military non-necessity may be construed.

2.3.1 Non-necessities Per Se: Futility and Purposelessness

First, non-necessity emanates from the lack of cogency intrinsic to the end sought or the means taken. Consider futility and purposelessness. Futility

[51] De Lee, 'Moral Ambiguities', at 133, 137. See also Brigety, 'Moral Ambiguities', at 140: 'In other words, De Lee suggests that the primary moral difficulty of the Cassino case is that the attack caused more damage than it might have done if it were carried out in a more expert and discriminate manner.'

[52] Ineffectiveness may be blamed on factors such as: misguided leadership; political-ideological preconceptions; doctrinal rigidity; defective communication and coordination; unimaginativeness, distraction and indecision at the tactical, operational and/or strategic levels; poor intelligence; incompetent planning; inadequate training; lack of equipment; wasteful allocation and expenditure of resources; reckless bravery and adventurism; indiscipline; cowardice; low morale; defeatism. Dixon, *Military Incompetence*, pp. 50 ('poor planning, unclear orders, lack of intelligence (in both senses of the word) and fatal acquiescence to social pressures'), 66 ('unrelieved stupidity' and generals being 'inexperienced, irresolute and lacking moral courage'), 144 ('passivity and courtesy, rigidity and obstinacy, procrastination, gentleness and dogmatism'), 148 ('inappropriate risk-taking, underestimation of the enemy, the neglect of unpalatable information and a failure of technology').

would arise where one identifies an end (Y) that is so patently unattainable at the relevant time that none of the means then available (X_1, X_2, X_3, ... X_n) would have any reasonable prospects of success. This occurs when, odd as it may sound, only refraining from any of these *X*s can be said to constitute a military necessity for *Y*, or when *Y* ought to be modified until at least one *X* does become a military necessity for it. Examples include launching assaults with an insufficient amount of resources in the knowledge that the objectives sought would remain unaccomplished as a result. Such was arguably the case with numerous instances of kamikaze attacks and Hitler's order to defend Berlin to the last man.

Where there is no rational military end set, the act in question might be purposeless and incapable of being materially necessary in any meaningful sense of the expression. The Rape of Nanking may be noted in this regard.

2.3.2 *Relative Non-necessities*

Second, non-necessity emanates from the lack of cogency under the circumstances between an otherwise reasonably attainable end sought and an otherwise reasonably actionable means taken.[53] Examples include wastefulness, excessiveness, and inappositeness.

2.3.2.1 Wastefulness

Wastefulness means expending more resources than would be reasonably required to accomplish a military goal under the prevailing circumstances.[54] Failing to achieve an economy of force[55] typifies a non-necessity

[53] As noted earlier, however, the mere fact that certain Clausewitzian friction attends a given act in war is not itself indicative of the act's lack of military necessity. The relevant comparison is not between paper-perfect, arm-chair alternatives, but between those that are reasonably actionable, friction having been taken into account. Nor, for that matter, is it perforce the case that a measure's non-necessity derives from it not being the least injurious amongst those reasonably available courses of action that are similarly conducive towards the end's attainment, or from it not retaining some acceptable ratio between the gain sought and the harm occasioned. Limiting injury and proportion are elements of what might be termed 'juridical' military necessity. See Chapter 10.

[54] Chris af Jochnick and Roger Normand, 'The Legitimation of Violence: A Critical History of the Laws of War' (1994) 35 *Harvard International Law Journal* 49, at 53–54: 'Belligerents tend to use the minimal force necessary to achieve their political objectives'.

[55] Joint Chiefs of Staff, *Joint Operation (Joint Publication 3-0)* (2008), appendix A, at A-2: 'The purpose of the economy of force is to allocate minimum essential combat power to secondary efforts. Economy of force is the judicious employment and distribution of forces. It is the measured allocation of available combat power to such tasks as limited

of this nature. Admittedly, calculating economy of force in military operations, as well as determining what makes particular belligerent conduct economical as opposed to wasteful, would be anything but straightforward. Nevertheless, several formulas, such as Lanchester's Square Law for a given sector of ground combat and its variations, have been suggested.[56]

During World War II, Lieutenant General Lloyd Fredendall of the US Army received criticism for what may be characterised as the wasteful – not to mention ineffectual – expenditure of resources over the command post he had constructed near Tebessa. According to one account:

> Commanders usually try to establish their headquarters near a road, adjacent to existing communications facilities and close enough to the combat units for convenient visits. Fredendall's was distant from the front and far up a canyon, a gulch that could be entered only by a barely passable road constructed by his corps engineers. Though towering mountains and wooded hillsides concealed his presence, he had underground shelters dug and blasted for himself and his staff. Two hundred engineers would work for more than three weeks on this project, then abandon it unfinished under the German threat at Kasserine . . . To those who asked, Fredendall explained that German aircraft were active over the area and that they made special efforts to destroy command posts. He had gone underground because he had no intention of having his activities disrupted. Though sixty or seventy miles behind the front was rather far for frequent visits to the combat units, he saw no need to be closer. He would run the battle by telephone and radio.[57]

Fredendall also had an entire anti-aircraft battalion emplaced to protect his command post.[58] General Dwight D. Eisenhower was quoted as saying: 'It was the only time during the war that I ever saw a higher headquarters so concerned over its own safety that it dug itself underground shelters.'[59] Fredendall sought the protection of his headquarters

attacks, defense, delays, deception, or even retrograde operations to achieve mass elsewhere at the decisive point and time.' See also Michael N Schmitt, 'The Interpretive Guidance on the Notion of Direct Participation in Hostilities: A Critical Analysis' (2010) 1 *Harvard National Security Journal* 5, at 33 n.92; Office of General Counsel, Department of Defense, *Department of Defense Law of War Manual* (2015), pp. 60, 1056.

56 Paul K Davis, *Aggregation, Disaggregation, and the 3:1 Rule in Ground Combat* (Santa Monica: RAND, 1995), pp. 2–6.

57 Martin Blumenson, *Kasserine Pass: Rommel's Bloody, Climactic Battle for Tunisia* (Boston: Houghton Mifflin Company, 1967), pp. 86–87.

58 Stephen E Ambrose, *D-Day, June 6, 1944: The Climactic Battle of World War II* (New York, London, Toronto and Sydney: Simon & Schuster, 1994), p. 361.

59 Richard Collier, *The War in the Desert* (Alexandria: Time-Life Books, 1977), p. 162.

against detection and attack by German aircraft.[60] He endeavoured to accomplish this objective by choosing the particular location for it and by expending considerable military resources – such as engineers for its construction and anti-aircraft batteries for its defence.[61] Some degree of protection from aerial threats, as well as some corresponding resource expenditure, may be reasonable for any military headquarters. It is arguable, however, that Fredendall's was both exaggerated in the end sought and wasteful in the means taken.

During the Cuban Revolution, Che Guevara apparently came to regard targeted assassinations – he called it 'terrorism'[62] – as a wasteful tactic. Thus,

> In special circumstances, after careful analysis, assaults on persons will be used. In general, we consider that it is not desirable except for the purpose of eliminating some figure who is notorious for his villainies against the people and the virulence of his repression. Our experience in the Cuban struggle shows that it would have been possible to save the lives of numerous fine comrades who were sacrificed in the performance of missions of small value. Several times these ended with enemy bullets of reprisal on combatants whose loss could not be compared with the results obtained. Assaults and terrorism in indiscriminate form should not be employed.[63]

Here, targeted assassination was a means being considered for the purpose of eliminating individual figures notorious for their villainies against the people. For Guevara, the wastefulness of this tactic would issue from his conclusion that 'it would have been possible to save the

[60] Blumenson, *Kasserine Pass*, pp. 86–87.

[61] Collier, *War in the Desert*, p. 162.

[62] Che Guevara, *Guerrilla Warfare*, JP Morray (trans.) (New York: Vintage Books, 1961), pp. 139–40: 'Sabotage has nothing to do with terrorism; terrorism and personal assaults are entirely different tactics. We sincerely believe that terrorism is of negative value, that it by no means produces the desired effects, that it can turn a people against a revolutionary movement, and that it can bring a loss of lives to its agents out of proportion to what it produces. On the other hand, attempts to take the lives of particular persons are to be made, though only in very special circumstances; this tactic should be used where it will eliminate a leader of the oppression. What ought never to be done is to employ specially trained, heroic, self-sacrificing human beings in eliminating a little assassin whose death can provoke the destruction in reprisal of all the revolutionaries employed and even more.'

[63] Ibid, p. 131. Guevara goes on to state: 'More preferable is effort directed at large concentrations of people in whom the revolutionary idea can be planted and nurtured, so that at a critical moment they can be mobilized and with the help of the armed forces contribute to a favorable balance on the side of the revolution.'

lives of numerous fine comrades who were sacrificed in the performance of missions of small value'.[64]

2.3.2.2 Excessiveness[65]

As a type of relative non-necessity, excessiveness would imply the combination of two things. First, the means taken accomplishes its end. Second, the means also generates externalities. Expending more resources than would otherwise be reasonably required to accomplish a military goal would be excessive if, by doing so, the expender achieves that goal as well as some other consequences immaterial to the goal's accomplishment. Understood thus, it might be said that excessiveness is a species of wastefulness.

Concentrated artillery bombardment commonly practised by the Allies during World War I is a case in point. In March 1915, the Battle of Neuve Chapelle saw the concentration of artillery fire reach one gun for four yards of attacking front.[66] The then-prevailing doctrine emphasised the importance of maximising the volume of shells falling per unit of space (i.e., the means taken) with a view to destroying as many physical obstacles on it as possible (i.e., the end sought) ahead of an infantry advance.[67] Inevitably, those shells that successfully eliminated obstacles such as barbed wire would come at the expense of numerous others that hit surfaces not, or no longer, containing any obstacle.[68]

The inefficient excessiveness of bombarding Neuve Chapelle led to an adjustment in the barrage technique. At the Battle of Aubers in May 1915, 'the bombardment before the attack on the ridge was more deliberate, and primarily concerned with accurate wire-cutting'.[69] This shift may have reduced the bombardment's excessiveness vis-à-vis its stated purpose. One commentator notes, however, that what was really needed, and later implemented for efficiency, is a shift in the purpose sought

64 Ibid.

65 To be abundantly clear, the expression 'excessiveness' here is used in a strictly material sense. Of interest is *not* excessiveness of the sort prohibited, inter alia, in Article 51(5)(b), Protocol Additional to the Geneva Conventions of 12 August 1949, and Relating to the Protection of Victims of International Armed Conflicts (Protocol I), 8 June 1977, in force 7 December 1978, 1125 UNTS 3 (hereinafter Additional Protocol I).

66 Ian V Hogg, *Barrage: The Guns in Action* (New York: Ballantine Books, 1970), pp. 11–13.

67 Ibid, p. 15.

68 There were complaints in the aftermath that 'the wire cutting was patchy and the firing careless, one or two shells actually falling short during the barrage'. Ibid, p. 16.

69 Ibid.

(i.e., from maximum material damage to undermining enemy morale) and in the means taken (i.e., from the heaviest possible bombardment to one that catches the enemy by surprise and maximises intensity).[70]

2.3.2.3 Inappositeness

Inappositeness is what results where the stated and otherwise reasonably attainable objective would not be served in any meaningful way by pursuing, even successfully, the means chosen.

In 2007, the Ig Nobel Prize for Peace was awarded to the US Air Force Wright Laboratory 'for instigating research & development on a chemical weapon – the so-called "gay bomb" – that will make enemy soldiers become sexually irresistible to each other'.[71] The award was based on research proposed for the development, inter alia, of:

> Chemicals that effect [*sic*] human behavior so that discipline and morale in enemy units is adversely effected [*sic*]. One distasteful but completely non-lethal example would be strong aphrodisiacs, especially if the chemical also caused homosexual behavior. Another example would be a chemical that made personnel very sensitive to sunlight.[72]

Reportedly, however, the effort to develop weapons such as those which would simulate flatulence amongst enemy soldiers was not pursued when 'researchers concluded that the premise for such a device was fatally flawed because "people in many areas of the world do not find faecal odour offensive, since they smell it on a regular basis"'.[73] The concern expressed by the Ig Nobel laureates might be reformulated as follows. There is a danger that the stated objective of adversely affecting enemy discipline and morale will not be pertinently served even if the bomb does simulate flatulence amongst enemy soldiers as intended.

Although it may come across as harsh second-guessing, being confronted with paradigm-changing weapons and tactics sometimes prompted warring parties to take courses of action which were inapposite vis-à-vis their military goals. At Agincourt in 1415, the numerically superior French men-at-arms charged 'like lemmings' into their deaths at the hands of English longbows raining on them in a highly confined

[70] Ibid, pp. 14–15.

[71] 'Winners of the Ig® Nobel Prize', Improbable Research (http://improbable.com/ig/winners). See also '"Gay Bomb" Scoops Ig Nobel Award', BBC News, 4 October 2007.

[72] US Air Force Wright Lab., *Harassing, Annoying, and 'Bad Guy' Identifying Chemicals* (1994) (www.sunshine-project.org/incapacitants/jnlwdpdf/wpafbchem.pdf).

[73] 'US Military Pondered Love Not War', BBC News, 15 January 2005.

and increasingly crowded 'killing zone'.[74] Military historians observe that the disjoint between the victory clearly sought (and assumed) by the French and their seemingly inapposite battlefield behaviour, especially the eschewal of their own longbows, was attributable to the 'confrontational ethos of the feudal warrior'.[75] Such ethos encompassed the traditional skills, weapons and education by which the feudal warrior identified himself, as well as 'the alleged unwillingness of men-at-arms to cross weapons with archers, their social inferiors, when the chance to win glory, and prisoners, in combat with other men-at-arms presented itself'.[76] Agincourt arguably exemplifies a non-necessity where the tactics were *not* cogently chosen in view of a military purpose, but driven in reality by inapposite considerations such as social status and personal gain.

2.4 Conclusion

Material military necessity is an element of belligerent conduct separating fighting that is effective and conducive to success from fighting that is neither. The notion merely entails the truism that it is in each belligerent's self-interest to maximise his or her abilities and that it is similarly in each belligerent's self-interest to avoid failures.

Indeed, to the consummate soldier of a Clausewitzian cast,[77] a good war is one in which every act constitutes a material military necessity – that is, executed both professionally and with the optimal resource mobilisation, and directed towards a clearly defined, strategically sound and reasonably attainable military goal under the circumstances.[78] Of course, as noted earlier, it is eminently possible that a soldier acts in accordance with material military necessity in a given situation without attaining his or her military goal. Despite the soldier's unsparing efforts to the best of his or her occupational competence, he or she may simply

74 Robert L O'Connell, *Of Arms and Men: A History of War, Weapons, and Aggression* (New York and Oxford: Oxford University Press, 1989), p. 104.

75 Ibid.

76 John Keegan, *The Face of Battle* (London: Jonathan Cape, 1976), p. 98.

77 Von Clausewitz, *On War*, p. 187: 'An army's military qualities are based on the individual who is steeped in the spirit and essence of [war]; who trains the capacities it demands, rouses them, and makes them his own; who applies his intelligence to every detail; who gains ease and confidence through practice, and who completely immerses his personality in the appointed task.'

78 Ibid, pp. 102–04, 697–771.

fall victim to war's inevitable friction – in other words, without anyone, himself or herself, or indeed anybody else, failing to act in accordance with military necessity. Acting in accordance with it is not, and need not be, a guarantee of success.

As is the case with any other occupation, pursuing material military necessities and avoiding non-necessities is first and foremost a component of vocational competence. This component involves assessing the relationship between the various means available and the various goals that might be pursued in the specific set of circumstances prevailing at the time. The component in question here is also essentially *a*moral. For our present purposes, the component's amorality arises from its capacity to be ethically sound as well as unsound. Consequences of ethically pertinent belligerent conduct are readily convertible into material military costs and benefits.[79] In particular, amorality here denotes the idea that affirmatively unethical actions can also be seen as materially competent.[80]

In the next chapter, we will address three major objections that may be raised against this line of reasoning. First, there can be something moral even about evaluating the material necessity or non-necessity of a belligerent act. Second, it is arguably part of a soldier's ethical virtue to fight competently. Third, a soldier's unethical conduct may not really constitute his or her truly professional conduct, all things considered.

[79] Fighting ethically in counterinsurgency exemplifies materially competent and morally beneficial belligerent behaviour. US Army and Marine Corps, *Counterinsurgency Field Manual* (2007), para. 7-25, at 7-5: 'A key part of any insurgent's strategy is to attack the will of the domestic and international opposition. One of the insurgents' most effective ways to undermine and erode political will is to portray their opposition as untrustworthy or illegitimate. These attacks work especially well when insurgents can portray their opposition as unethical by the opposition's own standards. To combat these efforts, Soldiers and Marines treat noncombatants and detainees humanely, according to American values and internationally recognized human rights standards. In [counter-insurgency operations], preserving noncombatant lives and dignity is central to mission accomplishment. This imperative creates a complex ethical environment.'

[80] Take the Holocaust and the Rwandan genocide, for example. Assuming that those who committed these atrocities intended to destroy the targeted groups, they were, in their own frighteningly appalling way, quite efficient in exterminating a very large number of victims.

3

Objections and Responses

The material component of the belligerent conduct's fitness as a means towards an end is separable from its meta-material components such as ethics. This remains so, although the two components may admittedly coincide, overlap or even entail each other in certain specific settings.

The 'separability' of these components entails three major tenets. First, military necessity in its material sense is conceivable independently of whatever other meta-material sense or senses it may be seen to carry. Second, military necessity is conceivable in the manner just described, even though it does not exclude the possibility that material competence can form an innate part of ethical competence. Third, their separability remains true, even though it may also be true that ethical competence can form an innate part of material competence.

These three major tenets invite three corresponding objections. Is it not true that military necessity's supposedly amoral component involves evaluations of some description and that, as such, it is moral in character after all? Is the narrow vocational competence of a soldier not merely part of the broader ethical competence of a patriotic citizen? Can it be that only ethically competent fighting counts as truly vocationally competent fighting, all things considered? This chapter considers these objections in turn.

3.1 Military Competence vs. Ethical Competence

Does it not follow from the very use of evaluative terms, such as 'good' war and 'bad' war,[1] that there are similarly evaluative statements such as

[1] Judith Jarvis Thomson, *Normativity* (Peru: Open Court Publishing Company, 2008), p. 17: 'I asked earlier: which judgments are the evaluatives? I gave three examples, namely that D is a good person, E is a good tennis player, and F is a good toaster. They are obviously judgments to the effect that a certain thing is good in a certain respect. We also took note of the existence of such judgments as that G is good at doing crossword puzzles, H is good

'sound' and 'unsound' military decisions? Does this not mean, then, that there is something innately moral about this fighting being 'competent', or that fighting being 'incompetent' – that is, fighting or not fighting as a good soldier *should*?[2]

Indeed, there may be something innately moral here. It is submitted, however, that the innate morality of vocationally competent war-fighting is not inherently one of ethical behaviour. In *On War*, von Clausewitz spoke of 'moral factors',[3] 'principal moral elements'[4] and 'military virtues'.[5] Of an army's military virtues, he wrote:

> No matter how clearly we see the citizen and the soldier in the same man, how strongly we conceive of war as the business of the entire nation, opposed diametrically to the pattern set by the *condottieri* of former times, the business of war will always remain individual and distinct. Consequently for as long as they practice this activity, soldiers will think of themselves as members of a kind of guild, in whose regulations, laws, and customs the spirit of war is given pride of place. No matter how much one may be inclined to take the most sophisticated view of war, it would be a serious mistake to underrate professional pride (*esprit de corps*) as something that may and must be present in an army to the greater or

for England, and I is good for use in making cheesecake. These too are evaluative judgments to the effect that a certain thing is good in a certain respect. We can surely say that all judgments to the effect that a certain thing is good in a certain respect are evaluative judgments.'

2 Ibid, pp. 1–2 (emphasis in original): 'I suggest that we should focus on a different difference among our normative judgments. I will call our judgments that A ought to be kind to his little brother, that B ought to move his rook, and that C ought to get a haircut, *directives*. Intuitively, they differ from our judgment that D is a good person, that E is a good tennis player, and that F is a good toaster, which I will call *evaluatives*. We will want to attend to both kinds of normative judgment.'

3 Von Clausewitz, *On War*, p. 184: '[The moral elements] constitute the spirit that permeates war as a whole, and at an early stage they establish a close affinity with the will that moves and leads the whole mass of force, practically merging with it, since the will is itself a moral quantity. Unfortunately they will not yield to academic wisdom. They cannot be classified or counted. They have to be seen or felt. The spirit and other moral qualities of an army, a general or a government, the temper of the population of the theater of war, the moral effects of victory or defeat – all these vary greatly. They can moreover influence our objective and situation in very different ways . . . If the theory of war did no more than remind us of these elements, demonstrating the need to reckon with and give full value to moral qualities, it would expand its horizon, and simply by establishing this point of view would condemn in advance anyone who sought to base an analysis on material factors alone.'

4 Ibid, p. 186. These elements, according to von Clausewitz, are the following: 'the skill of the commander, the experience and courage of the troops, and their patriotic spirit'.

5 Ibid, pp. 184–89.

> lesser degree. Professional pride is the bond between the various natural forces that activate the military virtues; in the context of this professional pride they crystallize more readily.[6]

It is unlikely that von Clausewitz used the expressions 'moral' and 'virtue' in a manner similar to the same expressions understood in ethical terms. In Ulrike Kleemeier's words:

> Originally, I used the term 'moral virtues' instead of 'moral forces'. The word 'virtue' is not morally neutral in the widespread sense of the expression 'moral'. To say of somebody that he or she possesses certain virtues means that we praise him or her for being just or kind, etc. The term 'force' seems to be more neutral. To push matters to the extreme: perhaps a (war) criminal can have moral forces in the Clausewitzian sense.[7]

Kleemeier lists the 'faculty of judgment',[8] 'bravery' or 'courage',[9] and 'a passion for reason'[10] as components of Clausewitzian 'moral forces'. It would appear that qualities such as these are merely descriptions – or prerequisites – of excellence in soldiering or effective fighting, rather than those in ethical conduct. The difference, then, would be one between what might be termed *military* virtues, with which von Clausewitz was concerned, on the one hand, and *ethical* virtues, on the other.[11]

6 Ibid, p. 187. See also ibid, pp. 187–88: 'An army that maintains its cohesion under the most murderous fire; that cannot be shaken by imaginary fears and resists well-founded ones with all its might; that, proud of its victories, will not lose the strength to obey orders and its respect and trust for its officers even in defeat; whose physical power, like the muscles of an athlete, has been steeled by training in privation and effort; a force that regards such efforts as a means to victory rather than a curse on its cause; that is mindful of all these duties and qualities by virtue of the single powerful idea of the honor of its arms – such an army is imbued with the true military spirit.'

7 Ulrike Kleemeier, 'Moral Forces in War' in Hew Strachan and Andreas Herberg-Roth (eds), *Clausewitz in the Twenty-First Century* (Oxford: Oxford University Press, 2007) 107, p. 107 n.5.

8 Ibid, p. 113.

9 Ibid, p. 114.

10 Ibid, pp. 118–19.

11 Contrary to popular belief, it may be doubted whether von Clausewitz really excluded the possibility of real-life warfare being amenable to ethical constraints. Geoffrey Best, 'The Restraint of War in Historical and Philosophical Perspective' in Astrid JM Delissen and Gerard J Tanja (eds), *Humanitarian Law of Armed Conflict: Challenges Ahead, Essays in Honour of Frits Kalshoven* (Dordrecht: Martinus Nijhoff Publishers, 1991) 3, p. 5; Paul Cornish, 'Clausewitz and the Ethics of Armed Force' (2003) 2 *Journal of Military Ethics* 213, at 219; Michael Howard, '*Temperamenta Belli*: Can War Be Controlled?' in Michael Howard (ed), *Restraints on War: Studies in the Limitation of Armed Conflict* (Oxford: Oxford University Press, 1979) 1, p. 1; David J Lonsdale, 'A View from Realism' in David

Judith Jarvis Thomson suggests a similar distinction:

> Let us now look again at 'Smith is a good liar.' My characterization of the notions 'praise/dispraise *simpliciter*' and 'praise/dispraise *qua*' yields the following. Saying 'Smith is a good liar' is dispraising Smith *simpliciter*, since it is or would be dispraiseworthy in Smith to be a liar. But it is also praising Smith *qua* liar, since it is saying that as liars go, Smith is a good one. So also for 'Jones is good at avoiding responsibility for what he does.' Saying that is dispraising Jones *simpliciter*, since it is or would be dispraiseworthy in Jones to avoid responsibility for what he does. But it is also praising Jones *qua* person who avoids responsibility for what he does, since it is saying that as people who do that go, he is good at it.[12]

In relation to virtues,[13] Thomson observes:

> We should notice ... that ... being a clever liar is a virtue in a liar. (The following is plainly true: a liar is as good a liar as a liar can be only if he or she is a clever liar. And it hardly needs saying that some liars are clever liars.) So be it. Being a clever liar is certainly not a moral [read 'ethical' for the purposes of this book] virtue in a liar. But our use of 'virtue' here is the broad one, and being a clever liar *is* in that broad use a virtue in a liar – just as while being a sharp carving knife is not [an ethical] virtue in a carving knife, it is a virtue in a carving knife.[14]

Thomson speaks of desirable qualities in a soldier as 'virtues': 'No doubt it is *a* virtue of a soldier to fight well; another is to obey appropriate orders.'[15] Here, 'fight well' may be understood in comparison to Thomson's discussion of 'play chess well'.[16] Thus, 'a chess move is

Whetham (ed), *Ethics, Law and Military Operations* (Basingstoke: Palgrave Macmillan, 2011) 29, p. 34.

12 Thomson, *Normativity*, pp. 57–58.

13 Ibid, p. 73: 'For F to be a virtue in a K is for it to be the case that (i) K is a goodness-fixing kind, and (ii) a K is as good a K as a K can be only if it has F, and (iii) it is possible for there to be a K that lacks F, and (iv) it is not nomologically impossible for there to be a K that has F.'

14 Ibid, p. 74. See also ibid, p. 81: '[T]here may be strategic, tactical, and political virtues in a plan or act.'

15 Ibid, p. 69 n.1 (emphasis in original). Let 'F' denote being a soldier who fights well, 'K' the kind soldier, and 'a K' a soldier, within the meaning of the terms used by Thomson. It follows that '[f]or F [being a soldier who fights well] to be a virtue in a K [a soldier] is for it to be the case that (i) that K [the kind soldier] is a goodness-fixing kind, and (ii) a K [a soldier] is as good a K [a soldier] as a K [a soldier] can be only if it has F [being a soldier who fights well], and (iii) it is possible for there to be a K [a soldier] who lacks F [being a soldier who fights well], and (iv) it is not nomologically impossible for there to be a K [a soldier] that has F [being a soldier who fights well]'. Ibid, p. 71.

16 Ibid, p. 169 n.3.

strategically correct if and only if it is a move conducive to winning'.[17] So is, it would stand to reason, a belligerent move. It may be said that 'rules' of chess strategy[18] are analogous to 'rules' of military strategy. Strategic correctness in war would simply mean pursuing military necessities and avoiding non-necessities.

Thomson uses the expression 'virtue' broadly[19] and, more importantly, distinguishes a 'virtue' in a thing or a person of a particular functional nature from a 'moral virtue' (again, read 'ethical virtue' here) in a person *simpliciter*.[20] Thus, being a soldier who fights well is a military virtue in a soldier[21]; being an ethical person is an ethical virtue in a person.[22]

It is entirely conceivable that military virtues and ethical virtues coincide in a person. What is not so is the idea that one type of virtues necessarily matches or always entails the other. In Thomson's view, for the statement 'A ought to V' to be true is for it to be true that 'if a K doesn't V, then it is a defective K'.[23] Let 'A' denote a soldier, 'K' the kind soldier and 'V' pursuing military necessities and avoiding non-necessities. For the statement 'a soldier ought to pursue material military necessities and avoid non-necessities' to be true, is for it to be true that 'if a soldier does not pursue military necessities and/or avoid non-necessities, then he or she is a defective soldier'. In other words, 'being a soldier who pursues military necessities and avoids non-necessities' is a military virtue in a soldier.

As it turns out, Thomson's formula for the truth of an 'A ought to V' statement includes an additional condition:

> [T]here is no directive kind K+ such that K is a sub-kind of K+, and such that if a K+ does V, then it is a defective K+.[24]

In other words, for the statement 'A ought to V' to be true is for the following to be true, that:

17 Ibid.
18 Ibid.
19 Ibid, p. 69.
20 Ibid, pp. 79–81.
21 Ibid, pp. 80–81.
22 Ibid, pp. 79–80.
23 Ibid, pp. 212, 214. 'K' denotes a function-kind, 'A' a member of K and 'V' a verb-phrase. This also means that K is what Thomson calls a 'directive kind' as well. Ibid, p. 209: 'Let us say that a kind K is a directive-generating kind – a directive kind, for short – just in case there is such a property as being a defective K.'
24 Ibid, p. 214.

> If a K doesn't V, then it is a defective K; and there is no directive kind K+ such that K is a sub-kind of K+, and such that if a K+ does V, then it is a defective K+.

Let 'K+' denote the directive kind human being, and 'K' the sub-kind soldier. Revised thus, for the statement 'a soldier ought to pursue military necessities and avoid non-necessities' to be true, is for it to be true that 'if a soldier does not pursue military necessities and/or avoid non-necessities, then he or she is a defective soldier; and there is no directive kind human being such that the kind soldier is a sub-kind of the kind human being, and such that if a human being pursues military necessities and avoids non-necessities, then he or she is a defective human being'.

Consider the Malmédy Massacre of December 1944. During their dash to the Meuse River, elements of Schutzstaffel (SS) Obersturmbannführer Joachim Peiper's unit killed hundreds of American prisoners of war (POWs) at various locations.[25] An order had apparently come all the way from Hitler, via Colonel General Josef Dietrich, commander of the 6th SS Panzer Army.[26] It was ordered that the German forces 'act with brutality and show no humane inhibitions', that 'a wave of fright and terror' should precede the attack, and that 'the enemy's resistance was to be broken by terror'.[27]

Taking the creation of terror as their stated purpose yields the result that giving no quarter was arguably a material military necessity.[28] It is also possible that the expected pace of Peiper's advance made it undesirable to care for enemy soldiers taken prisoner. Peiper is quoted as seeking to have the killings excused 'by the rapid movement of his kampfgruppe and its inability to retain prisoners under guard'.[29] Peiper's objective would be to maintain the momentum of his advance, and dispatching surrendered enemy soldiers would arguably constitute a military

[25] CE Straight, Office for Judge Advocate General for War Crimes, *Report of the Deputy Judge Advocate for War Crimes, European Command* (1948), p. 48. See generally Richard Gallagher, *Malmédy Massacre* (New York: Paperback Library, 1964), pp. 55–72.

[26] Straight, *Report of the Deputy Judge Advocate*, p. 48.

[27] Hugh M Cole, *The Ardennes: Battle of the Bulge* (Washington, DC: Chief of Military History, Department of the Army, 1965), pp. 262–63; Gallagher, *Malmédy Massacre*, p. 111.

[28] In the event, the terror did not produce the hoped-for breakdown of Allied resistance. On the contrary, the news of Malmédy 'undoubtedly stiffened the will of the American combatants'. Cole, *Battle of the Bulge*, p. 261. See also ibid, p. 264: 'There were American commanders who orally expressed the opinion that all SS troops should be killed on sight and there is some indication that in isolated cases express orders for this were given.'

[29] Ibid, p. 263.

necessity for it. Such construal is contemplated, if not endorsed, in one account of the event:

> It has to be noted that Peiper's men faced a very real problem in deciding what to do with the large number of prisoners taken in the Baugnez area. According to all German reports, Peiper was in a hurry to get to Ligneuville and capture the U.S. headquarters there, and he ordered the rest of the *Kampfgruppe* to follow up as quickly as possible. Faced with mounting delays and an irate commander, what were those at the crossroads to do with the prisoners? Armored columns had no spare manpower to look after POWs, and none of the follow-up infantry formation were anywhere near Five Points at the time. More than 100 men, even if they have surrendered and been disarmed, cannot be left to their own devices for long. Nor could they be ordered to start marching to the rear into captivity, as is usual in such circumstances, because there was a simple problem of geography. Peiper had penetrated the American lines on a very narrow front – a single road – and this meant that as far as the Germans were concerned the enemy lay along the N-23 to the northwest in Malmédy, the N-32 to the northeast in Waimes and the N-23 to the south in Ligneuville. There was therefore no road along which they could order the prisoners to set off. And it was more than possible that American combat units would move south out of Malmédy at any moment. A combination of all these factors – an angry SS lieutenant colonel in a hurry, no spare men to guard the prisoners, no easily available route to the rear and the possibility of American combat troops arriving at any moment – must have created a nightmare scenario for the officer in charge. It is therefore quite possible that he decided to take the simplest and most practical way out of his dilemma by giving an order to shoot the prisoners.[30]

Given Peiper's objectives and the circumstances prevailing at the time, killing the American POWs in Malmédy might have signalled a military virtue and failing to do so a military defect. If Peiper's men were to act not as soldiers (i.e., Ks) but as human beings (i.e., K+s), however, it is arguable that the second condition for the truth of Thomson's statement 'A ought to V' was not satisfied.[31] It follows, then, that evaluating the

[30] Michael Reynolds, 'Massacre at Malmédy during the Battle of the Bulge', *World War II* (February 2003) 43, at 48–49.

[31] Another way of putting it would be to point out the fact that, regarding those 'ought' statements involving the kind human being, Thomson proposes a special normative thesis. Thomson, *Normativity*, p. 216: 'If A is a human being, then for it to be the case that A ought to V_{act} is for it to be the case that if A knows at the time what will probably happen if he V_{act}s and what will probably happen if he does not, then he is a defective human being if he does not.' There are many possible kinds of defects in a human being. Thomson lists, among other things: being malicious, callous, lazy, greedy, unjust, reckless, imprudent, ruthless, cruel, sanctimonious, jealous, rude, weak-willed, unscrupulous,

virtues of the function-kind soldier is not the same as evaluating the virtues of the directive kind human being. What is important for our purposes is that the former is capable of consideration, at least conceptually, without reference to the latter.

3.2 Military Competence as Ethical Competence

This book proceeds on the assumption that prosecuting war is a purposive activity.[32] In other words, the soldier being called upon to pursue military necessities and avoid non-necessities actually wants to succeed in what he or she has set out to do. Of playing chess, Thomson notes:

> When we say, 'Alfred ought to move his queen,' . . . [w]e are also *assuming* that Alfred wants to win the game. We normally make these two assumptions when watching chess players, and we are normally right to make them. If we weren't making them, we wouldn't say, 'Alfred ought to move his queen.' At any rate, we would take a closer look at Alfred's circumstances and wants and weigh one thing against another before saying those words.[33]

This purposive assumption leads us to the second major objection to the idea that material military necessity is amoral. There is perhaps something ethical even about being good *qua* soldier. It is indeed possible that a military competence may *itself* be an ethical competence.

The United States has long maintained a Code of Conduct for Members of United States Armed Forces.[34] It admonishes, among other things, that the US soldier 'make every effort to escape' and 'accept

vengeful, petty, intemperate, cowardly, irresolute, misanthropic, irresponsible, lacking in self-respect and lacking in generosity. Ibid, p. 218. Plainly, some – though perhaps not all – of these defects are properly seen as ethical in nature. Moreover, some of these same defects clearly exemplify instances where military defects and ethical defects overlap each other.

32 So did von Clausewitz, albeit implicitly. Clausewitzian theory makes no sense whatsoever, unless one proceeds on the basis that each belligerent party wants to bring the war it fights to a conclusion on its own terms. Von Clausewitz, *On War*, pp. 90–99 (regarding purpose and means in war).

33 Thomson, *Normativity*, p. 172 (emphasis in original).

34 Code of Conduct for Members of the Armed Forces of the United States, Executive Order No. 10631 (17 August 1955; amended 1977, 1988):

I. I am an American, fighting in the forces which guard my country and our way of life. I am prepared to give my life in their defense.

II. I will never surrender of my own free will. If in command, I will never surrender the members of my command while they still have the means to resist.

neither parole nor special favors from the enemy' if captured. As a POW, he or she is to 'give no information or take part in any action which might be harmful to [his or her] comrades', 'evade answering further questions to the utmost of [his or her] ability' and 'make no oral or written statements disloyal to [his or her] country and its allies or harmful to their cause'. Implicit in this code of conduct is the idea that refusing to divulge accurate intelligence to the enemy is not only a military necessity, but also a sign of loyalty to comrades-in-arms as well as patriotic devotion to the nation. Does it not follow, then, that the ethical competence of a patriotic citizen includes his or her military competence as a soldier?

It may do so. Michael Walzer speaks of the two-fold responsibility that a mid-level field commander has through the chain of command. Of the upward variety, Walzer observes:

> [The mid-level field commander's] obligation is to win the battles that he fights or, rather, to do his best to win, obeying the legal orders of his immediate superiors, fitting his own decisions into the larger strategic plan, accepting onerous but necessary tasks, seeking collective success rather than individual glory. He is responsible for assignments unperformed or badly performed and for all avoidable defeats. And he is responsible up the chain to each of his superiors in turn and ultimately to the ordinary citizens of his country who are likely to suffer for his failures.[35]

Of the commander's downward responsibility, Walzer notes:

> His soldiers are in one sense the instruments with which he is supposed to win victories, but they are also men and women whose lives, because they are his to use, are also in his care. He is bound to minimize the risks his

III. If I am captured I will continue to resist by all means available. I will make every effort to escape and aid others to escape. I will accept neither parole nor special favors from the enemy.
IV. If I become a prisoner of war, I will keep faith with my fellow prisoners. I will give no information or take part in any action which might be harmful to my comrades. If I am senior, I will take command. If not, I will obey the lawful orders of those appointed over me and will back them up in every way.
V. When questioned, should I become a prisoner of war, I am required to give name, rank, service number and date of birth. I will evade answering further questions to the utmost of my ability. I will make no oral or written statement disloyal to my country and its allies or harmful to their cause.
VI. I will never forget that I am an American, fighting for freedom, responsible for my actions, and dedicated to the principles which made my country free. I will trust in my God and in the United States of America.

[35] Michael Walzer, *Arguing About War* (New Haven: Yale University Press, 2004), pp. 23–24.

> soldiers must face, to fight carefully and prudently, and to avoid wasting their lives, that is, not to persist in battles that cannot be won, not to seek victories whose costs overwhelm their military value, and so on. And his soldiers have every right to expect all this of him and to blame him for every sort of omission, evasion, carelessness, and recklessness that endangers their lives.[36]

In other words, it is the ethical duty of a soldier to fight competently by doing his or her best to pursue military necessities and avoid non-necessities. It would appear, however, that the ethical competence of the kind being articulated by Walzer here emanates from the particular community for which a soldier fights.[37] Nothing in the community-specific ethical competence makes the strictly amoral construal of military competence unintelligible. The strictly military competence may also constitute a community-specific ethical competence, but this is a matter of contingency. Walzer's depiction does not show that it must be inevitable, i.e., true for all real as well as hypothetical communities. Nor, more importantly, does it show that the military competence of a soldier inescapably forms part of the general ethical competence of a human being. To use Thomson's terminologies: 'it may be, and in some specific situations is, the case that being a soldier who pursues military necessities and avoids non-necessities is a military virtue in a soldier and a patriotic virtue in a citizen'.[38] The fact that military competence can entail community-specific ethical significance merely shows that the former competence is amenable to being understood 'on its own terms', as it were, in the first place. And it is precisely in this sense that material military necessity can be usefully and illuminatingly understood on its own terms.

3.3 Ethical Competence as Military Competence

There is a more serious objection to separability as an idea. Is there not something more to a soldier's vocational competence than his or her mere ability to fight effectively and 'get the job done'? Is it not true that a soldier would not even be a vocationally competent soldier unless he or

[36] Ibid, p. 24.

[37] In a perverse way, one could even say that terrorists might have moral virtues particular to the community or communities in whose name or on whose behalf they commit their acts. Avishai Margalit and Michael Walzer, 'Israel: Civilians & Combatants', *New York Review of Books*, 14 May 2009.

[38] Thomson, *Normativity*, p. 69.

she is also an ethically competent soldier? Where performing *X* is consistent with material military necessity yet inconsistent with what is ethically expected of a soldier, should that soldier's competence *qua* soldier ultimately not depend on his or her refraining from *X*?

Both ethical and military competences sometimes point the soldier in the same behavioural direction. In Iraq, fighting insurgents in such a way to garner the support of local residents proved not only strategically sound but also ethically important. For instance, a degree of success in stabilising Mosul in 2003 was largely attributed to the adoption of the methods advocated later in the US counterinsurgency manual.[39] Conversely, destroying the cognitive faculties of Mohammed al-Qahtani, a high-value intelligence detainee, through harsh interrogation methods was arguably both unethical and lacking in military necessity.[40]

The objection at issue, however, is not with such instrumentalist 'strategic necessity' or expedient attention to ethical considerations.[41] Rather, it asserts that only ethically competent belligerent conduct counts – or should count, at any rate – as *truly* vocationally competent belligerent conduct. To begin with, it may be unethical to do what would otherwise be materially competent. At a 1943 speech before SS officers, Heinrich Himmler stated: 'Whether 10,000 Russian females fall down from exhaustion while digging an anti-tank ditch interests me only in so far as the anti-tank ditch for Germany is finished'.[42] Forcing the 10,000 Russian women in captivity to perform physical labour to exhaustion may have arguably constituted a military necessity for its objective, namely an anti-tank ditch being completed. The question is whether such a clearly unethical course of action can ever be said to be militarily competent, all things considered.

Conversely, it might be unethical to avoid what would be materially incompetent. Frank Richards, a World War I veteran, recalled his

[39] US Army and Marine Corps, *Counterinsurgency Field Manual*, p. xv. Such attribution is by no means unanimous, however. Martin van Creveld, *The Changing Face of War: Lessons of Combat, from the Marne to Iraq* (New York: Presidio Press, 2006), p. 270; Bradley Graham, 'A Sharp Shift from Killing to Kindness', *The Washington Post*, 4 December 2004.

[40] Bob Woodward, 'Detainee Tortured, Says U.S. Official', *The Washington Post*, 14 January 2009. Al-Qathani's lawyer reportedly described him as '"paranoid," "incoherent," "cracked"'. Washington Media Associations, *Torturing Democracy* (2008).

[41] Lonsdale, 'View from Realism', pp. 39–40.

[42] Office of US Chief of Counsel for Prosecution of Axis Criminality, *Nazi Conspiracy and Aggression*, 8 vols. (1946), vol. V, p. 559.

November 1914 action in northern France at a village called Englefontaine:

> When bombing dug-outs or cellars it was always wise to throw bombs into them first and have a look around them after. But we had to be very careful in this village as there were civilians in some of the cellars. We shouted down them to make sure. Another man and I shouted down one cellar twice and receiving no reply were just about to pull the pins out of our bombs when we heard a woman's voice cry out and a young lady came up the cellar steps. As soon as she saw us she started to speak rapidly in French and gave the both of us a hearty kiss. She and the members of her family had their beds, stove and everything else of use in the cellar which they had not left for some days. They guessed an attack was being made and when we first shouted down had been too frightened to answer. If the young lady had not cried out when she did we would have innocently murdered them all.[43]

Richards considered it 'wise' – or perhaps militarily necessary or materially competent, to use the expression adopted in this book – 'to throw bombs into cellars first and have a look around them after'.[44] At the same time, however, he clearly found it ethically troubling to do so. In fact, he found it so ethically troubling that he decided *not* to do the wise thing.[45] Instead, Richards, together with his colleague, chose to shout several times into the cellar.[46] Walzer observes:

> *Innocently murdered*, because they had shouted first; but if they had not shouted, and then killed the French family, it would have been, Richards believed, murder simply. And yet he was accepting a certain risk in shouting, for had there been German soldiers in the cellar, they might have scrambled out, firing as they came. It would have been more prudent to throw the bombs without warning, which means that military necessity would have justified him in doing so ... And yet Richards was surely doing the right thing when he shouted his warning. He was acting as a moral man ought to act; his is not an example of fighting heroically, above and beyond the call of duty, but simply of fighting well. It is what we expect of soldiers.[47]

43 Frank Richards, *Old Soldiers Never Die* (New York: Berkeley Publishing Corporation, 1966), pp. 198–99. For further discussion of Richards's story, see Michael Walzer, *Just and Unjust Wars: A Moral Argument with Historical Illustrations*, 4th ed. (New York: Basic Books, 2006), pp. 152, 154.

44 Richards, *Old Soldiers Never Die*, pp. 198–99.

45 Ibid.

46 Ibid.

47 Walzer, *Just and Unjust Wars*, pp. 152, 154 (quoting Richards, *Old Soldiers Never Die*, p. 199). In contemporary terms, the 'wise' thing to do in Richards's situation is akin to

The objection holds that, where it appears to be vocationally competent *qua* soldier yet it is unethical *qua* human being to perform *X*, true vocational competence *qua* soldier, all things considered, lies with refraining from *X*. This is so, because ethical competences form an integral component of military competences. It follows that separability as an idea cannot stand.

There may be military competences 'in the narrow, material sense' and military competences 'in the broad, holistic sense'. In the former, military competences basically mean one's ability to 'get the job done', whereas in the latter, military competences include one's ability and inclination to preserve humanity such as retaining one's autonomous moral agency. It has been suggested that being a vocationally competent officer entails preserving the humanity of those under his or her command. Accordingly,

> we can ... attribute to officers some level of control – and therefore responsibility – over the specific actions of their troops that might place the troops' humanity in jeopardy ... A warrior's humanity is most obviously at risk when he or she participates in an atrocity. Vile actions such as rape, the intentional slaughter of civilians, or the torture of prisoners of war dehumanize the victims and degrade the perpetrators. We require officers not to lead or order their subordinates to commit criminal actions such as these.[48]

Perhaps military necessity in this 'broad, holistic sense' may entail always acting in a manner that promotes or preserves humanity. Even if ethical competences are intrinsic to the holistic construal of military competences, however, some separate consideration of those remaining bits of the latter not entailing ethics is still possible. It is in this narrow sense that this book uses the term 'material military necessity'.

3.4 Conclusion

The idea that the material and meta-material components of military necessity are separable is a modest one. The former component is capable of apprehension and evaluation without reference to the latter component. Strict materiality is but one dimension in our understanding of

ensuring force protection. Force protection is a matter that raises questions of risk-taking and involves an ethical principle known as the double effect. See Chapter 7 and Chapter 8.

48 Shannon E French, 'Sergeant Davis's Stern Charge: The Obligation of Officers to Preserve the Humanity of Their Troops' (2009) 8 *Journal of Military Ethics* 116, at 121–22.

military necessity; it insists neither that there can be no other dimensions, nor that it never overlaps with such dimensions.

A given belligerent act can be considered militarily necessary from a strictly *a*moral point of view, though perhaps not so from a morally engaged one. We should be mindful of these possibilities, lest we speak at cross-purposes while debating the military necessity of a belligerent act. This awareness becomes all the more important as we will soon begin approaching military necessity normatively and juridically.

This concludes Part II's discussion of military necessity in its strictly material context. Part III proceeds with 'normative' military necessity, i.e., military necessity understood in the context of IHL norm-creation. In that context, military necessity is generalised and stipulatory. The material question was whether a given act was or would be militarily necessary, in view of its particular purpose and circumstances. The question in Part III will be what the framers of IHL should do about this kind of act, *once* it is agreed that it would in general be materially necessary or unnecessary for an otherwise legitimate kind of military purpose.

Part III's central assertion is that military necessity is normatively indifferent. Conduct is normatively indifferent where the two propositions – 'It is permitted to perform it', and 'It is permitted to refrain from it' – are both true simultaneously. Military necessity permits the belligerent to pursue what is materially necessary and to avoid what is unnecessary. It also leaves the belligerent at liberty to miss opportunities and commit blunders, because neither victory nor defeat is per se of concern to IHL. The law does not make it its business to ensure that each belligerent maximise its prospect of success or minimise its prospect of failure. IHL framers have no reason to obligate militarily necessary behaviour or prohibit militarily unnecessary behaviour.

PART III

Military Necessity in Its Normative Context

4

Military Necessity and Legitimacy Modification

Part III of this book investigates military necessity in its normative context. This context is where military necessity appears as a weighty consideration in the process of IHL norm-creation.

We are no longer concerned as to whether a given course of action constitutes, or would constitute, a material military necessity or non-necessity, in view of its specific objective and circumstances. At issue here is whether a certain kind of conduct tends to constitute, or is deemed capable of constituting, a material military necessity or non-necessity; and whether, given the said tendency or capability, IHL should obligate, permit, restrict or prohibit this kind of conduct.

4.1 From Materiality to Normativity

This contextual shift in our discussion is accompanied by two related shifts. The first is a shift from assessing particular events to assessing patterns or kinds of events. For our purposes, descriptions of particular acts, such as 'torturing Mohammed al-Qahtani',[1] are replaced by those of generalised kinds of acts, such as 'torturing an intelligence detainee'. Similarly, descriptions of particular purposes, such as 'extracting reliable and actionable intelligence regarding al-Qaida', are replaced by those of generalised kinds of purposes, such as 'extracting reliable and actionable intelligence regarding an adversary'.

The other related shift involves the evaluative nature of material military necessity. The question in Part II was whether a given act did or would constitute a material military necessity or non-necessity, in view of its particular purpose and circumstances. The question in Part III is

[1] In 2009, Susan Crawford, a Bush administration official then in charge of convening military commissions, admitted that al-Qahtani's treatment had satisfied even the definition of torture as understood by the administration itself. Woodward, 'Detainee Tortured'.

what IHL should do about a given kind of act, *if*, or *once*, it is deemed materially necessary or unnecessary for a given kind of military purpose. For instance, there may well be no material military necessity to intern this or that particular POW given the circumstances of his or her capture. Nevertheless, interning POWs is generally deemed militarily necessary.[2] Normative military necessity prompts the framers of IHL rules to leave the belligerent at liberty to intern, or decline to intern, POWs.[3]

Discussions of military necessity in the context of IHL norm-creation involve *stipulating* the material military necessity or non-necessity of kinds of conduct, rather than *evaluating* that of instances of conduct. As R. B. Brandt observed:

> We should notice that the question which rules of war would be preferred by rational persons choosing behind a [Rawlsian] veil of ignorance is roughly the question that bodies like the Hague Conventions tried to answer. For there were the representatives of various nations, gathered together, say, in 1907, many or all of them making the assumption that their nations would at some time be at war. And, presumably in the light of calculated national self-interest and the principles of common humanity, they decided which rules they were prepared to commit themselves to follow, in advance of knowing how the fortunes of war might strike them in particular.[4]

It would appear reasonable to assume that the kind of act 'disabling an able-bodied, non-surrendering enemy combatant' is generally deemed conducive towards the materialisation of the kind of belligerent purpose 'weakening the military forces of the enemy'.[5] In other words, it would appear reasonable to stipulate the material military necessity of this kind of belligerent conduct. Stipulated thus, should IHL have any reason to

[2] Sibylle Scheipers, 'Introduction: Prisoners of War' in Sibylle Scheipers (ed), *Prisoners in War* (Oxford: Oxford University Press, 2010) 1, pp. 7–8; Office of General Counsel, *Law of War Manual*, p. 58.

[3] Article 5, Regulations Respecting the Laws and Customs of War on Land, annexed to Convention (IV) Respecting the Laws and Customs of War on Land, 18 October 1907, in force 26 January 1910 (hereinafter Hague Regulations [1907]); Article 21, Geneva Convention Relative to the Treatment of Prisoners of War, 12 August 1949, in force 21 October 1950, 75 UNTS 135 (hereinafter Geneva Convention III). But see Article 41(3), Additional Protocol I.

[4] RB Brandt, 'Utilitarianism and the Rules of War' (1972) 1 *Philosophy and Public Affairs* 145, at 151.

[5] This is the premise upon which the 1868 St. Petersburg Declaration rests. Declaration Renouncing the Use, in Time of War, of Explosive Projectiles Under 400 Grammes Weight, 11 December 1868, in force 11 December 1868 (hereinafter St. Petersburg Declaration).

obligate, permit, restrict or prohibit it? To use another example, it may be argued that 'destroying property in occupied territory' is a kind of belligerent conduct that in principle lacks material military necessity. Would this arguable material military non-necessity furnish IHL framers with any reason to obligate, permit, restrict or prohibit the kind of belligerent conduct in question?[6]

Normative military necessity refers to this reason-giving function[7] that stipulated material military necessity or non-necessity acquires in IHL norm-creation. It should be noted that military necessity is only one of many considerations that the framers of IHL rules would take into account.[8] Other reason-giving considerations include humanity, chivalry, fairness, justice, good faith, reciprocal self-interest, sovereignty, economic gain, religious beliefs, culture and the like. The following pages elucidate in greater detail the interplay between normative military necessity and humanity as weighty reason-giving considerations in IHL norm-creation.[9]

[6] Unless otherwise noted, whenever the remainder of Part III refers to 'conduct', it refers to the *kind* of conduct rather than its *instance*. The same goes for 'purposes' and 'circumstances'.

[7] Or, 'legislative policy' as Diane A. Desierto puts it. Desierto, *Necessity and National Emergency Clauses*, p. 326.

[8] Janina Dill and Henry Shue, 'Limiting the Killing in War: Military Necessity and the St. Petersburg Assumption' (2013) 26 *Ethics & International Affairs* 311.

[9] *Shimoda v State*, Case No. 2,914 (wa) of 1955 and Case No. 4,177 (wa) of 1957, Tokyo District Court, 7 December 1963, in 8 *Japanese Annual of International Law* 212 (1964), at 240; Yoram Dinstein, *The Conduct of Hostilities under the Law of International Armed Conflict*, 2nd edn (Cambridge: Cambridge University Press, 2010), pp. 4–5; Claude Pilloud and Jean Pictet, 'Article 57 – Precautions in Attack' in Yves Sandoz et al. (eds), *Commentary on the Additional Protocols of 8 June 1977 to the Geneva Conventions of 12 August 1949* (Geneva: International Committee of the Red Cross and Martinus Nijhoff Publishers, 1987) 677, p. 683; Schwarzenberger, *International Law as Applied by Courts and Tribunals* (vol. II), p. 135; GIAD Draper, 'Military Necessity and Humanitarian Imperatives' (1973) 12 *Military Law and Law of War Review* 129, at 141; Nico Keijzer, 'Réponses à la Question 2' (2000) 33 *Revue belge de droit international* 440, at 442; Marco Pertile, 'Legal Consequences of the Construction of a Wall in the Occupied Palestinian Territory: A Missed Opportunity for International Humanitarian Law?' (2004) 14 *Italian Yearbook of International Law* 121, at 149–50; Yoram Dinstein, 'Military Necessity', *Max Planck Encyclopedia of Public International Law* (2009). According to Riccardo Mazzeschi, Enzo Cannizzaro holds the view that weighing military necessity vis-à-vis humanitarian considerations is what the principle of proportionality entails in a unitary system of international law. Riccardo Pisillo Mazzeschi, 'Book Review: Il principio della proporzionalità nell'ordinamento internazionale' (2002) 13 *European Journal of International Law* 1031, at 1034 (reviewing Enzo Cannizzaro, *Il principio della proporzionalità nell'ordinamento internazionale* [Milano: Giuffrè, 2000]).

4.2 Necessity, Evil and Legitimacy

War being a necessary evil par excellence,[10] it may be felt that anything that is unnecessary in it would *ipso facto* be evil and therefore illegitimate. That is not so. Things in war can be neither necessary nor evil; nor need those that are unnecessary always be illegitimate. This chapter will show that the mere fact that a particular belligerent act is deemed lacking in material military necessity for its legitimate military purpose does not mean that the act becomes illegitimate *for that reason alone.* In IHL norm-creation, material military necessity or non-necessity is indeed an element in the legitimacy modification of an act that is seen as evil. It will be argued, however, that it is not an element in the legitimacy modification of *any* belligerent act, much less an act that is considered un-evil.

Here, one detects two sets of reference points. The first set is the legitimacy or illegitimacy of the military purpose that the actor seeks to attain. It would be fair to say that the illegitimacy of a purpose, once established, predetermines the illegitimacy of any act taken for it. This act's illegitimacy would remain unaffected even if it were deemed materially necessary in order to achieve that purpose.

An act's legitimacy is not a foregone conclusion, however, where its military purpose is legitimate. The act's legitimacy or illegitimacy would rather depend on a second set of reference points. This set consists of the various combinations between the act's evil or non-evil, on the one hand, and its material military necessity or non-necessity for the purpose's achievement, on the other.

Normative military necessity does offer weighty reasons for the particular manner in which the framers of IHL decide to formulate its rules. Nevertheless, the reasons that this necessity offers are not conclusive. The mere fact that certain behaviour is considered consistent with material military necessity does not necessarily mean that it becomes legitimate, or that IHL framers would make it lawful. Nor, more importantly here, does the mere fact that certain conduct is deemed materially unnecessary perforce mean that it becomes illegitimate or that it would be forbidden.

4.3 Purpose vis-à-vis Conduct

Let us first consider how the legitimacy of a military purpose may or may not affect the legitimacy of a belligerent act taken for its fulfilment.

[10] Jimmy Carter, 'Nobel Lecture', 10 December 2002.

The act's illegitimacy inevitably follows wherever the purpose is illegitimate. Questions of material military necessity no longer matter to such an act. Where the purpose itself is legitimate, evaluating the act's legitimacy requires looking into the interplay between the material military necessity with which the act may or may not be consistent and the evil that it may or may not entail.

4.3.1 *Where the Purpose Sought Is Illegitimate*

The idea that, where the purpose is illegitimate, whatever is done in its pursuit is likewise illegitimate[11] seems intuitively sound. Thomson argues:

> Suppose V_{act}-1-ing and V_{act}-2-ing are two distinct act-kinds. Let us ask what the conditions are under which the following is true: A ought not V_{act}-1 in order to V_{act}-2. One thing that would plainly make it true is its being the case that A ought not V_{act}-1. (If you ought not do a thing, then a fortiori, you ought not do it in order to bring such and such about.) I suggest that there is one other thing that would make it true, namely its being the case that A ought not V_{act}-2. (If you ought not bring such and such about, then you ought not try to.) In sum, I suggest that we should accept: For it to be the case that A ought not V_{act}-1 in order to V_{act}-2 is for the following to be the case: either A ought not V_{act}-1, or A ought not V_{act}-2.[12]

At issue here is Thomson's second consideration. Thus, the truth of 'A ought not V_{act}-2' is a sufficient condition, though not a necessary condition, for the truth of 'A ought not V_{act}-1'. In other words, whenever 'A ought not V_{act}-2' is true, 'A ought not V_{act}-1' is also true.

In his criticism of what Lon Fuller termed 'internal morality of law',[13] Hart observed that it is vital to distinguish between purposive activity and morality:

> Poisoning is no doubt a purposive activity, and reflections on its purpose may show that it has its internal principles. ('Avoid poisons however lethal if they cause the victim to vomit', or 'Avoid poisons however lethal if their shape, color, or size is likely to attract notice.') But to call these principles of the poisoner's art 'the morality of poisoning' would simply

[11] Henry Shue, 'Civilian Protection and Force Protection' in Whetham (ed), *Ethics, Law and Military Operations* 135, p. 137.

[12] Thomson, *Normativity*, p. 222.

[13] Lon L Fuller, *The Morality of Law*, rev. edn (New Haven: Yale University Press, 1969), p. 4.

> blur the distinction between the notion of efficiency for a purpose and those final judgments about activities and purposes with which morality in its various forms is concerned.[14]

Thomson's 'V_{act}-2' would correspond to Hart's 'poison the victim', and 'V_{act}-1' to 'avoid poisons however lethal if they cause the victim to vomit' and the like. Let 'V_{act}-1*bis*' denote 'choose and administer only that kind and amount of poison, and only in such a manner, so as to poison the victim effectively'. Once it is accepted that 'A ought not to poison B', it follows that 'A ought not to choose and administer that kind and amount of poison in such a manner so as to poison B effectively'.

Albeit in a slightly different context of justificatory self-defence, Walzer senses the same normative consequence that the illegitimacy of a purpose has on an agent's action:

> In the course of a bank robbery, a thief shoots a guard reaching for his gun. The thief is guilty of murder, even if he claims that he acted in self-defense. Since he had no right to rob the bank, he also had no right to defend himself against the bank's defenders. He is no less guilty for killing the guard than he would be for killing an unarmed bystander ... The thief's associates might praise him for the first killing, which was in their terms necessary ... But we won't judge him in that way, because the idea of necessity doesn't apply to criminal activity: it was not necessary to rob the bank in the first place.[15]

The same may be said, *mutatis mutandis*, of belligerent conduct. According to the 1868 St. Petersburg Declaration, 'the only legitimate object which States should endeavor to accomplish during war is to weaken the military forces of the enemy'.[16] The declaration delegitimises any object in war – no matter how rational it may otherwise be – that is *not* concerned with weakening the military forces of the enemy. In other words, the declaration delegitimises any purpose that is more or other than the weakening of the military forces of the enemy.[17] It would follow,

[14] HLA Hart, 'Book Review' (1965) 78 *Harvard Law Review* 1281, at 1286 (reviewing Lon L Fuller, *The Morality of Law* [New Haven: Yale University Press, 1964]). See also HLA Hart, 'Lon L. Fuller: The Morality of Law' in HLA Hart, *Essays in Jurisprudence and Philosophy* (Oxford: Oxford University Press, 1983) 343, p. 350.

[15] Walzer, *Just and Unjust Wars*, p. 128.

[16] Preamble, St. Petersburg Declaration. For a similar but broader formulation, see Final Protocol of the Brussels Conference of 1874, 27 August 1874 (hereinafter Brussels Declaration): 'the only legitimate object which States should have in view during war is to weaken the enemy without inflicting upon him unnecessary suffering'.

[17] Understood thus, illegitimate purposes would include strictly personal gain, *Lebensraum*, racial extermination and so on.

then, that any belligerent action taken in pursuit of such an illegitimate purpose in war is similarly illegitimate, even if it is otherwise deemed consistent with material military necessity.

It might be thought that the same reasoning would, or should, subsume the legitimacy of an act *in bello* to the legitimacy of an end *ad bellum*. Whether the strict separation between *jus ad bellum* and *jus in bello* is always or everywhere advisable is an issue that is highly contentious but not addressed further in this book.[18] Suffice it to note here that contemporary *jus in bello* does not yet appear to have reached that stage of subsumption.[19]

18 JHH Weiler and Abby Deshman, 'Far Be It from Thee to Slay the Righteous with the Wicked: An Historical and Historiographical Sketch of the Bellicose Debate Concerning the Distinction between *Jus ad Bellum* and *Jus in Bello*' (2013) 24 *European Journal of International Law* 25; Marko Milanović, 'A Non-response to Weiler and Deshman' (2013) 24 *European Journal of International Law* 63; Terry D Gill, 'Some Considerations Concerning the Role of *Ius ad Bellum* in Targeting' in Paul AL Ducheine, Michael N Schmitt and Frans PB Osinga (eds), *Targeting: The Challenges of Modern Warfare* (The Hague: TMC Asser Press, 2016) 101. At one end, in favour of maintaining the traditional separation, are Jasmine Moussa, 'Can *Jus ad Bellum* Override *Jus in Bello*? Reaffirming the Separation of the Two Bodies of Law' (2008) 90 *International Review of the Red Cross* 963; Jasmine Moussa, 'Nuclear Weapons and the Separation of *Jus ad Bellum* and *Jus in Bello*' in Gro Nystuen et al. (eds), *Nuclear Weapons under International Law* (Cambridge: Cambridge University Press, 2014) 59; Robert Kolb and Richard Hyde, *An Introduction to the International Law of Armed Conflict* (Oxford and Portland: Hart Publishing, 2008), pp. 21–27; Adam Roberts, 'The Equal Application of the Laws of War: A Principle under Pressure' (2008) 90 *International Review of the Red Cross* 931; Adam Roberts, 'The Principle of Equal Application of the Laws of War' in David Rodin and Henry Shue (eds), *Just and Unjust Warriors: The Moral and Legal Status of Soldiers* (Oxford: Oxford University Press, 2008) 226; Robert D Sloane, 'The Cost of Conflation: Preserving the Dualism of *Jus ad Bellum* and *Jus in Bello* in the Contemporary Law of War' (2009) 34 *Yale Journal of International Law* 47; Laurie Blank, 'A New Twist on an Old Story: Lawfare and the Mixing of Proportionalities' (2010–2011) 43 *Case Western Reserve Journal of International Law* 707. Those at the other end include Jeff McMahan, *Killing in War* (Oxford: Oxford University Press, 2009); Anthony Coates, 'Is the Independent Application of *Jus in Bello* the Way To Limit War?' in Rodin and Shue (eds), *Just and Unjust Warriors* 176; Christopher Kutz, 'Fearful Symmetry' in Rodin and Shue (eds), *Just and Unjust Warriors* 69; Jeff McMahan, 'The Morality of War and the Law of War' in Rodin and Shue (eds), *Just and Unjust Warriors* 19; David Rodin, 'The Moral Inequality of Soldiers: Why *Jus in Bello* Asymmetry Is Half Right' in Rodin and Shue (eds), *Just and Unjust Warriors* 44; Rotem M Giladi, 'Reflections on Proportionality, Military Necessity and the Clausewitzian War' (2012) 45 *Israel Law Review* 323.

19 O'Brien, 'Meaning of Military Necessity', at 142–44. De Menthon, a French prosecutor at Nuremberg, made unsuccessful assertions to this effect. It was a popular theme among Allied prosecutors in various other post-World War II war crimes trials as well.

4.3.2 *Where the Purpose Sought Is Legitimate*

The situation changes where the military purpose is legitimate. Thomson appears ambivalent about what role, if any, a legitimate purpose plays in the legitimacy or otherwise of the conduct chosen:

> Are there also truths of the form: A ought to V_{act}-1 in order to V_{act}-2? Alice ought not give her child an alpha-pill in order to kill it. Ought she give her child an alpha-pill in order to cure it? I don't myself think it matters much to what she ought to do for what V_{act}-2-ing it is such that she gives her child an alpha-pill in order to V_{act}-2, so long as it is not the case that she ought not V_{act}-2. (Though it might well matter to our assessment of how good a mother she is.) But others may think otherwise, and I therefore leave it open.[20]

Here, the familiar adage – 'the end justifies the means' – comes to mind. It may be said that this adage embodies utilitarian thinking. According to one commentator: 'Classical utilitarianism . . . states that morally just is that course of action that creates the greatest amount of good for the largest number of people. When an agent considers his options, he is obligated to choose that option, which leads to this result.'[21]

It is not our purpose to explore the philosophical terrain of utilitarianism. Of interest here is rather the specific manners in which military necessity reveals its relationship to utilitarianism in IHL norm-creation. Five such manners may be highlighted.[22] The first is utilitarianism's normative relation to *jus ad bellum* that we noted above. Ultimately, espousing thoroughgoing utilitarianism[23] would amount to abandoning the separation between *jus ad bellum* and *jus in bello*, and to subsuming all questions of *jus in bello* under those of *jus ad bellum*. For the outcome of this version of utilitarian thinking would be that *any* belligerent conduct that is materially necessary for victory in a just war is *ipso facto* legitimate; and that, contrariwise, *any*

[20] Thomson, *Normativity*, pp. 222–23.

[21] ThA van Baarda, 'Moral Ambiguities Underlying the Laws of Armed Conflict: A Perspective from Military Ethics' (2008) 11 *Yearbook of International Humanitarian Law* 3, at 5–6.

[22] Admittedly, there are also ways in which utilitarianism becomes relevant to IHL in addition to those discussed here. Ibid, at 10–12.

[23] In other words, utilitarianism that is neither of a rule-based variety, nor of a variety to which side constraints are attached. See below.

belligerent act that is materially unnecessary for victory in a just war is *ipso facto* illegitimate.

Here, brief mention may be made of the *Nuclear Weapons Advisory Opinion* rendered by the International Court of Justice (ICJ) in 1996.[24] This opinion contains a controversial disclaimer:

> [I]n view of the current state of international law ... the Court cannot conclude definitively whether the threat or use of nuclear weapons would be lawful or unlawful in an extreme circumstance of self-defence, in which the very survival of a State would be at stake.[25]

Commentators note with concern that this passage may leave open the possibility that the lawfulness *ad bellum* of use or threat of armed force in extreme self-defence may effectively set its unlawfulness *in bello* aside.[26]

Second, strictly within *jus in bello*, unfettered utilitarianism would assert that every kind of belligerent conduct that is conducive to military success maximises utility and therefore merits IHL protection or promotion. Conversely, every kind of material military non-necessity would represent disutility that IHL should prohibit or restrict.[27]

As will be seen below, IHL norm-creation appears to take the intrinsic utility of material military necessity seriously, though not conclusively. What it does *not* do, at any rate, is to treat material military non-necessity

[24] *Legality of the Threat or Force of Nuclear Weapons, Advisory Opinion, ICJ Reports 1996*, p. 226.

[25] Ibid, para. 105(2)(E).

[26] Ibid, *Separate Opinion of Judge Fleischhauer*, p. 305, paras 2–3; ibid, *Dissenting Opinion of Judge Higgins*, p. 583, paras 28–29; Rein Müllerson, 'On the Relationship between *Jus ad Bellum* and *Jus in Bello* in the General Assembly Advisory Opinion' in Laurence Boisson de Chazournes and Philippe Sands (eds), *International Law, the International Court of Justice and Nuclear Weapons* (Cambridge: Cambridge University Press, 1999) 267, pp. 268–72; Judith Gardam, 'Necessity and Proportionality in *Jus ad Bellum* and *Jus in Bello*' in Boisson de Chazournes and Sands (eds), *International Law, the International Court of Justice and Nuclear Weapons* 275, pp. 289–91; Luigi Condorelli, 'Nuclear Weapons: A Weighty Matter for the International Court of Justice – Jura Non Novit Curia?' (1997) 37 *International Review of the Red Cross* 9; Stefan Kandelbach, 'Nuclear Weapons and Warfare', *Max Planck Encyclopedia of Public International Law* (2009), para. 47; Michael Bothe, 'Nuclear Weapons Advisory Opinions', *Max Planck Encyclopedia of Public International Law* (2011), para. 19. But see Christopher Greenwood, '*Jus ad Bellum* and *Jus in Bello* in the Nuclear Weapons Advisory Opinion' in Boisson de Chazournes and Sands (eds), *International Law, the International Court of Justice and Nuclear Weapons* 247, pp. 263–64.

[27] Eric David, *Principes de Droit des conflits armés*, 3rd edn (Bruxelles: Bruylant, 2002), p. 273; Dill and Shue, 'Limiting the Killing in War', at 320.

as an intrinsic disutility that should be prohibited or restricted.[28] It is more likely that IHL is a system of norms in which the relationship between pursuing legitimate purposes and taking militarily necessary actions is characterised by a form of rule-utilitarianism,[29] or a form of utilitarianism to which what Robert Nozik calls 'side constraints'[30] are attached.[31]

The third way in which utilitarian thinking becomes relevant to IHL is in the law's relation to *Kriegsräson*. Simply put, *Kriegsräson*'s rationale is that a great deal of evil may need to be endured for a greatly important end in war, and that law cannot meaningfully – or should not, in any event – pre-empt high-utility actions. Holding otherwise, in Larry May's words, would amount to being a 'rule fetishist'.[32] Martti Koskenniemi explains this rationale thus:

> If . . . it is pragmatically unthinkable that a statesman might be deterred from using the weapon in a situation of extreme national danger (for instance, in order to prevent the killing of his or her innocent compatriots) merely because of what the legal adviser might say, then an opinion [such as *Nuclear Weapons*] underwriting such an absolute prohibition would have condemned the law to irrelevance already in advance.[33]

Koskenniemi continues:

> But I cannot see such an absolute rule as rationally justifiable either (or, indeed, justifiable by reference to recent history of warfare). If the law's purpose is to protect the innocent (and it is hard to see a more basic purpose for it in a system that excludes reference to personal virtue), and the launching of a nuclear strike would be the only means to attain this, then I cannot see how it could be excluded. In this sense, at least *prima facie*, the use of nuclear weapons in self-defence could not be excluded.[34]

[28] APV Rogers, 'What Is a Legitimate Military Target?' in Richard Burchill et al. (eds), *International Conflict and Security Law: Essays in Memory of Hilaire McCoubrey* (Cambridge: Cambridge University Press, 2005) 160, p. 177.

[29] Brandt, 'Utilitarianism', at 146–47.

[30] Robert Nozik, *Anarchy, State, and Utopia* (New York: Basic Books, 1974), p. 29.

[31] Shue, 'Civilian Protection and Force Protection', at 136.

[32] Larry May, *War Crimes and Just War* (New York: Cambridge University Press, 2007), pp. 196–97. But see Walzer, *Just and Unjust Wars*, pp. 251–63.

[33] Martti Koskenniemi, 'Faith, Identity, and the Killing of the Innocent: International Lawyers and Nuclear Weapons' (1997) 10 *Leiden Journal of International Law* 137, at 142.

[34] Ibid, at 145–46 (emphasis in original; footnote omitted).

Plainly, the utilitarian rationale implicit in *Kriegsräson* – although certainly *not* the doctrine's notorious *modus operandi* – is present in the very idea of regulating belligerent conduct through norms.[35] IHL norm-creation is a process that is well placed to deal with, and indeed contains, such a rationale.[36] This process is driven by IHL framers' desire to reduce, as far as possible, the range of belligerent conduct whose compliance or non-compliance with the law is left to a crude utilitarian interest-balancing exercise done by the law's addressees.[37]

Fourth, *reducing* this range is not the same as *eliminating* it altogether. Unsatisfactory as it may be, some rules of positive IHL amount to little more than what Nigel Simmonds calls 'a residual provision' that creates 'a general legal duty always to act for the greater good'.[38] Gary D. Solis explains: 'In these allowances, terms like "if possible," "as far as possible," and "if urgent," introduce elements of uncertainty and risks of arbitrary conduct. Without these concessions, which take reality into account, the allowances could not have been formulated and approved in the first place.'[39]

This residual utility-maximising duty has been variously described in ethics as the 'principle of double effect'[40] and the 'principle of double intention'.[41] The manner in which IHL deals

[35] Frits Kalshoven, 'Grotius' *Jus in Bello*, with Special Reference to Ruses of War and Perfidy' in Frits Kalshoven, *Reflections on the Law of War: Collected Essays* (Leiden and Boston: Martinus Nijhoff, 2007) 327, pp. 327–28. What is at stake in the context of IHL norm-creation is not so much *Kriegsräson*'s actual operation. The latter is a matter discussed in greater detail below, in connection with the invocation of military necessity considerations against absolute prohibitions of positive IHL. See Chapter 8.

[36] NE Simmonds, *Central Issues in Jurisprudence: Justice, Law and Rights*, 2nd edn (London: Sweet & Maxwell, 2002), pp. 37–40; Manuel Atienza, 'Reasoning and Legislation' in Luc J Wintgens et al. (eds), *The Theory and Practice of Legislation: Essays in Legisprudence* (London and New York: Routledge, 2005) 297, pp. 303–04.

[37] Simmonds, *Central Issues*, pp. 37–40.

[38] Ibid, p. 39. See also Schmitt, 'Military Necessity and Humanity', at 804–05.

[39] Solis, *Law of Armed Conflict*, p. 269.

[40] Henry Sidgwick, *The Elements of Politics* (London and New York: Macmillan and Co., 1891), p. 254; Joseph T Mangan, 'An Historical Analysis of the Principle of Double Effect' (1949) 10 *Theological Studies* 41, at 43; James F Keenan, 'The Function of the Principle of Double Effect' (1993) 54 *Theological Studies* 294; Colm McKeogh, *Innocent Civilians: The Morality of Killing in War* (London: Palgrave and Macmillan, 2002), pp. 64–65; Walzer, *Just and Unjust Wars*, p. 153; Noam Neuman, 'Applying the Rule of Proportionality: Force Protection and Cumulative Assessment in International Law and Morality' (2004) 7 *Yearbook of International Humanitarian Law* 79, at 104–05.

[41] Walzer, *Just and Unjust Wars*, pp. 155–56.

with attacks in hostilities exemplifies how such a principle operates on the ground.[42]

Fifth, humanity appears to occupy an increasingly privileged place in the utility calculus of IHL. This idea found its first treaty expression in the St. Petersburg Declaration.[43] Hague Convention II (1899) struck a somewhat less enthusiastic tone by stressing the parameters of military requirements within which war's evils would be diminished, rather than the other way around.[44] Humanity's prominence has since gained traction, however. The ICJ held:

> Certainly, as the Court has already indicated, the principles and rules of law applicable in armed conflict – at the heart of which is the overriding consideration of humanity – make the conduct of armed hostilities subject to a number of strict requirements.[45]

This sentiment is echoed in the historic *Tadić* Jurisdiction Decision that the ICTY Appeals Chamber issued in 1995:

> [T]he impetuous development and propagation in the international community of human rights doctrines, particularly after the adoption of the Universal Declaration of Human Rights in 1948, has brought about significant changes in international law, notably in the approach to problems besetting the world community. A State-sovereignty-oriented approach has been gradually supplanted by a human-being-oriented approach. Gradually the maxim of Roman law *hominum causa omne jus constitutum est* (all law is created for the benefit of human beings) has gained a firm foothold in the international community as well.[46]

[42] Articles 51(5)(b), 57(2)(a)(iii), 57(2)(b), Additional Protocol I; Neuman, 'Force Protection and Cumulative Assessment', at 102–05; Kenneth Watkin, 'Assessing Proportionality: Moral Complexity and Legal Rules' (2005) 8 *Yearbook of International Humanitarian Law* 3, at 26–30; Schmitt, 'Military Necessity and Humanity', at 804–05.

[43] St. Petersburg Declaration: '[T]he progress of civilization should have the effect of alleviating as much as possible the calamities of war . . .'

[44] Convention (II) with Respect to the Laws and Customs of War on Land, 29 July 1899, in force 4 September 1900 (hereinafter Hague Convention II [1899]). Its provisions had been 'inspired by the desire to diminish the evils of war so far as military necessities permit'.

[45] *Nuclear Weapons*, para. 95.

[46] *Prosecutor v Duško Tadić a/k/a 'Dule'*, Case No. IT-94-1, *Decision on the Defence Motion for Interlocutory Appeal on Jurisdiction*, 2 October 1995 (hereinafter *Tadić Jurisdiction Decision*), para. 97.

International manuals[47] and scholarly works[48] concur. The celebrated Martens Clause[49] anchors humanity's relevance in IHL norm-creation, although the clause's precise role therein remains a matter of debate.[50]

47 San Remo Manual on International Law Applicable to Armed Conflicts at Sea, 12 June 1994 (hereinafter San Remo Manual on Maritime Warfare), para. 2; Manual on International Law Applicable to Air and Missile Warfare, 15 May 2009 (hereinafter Manual on Air and Missile Warfare), para. 2(c). See also Louise Doswald-Beck (ed), *San Remo Manual on International Law Applicable to Armed Conflicts at Sea* (Cambridge: Cambridge University Press, 1995), p. 74; Program on Humanitarian Policy and Conflict Research, *Commentary on the HPCR Manual on International Law Applicable to Air and Missile Warfare* (Cambridge, MA: Harvard University, 2010), pp. 59–60.

48 Hersch Lauterpacht, 'The Problem of the Revision of the Law of War' (1952) 29 *British Yearbook of International Law* 360, at 363–64; Theodor Meron, 'The Humanization of Humanitarian Law' (2000) 94 *American Journal of International Law* 239, at 243; Emily Camins, 'The Past as Prologue: The Development of the "Direct Participation" Exception to Civilian Immunity' (2008) 90 *International Review of the Red Cross* 853, at 878–89; May, *War Crimes and Just War*, pp. 53–57, 67–90; Robert Kolb, 'The Main Epochs of Modern International Humanitarian Law Since 1864 and Their Related Dominant Legal Constructions' in Kjetil Mujezinović Larsen et al. (eds), *Searching for a 'Principle of Humanity' in International Humanitarian Law* (Cambridge: Cambridge University Press, 2013) 23, pp. 52–55.

49 See the preambles of various instruments in which the Martens Clause appears, e.g., Hague Convention II (1899); Hague Convention IV (1907); Protocol Additional to the Geneva Conventions of 12 August 1949, and Relating to the Protection of Victims of Non-international Armed Conflicts (Protocol II), 8 June 1977, in force 7 December 1978, 1125 UNTS 609 (hereinafter Additional Protocol II); Convention on Prohibitions or Restrictions on the Use of Certain Conventional Weapons Which May Be Deemed to Be Excessively Injurious or To Have Indiscriminate Effects, 10 October 1980, in force 2 December 1983, 1342 UNTS 137 (hereinafter Conventional Weapons Convention); Convention on Cluster Munitions, 30 May 2008, in force 1 August 2010, 2688 UNTS 39. See also, e.g., Article 63, Geneva Convention for the Amelioration of the Condition of the Wounded and Sick in Armed Forces in the Field, 12 August 1949, in force 21 October 1950, 75 UNTS 31 (hereinafter Geneva Convention I); Article 62, Geneva Convention for the Amelioration of the Condition of Wounded, Sick and Shipwrecked Members of Armed Forces at Sea, 12 August 1949, in force 21 October 1950, 75 UNTS 85 (hereinafter Geneva Convention II); Article 142, Geneva Convention III; Article 158, Geneva Convention Relative to the Protection of Civilian Persons in Time of War, 12 August 1949, in force 21 October 1950, 75 UNTS 287 (hereinafter Geneva Convention IV); Article 1(2), Additional Protocol I.

50 See Chapter 7. See also Shigeki Miyazaki, 'The Martens Clause and International Humanitarian Law' in Christophe Swinarski (ed), *Studies and Essays on International Humanitarian Law and Red Cross Principles in Honour of Jean Pictet* (Geneva and The Hague: International Committee of the Red Cross and Martinus Nijhoff, 1984) 432; Antonio Cassese, 'The Martens Clause: Half a Loaf or Simply Pie in the Sky?' (2000) 11 *European Journal of International Law* 187; Theodor Meron, 'The Martens Clause, Principles of Humanity, and Dictates of Public Conscience' (2000) 94 *American Journal of International Law* 78; Dinstein, *Conduct of Hostilities*, 2nd edn, pp. 8–9; Schmitt, 'Military Necessity and Humanity', at 800–01; Kolb and R Hyde, *International Law of*

Thus, for instance, a net increase in humanity – or a net reduction in inhumanity, as the case may be – is sometimes considered weightier[51] than, say, a net increase in the satisfaction of other considerations such as material military necessity and sovereignty. The military necessity–humanity interplay in the process of IHL norm-creation is a complex one that we will investigate in Chapter 7.

What follows now is a detailed assessment of the relationship *in bello* between legitimate purposes and the legitimacy or illegitimacy of various kinds of belligerent conduct taken to fulfil them.

4.4 Conduct vis-à-vis Purpose

As noted earlier, the purpose's legitimacy subjects the legitimacy or illegitimacy of the conduct to two reference points. They are, respectively, whether the conduct itself is seen as evil or un-evil, and whether it is deemed materially necessary or unnecessary for that purpose.

These two reference points can be combined in four ways, namely:

1. The conduct is deemed evil yet consistent with material military necessity;
2. The conduct is deemed evil and lacking in material military necessity;
3. The conduct is deemed un-evil and consistent with material military necessity; and
4. The conduct is deemed un-evil and lacking in material military necessity.

Let us examine these in turn.

4.4.1 The Conduct Is Deemed Evil

Where an act is deemed evil, its material military necessity or non-necessity is indeed one element in the act's legitimacy modification.

Let us assume for the moment that this evil act is necessary for the attainment of its legitimate purpose. Our reasoning here would proceed, roughly, as follows. We would compare the urge to reduce the evil this

Armed Conflict, p. 63; Jochen von Bernstorff, 'Martens Clause', *Max Planck Encyclopedia of Public International Law* (2009); MN Hayashi, 'Martens Clause and Military Necessity'.

51 Jean de Preux, 'Article 35 – Basic Rules' in Sandoz et al. (eds), *Commentary on Additional Protocols* 389, p. 395.

act entails, on the one hand, and the *ex hypothesi* concession that the act is materially necessary, on the other. Should the act's material military necessity outweigh its evil, its claim to legitimacy would strengthen. Conversely, if the act were more evil than necessary, its claim to legitimacy would diminish. Should the relative weight be indeterminate, the act's legitimacy would remain uncertain.

In contrast, an act that is deemed evil and lacking in material military necessity is plainly illegitimate. For unnecessary evil is evil *simpliciter*, and evil *simpliciter* is illegitimate. Crucially, even in such cases, the act's illegitimacy does *not* emanate from its non-necessity. Rather, the act's illegitimacy emanates from its evil, an evil that is now laid bare and unmitigated by considerations of military necessity.

Let an axiomatic example illustrate this reasoning. In his autobiography, Raleigh Trevelyan, a British Army veteran during World War II, recalled an encounter with a German soldier:

> There was a wonderfully vulgar sunshine. Everything was the colour of pink geraniums, and birds were singing. We felt like Noah must have done when he saw his rainbow. Suddenly Viner pointed across the stretch of scrubby heath. An individual, dressed in German uniform, was wandering like a sleep-walker across our line of fire. It was clear that for the moment he had forgotten war, and – as we had been doing – was revelling in the promise of warmth and spring. 'Shall I bump him off?' asked Viner, without a note of expression in his voice. I had to decide quickly. 'No,' I replied, 'just scare him away.' Viner aimed above the man's head, and fired. The Jerry turned for a moment or two, stared at us with mouth open, then went bounding through the trees, waving his rifle above his head. 'Another bomb-happy,' said Bishop, who happened to be standing by us, and he gave him a parting shot. Only Sergeant Chesterton didn't laugh. He said that we should have killed the fellow, since his friends would now be told precisely where our trenches were.[52]

Sergeant Chesterton thought the German soldier should have been killed. Here, Chesterton's purpose might be formulated as 'keeping the location of his unit's trenches concealed from the Germans'.[53] With a view to accomplishing this purpose, he advocated a particular act, namely, 'shooting to kill the German soldier who had noticed the unit's presence'. Here, the corresponding *kinds* of purpose and act would be

[52] Raleigh Trevelyan, *The Fortress: A Dairy of Anzio & After* (Glasgow: Collins, 1956), p. 23. See also Walzer, *Just and Unjust Wars*, pp. 140–41.

[53] Note here that we are *not* treating 'disabling the German soldier' as Chesterton's purpose.

'keeping the location of the trenches of one's unit concealed from the enemy',[54] and 'shooting to kill an enemy combatant who has noticed the presence of one's unit', respectively.

It would appear that this kind of purpose, so formulated, is legitimate. Also, as phrased, the kind of act in question would seem clearly evil, insofar as it involves the taking of human life. The variable that remains to be fixed is whether this kind of act would be deemed consistent with or lacking in material military necessity for the kind of purpose at issue.

4.4.1.1 The Conduct Is Deemed Evil yet Necessary

Suppose now that, as was apparently the case in the episode, the German soldier was able-bodied and not offering to surrender. In other words, he was not *hors de combat* at the time.[55]

Arguably, the act that Chesterton advocated, i.e., 'shooting to kill the German soldier who had noticed the presence of Chesterton's unit and was not placed *hors de combat* at that particular moment', was materially necessary in order to achieve his purpose. Similarly, the corresponding kind of act, i.e., 'shooting to kill an enemy combatant who has noticed the presence of one's unit and is not placed *hors de combat* at the time', would be deemed materially necessary for the corresponding kind of purpose.

It appears that those involved in IHL norm-creation to date have declined to consider it illegitimate to disable enemy combatants not placed *hors de combat*.[56] Arguably, according to today's positive IHL, it is not unlawful to disable these combatants by way of killing.[57]

This does *not* mean, however, that the material military necessity of any belligerent behaviour always trumps its evil. Marshall Cohen notes:

[54] Similarly, we are *not* treating 'disabling an enemy combatant' as the relevant kind of purpose.

[55] For an indicative treaty definition of a person placed *hors de combat* under IHL, see Article 41, Additional Protocol I. See also Avril McDonald, '*Hors de Combat*: Post-September 11 Challenges to the Rules' in Hensel (ed), *Legitimate Use of Military Force* 219.

[56] Office of General Counsel, *Law of War Manual*, p. 58.

[57] Here, the so-called 'capture rather than kill' debate springs to mind. Some commentators have argued that, where two courses of action equally conducive to the attainment of a military purpose are available, IHL obligates the belligerent to take the one that is less injurious than the other. Moreover, on this view, the belligerent's failure to do so amounts to a breach of the law, even if the law does not separately prohibit the more injurious course of action. See Chapter 8.

> The [Hague] conception permits the interests of humanity to carry enough weight so that they can sometimes inhibit the operation of the principle of military necessity. On this conception, therefore, the appeal to military necessity is by no means always a legitimate one; indeed, it is sometimes plainly ruled out.[58]

The fact that an act is deemed evil yet materially necessary does not settle the matter as to whether it becomes conclusively legitimate or illegitimate. The process of IHL norm-creation involves the weighing of the general value that is, or would be, harmed by the act's evil, and the need for this act to be adopted if the realisation of its legitimate purpose were to be attempted. The existence of this interplay is implied in various parts of IHL.[59]

It may happen that an act's evil outweighs its material military necessity and renders it illegitimate as a result. The unqualified[60] IHL prohibition against torture – underpinning our conviction that even effective tortures are deemed much too cruel to be permitted – is a case in point. It has been suggested that '[w]e do not have to do a cost–benefit analysis to determine whether such [acts] are impermissible in warfare: we already judge such acts to be heinous crimes because of their very nature'.[61]

Conversely, an act's material military necessity may outweigh its evil and render it legitimate as a result. Such is arguably the case, for instance, with Chesterton's suggested action.

4.4.1.2 The Conduct Is Deemed Evil and Unnecessary

Let us now alter the episode somewhat. Assume that the German soldier dropped his rifle, threw his hands up and unambiguously offered to

[58] Marshall Cohen, 'Morality and the Laws of War' in Virginia Held et al. (eds), *Philosophy, Morality, and International Affairs: Essays Edited for the Society of Philosophy and Public Affairs* (New York: Oxford University Press, 1974) 71, p. 74.

[59] For a further discussion on the military–humanity interplay in IHL norm-creation, see Chapter 7.

[60] In this book, the expression 'unqualified' refers to those rules to which no exceptional clauses are attached. IHL rules can be 'unqualified' in a general way, i.e., unqualified by *any* exceptional clauses. Alternatively, IHL rules can be 'unqualified' in a limited way, i.e., qualified by certain exceptional clauses but not, for example, by exceptional clauses emanating from military necessity. See Chapters 8 and 9.

[61] Brian Orend, *The Morality of War* (Toronto: Broadview Press, 2006), p. 123. See also David Whetham, 'The Just War Tradition: A Pragmatic Compromise' in Whetham (ed), *Ethics, Law and Military Operations* 65, p. 82: '[T]he principle of proportionality and also the idea of *mala in se* ... recognizes that some methods of war are simply evil in themselves, and cannot be justified under any circumstances.'

surrender to Chesterton's unit. In effect, he had placed himself *hors de combat* at the time.[62]

Arguably, in those modified circumstances, shooting to kill the German soldier would be materially unnecessary in order to keep the location of the trenches used by Chesterton's unit concealed from the Germans. All else being equal, taking the German prisoner – who would then be removed from the battlefield[63] and detained in the rear area – would be more consistent with material military necessity for Chesterton's unit, than shooting to kill that soldier.[64] That would be so, at a minimum, in view of the ammunitions spared and the German soldier's life saved.[65]

Conversely, given this alternative, shooting to kill the German would be materially wasteful (ammunition-wise) and excessive (death being an externality). The evil entailed by shooting to kill the German soldier remains the same in kind and amount; it is the lethal shooting's material military necessity that now ceases to exist. The evil act has moved from being a material military necessity to being a material military non-necessity for its legitimate purpose.

The corresponding *kind* of belligerent conduct, namely, 'shooting to kill an enemy combatant who has noticed the presence of one's unit and is placed *hors de combat* at the time', would lack material military necessity for the corresponding *kind* of belligerent purpose, namely, 'keeping the location of the trenches used by one's unit concealed from the enemy'. It seems uncontroversial that a kind of act deemed evil and lacking in material military necessity for its otherwise legitimate kind of purpose is plainly illegitimate. According to Michael Schmitt, it is illegitimate to commit 'destructive or harmful acts that are unnecessary to secure a military advantage'.[66] Here, the expression 'destructive or

62 Article 41(2)(b), Additional Protocol I.

63 As required, e.g., by Article 7, Convention Relative to the Treatment of Prisoners of War, 27 July 1929, 19 June 1931 (no longer in force) (hereinafter POW Convention [1929]); Article 19, Geneva Convention III.

64 In this chapter, we are *not* assuming that the conditions of combat in which Chesterton's unit found itself were of the kind covered by Article 41(3) of Additional Protocol I.

65 Admittedly, it is still possible that the German soldier's unexplained and prolonged disappearance might alert his comrades to the potential presence of enemies nearby.

66 Michael N Schmitt, 'Book Review: *Law on the Battlefield*' (1997) 8 *U.S. Air Force Academy Journal of Legal Studies* 255, at 258 (reviewing A.P.V. Rogers, *Law on the Battlefield* [Manchester and New York: Manchester University Press, 1996]). See also Michael N Schmitt, 'Green War: An Assessment of the Environmental Law of International Armed Conflict' (1997) 22 *Yale Journal of International Law* 1, at 52.

harmful' may indicate the evilness of the act taken, and the expression 'unnecessary' the lack of material military necessity for the act's legitimate end.

This idea finds support amongst commentators,[67] as well as a number of national military manuals. Thus, in the words of the *US Navy Commanders' Handbook*:

> [The law's] purpose is to ensure that the violence of hostilities is directed toward the enemy's war efforts and is not used to cause unnecessary human misery and physical destruction. The principle of military necessity recognizes that force resulting in death and destruction will have to be applied to achieve military objectives, but its goal is to limit suffering and destruction to that which is necessary to achieve a valid military objective.[68]

Other manuals treat humanity as effectively rendering unnecessary evil illegitimate.[69]

Where given conduct is considered illegitimate for the evil it entails, and the lack of its material military necessity leaves its illegitimacy unmitigated, the relevant IHL rule would unqualifiedly prohibit it. Such is the case, for example, with the conduct unqualifiedly prohibited under Article 25 of the 1907 Hague Regulations. This article stipulates that '[t]he attack or bombardment, by whatever means, of towns, villages, dwellings, or buildings which are undefended is prohibited'.[70] According to the United Kingdom (UK)'s *Joint Service Manual*:

[67] Geoffrey Best, *War and Law Since 1945* (Oxford: Clarendon Press, 1994), p. 242; de Preux, 'Basic Rules', p. 396; Archer Polson, *Principles of the Law of Nations, with Practical Notes and Supplementary Essays on the Law of Blockade and on Contraband of War* (London: Griffin, 1853), p. 42; Bill Rhodes, *An Introduction to Military Ethics: A Reference Handbook* (Sanda Barbara, Denver and Oxford: Praeger Security International, 2009), p. 105; Sidgwick, *Elements of Politics*, pp. 255, 257; Solis, *Law of Armed Conflict*, p. 258; Telford Taylor, *Nuremberg and Vietnam: An American Tragedy* (Chicago: Quadrangle Books, 1970), p. 20; Draper, 'Military Necessity and Humanitarian Imperatives', at 135; Waldemar A Solf, 'Protection of Civilians Against the Effects of Hostilities under Customary International Law and Protocol I' (1986) 1 *American University Journal of International Law and Policy* 117, at 117; Richard Wasserstrom, 'The Responsibility of the Individual for War Crimes' in Held et al. (eds), *Philosophy, Morality, and International Affairs* 47, p. 49; William H Boothby, *The Law of Targeting* (Oxford: Oxford University Press, 2012), p. 60.

[68] US Department of the Navy et al., *The Commander's Handbook on the Law of Naval Operations* (2007), p. 5-2.

[69] Canadian JAG, *Law of Armed Conflict*, p. 2-1; UK Defence Ministry, *Joint Service Manual*, p. 23; Office of General Counsel, *Law of War Manual*, p. 59.

[70] Article 25, Hague Regulations (1907). See also Article 59, Additional Protocol I.

> The reason for this rule is that there is no military need to attack a place that is not being defended. It can simply be occupied without resistance or bypassed. Enemy armed forces are likely to have withdrawn. Any remaining members of the enemy armed forces in the place can be taken prisoner of war and their weapons and military equipment captured.[71]

Here, occupying or bypassing an undefended locality is a legitimate purpose. Attacking or bombarding such a locality is an act that is deemed evil and lacking in material military necessity for it.

4.4.1.3 Preamble of the 1868 St. Petersburg Declaration: Evil Conduct Is Illegitimate if It Is Unnecessary

The St. Petersburg Declaration states: '*the only legitimate object* which States should endeavor to accomplish during war is to weaken the military force of the enemy'.[72] The declaration goes on to proclaim that, '*for this purpose*, it is *sufficient* to disable the greatest possible number of men'.[73] Disabling the greatest number of men is thereby held to be all that any belligerent should ever need to do in order to weaken the military forces of its enemy. Accordingly, though clearly evil and part of the 'calamities of war',[74] the disablement of such men remains legitimate, as far as the St. Petersburg Declaration is concerned. This first part of the declaration's preamble deals with conduct that is considered evil yet materially necessary.

There is one further step in the text, where disablement by way of injury or death now becomes the purpose and the employment of certain projectiles becomes the act taken for its fulfilment. The declaration finds that its drafters have 'by common accord fixed the technical limits within which the necessities of war ought to yield to the demands of humanity'.[75] There is no indication, however, that the drafters decided to let the 'demands of humanity' perforce trump the 'necessities of war'. Nor is there any indication that the drafters intended categorically to outlaw the employment of means of combat that are deemed evil yet materially necessary for their legitimate ends.[76]

71 UK Defence Ministry, *Joint Service Manual*, p. 91. See also Dinstein, 'Military Necessity' (2nd edn 2009), para. 3.

72 Preamble, St. Petersburg Declaration (emphasis added).

73 Ibid (emphasis added).

74 Ibid.

75 Ibid.

76 Schmitt, 'Military Necessity and Humanity', at 803.

On the contrary, the declaration's drafters appear to have declined to delegitimise such behaviour. The declaration itself falls short of delegitimising acts such as disabling the greatest number of men per se and using explosive projectiles 400 grams or more in weight generally. What this implies is two-fold. First, there may be suffering that is aggravating yet arguably not useless (e.g., suffering that disablement itself entails); there may also be death that is inevitable but arguably not useless (e.g., death as a form of disablement itself).[77] Similarly, there may be injury that is not superfluous, and suffering that is not unnecessary.[78] Second, cruel as it may be if used against soldiers, heavier explosive projectiles may prove materially necessary for the attainment of some other legitimate purpose (e.g., explosives in shells[79]).

Needless to say, the mere fact that the St. Petersburg Declaration declines to delegitimise these acts does not mean that IHL conclusively legitimises them. Nothing in the declaration precludes the possibility that such acts can become illegitimate on grounds that are established independently of, or subsequently to, the declaration itself. Such grounds may very well arise, for instance, from the scope of evil broadening, or the requisite thresholds of material military necessity heightening – or both, as the case may be – over time.

As noted earlier, excessiveness is a species of material military non-necessity.[80] The St. Petersburg Declaration essentially stipulates that the employment of explosive projectiles weighing under 400 grams produces two kinds of evil, namely, evil that is necessary to effect disablement, and evil that is external to disablement. The declaration proclaims that the disablement of the greatest number of men 'would be *exceeded* by the employment of arms which *uselessly* aggravate the sufferings of disabled men, or render their death inevitable'.[81] At stake here is evil entailed by the suffering of *disabled* men – i.e., those men who are already disabled

[77] Dinstein, *Conduct of Hostilities* (2nd edn), pp. 64–66; Simon O'Connor, 'Nuclear Weapons and the Unnecessary Suffering Rule' in Nystuen et al. (eds), *Nuclear Weapons* 128, p. 131.

[78] Christopher Greenwood, 'The Law of Weaponry at the Start of the New Millennium' in Christopher Greenwood, *Essays on War in International Law* (London: Cameron May, 2006) 223, p. 236.

[79] Adam Roberts and Richard Guelff (eds), *Documents on the Laws of War*, 3rd edn (Oxford: Oxford University Press, 2000), p. 53.

[80] See Chapter 2.

[81] Preamble, St. Petersburg Declaration (emphasis added).

but, presumably, alive.[82] Aggravating their suffering and/or rendering their death inevitable is declared illegitimate, insofar as such an act is deemed evil that is external to their disablement.[83] In the declaration's words, 'the employment of such arms would, *therefore*, be contrary to the laws of humanity'.[84]

This second part of the declaration's preamble deals with conduct that is considered evil and materially unnecessary for its otherwise legitimate purpose. Bereft of material military necessity, aggravating the suffering of disabled men is an act that is evil *simpliciter*, and it is therefore illegitimate. The declaration proceeds to ban the employment of explosive projectiles weighting less than 400 grams, an unnecessary evil.[85] As the ICJ noted in *Nuclear Weapons*:

> In conformity with the aforementioned principles [i.e., the principle of distinction, the prohibition against causing unnecessary suffering to combatants, and the Martens Clause], humanitarian law, at a very early stage, prohibited certain types of weapons either because of their indiscriminate effect on combatants and civilians or because of the unnecessary suffering caused to combatants, that is to say, a harm greater than that unavoidable to achieve legitimate military objectives.[86]

Where given conduct is deemed both evil and lacking in material military necessity, and where that conduct is held to be illegitimate as a result, this shows that material military non-necessity does not overrule or militate against what is already evil. What the material military non-necessity of an evil act does is simply to lay its evil bare, unmitigated. It is the act's evil, *not* its material military non-necessity, that delegitimises it.[87]

82 'Alive', so that they are susceptible to further suffering.

83 Frits Kalshoven, 'Arms, Armaments and International Law', *Collected Courses of the Hague Academy of International Law* (Leiden and Boston: Martinus Nijhoff, 1985), Vol. CXCI, 183, p. 206; Hans Blix, 'Means and Methods of Combat' in Henri Dunant Institute and UNESCO (eds), *International Dimensions of Humanitarian Law* (Geneva, Paris and Dordrecht: Henri Dunant Institute, UNESCO and Martinus Nijhoff, 1988) 135, pp. 138–39; William H Boothby, *Weapons and the Law of Armed Conflict* (Oxford: Oxford University Press, 2009), pp. 55–56.

84 Preamble, St. Petersburg Declaration (emphasis added).

85 Ibid. See also Dinstein, 'Military Necessity' (2nd edn 2009), para. 6: 'It is virtually a truism today that causing unnecessary suffering to enemy combatants cannot be a matter of military necessity.'

86 *Nuclear Weapons*, para. 78.

87 The same is true of superfluous injury and unnecessary suffering. Superfluousness is not what delegitimises injury. Causing injury is evil and superfluousness merely leaves its illegitimacy unmitigated. Similarly, causing suffering is evil and non-necessity only exposes its illegitimacy bare.

4.4.2 *The Conduct Is Deemed Un-evil*

Our discussion so far shows that the material military necessity or non-necessity of an *evil* act does play some role in its legitimacy modification. On the one hand, an evil act may become legitimate if it is deemed sufficiently necessary to attain a legitimate military purpose. On the other hand, if deemed unnecessary – or insufficiently necessary, at any rate – for a legitimate purpose, an evil act becomes illegitimate on account of its evilness.

The question, now, is this. Is the material military necessity or non-necessity of *any* act also an element in its legitimacy modification? In particular, is the fact that it is materially unnecessary to do something a sufficient reason for which it becomes illegitimate to do so?

These questions are to be answered in the negative. Plainly, it would be legitimate to do what is considered un-evil and materially necessary.[88] More importantly, it might be normatively indifferent, but would clearly not be illegitimate, to do what is deemed neither evil nor necessary. It is possible that there may be some third elements that modify the legitimacy of an unnecessary non-evil, but we are not concerned with such elements here.

Let us return to Sergeant Chesterton and his German soldier. Suppose that Chesterton advocates the German's non-lethal disablement by employing an entirely harmless yet effective weapon that happens to be at Chesterton's disposal. Two preliminary remarks are in order. First, whether 'non-lethal' weapons really exist is a matter of considerable controversy.[89] For our purposes, however, one can proceed on the assumption that there are indeed genuinely 'non-lethal' weapons if employed properly.[90] Second, strictly for the sake of our argument, we

[88] One further question involves whether IHL framers have any reason not only to permit acts deemed un-evil and materially necessary but also to obligate them. See Chapter 7.

[89] Lieutenant Colonel James C Duncan, 'A Primer on the Employment of Non-lethal Weapons' (1998) 45 *Naval Law Review* 1; David P Fidler, 'The Meaning of Moscow: "Non-Lethal" Weapons and International Law in the Early 21st Century' (2005) 87 *International Review of the Red Cross* 525, at 531, 550; Boothby, *Weapons and the Law of Armed Conflict*, pp. 246–50; Stephen Coleman, 'Discrimination and Non-lethal Weapons: Issues for the Future Military' in David W Lovell and Igor Primoratz (eds), *Protecting Civilians During Violent Conflict: Theoretical and Practical Issues for the 21st Century* (Surrey: Ashgate, 2012) 215.

[90] Consider sticky foam. During Operation United Shield in Somalia, the US Marine Corps reportedly employed sticky foam for blocking and access delay, with some success. Steven H Scott, 'Sticky Foam as a Less-than-Lethal Technology' (1997) 2934 *SPIE Proceedings: Security System and Nonlethal Technology for Law Enforcement* 96, at 96, 103. The foam's

are making further allowances that such weapons existed during World War II.

The conduct at issue, then, would be of the form 'non-lethally disabling the able-bodied, non-surrendering German soldier who has noticed the presence of Chesterton's unit'. This conduct's purpose remains the same, i.e., 'keeping the location of the trenches used by Chesterton's unit concealed from the Germans'.

Now we need to consider whether the kind of act 'non-lethally disabling an able-bodied, non-surrendering enemy soldier who has noticed the presence of one's unit' is deemed materially necessary or unnecessary for the kind of purpose 'keeping the location of the trenches used by one's unit concealed from the enemy'.

4.4.2.1 The Conduct Is Deemed Un-evil and Necessary

Let us say that the German soldier was able-bodied and not offering to surrender, i.e., not *hors de combat* at the relevant moment. Then, his non-lethal disablement would appear materially necessary in order to keep the location of the trenches used by Chesterton's unit concealed from the Germans.

Plainly, an act deemed neither evil nor lacking in material military necessity for a legitimate purpose would be legitimate.[91] The resulting IHL rule would most likely reflect this by authorising the act in question or by leaving the belligerent at liberty to perform it. Such would arguably be the case, for example, regarding the use of 'non-lethal' weapons in a manner that is indeed non-lethal.[92]

4.4.2.2 The Conduct Is Deemed Un-evil and Unnecessary

Now let us suppose, once again, that the German soldier dropped his rifle, threw his hands up and unambiguously offered to surrender, thereby placing himself *hors de combat* at the time.

effectiveness may have been less than stellar, however. Jon Ronson, *The Men Who Stare at Goats*, 2nd edn (New York: Simon & Schuster Paperbacks, 2009), p. 50.

91 That is, as noted earlier, unless there are some third elements in the act's legitimacy modification.

92 If sprayed on the target's mouth and/or nose, sticky foam may cause injury or even death. On such lethal effects that even 'non-lethal' weapons can have, see Boothby, *Weapons and the Law of Armed Conflict*, pp. 246–47, 249. It should also be noted that it is debatable whether a party that possesses non-lethal weapons is duty-bound to use them first. See ibid, p. 249; Chapter 8 in this volume.

Here, not even his non-lethal disablement would be materially necessary in order to keep the location of the trenches used by Chesterton's unit concealed from the Germans. All else being equal, non-lethally disabling the German soldier *hors de combat* would still involve wasting weapons, as opposed to simply taking him prisoner. The harmless character of his non-lethal disablement would remain the same in nature and degree; it is its material military necessity that would now disappear. The harmless conduct would move from embodying material military necessity to embodying non-necessity for its legitimate purpose. Would this, and other similarly harmless acts deemed materially unnecessary, become illegitimate by dint of their material military non-necessity *alone*?

I have argued elsewhere that military necessity helps distinguish acts in war that are deemed materially necessary and hence prima facie permissible, from those deemed materially unnecessary and hence impermissible.[93] Matters of rational conduct transform themselves into those of normative imperative – i.e., 'that which *can* be done without *must* be done without'.[94] So construed, normative military necessity would be a notion that provides framers of IHL rules with a reason to restrict or prohibit material military non-necessities per se.[95]

I no longer subscribe to this view. Its chain of reasoning lacks one component of a basic syllogism. Let the minor premise be 'it is materially unnecessary to do X_1', and let the conclusion be 'it is illegitimate to do X_1'. In order for these two propositions to form a complete syllogism, they need to be accompanied by a major premise of the sort 'it is illegitimate to do any X_n that is materially unnecessary'.

The proposition 'it is illegitimate to do any X_n that is materially unnecessary' would involve one of the two corollaries of thoroughgoing utilitarianism noted earlier, i.e., that disutilities are per se illegitimate.[96]

93 N Hayashi, 'Requirements of Military Necessity', at 45.

94 Ibid.

95 Dill and Shue, 'Limiting the Killing in War', at 320.

96 Nils Melzer, *Targeted Killing in International Law* (Oxford: Oxford University Press, 2008), pp. 281–82; Canadian JAG, *Law of Armed Conflict*, p. 2-1; de Preux, 'Basic Rules', p. 396; Phillipson, *International Law and the Great War*, p. 132; APV Rogers, *Law on the Battlefield*, 2nd edn (Huntington: Juris Publishing, 2004), p. 6; Solis, *Law of Armed Conflict*, p. 258; Taylor, *Nuremberg and Vietnam*, p. 34; UK Defence Ministry, *Joint Service Manual*, p. 22; UK Ministry of Defence, *Joint Services Publication 383: The Manual of the Law of Armed Conflict Amendment* 3 (2010), p. 5; US Department of the Navy et al., *Commander's Handbook*, p. 5-2; Burrus M. Carnahan, 'Lincoln, Lieber and the Laws of War: The Origins and Limits of the Principle of Military Necessity'

Yet, no cogent reason has been articulated for which IHL should prohibit material disutilities. There are, at best, only vague and oblique references. Thus, in R. B. Brandt's words:

> The position of a nation in a serious war is such, then, that it considers overpowering the enemy to be absolutely vital to its interests (and possibly to those of civilized society generally) – so vital, indeed, that it is willing to risk its very existence to that end. It is doubtful that both sides can be well justified in such an appraisal of the state of affairs. But we may assume that in fact they do make this appraisal. In this situation, we must simply take as a fact that neither side will consent to or follow rules of war which seriously impair the possibility of bringing the war to a victorious conclusion. This fact accounts for the restriction within which I suggested a choice of the rules of war must take place. We may notice that the recognized rules of war do observe this limitation: they are framed in such a way as not to place any serious obstacle in the way of a nation's using any available force, if necessary, to destroy the ability of another to resist. As Oppenheim has observed, one of the assumptions underlying the recognized rules of war is that 'a belligerent is justified in applying any amount and any kind of force which is necessary for . . . the overpowering of the opponent.' This limitation, however, leaves a good deal of room for rules of war which will maximize expectable long-range utility for all parties. This restriction, incidentally, itself manifests utilitarian considerations, for a nation is limited to the use of means *necessary* to overcome an opponent. Clearly it is contrary to the general utility that any amount or manner of force be employed when it is *not* necessary for victory.[97]

Contra Brandt, however, it would be of no concern to framers of IHL rules whether belligerents should or should not encumber themselves with material military non-necessities. Surely, neither victory nor defeat is per se of concern to IHL norm-creation. The law's framers do not make it their business to ensure that each belligerent maximise its prospect of success or minimise its prospect of failure. In other words, it would be of no concern to IHL norm-creation to protect or prohibit belligerents from engaging in unwise strategic, operational or tactical behaviour. Material wastefulness, excessiveness, inappositeness and the

(1998) 92 *American Journal of International Law* 213, at 230–31; Draper, 'Military Necessity and Humanitarian Imperatives', at 130; NCH Dunbar, 'Military Necessity in War Crimes Trials' (1952) 29 *British Yearbook of International Law* 442, at 444; Greenwood, 'Historical Development', pp. 36–37; Henri Meyrowitz, 'The Principle of Superfluous Injury or Unnecessary Suffering: From the Declaration of St. Petersburg of 1868 to Additional Protocol I of 1977' (1994) 34 *International Review of the Red Cross* 98, at 107.

97 Brandt, 'Utilitarianism', at 153–54 (emphasis in original). See also David, *Droit des conflits armé*, p. 273.

like[98] are, strictly speaking, matters of incompetence *qua* members of a function-kind.[99]

Consider falling for enemy deceptions, for example. From 26 February[100] until 8 September 1944,[101] the Allied forces conducted Operation Fortitude, a deception operation designed to strengthen Operation Overlord (Allied invasion of north-west Europe) by denying Germany knowledge of the true location and moment of their D-Day landing. Fortitude had three major components. Fortitude North simulated a threat of Allied landing on Norwegian coasts.[102] Fortitude South maintained the pre-D-Day illusion of an Allied assault on the Pas de Calais region of northern France,[103] while Fortitude South II sought to induce Germany into believing that Normandy was a diversion ahead of the main invasion at Pas de Calais.[104] A combination of wireless deception,[105] inclusion of false information in communication with Allied POWs in German custody and to resistance organisations,[106] concealment of real forces and display of decoys,[107] restriction on troop leave and postal services,[108] and, most importantly, double agents,[109] was used in the operation. While historical assessments of Fortitude's impact on Germany vary, they appear to agree that the deception did help the German High Command retain its major formations in the Pas de Calais area before and after the Allied forces landed at Normandy.[110]

Germany, for its part, sought to obtain the information on the invasion with a view to optimising its defence preparations.[111] In this Germany largely failed, due, among other things, to its overestimation of Allied strength,[112] its own preoccupations about an ideal landing

[98] See Chapter 2.
[99] Ibid, Chapter 3.
[100] Roger Hesketh, *Fortitude: The D-Day Deception Campaign* (New York: Overlook Press, 2000), p. 27.
[101] Ibid, at 290, 297.
[102] Mary Kathryn Barbier, *D-Day Deception: Operation Fortitude and the Normandy Invasion* (Westport and London: Praeger Security International, 2007), pp. 42, 45.
[103] Ibid, pp. 64–67.
[104] Ibid, pp. 127–31.
[105] Ibid, pp. 24–26.
[106] Ibid, p. 26.
[107] Ibid, pp. 26–30.
[108] Ibid, pp. 30–32.
[109] Ibid, pp. 32–39. See also Hesketh, *Fortitude*, pp. 46–57.
[110] Barbier, *D-Day Deception*, pp. 187–95.
[111] Ibid, pp. 148–81.
[112] Ibid, pp. 158–59.

site,[113] its internal disagreement and indecision,[114] as well as its generally inadequate intelligence.[115] Of the latter, one account states:

> According to John Masterman, who ran the Double-Cross Committee, the British captured and turned every agent whom the Germans sent to Great Britain. This could imply a certain degree of ineptitude on the part of the Germans either in the people whom they chose to be agents or in the level of training that they gave prospective agents. There is no denying that the British excelled at identifying possible enemy spies. The exploits of Garbo and Tricycle, as portrayed in their autobiographies and their case files, seem at times a bit far fetched; therefore, one has to wonder why the Germans failed to question their reliability and appeared to accept all of the information that these two and other spies provided. According to 'Johnny' Jebsen, a double agent known as Artist, Canaris 'did not care if all the agents in Britain were fakes as long as he could go to Field Marshal Keitel, the head of the German high command, and report that he had twelve agents in Britain, each of them writing a letter every week.' In addition, it is possible, by the end of the war, that several Abwehr officers were no longer employing agents despite the fact that they were still providing information from them. Several officers pocketed the money meant for the agents and either fabricated the information or obtained it from the newspapers.[116]

Germany's purpose might be described as 'discovering the true location and moment of the main Allied landing on north-west Europe in 1994', and one of the measures it took as 'choosing, training and monitoring Garbo and Tricycle as German agents operating in Great Britain'. Arguably, this action lacked material military necessity on account of its wastefulness and inappositeness. Moreover, its material military non-necessity was of a nature that revealed Germany's own improvable vocational incompetence and did not entail evil per se. Given the legitimacy of wartime espionage itself,[117] the framers of IHL rules have apparently seen no reason to protect or prohibit the belligerent

113 Ibid, pp. 149–50, 169–70.

114 Ibid, pp. 161, 165–67, 171–75.

115 Ibid, pp. 159–60, 167–68.

116 Ibid, pp. 159–60 (footnotes omitted).

117 Article 24, Hague Regulations (1907); Hersch Lauterpacht (ed), *Oppenheim's International Law: A Treatise*, 7th edn, 2 vols. (London: Longmans, 1952), vol. II, p. 419; Dinstein, *Conduct of Hostilities* (2nd edn), p. 241; Geoffrey S Corn et al., *The Law of Armed Conflict: An Operational Approach* (New York: Wolters Kluwer Law & Business, 2012), p. 226; Manual on Air and Missile Warfare, para. 119; UK Defence Ministry, *Joint Service Manual*, p. 63.

engaged in espionage from unnecessary non-evils, such as failing to select, train and handle its spies properly.

4.4.2.3 Preamble of the 1868 St. Petersburg Declaration: Is Un-evil Conduct Illegitimate if It Is Unnecessary?

Despite popular belief to the contrary,[118] the St. Petersburg Declaration does *not* encapsulate the idea that a belligerent act becomes illegitimate merely on account of its material military non-necessity. The declaration's drafters found to be 'contrary to the laws of humanity' excessive *evil* brought about by the employment of arms that either uselessly aggravate the suffering of disabled men or render their death uselessly inevitable.[119] Plainly, the reasoning underpinning the St. Petersburg Declaration does not address itself to situations where the conduct is considered un-evil in the first place.

Where an act that is deemed unnecessary becomes illegitimate for some reason, the reason is *not* its lack of material military necessity. At play here is rather the operation of some other element or elements in that conduct's legitimacy modification. Examples include conduct considered materially unnecessary that becomes illegitimate on account of its evil (e.g., maltreating persons *hors de combat*[120]); its lack of chivalry, unfairness or bad faith (e.g., improper use of enemy uniforms in certain situations of combat[121]); and so on.

4.5 Special Cases: Conduct Considered Evil in an Exclusively Self-Inflicted Way

Our discussion has so far proceeded on the assumption that evil encompasses all evil, regardless of who suffers it. It may be asked, however, whether this assumption is apposite always and everywhere. Does IHL norm-creation really concern itself with conduct that is deemed evil but in an exclusively self-inflicted way? If it does, does it juxtapose the conduct's exclusively self-inflicted evil vis-à-vis its material military

118 N Hayashi, 'Requirements of Military Necessity', at 47; Dill and Shue, 'Limiting the Killing in War', at 320.

119 Preamble, St. Petersburg Declaration. The prohibition against causing superfluous injury or unnecessary suffering – to which the declaration is often said to have given rise – deals with *injury* and *suffering*, not with acts that entail no evil. See also Chapter 8.

120 Article 41(1), Additional Protocol I. See also Chapter 7.

121 See Chapter 8.

necessity or non-necessity, as it would with conduct deemed evil but not in an exclusively self-inflicted way?

4.5.1 *Minding One's Own Business?*

There is no compelling reason why an act involving exclusively self-inflicted evil should fall outside the scope of IHL norm-creation. Humanity, if not military necessity, would call for the inclusion of such an act. Eyal Benvenisti notes that one vision of IHL 'highlights the overriding and unconditional humanitarian obligation toward civilians regardless of their nationality'.[122] The same would go even for the disabled soldier, whether he be 'friend or foe'.[123]

The conduct of hostilities is a major exception in this regard.[124] The Soviet Union and Germany refused to permit their own civilians in Stalingrad and Berlin, both besieged during World War II, to evacuate, so that locally raised units would 'defend the city more desperately'.[125]

Modern military campaigns are also replete with loss of life amongst one's own. Let us first highlight instances of losses that are arguably consistent with material military necessity. During the Axis advance towards Stalingrad in the summer of 1942, Joseph Stalin issued Order No. 227, which came to be known as 'Not One Step Backwards'. According to Antony Beevor:

> The order was to be read to all troops in the Red Army. 'Panic-mongers and cowards must be destroyed on the spot. The retreat mentality must be decisively eliminated. Army commanders who have allowed the voluntary abandonment of positions must be removed and sent for immediate trial by military tribunal.' Anyone who surrendered was 'a traitor to the Motherland.' Each army had to organize 'three to five well-armed detachments (up to 200 men each)' to form a second line to shoot down any

[122] Eyal Benvenisti, 'Human Dignity in Combat: The Duty to Spare Enemy Civilians' (2006) 39 *Israel Law Review* 81, at 82–83.

[123] Jean S Pictet (ed), *Commentary II Geneva Convention for the Amelioration of the Condition of Wounded, Sick and Shipwrecked Members of Armed Forces at Sea* (Geneva: International Committee of the Red Cross, 1960), p. 83; Jann K Kleffner, 'Protection of the Wounded, Sick, and Shipwrecked' in Fleck (ed), *Handbook of International Humanitarian Law* (2nd edn) 325, p. 331.

[124] Benvenisti, 'Human Dignity in Combat', at 87.

[125] Antony Beevor, *Stalingrad* (London: Viking Press, 1998), p. 106. See also Antony Beevor, *Berlin: The Downfall 1945* (London: Viking Press, 2002), p. 178.

> soldier who tried to run away. Zhukov implemented this order on the Western Front within ten days, using tanks manned by specially selected officers. They followed the first wave of an attack, ready 'to combat cowardice,' by opening fire on any soldiers who wavered.[126]

Beevor also recounts perhaps a somewhat 'milder' version of the same idea practised among the Allied forces. It can be seen in the orders reportedly given to airborne division sergeants dropping over Normandy:

> A sergeant mounted first to go to the front of the plane and the platoon commander last, as he would lead the way. The sergeant would bring up the rear so that he could act as 'pusher' to make sure that everyone had left and nobody had frozen. 'One trooper asked the sergeant if it was true that he had orders to shoot any man that refused to jump. "That's the orders I've been given." He said it so softly that everybody became quiet.'[127]

It has been suggested that the court martial, guilty verdict and execution of US Army Private Eddie Slovik on account of desertion had to do with the need to discourage further desertions, already a problem during the difficult 1944 Hürtgen Forest campaign.[128]

Sometimes, own-side losses are simply part and parcel of military operations. In his report on the evolution of artillery, Ian V. Hogg observed:

> By the time of the Somme, July 1916, more experience had been gained and more ammunition and guns amassed, and artillery support began to take on the shape with which it closed [World War I]. Moreover the infantry had become more used to the idea of close support and had realized the advantages of the curtain of fire. They began to speak of 'leaning on the barrage' by which they meant following close upon the bursting shells ... The French, with their greater elan and still-unconquered spirit of attack at all costs, were known to observe that unless the infantry suffered ten percent of their casualties from their own artillery, they weren't following the barrage close enough![129]

126 Beevor, *Stalingrad*, p. 85. See also ibid, p. 167: 'Blocking groups ... were placed behind [militia brigades] to prevent retreat'.

127 Antony Beevor, *D-Day: The Battle for Normandy* (London: Penguin Press, 2009), p. 28.

128 William Bradford Huie, *The Execution of Private Slovik: The Hitherto Secret Story of the Only American Soldier Since 1864 to Be Shot for Desertion* (London: Jarrolds, 1954), pp. 9–10, 12.

129 Hogg, *Barrage*, p. 21.

Also, at least hypothetically, soldiers may be ordered to allow their own deaths passively 'if the commander believes it is necessary for mission accomplishment'.[130]

Inevitably, however, soldiers may also die from actions of their own forces or governments that are lacking in material military necessity. During the Battle of the Somme in 1916, for example, thousands upon thousands of Allied infantry soldiers perished due to the incompetent decisions of their commanders.[131] Peter Rowe also notes that '[a]llied armed forces may mistake friendly forces as being those of the enemy and attack them. These, so-called "friendly fire" incidents have occurred to a greater or lesser extent in all modern armed conflicts.'[132] Furthermore, the deployment of faulty equipment may result in the gratuitous loss or reduction of fighting capabilities.[133]

Today's positive IHL regulates none of these acts. The underlying assumption for this omission seems to be as follows. As suggested earlier, it is not of concern to IHL norm-creation whether the belligerent fights competently and increases its prospects of success, or whether it fights incompetently and imperils itself with dangers of failure. If this is so, then it is likewise of little concern to IHL norm-creation whether the belligerent inflicts evil on itself, its co-belligerent or those associated with them while succeeding or failing in its endeavours.[134]

There is something faintly Millian about this assumption. John Stuart Mill posited:

> But if he refrains from molesting others in what concerns them, and merely acts according to his own inclination and judgment in things

[130] Richard V Meyer and Mark David Maxwell, 'The Natural Right to Intervene: The Evolution of the Concepts of Justification and Excuse for Both State and Individual' (2009) 7 *Journal of International Criminal Justice* 555, at 556 (citing Richard B Myers, Joint Chiefs of Staff, Standing Rules of Engagement of United States Forces § 3(a) (2005)) § 3(a) ('The previous Standing Rules of Engagement were promulgated in January 2000 (CJCSI 3121.01A)').

[131] Dixon, *Military Incompetence*, p. 388 (placing blame more on General Sir Douglas Haig than on General Sir Henry Rawlinson); Martin Middlebrook, *The First Day on the Somme: 1 July 1916* (New York: Norton, 1972), pp. 271–73 (placing blame more on Rawlinson than on Haig).

[132] Peter Rowe, *The Impact of Human Rights Law on Armed Forces* (Cambridge: Cambridge University Press, 2006), p. 139. See also *R. v Secretary of State for Defence* [2010] UKSC 29 [103] (Lord Hope).

[133] *R. v Secretary of State for Defence* [2010] UKSC 29 [127] (Lord Rodger).

[134] Arguably, international human rights law (IHRL) is making its inroads into the minimisation of *intra*-party evil. We will return to this theme shortly. See also Chapter 8.

> which concern himself, the same reasons which show that opinion should be free, prove also that he should be allowed, without molestation, to carry his opinions into practice at his own cost.[135]

Mill then reiterated the idea that a person should be able to act on his own judgement and 'stand the consequences' when his actions do not cause harm to others:

> If either a public officer or any one else saw a person attempting to cross a bridge which had been ascertained to be unsafe, and there were no time to warn him of his danger, they might seize him and turn him back, without any real infringement of his liberty; for liberty consists in doing what one desires, and he does not desire to fall into the river. Nevertheless, when there is not a certainty, but only a danger of mischief, no one but the person himself can judge of the sufficiency of the motive which may prompt him to incur the risk; in this case, therefore (unless he is a child, or delirious, or in some state of excitement or absorption incompatible with the full use of the reflecting faculty), he ought, I conceive, to be only warned of the danger; not forcibly prevented from exposing himself to it.[136]

Such an attitude arguably underpins the fact that IHL has been developed primarily to regulate inter-belligerent and belligerent-neutral relations – rather than, say, relations between co-belligerents, between a belligerent and persons and objects intrinsically affiliated with it, or between a belligerent and persons or objects similarly affiliated with its co-belligerent.

Article 4 of Geneva Convention IV is axiomatic in this respect. The provision reads, in relevant parts:

> Persons protected by the Convention are those who at a given moment and in any manner whatsoever, find themselves, in case of a conflict or occupation, in the hands of a Party to the conflict or Occupying Power of which they are not nationals.
>
> Nationals of a State which is not bound by the Convention are not protected by it. Nationals of a neutral State who find themselves in the territory of a belligerent State, and nationals of a co-belligerent State, shall not be regarded as protected persons while the State of which they are nationals has normal diplomatic representation in the State in whose hands they are.[137]

135 JS Mill, *On Liberty and Considerations on Representative Government* (Oxford: Basil Blackwell, 1948), p. 49. See also ibid, p. 67.

136 Ibid, p. 86.

137 Article 4, Geneva Convention IV.

During the 1974–77 Diplomatic Conference, Finland sought to specify in the *chapeau* of Additional Protocol I's Article 75 concerning fundamental guarantees that such guarantees apply to 'the Parties' own nationals and nationals of . . . co-belligerent States having normal diplomatic representation with the Party in whose power they are'.[138] Having failed to do so, Finland declared, upon ratification of the protocol: '[U]nder Article 72, the field of application of Article 75 shall be interpreted to include also the nationals of the Contracting Party applying the provisions of that Article'.[139]

The Red Cross commentary of the article notes ambiguities:

> Some claim that the fact that the reference to own nationals was deleted reveals an intention to exclude nationals from the application of the provisions of Article 75. Others believe that precisely by virtue of the wording of Article 72 (*Field of application*) and Article 75 there was no need to mention nationals of the Parties to the conflict explicitly.[140]

The commentary argues, on the one hand, that the fact that victims of a war of national liberation may technically be nationals of the state in whose power they find themselves should not deprive them of protection under Article 75, where they are 'not actually bound by a duty of allegiance'[141] vis-à-vis the state of their technical nationality. On the other hand, according to the Red Cross, the relevant provisions of Additional Protocol I 'apply to a Party to the conflict's own nationals, except where the article itself indicates otherwise'.[142]

4.5.2 *Are All War Crimes the Enemy's Crimes?*

This ambivalence closely mirrors the manner in which war crimes are often perceived. One party to the conflict habitually reserves the label 'war crimes' to describe acts that its adversary commits against persons and objects affiliated with it. Conversely, states may choose to deal with

138 Federal Political Department, *Official Records of the Diplomatic Conference on the Reaffirmation and Development of International Humanitarian Law Applicable in Armed Conflicts*, 3 vols. (Berne: Federal Political Department, 1978), vol. III, p. 295.

139 Claude Pilloud and Jean Pictet, 'Part IV, Section III – Treatment of Persons in the Power of a Party to the Conflict' in Sandoz et al. (eds), *Commentary on Additional Protocols* 837, p. 838.

140 Ibid, p. 868.

141 Ibid, p. 867.

142 Ibid, p. 838. See also René Provost, *International Human Rights and Humanitarian Law* (Cambridge: Cambridge University Press, 2002), pp. 40, 42.

comparable acts committed by their own personnel under their domestic law.[143] Ted van Baarda observes:

> While a violation of the *jus in bello* which has been committed by the enemy is likely to be portrayed as a typical example the less-than-human nature of the enemy, propaganda may also suggest that a violation of the *jus in bello* committed by one's own side is merely a mishap, an accident, or an act which was at the least justified by the pressure of enemy advances. One author on international criminal law was able to quote with irony a Minister of Defence who stated that a war crime is by definition an act which is committed by the enemy. The frightening result is that there develops a strong possibility that war crimes can be committed without them being recognized as such by the perpetrator. After all, it is apparently a good cause he is fighting for (at least, that is what the population is told by propaganda). The cause, the national interest, appears to justify the actions. The chances are that the nationalistic premise *in war, my country can do no wrong* will collide head-on with an international value system embodied in universally accepted Laws of Armed Conflict and core human rights.[144]

The significance of such labelling is not limited to propaganda. There is some weight of authority for the view that international law itself adheres to the exclusively inter-belligerent application of war crimes.[145] Commentators routinely cite *Pilz*[146] and *Motosuke*[147] as examples in support of this view.[148]

143 US Uniform Code of Military Justice, 10 USC §§ 801-946; Laurie R Blank and Gregory P Noone, *International Law and Armed Conflict: Fundamental Principles and Contemporary Challenges in the Law of War* (New York: Wolters Kluwer Law & Business, 2013), pp. 578–79. But see the UK International Criminal Court (ICC) Act 2001, and the cases held thereunder in which British military personnel were tried and convicted of war crimes properly so-called. Nathan Rasiah, 'The Court-Martial of Corporal Payne and Others and the Future Landscape of International Criminal Justice' (2009) 7 *Journal of International Criminal Justice* 177.

144 Ted van Baarda, 'The Ethical Challenges of a Complex Security Environment' in Whetham (ed), *Ethics, Law and Military Operations* 148, pp. 154–55 (footnote omitted; emphasis in original).

145 Antonio Cassese and Paola Gaeta, *Cassese's International Criminal Law*, 3rd edn (Oxford: Oxford University Press, 2013), p. 67.

146 *In re Pilz*, 17 *International Law Reports* [1956] 391; Göran Sluiter, 'Pilz' in Antonio Cassese (ed), *The Oxford Companion to International Criminal Justice* (Oxford: Oxford University Press, 2009) 872.

147 *Trial of Susuki Motosuke*, United Nations War Crimes Commission, *Law Reports of Trials of War Criminals*, 15 vols. (London: His Majesty's Stationery Office, 1949), vol. XIII, 126; Jonas Nilsson, 'Motosuke' in Cassese (ed), *Oxford Companion to International Criminal Justice* 816.

148 Cassese and Gaeta, *Cassese's International Criminal Law*, p. 67 n.7; Jann K Kleffner, 'Friend or Foe? On the Protective Reach of the Law of Armed Conflict: A Note on the

Grave breaches of Geneva Conventions III and IV formally require the absence of shared allegiance between the perpetrator and the victim.[149] As noted earlier, Article 4 of Geneva Convention IV excludes the perpetrator's own nationals from that convention's protection, and hence from its grave breaches provisions.[150] While the 1999 *Tadić* Appeal Judgment dispenses with the strict interpretation of *de jure* nationality, it merely replaces that interpretation with one based on ethnic allegiance.[151] In other words, the latter construal still retains the requirement of a hostile or adverse affiliation between the perpetrator and the victim.[152]

The same would be true, *mutatis mutandis*, of Article 4 of Geneva Convention III concerning the protection of POWs[153] and its grave breaches provisions.[154] Whether a flexible interpretation of the expression 'enemy' found in Article 4 of Geneva Convention III along the lines suggested in *Tadić* finds widespread support remains to be seen.[155]

SCSL Trial Chamber's Judgment in the Case of *Prosecutor v Sesay, Kallon and Gbao*' in Mariëlle Matthee et al. (eds), *Armed Conflict and International Law: In Search of the Human Face Liber Amicorum in Memory of Avril McDonald* (The Hague: TMC Asser Press, 2013) 285, p. 299; Joanna Nicholson, 'Fighters as Victims in International Criminal Law', PhD thesis, University of Oslo (2014), p. 154; Joanna Nicholson, *Fighting and Victimhood in International Criminal Law* (Oxford: Routledge, 2018), p. 81.

149 Héctor Olásolo, *Unlawful Attacks in Combat Situations: From the ICTY's Case Law to the Rome Statute* (Leiden: Martinus Nijhoff, 2008), pp. 61–62. *Contra* Olásolo, however, the grave breaches provisions of Geneva Conventions I and II arguably operate on a different basis. See below.

150 Article 147, Geneva Convention IV: 'Grave breaches to which the preceding Article refers shall be those involving any of the following acts, if committed against persons or property protected by the present Convention . . .'

151 *Prosecutor v Duško Tadić*, Case No. IT-94-1-A, *Judgment*, 15 July 1999, paras 164–69. See also *Prosecutor v Zejnil Delalić et al.*, Case No. IT-96-21-T, *Judgment*, 16 November 1998, paras 259, 263–66; *Prosecutor v Zejnil Delalić et al*, Case No. IT-96-21-A, *Judgment*, 20 February 2001, paras 52–106; *Prosecutor v Dario Kordić and Mario Čerkez*, Case No. IT-95-14/2-A, *Judgment*, 17 December 2004, paras 322–23, 328–30.

152 Kleffner, 'Friend or Foe?', p. 292. But see Nicholson, 'Fighters as Victims', pp. 153–64.

153 Judicial Committee of the Privy Council (UK), *Public Prosecutor* v. *Oie Hee Koi* and the connected appeals, 4 December 1967 [1968] AC 829 (finding it 'trite law that an armed group cannot hold its own members as prisoners of war').

154 Article 130, Geneva Convention III: 'Grave breaches to which the preceding Article refers shall be those involving any of the following acts, if committed against persons or property protected by the Convention . . .'

155 *Prosecutor v Jadranko Prlić et al*, Case No. IT-04-74-T, *Judgment*, 6 vols., 29 May 2013, vol. III, para. 604.

As regards other war crimes, the absence of shared allegiance is either spelled out explicitly,[156] or frequently taken for granted in the formulation of a requisite nexus.[157] Similar assumptions appear to pervade even those war crimes that are committed in non-international armed conflicts.[158] The *Sesay et al.* Trial Judgment of the Special Court for Sierra Leone[159] is quite explicit on this point. In a somewhat puzzling ruling that purportedly encompasses both the laws of international and non-international armed conflicts,[160] the *Sesay et al.* Trial Chamber held:

> The Chamber is of the opinion that the law of armed conflict does not protect members of armed groups from acts of violence directed against them by their own forces.
>
> The law of international armed conflict regulates the conduct of combatants *vis-à-vis* their adversaries and persons *hors de combat* who do not belong to any of the armed groups participating in hostilities. In this respect, we recall that the field of application of the Third Geneva Convention is restricted to persons 'who have fallen into the power of the enemy'.
>
> It is trite law that an armed group cannot hold its own members as prisoners of war. The law of international armed conflict was never intended to criminalise acts of violence committed by one member of an armed group against another, such conduct remaining first and foremost the province of the criminal law of the State of the armed group concerned and human rights law. In our view, a different approach would

156 A number of war crimes within the jurisdiction of the ICC contain explicit references to hostile and adverse affiliation of the persons and objects protected. See Articles 8(2)(b)(x), 8(2)(b)(xi), 8(2)(b)(xiii), 8(2)(b)(xiv), 8(2)(b)(xv), 8(2)(e)(ix), 8(2)(e)(xi), 8(2)(e)(xii), Rome Statute of the International Criminal Court, 17 July 1998, in force 1 July 2002, 2187 UNTS 3 (hereinafter Rome Statute), and their corresponding elements.

157 Michael Cottier, '(vi)' in Otto Triffterer (ed), *Commentary on the Rome Statute of the International Criminal Court: Observers' Notes, Article by Article*, 2nd edn (München, Oxford and Baden-Baden: C.H. Beck, Hart and Nomos, 2008) 275, p. 344 (regarding the war crime of 'killing or wounding a combatant who, having laid down his arms or having no longer means of defence, has surrendered at his discretion' under Article 8(2)(b)(vi), Rome Statute); *Prosecutor v Gragoljub Kunarac et al*, Case No. IT-96-23 & IT-96-23/1-A, *Judgment*, 12 June 2002, paras 58–59.

158 *Prosecutor v Ramush Haradinaj et al*, Case No. IT-04-84-T, *Judgment*, 3 April 2008, para. 1 (describing how Kosovar Albanians were charged with war crimes against Kosovar Albanian victims because of the latter's 'collaboration' with the Serbian authorities); *Prosecutor v Fatmir Limaj et al*, Case No. IT-03-66-T, *Judgment*, 30 November 2005, paras 1, 36, 45.

159 *Prosecutor v Issa Hassan Sesay et al*, Case No. SCSL-04-15-T, *Judgment*, 2 March 2009.

160 Ibid, paras 977 (finding that 'the armed conflict in Sierra Leone was of a non-international character'), 1452 (referring to 'the law of international armed conflict' and to Geneva Convention III).

> constitute an inappropriate reconceptualisation of a fundamental principle of international humanitarian law.[161]

Recent international jurisprudence is not entirely consistent, however. With regard to certain types of war crimes committed in non-international armed conflicts, several rulings reveal a tendency towards disregarding hostile or adverse affiliations. For instance, the ICTY's *Kvočka et al.* Appeal Judgment dismisses as 'irrelevant' for serious violations of common Article 3 the different ethnic groups to which the perpetrator and the victim belonged.[162] Nor, perhaps understandably, does the ICC consider such affiliations material to charges relating to the enlistment, conscription and use of child soldiers.[163] In *Ntaganda*, the ICC's Trial Chamber held that child soldiers and others may become victims of sexual violence committed by members of their own forces.[164] The *Ntaganda* Appeals Chamber went one step further: 'Upon closer examination of the principles and the cases, the Appeals Chamber is persuaded that international humanitarian law does not contain a general rule that categorically excludes members of an armed group from protection against crimes committed by members of the same armed group.'[165]

161 Ibid, paras 1451–53 (footnote omitted). For a sustained criticism of this ruling, see Kleffner, 'Friend or Foe?'; Nicholson, 'Fighters as Victims', pp. 154–60; Nicholson, *Fighting and Victimhood*, pp. 81–88.

162 *Prosecutor v Miroslav Kvočka et al*, Case No. IT-98-30/1-A, *Judgment*, 28 February 2005, para. 561.

163 *Prosecutor v Thomas Lubanga Dyilo*, Case No. ICC-01/04-01/06, *Judgment pursuant to Article 74 of the Statute*, 14 March 2012, paras 37–51 (raising at no point the possibility that the victims' ethnic or other bases of allegiance might not diverge from that of their victimisers as an issue); *Prosecutor v Germain Katanga and Mathieu Ngudjolo Chui*, Case No. ICC-01/04-01/07, *Decision on the Confirmation of Charges*, 30 September 2008, para. 248 ('this war crime can be committed by a perpetrator against individuals in his own party to the conflict. Thus, the allegiance of the child who is used in hostilities is not relevant for the purposes of this provision, as long as the child in question is under the age of fifteen'); *Prosecutor v Bosco Ntaganda*, Case No. ICC-01/04-02/06, *Decision Pursuant to Article 61(7) of the Rome Statute on the Charges of the Prosecutor Against Bosco Ntaganda*, 9 June 2014, paras 74–96, esp. 86 ('As part of its recruitment campaign, the [Hema-dominated armed formations with which Ntaganda was found to be affiliated] also implemented a policy of asking Hema families to contribute a child to the movement . . .').

164 *Prosecutor v Bosco Ntaganda*, Case No. ICC-01/04-02/06, *Second Decision on the Defence's Challenge to the Jurisdiction of the Court in Respect of Counts 6 and 9*, 4 January 2017, paras 45–54.

165 *Prosecutor v Bosco Ntaganda*, Case No. ICC-01/04-02/06, *Judgment on the Appeal of Mr Ntaganda Against the 'Second Decision on the Defence's Challenge to the Jurisdiction of the Court in Respect of Counts 6 and 9'*, 15 June 2017, para. 63.

It may be said that the so-called 'auto-genocide' as a species of genocide is undergoing a similar transformation.[166] This stands in contrast to crimes against humanity, a class of international crimes that have since their inception been specifically intended to cover, among other things, evil inflicted by authorities against their own nationals.[167]

4.5.3 *Life of a Soldier*

Belligerent acts involving exclusively self-inflicted evil are often closely linked to what a party to the conflict owes those who support it and the sacrifice it demands from them.[168] We may ask whether one form of exclusively self-inflicted evil, i.e., a soldier's death caused by the incompetence of his or her commander, can amount to an arbitrary deprivation of life. According to Rowe:

> Depending upon the degree of risk of loss of life and the nature of the compulsion (through the medium of military punishment for refusing to obey orders) it is possible to foresee a situation where a solider may arbitrarily be deprived of his life. An extreme example may illustrate the point. A commander has taken very little care over a plan to attack an enemy military installation with large numbers of his own soldiers. He expects that very many of them will be killed in the attack. If, however, any reasonable commander had thought through the planned operation he would have concluded that the loss of life of his own soldiers would clearly be excessive compared with the concrete and direct military advantage to be gained from the attack. It might not be difficult to conclude here that some of his men have been deprived of their lives arbitrarily.[169]

[166] Florian Jessberger, 'The Definition and the Elements of the Crime of Genocide' in Paola Gaeta (ed), *The Genocide Convention – A Commentary* (Oxford: Oxford University Press, 2009) 87, p. 110. William Schabas was initially sceptical of the notion, but he appears to have rescinded this scepticism. Compare William A Schabas, *Genocide in International Law: The Crime of Crimes* (Cambridge: Cambridge University Press, 2000), pp. 119–20, 148–49, with William A Schabas, *Genocide in International Law: The Crime of Crimes*, 2nd edn (Cambridge: Cambridge University Press, 2009), pp. 138–40.

[167] M Cherif Bassiouni, *Crimes Against Humanity in International Criminal Law*, 2nd rev. edn (The Hague: Kluwer Law International, 1999), p. 72; Geoffrey Robertson, *Crimes Against Humanity: The Struggle for Global Justice*, 3rd edn (London: Penguin Books, 2006), p. 260; Egon Schwelb, 'Crimes Against Humanity' (1946) 23 *British Yearbook of International Law* 178, at 182.

[168] Walzer, *Arguing About War*, p. 24.

[169] Rowe, *Impact of Human Rights Law on Armed Forces*, pp. 138–39 (footnotes omitted).

Rowe's view here is deeply problematic, for two reasons. First, it is not unusual that a commander may find himself ordering his soldiers to launch a dangerous and risky assault, fully expecting many of them to lose their lives doing it. The extent to which the commander takes care over his plans may be a matter of his personality (some commanders are more cautious than others). Besides, speaking of cautious versus audacious styles of commanding, would it make any difference if the commander himself expected to lose his life during the planned assault, given its high risk, and nevertheless led the way? Such a situation might well materialise, for example, where an encircled or invested unit were to choose between a surrender in order to save lives and a last-ditch attempt to breakout. Would it not be possible that, if the commander had chosen the latter, he might have acted negligently as far as his own life and those of his subordinates were concerned, but might have nevertheless earned praise for bravery and leadership rather than blame for the deaths of his soldiers?

Second, even if, *arguendo*, a state were duty-bound not to let its commanders launch attacks that are too risky, how would it follow *from this* that the death of its own soldiers in such attacks would become a breach of their right to life where such losses 'would clearly be excessive compared to the concrete and direct military advantage to be gained'? This is evidently a formulation borrowed from the test of proportionality *in bello* applicable to attacks.[170] But the relevant 'loss' variable for determining the proportionality or otherwise of such attacks is that of civilian life[171] – not one's own soldiers, much less those who are not placed *hors de combat*.[172] Why should the human rights standard for determining the arbitrary loss of a soldier's life in an attack depend on whether this loss was excessive compared to the concrete and direct military advantage anticipated from that attack?[173]

In other ways, however, grossly negligent combat decisions of a commanding officer imperilling the life of his subordinates may indeed constitute breaches of the latter's human right to life. Of an incident

[170] Rowe himself admits this. Ibid, at 138 n.102.

[171] Articles 51(5)(b), 57(2)(a)(iii), 57(2)(b), Additional Protocol I.

[172] Rogier Bartels, 'Dealing with the Principle of Proportionality in Armed Conflict in Retrospect: The Application of the Principle in International Criminal Trials' (2013) 46 *Israel Law Review* 271, at 304.

[173] *R. v Secretary of State for Defence* [2010] UKSC 29 [120-124] (Lord Rodger).

involving the death of a soldier caused by heatstroke while serving in Iraq,[174] the UK Supreme Court said:

> If armed forces on active service abroad are within a State's jurisdiction for purposes of article 1 [of the European Convention on Human Rights], the question arises of the scope of the substantive obligations imposed by article 2 [of the same convention]. Would the Strasbourg Court hold that they extend to the adequacy of the equipment with which the forces are provided; to the planning and execution of military manoeuvers? These questions are not easy to address, but an affirmative answer certainly cannot be excluded.[175]

A government's failure adequately to budget its military procurement programmes, train its troops and ensure competent combat decisions by its commanders, and so on, may properly be a matter of domestic accountability.[176] It may, perhaps, even be a matter of accountability under international human rights law (IHRL).[177]

4.5.4 Delegitimising Self-Inflicted Evil in War

The question, then, is whether the reduction of exclusively self-inflicted evil is – or should be – of concern to IHL.[178] There are signs, however modest, that it is so. Where an act involving such evil is also deemed lacking in material military necessity, its illegitimacy appears to be readily affirmed and contrary action unhesitatingly demanded.

Consider, for example, the belligerent's failure to protect and humanely treat helpless victims (including those of its own), contrary to Articles 73 through 77 and 79 of Additional Protocol I,[179] common

174 'Army Blamed for Iraq Heat Death', BBC News, 10 November 2006.

175 *R. v Secretary of State for Defence* [2010] UKSC 29 [79] (Lord Phillips), [100-106] (Lord Hope), [118-119] (Lord Rodger). But see ibid [214], [216-217] (Lord Mance).

176 'Soldiers' Families "Losing Faith" in MoD', BBC News, 7 December 2004; 'MoD Budget "Harm" Claims Denied', BBC News, 23 August 2009; 'Family Sues MoD Over Marine Death', BBC News, 12 October 2009.

177 Peter Rowe, 'Members of the Armed Forces and Human Rights Law' in Andrew Clapham and Paola Gaeta (eds), *The Oxford Handbook of International Law in Armed Conflict* (Oxford: Oxford University Press, 2014) 521, pp. 537–40.

178 Peter Rowe, 'The Obligation of a State Under International Law to Protect Members of Its Own Armed Forces during Armed Conflict or Occupation', 9 *Yearbook of International Humanitarian Law* 3 (2006), at 16–24.

179 As noted earlier, according to the Red Cross commentary, these rules protect not only victims in the hands of their adversary but also those in the hands of their own state. Pilloud and Pictet, 'Treatment of Persons in the Power of a Party to the Conflict', p. 838.

Article 3[180] or Geneva Conventions I and II.[181] Article 54 of Additional Protocol I may also be mentioned here. That article's second paragraph prohibits the belligerent from attacking, destroying, removing or rendering useless objects that are indispensable to the survival of the civilian population. Paragraph five of the same article qualifies this prohibition, by recognising 'vital requirements of any Party to the conflict in the defence of its national territory against invasion' and authorising derogation therefrom. This derogation is limited to objects located 'within such territory under [the derogating party's] own control' and to situations where derogation is 'required by imperative military necessity'.[182] Article 54 shows, in principle, that it is illegitimate to cause self-inflicted evil in the form of scorched earth from which one's own population will suffer.[183] This evil exceptionally ceases to be illegitimate, but only in the event of imperative military necessity.[184]

Initially, a number of states present in Geneva during the negotiations of Article 54 took it for granted that the rule would only apply where one party to the conflict inflicted the evil in question and another party suffered it.[185] Authorising scorching one's own territory if imperatively

[180] Jean S Pictet (ed), *Commentary IV Geneva Convention Relative to the Protection of Civilian Persons in Time of War* (Geneva: International Committee of the Red Cross, 1958), p. 40; Sylvie-S. Junod, 'Article 2 – Personal Field of Application' in Sandoz et al. (eds), *Commentary on Additional Protocols* 1357, pp. 1359, 1369–70; Lindsey Cameron et al., 'Conflicts Not of an International Character' in Knut Dörmann et al. (eds), *Commentary on the First Geneva Convention* (Cambridge: Cambridge University Press, 2016) 126, paras 545–49.

[181] Kleffner, 'Friend or Foe?', pp. 294–96; Robin Geiss, 'Protection and Care of the Wounded and Sick' in Dörmann et al. (eds), *Commentary First Geneva Convention* 471, paras 1337, 1368, 1370; Robin Geiss, 'Protection and Care of the Wounded, Sick and Shipwrecked' in Knut Dörmann et al. (eds), *Commentary on the Second Geneva Convention* (Cambridge: Cambridge University Press, 2017) 483, paras 1369, 1414, 1416.

[182] Article 54(5), Additional Protocol I. See also Louise Doswald-Beck and Sylvain Vité, 'International Humanitarian Law and Human Rights Law' (1993) 33 *International Review of the Red Cross* 94, at 100. The British Manual refers to 'the flooding of low-lying areas to impede invading forces' as an example of conduct falling within the scope of Article 54(5) exceptions. UK Defence Ministry, *Joint Service Manual*, p. 74.

[183] See Chapter 7.

[184] See ibid; Claude Pilloud and Jean Pictet, 'Article 54 – Protection of Objects Indispensable to the Survival of the Civilian Population' in Sandoz et al. (eds), *Commentary on Additional Protocols* 651, p. 659 ('in an extreme case'); Dinstein, 'Military Necessity' (2nd ed. 2009), para. 8.

[185] Federal Political Department, *Official Records of the Diplomatic Conference on the Reaffirmation and Development of International Humanitarian Law Applicable in Armed Conflicts*, 17 vols. (Berne: Federal Political Department, 1978), vol. XV, pp. 280, 350.

demanded by military necessity was an unavoidable trade-off in order to secure an otherwise unqualified prohibition against the destruction of objects indispensable to the survival of the civilian population – including, presumably, one's own civilian population.[186]

The separation of cultural property from military objectives under one's own control is another example.[187] Each party remains bound by this duty, until and unless 'military necessity imperatively requires' the infliction of a self-inflicted evil in the form of its cultural property being exposed to harmful consequences of armed hostilities.[188] In addition, when compelled to abandon its wounded and sick to an adversary, each belligerent is duty-bound to reduce self-inflicted evil by leaving elements of its medical personnel and *materiél* with them to assist in their care. This duty remains in place as far as 'military considerations permit'.[189]

Similarly, Article 58 of Additional Protocol I obligates each belligerent, though only 'to the maximum extent feasible':

(a) To endeavour, without prejudice to Article 49 of Geneva Convention IV,[190] to remove the civilian population, individual civilians and civilian objects under its control from the vicinity of military objectives;

186 Ibid, pp. 462, 516.

187 Article 4(1), Convention for the Protection of Cultural Property in the Event of Armed Conflict, 14 May 1954, in force 7 August 1956, 249 UNTS 215 (hereinafter Hague Cultural Property Convention). It appears that it is the avoidance of evil inflicted upon such property as a 'universal' concern, rather than that seen from a strictly self-interested point of view, that is at stake. See Jiří Toman, *The Protection of Cultural Property in the Event of Armed Conflict: Commentary on the Convention for the Protection of Cultural Property in the Event of Armed Conflict and Its Protocol, Signed 14 May, 1954 in the Hague, and on Other Instruments of International Law Concerning Such Protection* (Brookfield: Dartmouth Publishing Company, 1996), pp. 68–69.

188 Article 4(2), Hague Cultural Property Convention.

189 Article 1, Convention for the Amelioration of the Condition of the Wounded and Sick in Armies in the Field, 6 July 1906, in force 9 August 1907 (no longer in force) (hereinafter Wounded and Sick Convention [1906]); Article 1, Convention for the Amelioration of the Condition of the Wounded and Sick in Armies in the Field, 27 July 1929, in force 19 June 1931 (no longer in force) (hereinafter Wounded and Sick Convention (1929); Article 12, Geneva Convention I. This rule, according to the ICRC, meets a 'humanitarian requirement so obviously necessary'. See Jean S Pictet (ed), *Commentary I Geneva Convention for the Amelioration of the Condition of Wounded and Sick in Armed Forces in the Field* (Geneva: International Committee of the Red Cross, 1952), p. 141.

190 Article 49 of Geneva Convention IV principally prohibits forcible transfers and deportations of protected persons from occupied territory.

(b) To avoid locating military objectives within or near densely populated areas; and
(c) To take the other necessary precautions to protect the civilian population, individual civilians and civilian objects under its control against the dangers resulting from military operations.[191]

In this connection, reference may also be made to Article 51(7) of Additional Protocol I that prohibits the use of civilian persons – including one's own – as human shields.[192]

4.6 Conclusion

This chapter shows that military necessity can indeed affect the legitimacy of a belligerent act where the act is deemed evil and its purpose is considered legitimate. As we have seen, however, in no other circumstances does an act's legitimacy depend on whether it is materially necessary. In particular, material military necessity or non-necessity is *not* an element in the legitimacy modification of the following types of conduct:

1. Wherever it is taken for a military purpose that is considered illegitimate – the act at issue is *ipso facto* illegitimate in that case; and
2. Wherever, while taken for a legitimate military purpose, it is deemed un-evil to begin with – the act at issue is *ipso facto* legitimate in that case.[193]

More importantly, this chapter has demonstrated that the lack of material military necessity, as such, is *never* a reason for a belligerent act's illegitimacy as far as IHL norm-creation is concerned. That the framers of IHL rules take the intrinsic material utility of a given belligerent act seriously, if not conclusively, is intuitively sound. It would be an error to assume that they also took military disutilities per se seriously.

[191] The duty Article 58 creates for a belligerent party is predicated, at least vis-à-vis its own population, on self-interest. Pictet (ed), *Commentary Geneva Convention I*, pp. 692, 694; UK Defence Ministry, *Joint Service Manual*, p. 89.

[192] Claude Pilloud and Jean Pictet, 'Article 58 – Precautions against the Effects of Attacks' in Sandoz et al. (eds), *Commentary on Additional Protocols* 691, at 692. For an illustration of using one's own civilians as human shields, see Human Rights Watch, *Off Target: The Conduct of the War and Civilian Casualties in Iraq* (New York, Washington, DC, London and Brussels: Human Rights Watch, 2003), pp. 67–69.

[193] That is, subject to the involvement of some third element in the act's legitimacy modification.

For, although IHL endeavours to accommodate the pursuit of military necessities, the law does not make it its business to save incompetent belligerents from themselves. After all, if a warring party encumbers itself with missed opportunities and mounting blunders, it has only itself to blame.

Nevertheless, we should not take these Millian underpinnings too far. Albeit in a limited set of circumstances, the law does delegitimise exclusively self-inflicted evil, and it does mandate action with a view to reducing such evil. Our discussion in this chapter has indicated the involvement of third elements in the legitimacy modification of numerous belligerent acts, including those that entail exclusively self-inflicted evil.

How, then, does normative military necessity interact with other reason-giving considerations, such as humanity and chivalry, in the process of IHL norm-creation? It is to this question that we turn in Chapter 5.

5

Inevitable Conflict Thesis

IHL has been developed with a view to striking a realistic and meaningful balance between military necessity and humanity. It would follow, then, that the law has accounted for these considerations. This is a widely held view indeed.[1] Troublingly, however, what accounting for military necessity and humanity really means has remained obscure. This obscurity has given rise to different opinions.

These opinions may be grouped around two major sets of internally coherent ideas. Let us call the first set an 'inevitable conflict thesis'. On this view, accounting for military necessity and humanitarian considerations amounts to treating them as inevitably in conflict with each other. In other words, no belligerent conduct is capable of jointly satisfying them.

The truth of this assertion is predicated on three notions. First, acts deemed materially necessary are always deemed inhumane and those considered humane are always considered unnecessary. Second, as reason-giving considerations in IHL norm-creation, both military necessity and humanity generate imperatives. Third, these imperatives always create norm conflicts with regard to a given act. Such would be the case,

[1] Preamble, St. Petersburg Declaration; preamble, Hague Convention IV (1907); *von Lewinski (called Manstein)*, p. 512; US Department of the Army, *The Law of Land Warfare* (1956), p. 4; UK Defence Ministry, *Joint Service Manual*, pp. 23, 444; de Preux, 'Basic Rules', pp. 392–93; Thomas Erskine Holland, *The Laws of War on Land (Written and Unwritten)* (Oxford: Clarendon Press, 1908), p. 13; Dunbar, 'Significance of Military Necessity', at 212; Draper, 'Military Necessity and Humanitarian Imperatives', at 142; Frédéric de Mulinen, *Handbook on the Law of War for Armed Forces* (Geneva: International Committee of the Red Cross, 1987), p. 83; Ingrid Detter de Lupis, *The Law of War* (Cambridge: Cambridge University Press, 1987), p. 334; Best, 'Restraint of War', p. 5; Jochnick and Normand, 'Legitimation of Violence', at 53; Melzer, *Targeted Killing*, p. 290; Rogers, *Law on the Battlefield* (2nd edn), p. 4; Benvenisti, 'Human Dignity in Combat', at 81; Greenwood, 'Historical Development', pp. 37–38; Christine Byron, 'Von Lewinski' in Cassese (ed), *Oxford Companion to International Criminal Justice* 966, p. 967; Schmitt, 'Military Necessity and Humanity', at 798; Solis, *Law of Armed Conflict*, p. 269.

for instance, between propositions of the sort 'occupying powers must detain persons who threaten their security' and 'occupying powers must not detain such persons'. What results is a zero-sum game where obeying one imperative always comes at the expense of disobeying the other imperative.

For proponents of the inevitable conflict thesis, weaving into IHL a workable compromise between fundamentally irreconcilable demands of military necessity and humanity is what accounting for them really means. Thus, a positive IHL rule may create a principal obligation, and then subject it to exceptions on grounds of military necessity and/or humanity. Consider Article 49 of Geneva Convention IV, for example:

> Individual or mass forcible transfers, as well as deportations of protected persons from occupied territory to the territory of the Occupying Power or to that of any other country, occupied or not, are prohibited, regardless of their motive.
>
> Nevertheless, the Occupying Power may undertake total or partial evacuation of a given area if the security of the population or imperative military reasons so demand.[2]

Here, the rule's framers have struck the compromise between military necessity and humanity in such a way that pleas arising from either one of these grounds are admissible. There are also instances where the drafters have chosen to admit military necessity pleas only,[3] or humanity pleas only.[4] Leaving the rule unqualified elsewhere[5] implies that its framers intended to exclude such pleas. Consequently, no positive IHL rule admits military necessity pleas, unless the rule itself envisages their admissibility expressly and in advance. The same exclusion also applies, *mutatis mutandis*, to humanity pleas.

2 Article 49, Geneva Convention IV.

3 Article 143, Geneva Convention IV: 'Such visits [by representatives or delegates of the protecting power] may not be prohibited except for reasons of imperative military necessity, and then only as an exceptional and temporary measure.'

4 Article 127, Geneva Convention IV: 'Sick, wounded or infirm internees and maternity cases shall not be transferred if the journey would be seriously detrimental to them, unless their safety imperatively so demands. If the combat zone draws close to a place of internment, the internees in the said place shall not be transferred unless their removal can be carried out in adequate conditions of safety, or unless they are exposed to greater risks by remaining on the spot than by being transferred.'

5 Article 3 common to Geneva Conventions I–IV: '[T]he following acts are and shall remain prohibited at any time and in any place whatsoever with respect to the above-mentioned persons [i.e., those taking no active part in the hostilities].'

We may style the second set of ideas – to which the inevitable conflict thesis will be contrasted – a 'joint satisfaction thesis'.[6] In a nutshell, the latter thesis asserts that it is always possible for the belligerent to act in a manner that jointly satisfies military necessity and humanity. This is so, because military necessity is normatively indifferent. For the purposes of IHL norm-creation, neither the military necessity nor the military non-necessity of a belligerent act really makes its performance or forbearance mandatory.

Humanity does demand some belligerent acts and condemn others. In some situations, humanity affirmatively demands what military necessity indifferently permits (e.g., 'Belligerents must limit their attacks to legitimate military targets', and 'Belligerents may limit their attacks to such targets'). Here, it is plain that the belligerent satisfies both considerations by acting in conformity with humanity. There are also circumstances in which this kind of joint satisfaction is unavailable – e.g., 'POWs must be released where unusual conditions of combat make their evacuation to the rear area impractical', as opposed to 'POWs may be killed in such conditions'. Even there, however, what the addressee of these propositions experiences is a norm contradiction, not a norm conflict. The belligerent can still satisfy military necessity and humanity by acting as directed by the latter.

According to the joint satisfaction thesis, IHL norm-creation accounts for military necessity in two ways. The first is by positing rules that make the pursuit of joint satisfaction unqualifiedly, principally, indeterminately or exceptionally obligatory. The other is by declining or failing to posit such rules. Unqualified IHL obligations extinguish all contrary liberties and render inadmissible all indifference pleas that might otherwise be invoked in defence of deviant behaviour. Crucially, it is possible that those pleas that are not normatively indifferent remain admissible even vis-à-vis unqualified IHL rules.

What the joint satisfaction thesis shows is three-fold. First, normative military necessity furnishes the framers of IHL rules with robust reason to leave the belligerent at liberty to pursue material military necessities and to avoid non-necessities. Second, it also offers moderate reason for which the framers should consider leaving the belligerent at liberty to forgo necessities and suffer non-necessities. Third, and most importantly,

[6] See Chapters 6–8.

no positive IHL rules obligate or prohibit any belligerent action on account of its military necessity or non-necessity alone.

In this chapter, we will familiarise ourselves with the inevitable conflict thesis. Let us first take an overview of its main features. Our discussion will then concentrate on the thesis's two central assertions, namely, that a norm conflict between military necessity and humanity is inevitable, and that unqualified IHL rules exclude both military necessity and humanity pleas.

5.1 Overview

In truth, the inevitable conflict thesis is a collated summation of the positions taken by commentators and authorities on normative military necessity that are disparate, fragmented and sometimes inconsistent. Those to whom the thesis is attributed do not necessarily embrace it in all its aspects. Nevertheless, several major proponents, such as Yoram Dinstein and Michael Schmitt, are readily identifiable.

Dinstein championed the thesis in his earlier work. His 1982 *Max Planck Encyclopaedia* entry on military necessity states:

> The laws of war are all based on a subtle balance between two opposing considerations: military necessity, on the one hand, and humanitarian sentiments, on the other ... Each one of the laws of war discloses a balance between military necessity and humanitarian sentiments, as produced by the framers of international conventions or as crystallized in the practice of States. The equilibrium may be imperfect, but it is legally binding in the very form that it is constructed. It is not the privilege of each belligerent, let alone every member of its armed forces, to weigh the opposing considerations of military necessity and humanitarianism so as to balance the scales anew. *A fortiori*, it is not permissible to ignore legal norms on the ground that they are overridden by one of the two sets of considerations.[7]

A similar sentiment is reiterated in Dinstein's 2004 *Conduct of Hostilities* book:

> LOIAC [the law of international armed conflict] in its entirety is predicated on a subtle equilibrium between two diametrically opposed impulses: military necessity and humanitarian considerations ... In actuality,

[7] Yoram Dinstein, 'Military Necessity', *Max Planck Encyclopedia of Public International Law* (Amsterdam, New York and Oxford: North-Holland Publishing, 1982), vol. III, 274, p. 274.

> LOIAC takes a middle road, allowing belligerent States much leeway (in keeping with the demands of military necessity) and yet circumscribing their freedom of action (in the name of humanitarianism) . . . Every single norm of LOIAC is moulded by a parallelogram of forces: it confronts a built-in tension between the relentless demands of military necessity and humanitarian considerations, working out a compromise formula. The outlines of the compromise vary from one LOIAC norm to another. Still, in general terms, it can be stated categorically that no part of LOIAC overlooks military requirements, just as no part of LOIAC loses sight of humanitarian considerations. All segments of this body of law are stimulated by a realistic (as distinct from a purely idealistic) approach to armed conflict.[8]

The main contours of the inevitable conflict thesis are already visible in these passages. Thus, IHL strikes a 'subtle equilibrium' between military necessity and humanity. These are 'diametrically opposed' considerations. 'No part' of IHL loses sight of this equilibrium. No deviation from positive IHL rules is therefore permissible by dint of 'one of the two sets of considerations' – in other words, neither military necessity pleas nor humanity pleas are admissible.

Dinstein's views have remained largely unchanged over the years.[9] Two recent modifications may be noted, however. He now acknowledges the existence of 'rare occasions upon which the demands of military necessity converge with humanitarian considerations'.[10] He cites the unqualified prohibition against attacking undefended towns, villages or buildings, as an example.[11] Still, according to Dinstein, this 'is not the normal situation. Ordinarily, military necessity will point in one direction and humanitarian considerations in another'.[12] The other modification involves a change in the emphasis that he places on the inadmissibility of pleas. Although he stands by the idea, he now says: 'In particular, [belligerent parties] cannot try to avoid implementation of

[8] Yoram Dinstein, *The Conduct of Hostilities under the Law of International Armed Conflict* (Cambridge: Cambridge University Press, 2004), pp. 16–17 (footnotes omitted).

[9] Dinstein, *Conduct of Hostilities* (2nd edn), pp. 4–5; Dinstein, 'Military Necessity' (2nd edn 2009); Yoram Dinstein, 'Military Necessity', *Max Planck Encyclopedia of Public International Law* (2015); Yoram Dinstein, *The Conduct of Hostilities under the Law of International Armed Conflict*, 3rd edn (Cambridge: Cambridge University Press, 2016), pp. 9–12.

[10] Dinstein, 'Military Necessity' (2nd edn 2009), para. 3.

[11] Ibid.

[12] Ibid, para. 4.

a given norm in the name of military necessity'.[13] Omitted here is the notion that the parties cannot try to do so in the name of humanity.

Schmitt's positions closely echo those of Dinstein. Thus, Schmitt recently advocated:

- That 'IHL represents a carefully thought out balance between the principles of military necessity and humanity';[14]
- That these principles are 'opposing forces';[15]
- That '[e]very one of [IHL's] rules constitutes a dialectical compromise' between them;[16] and
- That 'neither [military necessity nor humanity] independently justifies departure from its provisions, unless otherwise specifically provided for in the law'.[17]

Schmitt, much like Dinstein, also acknowledges a limited possibility that military necessity and humanity may coincide:

> Consider a military objective in a concentration of civilians that would release chemicals harmful to the civilian population if attacked with regular explosive bombs. For the sake of analysis, assume that despite the expected incidental harm to civilians, the anticipated military advantage is great enough to comply with the proportionality principle. However, if incendiary weapons are employed, the resulting fire will consume the chemicals, thereby lessening the civilian impact and keeping the area accessible to ground forces.[18]

Here, Schmitt hypothesises a military purpose in the form of 'destroying a military objective in a concentration of civilians that would release chemicals harmful to the civilian population if attacked by regular explosive bombs'. Then, vis-à-vis this purpose, he proposes to compare two alternative courses of action. The first course of action may be described as 'employing regular explosive bombs', and the other 'employing incendiary weapons'. Assuming that both are similarly

[13] Ibid, para. 7.

[14] Schmitt, 'Military Necessity and Humanity', at 798. See also Schmitt, 'Interpretive Guidance', at 6.

[15] Schmitt, 'Military Necessity and Humanity', at 798.

[16] Ibid, at 798. See also Schmitt, 'Interpretive Guidance', at 6; Michael N. Schmitt, 'Discriminate Warfare: The Military Necessity-Humanity Dialectic of International Humanitarian Law' in Lovell and Primoratz (eds), *Protecting Civilians during Violent Conflict* 85, pp. 88, 102.

[17] Schmitt, 'Military Necessity and Humanity', at 801.

[18] Ibid, at 816.

conducive to the accomplishment of the said purpose, one may say that the latter is more consistent with material military necessity than the former. That is so, according to Schmitt, inasmuch as the resulting fire consumes the chemicals and keeps the area accessible to ground forces.[19]

Schmitt argues that, in the situation at hand, incendiary weapons are also more humane than regular explosive bombs. Incendiary weapons lessen the harmful chemicals' impact on the surrounding civilian population, whereas regular weapons do not. 'In this scenario', Schmitt continues, 'the use of incendiary weapons would serve both humanitarian and military ends'.[20]

5.2 Inevitability of Norm Conflicts

What relationship do proponents of the inevitable conflict thesis see between military necessity and humanity in the process of IHL norm-creation? What could Dinstein's 'diametrical opposition'[21] between military necessity and humanity, or Schmitt's 'dialectical compromise'[22] between them, really mean?

In my view, Dinstein and Schmitt can only be regarded as denying the possibility of a joint satisfaction between military necessity and humanity. In other words, humanity always demands what military necessity spurns, and the former always condemns what the latter requires. The belligerent must *always* choose between acting as required by military necessity at the expense of humanity, on the one hand, and acting as demanded by humanity at the expense of military necessity, on the other. Similarly, the framers of IHL rules must *always* choose between prioritising humanity over military necessity, prioritising the latter over the former, and striking a compromise between them.

All positive IHL rules embody a choice of this character their framers have made. For, as Dinstein notes in his revised 2010 *Conduct of Hostilities* book:

[19] Presumably, these forces are unequipped with protective gear.

[20] Schmitt, 'Military Necessity and Humanity', at 816.

[21] Dinstein, *Conduct of Hostilities* (1st edn), p. 16; Dinstein, *Conduct of Hostilities* (2nd edn), p. 5.

[22] Schmitt, 'Military Necessity and Humanity', at 798. See also Schmitt, 'Interpretive Guidance', at 6; Schmitt, 'Discriminate Warfare', p. 102.

> Every single norm of LOIAC is moulded by a parallelogram of forces: it confronts an inveterate tension between the demands of military necessity and humanitarian considerations, working out a compromise formula.[23]

We may think of the picture here as a tug of war, with military necessity pulling the rope of IHL norm-creation in one direction, and humanity pulling it in the other direction.[24]

In order for their positions to make sense, proponents of the inevitable conflict thesis must also uphold the combined truth of three subsidiary propositions, namely:

1. That military necessity and humanity in their material sense never coincide;
2. That, normatively speaking, both military necessity and humanity offer reasons for which the framers of IHL rules should obligate obedience with the imperatives that the two considerations respectively generate; and
3. That obeying the imperatives of military necessity and obeying those of humanity always conflict with each other.

5.2.1 Non-coincidence of Military Necessity and Humanity in Their Material Sense

The inevitability of conflict between military necessity and humanity in IHL norm-creation entails the notion that their material counterparts never coincide. Every kind of belligerent conduct is deemed either inhumane yet militarily necessary, or humane yet militarily unnecessary. Conversely, no act can be both humane and necessary, or both inhumane and unnecessary.

Consider the treatment of POWs in unusual conditions of combat. Dinstein discusses the matter thus:

> A good example for LOIAC rejecting military necessity in favour of humanitarian considerations pertains to the capture of prisoners of war. Under Geneva Convention (III) of 1949, prisoners of war in custody must not be put to death, and, as soon as possible after capture, they have to be evacuated to camps situated in an area far from the combat zone. As a rule, this will be done by assigning an escort to carry out the process of

[23] Dinstein, *Conduct of Hostilities* (2nd edn), p. 5.

[24] Judith Gardam, *Necessity, Proportionality and the use of Force by States* (Cambridge: Cambridge University Press, 2004), p. 8; Camins, 'Past as Prologue', at 879.

> evacuation, ensuring that the prisoners of war will not be able to escape en route. The question is what happens when enemy combatants are captured by a small light unit (of, e.g., commandos or Special Forces), which can neither handicap the mission by encumbering itself with prisoners of war nor detach guards for their proper evacuation. Can the prisoners of war be shot by dint of military necessity? The answer is unequivocally negative. Article 41(3) of Additional Protocol I addresses the issue forthrightly, prescribing that – in these unusual conditions – the prisoners of war must be released. This had actually been the law long before the Protocol was adopted. Customary international law proscribes the killing of prisoners of war, 'even in cases of extreme necessity', when they slow up military movements or weaken the fighting force by requiring an escort. Military necessity cannot override the rule, since it is already factored into it. The legally binding compromise between military necessity and humanitarian considerations has been worked out in such a way that prisoners of war must either be kept safely in custody or released.[25]

Here, Dinstein apparently considers an act of the sort 'killing a POW in unusual conditions of combat' inhumane yet consistent with material military necessity. Refraining from such killing, in contrast, would be deemed humane yet lacking in material military necessity.

As noted earlier, Dinstein concedes the existence of 'rare' occasions where performing certain conduct, e.g., attacking undefended localities, can be regarded as both inhumane and materially unnecessary.[26] It does not appear, however, that he envisages any occasion, even exceptionally, where a given belligerent act can be deemed both humane and materially necessary. For that, one must turn to Schmitt's example of incendiary weapons noted above.[27]

5.2.2 *Military Necessity and Humanity as Generators of Imperatives*

If – or once – it is agreed that a particular kind of belligerent conduct tends to be consistent with humanity, the framers of IHL rules will have very good reason to obligate its performance. They will also consider prohibiting acts that are deemed inhumane. Indeed, proponents of the inevitable conflict thesis appear to take this imperative-generating character of humanitarian considerations for granted.

[25] Dinstein, *Conduct of Hostilities* (2nd edn), p. 7 (footnotes omitted).
[26] Dinstein, 'Military Necessity' (2nd edn 2009), para. 3.
[27] Schmitt, 'Military Necessity and Humanity', at 816.

Whether they also treat military necessity as imperative-generating is unclear. It would be essential that they do so, however, if the inevitability of norm conflict between military necessity and humanity were to make any sense. Military necessity's mandatory character would take two specific forms. First, acts deemed materially necessary ought to be performed. Second, those deemed materially unnecessary ought to be forborne.

5.2.2.1 Obligating Materially Necessary Acts

Dinstein states: 'The dynamics of the law are such that whatever is required by military necessity, and is not excluded on the ground of humanitarianism, is permissible'.[28] His reference to 'whatever is required by military necessity' may be taken as indicating his appreciation of a given act being deemed materially necessary. Similarly, by 'whatever is [so required] ... is permissible', one may understand Dinstein's appreciation of normative military necessity as permitting, rather than demanding, the act's performance.

In fact, nowhere does Dinstein – nor does Schmitt, for that matter – appear to assert that the framers of IHL rules should consider making the performance of material military necessities obligatory. Indeed, the very idea feels odd. We saw earlier how the intrinsic utility of material military necessity is a serious reason-giving consideration in IHL norm-creation.[29] What this means is that the framers of IHL rules have good reason to leave the belligerent at liberty, rather than place it under an obligation, to pursue what is materially necessary. There is no reason why it should be of any concern to IHL to ensure that everything done by belligerents conduce towards military success.[30]

Surprisingly, however, assertions that there is an obligation to perform material military necessities are not entirely unheard of. The 2007 *Al-Jedda* decision of the UK House of Lords[31] is a case in point. In that case, the Law Lords were asked to clarify, inter alia, the relationship between the European Convention on Human Rights[32] and the Charter of the

[28] Dinstein, *Conduct of Hostilities* (2nd edn), p. 6. See also Dinstein, *Conduct of Hostilities* (1st edn), p. 18.
[29] See Chapter 4.
[30] See Chapter 4.
[31] *R. v Secretary of State for Defence* [2007] UKHL 58 (hereinafter *Al-Jedda UKHL*).
[32] Convention for the Protection of Human Rights and Fundamental Freedoms, 4 November 1950, in force 3 September 1953, 213 UNTS 221 (hereinafter European Convention on Human Rights).

United Nations (UN).[33] On the one hand, Article 5(1) of the European Convention stipulates the principal duty of non-detention,[34] followed by a list of six grounds on which a limited power of detention may be inferred.[35] It is generally agreed that this list is 'exhaustive'[36] and excludes detention 'where there is no intention to bring criminal charges within a reasonable time'.[37] On the other hand, Article 103 of the UN Charter establishes a hierarchy, whereby a Charter obligation prevails over conflicting obligations arising from other international agreements.[38] The UK government, respondent in the case, argued that a series of Security Council resolutions adopted under Chapter VII of the UN Charter bound it with an affirmative duty to detain Al-Jedda.[39] By virtue of the Charter's Article 103, this counter-duty of security detention displaced the United Kingdom's conflicting duty of non-detention arising under the European Convention.[40]

Lord Bingham found that the relevant Security Council resolutions 'use the language of authorisation, not obligation', and that, '[i]n ordinary speech to authorise is to permit or allow or license, not to require or oblige'.[41] In other words, no conflicting duties under Article 5(1) of the European Convention and Article 103 of the UN Charter existed for the United Kingdom vis-à-vis Al-Jedda.

Lord Bingham then examined the law of belligerent occupation. Citing Article 43 of the 1907 Hague Regulations,[42] he held that the United Kingdom, as an occupying power, 'was obliged ... to take necessary

33 Charter of the United Nations, 26 June 1945, in force 24 October 1945, 1 UNTS 16 (hereinafter UN Charter).

34 Namely, that '[n]o one shall be deprived of his liberty'.

35 Namely, 'save in the following cases and in accordance with a procedure prescribed by law'.

36 *Al-Jedda v UK* App. No. 27021/08 (ECtHR, 7 July 2011) (hereinafter *Al-Jedda ECtHR*), para. 99.

37 Ibid, para. 100.

38 Article 103 of the UN Charter reads: 'In the event of a conflict between the obligations of the Members of the United Nations under the present Charter and their obligations under any other international agreement, their obligations under the present Charter shall prevail.'

39 *Al-Jedda UKHL*, para. 26 (Lord Bingham).

40 Ibid.

41 Ibid, para. 31 (Lord Bingham).

42 Article 43, Hague Regulations (1907). This provision reads: 'The authority of the legitimate power having in fact passed into the hands of the occupant, the latter shall take all the measures in his power to restore, and ensure, as far as possible, public order and safety, while respecting, unless absolutely prevented, the laws in force in the country.'

measures to protect the safety of the public and its own safety'.[43] Elsewhere in the case,[44] Al-Jedda, a British national at the time of his detention in Iraq, was found not to have been a 'protected person' within the meaning of Article 4 of Geneva Convention IV.[45] Lord Bingham observed that the convention's Articles 41,[46] 42[47] and 78:[48]

> [S]how plainly that there is a power to intern persons who are not protected persons, and it seems to me that if the occupying power considers it necessary to detain a person who is judged to be a serious threat to the safety of the public or the occupying power there must be an obligation to detain such person.[49]

Al-Jedda took his case to the European Court of Human Rights.[50] The court found – correctly, in my view[51] – that the law of belligerent occupation empowers as a last resort, but it does not obligate, the occupying power to detain persons present in the territory that it administers solely on security grounds.[52]

Lord Bingham's reasoning has two, arguably distinct, prongs. One is the safety of the public, and the other is the occupying power's own safety. We are not presently concerned with the former. Suffice it to say that, while

43 *Al-Jedda UKHL*, para. 32 (Lord Bingham).
44 Ibid, para. 128 (Baroness Hale).
45 Article 4 of Geneva Convention IV reads, in relevant parts: 'Persons protected by the convention are those who, at a given moment and in any manner whatsoever, find themselves, in case of a conflict or occupation, in the hands of a Party to the conflict or Occupying Power of which they are not nationals.'
46 Article 41 of Geneva Convention IV reads, in relevant parts: 'Should the Power in whose hands protected persons may be consider the measures of control mentioned in the present Convention to be inadequate, it may not have recourse to any other measure of control more severe than that of assigned residence or internment.'
47 Article 42 of Geneva Convention IV reads, in relevant parts: 'The internment or placing in assigned residence of protected persons may be ordered only if the security of the Detaining Power makes it absolutely necessary.'
48 Article 78 of Geneva Convention IV reads, in relevant parts: 'If the Occupying Power considers it necessary, for imperative reasons of security, to take safety measures concerning protected persons, it may, at the most, subject them to assigned residence or to internment.'
49 *Al-Jedda UKHL*, para. 32 (Lord Bingham).
50 *Al-Jedda ECtHR*.
51 Nobuo Hayashi, 'Do the Good Intentions of European Human Rights Law Really Pave the Road to IHL Hell for Civilian Detainees in Occupied Territory?' (2015) 20 *Journal of Conflict & Security Law* 133, at 140.
52 *Al-Jedda ECtHR*, para. 107: 'In the Court's view it would appear from the provisions of the Fourth Geneva Convention that under international humanitarian law internment is to be viewed not as an obligation on the Occupying Power but as a measure of last resort.'

Article 43 of the 1907 Hague Regulations does create an affirmative duty to restore and ensure public order and safety, it is far from clear whether this necessarily translates into an affirmative duty of security detention.[53]

More importantly for our discussion here, the law of belligerent occupation clearly does not obligate the occupying power to protect its own safety. That remains the case, although it is also clearly in the occupier's own strategic interest, and hence consistent with material military necessity, to do so. Now, let us say that protecting an occupying power's own safety is a legitimate military purpose. Two questions arise. First, can detaining persons solely on security grounds be deemed consistent with material military necessity for that particular purpose? I am of the view that it can. Second, does it follow that the framers of IHL rules should consider making security detention obligatory? Lord Bingham, it appears, felt so. '[I]t seems to me', he stated, 'that if the occupying power considers it necessary to detain a person who is judged to be a serious threat to the safety of . . . the occupying power there must be an obligation to detain such person'.[54]

The expression that Lord Bingham used here – 'there must be an obligation' – is somewhat ambiguous. It could be interpreted as suggesting that, in order to proceed with security-based detentions, an occupying power must first demonstrate the existence of an obligation to do so. Alternatively, Lord Bingham could have meant that an occupying power that finds it necessary to detain persons on security grounds is duty-bound to do so. In the context of our discussion, it is more likely that he meant the latter.

5.2.2.2 Prohibiting Materially Unnecessary Acts

The notion that the framers of IHL rules should consider prohibiting materially unnecessary action is very widely supported.[55] Some

[53] In upholding an affirmative duty of security detention under the 1907 Hague Regulations, Lord Bingham cited *Armed Activities on the Territory of the Congo (Democratic Republic of the Congo v Uganda), Judgment, ICJ Reports 2005*, p. 168, para. 178. In that paragraph, the ICJ held: 'This obligation [under Article 43 of the Hague Regulations] comprised the duty to secure respect for the applicable rules of international human rights law and international humanitarian law, to protect the inhabitants of the occupied territory against acts of violence, and not to tolerate such violence by any third party.' See *Al-Jedda UKHL*, para. 32 (Lord Bingham).

[54] *Al-Jedda UKHL*, para. 32 (Lord Bingham).

[55] That is so, notwithstanding the fact that the mere lack of material military necessity does not signify an act's illegitimacy. See Chapter 4.

authorities appear to assume that unnecessary acts deserve to be banned, because only necessary ones deserve to be permitted. Thus, in D. I. A. D. Draper's words: 'The law of war ... accepts that in achieving victory ... there is to be the minimum expenditure of blood, treasure, resources and time. That may have nothing whatever to do with humanitarian considerations and may be styled "the doctrine of military economy".'[56] A. P. V. Rogers argues, as a foremost characteristic of military necessity in the law of war, that what military commanders do 'must be justified in every case by military necessity',[57] and that 'no action may be taken which is not militarily necessary'.[58]

For others, non-necessities ought to be prohibited because armed force equals, or entails, the infliction of evil. According to the *US Navy Commander's Handbook*, the goal of military necessity is:

> [T]o limit suffering and destruction to that which is necessary to achieve a valid military objective. Thus it prohibits the use of any kind or degree of force not required for the partial or complete submission of the enemy with a minimum expenditure of time, life, and physical resources.[59]

Seen in isolation, the second sentence of this passage might suggest that 'any kind or degree of force', evil or otherwise, would be prohibited if materially unnecessary. Such a view would come closer to that put forth by Draper and Rogers.

This apparent similarity becomes somewhat less definite when one looks at the first sentence. That sentence appears to indicate the manual drafters' belief that force, whatever its kind or degree, tends to generate 'suffering and destruction'. It is, according to the drafters, with a view to limiting this tendency – '[t]hus' is the expression used – that military necessity prohibits unnecessary acts. In a similar spirit, several authors equate force with 'injury',[60] 'damage'[61] and 'violence'.[62]

56 Draper, 'Military Necessity and Humanitarian Imperatives', at 130.

57 Rogers, *Law on the Battlefield* (2nd edn), p. 5. See also Melzer, *Targeted Killing*, p. 286 (emphasis in original): '[T]he principle of military necessity reduces the sum total of lawful military action from that which positive IHL does not prohibit *in abstracto* to that which is actually required *in concreto*.'

58 Rogers, *Law on the Battlefield* (2nd edn), 6.

59 US Department of the Navy et al., *Commander's Handbook*, p. 5-3-1.

60 Phillipson, *International Law and the Great War*, p. 131; Dunbar, 'Military Necessity in War Crimes Trials', at 444 (quoting ibid, p. 132).

61 Phillipson, *International Law and the Great War*, p. 131.

62 Ibid, p. 132; Dunbar, 'Military Necessity in War Crimes Trials' at 444; de Preux, 'Basic Rules', p. 396.

Schmitt once belonged to this group. While reviewing the first edition of Rogers' *Law on the Battlefield*, Schmitt noted:

> To exist as a principle of law, military necessity must have independent legal valence. That can, by definition, only occur when it is characterized as a limitation ... As a principle, military necessity prohibits destructive or harmful acts that are unnecessary to secure a military advantage.[63]

He also asserted that '[m]ilitary necessity operates ... to prohibit acts that are not militarily necessary; it is a principle of limitation, not authorization. In its legal sense, military necessity justifies nothing.'[64] Schmitt has since expressly repudiated this idea.[65]

As for Dinstein, there is no indication that he ever accepted the mere lack of material military necessity as a reason for prohibiting an act under IHL.

5.2.3 *Inevitable Conflict between Imperatives of Military Necessity and Imperatives of Humanity*

Combining the non-coincidence between military necessity and humanity in their material context, with the idea that they both generate imperatives in IHL norm-creation, yields the result that these imperatives inevitably conflict. Put another way, military necessity and humanity inevitably conflict with each other, because they always describe and demand belligerent acts in opposite directions.

5.2.3.1 Norm Conflicts and Their Pre-emption Generally

A norm conflict exists where a particular act is subject simultaneously to mandatory performance and mandatory forbearance.[66] Thus, according to Hart:

> Many writers favour the idea (which seems intuitively acceptable) that conflict between two rules requiring or prohibiting actions is to be understood in terms of the logical possibility of joint obedience to them. Two such rules conflict if and only if obedience to them both ('joint obedience') is logically impossible. The crudest case of such a conflict are

[63] Schmitt, 'Book Review', at 257, 258.
[64] Schmitt, 'Green War', at 54.
[65] Schmitt, 'Military Necessity and Humanity', at 799 n.9.
[66] Admittedly, this is a simplified version. Chapter 7 will present a more refined account of norm conflicts.

> rules which respectively require and forbid the same action on the part of the same person at the same time or times. The logical impossibility of joint obedience may be exhibited in the following way. For any rule requiring or prohibiting action, we can form a statement (an 'obedience statement') asserting that the action that is required by the rule is done, or the action prohibited by the rule is not done. Two such rules conflict if their respective obedience statements are logically inconsistent and so cannot both be true. Thus (to take one of Kelsen's examples), suppose one rule requires certain persons to kill certain other human beings, and another rule prohibits the same persons from killing the same other human beings, the obedience statements corresponding to those rules would be of the general form, 'killing is done', and 'killing is not done'. Of course, before we can determine whether two statements of this general form are logically inconsistent or not, they would have to be filled out with specifications of the agents and victims and times to which the rules, explicitly or implicitly, related. If the same agents are required by one rule to do, and by another rule to abstain from, the same action at the same time this will be reflected in the corresponding obedience statements which would be logically inconsistent. Joint obedience to the rules would be logically impossible.[67]

Hart cautions, however, that the logical impossibility of joint obedience to which two conflicting norms give rise does not preclude the logical impossibility of their valid co-existence:

> It is to be observed that this definition of conflict between rules leaves entirely open the question whether or not it is logically possible for two conflicting rules to coexist as valid rules of the same or different systems. To most people it would certainly seem possible for a law of one legal system made by one set of legislators to conflict with the law of another legal system made by another set of legislators; and it would perhaps seem equally obvious that one such law could conflict with some moral rule or principle. Joint obedience to these rules would be logically impossible, but their coexistence as valid rules would be logically possible. Further, though it would certainly be deplorable on every practical score if laws of a single legal system conflicted and the system provided no way of resolving such conflicts, it is still far from obvious that even this is a logical impossibility.[68]

[67] HLA Hart, 'Kelsen's Doctrine of the Unity of Law' in Hart, *Jurisprudence and Philosophy* 309, p. 325 (footnotes omitted). See also Hans Kelsen, *General Theory of Norms*, Michael Hartney (trans.) (Oxford: Clarendon Press, 1991), p. 191; Bruno Celano, 'Norm Conflicts: Kelsen's View in the Late Period and a Rejoinder' in Paulson and Paulson (eds), *Normativity and Norms* 343, pp. 346–53.

[68] Hart, 'Kelsen's Doctrine', pp. 325–26.

That two conflicting norms may validly co-exist, even within one legal system, is indeed a logical possibility.[69] It would still be a functional shortcoming of that legal system to contain valid yet conflicting norms. Thus, if for nothing else, it would be in the practical interest of a legal system to pre-empt norm conflicts between its positive rules by coordinating its legislative processes.

5.2.3.2 Norm Conflicts between Military Necessity and Humanity, and Their Pre-emption in IHL Norm-Creation

We have so far established the following chain of reasoning underlying the inevitable conflict thesis. If a given belligerent act is deemed materially necessary, it is always deemed inhumane. Military necessity demands this act, whereas humanity condemns it. Conversely, if an act is considered humane, it is always considered materially unnecessary. Humanity makes its performance mandatory, while military necessity makes its forbearance mandatory. Obeying humanity always entails disobeying military necessity, and vice versa. Consequently, military necessity and humanity always result in norm conflicts.

Now imagine a situation where either military necessity or humanity, but not both, were the only set of reason-giving considerations for the framers of IHL rules. Arguably, in such a situation, no danger of norm conflict among the resulting rules would arise. Since both are relevant, however, and since, according to the inevitable conflict thesis, they always generate norm conflicts, it would be seriously detrimental to the functionality of IHL if these conflicting considerations led to the adoption of conflicting rules.

The process of IHL norm-creation endeavours to pre-empt such eventualities by striking a compromise between military necessity and humanity.[70] For proponents of the inevitable conflict thesis, this is what accounting for these considerations really means. The framers of IHL rules endeavour to do so:

1. By letting humanity trump military necessity;
2. By letting military necessity trump humanity; or
3. By working out some middle ground between the two.

[69] Georg Henrik von Wright, 'Value, Norm, and Action in My Philosophical Writings' in Georg Meggle (ed), *Actions, Norms, Values: Discussions with Georg Henrik von Wright* (Berlin and New York: Walter de Gruyter, 1999) 11, p. 21; Ota Weinberger, 'Logical Analysis in the Realm of the Law' in Meggle (ed), *Actions, Norms, Values* 291, p. 300.

[70] It might be felt that techniques such as *lex specialis* and *jus cogens* would also be available. They are *not* the relevant techniques for our present purposes, however. See Chapter 8.

Let us consider a belligerent act that is deemed inhumane yet materially necessary, e.g., detaining persons based exclusively on the security threats they pose to the occupying power. Letting humanity trump military necessity would result in the creation of an unqualified IHL rule of the form 'the occupying power shall not detain persons on security grounds alone'. Should military necessity prevail over humanity, the resulting IHL rule would make their detention obligatory instead.

Applying the same line of reasoning to acts deemed humane yet materially unnecessary is bound to come across as awkward. Take the treatment of POWs in unusual conditions of combat, for example. On the one hand, were the framers of IHL rules to let humanity trump military necessity, they would validly posit an unqualified obligation of the form 'POWs shall be released in unusual conditions of combat'. On the other hand, letting military necessity prevail over humanity could very well lead to a strange obligation to kill them. After all, compared to killing them outright, neither dragging them around nor releasing them, thereby exposing their captor to dangers of detection by enemy forces nearby, seems consistent with material military necessity.

Bizarre as it may be, the inevitable conflict thesis commits its adherents to accepting the possibility of these contrasting IHL obligations. Holding otherwise would amount to conceding that military necessity does not generate imperatives. Conceding thus would, in turn, amount to acknowledging that a conflict between military necessity and humanity is not inevitable.

Where a middle ground is worked out, the resulting rule is likely to contain a principal obligation to perform humane acts – or materially necessary acts, as the case may be – followed by an exceptional obligation to abstain from such acts if military necessity or humanity so demands. Thus, for example, Article 143 of Geneva Convention IV obligates the detaining power to permit visits by representatives or delegates of the protecting power, 'except for reasons of imperative military necessity'.[71] Alternatively, the resulting rule may principally prohibit inhumane or materially unnecessary acts, and yet exceptionally obligate such acts should the latter be demanded by humanity and/or military necessity. One may recall Article 49 of Geneva Convention IV discussed at the outset of this chapter.

[71] Article 143, Geneva Convention IV. As discussed earlier, the inevitable conflict thesis would insist that reasons of imperative military necessity obligate the detaining power to refuse visits by representatives or delegates of the protecting power.

5.3 Inadmissibility of Military Necessity and Humanity Pleas vis-à-vis All Unqualified IHL Rules

The inevitable conflict thesis is remarkable for the starkly contrasting manner in which it juxtaposes military necessity with humanity in IHL norm-creation. Its significance does not end there, however. The thesis also claims that unqualified rules of positive IHL exclude all military necessity pleas,[72] as well as all humanity pleas.

This latter claim stems from two assertions. First, the existence of exceptional clauses on grounds of military necessity and/or humanity reveals the framers' intention to withhold them elsewhere. Second, every valid IHL rule embodies a compromise between military necessity and humanity.

5.3.1 *Excluding Military Necessity and Humanity Pleas Alike*

Express military necessity exceptions are attached to some positive IHL rules.[73] This clearly indicates the framers' intention to admit military necessity pleas vis-à-vis these rules. It follows that the framers intended to disallow deviations from the prescriptions of unqualified rules on account of military necessity. Had it been otherwise, they would surely have qualified these rules by adding exceptional clauses expressly authorising such deviations. It can therefore be inferred that the exclusion of military necessity pleas is generally intended.[74]

[72] The idea that military necessity may not be invoked vis-à-vis unqualified rules of positive IHL is not controversial. To hold otherwise – i.e., whether it be military necessity as an additional layer of permission, or as an additional layer of restriction – is to conflate military necessity in its normative and juridical contexts. The joint satisfaction thesis also arrives at the same conclusion. What distinguishes the joint satisfaction thesis from the inevitable conflict thesis is the chain of reasoning used when reaching this conclusion and the further consequences to which it gives rise. See Chapters 6, 7 and 8.

[73] Article 23(g), Hague Regulations (1907); Articles 8, 33, 34, 50, Geneva Convention I; Articles 8, 28, 51, Geneva Convention II; Article 126, Geneva Convention III; Articles 49, 53, 143, 147, Geneva Convention IV; Articles 4(2), 11(2), Hague Cultural Property Convention; Articles 54(5), 62(1), 67(4), 71(3), Additional Protocol I; Article 17(1), Additional Protocol II; Articles 8(2)(b)(xiii), 8(2)(e)(viii), 8(2)(e)(xii), Rome Statute; Article 6, Second Protocol to the Hague Convention of 1954 for the Protection of Cultural Property in the Event of Armed Conflict, 26 March 1999, in force 9 March 2004, 2253 UNTS 172 (hereinafter Hague Cultural Property Protocol II).

[74] Draper, 'Military Necessity and Humanitarian Imperatives', at 138; Greenwood, 'Historical Development', pp. 37–38; Gerald J. Adler, 'Targets in War: Legal Considerations' (1970–1971) 8 *Houston Law Review* 1, at 16.

This also means that, other than those reflected in exceptional clauses, no considerations of military necessity escape exclusion – or 'survive' – during the process of IHL norm-creation into positive IHL. Used in this fashion as an inferential technique, *argumendum a contrario* excludes military necessity in its juridical context in two important ways – namely, as a supposedly additional layer of normative restraint, and as a purported exception, justification or excuse.[75] Dinstein explains:

> Either way, the solution chosen by the framers of the treaty – or consolidated in the general practice of States – must be viewed as binding on Contracting Parties to the treaty, or on the entire international community, in the very form in which it is constructed. Belligerent parties are not free to question the manner in which the compromise between military necessity and humanitarian considerations was forged by the framers. In particular, they cannot try to avoid implementation of a given norm in the name of military necessity.[76]

Somewhat oddly, the same logic would also exclude humanity, both as a supposedly additional layer of normative restraint and as a purported exception, justification or excuse, vis-à-vis unqualified IHL rules. For there are positive IHL rules that expressly provide for exceptions on humanitarian grounds or, at any rate, on grounds that are arguably analogous. Article 127 of Geneva Convention IV prohibits, inter alia:

- The transfer of sick, wounded, or infirm internees and maternity cases involving arduous journeys, 'unless their safety imperatively so demands'; and
- The transfer of internees in the event of the combat zone drawing close to their place of internment, 'unless they are exposed to greater risks by remaining on the spot than by being transferred'.[77]

Clearly, Article 127's framers intended to admit humanity pleas as an exception to the principal obligation of non-transfer. The absence of similar exceptions in unqualified IHL rules indicates that their framers intended to disallow deviations on account of humanity. Accordingly, the general intention is to exclude humanity as an implicit exception, justification or excuse.

As noted above, Dinstein appears to have toned down from his earlier position that 'it is not permissible to ignore legal norms on the ground

[75] See Chapters 8 and 9.
[76] Dinstein, 'Military Necessity' (2nd edn 2009), para. 7.
[77] Article 127, Geneva Convention IV.

that they are overridden by [humanitarian] considerations'.[78] Schmitt, in contrast, insists on the inadmissibility of both military necessity and humanity pleas, at least as far as treaty law is concerned:

> Extant treaty law therefore reflects an agreed-upon balance between military necessity and humanity, such that *neither independently justifies departure from its provisions*, unless otherwise specifically provided for in the law ... At times the express or inherent balance between military necessity and humanity may appear illogical, such that one or the other ought to be invoked to rebalance an existing rule. But any such rebalancing would be without justification insofar as the new balance deviates from that which states have agreed upon.[79]

5.3.2 Military Necessity and Humanity Accounted for in All Positive IHL Rules

Neither military necessity nor humanity may be invoked vis-à-vis unqualified IHL rules, because the process of their norm-creation already accounts for both considerations. What would happen, however, if it could be shown that this process does *not* always account for military necessity and/or humanity in the way just described? Would it follow that, in such cases, military necessity and/or humanity pleas might conceivably be admissible even vis-à-vis unqualified IHL rules?

Dinstein and Schmitt flatly deny such a possibility. For them, no positive IHL rule leaves military necessity and humanity unaccounted for. On the contrary, they are quite emphatic that 'every single norm'[80] of IHL, and 'every one of its rules',[81] embodies a compromise between military necessity and humanity.[82] It would appear that, to Dinstein and Schmitt at least, the admissibility of military necessity and humanity

[78] Dinstein, 'Military Necessity' (1st edn), p. 274 (emphasis added). Compare this with Dinstein, *Conduct of Hostilities* (1st edn), pp. 18–19; Dinstein, 'Military Necessity' (2nd edn 2009), para. 7; Dinstein, *Conduct of Hostilities* (2nd edn), pp. 6–7.

[79] Schmitt, 'Military Necessity and Humanity', at 801, 805 (emphasis added).

[80] Dinstein, *Conduct of Hostilities* (2nd edn), p. 5; Dinstein, *Conduct of Hostilities* (3rd edn), p. 10. See also Dinstein, 'Military Necessity' (2nd edn 2009), para. 7.

[81] Schmitt, 'Military Necessity and Humanity', at 798. See also Schmitt, 'Interpretive Guidance', at 6.

[82] Robert Kolb, 'La nécessité militaire dans le droit des conflits armés: essai de clarification conceptuelle' in Sociéte française pour le droit international, *Colloque de Grenoble, La nécessité en droit international* (Paris: Pedone, 2007) 151, p. 158: '[i]l n'y a pas une seule norme du droit des conflits armés qui ne réponde à une mise en balance entre les intérêts humanitaires et les intérêts issus des nécessités de la situation de belligérance'.

pleas vis-à-vis unqualified IHL rules is an academic question – that is, unless and until such rules are discovered or newly created.

5.4 Conclusion

In this chapter, we have canvassed some salient features of one internally coherent theory that best explains, or would best explain, the various positions taken by weighty IHL authorities. Thus, to say that IHL accounts for military necessity and humanity is to treat them as generators of mutually incompatible imperatives. If left unaddressed by the law's framers, these imperatives would inevitably result in conflicting IHL rules with which the belligerent is unable to comply simultaneously. Pre-empting such functional defects involves striking a compromise between military necessity and humanity. Since this compromise permeates the entire *corpus juris* of positive IHL, all military necessity and humanity pleas are excluded save where the rule itself envisions their admissibility expressly and in advance.

Securing the logical consistency of this theory has come at a price. First, the theory requires materially necessary acts to be always inhumane, and humane acts to be always materially unnecessary. And yet, as Dinstein and Schmitt themselves acknowledge, the non-coincidence of military necessity and humanity in their material sense sits uncomfortably with the fact that some belligerent acts can be both inhumane and unnecessary, or both materially necessary and humane. Second, military necessity and humanity would normatively conflict with each other only if they both generated imperatives; but it is difficult to see why the framers of IHL rules should consider obligating materially necessary acts and prohibiting unnecessary ones. Third, treating military necessity – or humanity, for that matter – as a generator of imperatives would imply that exceptional clauses attached to positive IHL rules should take the form of obligations. That, however, is plainly not the case. Fourth, it simply seems too inflexible to hold the belligerent to the letter of unqualified IHL rules, even against genuine and urgent humanitarian considerations.

I submit that we can, and should, remedy these flaws. It is, in essence, their rectification that transforms the inevitable conflict thesis into the joint satisfaction thesis. Let us see how this transformation occurs in the next three chapters.

6

Joint Satisfaction Thesis I

Alignment and Indifference

The joint satisfaction thesis rejects the idea that materially necessary acts are always inhumane, and humane acts are always materially unnecessary. On the contrary, numerous belligerent acts reveal an alignment between military necessity and humanity in their material context. This alignment can be characterised either as 'necessary-humane' or as 'unnecessary-inhumane'.

The thesis also asserts that neither military necessity nor humanity always generates imperatives. Humanity does demand some acts and condemn others. Nevertheless, it leaves certain kinds of belligerent conduct to matters of permission and tolerance. Military necessity, for its part, never prompts the framers of IHL rules to consider obligating materially necessary acts or prohibiting unnecessary ones.

In the event of a necessary-humane alignment, military necessity permits, and humanity often demands, the act's performance. Conversely, an unnecessary-inhumane alignment suggests that military necessity permits, and humanity frequently demands, the act's forbearance. Either way, by acting in accordance with the alignment, the belligerent satisfies both sets of considerations.

Admittedly, not all belligerent acts are subject to such an alignment. Some may be deemed materially necessary yet inhumane, or humane yet materially unnecessary. Even in these cases, however, joint satisfaction of a somewhat more limited character is always available. That is so, because military necessity is normatively indifferent. Thus, even where military necessity merely tolerates what humanity demands, or where the former permits what the latter condemns, the belligerent still satisfies both considerations jointly, by acting in accordance with humanity's imperatives.

Consequently, where an act involves considerations of military necessity and humanity,[1] their joint satisfaction is always possible. A norm conflict between them is therefore not inevitable.

[1] We will see in Chapter 8 that not all belligerent acts in fact involve considerations of military necessity and humanity.

In this chapter, we will see how military necessity and humanity in their material sense may, and frequently do, align with each other. In addition, it will be shown that normative military necessity not only permits materially necessary acts, but it also tolerates unnecessary ones. Nor, for that matter, does humanity demand all humane acts or condemn all inhumane acts – although, admittedly, it often does.

6.1 Military Necessity-Humanity Alignment in Their Material Context

Dinstein concedes that a belligerent act can on 'rare' occasions be both materially unnecessary and inhumane.[2] While clearly a welcome improvement on his earlier position, Dinstein ought to accept the possibility of such occasions far beyond that of rarity.

On the one hand, Dinstein's failure to do so is unfortunate, given his otherwise apposite observation:

> Military commanders are often the first to appreciate that their professional duties can, and should, be discharged without causing pointless distress to the troops.[3]

Presumably, pointless distress of the kind that Dinstein has in mind includes exposure to situations of needless inhumanity. On the other hand, even conceding this latter point so forthrightly would render a principal component of the inevitable conflict thesis untenable.

It appears that Dinstein's refusal to recognise the possibility of a necessary-humane alignment remains firm.[4] He thereby locks himself further into the inevitable conflict thesis. Schmitt, in contrast, at least acknowledges situations where using incendiary weapons may be both more humane and more consistent with material military necessity than using ordinary explosives.[5] Schmitt's concession is far from adequate, however. As will be seen below, there are numerous other, more intuitive, examples.

Let us first highlight those belligerent acts that typify the unnecessary-inhumane alignment. Our discussion will then turn to those characterised by the necessary-humane alignment.

[2] Dinstein, 'Military Necessity' (2nd edn 2009), para. 3.
[3] Dinstein, *Conduct of Hostilities* (2nd edn), p. 5.
[4] See Chapter 5.
[5] See Schmitt, 'Military Necessity and Humanity', at 816.

6.1.1 Unnecessary and Inhumane

Al-Qahtani was captured in Afghanistan, and brought to Guantánamo in November 2002.[6] While in detention, he was repeatedly subjected to harsh interrogation techniques.[7] Extracting actionable intelligence regarding al-Qaida's activities was among those ostensible purposes for which these techniques were administered.[8] In 2009, Susan Crawford, a Bush administration official then in charge of convening military commissions, admitted that al-Qahtani's treatment had satisfied even the definition of torture as understood by the administration itself.[9] Al-Qahtani's lawyer reportedly described him as '"paranoid", "incoherent", "cracked"'.[10]

One would agree that the act 'torturing Mohammed al-Qahtani to the point of incoherence' was not only inhumane but also materially unnecessary for its purpose 'extracting actionable intelligence regarding al-Qaida's activities from him'. It would follow that the kind of act 'torturing a detainee of intelligence value to the point of incoherence' might be deemed both inhumane and materially unnecessary for the kind of purpose 'extracting actionable intelligence regarding enemy activities from a detainee of intelligence value'.

In the early phases of the Iraq War, US soldiers killed an increasing number of civilians. Such killings fuelled anti-American sentiments amongst the very people the United States claimed to have come to protect.[11] These incidents are indicative of inhumanity as well as a lack of material military necessity.

The idea that belligerent acts can be deemed both inhumane and materially unnecessary is an old one indeed.[12] According to Henry Sidgwick, a nineteenth-century utilitarian thinker, the belligerent 'may be expected to abstain from recruiting his army compulsorily out of the

[6] Adam Zagorin and Michael Duffy, 'Inside the Interrogation of Detainee 063', *Time*, 20 June 2005.

[7] Ibid.

[8] Ibid.

[9] Woodward, 'Detainee Tortured'.

[10] Washington Media Association, *Torturing Democracy*, p. 52.

[11] Richard C Paddock, 'Shots to the Heart of Iraq', *Los Angeles Times*, 25 July 2005.

[12] Stephen C Neff, 'Prisoners of War in International Law: The Nineteenth Century' in Scheipers (ed), *Prisoners in War* 57, pp. 63–64 (citing Emmerich de Vattel, *The Law of Nations; or, the Principles of Natural Law Applied to Conduct and to the Affairs of Nations and Sovereigns*, 3 vols., Charles G. Fenwrick (trans.) [Washington, DC: Carnegie Institution of Washington, 1916], vol. III, pp. 280, 284–86).

population of an invaded country'.[13] Here, the lack of material military necessity would emanate from the fact that 'the modern sense of nationality would not only excite a strong reprobation for such conduct, but would also make the forced recruits a bad element of the army'.[14]

It is somewhat less clear whether, at the time of his writing in 1891, Sidgwick himself considered it inhumane to force persons to serve in the armed forces of a hostile power. All that Sidgwick noted is:

> [T]here has been a considerable change since the now prohibited practice was largely carried on by the Prussians in Saxony in 1756; owing to the general growth of national sentiment that has taken place in the interval.[15]

Be that as it may, the notion that forced recruitment of residents in occupied territory – or, indeed, that of enemy nationals generally – is inhumane appears to have become evident over time. This notion had already appeared in Articles 36 and 37 of the 1874 Brussels Declaration,[16] and Articles 47 and 48 of the 1880 Oxford Manual.[17] Articles 44 and 45 of the 1899 Hague Regulations[18] were adopted at the first Peace Conference without much dissent.[19] Nor was there any significant debate at the 1949 Diplomatic Conference[20] where Articles 51 and 147 of Geneva Convention IV[21] were negotiated. The Red Cross commentary on Article 51 notes:

13 Sidgwick, *Elements of Politics*, p. 255.

14 Ibid.

15 Ibid.

16 Articles 36, 37, Brussels Declaration.

17 Articles 47, 48, The Laws of War on Land, 9 September 1880 (hereinafter Oxford Manual).

18 Article 44, Regulations Respecting the Laws and Customs of War on Land, annexed to Convention Respecting the Laws and Customs of War on Land, 29 July 1899, in force 4 September 1900 (hereinafter Hague Regulations [1899]). See also Articles 23(h), 45, Hague Regulations (1907).

19 Carnegie Endowment for International Peace, *The Proceedings of the Hague Peace Conferences Translation of the Official Texts: The Conference of 1899* (New York: Oxford University Press, 1920), pp. 63, 427–28, 487, 557–58.

20 Federal Political Department, *Final Record of the Diplomatic Conference of Geneva of 1949*, 3 vols. (Berne: Federal Political Department, 1949), vol. II-A, pp. 665, 776–77, 799–800, 809, 828–29; Federal Political Department, *Final Record of the Diplomatic Conference of Geneva of 1949*, 3 vols. (Berne: Federal Political Department, 1949), vol. II-B, pp. 193–94, 416–17; Pictet (ed), *Commentary Geneva Convention IV*, pp. 292–93, 600.

21 Articles 51, 147, Geneva Convention IV. See also Article 130, Geneva Convention III; Jean S. Pictet (ed), *Commentary III Geneva Convention Relative to the Treatment of Prisoners of War* (Geneva: International Committee of the Red Cross, 1960), p. 628.

> [The prohibition's] object is to protect the inhabitants of the occupied territory from actions offensive to their patriotic feelings or from attempts to undermine their allegiance to their own country.[22]

Several German accused were convicted of similar acts committed during World War II.[23] Those involved in the adoption and articulation of Articles 8(2)(a)(v) and 8(2)(b)(xv) of the Rome Statute[24] apparently found it unnecessary to revisit the sense of inhumanity underlying these crimes.[25]

Elsewhere, Sidgwick clearly deemed acts of the sort 'harsh[ly] treat[ing . . .] non-combatants' both inhumane, and materially unnecessary for purposes of the sort 'scaring the enemy into submission'.[26] In view of such purposes, Sidgwick continued, the acts concerned would 'on the whole' be:

> [T]oo uncertain and remote to outweigh (1) the danger of rousing the sympathetic indignation of neutrals, together with (2) the serious inconveniences to which an invading army is exposed in the midst of a population embittered by private injuries.[27]

Sidgwick also offered analogous reasons when explaining the grounds on which indiscriminate pillage had come to be prohibited.[28]

Brandt also suggests a possible link between an act's inhumanity and its lack of material military necessity. For Brandt:

> There are some things that troops may be tempted to do which are at best of negligible utility to their nation but which cause serious loss to enemy civilians, although not affecting the enemy's power to win the war.[29]

22 Pictet (ed), *Commentary Geneva Convention IV*, p. 293.

23 *Robert Wagner et al.*, in which a Permanent Military Tribunal at Strasbourg convicted Wagner, Röhn and Schuppel, under Article 75 of the French penal code then in force. See *Trial of Robert Wagner et al.*, UN War Crimes Commission, *Law Reports of Trials of War Criminals*, 15 vols. (London: His Majesty's Stationery Office, 1948), vol. III, 23, pp. 40–41, 51. See also *Trial of Erhard Milch*, UN War Crimes Commission, *Law Reports of Trials of War Criminals*, 15 vols. (London: His Majesty's Stationery Office, 1948), vol. VII, 27, pp. 38–40, 53–61.

24 Articles 8(2)(a)(v), 8(2)(b)(xv), Rome Statute.

25 Knut Dörmann, *Elements of War Crimes under the Rome Statute of the International Criminal Court: Sources and Commentary* (Cambridge: Cambridge University Press, 2003), pp. 97–99, 269–71.

26 Sidgwick, *Elements of Politics*, p. 256.

27 Ibid.

28 Ibid. See also Doswald-Beck and Vité, 'International Humanitarian Law and Human Rights Law', at 99.

29 Brandt, 'Utilitarianism', at 154.

It seems clear that these 'things' constitute various kinds of belligerent conduct 'troops may be tempted' to perform. We may also treat 'bringing tangible utility to one's nation', and 'adversely affecting the enemy's power to win the war', as the relevant kinds of purpose. Arguably, Brandt deems performing the former materially unnecessary in relation to the latter.[30] It also appears that he considers the 'serious loss to enemy civilians' entailed by the acts in question to be inhumane.

Brandt then enumerates, as examples of acts deemed both materially unnecessary and inhumane, murdering POWs[31]; plundering private or public property[32]; raping women and ill-treating populations of occupied territories[33]; and wantonly destroying cities, towns or villages, as well as committing devastation.[34] As will be seen below, these kinds of conduct typically find their corresponding prohibitions in positive IHL.[35]

Other commentators add yet more examples to the list. L. B. Schapiro maintained that repatriating deserters in the aftermath of hostilities would be not only inhumane but also materially unnecessary:

> [W]ars have often been fought over issues of principle. Desertion from the ranks of one belligerent may in such circumstances be an act not of cowardice but of political faith, an act which not only weakens the moral case of the belligerent from which the desertion takes place but also strengthens the moral case of the belligerent to which the deserter flees. To surrender a deserter in such circumstances may be not only an act of bad faith and akin to the surrender of a political refugee, but also an act of bad policy, since it may discourage others from doing the same in any future war.[36]

There is arguably a dissonance between the unnecessary-inhumane alignment that Schapiro found here, on the one hand, and the positive IHL rule regarding the post-hostilities repatriation of deserters, on the other.

The first paragraph of Article 118 of Geneva Convention III provides that 'prisoners of war shall be released and repatriated without delay after

30 Doswald-Beck and Vité, 'International Humanitarian Law and Human Rights Law', at 99.
31 Brandt, 'Utilitarianism', at 154–55.
32 Ibid, at 155. See also Doswald-Beck and Vité, 'International Humanitarian Law and Human Rights Law', at 99.
33 Brandt, 'Utilitarianism', at 155.
34 Ibid.
35 See Chapter 7.
36 LB Schapiro, 'Repatriation of Deserters' (1952) 29 *British Yearbook of International Law* 310, at 311. But see JAC Gutteridge, 'The Repatriation of Prisoners of War' (1953) 2 *International and Comparative Law Quarterly* 207, at 214.

the cessation of active hostilities'.[37] This provision makes no reference to deserters; nor, for that matter, do deserters appear to be treated on a different footing from POWs elsewhere in the convention.[38] Nevertheless, according to the Red Cross commentary, deserters should be excluded from the scope of Article 118.[39] The commentary expresses the humanitarian rationale for this exclusion as follows:

> Enemy military personnel who have been illegally enrolled in the armed forces cannot be treated on the same basis as other prisoners of war, nor can those who go over to the other side. Although many countries, for instance Great Britain, treated the latter as prisoners of war, this does not mean that they are entitled to that status. The Detaining Power is under no obligation to repatriate persons who have deserted to the other side. Similarly, their names are not usually notified to their country of origin. It should, however, be noted that the status of a deserter who has gone over to the other side must be determined by the way in which he surrendered or by his statements during initial questioning. A prisoner of war does not become a deserter merely because he makes a statement in the course of captivity.[40]

In truth, the pervasive room for an unnecessary-inhumane alignment is but a reflection of what von Clausewitz advocated nearly two centuries ago:

> If, then, civilized nations do not put their prisoners to death or devastate cities and countries, it is because intelligence plays a larger part in their methods of warfare and has taught them more effective ways of using force than the crude expression of instinct.[41]

For von Clausewitz, committing needless brutalities, such as putting prisoners to death and devastating cities and countries, was first and foremost a sign of ineffective and unintelligent fighting.[42] Numerous

[37] Article 118, Geneva Convention III.

[38] The same goes, *mutatis mutandis*, for those POWs who have expressed their wish not to be repatriated after the cessation of active hostilities. We shall return to this particular type of POWs in Chapter 8.

[39] Pictet (ed), *Commentary Geneva Convention III*, p. 549. See also Marco Sassoli, 'The Status, Treatment and Repatriation of Deserters under International Humanitarian Law' (1985) *Yearbook of the International Institute of Humanitarian Law* 9, at 35–36.

[40] Ibid.

[41] Von Clausewitz, *On War*, p. 85. See also Doswald-Beck and Vité, 'International Humanitarian Law and Human Rights Law', at 99 (referring to 'sadistic acts of cruelty').

[42] Myres S. McDougal and Florentino P. Feliciano, 'International Coercion and World Public Order: The General Principles of the Law of War' (1958) 67 *Yale Law Journal* 771, at 812.

commentators have since echoed this Clausewitzean thinking.[43] For Geoffrey S. Corn and Gary P. Corn, IHL is

> replete with examples of the symmetry between regulation and operational logic. A quintessential example is the prohibition against the infliction of superfluous or unnecessary suffering . . . By prohibiting the calculated inflection of superfluous suffering or injury, the principle advances not only a humanitarian purpose, but also the military logic reflected in the concept of economy of force. There is no military value in wasting resources for the purpose of exacerbating the suffering of an opponent already rendered combat ineffective; the principle of law is consistent with this logic . . . Another example is the law of military objective. While there may be definitional uncertainty on the fringes of the rule when it is operationally applied, the underlying premise is militarily sound: the application of combat power should be limited only to those persons, places, or things that contribute to the achievement of operational objectives. This rule is consistent with the logic that a resource-conscience commander should instinctively avoid wasting resources on targets of no operational or tactical significance.[44]

Indeed, Corn and Corn call it 'the reasoned judgment of the profession-at-arms' that 'unnecessary violence, destruction, and suffering will not only waste limited and valuable resources, but will also ultimately undermine the strategic purpose of armed conflict: restoration of peace'.[45]

To be abundantly clear, what is suggested in this chapter is *not* that no brutalities may ever be deemed materially necessary (some plainly are),

[43] Ernst H Feilchenfeld, *Prisoners of War* (Washington, DC: Institute of World Polity, 1948), p. 97; Robert E Osgood, *Limited War: The Challenges to American Strategy*, 5th edn (Chicago: University of Chicago Press, 1957), p. 18; Myres S McDougal and Florentino P Feliciano, *Law and Minimum World Public Order: The Legal Regulation of International Coercion* (New Haven: Yale University Press, 1961), pp. 811–13; WT Mallison, Jr, 'The Laws of War and the Juridical Control of Weapons of Mass Destruction in General and in Limited Wars' (1967) 36 *George Washington Law Review* 308, at 314–15; Jean Pictet, *Humanitarian Law and the Protection of War Victims* (Leiden and Geneva: A.W. Sijhoff and Henri Hunant Institute, 1975), p. 30; Department of the Air Force, *Judge Advocate General Activities: International Law – The Conduct of Armed Conflict and Air Operations* (1976), pp. 1–12; Jochnick and Normand, 'Legitimation of Violence', at 53–54.

[44] Geoffrey S Corn and Lieutenant Colonel Gary P Corn, 'The Law of Operational Targeting: Viewing the LOAC Through an Operational Lens' (2012) 47 *Texas International Law Journal* 337, at 359–60.

[45] Ibid, at 358–59. See also Kenneth J Keith, 'The Present State of International Humanitarian Law' (1980) 9 *Australian Yearbook of International Law* 13, at 34 (suggesting that 'attacks directed at civilians can be counterproductive').

or that no effective armies ever commit needless brutalities (some plainly do). The point here is rather that it is erroneous to insist on the total absence, or even the rarity as Dinstein does, of belligerent acts that can be deemed inhumane and materially unnecessary at the same time.

6.1.2 Necessary and Humane

While serving as commander of the US Army's 101st Airborne Division in northern Iraq, Lieutenant General David Petraeus stressed the importance of 'selective use of force' during raids.[46] Rather than bursting in, for instance, his soldiers would 'surround the house and then go to the door and knock'.[47] Petraeus was praised, though by no means exclusively or uncontestedly,[48] for a degree of success that he had achieved in stabilising Mosul in 2003.[49]

Petraeus's action exemplifies the idea of ethical fighting in counterinsurgency. Indeed, the notion that it is strategically expedient to counter insurgencies ethically, with a view to earning the support of local residents, is hardly new. The British practised it in Malaya.[50] David Galula, a theorist, proclaimed it the first law of counterinsurgency warfare.[51]

Building on their own experience in Iraq since 2003, the US Army and Marine Corps issued the oft-cited *Counterinsurgency Field Manual* in 2007.[52] Although presented in the manual as 'paradoxes' and 'counterintuitive to the traditional US view of war',[53] the following propositions merely encapsulate the necessary-humane alignment that pervades in counterinsurgency warfare:

1. The '[u]ltimate success in COIN [counterinsurgency] is gained by protecting the populace';[54]

[46] Michael R Gordon, 'The Struggle for Iraq: Reconstruction; 101st Airborne Secures Success in Northern Iraq', *The New York Times*, 4 September 2003.
[47] Ibid.
[48] Graham, 'Sharp Shift'; van Creveld, *Changing Face of War*, p. 270.
[49] US Army and Marine Corps, *Counterinsurgency Field Manual*, p. xv.
[50] John A Nagl, *Counterinsurgency Lessons from Malaya and Vietnam: Learning to East Soup with a Knife* (Westport and London: Praeger Publications, 2002), pp. 87–107.
[51] David Galula, *Counterinsurgency Warfare: Theory and Practice* (Westport and London: Praeger Security International, 1964), p. 52.
[52] US Army and Marine Corps, *Counterinsurgency Field Manual*. See also Colombian Ministry of National Defence, *Comprehensive Human Rights and IHL Policy* (2008), paras 11–17.
[53] US Army and Marine Corps, *Counterinsurgency Field Manual*, p. 47.
[54] Ibid, p. 48.

2. '[U]sing force precisely and discriminately strengthens the rule of law that needs to be established';[55] and
3. 'Counterinsurgents often achieve the most meaningful success in garnering public support and legitimacy for the [host nation] government with activities that do not involve killing insurgents'.[56]

The field manual goes on to explain:

> Insurgents use unlawful violence to weaken the [host nation] government, intimidate people into passive or active support, and murder those who oppose the insurgency ... Kindness and compassion can often be as important as killing and capturing insurgents.[57]

The manual admonishes that those leading counterinsurgency efforts display qualities such as '[g]enuine compassion and empathy for the populace'[58] and 'serve as a moral compass',[59] so that 'the populace must feel protected, not threatened, by COIN forces' actions and operations'.[60] More specifically:

> A key part of any insurgent's strategy is to attack the will of the domestic and international opposition. One of the insurgents' most effective ways to undermine and erode political will is to portray their opposition as untrustworthy or illegitimate. These attacks work especially well when insurgents can portray their opposition as unethical by the opposition's own standards. To combat these efforts, Soldiers and Marines treat noncombatants and detainees humanely, according to American values and internationally recognized human rights standards. In COIN, preserving noncombatant lives and dignity is central to mission accomplishment. This imperative creates a complex ethical environment.[61]

Much the same can be said of the evolution in the American doctrine of aerial warfare known as effects-based operations[62]:

> Effects-based operations (EBO) are operations that are planned, executed, assessed, and adapted to influence or change systems or capabilities in order to achieve desired outcomes ... The key insights are: that effective

[55] Ibid.
[56] Ibid, p. 49.
[57] Ibid, p. 167.
[58] Ibid, p. 239.
[59] Ibid.
[60] Ibid, p. 238.
[61] Ibid, pp. 245–46.
[62] David A Deptula, *Effects-Based Operations: Change in the Nature of Warfare* (Arlington: Aerospace Education Foundation, 2001).

> operations must be part of a coherent plan that logically supports and ties all objectives and the end state together; that the plan to achieve the objectives must guide employment ... EBO is focused upon desired outcomes – objectives and the end state – and all efforts should be directed in a logically consistent manner toward their attainment ... EBO seeks to attain objectives efficiently, but the availability of resources may constrain the options. That is, commanders must accomplish their assigned missions, but within that constraint, they should be accomplished for as little 'cost' (in terms of lives, treasure, time, and/or opportunities) as possible.[63]

EBO efforts are characterised, first and foremost, by their aspiration to maximise consistency with material military necessity.[64]

EBO, to be sure, has come under sustained criticism in the context of land warfare.[65] The US Army[66] and the Joint Command[67] abandoned this doctrine. It appears, however, that the US Air Force continues to embrace it.[68] According to a recent Air Force document, applying the effects-based approach successfully to strategic attacks yields, among other things, the following result:

> [Strategic attacks] of valid military objectives can have the coercive effect of creating unrest among an enemy's population and/or weakening of the enemy's infrastructure. These mechanisms are aimed at impacting the enemy's popular will or perception. In the past, these mechanisms have involved directly targeting civilian populations to increase disaffection and pressure the adversary leadership to accept the demands of the coercer. However, the law of war, which is legally binding on the US, prohibits making civilians and civilian objects the object of attack. The US remains committed to the principles that support these laws.

63 US Air Force, *Operations and Organization: Air Force Doctrine Document 2* (2007), pp. 13–14.

64 Ibid, pp. 15–17. See also Claude Pilloud and Jean Pictet, 'Article 51 – Protection of the Civilian Population' in Sandoz et al. (eds), *Commentary on Additional Protocols* 613, p. 621; Blix, 'Means and Methods', p. 145.

65 Matt M Matthews, *We Were Caught Unprepared: The 2006 Hezbollah-Israeli War* (Fort Leavenworth: Combat Studies institute Press, 2006), pp. 61–65; Justin Kelly and David Kilcullen, 'Chaos Versus Predictability: A Critique of Effects-Based Operations' (2004) 2 *Australian Army Journal* 87; Milan N Vego, 'Effects-Based Operations: A Critique' (2006) 41 *Joint Forces Quarterly* 51; Ron Tira, 'Breaking the Amoeba's Bones' (2006) 9 *Strategic Assessment* no. 3; Avi Kober, 'The Israel Defense Forces in the Second Lebanon War: Why the Poor Performance?' (2008) 31 *Journal of Strategic Studies* 3, at 32–33.

66 US Army Combined Arms Center, *Army Doctrine Update #1* (2007), pp. 4–5.

67 James N Mattis, 'USJFCOM Commander's Guidance for Effects-Based Operations' (2008) 38 *United States Army War College Quarterly* 18.

68 US Air Force, *US Air Force Doctrine: Doctrine Annex 3-60 – Targeting* (2019), pp. 13–14.

> Additionally, historical evidence suggests that strategies directed against an enemy's population seldom succeed . . . Now, however, with the advent of precision weaponry, the US is capable of carefully managing the destructive effects of [strategic attacks], thereby significantly reducing collateral damage, especially against non-[chemical, biological, radiological, and nuclear] targets. This capability enables the US to use these coercive mechanisms in a way that better complies with the international laws of war . . . and enables a more discriminate use of airpower, improving [strategic attacks]' coercive ability.[69]

EBO shows that military thinkers of some technologically advanced air forces consider it strategically expedient to be humane by carefully regulating the destructive effects of attacks and minimising collateral damage. Similarly, by using the example of incendiary weapons, Schmitt acknowledges that the more technologically advanced party in an asymmetrical conflict has 'little incentive . . . to deviate from IHL – at least until its opponent does'.[70] He also foresees EBO's 'potential of enhancing the humanitarian ends of IHL with no detriment to military necessity'.[71] Here, Schmitt is only a small step away from joining those[72] who argue that the necessary-humane alignment can manifest itself in numerous other acts, too.

6.1.3 *Effective Armies Committing Atrocities: Do They Invalidate the Possibilities of Military Necessity-Humanity Alignment?*

In one of his addresses to those attending the 1899 Hague Peace Conference, Friedrich Fromhold von Martens declared:

> Those who have caused the idea of humanity to progress in the practice of war are not so much the philanthropists and publicists as the great

[69] US Air Force, *US Air Force Doctrine: Doctrine Annex 3-70 – Strategic Attack* (2017), pp. 46–47.

[70] Michael N Schmitt, 'Asymmetrical Warfare and International Humanitarian Law' in Wolff Heintschel von Heinegg and Volker Epping (eds), *International Humanitarian Law Facing New Challenges: Symposium in Honour of Knut Ipsen* (Berlin and New York: Springer, 2007) 11, p. 21.

[71] Ibid, p. 37. In fairness, he also notes the danger of the doctrine adversely affecting IHL compliance. Ibid, pp. 37–38; Michael N Schmitt, 'Effects-Based Operations and the Law of Aerial Warfare' (2006) 5 *Washington University Global Studies Law Review* 265. See also Boothby, *Law of Targeting*, pp. 489–511.

[72] Geoffrey Best, 'Restraints on War by Land Before 1945' in Howard (ed), *Restraints on War* 17, pp. 28–30; Brandt, 'Utilitarianism', at 154–55; Gardam, *Necessity, Proportionality and the use of Force by States*, p. 7; Greenwood, 'Historical Development', p. 38.

> captains, such as Gustavus Adolphus, who have seen war with their own eyes. Being obliged to place a curb on the inflamed passions of their soldiers, they inaugurated a discipline in their armies, which was the source of the regulation of the usages of war, which discipline was all the more necessary in case of invasion of a hostile territory.[73]

In a somewhat similar vein, Christopher Greenwood suggests that 'most rules of humanitarian law reflect good military practice, and adherence by armed forces to those rules is likely to reinforce discipline and good order within the forces concerned'.[74] In Greenwood's view, the kind of belligerent behaviour that is IHL-compliant (and, arguably, humane) also tends to be disciplinarily sound (and, arguably, consistent with material military necessity). That this is so, according to Corn and Corn, is a fact that is 'often overlooked in contemporary scholarship and commentary'.[75]

It may be objected that some of the most horrific atrocities in history have been committed by well-disciplined armed forces. Indeed, as Michael Howard warned:

> Military activity thus carries an intrinsic imperative towards control; an imperative derived from the need to maintain order and discipline, to conserve both moral and material forces and ensure that these are always responsive to direction. These military criteria however will not necessarily coincide with the dictates of humanity … The military principle of 'economy of force' may sometimes conveniently coincide with the dictates of transcendent moral values, but there is little historical justification for assuming that this will always be the case.[76]

Take, for example, the notoriously brutal tactics, such as the beheadings of hostages, to which the so-called 'Islamic State' (IS) resorts. Robert McFadden, an intelligence security consultant, is quoted as saying that IS 'can easily broadcast their atrocities to the world, which serves the dual purpose of instilling terror in their enemies and enticing new recruits inspired by the cult of martyrdom'.[77] Acts deemed consistent with

[73] Carnegie Endowment, *Proceedings of the Hague Peace Conference 1899*, p. 506. See also preface, Oxford Manual.

[74] Greenwood, 'Historical Development', 38. See also Martin van Creveld, *The Transformation of War* (New York: The Free Press, 1991), pp. 89–90; Doswald-Beck and Vité, 'International Humanitarian Law and Human Rights Law', at 99.

[75] Corn and Corn, 'Law of Operational Targeting', at 359.

[76] Howard, '*Temperamenta Belli*', pp. 3–4. But see van Creveld, *Transformation of War*, pp. 88–89.

[77] Graeme Hamilton, 'ISIS Uses Gruesome Social Media Posts to Recruit More "Blood-Thirsty" Jihadists and Instill Terror in Enemies', *National Post*, 11 August 2014. See also

material military necessity need not be deemed consistent with humanity; on the contrary, they may well display the exact opposite characteristics.

Is this possibility, admittedly on point, such that it invalidates Greenwood's observations? It is submitted here that it does not. His thesis is that acting humanely is likely to strengthen discipline, whereas the objection merely asserts that good discipline does not necessarily lead to humane behaviour. Both of these propositions can be simultaneously true, and the truth of one proposition does not negate the truth of the other.

Greenwood's statements have two essential components. The first is the correlational idea that 'most rules of humanitarian law reflect good military practice'. In this proposition, one finds two variables, namely: (a) observing or disregarding IHL rules, and (b) exhibiting good or bad military practice. From these variables follow four possible combinations:

1. That observance of IHL rules reflects good military practice;
2. That observance of IHL rules reflects bad military practice;
3. That disregard of IHL rules reflects good military practice; and
4. That disregard of IHL rules reflects bad military practice.[78]

Greenwood offers two assertions, and two assertions only. He clearly affirms the truth of the first combination, namely that observance of IHL rules reflects good military practice. He also clearly rejects the truth of the second combination. For Greenwood, observance of IHL rules cannot be a reflection of bad military practice.

Objections of the sort in consideration here purport to have the third combination – i.e., that disregard of IHL rules reflects good military practice – undermine Greenwood's view. In this, however, they do not succeed. What the objection really says is that good military discipline does not necessarily reflect observance of IHL rules, since even effective armies can commit atrocities. Greenwood's claim simply does not comment on disregard of IHL rules at all, let alone how such disregard might reflect the quality of military practice.

Fawaz A Gerges, 'Islamic State: Can Its Savagery be Explained?', *BBC News*, 9 September 2014; Frank Gardner, 'Islamic State Message Shows Desire for US Boots on the Ground', *BBC News*, 22 September 2014.

[78] According to Sidgwick, W.E. Hall apparently asserted the truth of this last combination, at least as regards the relationship between troops committing indiscriminate pillage and maintaining discipline among them. See Sidgwick, *Elements of Politics*, p. 258.

That this objection misfires may also be seen from another, more causal angle. Greenwood's second proposition holds that 'adherence by armed forces to those [IHL] rules is likely to reinforce discipline and good order within the forces concerned'. Here, too, there are two variables: (a) armed forces adhering or not adhering to IHL rules; and (b) armed forces reinforcing or not reinforcing discipline and good order. The four resulting combinations are:

1. That IHL-adherent armed forces are likely to reinforce discipline and good order;
2. That IHL-adherent armed forces are *un*likely to reinforce discipline and good order;
3. That *non*-IHL-adherent armed forces are likely to reinforce discipline and good order; and
4. That *non*-IHL-adherent armed forces are *un*likely to reinforce discipline and good order.

Greenwood clearly affirms the truth of the first combination and rejects the truth of the second. Just as evidently, he does not address himself to the third or fourth combination, because he simply does not discuss what happens to non-IHL-adherent armed forces. And yet, the aforementioned objection would have us believe that the third combination can be true, and that it invalidates the position Greenwood takes.

Plainly, it does not. The fact that some highly disciplined armed forces are capable of committing large-scale IHL breaches only establishes that being IHL-adherent is not a *conditio sine qua non* for reinforced discipline and good order. This fact is immaterial to Greenwood's assertions, however. For him, as long as it remains true that adherence to IHL rules is likely to reinforce discipline and good order, and that it is unlikely to undermine discipline and good order, it makes strategic sense for armed forces to promote such adherence. This remains so, whatever consequence non-adherence to IHL rules may entail for the quality of military discipline and order.

Other commentators, such as Geoffrey Best and Brandt, describe certain measures taken during belligerent occupation in similar terms.[79] Article 49 of Geneva Convention IV envisages situations where the total or partial evacuation of a given area may be humane or materially necessary – or both, as the case may be. The provision reads, in relevant parts:

[79] Best, 'Restraints on War by Land', pp. 28–29; Brandt, 'Utilitarianism', at 155.

> Individual or mass forcible transfers, as well as deportations of protected persons from occupied territory to the territory of the Occupying Power or to that of any other country, occupied or not, are prohibited, regardless of their motive.
>
> Nevertheless, the Occupying Power may undertake total or partial evacuation of a given area if the security of the population or imperative military reasons so demand.[80]

According to the Red Cross commentary, the latter demands may include situations in which 'an area is in danger as a result of military operations or is liable to be subjected to intense bombing' and 'the presence of protected persons in [the] area hampers military operations'.[81]

6.2 Military Necessity as Normative Indifference

The inevitable conflict thesis holds that, as a set of reason-giving considerations in IHL norm-creation, humanity always demands humane acts and condemns inhumane acts.[82] The said thesis also asserts that military necessity always demands acts that are deemed materially necessary and condemns those deemed unnecessary.[83] In other words, in their normative context, both humanity and military necessity always generate imperatives.

The joint satisfaction thesis refutes these assertions in two ways. First, normative military necessity provides the framers of IHL rules with no reason to obligate materially necessary acts per se. Rather, it merely endeavours to ensure that such acts' performance remains permitted and their forbearance tolerated. Nor does military necessity urge the framers to prohibit or restrict materially unnecessary acts. It simply encourages the framers to permit their forbearance and tolerate their performance. In other words, military necessity is normatively indifferent.

Second, while humanity can be a generator of imperatives in many cases, it is not necessarily so in others. Humanity, in fairness, is likely to prompt the framers of IHL rules to forbid inhumane acts. Nevertheless, some such acts may very well remain tolerated by it. Whether humanity demands the performance of all humane acts is even less clear. It does appear to do so sometimes, but numerous acts deemed evidently humane give rise to humanitarian permissions rather than humanitarian demands.

[80] Article 49, Geneva Convention IV.
[81] Pictet (ed), *Commentary Geneva Convention IV*, p. 280.
[82] See Chapter 5.
[83] See ibid.

6.2.1 *Normative Indifference Generally*

I submit that military necessity promotes only what Georg Henrik von Wright called morally indifferent forms of behaviour. The Finnish philosopher explained these forms of behaviour thus:

> If the negation of an act is forbidden, the act itself is called obligatory. For instance: it is forbidden to disobey the law, hence it is obligatory to obey the law. We *ought* to do that which we are *not allowed not to* do. If an act and its negation are both permitted, the act is called (morally) indifferent. For instance: in a smoking compartment we may smoke, but we may also not smoke. Hence smoking is here a morally indifferent form of behaviour.[84]

Von Wright subsequently revised his position regarding the relationship between permissions, prohibitions and obligations. According to his revised view, 'the negation of an obligation is a permission "to the contrary"; and the negation of a permission is an obligation to the contrary'.[85] Be that as it may, the essence of von Wright's observations regarding the relationship between obligations and permissions, as well as those regarding morally indifferent behaviour, remains valid for our purposes here.

6.2.2 *Normative Indifference towards Military Success or Failure*

It is strictly in the belligerent's self-interest to do what is materially necessary, and to avoid what is unnecessary.[86] Insofar as this is the case, it may be said that normative military necessity 'robustly' permits the performance of materially necessary acts, as well as the forbearance of

[84] Georg Henrik von Wright, 'Deontic Logic' (1951) 60 *Mind* 1, at 3–4 (emphasis in original).

[85] Georg Henrik von Wright, 'Ought to Be – Ought to Do' in Meggle (ed), *Actions, Norms, Values* 3, p. 6. Von Wright continued (ibid, pp. 4, 5–6): 'Most deontic logics use two operators: *O* for obligation ("ought") and *P* for permission ("may"). On what may be called a received view, the operators are interdefinable with the aid of the symbol of negation ~, $O = \sim P \sim$ and $P = \sim O \sim$. This view I do no longer find acceptable. A special symbol for prohibition, however, is not needed, since a prohibition may be defined as an obligation to the contrary ($O \sim$) and an obligation as a prohibition to the contrary ($O \sim \sim p = Op$). This I find acceptable . . . By the negation-norm of a [*sic*] *O*-norm I understand a *P*-norm, the content of which is the negation of the content of the *O*-norm. Similarly, the negation-norm of a *P*-norm is a *O*-norm, the content of which is the negation of the content of the *P*-norm.'

[86] See Chapter 2.

unnecessary ones. Conversely, it is strictly against one's self-interest to forgo material military necessities, or to endure non-necessities.[87] Military necessity may still be said to permit him or her to do so, if only 'moderately' – although it is perhaps more apt to say that military necessity merely 'tolerates' such behaviour.

All these are, nevertheless, permissions. Indeed, in IHL norm-creation, military necessity becomes relevant only to the extent that it seeks to render the maximum possible range of belligerent acts what Wesley Newcomb Hohfeld called 'privileges'[88] and subsequently came to be known as Hohfeldian 'liberties'.[89] As such, military necessity does not prohibit or restrict. It only – and therefore indifferently – permits.[90]

Dinstein observes that '[t]he dynamics of the law are such that whatever is required by military necessity, and is not excluded on the ground of humanitarianism, is permissible'.[91] This statement, while true, does not present a complete picture. It needs to be supplemented with: 'Or, for that matter, whatever is *not* required by military necessity, and is not excluded on the ground of humanitarianism, is *also* permissible.' Thus, if IHL were an autonomous system of rules wherein only military necessity operated as reason-giving considerations, this law would contain nothing but permissions.[92]

IHL does prohibit numerous acts that happen to be deemed materially unnecessary. As seen earlier, however, the lack of material military necessity is *not* the reason for their prohibition.[93] Similarly, although

[87] See ibid.

[88] Wesley Newcomb Hohfeld, 'Fundamental Legal Concepts as Applied in Judicial Reasoning' (1919) 26 *Yale Law Journal* 710, at 710.

[89] John Finnis, 'Some Professional Fallacies about Rights' (1971) 4 *Adelaide Law Review* 377, at 377; John Finnis, *Natural Law and Natural Rights* (Oxford: Clarendon Press, 1980), p. 199; Matthew H Kramer, 'Rights Without Trimmings' in Matthew H Kramer et al., *A Debate Over Rights: Philosophical Enquiries* (Oxford: Oxford University Press, 1998) 7, pp. 10–20.

[90] Jens D Ohlin, 'The Duty to Capture' (2013) 97 *Minnesota Law Review* 1268, at 1304 (footnote omitted): 'military necessity tracks the licencing function of IHL more than it tracks the regulating function of IHL, the latter being carried by more specific prohibitory rules'.

[91] Dinstein, *Conduct of Hostilities* (2nd edn), p. 6.

[92] Raz, *Practical Reason and Norms*, pp. 85–87, 90; Weinberger, 'Logical Analysis', p. 292. Dinstein *is* therefore correct when he says (Dinstein, *Conduct of Hostilities* (2nd edn), p. 4): '[I]f military necessity were the sole beacon to guide the path of armed forces in wartime, no limitation of any significance would have been imposed on the freedom of action of Belligerent Parties'.

[93] See Chapter 4.

the law obligates the performance of some acts that happen to be militarily necessary,[94] their consistency with material military necessity is *not* what explains the existence of these obligations.

6.2.3 *Disabling 'Naked' Soldiers*

Holding otherwise would generate consequences that are highly counter-intuitive. Consider Michael Walzer's discussion of 'naked' soldiers,[95] for example. By this expression, he refers to those soldiers 'who look funny, who are taking a bath, holding up their pants, reveling in the sun, smoking a cigarette'.[96] Walzer notes that it is 'not against the rules of war' to kill such soldiers.[97] He then recounts the stories of five men during the two World Wars who declined to kill naked soldiers,[98] adding:

> Their refusals seem, even to them, to fly in the face of military duty. Rooted in a moral recognition, they are nevertheless more passionate than principled decisions. They are acts of kindness, and insofar as they entail any danger at all or lower minutely the odds for victory later, they may be likened to superogatory acts. Not that they involve doing more than is morally required; they involve doing less than is permitted.[99]

At issue here is *not* whether declining to kill naked soldiers is consistent with humanity (which it clearly is). Rather, we are presently concerned as to whether killing such soldiers may be materially necessary and, if so, whether normative military necessity demands killing them.

A clear distinction should be drawn between what Walzer calls 'the rules of war' and 'military duty'. It appears evident that the latter is what each of Walzer's five protagonists owes his respective state *qua* citizen-soldier under that state's domestic law.[100] It seems equally evident, however, that they owed no such duty towards the international community – such as it was in those days, at any rate – *qua* combatants under that community's laws and customs of war.[101] The prominence of their national military duty is also highlighted by the fact that what Walzer

[94] See Chapter 7.
[95] Walzer, *Just and Unjust Wars*, pp. 138–43.
[96] Ibid, p. 142.
[97] Ibid. This, it is submitted here, is also the correct view of positive IHL. See Chapter 7.
[98] These five men are: Wilfred Owen, Robert Graves, George Orwell, Raleigh Trevelyan and Emilio Lussu. See Walzer, *Just and Unjust Wars*, pp. 139–43.
[99] Ibid, p. 143.
[100] See Chapter 3.
[101] See ibid.

describes by reference to these men is the moral landscape of typical conscripts serving in mass national armies of the early 20th century.[102]

We may also consider Walzer's expression 'doing less than permitted' analogous to 'declining to perform what normative military necessity permits'. Implicit in his view, in other words, is the idea that military necessity permits the killing of naked soldiers, since it is deemed materially necessary.

Two questions arise here. First, should it really be deemed consistent with material military necessity to kill naked soldiers? For Walzer, shooting even a naked soldier is materially necessary because, in a nutshell, that soldier has allowed himself 'to be made into a dangerous man'.[103] It is submitted here that a soldier's role as a dangerous man does *not* have to do with the danger the soldier actually poses to his or her enemy at a specific moment via a specific act. Rather, it has to do with the fact that being a soldier means being a member of a dangerous function-kind.[104]

May criticises Walzer for defending 'the justifiability of shooting the naked soldier; indeed, [Walzer] says that it is, strictly speaking, impermissible not to shoot [that naked soldier]'.[105] May's objection is based on the idea that not all members of the soldier class are dangerous all the time to their enemy soldiers or to their enemy states.[106] Thus, while they are in fact naked, and therefore posing no requisite danger, it should not be permitted to shoot them. In so arguing, however, May invokes 'the principle of humanity'[107] rather than, say, the momentary lack of the said act's material military necessity. Furthermore, May asks:

> Walzer may think that by not surrendering, the naked soldier indicates that he is still a member of the group and thus without immunity from being killed. But why are all of the members of the group to be treated the same? Why is the only way to regain one's immunity completely to remove oneself from the group? [W]hat do we do with the fact that even those who surrender are legitimately seen as required to try to escape so that they can rejoin their military units [?][108]

[102] Walzer, *Just and Unjust Wars*, pp. 142–43, 305–06. It should be noted that, in his more recent reflections, Walzer does include members of professional armed forces. See Walzer, *Arguing About War*, pp. 23–24.

[103] Walzer, *Just and Unjust Wars*, p. 145.

[104] See Chapter 3.

[105] May, *War Crimes and Just War*, p. 109 (footnote omitted).

[106] Ibid, pp. 109–12.

[107] Ibid, p. 111. See also ibid, pp. 172–89.

[108] Ibid, p. 111.

'[T]hose who surrender', according to May, 'are legitimately seen as required' to escape and rejoin their military units – but *in whose eye* are they so seen? As noted earlier, escape and non-cooperation with the captor arguably constitute ethical virtues that are community-specific[109] and duties that a surrendering soldier may owe towards the specific community for which he or she fights. The framers of IHL rules, in contrast, have no reason of their own to expect such virtues of POWs, and therefore no reason to impose corresponding duties on them. It appears that this particular basis for May's criticism of Walzer unhelpfully conflates distinct moral constituencies.

It seems to me that, as Walzer apparently suggests, killing even a naked soldier can indeed be deemed materially necessary.[110] In any event, however, it is, *contra* May, clearly not Walzer's assertion that the 'rules of war' make it impermissible not to kill such a soldier.

The second question is whether, regardless of Walzer and May's views on the matter, killing eligible enemy combatants in active hostilities somehow becomes an act military necessity demands rather than merely permits. Bill Millin was a Scottish combat bagpiper during the D-Day landings.[111] Indications are that Millin's work boosted the morale among members of his unit:

> And ['Ladies from Hell'] raised the hearts and minds of the home side, so much so that when Mr Millin played on June 5th, as the troops left for France past the Isle of Wight and he was standing on the bowsprit just about keeping his balance above the waves getting rougher, the wild cheers of the crowd drowned out the sound of his pipes even to himself.[112]

For the Germans, undermining the morale of Millin's comrades would have been materially necessary. Assuming that Millin was indeed a combatant, and hence a lawful target according to the laws and customs of war then in force, he would have been liable to attacks by German defenders of the Normandy beaches. And yet, according to one account, '[a]ll the way, [Millin] learned later, German snipers had had him in their sights but, out of pity for this madman, had not fired'.[113]

109 See Chapter 3.
110 Here, too, we are immediately drawn to the 'capture rather than kill' debate. See Chapter 8.
111 'Bill Millin, Piper at the D-Day Landings, Died on August 17th, Aged 88', *The Economist*, 26 August 2010.
112 Ibid.
113 Ibid.

It might appear that, in one sense, Millin was naked in the eyes of those German snipers, even during active combat, because of his 'madman' behaviour. In another sense, however, he was perhaps not truly naked. After all, the tunes he played during the D-Day invasion were not exactly unguarded revelations of his vulnerability as 'a man'.[114]

Be that as it may, by declining to take Millin out, the Germans might have ultimately failed in their national duty. It would be odd to say, however, that they failed to act as demanded by military necessity. Although contrary to material military necessity, a failure of this kind is something that normative military necessity simply tolerates. The framers of IHL rules have no reason to forbid it. Rather, they have reason to leave the belligerent at liberty to do it – at its own peril and to its own detriment.

6.2.4 High-Altitude Aerial Bombardment

The same is true of other materially necessary acts, such as reducing risks of self-endangerment. The altitude of 15,000 feet at which North Atlantic Treaty Organization (NATO) bombers flew during the early phases of the 1999 Kosovo crisis became a highly contentious issue.[115] Rogers notes:

> Humanitarian considerations would require the pilot to get close to the target to identify it properly; military considerations would require the pilot to fly at a safe height to be at reduced risk from anti-aircraft fire.[116]

Let us leave aside, for the moment, what humanity would have to say about pilots exposing themselves to the dangers of anti-aircraft fire while endeavouring to verify their targets.[117]

[114] Emilio Lussu, *Sardinian Brigade* (New York: Alfred A. Knopf, 1939), p. 170. See also Walzer, *Just and Unjust Wars*, p. 142.

[115] Amnesty International, *NATO/Federal Republic of Yugoslavia 'Collateral Damage' or Unlawful Killings? Violations of the Laws of War by NATO during Operation Allied Force* (2000), pp. 16–17; Human Rights Watch, *Civilian Death in the NATO Air Campaign* (2000), p. 23; International Criminal Tribunal for the Former Yugoslavia, *Final Report to the Prosecutor by the Committee Established to Review the NATO Bombing Campaign Against the Federal Republic of Yugoslavia* (2000), para. 56; WJ Fenrick, 'Targeting and Proportionality during the NATO Bombing Campaign against Yugoslavia' (2001) 12 *European Journal of International Law* 489, at 501; Colonel Frederic L Borch, 'Targeting After Kosovo: Has the Law Changed for Strike Runners?' (2003) 56 *Naval War College Review* 64; Neuman, 'Force Protection and Cumulative Assessment', at 94; Boothby, *Law of Targeting*, pp. 185–87.

[116] APV Rogers, 'Zero-Casualty Warfare' (2000) 82 *International Review of the Red Cross* 165, at 175.

[117] See Chapter 8.

Of immediate concern to us here is the notion that 'military considerations would require the pilot to fly at a safe height to be at reduced risk from anti-aircraft fire'. Rogers appears to be using the word 'require' in the sense that climbing to a higher altitude is what one would have to do if he or she were to act consistently with material military necessity. One would agree that belligerent acts of the kind 'fly[ing] at a safe height to be at reduced risk' might be conducive towards military purposes of the sort 'preserving one's military strength'. In other words, it would be strictly in the belligerent's self-interest to minimise risks of self-endangerment.

Rogers clearly does not use the word 'require' in the sense that military necessity would prompt the framers of IHL rules to bind combat aircrews in a duty to fly at a sufficiently high altitude for their own safety. Nor should there be any reason for the situation to be otherwise. Military necessity merely gives the law's framers weighty reason to permit this conduct. Here, too, reducing safety for some reason – for example, out of humanitarian concern for the civilians on the ground – is an option military necessity tolerates and the law leaves the belligerent entirely at liberty to choose.

6.2.5 Recruiting Child Soldiers

Even weirder consequences would await if it were the case that normative military necessity turns an act's consistency with material military necessity into a reason for which IHL should obligate its performance.

Studies show that some warring parties recruit child soldiers and use them in hostilities on the grounds that children's superior stamina[118] and reduced fear or revulsion for atrocities,[119] as well as their abundance and economy,[120] make their recruitment and use strategically advantageous. It could therefore be argued that recruiting child soldiers and using them in hostilities is materially necessary.

Even if, *arguendo*, it were the case, the framers of IHL rules would still have no reason whatsoever to make the recruitment and use of child soldiers in hostilities obligatory.

[118] Ilene Cohn and Guy S Goodwin-Gill, *Child Soldiers: The Role of Children in Armed Conflict* (Oxford: Clarendon Press 1994), p. 26.

[119] Ibid.

[120] PW Singer, *Children at War* (Berkeley and Los Angeles: University of California Press, 2006), pp. 52–56.

6.3 Nor Does Humanity Always Generate Imperatives

The situation is somewhat more nuanced for humanity. Acts such as assuming certain risks of self-endangerment in favour of civilians and caring for the wounded and sick in the battlefield would be deemed humane, and humanity would readily demand their performance. Yet some other humane acts may remain permitted, rather than demanded. Similarly, humanity does not condemn all acts that are, or would be, deemed inhumane.

6.3.1 Humanity's Permission and Tolerance

Concluding agreements on the recognition of hospital zones and localities is a case in point. Article 23 of Geneva Convention I provides, in relevant parts:

> In time of peace, the High Contracting Parties and, after the outbreak of hostilities, the Parties to the conflict, may establish in their own territory and, if the need arises, in occupied areas, hospital zones and localities so organized as to protect the wounded and sick from the effects of war, as well as the personnel entrusted with the organization and administration of these zones and localities and with the care of the persons therein assembled.
>
> Upon the outbreak and during the course of hostilities, the Parties concerned may conclude agreements on mutual recognition of the hospital zones and localities they have created.[121]

The Red Cross commentary on this article observes:

> The 1947 Conference of Government Experts showed that States were not inclined to adopt clauses of a mandatory nature in this matter. The most the experts would agree to was that the Geneva Conventions should provide for the possible creation of such places of refuge; their recognition by the enemy was, however, to be dependent upon the conclusion of special agreements . . . Article 23 . . . of the 1949 Convention is optional in character. It should be noted, however, that the object of international Conventions is to define the obligations which States contract towards one another. It is not customary for them to include mere suggestions, although examples of this do exist. *The above course has been adopted in the case of hospital zones, because the authors of the Convention wished to draw attention to their importance from the humanitarian point of view, and to recommend their adoption in practice.* The responsible authorities

[121] Article 23, Geneva Convention I.

> in each country should not, therefore, regard Article 23 as being a mere reference to a possible solution; they should look upon it as a recommendation to make every effort to apply that solution in practice.[122]

It was noted elsewhere that, '[w]hile these provisions are not mandatory, they nevertheless serve as the basis for procedures, the desirability of which, from a humanitarian standpoint, cannot be gainsaid'.[123] The foregoing shows that the humanitarian desirability of such procedures alone does not compel the conclusion that humanity demands their implementation. On the contrary, regrettable as it may otherwise be, declining or failing to conclude agreements recognising hospital zones and localities is a less-than-ideal act that humanity tolerates.

Plunder, torture and the like would be deemed inhumane and unhesitatingly condemned. Yet, humanity might tolerate some relatively minor acts of inhumanity. Examples include limiting[124] and censoring[125] communications between POWs and the exterior. The Red Cross commentary on Geneva Convention III explains the underlying rationale thus:

> In principle, prisoners of war are entitled to send and receive an unlimited number of letters and cards which may be sent to any destination or may come from any part of the world, without any distinction of a national kind.
>
> This is the principle, but one can easily understand that its full application must inevitably be restricted, whether because of transport difficulties or because of the military security of the Detaining Power.[126]

From the standpoint of strictly humanitarian ideals, those held in custody exclusively on non-penal grounds[127] should be allowed to

[122] Pictet (ed), *Commentary Geneva Convention I*, pp. 210, 211–12 (emphasis added).

[123] Raymund T Yingling and Robert W Ginnane, 'The Geneva Conventions of 1949' (1952) 46 *American Journal of International Law* 393, at 400.

[124] Article 71, Geneva Convention III.

[125] Ibid, Article 76.

[126] Pictet (ed), *Commentary Geneva Convention III*, p. 345.

[127] The notion that POW internment is entirely non-penal in character is well established in modern IHL. Article 61, Oxford Manual. This has given rise to a degree of awkwardness vis-à-vis Article 5(1) of the European Convention on Human Rights. *Cyprus v Turkey* decided by the European Human Rights Commission (App. No. 6780/74 & 6950/75); Françoise J Hampson, 'The Relationship between International Humanitarian Law and Human Rights Law from the Perspective of a Human Rights Treaty Body' (2008) 90 *International Review of the Red Cross* 549, at 565 (calling *Cyprus v Turkey* 'absurd'). The terrorist attacks on 11 September 2001 ushered in a series of contentious debates regarding the non-penal character of POW internment. Derek Jinks, 'The Applicability

establish and maintain communication with the outside world. If so, declining or failing to facilitate such communication would be contrary to those humanitarian ideals.

Nevertheless, Article 71 of Geneva Convention III concedes that the volume of correspondence may be limited to two letters and four cards monthly, 'if the Detaining Power deems it necessary' to do so.[128] Significantly, this article does not restrict such limitations to any specific grounds.[129] Similarly, Article 76 of the same convention appears reconciled with the inevitability of censoring POW correspondence. The provision imposes no restriction whatsoever on the permissible reasons for censorship to be carried out; the rule only stipulates that it 'shall be done as quickly as possible'.[130] It would appear, then, that humanity tolerates this somewhat inhumane course of action.

In other words, although what humanity demands or condemns is not a matter of normative indifference, what it merely permits or tolerates is.

6.3.2 Demanding vs. Praising Humane Acts

That this is so should not be surprising. Philosophers acknowledge that ethics and morality in society encompass not only duties and obligations but also qualities that go beyond them. Thus, according to Hart:

> [E]ven within the morality of a particular society, there exist side by side with the structure of mandatory moral obligations and duties and the relatively clear rules that define them, certain moral *ideals*. The realization

of the Geneva Conventions to the "Global War on Terrorism"' (2005–2006) 46 *Virginia Journal of International Law* 165; Sean D Murphy, 'Evolving Geneva Convention Paradigms in the "War on Terrorism": Applying the Core Rules to the Release of Persons Deemed "Unprivileged Combatants"' (2006–2007) 75 *George Washington Law Review* 1105; David E Graham, 'The Dual U.S. Standard for the Treatment and Interrogation of Detainees: Unlawful and Unworkable' (2008–2009) 48 *Washburn Law Journal* 325; Emily Crawford, *The Treatment of Combatants and Insurgents under the Law of Armed Conflict* (Oxford: Oxford University Press, 2010); Helen Duffy, *The 'War on Terror' and the Framework of International Law*, 2nd edn (Cambridge: Cambridge University Press, 2015).

128 Article 71, Geneva Convention III.

129 Ibid. In contrast, this article restricts *further* limitations on the volume to situations where 'the Protecting Power is satisfied that it would be in the interests of the prisoners of war concerned to do so owing to difficulties of translation caused by the Detaining Power's inability to find sufficient qualified linguists to carry out the necessary censorship'.

130 Ibid, Article 76.

> of these is not taken, as duty is, as a matter of course, but as an achievement deserving praise. The hero and the saint are extreme types of those who do *more* than their duty. What they do is not like obligation or duty, something which can be demanded of them, and failure to do it is not regarded as wrong or matter for censure. On a humbler scale than the saint or hero, are those who are recognized in a society as deserving praise for the moral virtues which they manifest in daily life such as bravery, charity, benevolence, patience, or chastity. The connection between such socially recognized ideals and virtues and the primary mandatory forms of social obligation and duty is fairly clear. Many moral virtues are qualities consisting in the ability and disposition to carry forward beyond the limited extent which duty demands, the kind of concern for others' interests or sacrifice of personal interest which it does demand. Benevolence and charity are examples of this. Other moral virtues like temperance, patience, bravery, or conscientiousness are in a sense ancillary: they are qualities of character shown in exceptional devotion to duty or in the pursuit of substantive moral ideals in the face of special temptation or danger.[131]

One may also recall Fuller's celebrated distinction between what he called 'morality of duty' and 'morality of aspiration'.[132] His theory explains why certain morally relevant conduct is treated as a matter of duty[133] whereas some other morally relevant conduct is treated as a matter of aspiration,[134] and how it is that the former engages penalties whereas the latter engages rewards.[135]

And so, *mutatis mutandis*, it is the case with humanity in IHL norm-creation. Humanity expects the performance of some humane acts as a matter of course, and one's refusal or failure to do so would attract censure. In contrast, humanity places the performance of many other humane acts beyond one's call of duty and renders them praiseworthy rather than mandatory. Similarly, while humanity would forthrightly

131 Hart, *Concept of Law* (2nd edn), pp. 182–83 (emphasis in original). For a slightly different take of supererogation, see Raz, *Practical Reason and Norms*, pp. 91–95, esp. 94 (footnote omitted): '[H]ow can one be permitted to refrain from action which is required by reason? The solution is to be found in the notion of an exclusionary permission. The permission to refrain from performing an act supererogation is an exclusionary permission, a permission not to act on certain reasons. An act is a supererogatory act only if it is an act which one ought to do on the balance of reasons and yet one is permitted not to act on the balance of reasons.'

132 Fuller, *Morality of Law* (rev. edn), p. 4.

133 Ibid, pp. 19–27.

134 Ibid, pp. 15–19.

135 Ibid, pp. 30–32.

demand the forbearance of numerous inhumane acts, it would decline to condemn a limited number of other such acts.

The point at which the 'humanity of duty' ends and the 'humanity of aspiration' begins, as it were, is bound to be highly contentious. Fuller himself conceded as much, at least in relation to the 'pointer' where the morality of duty yields to the morality of aspiration.[136]

Recall here Richards's action at the northern French village of Englefontaine[137]:

> When bombing dug-outs or cellars it was always wise to throw bombs into them first and have a look around them after. But we had to be very careful in this village as there were civilians in some of the cellars. We shouted down them to make sure. Another man and I shouted down one cellar twice and receiving no reply were just about to pull the pins out of our bombs when we heard a woman's voice cry out and a young lady came up the cellar steps. As soon as she saw us she started to speak rapidly in French and gave the both of us a hearty kiss. She and the members of her family had their beds, stove and everything else of use in the cellar which they had not left for some days. They guessed an attack was being made and when we first shouted down had been too frightened to answer. If the young lady had not cried out when she did we would have innocently murdered them all.[138]

Richards considered it 'wise' to 'throw bombs into [cellars] first and have a look around them after'. It may be said that, by calling this course of action 'wise', he essentially meant that it would be consistent with material military necessity, and therefore something in his strictly *a*moral self-interest to do.

At the same time, however, Richards clearly found it morally troubling to do the 'wise' thing. Instead, together with his colleague, Richards chose to shout several times into the cellar. In Walzer's words: '[H]e was accepting a certain risk in shouting, for had there been German soldiers in the cellar, they might have scrambled out, firing as they came. It would have been more prudent to throw the bombs without warning, which means that military necessity would have justified him in doing so.'[139] Contemporary thinkers debate whether the risk of self-

[136] Ibid, pp. 9–13, 27–30.
[137] See Chapter 3.
[138] Richards, *Old Soldiers Never Die*, p. 310. See also Walzer, *Just and Unjust Wars*, pp. 152, 154.
[139] Walzer, *Just and Unjust Wars*, p. 152.

endangerment of the kind assumed by Richards is what humanity merely permits or demands.[140]

6.4 Conclusion

This chapter has refuted two salient features of the inevitable conflict thesis. They are, first, that military necessity and humanity in their material context never coincide with each other and, second, that their normative counterparts always generate imperatives. Our discussion reveals how necessary-humane and unnecessary-inhumane alignments are not only intuitively sound but also widely accepted. It also becomes clear that military necessity is always normatively indifferent, while humanity is so in respect of certain acts but not so in respect of others.

What do these revelations mean for the idea that a norm conflict between military necessity and humanity is inevitable and that IHL norm-creation is about pre-empting such conflicts from finding their way into positive IHL rules? We will consider this question in Chapter 7.

[140] For further discussions of this debate, see Walzer, *Just and Unjust Wars*, pp. 152, 154, 305–06; Thomas W Smith, 'Protecting Civilians . . . or Soldiers? Humanitarian Law and the Economy of Risk in Iraq' (2008) 9 *International Studies Perspectives* 144; Margalit and Walzer, 'Civilians & Combatants'; Whetham, 'Pragmatic Compromise', p. 83; Peter Margulies, 'Valor's Vices: Against a State Duty to Risk Forces in Armed Conflict' (2012) 37 *Vermont Law Review* 271; Ziv Bohrer and Mark Osiel, 'Proportionality in Military Force at War's Multiple Levels: Averting Civilian Casualties *v.* Safeguarding Soldiers' (2013) 46 *Vanderbilt Journal of Transnational Law* 747; Ziv Bohrer and Mark Osiel, 'Proportionality in War: Protecting Soldiers from Enemy Captivity, and Israel's Operation Cast Lead – "The Soldiers Are Everyone's Children"' (2013) 22 *Southern California Interdisciplinary Law Journal* 637; Cheryl Abbate, 'Assuming Risk: A Critical Analysis of a Soldier's Duty to Prevent Collateral Casualties' (2014) 13 *Journal of Military Ethics* 70; Seth Lazar, 'Necessity and Non-combatant Immunity' (2014) 40 *Review of International Studies* 53; David Luban, 'Risk Taking and Force Protection' in Yitzhak Benbaji and Naomi Sussmann (eds), *Reading Walzer* (London and New York: Routledge, 2014) 277; Nancy Sherman, 'The Moral Psychic Reality of War' in Benbaji and Sussmann (eds), *Reading Walzer* 302, pp. 320–21; Michael Walzer, 'Response' in Benbaji and Sussmann (eds), *Reading Walzer* 328, pp. 328–29; Robert D Sloane, 'Puzzles of Proportion and the "Reasonable Military Commander": Reflections on the Law, Ethics, and Geopolitics of Proportionality' (2015) 6 *Harvard National Security Journal* 299.

7

Joint Satisfaction Thesis II

Accounting for the Military Necessity-Humanity Interplay in IHL Norm-Creation

According to the inevitable conflict thesis, humanity always demands what military necessity spurns, and humanity always condemns what military necessity requires. In Chapter 6, however, we saw that some acts can be both humane and materially necessary, or both inhumane and materially unnecessary. Nor, despite the inevitable conflict thesis's suggestion to the contrary, does military necessity and humanity always generate imperatives. It was shown, in particular, how military necessity is always normatively indifferent.

The stage is now set for the joint satisfaction thesis to refute the notion that the two sets of considerations inevitably conflict with each other. Because military necessity is normatively indifferent, it never conflicts with humanity. Where military necessity permits what humanity demands, or where military necessity merely tolerates what humanity condemns, it always remains open to the belligerent to satisfy them both by acting as directed by humanity. The question, then, is how the framers of IHL rules choose to regulate conduct where such a possibility exists. We will see that the framers are likely to impose unqualified prohibitions against acts that are deemed unnecessary and inhumane. It is somewhat less likely that the framers will obligate necessary and humane acts.

We will then consider two less straightforward situations. Thus, military necessity may permit, whereas humanity may condemn, the same conduct. Conversely, a given act may be tolerated by military necessity yet demanded by humanity. Even in these situations, however, the belligerent satisfies both considerations jointly, albeit limitedly, by acting as directed by humanity. It is for the IHL framers to decide whether to obligate such jointly satisfactory behaviour, and, if so, whether to obligate it unqualifiedly, principally, indeterminately or exceptionally.

7.1 Joint Satisfaction Thanks to Military Necessity-Humanity Alignment

Where an act is condemned by humanity and tolerated by military necessity, the belligerent satisfies both by refraining from that act. Where humanity demands and military necessity permits an act, the belligerent satisfies both by performing that act.

These types of joint satisfaction might be characterised, metaphorically, as 'firm'. Their 'firmness' emanates from the fact that the underlying acts exhibit an unnecessary-inhumane or necessary-humane alignment.[1] How do the framers of IHL rules approach possibilities of such jointly satisfactory behaviour? Do they prohibit what humanity condemns and military necessity tolerates? Do they obligate what humanity demands and military necessity permits? What explains situations where the framers do not do so?

7.1.1 Unqualified Obligations to Pursue Joint Satisfaction that Is Based on Forbearance

Let us begin with acts that humanity condemns and military necessity tolerates. Typically, IHL accounts for the possibility of joint satisfaction when its rules unqualifiedly prohibit this kind of belligerent conduct.[2]

We have already considered several paradigmatic examples of belligerent conduct that fall within this category. They include: using explosive projectiles weighing less than 400 grams;[3] bombarding undefended localities;[4] and shooting to kill a person placed *hors de combat*.[5] To these, one may add shooting persons descending from aircraft in distress.[6]

1 See Chapter 6.

2 Brandt, 'Utilitarianism', at 154–55.

3 See Chapter 4. The prohibition appears in the St. Petersburg Declaration. See also Jean-Marie Henckaerts and Louise Doswald-Beck, *Customary International Humanitarian Law*, 2 vols. (Cambridge: Cambridge University Press, 2005), vol. I, pp. 272–74; Jochnick and Normand, 'Legitimation of Violence', at 66–67 (calling it 'an unreliable and already obsolete weapon'). But see Boothby, *Weapons and the Law of Armed Conflict*, pp. 141–44.

4 See Chapter 4. The prohibition appears in Article 15, Brussels Declaration; Article 25, Hague Regulations (1907); Article 59, Additional Protocol I; Article 3(c), Statute of the International Criminal Tribunal for the Former Yugoslavia, 22 May 1993 (hereinafter ICTY Statute); Article 8(2)(b)(v), Rome Statute. See also Henckaerts and Doswald-Beck, *Customary International Humanitarian Law* (vol. I), pp. 164–70.

5 See Chapter 4. The prohibition appears in Article 41(1), Additional Protocol I; Article 8(2)(b)(vi), Rome Statute. See also Chapter 8 for a debate concerning the somewhat flexible scope of what constitutes *hors de combat*.

6 Article 42(1), Additional Protocol I. See also W Hays Parks, 'Air War and the Laws of War' (1990) 32 *Air Force Law Review* 1, at 108–11; Henckaerts and Doswald-Beck,

Prohibitions of this type extinguish all contrary liberties to behave otherwise (i.e., to perform the prohibited acts). These prohibitions are *unqualified*. In other words, under no circumstances are they subject to modification on account of countervailing considerations that are normatively indifferent. This signifies two things. First, IHL framers exclude all such considerations when positing unqualified prohibitions.[7] Second, invoking these considerations does not repair breaches of unqualified prohibitions.[8]

Neither what humanity condemns, nor what military necessity tolerates, is immutable to the passage of time. Nor, for that matter, is the manner of their interplay. Schmitt notes:

> Of course, all policy decisions are contextual in the sense of being based on past, existing, or anticipated circumstances. When circumstances change, the perceived sufficiency of a particular balancing of military necessity and humanity may come into question.[9]

Accordingly, a given act may be deemed materially necessary at one moment in history yet unnecessary at another. Similarly, our understanding of what is humane and inhumane may evolve over time, rendering certain conduct newly consistent – or inconsistent, as the case may be – with humanity. These fluctuations affect when an act becomes a matter of forbearance-based joint satisfaction and when IHL framers choose unqualifiedly to prohibit it.

Customary International Humanitarian Law (vol. I), pp. 170–72; Federal Political Department, *Official Records of the Diplomatic Conference on the Reaffirmation and Development of International Humanitarian Law Applicable in Armed Conflicts*, 17 vols. (Berne: Federal Political Department, 1978), vol. VI, pp. 108–10; Federal Political Department, *Official Records of the Diplomatic Conference* (vol. XV), pp. 94–95, 97, 99. But see ibid, pp. 97, 104–05, 386, 429; LR Penna, 'Customary International Law and Protocol I: An Analysis of Some Provisions', Swinarski (ed), *Studies and Essays on International Humanitarian Law* 201, pp. 212–14.

7 As will be seen in Chapter 8, however, the joint satisfaction thesis leaves open the possibility whereby considerations that are normatively *not* indifferent, such as humanitarian imperatives, may avoid exclusion during the process of IHL norm-creation. Consequently, they may act as an additional layer of restraint or obligation over and above positive IHL rules.

8 Here, too, pleas emanating from non-indifferent considerations may be admissible even vis-à-vis unqualified prohibitions. See Chapter 8.

9 Schmitt, 'Military Necessity and Humanity', at 799. See also Alain Pellet, 'The Destruction of Troy Will Not Take Place' in Emma Playfair (ed), *International Law and the Administration of Occupied Territories: Two Decades of Israeli Occupation of the West Bank and Gaza Strip* (Oxford: Clarendon Press, 1992) 169, pp. 170, 194–95; Schwarzenberger, *International Law as Applied by Courts and Tribunals* (vol. II), p. 135.

7.1.1.1 Using Banned Weapons

Over the course of history, numerous types of weapons have seen their effectiveness and utility diminish due to technological advances and tactical evolutions.[10] Such is the case with siege weapons,[11] anti-armour weapons,[12] the dum-dum bullet[13] and certain incendiary weapons,[14] just to name a few. A weapon's diminished utility has in turn hastened its ripeness for restriction or outright prohibition.[15] Chris af Jochnick and Roger Normand were therefore correct when they stated:

> After heated debate, the delegates at the [1899] Hague Conference managed to prohibit the use of only three weapons, all of dubious military value: Asphyxiating gases, dum dum bullets, and balloon-launched munitions. Prohibitions on these weapons received widespread support among delegates eager to demonstrate humanitarian motives but reluctant to compromise military interests.[16]

Three questions arise here. The first question concerns the unnecessary-inhumane alignment. If it is true that weapons of diminishing utility are correspondingly susceptible to bans, would the same apply to inhumane methods of combat more broadly and, indeed, to inhumane conduct generally? In other words, would it be the case that IHL framers would ban all acts that are unnecessary and inhumane? If not, what explains it?

[10] Boothby, *Weapons and the Law of Armed Conflict*; Leslie C Green, 'What One May Do in Combat – Then and Now' in Delissen and Tanja (eds), *Humanitarian Law of Armed Conflict* 269, pp. 274, 293–94.

[11] That is so, according to Leslie C Green, since siege had become less frequent. Leslie C Green, *The Contemporary Law of Armed Conflict*, 3rd edn (Manchester: Manchester University Press, 2008), p. 34.

[12] Similarly, since knightly heavy metal armour had gone out of fashion. Ibid, pp. 38, 156 n.70.

[13] Although its ban was resisted for a while by some states insisting on its lawful use against 'savages'. Jochnick and Normand, 'Legitimation of Violence', at 73; Henckaerts and Doswald-Beck, *Customary International Humanitarian Law* (vol. I), pp. 268–71; Green, *Contemporary Law of Armed Conflict*, pp. 38, 158. William Hays Parks notes that most armed forces use only full-metal jacketed bullets, because only they would be reliably fired from military weapons. W Hays Parks, 'Conventional Weapons and Weapon Reviews' (2005) 8 *Yearbook of International Humanitarian Law* 55, p. 69. See also Boothby, *Weapons and the Law of Armed Conflict*, pp. 145–46.

[14] Since they had become less relevant in mechanised warfare. Green, *Contemporary Law of Armed Conflict*, pp. 64, 165–66.

[15] Julius Stone, *Legal Controls of International Conflict: A Treatise on the Dynamics of Disputes- and War-Law* (London: Stevens and Sons, 1954), pp. 550–51.

[16] Jochnick and Normand, 'Legitimation of Violence', at 72.

Let us defer a full discussion of this particular matter until later in this chapter. Suffice it to note here that not all instances of conduct exhibiting the unnecessary-inhumane alignment are unqualifiedly prohibited. There are several reasons for this, including the largely self-inflicted character of the evil the relevant acts typically entail, and the existence of sovereign interests favouring maximum freedom of action.

The second question concerns weapons that are deemed inhumane yet necessary. If useless weapons have typically become the subject of an IHL ban, would it mean, *a contrario*, that those weapons deemed materially necessary would be incapable of IHL prohibition? Nuclear weapons – one class of weapons of mass destruction that has so far escaped a universal ban, despite the ICJ's 1996 advisory opinion and the 2017 ban treaty[17] – come to mind.

This is also a matter explored in greater detail below. We will see how IHL framers may choose to posit an unqualified prohibition on account of its inconsistency with humanitarian imperatives even where military necessity permits contrary behaviour.

The third question concerns how Jochnick and Normand arguably exaggerated the correlation between the diminishing utility of a means or method of warfare, on the one hand, and its susceptibility to restriction or prohibition, on the other.[18] The two commentators effectively asserted that, insofar as a given means or method of warfare retains its utility, it is *in*susceptible to meaningful restriction or prohibition.

To be sure, Jochnick and Normand are not the first to espouse such a view. They largely echo M. W. Royse, according to whom:

> [T]he two great peace conferences of modern times [in The Hague, in 1899 and 1907], along with their lesser predecessors, did not succeed in reducing armaments, or in restricting the development and improvement of weapons, or in prohibiting or restricting the use of any effective weapon or method of warfare ... The proceedings of the Hague Conference demonstrate rather that a weapon will be restricted in inverse proportion, more or less, to its effectiveness; that the more efficient a weapon or method of warfare the less likelihood there is of its being restricted in action by rules of war.[19]

[17] Treaty on the Prohibition of Nuclear Weapons, 7 July 2017, not yet in force.

[18] Jochnick and Normand, 'Legitimation of Violence', at 67, n.72, 68–69. See also Townsend Hoopes, 'Comments' in Peter D Trooboff (ed), *Law and Responsibility in Warfare: The Vietnam Experience* (Chapel Hill: University of North Carolina Press, 1975) 142.

[19] MW Royse, *Aerial Bombardment and the International Regulation of Warfare* (New York: Harold Vinal, 1928), pp. 131–32 (quoted in Jochnick and Normand, 'Legitimation of Violence', at 76 n.123).

Some weapons did, however, become the subject of an unqualified ban despite their perceived or arguable utility. Poison and poisonous weapons, including asphyxiating and other gases,[20] are a case in point. For, after all, it is not entirely inconceivable for them to be delivered against the right target, in the right doses, and at the right moment, and be effective as a result.[21] According to William H. Boothby, Hersch Lauterpacht admitted this possibility when he observed:

> Oppenheim refers to the practice of diffusing poisonous and asphyxiating gases from cylinders or otherwise than by projectiles during World War I, and concludes that, irrespective of whether that practice breached the prohibition on poisons and poisonous weapons, it was illegal to the extent that it exposed combatants to unnecessary suffering.[22]

On this view, diffusion of poisonous and asphyxiating gases from cylinders and so on would be illegal *to the extent* such diffusion exposed combatants to unnecessary suffering.

One might debate whether the prohibitions contained in Article 23(a) and (e) of the 1907 Hague Regulations[23] really encompassed this kind of diffusion during World War I.[24] What is significant for our purposes, however, is two-fold. First, Lauterpacht, at least as described by Boothby, conceded that not all parts of the suffering to which the diffusion of these gases exposed combatants might be unnecessary. In other words, only that part of suffering considered unnecessary would render the diffusion unlawful.[25] Second, despite this room for consistency with material military necessity, positive IHL has prohibited the diffusions of poisonous and asphyxiating gases, together with the use of gases generally.[26]

[20] Boothby, *Weapons and the Law of Armed Conflict*, pp. 117–21.

[21] Of course, these can also be employed in a manner that renders them ineffective. See Roberts Graves, *Good-Bye to All That* (London: Jonathan Cape, 1929), pp. 198–211.

[22] Boothby, *Weapons and the Law of Armed Conflict*, p. 119 (quoting Lauterpacht [ed], *Oppenheim's International Law* [7th edn], p. 340 n.6).

[23] The provisions read, in relevant parts: 'In addition to the prohibitions provided by special Conventions, it is especially forbidden . . . (a) [t]o employ poison or poisonous weapons [and] (e) [t]o employ arms, projectiles, or material calculated to cause unnecessary suffering.'

[24] Garner, *International Law and the World War* (vol. I), pp. 271–78.

[25] Indeed, some commentators suggest that gases were no more inhumane than other weapons. Stone, *Legal Controls of International Conflict*, p. 554.

[26] Article 13(a), Brussels Declaration; Article 8(a), Oxford Manual; Article 23(a), Hague Regulations (1899); Article 23(a), Hague Regulations (1907); Article 8(2)(b)(xvii), 8(2)(b)(xviii), Rome Statute; *United States of America et al. v Hermann Wilhelm Göring et al.*, *Trial of the Major War Criminals Before the International Military Tribunal*, 42 vols.

7.1.1.2 Killing POWs

Geneva Convention III unqualifiedly prohibits the killing of POWs.[27] Historically, however, the notion of sparing POWs' lives had little to do with humanity.

In medieval Europe, for instance, sparing POWs had more to do with other political, strategic and practical reasons – including, in particular, their captors' decidedly selfish and un-humanitarian interests such as pecuniary gain and prestige.[28] It is only later in time that humanitarian sentiments came to match such practice. Thus, as observed by G. I. A. D. Draper:

> It may well be that much of the Law of Arms of the pre-Grotian period imposed binding legal restrictions, well understood by those engaged in warfare, for reasons that had little to do with our modern philosophy of humanitarianism. The sparing of prisoners and the system of parole had little basis in humanitarian considerations. Dead prisoners cannot pay ransom and a prisoner cannot raise the ransom unless he has the chance to go home and persuade his family and friends to put up the money for his liberty. Later, as so often in the passage of legal history, these same legal institutions, quarters and parole, get viewed in quite another light, i.e., the changing morality of a later age when humanitarianism in warfare becomes acceptable and demanded.[29]

(Nuremberg: International Military Tribunal, 1947), vol. I, 171, p. 220; Henckaerts and Doswald-Beck, *Customary International Humanitarian Law* (vol. I), pp. 251–54, 259–63; Jean Pascal Zanders, 'International Norms against Chemical and Biological Warfare: An Ambiguous Legacy' (2003) 8 *Journal of Conflict & Security Law* 391, at 392–94; Green, *Contemporary Law of Armed Conflict*, pp. 161, 167–68. See also Stone, *Legal Controls of International Conflict*, pp. 555–56; Kalshoven, 'Arms, Armaments and International Law', p. 216 n.33 (quoted in Boothby, *Weapons and the Law of Armed Conflict*, p. 122); Boothby, *Weapons and the Law of Armed Conflict*, pp. 121–25.

27 Article 4, Hague Regulations (1899); Article 4, Hague Regulations (1907); Article 2, POW Convention (1929); Article 13, Geneva Convention III. See also Article 23, Brussels Declaration; Article 63, Oxford Manual; Pictet (ed), *Commentary Geneva Convention III*, p. 140; Article 41(3), Additional Protocol I; Article 8(2)(a)(i), Rome Statute. See Chapter 8 for a discussion concerning the unqualified prohibition against killing POWs out of mercy.

28 Percy Bordwell, *The Law of War between Belligerents: A History and Commentary* (Chicago: Callaghan & Co., 1908), pp. 20–21; Peter H Wilson, 'Prisoners in Early Modern European Warfare' in Scheipers (ed), *Prisoners in War* 39, pp. 44–53.

29 Draper, 'Military Necessity and Humanitarian Imperatives', at 129. See also Geoffrey Butler and Simon MacCoby, *The Development of International Law* (London: Longmans, Green and Co., 1928), pp. 122–23; MH Keen, *The Laws of War in the Late Middle Ages* (London and Toronto: Routledge and Kegan Paul, University of Toronto Press, 1965), pp. 156–85; Neff, 'Prisoners of War in International Law', p. 57.

By the eighteenth century, the Grotian notion that POWs should be spared[30] found resonance in Jean-Jacque Rousseau's writings:

> War, then, is not a relation between man and man, but a relation between state and state, in which individuals are enemies only by accident, not as men, nor even as citizens, but as soldiers; not as members of the fatherland, but as its defenders ... The aim of war being the destruction of the hostile state, we have a right to slay its defenders so long as they have arms in their hands; but as soon as they lay them down and surrender, ceasing to be enemies or instruments of the enemy, they become again simply men, and no one has any right over their lives.[31]

This 'liberal'[32] tendency consolidated in the nineteenth century with the Lieber Code in 1863[33] and the Brussels Declaration in 1874,[34] followed by the adoption of the 1899 and 1907 Hague Regulations.[35]

7.1.1.3 Committing Rape

The unqualified prohibition against rape also shows how the military necessity-humanity interplay may evolve over time.[36]

In medieval Europe, rape in the aftermath of the conquest of a city by storm was lawful. This was permitted by military necessity, notwithstanding its evident inhumanity.[37] According to M. H. Keen:

> Women could be raped ... The prospect of this free run of his lusts for blood, spoil and women was a major incentive to a soldier to persevere in the rigours which were likely to attend to a protracted siege.[38]

30 Hugo Grotius, *De Jure Belli Ac Pacis Libri Tres*, 2 vols., Francis W Kelsey (trans.) (Oxford: Clarendon Press, 1925), vol. II, pp. 737–39.

31 Jean-Jacques Rousseau, *The Social Contract or Principles of Political Right*, HJ Tozer (trans.) (Ware: Wordsworth Editions Limited, 1998), pp. 10–11. See also Emer de Vattel, *The Law of Nations; or Principles of the Law of Nature, Applied to the Conduct and Affairs of Nations and Sovereigns*, Joseph Chitty (trans.) (Philadelphia: T. & J.W. Johnson, 1844), pp. 63, 68–70; Neff, 'Prisoners of War in International Law', p. 70.

32 Claude Pilloud, 'Protection of the Victims of Armed Conflicts' in Henri Dunant Institute and UNESCO (eds), *International Dimensions of Humanitarian Law* 167, p. 168.

33 Article 56, Lieber Code.

34 Article 23, Brussels Declaration. See also Article 63, Oxford Manual.

35 Article 4, Hague Regulations (1899); Article 4, Hague Regulations (1907). See also Pictet, *Commentary III Geneva Convention*, at 140; Sibylle Scheipers, 'Prisoners and Detainees in War', *European History Online* (Mainz: Institute of European History, 2011).

36 Pellet, 'Destruction of Troy Will Not Take Place', pp. 170, 194–95; Schmitt, 'Military Necessity and Humanity', at 799; Schwarzenberger, *International Law as Applied by Courts and Tribunals* (vol. II), p. 135.

37 Keen, *Law of War in the Late Middle Ages*, pp. 121–22.

38 Ibid.

Today's IHL unqualifiedly prohibits rape.[39] This change may be due to the fact that rape's inhumanity has become universally acknowledged. It can also be argued that the military utility attributed to rape has diminished if not entirely eliminated,[40] and that military necessity has shifted from permitting rape to (merely) tolerating it. Indeed, Brandt observed: 'And the rape of women ... of occupied countries serves no military purpose. On the contrary, such behaviour arouses hatred and resentment and constitutes a military liability.'[41]

7.1.2 Unqualified Obligations to Pursue Joint Satisfaction that Is Based on Performance

Firm joint satisfaction also results where the belligerent performs what humanity demands and military necessity permits. Here, too, IHL accounts for the two sets of considerations when it imposes an unqualified obligation to perform the act in question.

This remains the case, although categorical IHL obligations that can be said to embody the necessary-humane alignment are limited in number. Our earlier discussion has highlighted the humane treatment of residents and their property in occupied territory as an example.[42] In Brandt's words: 'So utility is maximized, within our indicated basic limitations, by a strict rule calling for good treatment of the civilian population of an occupied territory.'[43]

It should be noted that treating civilians in occupied territory well in eighteenth and nineteenth-century wars had more to do with military

[39] Article 76(1), Additional Protocol I; Article 4(2)(e), Additional Protocol II; Article 8(2)(b)(xxii), 8(2)(e)(vi), Rome Statute. See also *Prosecutor v Jean-Paul Akayesu*, Case No. ICTR-96-4-T, *Judgment*, 2 September 1998, paras 596–98, 686–88; *Prosecutor v Anto Furundžija*, Case No. IT-95-17/1-T, *Judgment*, 10 December 1998, para. 185; *Prosecutor v Dragoljub Kunarac et al*, Case No. IT-96-23&23/1-T, *Judgment*, 22 February 2001, para. 460; *Kunarac et al Appeal Judgment*, paras 125–33; *Prosecutor v Mikaeli Muhimana*, Case No. ICTR-95-1B-T, *Judgment*, 28 April 2005, paras 547–51; Henckaerts and Doswald-Beck, *Customary International Humanitarian Law* (vol. I), pp. 323–27; Gloria Gaggioli, 'Sexual Violence in Armed Conflicts: A Violation of International Humanitarian Law and Human Rights Law' (2014) 96 *International Review of the Red Cross* 503, at 511–13.

[40] This is without prejudice to the *rhetoric* of rape as a 'weapon of war' or 'method of war'. Gaggioli, 'Sexual Violence in Armed Conflicts', at 517–19.

[41] Brandt, 'Utilitarianism', at 155. See also Gaggioli, 'Sexual Violence in Armed Conflicts', at 517–19.

[42] See Chapter 6.

[43] Brandt, 'Utilitarianism', at 155.

considerations than humanitarian ones. The latter essentially 'caught up' with the former – or so, at least, the theory would go.[44] In any event, today's IHL imposes a number of unqualified, affirmative obligations upon the belligerent in its administration of occupied territory.[45]

As with unqualified prohibitions, unqualified obligations extinguish all contrary liberties to behave otherwise (i.e., to refrain from the acts in question). Under no circumstances are they modifiable on account of countervailing indifferent considerations. Consequently, invoking such considerations does not repair failures or refusals to perform unqualified obligations.[46]

7.2 Paucity of Unqualified Obligations Despite Military Necessity-Humanity Alignment

We should not assume, too hastily, that possibilities of firm joint satisfaction *always* result in unqualified IHL rules. On the contrary, numerous acts exhibiting the military necessity-humanity alignment elude unqualified IHL regulation. This occurs where positive IHL contains no

[44] What happened in reality appears less auspicious. Best, 'Restraints on War by Land', pp. 27–28.

[45] Articles 46 (respecting family honour and rights), 55 (safeguarding the capital of public buildings), 56 (treating properties of municipalities and other entities as private property), Hague Regulations (1899); Articles 46 (respecting family honour and rights), 55 (safeguarding the capital of public buildings), 56 (treating properties of municipalities and other entities as private property), Hague Regulations (1907). No major debate regarding these provisions occurred at the 1899 and 1907 Hague Conferences, where delegates adopted them largely based on Article 38 of the Brussels Declaration. See also Articles 50 (facilitating the proper working of institutions for education and care of children), 58 (permitting spiritual assistance, and accepting consignments of religious material and facilitating their distribution), 59 (agreeing to relief schemes), Geneva Convention IV. Here, too, no major difficulties arose at the 1949 Diplomatic Conference regarding Articles 50 and 59 of Geneva Convention IV, drawn as they were from Articles 46 and 48 of the Draft Convention Relative to the Treatment of Prisoners of War (approved by the 1948 XVIIth International Red Cross Conference in Stockholm) (hereinafter Stockholm Draft). Article 58 was introduced by the Holy See and adopted without debate. Federal Political Department, *Final Record of the Diplomatic Conference* (vol. II-A), pp. 748, 831; Federal Political Department, *Final Record of the Diplomatic Conference* (vol. II-B), p. 421; Hans-Peter Gasser and Knut Dörmann, 'Protection of the Civilian Population' in Dieter Fleck (ed), *The Handbook of International Humanitarian Law*, 3rd edn (Oxford: Oxford University Press, 2013) 231, pp. 276–78; Henckaerts and Doswald-Beck, *Customary International Humanitarian Law* (vol. I), pp. 178–81.

[46] The joint satisfaction thesis envisions potential room where non-indifference pleas may in fact be admissible even vis-à-vis unqualified IHL obligations. See Chapter 8.

pertinent rules, or where, although the law does contain such rules, they have a narrow scope of application.

Three major explanations readily present themselves. First, some acts deemed both inhumane and unnecessary are of a nature that involves exclusively self-inflicted evil.[47] We saw earlier that, whereas IHL addresses itself to such acts in limited circumstances, it still remains heavily influenced by the Millian presumption of behavioural autonomy.[48]

Second, acts deemed humane and necessary are often aspirational rather than mandatory in character.[49] Since, with respect to such acts, neither military necessity nor humanity generates imperatives, it is unlikely that IHL framers will elect to make the pursuit of joint satisfaction obligatory. For example, Article 34 of Geneva Convention II strictly forbids the possession or use of a secret code by hospital ships for their wireless or other means of communication.[50] According to the Red Cross commentary:

> The fact that the use of any secret code is prohibited affords a guarantee to the belligerents that hospital ships will not make improper use of their transmitting apparatus or any other means of communication. Hospital ships may only communicate in clear, or at least in a code which is universally known, and rightly so, for the spirit of the Geneva Conventions requires that there should be nothing secret in their behaviour vis-à-vis the enemy.[51]

This prohibition was relaxed in paragraph 171 of the 1994 Sam Remo Manual on Maritime Warfare. That paragraph stipulates: 'In order to fulfil most effectively their humanitarian mission, hospital ships should be permitted to use cryptographic equipment. The equipment shall not be used in any circumstances to transmit intelligence data nor in any other way to acquire any military advantage.'[52] Arguably, the idea that hospital ships should now be permitted to use cryptographic equipment has to do with a combination of military necessity (i.e., warships cannot otherwise communicate in clear with hospital ships without revealing their own position) and humanity (i.e., only by communicating with

[47] See Chapter 4.
[48] See Chapter 4.
[49] See Chapter 6.
[50] Article 34, Geneva Convention II.
[51] Pictet (ed), *Commentary Geneva Convention II*, p. 193.
[52] San Remo Manual on Maritime Warfare, para. 171.

other warships can hospital ships effectively carry out their humanitarian mission in the modern world).[53] Importantly for our purposes here, modern IHL still does not obligate hospital ships to use cryptographic equipment.

Third, other considerations may prevent or discourage IHL framers from unqualifiedly obligating necessary and humane acts or prohibiting unnecessary and inhumane ones.[54] Take sovereign interests,[55] for instance. These interests have blocked or delayed the adoption of an unqualified IHL rule – or, in any event, the extension of an existing one's scope of application – even where it would otherwise accord with humanity and military necessity.

7.2.1 General Participation Clause

Clausula si omnes[56] typifies historical instances where considerations of sovereignty among warring states occasionally precluded the application of unqualified IHL rules obligating jointly satisfactory behaviour.[57] It is widely agreed that general participation no longer forms part of modern IHL.[58]

7.2.2 Non-international Armed Conflicts

Sovereign considerations have also hampered the adoption of treaty provisions unqualifiedly prohibiting inhumane and unnecessary acts in non-international armed conflicts.[59] The International Committee of the

[53] I am grateful to Charles Garraway for his insight on the matter. See also Wolff Heintschel von Heinegg, 'Maritime Warfare' in Clapham and Gaeta (eds), *Oxford Handbook of International Law in Armed Conflict* 145, pp. 157–59.

[54] On the significance of these considerations, see Chapter 8.

[55] Jochnick and Normand, 'Legitimation of Violence', at 71–72.

[56] Pictet (ed), *Commentary Geneva Convention III*, pp. 21–22; Philippe Gautier, 'General Participation Clause (Clausula si omnes)', *Max Planck Encyclopedia of Public International Law* (2006).

[57] Gautier, 'General Participation Clause', paras 4–6.

[58] Article 2, paragraph 3, common to Geneva Conventions I–IV. See also Georges Abi-Saab, 'The Specifics of Humanitarian Law' in Swinarski (ed), *Studies and Essays on International Humanitarian Law* 265, pp. 267–68; Gautier, 'General Participation Clause', paras 6–7; Theodor Meron, 'The Geneva Conventions and Public International Law' (2009) 91 *International Review of the Red Cross* 619, at 621.

[59] Alexander Zahar, 'Civilizing Civil War: Writing Morality as Law at the ICTY' in Bert Swart et al. (eds), *The Legacy of the International Criminal Tribunal for the Former Yugoslavia* (Oxford: Oxford University Press, 2011) 469, pp. 500–02; Dapo Akande,

Red Cross (ICRC) failed to rally state support for broadening the scope of application of the four Geneva Conventions in their entirety to cover non-international armed conflicts.[60] The same fate befell numerous would-be provisions of Additional Protocol II.[61]

Two appellate rulings in *Tadić* may be briefly noted here. In 1995, the ICTY Appeals Chamber found that 'the prohibition of means of warfare proscribed in international armed conflicts and ban of certain methods of conducting hostilities'[62] had by 1991 become customarily applicable in non-international armed conflicts. This ruling has been widely praised for its contribution to IHL development.[63] Predictably, however, it has

'Classification of Armed Conflicts: Relevant Legal Concepts' in Elizabeth Wilmshurst (ed), *International Law and the Classification of Conflicts* (Oxford: Oxford University Press, 2012) 32, pp. 37–39; Dieter Fleck, 'The Law of Non-international Armed Conflict' in Fleck (ed), *Handbook of International Humanitarian Law* (3d edn) 581, p. 590.

[60] Pictet (ed), *Commentary Geneva Convention I*, pp. 38–48; Frits Kalshoven, 'Applicability of Customary International Law in Non-international Armed Conflicts' in Kalshoven, *Collected Essays* 133, p. 140; Georges Abi-Saab, 'Non-international Armed Conflicts' in Henri Dunant Institute and UNESCO (eds), *International Dimensions of Humanitarian Law* 217, p. 220; David A Elder, 'The Historical Background of Common Article 3 of the Geneva Conventions of 1949' (1979) 11 *Case Western Reserve Journal of International Law* 37, at 41–54; Lindsay Moir, *The Law of Internal Armed Conflict* (Cambridge: Cambridge University Press, 2002), pp. 24–29; Rogier Bartels, 'Timelines, Borderlines and Conflicts: The Historical Evolution of the Legal Divide between International and Non-international Armed Conflicts' (2009) 91 *International Review of the Red Cross* 35, at 57–61; Sandesh Sivakumaran, *The Law of Non-international Armed Conflict* (Oxford: Oxford University Press, 2012), pp. 40–42; Anthony Cullen, *The Concept of Non-international Armed Conflict in International Humanitarian Law* (Cambridge: Cambridge University Press, 2010), pp. 44–49.

[61] Abi-Saab, 'Non-international Armed Conflicts', pp. 230–33; Moir, *Law of Internal Armed Conflict*, pp. 91–96; Lindsay Moir, 'Towards the Unification of International Humanitarian Law?' in Burchill et al. (ed), *International Conflict and Security Law* 108, pp. 111–13; Bartels, 'Times, Borderlines and Conflicts', at 61–64; Meron, 'Geneva Conventions', at 622–23; Sivakumaran, *Law of Non-international Armed Conflict*, pp. 49–52; Cullen, *Concept of Non-international Armed Conflict*, pp. 86–102; Michael Bothe, Karl Josef Partsch and Waldemar A Solf, *New Rules for Victims of Armed Conflicts: Commentary on the Two 1977 Protocols Additional to the Geneva Conventions of 1949*, 2nd rev. edn (Leiden and Boston: Martinus Nijhoff, 2013), pp. 714–20.

[62] *Tadić Jurisdiction Decision*, para. 127.

[63] Christopher Greenwood, 'International Humanitarian Law and the *Tadić* Case' in Greenwood, *Essays on War in International Law* 457, pp. 473–474; Christopher Greenwood, 'The Development of International Humanitarian Law by the International Criminal Tribunal for the Former Yugoslavia' (1998) 2 *Max Planck Yearbook of United Nations Law* 97, at 130; Theodor Meron, 'War Crimes Law Comes of Age' (1998) 92 *American Journal of International Law* 462, at 463; Allison Marston Danner, 'When Courts Make Law: How the International Criminal Tribunals Recast the Laws of War'

also attracted criticisms on account of its creative customary law methodologies[64] and threat to state sovereignty.[65]

In 1999, the Appeals Chamber effectively held that the Geneva Conventions apply to certain types of armed conflicts ordinarily deemed non-international in character,[66] and that Geneva Convention IV extends protection to some victims traditionally considered ineligible.[67] These findings, too, have received expressions of support[68] and concern[69] alike.

7.2.3 *Belligerent Reprisals*[70]

Sovereign prerogatives have delayed the establishment of a customary prohibition against subjecting civilian persons to belligerent reprisals during active hostilities in international armed conflicts.[71] As seen below, this technique is regarded as inhumane and of little or no material utility. The ICTY's *Martić Rule 61 Decision*[72] and *Kupreškić et al. Trial*

(2006) 59 *Vanderbilt Law Review* 1, at 25–26; Francoise Hampson, 'Relevance for the Prosecution of Violations of International Humanitarian Law' in Larry Maybee and Benarji Chakka (eds), *Custom as a Source of International Humanitarian Law* (no place: International Committee of the Red Cross, Asian and African Legal Consultative Organisation, 2006) 103, p. 109; Shane Darcy, 'Bridging the Gaps in the Laws of Armed Conflict? International Criminal Tribunals and the Development of Humanitarian Law' in Noëlle Quénivet and Shilan Shah-Davis (eds), *International Law and Armed Conflict: Challenges in the 21st Century* (The Hague: TMC Asser Press, 2010) 319, pp. 328–29.

64 Frits Kalshoven, 'Development of Customary Law of Armed Conflict' in Kalshoven, *Collected Essays* 321, p. 324; Schmitt, 'Military Necessity and Humanity', at 818–19.

65 Peter W Murphy, book review on 'Judging War Criminals' (2000) 35 *Texas International Law Journal* 325, at 332; Schmitt, 'Military Necessity and Humanity', at 819–20, 822.

66 *Tadić Appeal Judgment*, paras 83–162.

67 Ibid, paras 163–69.

68 Danner, 'When Courts Make Law', at 25–26; Darcy, 'Bridging the Gaps', pp. 326–28.

69 Murphy, book review, at 332; Frits Kalshoven, 'From International Humanitarian Law to International Criminal Law' in Kalshoven, *Collected Essays* 947, pp. 953–54.

70 For an earlier version of the following passages on belligerent reprisals, see Nobuo Hayashi, 'Is the Yugoslav Tribunal Guilty of Hyper-Humanising International Humanitarian Law?' in Nobuo Hayashi and Cecilia M Bailliet (eds), *The Legitimacy of International Criminal Tribunals* (Cambridge: Cambridge University Press, 2017) 179, pp. 182–86. See also Nobuo Hayashi, 'Performance of International Criminal Courts and Tribunals' in Theresa Squatrito et al. (eds), *The Performance of International Courts and Tribunals* (Cambridge: Cambridge University Press, 2018) 154, pp. 157–58, 174–75.

71 Henckaerts and Doswald-Beck, *Customary International Humanitarian Law* (vol. I), pp. 520–23; Meron, 'Geneva Conventions', at 623. The notion that states parties to Additional Protocol I without reservations are unqualifiedly forbidden to resort to this technique is uncontroversial. Article 51(6), Additional Protocol I.

72 *Prosecutor v Milan Martić*, Case No. IT-95-11-R61, *Decision*, 8 March 1996, para. 17.

Judgment[73] declare the technique customarily unlawful. Reactions to these decisions have nevertheless been largely disapproving.[74]

Article 51(6) of Additional Protocol I provides that '[a]ttacks against the civilian population or civilians by way of reprisals are prohibited'. Upon ratification, Italy, Germany and Egypt declared that they would react to violations of Additional Protocol I obligations with 'all means admissible under international law in order to prevent any further violation'.[75] The United Kingdom's 1998 ratification was explicitly on condition that it 'will regard itself as entitled to take measures otherwise prohibited by [Articles 51–55]', subject to a number of stringent conditions.[76] France appended a declaration to its 2001 instrument of

[73] *Prosecutor v Zoran Kupreškić et al*, Case No. IT-95-16-T, *Judgment*, 14 January 2000, para. 531.

[74] UK Defence Ministry, *Joint Service Manual*, p. 421; Payam Akhavan, 'The Dilemmas of Jurisprudence: The Contribution of the Ad Hoc Tribunals to International Humanitarian Law' (1998) 13 *American University International Law Review* 1518, at 1518–20; Greenwood, 'Development of International Humanitarian Law', at 123–25; Shane Darcy, 'The Evolution of the Law of Belligerent Reprisals' (2003) 175 *Military Law Review* 184; Frits Kalshoven, 'Reprisals and the Protection of Civilians: Two Recent Decisions of the Yugoslavia Tribunal' in Lal Chand Vohrah et al. (eds), *Man's Inhumanity to Man: Essays on International Law in Honour of Antonio Cassese* (The Hague: Kluwer Law International, 2003) 481; Christopher Greenwood, 'Belligerent Reprisals in the Jurisprudence of the International Criminal Tribunal for the Former Yugoslavia' in Greenwood, *Essays on War in International Law* 331; Robert Cryer, 'Of Custom, Treaties, Scholars and the Gavel: The Influence of the International Criminal Tribunals on the ICRC Customary Law Study' (2006) 11 *Journal of Conflict & Security Law* 239, at 255–56; Michael A Newton, 'Reconsidering Reprisals' (2009–2010) 20 *Duke Journal of Comparative and International Law* 361; Schmitt, 'Military Necessity and Humanity', at 820–22; Milan Kuhli and Klaus Günther, 'Beyond Dispute: International Judicial Institutions as Lawmakers: Judicial Lawmaking, Discourse Theory, and the ICTY on Belligerent Reprisals' (2011) 12 *German Law Journal* 1261; Brian San Yk, 'Legal Regulation of Belligerent Reprisals in International Humanitarian Law: Historical Development and Present Status' (2012) *African Yearbook on International Humanitarian Law* 134; Veronika Bílková, 'Belligerent Reprisals in Non-international Armed Conflicts' (2014) 63 *International and Comparative Law Quarterly* 31. But see Alexander Orakhelashvili, book review (2009) 79 *British Yearbook of International Law* 371, at 373; Jean-François Quéguiner, 'The Principle of Distinction: Beyond an Obligation of Customary International Humanitarian Law' in Hensel (ed), *Legitimate use of Military Force* 161; Brian D Lepard, 'Customary International Law as a Dynamic Process' in Curtis A Bradley (ed), *Custom's Future: International Law in a Changing World* (Cambridge: Cambridge University press, 2016) 62.

[75] Ratification and Accession, Italy, 27 February 1986, 1425 UNTS 438, p. 440; Ratifications and Accessions, Germany, 14 February 1991, 1607 UNTS 526, p. 529; Ratification and Accession, Egypt, 9 October 1992, 1712 UNTS 435, p. 439.

[76] Ratification (with declarations and reservations), United Kingdom of Great Britain and Northern Ireland, 28 January 1998, 2020 UNTS 75, p. 78.

accession to the effect that it will apply Article 51 in such a way that '*l'interprétation de celles-ci ne fait pas obstacle à l'emploi, conformément au Droit international, des moyens qu'il estimerait indispensables pour protéger sa population civile de violations graves, manifestes et délibérées des Conventions de Genève et du Protocole par l'ennemi*'.[77] The United States specified Article 51, especially its ban on belligerent reprisals against civilians in hostilities, as one of the reasons for refusing to ratify Additional Protocol I.[78] During the ICJ's *Nuclear Weapons* advisory proceedings, both the United States and the United Kingdom reiterated their position that the content of Article 51(6) had not passed into custom.[79] The prohibition's customary status in the pre-*Martić* and pre-*Kupreškić et al.* era was therefore debatable.

The *Martić* Rule 61 Chamber offered two problematic bases. The first is the so-called obligation 'to respect and to ensure respect' found in Article 1 common to all Geneva Conventions.[80] It is true that the ICJ invoked common Article 1 in its *Nicaragua Judgment*.[81] However, that court did not consider common Article 1 to contain new obligations or obligations that are more stringent than those that IHL already stipulates. It seems generally agreed that common Article 1 does not do so,[82] despite occasional suggestions to the contrary.[83] The *Martić* Rule 61 Chamber

[77] Reservations and declarations to the accession, France, 11 April 2001 (https://ihl-databases.icrc.org/applic/ihl/ihl.nsf/Notification.xsp?action=openDocument&documentId=D8041036B40EBC44C1256A34004897B2).

[78] Abraham D Sofaer, 'The Position of the United States on Current Law of War Agreements: Remarks of Judge Abraham D. Sofaer, Legal Adviser, United States Department of State, January 22, 1987' (1987) 2 *American University Journal of International Law and Policy* 460 at 469.

[79] *Written Statement of the Government of the United States of America*, 20 June 1995, pp. 25, 30–31; *Statement of the Government of the United Kingdom*, June 1995, para. 3.81.

[80] *Martić Rule 61 Decision*, para. 15.

[81] *Military and Paramilitary Activities in and against Nicaragua (Nicaragua v United States of America), Merits, Judgment, ICJ Reports 1986*, p. 14, para. 220 (cited in *Martić Rule 61 Decision*, para. 15).

[82] Adam Roberts, 'The Laws of War: Problems of Implementation in Contemporary Conflicts' (1995) *Duke Journal of Comparative and International Law* 13, at 29–30; Greenwood, 'Development of International Humanitarian Law', at 124; Carlo Focarelli, 'Common Article 1 of the Geneva Conventions: A Soap Bubble?' (2010) 21 *European Journal of International Law* 125, at 171.

[83] *Request by the United Nations General Assembly for an Advisory Opinion on the Legality of the Threat or Use of Nuclear Weapons: Written Observations Submitted by the Government of Solomon Islands to the International Court of Justice*, 20 June 1995, para. 3.10: 'The threat of [nuclear weapons'] use must be considered as totally incompatible with the solemn obligation undertaken by States under common Article 1 of the four

also invoked General Assembly Resolution 2675,[84] Article 51(6) of Additional Protocol I[85] and Article 4 of Additional Protocol II.[86] Together or individually, however, it does not appear that these authorities alone establish the existence of a customary IHL prohibition on belligerent reprisals against civilians in hostilities.[87]

In contrast to the *Martić Rule 61 Decision*, the *Kupreškić et al. Trial Judgment* approaches belligerent reprisals from four distinct angles. They are:

1. The Martens Clause as requiring restrictive interpretation;[88]
2. The Martens Clause as a basis for elevating *opinio necessitatis* above *usus*;[89]
3. Belligerent reprisals' deontological undesirability;[90] and
4. Belligerent reprisals' diminishing relative utility.[91]

The first angle stems from how one is to interpret IHL provisions granting belligerents discretionary powers and those extending protection to civilians, as well as the place the Martens Clause occupies therein. In the *Kupreškić et al.* Trial Chamber's words:

> However, this [Martens] Clause enjoins, as a minimum, reference to those principles [of humanity] and dictates [of public conscience] any time a rule of international humanitarian law is not sufficiently rigorous or precise: in those instances the scope and purport of the rule must be defined with reference to those principles and dictates. In the case under discussion, this would entail that the prescriptions of Articles 57 and 58 [of Additional Protocol I] (and of the corresponding customary rules) must be interpreted so as to construe as narrowly as possible the

Geneva Conventions of 1949 and Article 1(1) of the 1st 1977 Additional Protocol "to respect and ensure respect" of the four Conventions and the Protocol.' Nowhere in "the *Nuclear Weapons Advisory Opinion* itself", does the ICJ refer to common Article 1.

84 UN General Assembly Resolution 2675 (XXV), 9 December 1970 (cited in *Martić Rule 61 Decision*, para. 16).

85 Article 51(6), Additional Protocol I (cited in *Martić Rule 61 Decision*, para. 16).

86 Article 4, Additional Protocol II (cited in *Martić Rule 61 Decision*, para. 16).

87 Interestingly, both the *Martić Trial Judgment* and the *Martić Appeal Judgment* appear to accept that belligerent reprisals are not completely outlawed. See *Prosecutor v Milan Martić*, Case No. IT-95-11-T, *Judgment*, 12 June 2007, paras 465–68; *Prosecutor v Milan Martić*, Case No. IT-95-11-A, *Judgment*, 8 October 2008, paras 263–69.

88 *Kupreškić et al. Trial Judgment*, para. 525.

89 Ibid, paras 527, 531–33.

90 Ibid, paras 528–29.

91 Ibid, para. 530.

> discretionary power to attack belligerents and, by the same token, so as to expand the protection accorded to civilians.[92]

Does the Martens Clause require maximum restriction when interpreting the belligerent's discretionary power? If it does, then one should perhaps consider reprisals against civilians during hostilities unavailable given the technique's ambiguous customary status. Some argue that the Martens Clause effectively reverses any *Lotus*-esque *in dubio pro libertate* presumption under IHL.[93] For them, the clause is a 'safeguard of customary humanitarian law by supporting the argument that what is not prohibited by treaty may not necessarily be lawful'.[94] As will be seen below, however, it is not clear whether a *full* reversal – i.e., *in dubio pro prohibitione* – is what the Martens Clause gives us.[95]

Second, according to the *Kupreškić et al.* Trial Chamber, the lawfulness or unlawfulness of belligerent reprisals against civilians in combat zones is

> an area where *opinio juris sive necessitatis* may play a much greater role than *usus*, as a result of the aforementioned Martens Clause. In the light of the way States and courts have implemented it, this Clause clearly shows that principles of international humanitarian law may emerge through a customary process under the pressure of the demands of humanity or the dictates of public conscience, even where State practice is scant or inconsistent. The other element, in the form of *opinio necessitatis*, crystallising as a result of the imperatives of humanity or

[92] Ibid, para. 525. See also de Breucker's statement at the 1974 Diplomatic Conference (Federal Political Department, *Official Records of the Diplomatic Conference on the Reaffirmation and Development of International Humanitarian Law Applicable in Armed Conflicts*, 17 vols. [Berne: Federal Political Department, 1987], vol. VIII, p. 18); Cassese, 'Martens Clause', at 212.

[93] *Nuclear Weapons, Dissenting Opinion of Judge Shahabuddeen*, p. 375, pp. 394–96; ibid, *Dissenting Opinion of Judge Weeramantry*, p. 429, pp. 494–96; Louise Doswald-Beck, 'International Humanitarian Law and the Advisory Opinion of the International Court of Justice on the Legality of Threat or Use of Nuclear Weapons' (1997) 37 *International Review of the Red Cross* 35; Rupert Ticehurst, 'The Martens Clause and the Laws of Armed Conflict' (1997) 37 *International Review of the Red Cross* 125.

[94] Von Bernstorff, 'Martens Clause', para. 13. See also *Nuclear Weapons*, para. 84; *Legality of the Threat or use of Nuclear Weapons (Request for an Advisory Opinion by the United Nations General Assembly): Statement of the Government of the United Kingdom*, 16 June 1995, para. 3.58; International Court of Justice, *Verbatim Record*, 15 November 1995 (CR 95/34), p. 78; Abi-Saab, 'Specifics of Humanitarian Law', pp. 274–75; Georg Schwarzenberger, *The Legality of Nuclear Weapons* (Toronto: Carswell Co., 1958), at 10–11 (cited in Cassese, 'Martens Clause', at 189 n. 3).

[95] See below.

> public conscience, may turn out to be the decisive element heralding the emergence of a general rule of principle of humanitarian law.[96]

Note how the chamber subtly shifts its attention from *opinio juris sive necessitatis* to *opinio necessitatis*.[97] While the full Latin maxim encompasses both *opinio juris* and *opinio necessitatis*, international law authorities almost always refer to the underlying notion as *opinio juris*.[98] *Opinio necessitatis* may bring the matter closer to what 'needs' to be done, rather than law as it actually is. The chamber appears to be suggesting that, in IHL, the belief of the relevant law-making entities regarding the aforementioned 'need' is sufficient for the finding of custom. Crucially, on this view, such a finding is possible even where neither their corresponding belief regarding the law as it is, nor their corresponding behaviour on the ground, exists.[99]

This suggestion is quite novel, though not entirely without precedent.[100] Does the Martens Clause warrant a shift in our discussion of customary IHL from one based on *opinio juris* to that based on *opinio necessitates*?[101] To complicate the matter further, the *Kupreškić et al. Trial Judgement* enlists into the group of relevant *opinio*-holders not only states[102] – whose *opinio necessitatis* may be more ambiguous than it is

[96] *Kupreškić et al. Trial Judgment*, para. 527.

[97] Ibid, paras 531–33.

[98] *North Sea Continental Shelf, Judgment, ICJ Reports 1969*, p. 3, paras 71, 77. See also International Law Association, *Final Report of the Committee: Statement of Principles Applicable to the Formation of General Customary International Law* (2000), p. 7 (referring to the 'subjective' element of customary law as '*opinio juris sive necessitatis* (or *opinio juris* for short)'), 32–34.

[99] Martti Koskenniemi, *From Apology to Utopia: The Structure of International Legal Argument: Reissue with New Epilogue* (Cambridge: Cambridge University Press, 2005), p. 421; David J Bederman, *Custom as a Source of Law* (Cambridge: Cambridge University Press, 2010), pp. 20–22.

[100] Maurice H Mendelson, 'The Formation of Customary International Law', *Collected Courses of the Hague Academy of International Law* (Leiden and Boston: Martinus Nijhoff, 1998), vol. CCLXXII, 155, p. 271; Antonio Cassese, 'A Follow-Up: Forcible Humanitarian Countermeasures and *Opinio Necessitatis*' (1999) 10 *European Journal of International Law* 791, at 797–99.

[101] Robert Cryer et al. (eds), *An Introduction to International Criminal Law and Procedure*, 2nd edn (Cambridge: Cambridge University Press, 2010), p. 134 n.109; Achilles Skordas, 'Hegemonic Custom?' in Michael Byers and Georg Nolte (eds), *United States Hegemony and the Foundation of International Law* (Cambridge: Cambridge University Press, 2003) 317, pp. 325–30; Erik Vincent Koppe, *The Use of Nuclear Weapons and the Protection of the Environment during International Armed Conflict* (Oxford and Portland: Hart Publishing, 2008), p. 167.

[102] *Kupreškić et al. Trial Judgment*, paras 532–33.

presented to be in the decision[103] – but also the ICRC,[104] the *Martić* Rule 61 Chamber[105] and the International Law Commission (ILC).[106]

The third and fourth angles depart from public international law methodologies proper. The third angle is that, as a means of seeking compliance with international law, belligerent reprisals are inherently barbaric.[107] The judgment notes: 'The most blatant reason for the universal revulsion that usually accompanies reprisals is that they may not only be arbitrary but are also not directed specifically at the individual authors of the initial violation.'[108] Accordingly, 'the reprisal killing of innocent persons, more or less chosen at random, without any requirement of guilt or any form of trial, can safely be characterized as a blatant infringement of the most fundamental principles of human rights'.[109]

At issue here is belligerent reprisals' problematic deontological status,[110] whether they successfully compel the delinquent adversary to return to IHL compliance or not. Significantly, both the *Kupreškić et al. Trial Judgment* and its critics agree that the technique is inhumane.[111] The question is whether IHL should ban belligerent reprisals *because of* their inhumanity, or whether it should tolerate them *despite* their inhumanity.[112]

This leads us to the fourth angle from which the *Kupreškić et al. Trial Judgment* approaches belligerent reprisals. The judgment rejects the utilitarian arguments often offered in their support. Thus,

[103] Greenwood, 'Belligerent Reprisals', pp. 344–46; Schmitt, 'Military Necessity and Humanity', at 820–21.

[104] *Kupreškić et al. Trial Judgment*, para. 532.

[105] Ibid.

[106] Ibid, para. 534.

[107] Ibid, para. 528.

[108] Ibid.

[109] Ibid, para. 529.

[110] Robert Kolb calls it 'a translation of a Kantian categorical imperative into the law'. Robert Kolb, 'International Humanitarian Law and Its Implementation by the Court' in José Doria et al. (eds), *The Legal Regime of the International Criminal Court: Essays in Honour of Professor Igor Blishchenko* (Leiden and London: Martinus Nijhoff, 2009) 1015, p. 1032. See also ibid, pp. 1033–34.

[111] Frits Kalshoven, *Belligerent Reprisals* (Leiden: A.W. Sijthoff, 1971), pp. 42–44, 342–44; Kalshoven, 'Reprisals and the Protection of Civilians', at 481.

[112] Françoise Hampson, 'Belligerent Reprisals and the 1977 Protocols to the Geneva Conventions of 1949' (1988) 37 *International and Comparative Law Quarterly* 818; Frits Kalshoven, 'Belligerent Reprisals Revisited' in Kalshoven, *Collected Essays* 759, pp. 771–76.

> while reprisals could have had a modicum of justification in the past, when they constituted practically the only effective means of compelling the enemy to abandon unlawful acts of warfare and to comply in future with international law, at present they can no longer be justified in this manner. A means of inducing compliance with international law is at present more widely available and, more importantly, is beginning to prove fairly efficacious: the prosecution and punishment of war crimes and crimes against humanity by national or international courts.[113]

In truth, this angle is not really about belligerent reprisals or their efficaciousness. Neither the judgment nor its critics claim that belligerent reprisals are effective in achieving what they are intended to achieve. It is quite the contrary. By their proponents' own admission,[114] belligerent reprisals are fraught with risks of abuse and adverse consequences such as counter-reprisals. States rarely, if ever, resort to them these days.[115] In other words, all appear to agree that belligerent reprisals, including those against civilians during hostilities, are both inhumane and of questionable consistency with material military necessity.

Instead, the judgment focuses on the availability and efficaciousness of 'prosecution and punishment of war crimes and crimes against humanity by national or international courts' as an alternative.[116] All else being equal, the more efficacious such prosecution and punishment would become over time, the less justifiable belligerent reprisals would become by comparison.

Perhaps the judgment's first claim, i.e., the wider availability of war crimes prosecutions before national or international courts, has some grain of truth. Its second claim that their efficaciousness is also improving, however, may be suspect.[117] Here, a hint of naïveté vety – understandable though it may have been in 2000, given the optimism about international criminal justice that was still largely intact at the time – is difficult to dispel.

[113] *Kupreškić et al. Trial Judgment*, para. 530. See also Kalshoven, *Belligerent Reprisals*, pp. 370–71; Christopher Greenwood, 'Reprisals and Reciprocity in the New Law of Armed Conflict' in Michael A Meyer (ed), *Armed Conflict and the New Law: Aspects of the 1977 Geneva Protocols and the 1981 Weapons Convention* (London: British Institute of International and Comparative Law, 1989) 227, pp. 238–46.

[114] Kalshoven, *Belligerent Reprisals*, pp. 41–42; Greenwood, 'Reprisals and Reciprocity', at 295, 316.

[115] Writing in 1989, Christopher Greenwood predicted that 'belligerent reprisals will continue to enjoy a twilight existence'. Greenwood, 'Reprisals and Reciprocity', at 329.

[116] Kolb, 'International Humanitarian Law and Its Implementation by the Court', p. 1034.

[117] Schmitt, 'Military Necessity and Humanity', at 821.

Schmitt faults the *Martić* and *Kupreškić et al.* decisions with the unusual methodologies of public international law used, as well as the unsubstantiated optimism offered about the potential of war crimes prosecutions. In his words: 'When they engage in such activism, international tribunals supplant states in their role as the arbiter of the balance [between military necessity and humanity].'[118] This indicates two things. First, these rulings are seen as challenging the law's traditionally state-driven mode of norm-creation and adjustment. Second, judges are seen as taking the law into directions to which not all states, *qua* IHL framers, may be prepared to go.

In its 2004 manual, the United Kingdom stated its disagreement with *Kupreškić et al.* in no uncertain terms: 'the court's reasoning is unconvincing and the assertion that there is a prohibition in customary law flies into the face of most of the state practice that exists. The UK does not accept the position as stated in this judgment'.[119] The US Defence Department's 2015 manual does not criticise the judgment by name, but it reaffirms the United States' earlier view that belligerent reprisals retain significant deterrent value.[120]

France and Italy appear more equivocal. France's 2012 manual exhibits ambiguities on its view about belligerent reprisals against civilians in hostilities. The document nevertheless cites paragraphs from the *Kupreškić et al. Trial Judgment* that reject reciprocity, synallagmaticity and derogability as characteristics of IHL rules.[121] In its 1991 military manual, Italy merely reiterated the view it had expressed when ratifying Additional Protocol I.[122]

7.3 Joint Satisfaction amid Military Necessity-Humanity Contradiction

Not all belligerent acts are amenable to what we metaphorically called firm joint satisfaction at the outset of this chapter. Can we still speak of joint satisfaction, albeit of a more 'modest' character, with respect to these other acts?

118 Ibid, at 822.
119 UK Defence Ministry, *Joint Service Manual*, p. 423.
120 Office of General Counsel, *Law of War Manual*, pp. 1098–99.
121 Ministère de la défense, *Manuel du droit des conflits armés* (2012), p. 82.
122 Stato Maggiore della Difesa, *Manuale di diritto umanitario, Introduzione e Volume I, Usi e convenzioni di Guerra* (1991), §§ 23–26.

At stake here are situations in which a given act is amenable neither to an unnecessary-inhumane alignment nor to a necessary-humane alignment. One important tenet of the joint satisfaction thesis is that, even where this occurs, it is still always open to the belligerent to act in a jointly satisfactory manner. Accordingly, there is no norm conflict here, either.

7.3.1 Norm Contradiction Generally

Where there is neither any obligation to perform a given act nor any obligation to refrain from it, that act is a normatively indifferent form of behaviour.[123] If, then, one norm stipulates such indifference regarding a particular action, whereas another norm stipulates an obligation to perform it – or to refrain from it, for that matter – the two norms contradict each other.

Joint satisfaction nevertheless results when the addressee acts according to the latter obligation. Norm contradiction of the kind at issue in this book becomes problematic if, but only if, the addressee avails itself of the indifferent liberty in such a manner that leaves the contrary obligation unfulfilled.[124]

7.3.1.1 Liberty and Permission as the Absence of a Contrary Duty

In Hohfeld's first-order jural relations, a liberty to perform an act corresponds to the absence of a duty to refrain from that act.[125] This liberty is normatively contradictory to the latter duty, and vice versa. They contradict each other, because the following two statements – 'it is the case that there exists an affirmative duty to refrain from this act' and 'it is *not* the case that there exists an affirmative duty to refrain from this act' – cannot both be true at the same time, with respect to the same addressee, and for the same instance of the act. According to Matthew H. Kramer,

> As Hohfeld was fully aware, the contradiction lies ... between a duty to do ϕ and a liberty to *abstain from* ϕ – or between a duty to abstain from ϕ and a liberty to do ϕ. If *Y* has a duty to abstain from interfering with *Z*'s project ϕ, then *Y* does not have a liberty to interfere. Similarly, if *Y* has a

[123] See Chapter 6.

[124] In contrast, norm conflict of the sort that involves incompatible obligations always becomes problematic, no matter which obligation the address chooses to follow.

[125] See Chapter 6.

> duty to render certain assistance to *Z* for the doing of ϕ, then *Y* does not have a liberty to refuse to give such assistance. Conversely, if *Y* does have a liberty to interfere with *Z*'s doing of ϕ, then *Y* does not have a duty to refrain from interfering; and if *Y* does have a liberty to withhold assistance from *Z*, then *Y* does not have a duty to provide the assistance.[126]

In other words, where a person is duty-bound to perform ϕ and simultaneously at liberty to refrain from ϕ, there is a norm contradiction.

Much like the Hohfeldian liberty, a permission to perform an act, as understood by von Wright, equals the absence – or the negation – of a duty to refrain from it.[127] A permission to do something is contradictory to a duty to refrain from it.[128]

7.3.1.2 Overcoming Norm Contradiction Is Always a Matter of Choice

When a normatively indifferent norm ('you may kill this person, but you may also refrain from killing this person') stands alongside a contrary duty ('you must refrain from killing this person'), there is an element of norm contradiction ('you may kill this person' vs. 'you must refrain from killing this person').

The question now is whether joint satisfaction is or is not possible where this contradiction occurs. In Hart's view, joint conformity is logically impossible where there is a norm contradiction:

> The contradictory of '*A* ought not to be done' is 'it is not the case that *A* ought not to be done', and two ought-statements of this form would describe not two rules that require [*sic*] and prohibited the same action, but two rules, one of which prohibited and the other of which permitted the same action.[129]

Hart also observed:

> Laws and rules . . . instead of requiring or forbidding action, may either expressly permit action, or by not forbidding them, tacitly permit them; and it is clear that there may be conflicts between laws that forbid and laws or legal systems that expressly or tacitly permit. To meet such cases, we

126 Kramer, 'Rights Without Trimmings', p. 13 (footnote omitted).

127 Von Wright, 'Ought to Be – Ought to Do', pp. 5–6.

128 Ibid. See also Erich Vranes, 'The Definition of "Norm Conflict" in International Law and Legal Theory' (2006) 17 *European Journal of International Law* 395, at 409; Kelsen, *Pure Theory of Law*, pp. 205–08; Kelsen, *General Theory of Norms*, p. 189 (on logical contradiction as opposed to norm conflict).

129 Hart, 'Kelsen's Doctrine', pp. 330–31 (footnotes omitted; emphasis in original).

> should have to use not only the notion of obedience, which is appropriate to rules requiring or forbidding action, but the notion of acting on or availing oneself of a permission. We might adopt the generic term 'conformity' to comprehend both obedience to rules that require or prohibit and acting on or availing oneself of permission, and we could adopt the expression 'conformity statements' to cover both kinds of corresponding statement. In fact, the conformity statement showing that a permissive rule (e.g. permitting though not requiring killing) had been acted on will be of the same form as the obedience statement for a rule requiring the same action (killing is done). So if one rule prohibits and another rule permits the same action by the same person at the same time, joint conformity will be logically impossible and the two rules will conflict.[130]

There are two difficulties with Hart's reasoning. First, given the normatively indifferent manner in which he characterises permission above, it would be odd to treat 'acting on it' as conforming to the rule without also treating 'refraining from it' as conforming to the same rule. Yet Hart implicitly considers the latter non-conformity.[131] Treating refraining from a permitted act as non-conformity gives rise to Hart's second difficulty. He treated permission and its contrary duty as being in conflict with each other. The picture Hart paints here is somewhat simplistic – unless, as we will soon discover, one acknowledges two additional considerations.[132]

Compare Hart's joint conformity theory with Stephen Munzer's three rule-combinations. They are:

1. Where '[t]wo duty-imposing rules may require and forbid the same action by the same person at the same time';[133]
2. Where '[a] rule may impose a duty on certain persons to act (not to act) at a certain time, while another rule may permit such persons not to act (to act) at that time'[134] ('case (ii)', as Munzer called it); and
3. Where '[a] rule may allow certain persons to act at a certain time, and another may allow them not to act in that way at that time'[135] (similarly, 'case (iii)').

130 Ibid, pp. 326–27 (footnotes omitted).

131 It would indeed be non-conformity if the underlying rule were of a kind to *require* action.

132 First, being duty-bound to refrain from acting on a permission can mean failing to fulfil public expectations backed up with policy. Second, it can mean frustrating the exercise of a formally sanctioned freedom of choice. See below.

133 Stephen Munzer, 'Validity and Legal Conflicts' (1973) 82 *Yale Law Review* 1140, at 1142.

134 Ibid.

135 Ibid.

Of these three combinations, Munzer regarded only the first as properly embodying a norm conflict.[136] He went on to state that 'the joint conformity theory deals very awkwardly, if at all, with cases (ii) and (iii)',[137] adding:

> Now in case (ii) we might be willing to apply the word 'conflict' if the norm-subject acted on the permissive rule; for he would then have violated a duty-imposing rule. But if the norm-subject discharged his obligation under the duty-imposing rule, we would usually be reluctant to say that he was in a situation of 'conflict' merely because he did not simultaneously act on the permissive rule. So far as cases of type (iii) are concerned, our inclination would be to say ... that the two permissive rules do not conflict at all. Yet the joint conformity theory would commit us to precisely the opposite conclusion.[138]

Plainly, joint conformity is possible in both cases (ii) and (iii). For case (ii), joint conformity results just where the addressee acts according to the obligation. The *jointness* of the said conformity is lost just where the addressee acts upon the contradictory permission. For case (iii), joint conformity arises no matter which permission is acted upon.[139]

Munzer nevertheless recognised the existence, in certain circumstances, of something resembling a conflict with respect to cases (ii) and (iii). Thus, for case (ii):

> Normally, no conflict will exist on any occasion when the norm-subject discharges the obligation imposed by the duty-imposing rule and simply declines to act on the permissive rule. But the answer may be different if there is a strong pressure or policy, intimately related to the permission, for the norm-subject to avail himself of the permission. Suppose that ... one rule prohibits doctors from treating patients found injured on the roadway and another permits such treatment. Suppose that neglecting to treat such persons is a hideous violation of professional ethics, accepted morality, and express public policy to reduce roadway deaths. Assume further that the permission to treat such persons is corroborated by the law in various ways, *e.g.*, by depriving one treated of the right to sue for battery, by setting a lower standard of professional care for such treatment, or even by offering physicians some reward for saving injured persons. In this case, I think it is accurate to say that the rules 'clash' or 'collide' even when the norm-subject does not act on the permission. Certainly, on such an occasion the norm-subject is put in a quandary ... quite different from

[136] Ibid, at 1143.
[137] Ibid.
[138] Ibid.
[139] Vranes, 'Definition of "Norm Conflict"', at 409.

> the mere bafflement he might feel if simultaneously forbidden and permitted to do an act that neither law nor society seeks to promote.[140]

Here, there is indeed an informal norm conflict. Joint conformity is logically impossible. Similarly, for case (iii), Munzer envisaged conflict-like instances where 'the norm-subject acts on one permission and thereby fails to act on a different permission which is backed by a strong, intimately related pressure or policy'.[141]

This particular conclusion Munzer drew regarding case (iii) is incomplete, however. Rectifying this incompleteness requires adding two observations. First, even if one of the two permissions at issue is backed by a strong, intimately related pressure or policy, this and the other permission are still in a relationship of norm contradiction akin to case (ii). Second, joint conformity is possible just where the addressee acts in accordance with the permission backed by such a pressure or policy.

7.3.2 Frustration between a Duty and a Counter-Liberty

It might be thought that a norm conflict would still result where forcing the norm's addressee 'to refrain from exercising one of its rights could ... lead to the frustration of the permissive norm equally as with an obligatory one'.[142] I myself recently wrote:

> [F]rustration between a duty of non-detention [arising from Article 5(1) of the European Convention on Human Rights] and a counter-power of security detention [arising from the law of belligerent occupation] can constitute a norm conflict.[143]

140 Munzer, 'Validity and Legal Conflicts', at 1145–46 (footnote omitted).

141 Ibid, at 1146.

142 Marko Milanović, 'Norm Conflict in International Law: Whither Human Rights?' (2009) 20 *Duke Journal of Comparative and International Law* 69, at 73. See also Joost Pauwelyn, *Conflict of Norms in Public International Law: How WTO Law Relates to Other Rules of International Law* (Cambridge: Cambridge University Press, 2003), pp. 175–83; Martti Koskenniemi, 'Fragmentation of International Law: Difficulties Arising from the Diversification and Expansion of International Law' in International Law Commission, *Report of the Study Group of the International Law Commission*, A/CN.4/L.682, paras 24–25; Vranes, 'Definition of "Norm Conflict"'; François Bourdreault, 'Identifying Conflicts of Norms: The ICJ Approach in the Case of the *Jurisdictional Immunities of the State (Germany v Italy: Greece Intervening)*' (2012) 25 *Leiden Journal of International Law* 1003, at 1008–10; Valentin Jeutner, *Irresolvable Norm Conflicts in International Law: The Concept of a Legal Dilemma* (Oxford: Oxford University Press, 2017), pp. 10–11, 27–30, 34–37.

143 N Hayashi, 'Do the Good Intentions of European Human Rights Law Really Pave the Road to IHL Hell?', at 146.

I argued that meta-rules often invoked in order to resolve norm conflicts, such as *lex specialis*,[144] *lex superior*,[145] *lex posterior*[146] and *lex favorabilis*,[147] are highly ambiguous and ultimately inconclusive.[148] We should focus instead on the effects that the application of meta-rules produces on the affected norms.[149] The effects in question include: conflict avoidance through harmonisation or clarification[150]; conflict

[144] Article 31(3)(1), Vienna Convention on the Law of Treaties, 23 May 1969, in force 27 January 1980, 1155 UNTS 331; Article 55, Responsibility of States for Internationally Wrongful Acts, 12 December 2001, A/RES/56/83.

[145] Articles 53, 64, Vienna Convention on the Law of Treaties.

[146] Ibid. Articles 30, 59.

[147] Seyed-Ali Sadat-Akavi, *Methods of Resolving Conflicts between Treaties* (Leiden and Boston: Martinus Nijhoff, 2003), pp. 213–32; Anne-Laurence Graf-Brugère, 'A *Lex Favorabilis*? Resolving Norm Conflicts between Human Rights Law and Humanitarian Law' in Robert Kolb and Gloria Gaggioli (eds), *Research Handbook on Human Rights and Humanitarian Law* (Cheltenham: Edward Elgar, 2013) 251.

[148] N Hayashi, 'Do the Good Intention of European Human Rights Law Really Pave the Road to IHL Hell?', at 147–49. See also Marko Milanović, 'A Norm Conflict Perspective on the Relationship between International Humanitarian Law and Human Rights Law' (2010) 14 *Journal of Conflict & Security Law* 459, at 462, 482 (calling *lex specialis* 'descriptively misleading, vague in meaning, and of little practical use in application'); Nancie Prud'homme, '*Lex Specialis*: Oversimplifying a More Complex and Multifaceted Relationship?' (2007) 40 *Israel Law Review* 356, at 378–86; Kenneth Watkin, 'Use of Force during Occupation: Law Enforcement and Conduct of Hostilities' (2012) 94 *International Review of the Red Cross* 267, at 301–04.

[149] N Hayashi, 'Do the Good Intention of European Human Rights Law Really Pave the Road to IHL Hell?', at 148–49.

[150] Ibid, at 17–18. See also Article 31(3)(c), Vienna Convention on the Law of Treaties; *Nuclear Weapons*, para. 25; *Legal Consequences of the Construction of a Wall in the Occupied Palestinian Territory, Advisory Opinion, ICJ Reports 2004*, p. 136, para. 106; *Armed Activities*, para. 106; *Al-Adsani v UK* App. No. 35763/97 (ECtHR, 21 November 2001), para. 55; *Bankovic et al v Belgium et al* App. No. 2207/99 (ECtHR, 12 December 2001), para. 57; *Varnava et al v Turkey* App. Nos. 16064/90, 16065/90, 16066/90, 16068/90, 16069/90, 16071/90, 16072/90, 16073/90 (ECtHR, 18 September 2009), para. 185; *Nada v Switzerland* App. No. 10593/08 (ECtHR, 12 September 2012), para. 170; *Georgia v Russia* App. No. 38263/08 (ECtHR, 13 December 2011), para. 72; *Al-Saadon and Mufdhi v UK* App. No. 61498/08 (ECtHR, 2 March 2010), para. 126; *Hassan v UK* App. No. 29750/09 (ECtHR, 16 September 2014), paras 102–05; Cordula Droege, 'The Interplay between International Humanitarian Law and International Human Rights Law in Situations of Armed Conflict' (2007) 40 *Israel Law Review* 310, at 335; Noam Lubell, 'Parallel Application of International Humanitarian Law and International Human Rights Law: An Examination of the Debate' (2007) 40 *Israel Law Review* 648, at 655; Marco Sassòli and Laura M Olsen, 'The Relationship between International Humanitarian Law and Human Rights Law Where It Matters: Admissible Killing and Internment of Fighters in Non-international Armed Conflicts' (2008) 90 *International Review of the Red Cross* 599, at 605; Vaios Koutroulis, 'The Application of International Humanitarian Law and International Human Rights Law in Situation of Prolonged

elimination through invalidation, restriction or exception[151]; and conflict remedy through modification in the operation of secondary rules.[152]

Norm conflicts of a frustrating sort involve two rules, one containing an obligation and the other a counter-liberty, that are independently valid according to two unintegrated fields of law to which they respectively belong.[153] What we call norm contradictions in this chapter would be similar to norm conflicts of this sort, if:

- The 'law of humanity' and the 'law of military necessity' were two unintegrated fields of law; and
- We were confronted with an act that is prohibited by one valid rule of the 'law of humanity', yet permitted at the same time by another, equally valid rule of the 'law of military necessity'.

Occupation: Only a Matter of Time?' (2012) 94 *International Review of the Red Cross* 165, at 196–97; Milanović, 'Norm Conflict Perspective', at 463, 468; Andrea Gioia, 'The Role of the European Court of Human Rights in Monitoring Compliance with Humanitarian Law' in Orna Ben-Naftali (ed), *International Humanitarian Law and International Human Rights Law* (Oxford: Oxford University Press, 2011) 201, at 214; Oona A Hathaway et al., 'Which Law Governs during Armed Conflict? The Relationship between International Humanitarian Law and Human Rights Law' (2011–2012) 96 *Minnesota Law Review* 1883, at 1897–902; Jean d'Aspremont and Elodie Tranchez, 'The Quest for a Non-conflictual Coexistence between International Human Rights Law and International Humanitarian Law: Which Role for the *Lex Specialis* Principle?' in Kolb and Gaggioli (eds), *Research Handbook on Human Rights and Humanitarian Law* 223, at 234–38.

151 N Hayashi, 'Do the Good Intention of European Human Rights Law Really Pave the Road to IHL Hell?', at 150–151. See also William A Schabas, '*Lex Specialis*? Belt and Suspenders? The Parallel Operation of Human Rights Law and the Law of Armed Conflict, and the Conundrum of *Jus ad Bellum*' (2007) 40 *Israel Law Review* 592, at 597–98.

152 N Hayashi, 'Do the Good Intention of European Human Rights Law Really Pave the Road to IHL Hell?', at 151. See also Article 59, Articles on State Responsibility; International Law Commission, *Report on the Work of Its Fifty-Third Session (23 April–1 June and 2 July–10 August 2001)*, A/56/10, p. 143; Sir Humphrey Waldock, 'Second Report on the Law of Treaties' in International Law Commission, 2 *Yearbook of the International Law Commission 1963*, A/CN.4/SER.A/1963/ADD.1, 36, p. 55 (quoting Sir Gerald Fitzmaurice); Rudolf Bernhardt, 'Article 103' in Bruno Simma et al. (eds), *The Charter of the United Nations: A Commentary*, 2nd edn (Oxford: Oxford University Press, 2002) 1292, p. 1298; Koskenniemi, 'Fragmentation of International Law', paras 333–40; Rain Liivoja, 'The Scope of the Supremacy Clause of the United Nations Charter' (2008) 57 *International and Comparative Law Quarterly* 583, at 596–97; Milanović, 'Norm Conflict in International Law', at 76–77; Samantha A Miko, 'Norm Conflict, Fragmentation, and the European Court of Human Rights' (2013) *Boston College Law Review, Symposium Issue* 1351, at 1361.

153 Anja Lindroos, 'Addressing Norm Conflicts in a Fragmented Legal Order: The Doctrine of *Lex Specialis*' (2005) 74 *Nordic Journal of International Law* 27.

Jus ad bellum and *jus in bello* are prime examples of two unintegrated fields of international law. Hypothetically at least, a state under armed attack would be frustrated in the exercise of its right of self-defence if only unqualifiedly prohibited means and methods of warfare were at its disposal.[154] It could be said that domestic law and IHL also constitute two unintegrated fields. A state may empower its commanders to take measures with a view to reducing risks of self-endangerment.[155] Such empowerment would be frustrated if one were of the view that IHL obligates the armed forces to prioritise civilian protection over their own protection.[156] Conversely, a combatant may find him or herself simultaneously duty-bound *qua* citizen-soldier of a warring state to fire and at liberty to withhold fire under IHL. I have already alluded to European human rights law (imposing a duty of non-detention on security grounds) and IHL (granting a counter-power of security detention in occupied territory).[157]

Frustration would also result if, even as one system, positive IHL contained two equally valid rules, one prohibiting the belligerent from performing an act and the other simultaneously permitting the same addressee to perform it.

7.3.3 *Norm Contradiction between Military Necessity and Humanity*

We are, however, not concerned with two unintegrated fields of law or with two independently valid IHL rules containing an obligation and a counter-liberty. At issue here is rather the interplay between humanity and military necessity *qua* reason-giving considerations in IHL norm-creation. We want to understand how the framers take such

[154] Koskenniemi, 'International Lawyers and Nuclear Weapons', at 145 ('If the law's purpose is to protect the innocent (and it is hard to see a more basic purpose for it in a system that excludes reference to personal virtue), and the launching of a nuclear strike would be the only means to attain this, then I cannot see how it could be excluded'). See Chapter 8 for a discussion of self-preservation.

[155] Examples include 'avoidance of close contact with the enemy; and use of remote vehicles and remotely delivered weapons'. Roberts, 'Principle of Equal Application', p. 251. Some states consider themselves entitled under IHL to include considerations of the security of attacking forces in the military advantage calculus. Ratification, Australia, 21 June 1991, 1642 UNTS 473, p. 474; Ratification and Accession, New Zealand, 8 February 1988, 1499 UNTS 358, p. 358.

[156] See below.

[157] N Hayashi, 'Do the Good Intentions of European Human Rights Law Really Pave the Road to IHL Hell?', at 146.

considerations into account when positing one uniquely valid IHL rule on the matter.

To say that military necessity permits particular behaviour and tolerates contrary behaviour at the same time, is to say that the notion is normatively indifferent on the matter. Norm contradiction arises where humanity demands what military necessity tolerates, and where the former condemns what the latter permits.

During World War I, Emilio Lussu, an officer in the Italian army, spotted an Austrian officer while reconnoitring the enemy trench from a perfectly concealed position:

> The Austrian officer lit a cigarette. Now he was smoking. This cigarette formed an invisible link between us. No sooner did I see its smoke than I wanted a cigarette myself; which reminded me that I had some with me ... There was no doubt that I considered the war morally and politically justified. My conscience as a man and a citizen was not in conflict with my military duties. War was, for me, a hard necessity, terrible, to be sure, but one to which I submitted, as one of the many necessities, unpleasant but inevitable, of life. Moreover, I was on campaign and there were men fighting under my orders. That is to say, morally, I was fighting twice over. I had already taken part in many engagements. It was therefore quite logical for me to fire on an enemy officer. I insisted on my men keeping alert while on patrol, and shooting straight if the enemy offered them a target. Then why did I not fire on this officer? I knew it was my duty to fire. Otherwise it would have been monstrous for me to have continued to fight and to make others do so. There was no doubt about it: I ought to fire. And yet I did not ... In front of me I had a young officer who was quite unconscious of the danger that threatened him. I could not have missed him. I could have fired a thousand rounds at that range and never have missed once. All I had to do was to press the trigger and he would have fallen dead. The certainty that his life depended solely on my will made me hesitate. What I had in front of me was a man. A man! I could see his face perfectly clearly. The light was increasing and the sun was just becoming visible behind the tops of the mountains. Could I fire like this, at a few paces, on a man – as if he were a wild boar? I began to think that perhaps I ought not to do so. I reasoned like this: To lead a hundred, even a thousand, men against another hundred, or thousand, was one thing; but to detach one man from the rest and say to him, as it were: 'Don't move, I'm going to shoot you. I'm going to kill you' – that was different. Entirely different. To fight is one thing, but to kill a man is another. And to kill him like that is to murder him ... 'You can't kill a man like that!' I said to myself ... I could think of letting another do what I could not reconcile with my own conscience. I had the rifle with its barrel through the branches of the bush, and the butt resting on the ground. The corporal was close beside

> me. Signing to him to take the butt, I whispered: 'Look here – I'm not going to fire on a man, alone, like that. Will you?' The corporal took hold of the rifle-butt. Then he said: 'No, I won't either.' We crept back into our trenches, on all fours.[158]

It should be noted that Lussu's 'duty' to fire was one he owed, *qua* citizen-soldier, strictly towards Italy under its domestic law.[159]

Military necessity left Lussu at liberty to fire. 'It was *not* the case that Lussu ought to withhold fire', in other words. Military necessity also left him at liberty to withhold fire. Consequently, 'it was *not* the case that Lussu ought not to withhold fire', either. Humanity, for its part, demanded that Lussu avoid harming another human being. It would follow that, according to humanity, 'it was the case that Lussu ought to withhold fire'.

Take two of the three propositions, i.e., 'it was *not* the case that Lussu ought to withhold fire' and 'it was the case that Lussu ought to withhold fire'. These reveal a norm contradiction. Would joint satisfaction be possible between that part of military necessity according to which Lussu was at liberty to fire, and humanity according to which Lussu ought to withhold fire?

In the event, Lussu did withhold fire, as demanded by humanity. Since military necessity creates neither a corresponding duty nor a contrary duty upon Lussu, he also satisfied military necessity by withholding fire. Thus, Lussu acted in a manner that generated joint satisfaction of the two sets of considerations.

This joint satisfaction is modest in character, insofar as Lussu declined to act upon a liberty (i.e., to fire) that military necessity also permitted. Had Lussu chosen to fire, he would not have jointly satisfied both considerations. His pursuit of that liberty would have come at the expense of the contrary humanitarian demand left unfulfilled.

7.3.4 Permission and 'Strong Pressure or Policy'

Could military necessity be analogous to Munzer's 'strong pressure or policy'[160] and be intimately related to what it permits? If it were, then,

[158] Lussu, *Sardinian Brigade*, pp. 169–71. See also Walzer, *Just and Unjust Wars*, pp. 141–42.
[159] See Chapter 3.
[160] Munzer, 'Validity and Legal Conflicts', at 1145.

there could arguably be an informal norm conflict between that permission and humanity's contrary demand.

Munzer's description indicates that such a pressure or policy involves the combination of two elements. The first is what he called 'a hideous violation of professional ethics, accepted morality, and express public policy'[161] arising from the addressee's failure to act on the permission at hand. The other is the existence of various corroborations, such as legal protections and incentives in favour of acting on that permission.[162] It would appear that no such combination of analogous elements reveal themselves when IHL framers approach military necessity.[163]

In contrast, humanity might be deemed analogous to strong pressures or policies intimately related to what it permits. Humanitarian permissions might not entitle their satisfier to specific legal protection or incentive. In some circumstances, however, failing to satisfy them could be considered deplorable – if not, perhaps, quite 'hideous[ly]'[164] so – by accepted international morality or public policy. If, and to the extent that, such an analogy could be drawn, there might be possibilities of informal norm conflict between a liberty permitted by humanity and a contrary liberty permitted by military necessity.

7.4 Obligations to Pursue Joint Satisfaction amid Military Necessity-Humanity Contradiction

Joint satisfaction involving norm contradictions comes in two forms. First, where an act is condemned by humanity yet permitted by military necessity, the belligerent satisfies both considerations by refraining from it. Second, where humanity demands what military necessity tolerates, the belligerent satisfies both by performing the act.

How IHL norm-creation accounts for these possibilities of joint satisfaction varies from one type of conduct to another. Five distinct consequences are discernible. They are:

1. The law posits an *unqualified* obligation to pursue joint satisfaction;
2. The law posits a *principal* obligation to do so;

161 Ibid.

162 Ibid, at 1145–46.

163 Here, too, the picture can be quite different from a strictly community-specific point of view discussed in Chapter 3. States may very well enact laws affirmatively obligating their soldiers to pursue military necessities and avoid military non-necessities.

164 Munzer, 'Validity and Legal Conflicts', at 1145.

3. The law posits an *indeterminate* obligation to do so;
4. The law posits only an *exceptional* obligation to do so; and
5. The law *declines*, or *fails*, to posit an obligation to do so.

Each of these consequences reveals unique characteristics of the military necessity-humanity interplay involved. It also shows what becomes of military necessity's permission not to pursue joint satisfaction.

7.4.1 Unqualified Obligations

Today's IHL categorically prohibits attacks on the civilian population or individual civilians not directly participating in hostilities.[165] It has taken this prohibition a long time to develop, as the difficult history of restricting 'morale bombings' and indiscriminate attacks shows.[166] Here, the obligatory pursuit of joint satisfaction has arguably changed from principal to unqualified. According to Emily Camins:

> Protocol I went against the tide of history by expressly conferring civilian status on all those who were not combatants properly so called, regardless of whether or not they were harmless. The inclusive definition of 'civilian' in Article 50 of Protocol I meant that classes of people not fitting the traditional civilian mould were nonetheless entitled to immunity against attack. As a result of Protocol I's undifferentiating conception of civilians, international humanitarian law found itself, in the words of Best, 'teetering on the edge of a credibility gap', with the law bestowing on all classes non-combatants the same protection ... Notions of military necessity suggest that civilians whose actions are harmful to the enemy should lose their immunity from attack. In contrast with previous manifestations of the exception to civilian immunity, however, Article 51(3) does not permit the targeting of all civilians whose attack is necessary from a military perspective. Rather, only those who are participating directly in hostilities may be subject to attack.[167]

Similarly, IHL unqualifiedly prohibits methods or means of combat intended or expected to cause widespread, long-term and severe

[165] Article 51(1), 51(3), Additional Protocol I; Henckaerts and Doswald-Beck, *Customary International Humanitarian Law* (vol. I), pp. 3–8. See also Article 8(2)(b)(i), 8(2)(e)(i), Rome Statute. Generally, see also Judith Gardam, *Non-combatant Immunity as a Norm of International Humanitarian Law* (Dordrecht, Boston and London: Martinus Nijhoff, 1993).

[166] Jochnick and Normand, 'Legitimation of Violence', at 79–95.

[167] Camins, 'Past as Prologue', at 880–81 (footnote omitted).

damage to the environment.[168] Other examples of unqualified IHL prohibitions include those against denying quarter;[169] deliberately inflicting terror amongst civilians;[170] starving civilians as a method of combat;[171] recruiting children into the armed forces and using them in hostilities;[172] using biological and chemical weapons,[173] anti-personal

168 Articles 35(3), 55(1), Additional Protocol I; Henckaerts and Doswald-Beck, *Customary International Humanitarian Law* (vol. I), pp. 151–58. See also Stefan Oeter, 'Methods and Means of Combat' in Fleck (ed), *Handbook of International Humanitarian Law* (2nd edn) 119, at 132 (quoting de Preux, 'Basic Rules', pp. 410–11).

169 Article 23(c), Article 23(d), Hague Regulations (1907); Article 40, Additional Protocol I; Article 4(1), Additional Protocol II; Article 8(2)(b)(xii), Article 8(2)(e)(x), Rome Statute; Henckaerts and Doswald-Beck, *Customary International Humanitarian Law* (vol. I), pp. 161–63. See also Morris Greenspan, *The Modern Law of Land Warfare* (Berkeley and Los Angeles: University of California Press, 1959), at 111–12; Claude Pilloud, 'Article 40 - Quarter' in Sandoz et al. (eds), *Commentary on Additional Protocols* 473, p. 475 n.8; Dinstein, *Conduct of Hostilities* (2nd edn), p. 7. Bothe, Partsch and Solf, however, consider this rule a reflection of conduct deemed both inhumane and lacking in military necessity. Bothe, Partsch and Solf, *New Rules for Victims of Armed Conflicts* (2nd rev. edn), p. 249.

170 Article 51(2), Additional Protocol I; Henckaerts and Doswald-Beck, *Customary International Humanitarian Law* (vol. I), pp. 8–11; *Prosecutor v Stanislav Galić*, Case No. IT-98-29-T, *Judgment and Opinion*, 5 December 2003, paras 63–138; *Prosecutor v Stanislav Galić*, Case No. IT-98-29-A, *Judgment*, 30 November 2006, paras 69–109; ibid, *Separate and Partially Dissenting Opinion of Judge Schomburg*, p. 211, paras 4-22, 24; *Prosecutor v Dragomir Milošević*, Case No. IT-98-29/1-T, *Judgment*, 12 December 2007, paras 873–88; *Prosecutor v Dragomir Milošević*, Case No. IT-98-29/1-A, *Judgement*, 12 November 2009, paras 24–41; Frits Kalshoven, 'Bombardment: From "Brussels 1874" to "Sarajevo 2003"', Kalshoven, *Collected Essays* 431, at 455–63.

171 Article 54(1), Additional Protocol I; Article 8(2)(b)(xxv), Rome Statute; Henckaerts and Doswald-Beck, *Customary International Humanitarian Law* (vol. I), pp. 186–89. See also George A Mudge, 'Starvation as a Means of Warfare' (1970) 4 *International Lawyer* 228, at 228–51; Solf, 'Protection of Civilians Against the Effects of Hostilities', at 133.

172 Article 77(2), Additional Protocol I; Article 8(2)(b)(xxvi), Article 8(2)(e)(vii), Rome Statute; Henckaerts and Doswald-Beck, *Customary International Humanitarian Law* (vol. I), pp. 482–88; *Prosecutor v Sam Hinga Norman*, Case No. SCSL-04-14-AR72(E), *Decision on Preliminary Motion Based on Lack of Jurisdiction (Child Recruitment)*, 31 May 2004; *Lubanga Trial Judgment*. See also Peter Rowe, 'The Obligation of a State under International Law to Protect Members of its Own Armed Forces during Armed Conflict or Occupation' (2006) 9 *Yearbook of International Humanitarian Law* 3, at 17–18.

173 Article 1, Convention on the Prohibition of the Development, Production, Stockpiling and Use of Chemical Weapons and on Their Destruction, 3 September 1992, in force 29 April 1997, 1974 UNTS 45; Article 1, Convention on the Prohibition of Development, Production and Stockpiling of Bacteriological (Biological) and Toxin Weapons and on Their Destruction, 10 April 1972, in force 26 March 1975, 1015 UNTS 163; Article 8(2)(b)(xviii), Rome Statute; Henckaerts and Doswald-Beck, *Customary International Humanitarian Law* (vol. I), pp. 256–263. See also Josef Goldblat, 'The Biological Weapons Convention: An Overview' (1997) 79 *International Review of the Red Cross*

landmines[174] and poisoned weapons;[175] using POWs[176] or protected persons[177] as human shields; compelling residents of occupied territory to furnish information;[178] and taking hostages.[179]

As for performance-based joint satisfaction, one may cite, for example, the unqualified obligation in unusual conditions of combat to release captured enemies with safety provisions.[180] This particular obligation has also arguably changed from principal to unqualified, in two ways. The first involves denying quarter. According to the Lieber Code, military necessity exceptionally permitted the denial of quarter.[181] Julius Stone, writing in 1954, agreed, especially in situations 'where a State's principal forces cannot detain prisoners, and where their release would so reinforce the enemy as to make defeat inevitable'.[182] Modern IHL has

251, at 257; AV Lowe, '1972 Convention on the Prohibition of the Development, Production and Stockpiling of Bacteriological (Biological) and Toxin Weapons and their Destruction' in N Ronzitti (ed), *The Law of Naval Warfare: A Collection of Agreements and Documents with Commentaries* (Dordrecht, Boston and London: Martinus Nijhoff, 1988) 629, p. 643.

174 Article 1, Convention on the Prohibition of the Use, Stockpiling, Production and Transfer of Anti-Personnel Mines and on Their Destruction, 18 September 1997, in force 1 March 1999, 2056 UNTS 211.

175 Article 23(a), Hague Regulations (1907); Article 8(2)(b)(xvii), Article 8(2)(b)(xviii), Rome Statute; Henckaerts and Doswald-Beck, *Customary International Humanitarian Law* (vol. I), pp. 251–54. See also Doswald-Beck and Vité, 'International Humanitarian Law and Human Rights Law', at 99.

176 Article 23, Geneva Convention III. See also *High Command*, at 588.

177 Article 28, Geneva Convention IV; Article 51(7), Additional Protocol I; Henckaerts and Doswald-Beck, *Customary International Humanitarian Law* (vol. I), pp. 337–40; *Prosecutor v Tihomir Blaškić*, Case No. IT-95-14-T, *Judgment* 3 March 2000, para. 716; *Prosecutor v Dario Kordić and Mario Čerkez*, Case No. IT-95-14/2-T, *Judgment*, 26 February 2001, para. 57; *Prosecutor v Zlatko Aleksovski*, Case No. IT-95-14/1-T, *Judgment*, 25 June 1999, para. 229; *Adalah et al v GOC Central Command et al*, HCJ 3799/02, *Judgment*, 23 June 2005.

178 Article 44, Hague Regulations (1907).

179 Article 34, Geneva Convention IV; Henckaerts and Doswald-Beck, *Customary International Humanitarian Law* (vol. I), pp. 334–36. See also Dinstein, *Conduct of Hostilities* (1st edn), p. 227.

180 Article 41(3), Additional Protocol I. See also Dinstein, *Conduct of Hostilities* (2nd edn), p. 7.

181 Article 60, Lieber Code: '[A] command is permitted to direct his troops to give no quarter, in great straits, when his own salvation makes it *impossible* to cumber himself with prisoners' (emphasis in original).

182 Stone, *Legal Controls of International Conflict*, p. 558 n. 67. See also Taylor, *Nuremberg and Vietnam*, p. 36 n.

removed military necessity exceptions vis-à-vis its prohibition against denying quarter.

The second concerns killing POWs in captivity. During the Napoleonic Wars, POWs were killed en masse on account of military necessity.[183] Towards the end of World War II, General Maxwell Taylor reportedly said: 'if you were to take prisoners, they handicap our ability to perform our mission. We were going to have to dispose of prisoners as best we saw fit'.[184] By 1959, however, it had become widely accepted that

> [a] commander is not entitled to kill his prisoners to preserve his own forces, even in cases of extreme necessity. Neither may he do so because they slow up his movements, weaken his fighting force because they require a guard, consume supplies, or appear certain to be set free by their own forces.[185]

Since the belligerent may under no circumstances deny enemies quarter or kill them in captivity, it is unqualifiedly obligated to release them with provisions if they cannot be safely evacuated.

The fact that these IHL rules have been posited means that their framers have elected to let the demands of humanity trump the contrary permission of military necessity. In Marshall Cohen's words:

> [The Lieber-Hague conception of the laws of war] permits the interests of humanity to carry enough weight so that they can sometimes inhibit the operation of the principle of military necessity. On this conception, therefore, the appeal to military necessity is by no means always a legitimate one; indeed, it is sometimes plainly ruled out.[186]

The framers of unqualified IHL rules have chosen to rule out such an appeal for all circumstances where the belligerent is presented with an opportunity to perform the act in question or to refrain from it. By positing such rules, the law extinguishes any liberty on the belligerent's part to behave as might otherwise be permitted by military necessity.

183 Gunther Rothenberg, 'The Age of Napoleon' in Michael Howard et al. (eds), *The Laws of War: Constraints on Warfare in the Western World* (New Haven: Yale University Press, 1994) 86, at 90–91.

184 Beevor, *D-Day*, p. 24.

185 Greenspan, *Modern Law of Land Warfare*, p. 103 (footnote omitted). See also Cohen, 'Morality and the Laws of War', p. 77.

186 Cohen, 'Morality and the Laws of War', p. 74.

7.4.2 Principal Obligations

Article 53 of Geneva Convention IV prohibits the destruction of real or personal property in occupied territory 'except where such destruction is rendered absolutely necessary by military operations'.[187] The types of military operations envisaged in this exceptional clause are understood to include the so-called 'scorched earth' policy by an occupying force in retreat.[188] By virtue of Article 54(2) of Additional Protocol I, however, retreating occupiers are no longer eligible for this exception with respect to objects indispensable to the survival of the civilian population.[189]

Similarly, customary IHL principally prohibits the destruction of captured enemy and neutral merchant vessels, yet it exceptionally authorises their destruction.[190]

Some IHL obligations to pursue joint satisfaction have changed from unqualified to principal. The judge advocate in *von Lewinski (called Manstein)* opined that military necessity did not justify deportations of residents from occupied territories.[191] Article 49 of Geneva Convention IV exceptionally permits their temporary evacuations on account of imperative military reasons.[192] The *Krstić* Trial Chamber took issue with the judge advocate's conclusion:

[187] Article 53, Geneva Convention IV. See also Article 23(g), Hague Regulations (1907); Article 3(b), ICTY Statute; Article 8(2)(a)(iv), Rome Statute; Henckaerts and Doswald-Beck, *Customary International Humanitarian Law* (vol. I), pp. 175–82; Brandt, 'Utilitarianism', at 155–60; Doswald-Beck and Vité, 'International Humanitarian Law and Human Rights Law', at 100. This exception encompasses the destruction of cultural property and objects indispensable to the survival of the civilian population. For cultural property, see Article 4(2), Hague Cultural Property Convention; Article 6, Hague Cultural Property Protocol II; Doswald-Beck and Vité, 'International Humanitarian Law and Human Rights Law', at 100; Roger O'Keefe, *The Protection of Cultural Property in Armed Conflict* (Cambridge: Cambridge University Press, 2006), pp. 121–32. For objects indispensable to the survival of the civilian population, see Article 54(2) and Article 54(5), Additional Protocol I.

[188] Pictet (ed), *Commentary Geneva Convention IV*, p. 302.

[189] Article 54(2), Additional Protocol I; Henckaerts and Doswald-Beck, *Customary International Humanitarian Law* (vol. I), pp. 189–93.

[190] Procès-Verbal Relating to the Rules of Submarine Warfare Set Forth in Part IV of the Treaty of London of 22 April 1930, 6 November 1936, in force 6 November 1936; San Remo Manual on Maritime Warfare, para. 102; Wolff Heintschel von Heinegg, 'The Law of Armed Conflict at Sea' in Fleck (ed), *Handbook of International Humanitarian Law* (3rd edn) 464, pp. 490–91; Michael Bothe, 'The Law of Neutrality' in Fleck (ed), *Handbook of International Humanitarian Law* (3rd edn) 549, p. 571.

[191] *Von Lewinski (called Manstein)*, p. 523.

[192] Article 49, paragraph 2, Geneva Convention IV. See also Henckaerts and Doswald-Beck, *Customary International Humanitarian Law* (vol. I), pp. 457–62.

> Indeed, the judge advocate went so far as to suggest that deportation of civilians could never be justified by military necessity, but only by concern for the safety of the population ... This position, however, is contradicted by the text of the later Geneva Convention IV, which does include 'imperative military reasons', and the Geneva Convention is more authoritative than the view of one judge advocate.[193]

In fact, Erich von Manstein's verdict was announced in December 1949, several months after the Geneva Conventions were adopted.[194]

It may well be that the law espoused by the drafters of Geneva Convention IV, which allowed military necessity exceptions to the prohibition against deportation, was an improvement upon the law without such exceptions.[195] A clause alluding to military necessity exceptions first appeared in Article 27 of a 1947 document on the protection of civilians prepared by government experts.[196] It was reformulated into draft Article 45 at the Stockholm Red Cross Conference the following year, to the effect that '[t]he occupying Power shall not undertake total or partial evacuation of a given area, unless the security of the population or imperative military considerations demand'.[197] At no point do the preparatory works leading up to the 1949 Diplomatic Conference indicate where the idea of this exception originated or, once brought into the form of a draft provision, whether it was seriously debated.

Be that as it may, Geneva Convention IV was clearly not in force when von Manstein deported civilians from occupied Ukraine during World

193 *Prosecutor v Radislav Krstić*, Case No. IT-98-33-T, *Trial Judgment*, 2 August 2001, para. 526 n.1178.

194 *Von Lewinski (called Manstein)*, p. 510.

195 I am grateful to the late Frits Kalshoven for his input here.

196 International Committee of the Red Cross, *Report on the Work of the Conference of Government Experts for the Study of the Conventions for the Protection of War Victims (Geneva, April 14–26, 1947)* (Geneva: International Committee of the Red Cross, 1947), p. 288: 'This prohibition [against individual or collective deportations or transfers] applies to all persons in [occupied] territories. It shall not constitute an obstacle to the general evacuation of an area by the occupying Power, if military operations make it necessary.'

197 Federal Political Department, *Final Record of the Diplomatic Conference of Geneva of 1949*, 3 vols. (Berne: Federal Political Department, 1949), vol. I, at 120. The ICRC commented (*Draft Revised or New Conventions for the Protection of War Victims Established by the International Committee of the Red Cross with the Assistance of Government Experts, National Red Cross Societies and Other Humanitarian Associations* (1948), at 173): 'The evacuation of particular cases ... is permitted in two cases, namely by way of limitation: (1) if the security of the population requires; (2) if imperative military considerations demand.'

War II. It is unclear whether Article 49 of Geneva Convention IV codified a pre-existing customary rule. Nor is it clear whether the only pre-World War II articulation on the matter, Article 19(b) of the 1934 Tokyo draft, actually contained any military necessity exception.[198] Article 6(b) of the Nuremberg Charter and Article II(1)(b) of Control Council Law No. 10, both adopted in 1945, list 'deportation to slave labour or for any other purpose, of civilian population from occupied territory' as a war crime without qualification.[199]

Some IHL rules impose principal obligations to perform acts, while exceptionally authorising their forbearance. Thus, for instance, Article 15 of the 1907 Hague Regulations principally obligates the belligerent to allow, and even assist, humanitarian personnel in the discharge of their functions. And yet, that article exceptionally authorises the belligerent to restrict or prohibit such discharge if and to the extent required by military necessity.[200]

By virtue of Article 126 of Geneva Convention III, representatives of the Protecting Powers and ICRC delegates have the right of visits and private interviews with POWs.[201] The article's second paragraph contains a clause authorising the Detaining Power to block such visits, however, subject to the imperative character of the military necessity

198 ICRC, *Report on the Work of the Conference of Government Experts*, p. 288: 'Deportations outside the territory of the occupied State are forbidden, unless they are evacuations intended, on account of the extension of military operations, to ensure the security of the inhabitants.'

199 Article 6(2), Agreement by the Government of the United Kingdom of Great Britain and Northern Ireland, the Government of the United States of America, the Provisional Government of the French Republic and the Government of the Union of Soviet Socialist Republics for the Prosecution and Punishment of the Major War Criminals of the European Axis, 8 August 1945, in force 8 August 1945, 82 UNTS 279 (hereinafter Nuremberg Charter); Article II(1)(b), Control Council Law No. 10, 20 December 1945.

200 Article 15, Hague Regulations (1907). See also Article 71(3), Additional Protocol I; Henckaerts and Doswald-Beck, *Customary International Humanitarian Law* (vol. I), pp. 200–02.

201 Article 126, paragraph 1, Geneva Convention III: 'Representatives or delegates of the Protecting Powers shall have permission to go to all places where prisoners of war may be, particularly to places of internment, imprisonment and labour, and shall have access to all premises occupied by prisoners of war; they shall also be allowed to go to the places of departure, passage and arrival of prisoners who are being transferred. They shall be able to interview the prisoners, and in particular the prisoners' representatives, without witness, either personally or through an interpreter.' See also ibid, fourth paragraph: 'The delegates of the International Committee of the Red Cross shall enjoy the same prerogatives.'

invoked and the measure's exceptional and temporary nature.[202] Interestingly, this latter clause was inserted by the ICRC on its own initiative, and adopted without discussion at the 1949 Diplomatic Conference.[203] A substantially identical set of provisions is found in Geneva Convention IV.[204] Draper observed:

> This is perhaps the classical formula of the modern law of armed conflicts. It is a provision of paramount importance both for the ICRC upon whom the main duty of these visits devolves, and for the POW. Without the right to make such visits the supervisory system of the Geneva (POW) Convention is, in large part, rendered sterile. Places where such visits are likely to be subject to considerable restriction, certainly as to the timing of them, are interrogation centres and screening camps. It is in such places, frequently under the tight control of the Intelligence Services of the Detaining Power, that, experience shows, much of the unlawful treatment of POW takes place, generally under the desire to obtain military intelligence at all costs. When such places are freely accessible to non-military and para-military Intelligence Services the right of the Protecting Power or of the ICRC to make the visits envisaged in the Convention is the main humanitarian counter-balance to secret and cruel methods of interrogation.[205]

Other IHL rules also exhibit the same characteristics that combine principal obligations to perform an act with exceptional liberties to refrain from it. They include: rules principally obligating the Detaining Power to allow relief shipments, yet exceptionally authorising it to limit their quantity;[206] rules principally obligating combatants to distinguish themselves from the civilian population, yet exceptionally granting them partial waiver;[207] rules principally obligating attackers to give effective

[202] Ibid, second paragraph: 'Representatives and delegates of the Protecting Powers shall have full liberty to select the places they wish to visit. The duration and frequency of these visits shall not be restricted. Visits may not be prohibited except for reasons of imperative military necessity, and then only as an exceptional and temporary measure.'

[203] Pictet (ed), *Commentary Geneva Convention III*, p. 611. See also Pictet (ed), *Commentary Geneva Convention IV*, p. 576.

[204] Article 143, Geneva Convention IV.

[205] Draper, 'Military Necessity and Humanitarian Imperatives', at 139.

[206] Article 108, Geneva Convention IV. This provision envisages situations where 'military necessity require[s] the quantity of such shipments to be limited', implying that otherwise impermissible limitations are exceptionally permissible if and to the extent they actually constitute military necessities.

[207] Article 44(3), Additional Protocol I; Henckaerts and Doswald-Beck, *Customary International Humanitarian Law* (vol. I), pp. 384–89. This duty is partially waived when operating under special circumstances if and to the extent required by these

advance warning, yet exceptionally authorising them to withhold it;[208] and rules principally obligating belligerents to allow the performance of civil defence tasks, yet exceptionally releasing them from this obligation.[209]

Furthermore, at least by implication, IHL principally obligates the Detaining Power to allow POWs and internees to correspond with the exterior, yet exceptionally releases it from this obligation.[210] The law also principally obligates parties to ensure the conveyance of mail and relief shipment, yet exceptionally releases them from this obligation.[211]

The adoption of these rules shows that their framers have chosen, in principle, to let humanitarian demands take precedence over contrary liberties permitted by military necessity. The law makes the pursuit of joint satisfaction primarily obligatory whenever an opportunity to perform or refrain from the relevant act presents itself. The obligatory nature of this pursuit ceases, however, if and to the extent acting otherwise proves militarily necessary in a particular situation.[212]

The rules at issue forbid acts deemed inhumane yet materially necessary or obligate those deemed humane yet materially unnecessary. It is important to remember that, in some circumstances, acting in deviation from the principal rules can be, and sometimes is, materially necessary.[213] Each such instance exempts the belligerent from its

circumstances. Guerrillas are entitled to a looser self-distinction requirement in recognition of 'situations in armed conflicts where, owing to the nature of the hostilities an armed combatant cannot … distinguish himself' in accordance with a fuller self-distinction requirement. See also Camins, 'Past as Prologue', at 880–81.

208 Article 26, Hague Regulations (1907); Article 57(2)(c), Additional Protocol I; Henckaerts and Doswald-Beck, *Customary International Humanitarian Law* (vol. I), pp. 62–65. See also Stone, *Legal Controls of International Conflict*, pp. 622–23; Rogers, *Law on the Battlefield* (2nd edn), p. 88. Belligerents need not give such warning if 'circumstances do not permit' (such as assault requiring an element of surprise). Pnina Sharvit Baruch, 'The Obligation to Give Effective Warnings: Lessons Learned from Recent Conflicts' in Edoardo Greppi (ed), *Conduct of Hostilities: The Practice, the Law and the Future* (Milan: Franco Angeli, 2015) 115, at 118–19.

209 Article 62(1), Additional Protocol I. That is, 'except in case of imperative military necessity'.

210 Article 71, Geneva Convention III; Article 107, Geneva Convention IV. That is, unless it is temporarily necessary to prohibit such correspondence. See Article 76, Geneva Convention III; Article 112, Geneva Convention IV; Henckaerts and Doswald-Beck, *Customary International Humanitarian Law* (vol. I), pp. 445–47.

211 Article 111, Geneva Convention IV. That is, unless prevented by military operations.

212 Office of General Counsel, *Law of War Manual*, p. 55.

213 Indeed, the very fact that acting in such a manner is permitted by military necessity means that this kind of conduct is deemed materially necessary.

otherwise principal obligation to pursue joint satisfaction. In other words, through these rules, the law limits the belligerent's liberty to act as permitted by military necessity to specific situations where it is, in fact, materially necessary to do so.

7.4.3 Indeterminate Obligations

Some IHL rules indeterminately obligate the pursuit of joint satisfaction. The interplay between military necessity and humanity involved leaves their precedence vis-à-vis each other unsettled. The resulting rule authorises the non-pursuit of joint satisfaction if and to the extent military necessity permits it; the same rule also obligates pursuit insofar as humanity demands it.[214] In so doing, the rule does not specify the point at which the authorised non-pursuit gives way to the obligatory pursuit. IHL framers effectively transfer the burden of discovering this point to those adjudicating, or governed by, the rule in question.

This outcome can be seen, e.g., in rules concerning proportionality in attacks[215] and the use of weapons of a nature to cause superfluous injury and unnecessary suffering.[216] Similarly, with respect to the use of

[214] Office of General Counsel, *Law of War Manual*, pp. 55–56.

[215] Article 51(5)(b), Article 57(2)(a)(iii) and Article 57(2)(b), Additional Protocol I; Article 8(2)(b)(iv), Rome Statute. See also Lieutenant Colonel William J Fenrick, 'The Rule of Proportionality and Protocol I in Conventional Warfare' (1982) 98 *Military Law Review* 91; Watkin, 'Assessing Proportionality'; Stefan Oeter, 'Methods and Means of Combat' in Fleck (ed), *Handbook of International Humanitarian Law* (3rd edn) 115, p. 122; Office of General Counsel, *Law of War Manual*, pp. 51, 60–62; Doswald-Beck and Vité, 'International Humanitarian Law and Human Rights Law', at 100; Schmitt, 'Military Necessity and Humanity', at 804–05; Luban, 'Risk Taking and Force Protection', pp. 294–97; Walzer, 'Response', p. 329.

[216] St. Petersburg Declaration; Article 23(e), Hague Regulations (1907); Article 35(2), Additional Protocol I; preamble, Conventional Weapons Convention; Article 6(2), Protocol on Prohibitions or Restrictions on the Use of Mines, Booby-traps and Other Devices as Amended on 3 May 1996 (Protocol II as Amended on 3 May 1996) Annexed to the Convention on Prohibitions or Restrictions on the Use of Certain Conventional Weapons Which May Be Deemed to Be Excessively Injurious or to Have Indiscriminate Effects, 3 May 1996, in force 3 December 1998, 2048 UNTS 93; Article 3(a), ICTY Statute; Article 8(2)(b)(xx), Rome Statute (subject to the adoption of an annex). See also de Preux, 'Basic Rules', pp. 399–410; Meyrowitz, 'Principle of Superfluous Injury or Unnecessary Suffering'; *Dissenting Opinion of Judge Shahabuddeen, Nuclear Weapons* 375, pp. 402–05; *Dissenting Opinion of Judge Weeramantry, Nuclear Weapons* 429, pp. 497–99; *Dissenting Opinion of Judge Higgins, Nuclear Weapons* 583, at 585–87; Yves Sandoz, 'International Humanitarian Law in the Twenty-First Century' (2003) 6 *Yearbook of International Humanitarian Law* 3, at 8; W Hays Parks, 'Means and Methods of

incendiary weapons, the *UK Joint Service Manual* observes: 'Although these weapons can cause severe injury to personnel, their use is lawful provided the military necessity for their use outweighs the injury and suffering which their use may cause.'[217] Reference may also be made to rules obligating humane yet militarily unnecessary action 'as far as military considerations permit',[218] 'whenever circumstances permit'[219] and 'to the maximum extent feasible'.[220]

7.4.4 Exceptional Obligations

Customary IHL principally authorises the declaration and establishment of blockades.[221] Conversely, in principle, the blockading party is

Warfare' (2006) 38 *George Washington International Law Review* 511, at 517 n.25; Frits Kalshoven, 'Conventional Weaponry: The Law from St. Petersburg to Lucerne and Beyond' in Kalshoven, *Collected Essays* 377, pp. 386–87; Théo Boutruche, 'L'Interdiction des Maux Superflus: Contribution á l'Études des Principes et Règles Relatifs aux Moyens et Méthodes de Guerre en Droit International Humanitaire', PhD thesis, The Graduate Institute of International and Development Studies (2008); Program on Humanitarian Policy and Conflict Research, *Commentary on Air and Missile Warfare Manual*, pp. 65–67.

217 UK Defence Ministry, *Joint Service Manual*, p. 111.

218 That is, for example, leaving elements of a party's medical personnel and *materiél* with the wounded and sick to assist in the latter's care, should the party in question be compelled to abandon them to the enemy. See Article 12, Geneva Convention I. See also Article 1, Wounded and Sick Convention (1906) ('so far as military conditions permit'); Article 1, Wounded and Sick Convention (1929) ('as far as military exigencies permit'); Pictet (ed), *Commentary Geneva Convention I*, pp. 141–42.

219 That is, for example, searching, collecting and evacuating the wounded, sick, shipwrecked and dead. See Article 15, Geneva Convention I; Article 18, Geneva Convention II; Henckaerts and Doswald-Beck, *Customary International Humanitarian Law* (vol. I), pp. 396–99, 406–08; Doswald-Beck and Vité, 'International Humanitarian Law and Human Rights Law', at 100.

220 That is, for example, removing movable cultural property from the vicinity of military objectives and avoiding locating military objectives near cultural property. See Article 8, Hague Cultural Property Protocol II.

221 That is, unless it has the sole purpose of starving the civilian population or is disproportionately injurious to the civilian population. See San Remo Manual on Maritime Warfare, paras 93, 102; Peter Macalister-Smith, 'Protection of the Civilian Population and the Prohibition of Starvation as a Method of Warfare: Draft Texts on International Humanitarian Assistance' (1991) 31 *International Review of the Red Cross* 440, at 445; Wolff Heintschel von Heinegg, 'Naval Blockade' in Michael N Schmitt (ed), *International Law across the Spectrum of Conflict: Essays in Honour of Professor L.C. Green on the Occasion of His Eightieth Birthday* (New Port: Naval War College, 2000) 203, p. 216; von Heinegg, 'Law of Armed Conflict at Sea', pp. 535–36.

customarily authorised to deny free passage of essential goods to blockaded ports.[222]

One set of IHL rules stands out for their unusually high degree of convulsion. The rules in question are Article 33 of Geneva Convention I[223] and Article 28 of Geneva Convention II[224] regarding the treatment of certain medical facilities and equipment. These provisions principally authorise the commander to make use of the objects concerned in accordance with the 'laws of war'.[225] The rules then exceptionally obligate the commander to refrain from making such use, if and to the extent non-diversion proves humane – that is, insofar as the objects are required for the care of the wounded and sick. Intriguingly, this obligation of non-diversion is again subject to a further exception, if and to the extent required by urgent military necessity. The latter exception is available, however, only once humanity's demand, i.e., proper care of those nursed therein, has been ensured.[226]

By positing these rules, IHL framers have chosen principally to let military necessity's permission trump humanity's contrary demands (the latter being where the joint satisfaction lies). The belligerent's liberty to act as permitted by military necessity is no longer limited to specific situations where it is, in fact, materially necessary to do so. On the contrary, the liberty remains in place regardless. What matters instead is the fact that, in certain circumstances, the contrary action can be

222 That is, unless the civilian population is inadequately supplied. See San Remo Manual on Maritime Warfare, para. 103; Wolff Heintschel von Heinegg, 'Blockade', *Max Planck Encyclopaedia of Public International Law* (2015), paras 50–53.

223 Article 33, paragraph 2, Geneva Convention I: 'The buildings, material and stores of fixed medical establishments of the armed forces shall remain subject to the laws of war, but may not be diverted from that purpose as long as they are required for the care of wounded and sick. Nevertheless, the commander of forces in the field may make use of them, in case of urgent military necessity, provided that they make previous arrangements for the welfare of the wounded and sick who are nursed in them.'

224 Article 28, Geneva Convention II: 'Sick-bays and their equipment [on board a warship] shall remain subject to the laws of warfare, but may not be diverted from their purpose so long as they are required for the wounded and sick. Nevertheless, the commander into whose power they have fallen may, after ensuring the proper care of the wounded and sick who are accommodated therein, apply them to other purposes in case of urgent military necessity.'

225 On this expression, see Pictet (ed), *Commentary Geneva Convention I*, pp. 274–75; Pictet (ed), *Commentary Geneva Convention II*, pp. 176–77.

226 In Draper's words: 'To what extent this *via media* gains in value over the less sophisticated statement of the humanitarian dictate followed by the qualification of (urgent or imperative) military necessity is open to doubt.' Draper, 'Military Necessity and Humanitarian Imperatives', at 139.

humane.[227] Although principally optional, the pursuit of joint satisfaction becomes exceptionally obligatory, and the contrary liberty exceptionally unavailable, just in cases where the said pursuit proves humane.

It might be said that those in favour of upholding a duty to 'capture rather than kill' in combat are effectively seeking to have it recognised as a positive IHL rule under this heading.[228] On this view, IHL principally authorises the killing of enemy combatants. All else being equal, however, the law exceptionally obligates belligerents not to kill them where a more humane means of their disablement (i.e., capture) happens to be reasonably available. Opponents counter by claiming that the matter falls into situations described below, where positive IHL does not obligate non-killing.

7.5 No Obligation to Pursue Joint Satisfaction amid Military Necessity-Humanity Contradiction

One last set of consequences of interest to us remains. This set is marked by the absence of an IHL obligation to pursue jointly satisfactory behaviour.

We may interpret these consequences in two ways. One possibility is that IHL framers have declined to impose any obligation – be it an unqualified, principal, indeterminate or exceptional one. Evidently, no such obligation exists where the law expressly authorises the non-pursuit of joint satisfaction.

Alternatively, the framers may either fail to posit an obligation or choose to leave the matter unregulated.[229] We must then consider (a) whether permissive or prohibitive presumptions operate and (b) what role, if any, considerations of military necessity and humanity play in their operation.

7.5.1 Where the Law Affirmatively Authorises Non-pursuit of Joint Satisfaction

IHL framers have declined to obligate the pursuit of joint satisfaction where a rule affirmatively authorises contrary behaviour. Consider, e.g.,

[227] Indeed, the very fact that acting in such a manner is demanded by humanity means that this kind of conduct is deemed humane.

[228] For further discussion of 'capture rather than kill', see Chapter 8.

[229] The latter is akin in character to what Munzer called 'bare' permissions. See Munzer, 'Validity and Legal Conflicts', at 1141–42, 1145 n.13.

rules authorising the Detaining Power to intern POWs,[230] the belligerent to search and control medical vessels,[231] and the Occupying Power to confiscate such state property in occupied territory as may be used for military operations.[232] The same may be true where, for instance, the law expressly withholds the inviolability of postal correspondence in case of blockade violations.[233]

These rules' framers have chosen to grant military necessity permissions unfettered priority over contrary humanitarian demands. With respect to these acts, the law leaves the belligerent entirely at liberty to act as permitted by military necessity. It in no way matters whether acting in such a manner happens to be materially necessary or unnecessary at a particular moment. Nor does it matter whether contrary action in concrete situations proves humane or inhumane. Acting as demanded by humanity, and thereby acting in joint satisfaction, is now entirely optional whenever the belligerent is presented with an opportunity to do so.

7.5.2 *Where the Law Fails to Obligate Jointly Satisfactory Behaviour*

More often, however, the relevant acts are found through the absence of positive IHL rules. Examples include:

- The absence of prohibitions against forcibly displacing eligible enemy combatants through combat;[234]
- The absence of prohibitions against using artillery, either observed or unobserved, against lawful military objectives in civilian-populated areas;[235]

[230] Article 5, Hague Regulations (1907); Article 21, Geneva Convention III. See also Sandra Krähenmann, 'Protection of Prisoners in Armed Conflict' in Fleck (ed), *Handbook of International Humanitarian Law* (3rd edn) 359, at 366, 392; Office of General Counsel, *Law of War Manual*, p. 58.

[231] Article 31, Geneva Convention II.

[232] Article 53, Hague Regulations (1907).

[233] Article 1, Convention (XI) Relative to Certain Restrictions with Regard to the Exercise of the Right of Capture in Naval War, 18 October 1907, in force 26 January 1910.

[234] *Prosecutor v Vujadin Popović et al*, Case No. IT-05-99-A, *Judgment*, 30 January 2015, para. 774.

[235] This, at least, is the view advocated by Geoffrey S. Corn and Gary P. Corn. See Corn and Corn, 'Law of Operational Targeting', at 370. But see *Prosecutor v Ante Gotovina et al*, Case No. IT-06-90-T *Judgment*, 15 April 2011, para. 1906, n.932; Darren Valletgoed, 'The Last Round? A Post-Gotovina Reassessment of the Legality of Using Artillery Attack Against Built-Up Areas' (2013) 18 *Journal of Conflict & Security Law* 25, at 39.

- The absence of prohibitions against attacking or disabling eligible enemy combatants[236] (including airborne troops during their descent[237]);
- The absence of prohibitions against deliberately inflicting terror amongst enemy combatants;[238]
- The absence of prohibitions against starving enemy combatants as a method of combat;[239]
- The absence of prohibitions against lifting protection for medical units, personnel and *materiél*, as well as those belonging to civil defence organisations, that are used to commit acts harmful to the enemy;[240]
- The absence of prohibitions against the Detaining Power censoring correspondence between POWs[241] or internees[242] with the exterior;
- The absence of prohibitions against the Occupying Power collecting contributions and requisitions;[243] and
- The absence of rules obligating the belligerent to grant requests by its adversary for medical flights.[244]

These are arguable instances where the framers have left the non-pursuit of joint satisfaction 'barely' permitted.[245]

Elsewhere, the absence of a positive rule obligating jointly satisfactory conduct may imply the law's failure to do so. Arguably, the ICJ's agnosticism regarding the lawfulness of the use or threat of nuclear weapons in extreme self-defence is a case in point.[246] The ICRC conceded that it is

[236] Office of General Counsel, *Law of War Manual*, p. 58.

[237] Article 42(3), Additional Protocol I. See also Jean de Preux, 'Article 42 – Occupants of Aircraft' in Sandoz et al. (eds), *Commentary on Additional Protocols* 493, p. 501.

[238] Ibid, p. 618.

[239] Article 17, Lieber Code; Esbjörn Rosenblad, 'Starvation as a Method of Warfare – Conditions for Regulation by Convention' (1970) 7 *International Lawyer* 252, at 253, 254–55.

[240] Articles 21, 22, Geneva Convention I; Articles 34, 35, Geneva Convention II; Article 19, Geneva Convention IV; Articles 13, 65(1)-(2), Additional Protocol I.

[241] Article 76, Geneva Convention III.

[242] Article 107, Geneva Convention IV.

[243] Articles 49, 52, Hague Regulations (1907).

[244] Article 29(3), Additional Protocol I. But see Manual on Air and Missile Warfare, para. 78(c).

[245] Munzer, 'Validity and Legal Conflicts', at 1141–42, 1145 n.13.

[246] *Nuclear Weapons*, paras 95–97, 105(2)(E). See also Oeter, 'Methods and Means of Combat' (2nd edn), at 154–56.

unclear whether customary IHL permits or forbids belligerent reprisals against civilians during hostilities.[247]

It is unclear whether a party is duty-bound, in contact zones as well as areas it controls, to grant protection to medical flights of an adversary where no prior agreement has been reached to permit such flights and before they are recognised as such.[248] Nor is it clear whether a state party bound by Additional Protocol II is obligated to ensure supplies essential to the survival of the civilian population.[249] There is no clear IHL rule obligating civilians directly participating in hostilities, continuously or otherwise, to distinguish themselves from non-participating civilians;[250] or obligating parties with advanced precision-guided weapons to exhaust such weapons first.[251]

7.5.3 In dubio pro libertate *or* prohibitione?

Does IHL contain any permissive or prohibitive presumptions with respect to acts that are not specifically regulated by its positive rules? While the Martens Clause arguably reduces or extinguishes the *in dubio pro libertate* presumption articulated in the *Lotus* case,[252] the clause

247 Henckaerts and Doswald-Beck, *Customary International Humanitarian Law* (vol. I), pp. 520–23. See also UK Defence Ministry, *Joint Service Manual*, pp. 420–21; Quéguiner, 'The Principle of Distinction', pp. 174–75; Schmitt, 'Military Necessity and Humanity', at 820–22.

248 Articles 26, 27(2), Additional Protocol I; Manual on Air and Missile Warfare, para. 78(a).

249 Article 18(2), Additional Protocol II. See also Pictet (ed), *Commentary Geneva Convention I*, pp. 1478–80.

250 Nobuo Hayashi, 'Continuous Attack Liability Without Right or Fact of Direct Participation in Hostilities – The ICRC *Interpretive Guidance* and Perils of a Pseudo-Status' in Joanna Nowakowska-Małusecka (ed), *International Humanitarian Law: Antecedences and Challenges of the Present Time* (Bydgoszcz-Katowice: Oficyna Wydawnicza Branta, 2010) 56, at 75–76.

251 Manual on Air and Missile Warfare, para. 8. On a variation of this theme, i.e., whether states are duty-bound to use non-lethal weapons, see Boothby, *Weapons and the Law of Armed Conflict*, p. 249.

252 *The Case of the S.S. 'Lotus'*, 1927 PCIJ Series A, No. 10. See also Ole Spiermann, '*Lotus* and the Double Structure of International Legal Argument' in Boisson de Chazournes and Sands (eds), *International Law, the International Court of Justice and Nuclear Weapons* 131; Daniel Bodansky, '*Non Liquet* and the Incompleteness of International Law' in Boisson de Chazournes and Sands (eds), *International Law, the International Court of Justice and Nuclear Weapons* 153, pp. 161–65; Hugh Thirlway, 'The Nuclear Weapons Advisory Opinions: The Declarations and Separate and Dissenting Opinions'

does not appear to replace it with an *in dubio pro prohibitione* presumption.

In our context, *in dubio pro libertate* asserts that it is lawful to act in a given manner unless specifically prohibited by positive IHL rules. Such a permissive presumption resonates with those who believe that, '[i]n the simplest terms, nations do not legislate self-denying restrictions on those weapons and techniques that they judge their survival to depend upon'.[253]

Others argue that the Martens Clause reverses this presumption.[254] No major problem would arise if reversal simply meant the presumption's diminishment or removal. It would be more contentious, however, to regard the Martens Clause not only as extinguishing *in dubio pro libertate* but also substituting it with *in dubio pro prohibitione*. The latter would assert that it is unlawful to act in a given manner unless expressly authorised by positive IHL rules.

Commentators identify at least four possible interpretations of the Martens Clause:[255]

1. As a safeguard of customary international law, to the effect that what is not prohibited by treaty may not be necessarily lawful;[256]
2. As an interpretive device, whereby *jus in bello* should in cases of doubt be interpreted according to the principles of humanity and dictates of public conscience;[257]

in Boisson de Chazournes and Sands (eds), *International Law, the International Court of Justice and Nuclear Weapons* 390, pp. 406–09.

[253] Jochnick and Normand, 'Legitimation of Violence', at 56 (citing Hoopes, 'Comments', p. 142), 68–69.

[254] *Nuclear Weapons Shahabuddeen Dissenting Opinion*, pp. 405–11; *Nuclear Weapons Weeramantry Dissenting Opinion*, pp. 492–96; Doswald-Beck, 'International Humanitarian Law and the Advisory Opinion', at 49.

[255] Cassese, 'Martens Clause'; Meron, 'Martens Clause', at 87; von Bernstorff, 'Martens Clause', para. 13. See also Michael Salter, 'Reinterpreting Competing Interpretations of the Scope and Potential of the Martens Clause' (2012) 17 *Journal of Conflict & Security Law* 403.

[256] *Nuclear Weapons*, paras 84, 87; *Statement of the Government of the United Kingdom*, para. 32; *Verbatim Record*, p. 78; Schwarzenberger, *Legality of Nuclear Weapons*, pp. 10–11 (cited in Cassese, 'Martens Clause', at 189 n.3); Mary Ellen O'Connell, 'Historical Development and Legal Basis' in Fleck (ed), *Handbook of International Humanitarian Law* (3rd edn) 1, p. 34. Stephan Michel and Claude Schenker, with contributions from Iris Müller, 'Denunciation' in Dörmann et al. (eds), Commentary First Geneva Convention 1177, para. 3297.

[257] *Kupreškić et al. Trial Judgment*, para. 525; Cassese, 'Martens Clause', at 189–90, 212; Michel and Schenker, 'Denunciation', para. 3294.

3. As an affirmation that the principles of humanity and dictates of public conscience constitute separate sources of international law, to be distinguished from treaty or customary law;[258] and
4. As a device in customary *jus in bello* that loosens the requirements normally prescribed for *usus* and elevates *opinio* to a rank higher than normally admitted.[259]

It is doubtful whether any of these interpretations, even if sound in themselves, warrants the conclusion that the Martens Clause injects *in dubio pro prohibitione* into IHL.[260] Nor would the law's increasing 'homo-centricity'[261] alone generate such an effect. It is, if anything, humanity, the dictates of public conscience, and the like that would have more potential in this regard.[262] The Martens Clause would simply be a conduit through which they would shape substantive IHL rules.

7.6 Conclusion

The inevitable conflict thesis insists that obeying the imperatives of military necessity and obeying those of humanity always conflict with each other. IHL norm-creation is about pre-empting these considerations from giving rise to conflicting rules of positive IHL.

This chapter shows both propositions to be false. To begin with, possibilities of joint satisfaction are plain where humanity demands what military necessity permits, and where humanity condemns what military necessity tolerates. Even for conduct that is not amenable to the unnecessary-inhumane or necessary-humane alignment, the belligerent still satisfies both considerations by acting in accordance with humanity.

Moreover, IHL norm-creation is about obligating or not obligating jointly satisfactory behaviour. Where joint satisfaction is firm, it often

[258] Meron, 'Martens Clause', at 81 nn.20, 22 (citing *Nuclear Weapons Shahabuddeen Dissenting Opinion*, p. 406), 86 n.55 (citing *Nuclear Weapons Shahabuddeen Dissenting Opinion*, p. 408); Cassese, 'Martens Clause', at 190–92; Michel and Schenker, 'Denunciation', paras 3291–92.

[259] *Kupreškić et al. Trial Judgment*, para. 527; Meron, 'Martens Clause', at 88; Cassese, 'Martens Clause', at 214; Michel and Schenker, 'Denunciation', para. 3293.

[260] Meron, 'Martens Clause', at 86 (citing Ticehurst, 'Martens Clause and the Laws of Armed Conflict', at 126), 88 (citing Doswald-Beck, 'International Humanitarian Law and the Advisory Opinion', at 49).

[261] Kolb, 'Main Epochs', pp. 24, 52; Meron, 'Martens Clause', at 88.

[262] Meron, 'Martens Clause', at 86 (citing Ticehurst, 'Martens Clause and the Laws of Armed Conflict', at 126), 88 (citing Doswald-Beck, 'International Humanitarian Law and the Advisory Opinion', at 49). See also Chapter 8.

results in the adoption of an unqualified IHL obligation to pursue that satisfaction. Where such an obligation is absent, this can be explained by reference to considerations other than humanity or military necessity. Where military necessity and humanity contradict each other, IHL framers decide whether to obligate the pursuit of modest joint satisfaction and, if so, whether to do so unqualifiedly, principally, indeterminately or only exceptionally. This process is what accounting for the military necessity-humanity interplay in IHL norm-creation really means.

This concludes Part III's discussion of military necessity in its normative context. In Part IV, we will begin investigating military necessity in its juridical context. Its first chapter, Chapter 8, examines how the joint satisfaction thesis transforms one final aspect of the inevitable conflict thesis. The latter thesis claims that neither military necessity pleas nor humanity pleas are admissible vis-à-vis unqualified IHL rules. That, according to the inevitable conflict thesis, is so because IHL framers intended to admit them elsewhere by inserting exceptional military necessity and humanity clauses.

The joint satisfaction thesis will demonstrate two things. First, unqualified IHL rules extinguish all indifferent considerations that might permit contrary behaviour. What precludes all indifference pleas is the unqualifiedly duty-imposing character of these rules. It is *not* the empirically troublesome claim of the inevitable conflict thesis that every positive IHL rule embodies the military necessity-humanity interplay.

Second, non-indifferent considerations, e.g., humanitarian imperatives, may escape exclusion when IHL framers posit unqualified rules. Non-indifferent considerations may therefore operate as an additional layer of permission or restraint *even over unqualified rules.* Where humanity condemns conduct that a positive rule unqualifiedly obligates, or where humanity demands conduct that a positive rule unqualifiedly prohibits, IHL may let the belligerent invoke humanity as a ground for declining to comply with the law.

PART IV

Military Necessity in Its Juridical Context

8

Joint Satisfaction Thesis III

Exclusionary and Non-exclusionary Effects

In Part IV, we investigate the legal consequences to which accounting for military necessity gives rise. Juridical military necessity concerns conventional or customary IHL rules that have been validly posited.

Whether certain kinds of conduct should be deemed militarily necessary or unnecessary, and how IHL framers should regulate them in view of their status as military necessities or non-necessities, are no longer in issue. Rather, our aim here is to tackle questions such as: How should we apply unqualified rules of positive IHL to situations where the rules' addressee invokes military necessity while engaging in deviant behaviour? Where a positive IHL rule contains an express military necessity clause, how should we interpret that clause in relation to the facts at hand? What place do military necessity pleas have, if any, in the adjudication of international crimes?

8.1 From Normativity to Juridicity

Moving from normative military necessity to juridical military necessity entails two related shifts. First, in principle, we do not assess patterns or kinds of conduct.[1] Instead, we are back to assessing specific acts, such as 'destroying the houses and their contents at Siboney, Cuba, in June 1898' during the Spanish–American War.[2] The same is true of the purposes for which specific acts are taken, e.g., 'preventing V Corps of the United States Army, Siboney's occupation force at the time, from decimation by a yellow fever epidemic feared'.[3] We are then to consider whether these specific acts constitute military necessity within the meaning of

[1] This chapter is a partial exception. See below.

[2] Paul G Pierpaoli Jr, 'Siboney, Cuba' in Spencer C Tucker (ed), *The Encyclopedia of the Spanish-American and Philippine-American Wars: A Political, Social, and Military History* (Santa Barbara, Denver and Oxford: ABC-CLIO, 2009) 590, pp. 590–91.

[3] Ibid.

applicable IHL rules. In the Siboney situation, a UK–US Arbitral Tribunal found that the destruction did indeed constitute military necessity.[4]

Second, within the normative context, we *stipulated* the material military necessity or non-necessity of a given kind of behaviour. Within the juridical context, we once again *evaluate* that of concrete instances.[5] Unlike Part II that looked at material military necessity, however, it is the relevant IHL provisions that furnish the basis of evaluation in Part IV. In other words, Part IV explores how the law's addressees, adjudicators and commentators *interpret* military necessity in its juridical context.

Juridical military necessity takes three forms. In one, it manifests itself through exclusion. The framers of unqualified IHL rules have accounted for all indifferent considerations, including military necessity, by setting them aside and obligating jointly satisfactory behaviour without exception. Rules of this type extinguish all counter-liberties to behave otherwise. Accordingly, pleas emanating from such considerations may not be invoked in support of conduct deviating from the prescriptions of unqualified IHL rules.

Juridical military necessity also takes the form of an exceptional clause attached to certain provisions of positive IHL. Where such a clause appears, it signifies the process of IHL norm-creation through which the framers have chosen specifically to authorise the belligerent to plead military necessity as a ground for exemption from the principal rule. What constitutes military necessity within the meaning of such a clause is a matter of legal interpretation.

The third form juridical military necessity takes is as a negative element of some war crimes and crimes against humanity. Several offences, such as those involving property destruction and forcible displacement, are built on substantive IHL rules that admit military necessity exceptions. When a rule envisages an exception, and when the rule's violation constitutes a crime, it is only logical that the absence of circumstances satisfying the exception's requirements is itself an element of that crime.

[4] *William Hardman (United Kingdom) v United States*, 18 June 1913 [2006] 6 *Reports of International Arbitral Awards* 25; (1913) 7 *American Journal of International Law* 879; (1921–1922) 2 *British Yearbook of International Law* 197. See also Schwarzenberger, *International Law as Applied by Courts and Tribunals* (vol. II), pp. 131–32; Hilaire McCoubrey, 'The Nature of the Modern Doctrine of Military Necessity' (1991) 30 *Revue de droit militaire et de droit de la guerre* 215, at 222–23.

[5] Here, too, this chapter is a partial exception. See below.

8.2 Perils of Excluding Military Necessity Pleas vis-à-vis Unqualified IHL Rules on Unsound Empirical Bases and *a contrario* Reasoning

This chapter deals with one difficulty associated with the inevitable conflict thesis that 'spills over' into the juridical context.

Both the inevitable conflict thesis and the joint satisfaction thesis hold that IHL accounts for military necessity once its framers have posited unqualified rules. Both of these theses also agree that one consequence of this is that military necessity does not operate as an additional layer of lawfulness-modification over such rules. Military necessity pleas are therefore inadmissible.

Nevertheless, the inevitable conflict thesis reaches this conclusion based on two problematic claims. One is *argumendum a contrario*.[6] The fact that some specific IHL rules contain exceptional clauses means that those without such clauses admit no exceptions. The soundness of this inferred intention hinges, in turn, on the notion that the framers of every positive IHL rule containing no exceptional clause considered adding such a clause, and then decided not to do so. This leads us to the inevitable conflict thesis's other contentious claim. The inferred exclusion holds if, but only if, it is true that the military necessity–humanity interplay underpins the creation of every positive IHL rule.[7] Conceding otherwise would amount to acknowledging that not all of these rules in fact account for military necessity or humanity. Those rules that do not account for them, including some unqualified rules, would arguably be susceptible to military necessity and/or humanity pleas.

The joint satisfaction thesis refutes both claims. Positing an unqualified IHL rule has the *logical* effect of precluding all pleas built on indifferent considerations. When IHL framers posit an unqualified rule, they account for indifferent considerations by setting them aside – even if such considerations do not specifically appear in the process of that rule's creation. Since military necessity in its normative context is a set of indifferent considerations,[8] pleas emanating from them are *ipso facto* inadmissible vis-à-vis unqualified rules. This outcome does not depend on IHL framers' exclusionary intention being inferred from the existence of some IHL rules that expressly envisage such pleas.

[6] See Chapter 5.
[7] See ibid.
[8] See Chapter 6.

The inevitable conflict thesis asserts that unqualified IHL rules exclude humanity pleas as well. Here, too, their exclusion is inferred, because some IHL rules do admit exceptions on account of humanity.[9] The joint satisfaction thesis shows flaws in this reasoning and proposes a more nuanced picture. Some humanitarian considerations are normatively indifferent[10] and, accordingly, inadmissible as bases for pleas vis-à-vis unqualified rules. Humanity also demands action and condemns others, however.[11] Since we have reason to believe that non-indifferent considerations may escape exclusion through IHL norm-creation, we also have reason to accept the possibility that they may modify an act's lawfulness over and above unqualified rules.

This chapter proceeds as follows. First, we will see that IHL norm-creation does not always involve the military necessity–humanity interplay. Examples will be given where at least one of the two sets of considerations is missing. Second, our discussion will demonstrate that unqualified IHL rules preclude all pleas that emanate from indifferent considerations. Their exclusion always results, because positing an unqualified obligation extinguishes its addressee's option to avail itself of any contrary liberties.[12] Inadmissible pleas include *Kriegsräson* as well as its variations, and what may be termed *Humanitätsräson.* Third, the chapter will show situations where the letter of unqualified rules may not be all there is to an act's IHL compliance. These situations reveal the existence of a genuine norm conflict between unqualified IHL obligations, on the one hand, and counter-imperatives that non-indifferent considerations generate, on the other. It is not inconceivable that acting as humanity demands may repair its unlawfulness otherwise established by unqualified IHL rules; or, conversely, acting in compliance with applicable IHL rules may be rendered unlawful if it contravenes what humanity demands.

8.3 IHL Norm-Creation Not Involving the Military Necessity–Humanity Interplay

The inevitable conflict thesis claims that *all* positive IHL rules embody the interplay between humanity and military necessity. In fact, some,

[9] See Chapter 5.
[10] See Chapter 6.
[11] See ibid.
[12] See Chapter 7.

including those creating unqualified obligations, do not. Several of those involve military necessity but *not* humanity,[13] whereas others involve humanity but *not* military necessity.[14]

8.3.1 *Involving Military Necessity But Not Humanity*

A number of positive IHL rules involve military necessity but not humanity in their creation. Where this occurs, military necessity is typically juxtaposed with considerations of fairness or chivalry, pecuniary gain, and sovereignty.

Consider, for instance, the IHL prohibition against the improper use of enemy uniforms.[15] Of relevance here is their use 'while engaging in attacks'.[16] Our discussion does not concern the use of enemy uniforms where there is no deceptive intention[17] or no intention to engage in hostile acts.[18] Rather, we are interested in acts such as 'using enemy uniforms with intention to deceive' with a view to achieving purposes

[13] Nils Melzer suggests that the interplay may involve military necessity, on the one hand, and considerations other than humanity, such as 'cultural, religious, political, environmental, and economic' ones, on the other. Melzer, *Targeted Killing*, p. 281. Perhaps religious considerations, including mercy and compassion, may at times be deemed humanity-equivalent. Carolyn Evans, 'The Double-Edged Sword: Religious Influences on International Humanitarian Law' (2005) 6 *Melbourne Journal of International Law* 1, at 12–27; Frédéric Mégret, 'A Cautionary Tale from the Crusades? War and Prisoners in Conditions of Normative Incommensurability' in Scheipers (ed), *Prisoners in War* 23, p. 23.

[14] Or, for that matter, the process may involve neither military necessity nor humanity. This particular possibility is not explored further here. In view of the claim made by the inevitable conflict thesis, we will have accomplished our purpose once it is shown that *some* positive IHL rules do not involve *either* military necessity *or* humanity in their creation.

[15] Article 13(f), Brussels Declaration; Article 23(f), Hague Regulations (1899); Article 23(f), Hague Regulations (1907). See also Rule 64, Manual on the International Law Applicable to Cyber Warfare, 15 March 2013; Michael N Schmitt (ed), *Tallinn Manual on the International Law Applicable to Cyber Warfare: Prepared by the International Group of Experts at the Invitation of the NATO Cooperative Cyber Defence Centre of Excellence* (Cambridge: Cambridge University Press, 2013), pp. 188–91.

[16] Article 39(2), Additional Protocol I. See also Bordwell, *Law of War between Belligerents*, p. 283.

[17] Holland, *Laws of War on Land*, p. 45; Dinstein, *Conduct of Hostilities* (2nd edn), p. 238; Office of General Counsel, *Law of War Manual*, p. 299.

[18] Dinstein, *Conduct of Hostilities* (2nd edn), p. 238. The British Manual holds that using enemy uniforms, e.g., in rear areas for training purposes, would not be improper. UK Defence Ministry, *Joint Service Manual*, p. 61. See also Office of General Counsel, *Law of War Manual*, p. 299.

such as 'obtaining tactical advantage over the enemy'. It should also be noted that we are looking exclusively at *enemy* uniforms.[19]

The expression 'improper' has divided opinions.[20] Nevertheless, there appear to be two distinct situations – i.e., during combat and in enemy-held territory – where the use of enemy uniforms is unqualifiedly banned. First, the law unqualifiedly prohibits the use of enemy uniforms in combat.[21] If some of those fighting for a party wore the uniforms of its adversary during combat, it would be unfair for that adversary. 'Fairness'[22] as a reason-giving consideration in IHL norm-creation would prompt the law's framers to consider banning such practice. Meanwhile, the tactic would be confusing for everyone[23] – including, self-defeatingly, those fighting for the very party that resorts to it. Normative military necessity would merely tolerate the use of enemy uniforms in combat.

A prospect of jointly satisfying fairness and military necessity arises here. By unqualifiedly obligating that satisfaction, the framers of IHL rules on the use of enemy uniforms have accounted for both considerations. In some situations of isolated, close-quarter combat where there is no real danger of confusion amongst one's own ranks, it may prove consistent with military necessity to wear enemy uniforms. If one does so, however, he or she will not be entitled to plead military necessity.

Second, IHL unqualifiedly prohibits the use of enemy uniforms in enemy-held territories.[24] Even if wearing enemy uniforms might prove materially necessary for the wearer,[25] it would be considered lacking in

[19] That is, rather than, e.g., neutral uniforms. See below.

[20] *Trial of Otto Skorzeny and Others*, United Nations War Crimes Commission, 9 *Law Reports of Trials of War Criminals*, vol. IX, 90, at 92–93; Ronald F Roxburgh (ed), *Oppenheim's International Law: A Treatise* 3rd edn, 2 vols. (London: Longmans, Green and Co., 1921), vol. II, p. 228; Jean de Preux, 'Article 39 – Emblems of Nationality' in Sandoz et al. (eds), *Commentary on Additional Protocols* 461, p. 466.

[21] Article 39(2), Additional Protocol I.

[22] Or, perhaps, chivalry. See below. The US Department of Defense calls it 'good faith'. See Office of General Counsel, *Law of War Manual*, p. 295.

[23] Roxburgh (ed), *Oppenheim's International Law* (3rd edn), p. 228: 'As regards the use of the national flag, the military ensigns, and the uniforms of the enemy, theory and practice are unanimous in prohibiting such use during actual attack and defence, since the principle is considered inviolable that during actual fighting belligerent forces ought to be certain who is friend and who is foe.'

[24] That is, unless the user is a POW wearing enemy uniform 'in order to conceal, facilitate or protect' his or her escape. See de Preux, 'Emblems of Nationality', p. 467.

[25] Wearing enemy uniforms while performing commando operations would constitute a breach of this prohibition, but not necessarily an act of espionage. See UK Defence Ministry, *Joint Service Manual*, p. 61.

fairness for the party to which the uniforms belong. Here, too, the framers of this unqualified prohibition have accounted for fairness and military necessity by setting military necessity aside.

Nowhere in this process does humanity appear. Improperly using enemy uniforms is distinct from improperly using the uniforms of 'neutral and other States not Parties to the conflict'.[26] That is so, because only the latter is

> of great concern to the Red Cross . . . [R]espect for the rules of neutrality is fundamental for carrying out the mandate of a Protecting Power . . . By sheltering a neutral State from military operations, this concept makes it possible to carry out humanitarian activities for the benefit of the States involved in the conflict.[27]

Unlike the improper use of neutral and non-party uniforms, the improper use of enemy uniforms is not enumerated as an example of perfidy in Article 37(1)(d) of Additional Protocol I.[28] Several states proposed its inclusion[29] – or, at any rate, other enemy markers such as distinctive emblems[30] – at the Diplomatic Conference. These proposals did not succeed for reasons that are not entirely clear. All that the preparatory works indicate is that '[e]xamples that were debatable or involved borderline cases were avoided'.[31]

Be that as it may, it makes sense to exclude the improper use of enemy uniforms from Article 37(1)(d). Perfidy's definition specifically involves

[26] Article 39(1), Additional Protocol I.

[27] De Preux, 'Emblems of Nationality', p. 465.

[28] The provision reads: 'the feigning of protected status by the use of signs, emblems or uniforms of the United Nations or of neutral or other States not Parties to the conflict'. But see Henckaerts and Doswald-Beck, *Customary International Humanitarian Law* (vol. I), pp. 1341–53 (citing Belgium, France, Germany, Greece, Hungary, Israel, Romania and Switzerland which treat improper use of enemy uniforms as perfidious).

[29] Federal Political Department, *Official Records of the Diplomatic Conference* (vol. III), p. 163 (Belgium).

[30] Ibid, p. 162 (Norway).

[31] Federal Political Department, *Official Records of the Diplomatic Conference* (vol. XV), p. 382. See also Article 21(d) of the ICRC's draft Additional Protocol II ('the use in combat of the enemy's distinctive military emblems') (Federal Political Department, *Official Records of the Diplomatic Conference on the Reaffirmation and Development of International Humanitarian Law applicable in Armed Conflicts*, 17 vols. (Berne: Federal Political Department, 1978), vol. I, p. 39). This draft article was deleted without discussion and by consensus at the conference's 52nd plenary meeting on 6 June 1977. Federal Political Department, *Official Records of the Diplomatic Conference on the Reaffirmation and Development of International Humanitarian Law applicable in Armed Conflicts*, 17 vols. (Berne: Federal Political Department, 1978), vol. VII, p. 128.

IHL 'protection'.[32] Plainly, enemy uniforms are not per se protected under IHL.[33] The law does not confer upon the wearer of a party's uniform any special protection vis-à-vis other members of its own armed forces.[34] It follows that 'feigning' membership in the enemy's armed forces does not amount to 'inviting the confidence of an adversary to lead him to believe that he is entitled to, or is obliged to accord, *protection under the rules of international law applicable in armed conflict*' as required by Article 37(1).[35]

This interpretation also accords with the proviso that is often added to Article 37(1)(d). The Red Cross commentary notes:

> With regard to the United Nations, it is appropriate to state that the wrongful use of its signs, emblems or uniforms can constitute an act of perfidy in the sense of Article 37 only in cases where the personnel of the United Nations have the status of neutral or protected persons, and not in situations where members of the United Nations armed forces intervene in a conflict as combatants, even when this is for peacekeeping purposes. However, this type of abuse remains unlawful.[36]

First, if feigning protected status by using the UN uniforms and other markers ceases to be perfidious where UN forces become involved as combatants, the same would a fortiori be true of feigning the status of enemy combatants by using their uniforms and markers. Second, whereas it is true that unauthorised use of the UN emblem remains unlawful, perfidy is not the basis for this prohibition.[37]

[32] This element was added at the suggestion of Canada, Ireland and the United Kingdom. Federal Political Department, *Official Records of the Diplomatic Conference* (vol. III), pp. 164; Federal Political Department, *Official Records of the Diplomatic Conference on the Reaffirmation and Development of International Humanitarian Law Applicable in Armed Conflicts*, 17 vols. (Berne: Federal Political Department, 1978), vol. XI, pp. 259–70. See also Mike Madden, 'Of Wolves and Sheep: A Purposive Analysis of Perfidy Prohibitions in International Humanitarian Law' (2012) 17 *Journal of Conflict & Security Law* 439; Richard B Jackson, 'Perfidy in Non-international Armed Conflicts' (2012) 88 *International Law Studies* 237.

[33] Office of General Counsel, *Law of War Manual*, p. 299.

[34] See Chapter 4. See also Sean Watts, 'Law-of-War Perfidy' (2014) 219 *Military Law Review* 106, at 114.

[35] Emphasis added. Terry Gill describes perfidy also as being contrary to chivalry. Terry Gill, 'Chivalry: A Principle of the Law of Armed Conflict?' in Matthee et al. (eds), *Armed Conflict and International Law* 33, pp. 41–42.

[36] Jean de Preux, 'Article 37 – Prohibition of Perfidy' in Sandoz et al. (eds), *Commentary on the Additional Protocols* 429, p. 439 (footnotes omitted). See also Federal Political Department, *Official Records of the Diplomatic Conference* (vol. XV), p. 382.

[37] Article 38(2), Additional Protocol I.

Adherents of the inevitable conflict thesis may disagree that humanity does not appear in the unqualified IHL prohibition against the improper use of enemy uniforms. Should they agree, however, they would be compelled to concede that humanity pleas in support of using enemy uniforms might be admissible in some situations (e.g., hostage rescue operations[38]).

There are further instances of IHL norm-creation that arguably embody the interplay between military necessity and considerations of fairness, chivalry or honour, but not humanity. Examples include the unqualified prohibition against active military service by paroled or repatriated POWs[39] and by those sick, wounded or shipwrecked who have been returned.[40] The framers of these rules juxtaposed considerations of chivalry or honour condemning such service[41] and those of military necessity permitting it. Elsewhere, IHL framers have occasionally decided to leave the belligerent at liberty to pursue military necessities despite their arguably unchivalrous or honourless character. Rules that authorise the detention and search of parlementaires,[42] and the absence of rules that prohibit espionage per se,[43] exemplify such occasions.

[38] We will soon discuss a real-life hostage rescue operation in which the Red Cross emblem was misused.

[39] Article 6, Convention for the Amelioration of the Condition of the Wounded in Armies in the Field, 22 August 1864, in force 22 June 1865 (no longer in force); Articles 31–33, Brussels Declaration; Articles 10–12, Hague Regulations (1899); Articles 10–12, Hague Regulations (1907); Article 74, POW Convention (1929); Article 117, Geneva Convention III. See also Evan J Wallach, 'Pray Fire First Gentlemen of France: Has 21st Century Chivalry been Subsumed by Humanitarian Law?' (2012) 3 *Harvard National Security Journal* 431.

[40] Article 16, Geneva Convention II; Roxburgh (ed), *Oppenheim's International Law* (3rd edn), p. 192.

[41] Gary D Brown, 'Prisoner of War Parole: Ancient Concept, Modern Utility' (1998) 156 *Military Law Review* 200, at 210–14; Office of General Counsel, *Law of War Manual*, p. 67.

[42] Articles 44–45, Brussels Declaration; Articles 33–34, Hague Regulations (1899); Articles 33–34, Hague Regulations (1907). See also Carnegie Endowment, *Proceedings of the Hague Peace Conference 1899*, pp. 60–61; Gill, 'Chivalry', p. 42; Office of General Counsel, *Law of War Manual*, pp. 832–33.

[43] Roxburgh (ed), *Oppenheim's International Law* (3rd edn), pp. 222–23. See also Manual on Air and Missile Warfare, para. 119; Dinstein, *Conduct of Hostilities* (2nd edn), p. 241. The absence of rules prohibiting espionage per se is to be distinguished from the status and treatment of persons caught engaging in acts of espionage. Roxburgh (ed), *Oppenheim's International Law* (3rd edn), p. 223; Bordwell, *Law of War between Belligerents*, p. 292.

Some positive IHL rules embody the interplay between military necessity, on the one hand, and considerations of pecuniary gain, prestige or sovereignty, on the other. Historically, those rules that obligate the sparing of POWs' lives and authorise their parole had little to do with humanity.[44] It may also be argued that a number of occupation-related rules account for the displaced state's interests[45] but not humanity. Much of the law on neutrality concerns itself with the safeguarding of neutral interests,[46] rather than humanitarian considerations.

8.3.2 *Involving Humanity But Not Military Necessity*

Conversely, there are positive IHL rules that involve humanity but not military necessity in their creation. In such situations, humanity is often compared to chivalry and honour. Sometimes, IHL rules juxtapose competing humanitarian imperatives.

By virtue of Article 49 of Geneva Convention III, officer POWs 'may in no circumstances be compelled to work'.[47] It appears that the rule's framers accounted for both chivalry or honour condemning such treatment and humanity permitting it, by imposing an unqualified ban on compulsory labour for officer POWs.

Neither the 1874 Brussels Declaration[48] nor the 1899 Hague Regulations[49] contain a categorical prohibition against compelling officer POWs to work. The expression 'officers excepted' was first added to Article 6 of the 1907 Hague Regulations, upon a Spanish proposal.[50]

44 See Chapter 7.
45 Best, 'Restraints on War by Land', pp. 28–29 (regarding requisitions).
46 Article 24, Hague Regulations (1907); Convention (V) Respecting the Rights and Duties of Neutral Powers and Persons in Case of War on Land, 18 October 1907, in force 26 January 1910; Convention (XIII) Concerning the Rights and Duties of Neutral Powers in Naval War, 18 October 1907, in force 26 January 1910; Roxburgh (ed), *Oppenheim's International Law* (3rd edn), pp. 400–04; Paul Seger, 'The Law of Neutrality' in Clapham and Gaeta (eds), *Oxford Handbook of International Law in Armed Conflict* 248, pp. 254–57.
47 Article 49, Geneva Convention III. See also Article 6, Hague Regulations (1907); Article 27, POW Convention (1929).
48 Article 25, Brussels Declaration.
49 Article 6, Hague Regulations (1899).
50 Carnegie Endowment for International Peace, *The Proceedings of the Hague Peace Conferences Translation of the Official Texts: The Conference of 1907*, 3 vols. (New York: Oxford University Press, 1921), vol. III, pp. 18, 103–04, 242. See also Article 41, Stockholm Draft: 'officers and persons of equivalent status excepted'.

At the 1949 Diplomatic Conference, Drafting Committee No. 1 proposed what became the final text of Article 49 of Geneva Convention III on officer exemption.[51] This unqualified prohibition stands, although compulsory labour would be considered humane for POWs in general.

The most logical explanation for this ban is that officer POWs are too senior in rank to be subjected to forced labour.[52] After all, labour may be imposed on POWs exclusively 'with a view to . . . maintaining them in a good physical and mental health'.[53] In the Red Cross commentary's words:

> Provision is made for prisoners of war to work because of humanitarian considerations and not on account of the economic interest of the Detaining Power; the primary purpose is, through work, to preserve the bodily health and morale of prisoners of war. In addition, camp administration is made easier and, lastly, the prisoners are materially better off because of the pay which they receive.[54]

When it comes to officer POWs, however, these humanitarian desiderata have been accounted for and set aside. Pleas emanating from them are therefore inadmissible vis-à-vis Article 49.

Article 118 of Geneva Convention III arguably imposes an unqualified obligation upon the Detaining Power to repatriate POWs after the cessation of active hostilities.[55] The article's drafters juxtaposed considerations of sovereignty – that is, of the home state – demanding repatriation[56] with humanity demanding non-repatriation in some

[51] Federal Political Department, *Final Record of the Diplomatic Conference* (vol. II-A), p. 361.

[52] Carnegie Endowment, *Proceedings of the Hague Peace Conference 1907* (vol. III), p. 103 (Spanish delegate explaining that officer POWs should not be compelled to perform 'annoying tasks'); Federal Political Department, *Final Record of the Diplomatic Conference* (vol. II-A), p. 361 (Soviet delegate describing how 'it would be wrong to place [regular non-commissioned officers who were often regarded as lower-ranking officers] on an equal footing with other [non-regular] non-commissioned officers').

[53] Article 49, Geneva Convention III.

[54] Pictet (ed), *Commentary Geneva Convention III*, p. 260.

[55] Article 118, Geneva Convention III: 'Prisoners of war shall be released and repatriated without delay after the cessation of active hostilities.'

[56] At the 1949 Diplomatic Conference, the Soviet delegate opposed the Austrian amendment, ostensibly on the ground that the possibility of non-repatriation 'could be used to the detriment of the prisoners themselves and of their country'. The US delegate agreed. Federal Political Department, *Final Record of the Diplomatic Conference* (vol. II-A), pp. 324, 462. See also Pictet (ed), *Commentary Geneva Convention III*, pp. 542–43. As will be seen below, the returning state's sovereign interests were disguised as concerns for the welfare of their soldiers taken prisoner.

circumstances,[57] and chose to set the latter aside in favour of the former.[58] As will be seen below, the role of humanitarian demands vis-à-vis unqualified IHL rules obligating contrary action raises complex issues.

Elsewhere, the juxtaposition may involve competing imperatives of humanity. For instance, positive IHL prohibits medical interference with POWs 'not justified by the medical, dental or hospital treatment of the prisoner concerned and carried out in his interest'.[59] Article 78(1) of Additional Protocol I prohibits the evacuation of children to a foreign country 'except for a temporary evacuation where compelling reasons of the health or medical treatment of the children or, except in occupied territory, their safety, so require'.[60]

In none of these cases does military necessity appear as reason-giving considerations. For adherents of the inevitable conflict thesis, accepting these characterisations would be tantamount to conceding the existence of unqualified IHL rules that do not account for military necessity. Consequently, military necessity pleas would be admissible vis-à-vis these rules. If militarily necessary, specific instances of compelling officer POWs to work, refusing to repatriate POWs or interfering with them medically, and evacuating children temporarily to a foreign country could all be lawful notwithstanding their otherwise unqualified prohibitions.

8.4 Excluding Indifference Pleas

The inevitable conflict thesis contends that all positive IHL rules embody the military necessity–humanity interplay. It is based on this assertion that neither military necessity nor humanity may be pleaded in defence of conduct deviating from unqualified rules. The previous section shows how problematic the first contention is, and how the second claim unravels as a result.

The joint satisfaction thesis also holds that unqualified rules exclude all pleas emanating from indifferent considerations. Accordingly,

[57] At the 1949 Diplomatic Conference, Austria proposed and Israel supported an amendment to this effect. Federal Political Department, *Final Record of the Diplomatic Conference* (vol. II-A), pp. 324, 462.

[58] Ibid, p. 462: 'The Austrian amendment was rejected by a large majority.'

[59] Article 13, Geneva Convention III.

[60] Article 78(1), Additional Protocol I. See also Article 24, Geneva Convention IV; Pictet (ed), *Commentary Geneva Convention IV*, pp. 909–13.

Kriegsräson, as well as its variations like self-preservation, and what might be termed *Humanitätsräson*, are inadmissible vis-à-vis such rules.[61] The reasons for this outcome, however, are quite different.

8.4.1 Exclusionary Basis

We are here concerned with the consequences of norm contradictions that occur in IHL norm-creation. As seen in Chapter 7, norm contradictions are distinct from norm conflicts. That remains so, whether the latter are full conflicts between duties and counter-duties, conflicts of a frustrating character between duties and counter-liberties that are already independently valid as legal rules, or informal conflicts between contradictory liberties where strong pressure or policy undergirds them.

When IHL framers posit a rule in unqualified terms, they logically exclude counter-liberties otherwise sanctioned by military necessity. Indeed, this logical exclusion applies to counter-liberties sanctioned by *any* indifferent considerations. Since humanity also remains normatively indifferent towards some acts,[62] pleas based on such considerations are inadmissible as grounds for deviation from unqualified IHL rules.

8.4.2 Kriegsräson *and Its Variations*

Kriegsräson's main claim in its juridical context may be summarised as follows. Although IHL accounts for military necessity, it cannot be construed in such a manner that the belligerent is denied the option to do what it needs to succeed. Where a positive IHL rule is formulated without an express military necessity exception, it merely signals agreement among its framers that deviation from the rule's prescriptions would ordinarily be lacking in military necessity. Neither the law nor its framers can be deemed to have foreseen all future events and legislated for them without the need for adjustments. Accordingly, whenever deviation happens to be militarily necessary, this necessity overrides and renders inoperative any provisions of the law that prescribe contrary action.[63]

61 McMahan, 'Morality of War and the Law of War', p. 37.

62 See Chapter 6.

63 Stone, *Legal Controls of International Conflict*, p. 352 (footnote omitted): 'the latter [*Kriegsmanier*, or "custom of war"] binding on a belligerent in ordinary circumstances, the former [*Kriegsräson*] overruling it in special circumstances, where necessary either for escaping military danger, or for attaining military success. It had the effect of reducing the Hague Regulations to merely moral authority.'

Kriegsräson is unacceptable because it purports to justify militarily necessary conduct even where positive IHL has already extinguished all indifferent counter-liberties. Rejecting *Kriegsräson* means rejecting the idea that material military necessity somehow rights or repairs the unlawfulness of such conduct. Insofar as they are variations of *Kriegsräson*, self-preservation,[64] self-defence[65] and impracticality[66] pleas are to be rejected for the same reason.

8.4.2.1 Consistency with Military Necessity as Conclusive Lawfulness, All Things Considered

It can be tempting for some – particularly those with consequentialist leanings to whom the adage 'the end justifies the means' rings true – to regard military necessity as a justification. The idea that a belligerent act is materially necessary for a legitimate military purpose tends to strengthen the idea that the act is, at least prima facie, legitimate as well.[67] Embracing these ideas is only one small step away from asserting that a given act's military necessity rights or repairs its illegality, even where such illegality is otherwise established in light of unqualified rules of positive IHL. What is crucial here, however, is the fact that the framers have already taken this step and extinguished counter-liberties for the law's addressees. Purporting to reinsert these liberties amounts to taking the same step *anew*, essentially negating the law's existence as an autonomous and previously agreed-upon body of binding norms.[68]

[64] Ibid, pp. 352–53. But see Dunbar, 'Military Necessity in War Crimes Trials', at 443; Schwarzenberger, *International Law as Applied by Courts and Tribunals* (vol. II), p. 136; Walzer, *Just and Unjust Wars*, p. 305; Cohen, 'Morality and the Laws of War', pp. 76–78; Dinstein, 'Military Necessity' (2nd edn 2009), paras 10–11.

[65] *Nuclear Weapons*, paras 95–96. But see ibid, *Higgins Dissenting Opinion*, paras 28–29; ibid, *Weeramantry Dissenting Opinion*, at 513–20; Luigi Condorelli, 'Le droit international humanitaire, ou l'exploration par la cour d'une terra à peu près incognita pour elle' in Boisson de Chazournes and Sands (eds), *International Law, the International Court of Justice and Nuclear Weapons* 229, pp. 244–45; Greenwood, '*Jus ad Bellum* and *Jus in Bello*', p. 264; Gardam, 'Necessity and Proportionality', p. 292; Marcelo G Kohen, 'The Notion of "State Survival" in International Law' in Boisson de Chazournes and Sands (eds), *International Law, the International Court of Justice and Nuclear Weapons* 293, p. 310; MN Hayashi, 'Martens Clause and Military Necessity', pp. 143–44; Dinstein, *Conduct of Hostilities* (2nd edn), pp. 85–86; Solis, *Law of Armed Conflict*, p. 269; Greenwood, 'Historical Development', pp. 36–37.

[66] McCoubrey, 'Modern Doctrine of Military Necessity', at 237.

[67] See Chapter 4.

[68] In the context of the so-called 'war on terror' championed by the Bush administration, controversial arguments were advanced with a view to effectively excepting, justifying

As noted earlier, *Kriegsräson* found increasing following in Germany during the late-nineteenth century and remained influential among German military and international lawyers until the end of World War II. Since its unambiguous rejection in post-World War II war crimes trials, *Kriegsräson* has been thoroughly discredited.[69] Most authorities now agree that juridical military necessity has no place outside the confines of specific exceptional clauses.[70]

8.4.2.2 Self-Preservation

Some commentators who reject *Kriegsräson* still defend a form of juridical military necessity that in certain circumstances goes beyond express exceptional clauses. At first sight, James Wilford Garner may come across as one of them. He stated:

> It must be admitted that within reasonable limits this much criticized theory [i.e., *Kriegsräson*] is legally defensible; that is to say, a belligerent is justified in disregarding a rule of war law whenever conformity to the rule would involve his destruction.[71]

Upon closer reading, however, it becomes apparent that Garner's support for self-preservation was more reserved.[72] Brandt is another:

> It is conceivable that ideal rules of war would include one rule to the effect that anything is allowable, if necessary to prevent absolute catastrophe. As Oppenheim remarks, it may be that if the basic values of society are threatened nations are possibly released from all the restrictions in order to do what 'they deem to be decisive for the ultimate vindication of the law of nations'.[73]

It is in Stone that we find self-preservation's perhaps most forceful advocate. In his view, military necessity does – or should, at any rate – entitle a state at war to depart from its duties under international law on

and/or excusing torture despite its unqualified prohibition under international law. Alberto Gonzales et al., White House Press Briefing, 22 June 2004; Henry, *Principe de nécessité militaire*, pp. 411–23. But see Scott Horton, '*Kriegsraison* or Military Necessity? The Bush Administration's Wilhelmine Attitude towards the Conduct of War' (2006) 30 *Fordham International Law Journal* 576.

69 See Chapter 1.

70 Ibid.

71 James Wilford Garner, *International Law and the World War*, 2 vols. (New York: Longmans, Green and Co., 1920), vol. II, pp. 196–97.

72 Ibid, pp. 193–95, 197.

73 Brandt, 'Utilitarianism', at 147 n.3 (citing Lauterpacht (ed), *Oppenheim's International Law* (7th edn), p. 351).

account of self-preservation.[74] Stone clearly accepted the criticism of what he called military necessity in 'such an extended German sense'.[75] His doubts concerned whether this criticism, while valid in relation to *Kriegsräson*, could be defensibly construed as excluding self-preservation:

> The central point of criticism of the German doctrine is undoubtedly the extended notion of 'necessity' held thus to justify the overriding of the law of war, a notion covering not merely the needs of military survival, but also lesser dangers, and even the needs of positive military success . . . This reasoning, however, would forbid departure from the rules of war-law even in face of the direst needs of survival. Yet it remains ground common to British, American, French, Italian and other publicists, as well as German, that a State is privileged, in title of self-preservation, to violate its ordinary duties under international law, even towards States with which it is at peace; and may also itself determine when its self-preservation is involved. Neither practice nor the literature explain satisfactorily how the privilege based on self-preservation in time of peace can be denied to States at war. If, as the Writer believes, the German doctrine is properly condemned, a frank review of the meaning of the self-preservation doctrine remains all the more urgent.[76]

Contrast Stone's position with N. C. H. Dunbar's. Dunbar urged that:

> [T]he phrase 'necessity in self-preservation' is more properly employed to describe a danger or emergency of such proportions as to threaten immediately the vital interests, and, perhaps, the very existence, of the state itself. Military necessity should be confined to the plight in which armed forces may find themselves under stress of active warfare.[77]

Be that as it may, self-preservation has no place in positive IHL as long as it is understood merely as a more radical version of *Kriegsräson*.[78]

[74] Stone, *Legal Controls of International Conflict*, pp. 352–53.

[75] Ibid, p. 352.

[76] Ibid, pp. 352–53. Footnotes omitted.

[77] Dunbar, 'Military Necessity in War Crimes Trials', at 443. See also Stone's response to Dunbar's criticism (Stone, *Legal Controls of International Conflict*, p. 353 n.24).

[78] The Department of Defense manual also observes: 'It is . . . unlawful for a commander to kill enemy prisoners in the force's custody on grounds of self-preservation.' Office of General Counsel, *Law of War Manual*, p. 525. Some commentators even question whether self-preservation should be discussed alongside justificatory military necessity in the first place. Schwarzenberger, *International Law as Applied by Courts and Tribunals* (vol. II), p. 136; Walzer, *Just and Unjust Wars*, p. 305; Cohen, 'Morality and the Laws of War', pp. 76–78; Dinstein, 'Military Necessity' (2nd edn 2009), paras 10–11; Kolb, 'La nécessité militaire', pp. 168, 170; Gabriella Venturini, 'Necessity in the Law of Armed Conflict and International Criminal Law' (2010) 41 *Netherlands Yearbook of International Law* 45, at 51.

This conclusion could change in two ways. One is where self-preservation in IHL might somehow be deemed normatively non-indifferent or, though indifferent, backed up with strong pressure or policy. There is no indication in the law that this is the case.

The other possibility is where self-preservation might constitute an established right outside of IHL, e.g., in *jus ad bellum*. *Nuclear Weapons* is particularly relevant here. In that opinion, the ICJ observed that the threat or use of nuclear weapons would *generally* be contrary to IHL.[79] The opinion goes on to state that the court 'cannot lose sight of the fundamental right of every State to survival, and thus its right to resort to self-defence ... when its survival is at stake'.[80] The court held, by seven votes to seven, with the President casting the deciding vote, that it 'cannot conclude definitively whether the threat or use of nuclear weapons would be lawful or unlawful in an extreme circumstance of self-defence, in which the very survival of a State would be at stake'.[81]

One may question whether the ICJ really acknowledged self-preservation as a rule of *jus ad bellum*.[82] If it were a valid norm, however, we might have a norm conflict of a frustrating kind. On the one hand, positive IHL imposes an unqualified duty to refrain from launching an indiscriminate attack on cities.[83] This duty, on the other hand, might frustrate the *ex hypothesi* right of self-preservation under *jus ad bellum* sanctioning a counter-liberty to launch such an attack in extreme cases.

As noted earlier, the relationship between *jus ad bellum* and *jus in bello* is not within this book's ambit.[84] The debate continues unabated,[85]

[79] *Nuclear Weapons*, para. 105(2)(E).
[80] Ibid, para. 96.
[81] Ibid, para. 105(2)(E). See also ibid, para. 96.
[82] Kohen, 'Notion of "State Survival"', p. 293.
[83] Henckaerts and Doswald-Beck, *Customary International Humanitarian Law* (vol. I), pp. 37–38.
[84] See Chapter 4.
[85] *Nuclear Weapons Higgins Dissenting Opinion*, para. 29; ibid, *Weeramantry Dissenting Opinion*, pp. 513–20; ibid, *Separate Opinion of Judge Ranjeva*, p. 294, pp. 301–02; Dinstein, *Conduct of Hostilities* (2nd edn), pp. 85–86; Greenwood, '*Jus ad Bellum* and *Jus in Bello*', pp. 249–50, 264; MN Hayashi, 'Martens Clause and Military Necessity', pp. 143–44; Condorelli, 'Le droit international humanitaire', pp. 244–45; Gardam, 'Necessity and Proportionality', p. 292; Kohen, 'Notion of "State Survival"', p. 310; Greenwood, 'Historical Development', pp. 36–37; Kolb and R. Hyde, *International Law of Armed Conflict*, pp. 21–28; Solis, *Law of Armed Conflict*, p. 269; Keiichiro Okimoto, *The Distinction and Relationship between* Jus ad Bellum *and* Jus in Bello (Oxford and Portland: Hart Publishing, 2011); Moussa, 'Nuclear Weapons and the Separation of *Jus ad Bellum* and *Jus in Bello*'.

despite the fairly uniform insistence among IHL specialists that the two fields remain separate. This separation would mean that lawful acts of self-defence under *jus ad bellum* ought not right or repair IHL violations (or vice versa);[86] and, conversely, that acts in breach of *jus ad bellum* ought not wrong or vitiate IHL-compliant behaviour (or vice versa). The enduring salience of this issue reveals the intractable character of norm conflicts between independently valid rules that belong respectively to two unintegrated fields of international law.[87]

8.4.2.3 Material Impossibility and Impracticality

According to Hilaire McCoubrey, Jean Pictet espoused a version of military necessity whereby non-compliance with a positive IHL rule would be tolerated in the event of genuine material impossibility. In McCoubrey's words:

> The second position … of military necessity appears to be reflected [into a] much more limiting model advanced by Jean Pictet … Here the doctrine of military necessity is reduced to an admission that in certain cases it may be 'impossible' to comply with legal norms in which case a 'defence' in respect of *prima facie* unlawful action will arise.[88]

It is doubtful, however, whether Pictet actually regarded 'genuine material impossibility' as a variant of juridical military necessity. All Pictet said is this:

> [T]here is an implicit clause in any law to the effect that no one is obliged to do what is impossible. This remains implicit because if it were stated openly the risks of abusive and tendentious interpretations would be too great … Thus, when we speak of what is 'impossible' we must refer only to a genuine material impossibility.[89]

Pictet's treatment of genuine material impossibility as an implicit clause stands in stark contrast to his thorough rejection of implicit military necessity clauses: 'We should emphasize that there is *no express*

[86] *Prosecutor v Nikola Šainović et al.*, Case No. IT-05-87-A, *Judgment*, 23 January 2014, para. 1662.

[87] Lindroos, 'Addressing Norm Conflicts in a Fragmented Legal Order', at 42, 44; Milanović, 'Norm Conflict Perspective', at 476, 482.

[88] McCoubrey, 'Modern Doctrine of Military Necessity', at 220 (footnotes omitted). See also Hilaire McCoubrey, *International Humanitarian Law: Modern Developments in the Limitation of Warfare*, 2nd edn (Aldershot and Brookfield: Ashgate, 1998), pp. 303–04.

[89] Jean Pictet, *Development and Principles of International Humanitarian Law* (Dordrecht, Boston and Manchester: Martinus Nijhoff, 1985), p. 88.

or implicit clause in the law of war giving priority to military necessity – otherwise there would be no such thing as the law of war!'[90] McCoubrey himself suggested that, for the purposes of military necessity, 'necessity connotes an immediate and overwhelming circumstance in military action, which renders [strict] compliance, upon rational [analysis], impractical rather than "impossible"'.[91]

There may be certain situations in which it is impractical to comply with unqualified IHL obligations. The mere fact that these situations exist, however, does nothing to change the fact that unqualified IHL rules exclude pleas emanating from indifferent permissions. In fact, McCoubrey's unfortunate allusion to impracticality conceals an idea that might otherwise deserve serious consideration. That idea would not entail a norm contradiction between an unqualified IHL rule and a counter-liberty on account of impracticality. Rather, it would entail a full conflict between the rule and a humanitarian counter-imperative.[92]

8.4.3 Humanitätsräson

Let us now consider the exclusionary effects unqualified IHL rules have vis-à-vis humanity's indifferent permissions. *Humanitätsräson* asserts that, although IHL accounts for humanity, it cannot be construed in a manner that deprives the belligerent of its liberty to act humanely. Where a positive IHL rule is formulated without an express humanitarian exception, it merely shows that the rule's framers considered deviation from its prescriptions generally inhumane. Neither the law nor its framers can be deemed to have foreseen all future events and legislated for them. Consequently, deviation that is in fact humane takes precedence over any provisions of the law that prescribe contrary action. 'Necessities of humanity override rules of war', in other words.

Humanitätsräson is irreparably flawed for exactly the same reason *Kriegsräson* is irreparably flawed. Holding otherwise would amount to accepting the idea that, like *Kriegsräson*, acting as permitted by humanity somehow rights or repairs the act's unlawfulness. The framers of

[90] Ibid (emphasis added).

[91] McCoubrey, 'Modern Doctrine of Military Necessity', at 237. McCoubrey went on to qualify his position (ibid): 'Impractical is a term here carefully chosen, it is by no means intended to imply the concession to tactical and strategic convenience which is implicit in the maxim *kriegsrason geht vor kriegsmanier*'.

[92] See below.

unqualified IHL rules have already accounted for humanity's indifferent considerations by excluding all counter-liberties emanating from them. Reinserting these liberties is tantamount to relegislating IHL to suit the inserter's circumstances.

8.4.3.1 Consistency with Humanity's Indifferent Permissions as Conclusive Lawfulness, All Things Considered

Humanitätsräson might appeal to those for whom the end does (or should) justify the means. If anything, *Humanitätsräson*'s case would be stronger than *Kriegsräson*'s. The end sought is not some legitimate belligerent purpose, but a humanitarian one. Who can object to that?

Gabriella Blum asserts that a humanitarian necessity defence should be available to justify deviations even from unqualified prohibitions of positive IHL. These prohibitions include, for example, Articles 3 (hostage taking), 8 (renunciation of rights), 27 (acts and threats of violence), 28 (human shields) and 51 (forced participation in military operations) of Geneva Convention IV; and Article 51(7) (human shields) of Additional Protocol I.[93] Blum also advocates this defence for the absolute IHL prohibitions against torture[94]; deliberate, indiscriminate or excessively injurious attacks on civilians; and the use of poisonous weapons.[95] Blum goes on to state: '[A]ssassinations of rogue leaders ... and, in some extreme cases, even the deliberate killing of civilians or combatants who are *hors de combat*, might be justified under a humanitarian necessity justification, provided they meet all the relevant conditions'.[96] The conditions are:

1. That the conduct in question was designed to minimise harm to individuals other than the defendant's compatriots;[97]
2. That the person could reasonably expect that his or her action would be effective as the direct cause of minimising the harm;[98] and
3. That there were no less harmful alternatives under the circumstances to produce a similar humanitarian outcome.[99]

[93] Blum, 'Laws of War and the "Lesser Evil"', at 16 (citing *Adalah et al.*). See also *Adalah et al.*, paras 20–23.
[94] Blum, 'Laws of War and the "Lesser Evil"', at 20.
[95] Ibid, at 25.
[96] Ibid, at 67.
[97] Ibid, at 63, 67.
[98] Ibid, at 64–65, 67.
[99] Ibid, at 66–67.

As these requirements indicate, and Blum freely admits, hers is a 'lesser-evil' or 'greater good' defence.[100] Diane A. Desierto mounts a convincing rebuttal of Blum's theory.[101] Desierto finds Blum's strict utilitarian metric plainly incompatible with the distinct institutional design and purposes of *jus in bello*.[102] Nor does Blum sufficiently describe the process of determining 'humanitarian' intentions for breaking *jus in bello* obligations during armed conflicts.[103] She fails to show why the current use of military necessity as both a *legislative policy* (i.e., what this book calls normative military necessity) and a *legislated norm* (similarly, juridical military necessity) in *jus in bello* is inadequate for her supposedly 'humanitarian' purposes.[104] Desierto concludes that, with her deontological, consequentialist and institutional reasons for modern *jus in bello*'s alleged deficiencies, Blum effectively sets up straw arguments nowhere in accord with the law's actual *legal* reasoning.[105]

Suffice it to note here that *Humanitätsräson* is no more persuasive for well-meaning humanitarians than *Kriegsräson* is for efficiency-maximising soldiers. Both *Humanitätsräson* and *Kriegsräson* hinge the lawfulness of given belligerent conduct on the legitimacy of its goal (net gain in humanity; net gain in military success). They are both prepared to let consequentialist considerations trump all contrary side-constraints.[106] In short, they both engage in exactly the same process of reasoning.

In fairness, Blum is neither alone nor the first to put forth humanity-driven consequentialism. Let us consider four examples where analogous views have been advanced. They are: misusing the Red Cross emblem in bloodless hostage rescue operations; killing persons placed *hors de combat* out of mercy; forcibly preventing civilians from leaving besieged localities with a view to expediting capitulation; and fighting shorter wars without moderation, rather than fighting longer wars with moderation.

8.4.3.2 Misusing the Red Cross Emblem in Bloodless Hostage Rescue Operations

On 2 July 2008,[107] Colombia carried out a daring operation codenamed 'Operation Jaque' in which it freed fifteen hostages held by the Fuerzas

[100] Ibid, at 35.
[101] Desierto, *Necessity and National Emergency Clauses*, pp. 333–47.
[102] Ibid, p. 343.
[103] Ibid.
[104] Ibid
[105] Ibid, p. 344.
[106] See Chapter 4.
[107] Tim Padgett, 'Colombia's Stunning Hostage Rescue', *Time*, 2 July 2008.

Armadas Revolucionarias de Colombia (FARC). Relevant facts are as follows.[108] Prior to the rescue, Colombia's military intelligence had infiltrated senior FARC leadership. Infiltrators successfully induced the guerrillas into arranging what they believed was a relocation of Ingrid Betancourt and fourteen other hostages. Colombian military agents, disguised as journalists and members of a fictitious humanitarian organisation, arrived at the designated collection point in two helicopters and brought the hostages on board. Shortly after take-off, two FARC members who boarded the helicopter alongside their hostages were overpowered by the Colombian agents.

In the aftermath, it was reported that at least one of the Colombian agents who arrived at the collection site wore a bib with the ICRC symbol printed on it, a claim initially denied by the Colombian authorities.[109] However, Álvaro Uribe, Colombia's then president, soon confirmed that one nervous soldier did so against orders and conveyed his government's apologies to the ICRC.[110] Video footage suggesting deliberate misuse of the emblem surfaced several weeks later, prompting the ICRC to express 'serious concern'.[111]

Under both conventional[112] and customary[113] law, misusing the Red Cross emblem has long been the subject of an unqualified prohibition. At stake here is the humanitarian demand that Red Cross workers be able to discharge their functions without hindrance or suspicion. It does not matter whether misusing the emblem can simultaneously be consistent with humanity's other indifferent permissions. It might be felt that the misuse in this particular case was harmless – if also conducive to the

108 'Colombia Hostage Betancourt Freed', BBC News, 3 July 2008; 'Colombia Tricks Rebels into Freeing Hostages', MSNBC, 3 July 2008; Simon Romero, 'Colombia Plucks Hostages from Rebels' Grasp', *The New York Times*, 3 July 2008.

109 Karl Penhaul, 'Colombian Military Used Red Cross Emblem in Rescue', CNN, 15 July 2008.

110 International Committee of the Red Cross, 'Colombia: ICRC Underlines Importance of Respect for Red Cross Emblem', News Release 08/129, 16 July 2008; 'Betancourt Rescuer Wore Red Cross', BBC News, 17 July 2008; 'Colombian Soldier Wore Red Cross Logo in Hostage Rescue', *The New York Times*, 17 July 2008.

111 International Committee of the Red Cross, 'Colombia: ICRC Deplores Improper Use of Red Cross Emblem', News Release 08/139, 6 August 2008.

112 Articles 39, 44, 53, 54, Geneva Convention I; Articles 41, 44, 45, Geneva Convention II; Article 38(1), Additional Protocol I; Article 12, Additional Protocol II; Articles 24, 28, Wounded and Sick Convention (1929); Article 23(f), Hague Regulations (1907); Articles 27, 28, Wounded and Sick Convention (1906); Article 23(f), Hague Regulations (1899).

113 Henckaerts and Doswald-Beck, *Customary International Humanitarian Law* (vol. I), pp. 207–09.

success of the operation's humanitarian ends[114] – and, consequently, that Colombia was at liberty to resort to it.[115] One might therefore be tempted to argue that the use of the Red Cross emblem in Operation Jaque should be deemed lawful, all things considered, despite its unqualified prohibition under positive IHL. These arguments would be immaterial because the rule's framers have extinguished such counter-liberties and excluded pleas emanating from them.

8.4.3.3 'Mercy Killing'

The next three examples are even more contentious, as it becomes increasingly less clear whether the conduct in question can be deemed humane to begin with. It is unclear whether humanity in its normative sense permits or even tolerates it. The fact remains, however, that humanity's indifferent permission has been invoked by those seeking to release themselves from their unqualified IHL obligation on the matter.

On 21 May 2004, Captain Rogelio 'Roger' Maynulet killed Karim Hassan in central Iraq.[116] While on patrol in Kufa, Maynulet's tank company chased and fired at a car thought to be carrying militants loyal to Muqtada Sadr. One passenger was killed immediately, while Hassan, who was driving the car, was badly injured. Maynulet then fatally shot Hassan. Maynulet was tried before a US court-martial sitting in Germany. The prosecution alleged that Maynulet, who had been trained in first aid, 'played God' by 'prescrib[ing] two bullets. He did not call his superiors for guidance, didn't consult with his medic'. Maynulet reportedly told a witness that Hassan 'had half his brain hanging out, there was nothing more that could be done for him'. In court, Maynulet argued that he shot the man to 'put him out of his misery'. The court martial found Maynulet guilty of assault with intent to commit manslaughter.

When viewed in the manner most favourable to Maynulet, the evidence might reveal a situation where hastening Hassan's death without

[114] Betancourt publicly praised the operation's bloodless success. 'Betancourt Rescue in Colombia: Israeli Connection', Ynet, 4 July 2008.

[115] Operation Jaque did, however, involve what might constitute a perfidious capture. John C Dehn, 'Permissible Perfidy? Analysing the Colombian Hostage Rescue, the Capture of Rebel Leaders and the World's Reaction' (2008) 6 *Journal of International Criminal Justice* 627, at 632–33, 644. See also Dinstein, *Conduct of Hostilities* (2nd edn), p. 229. Perfidy can arguably be contrary to humanity in general, if confidence in the rules protecting victims, relief personnel and the like were to be eroded. UK Defence Ministry, *Joint Service Manual*, p. 60; Dehn, 'Permissible Perfidy?', at 632–33.

[116] 'U.S. Army Captain Is Found Guilty in Shooting Death of Wounded Iraqi', Stars and Stripes, 31 March 2005; 'US Captain Guilty of Iraq Killing', BBC News, 31 March 2005.

additional pain was not inhumane or, in any event, no more inhumane than leaving him for dead without medical intervention such as the administration of morphine.

The idea that humanity should permit certain instances of mercy killing is not new. Sidgwick noted:

> In the Declaration of St. Petersburg, in 1868, the European powers laid down that it would be 'contrary to the laws of humanity to employ arms which render death inevitable'. I do not understand the principle on which this is laid down, since death is the most effectual kind of disablement; and if the process that made it inevitable also made dying more rapid, without making it more painful, the sufferings of a battlefield would be materially diminished.[117]

One senses a subtle misconstrual here. Of concern to the St. Petersburg Declaration was, inter alia, an act of the kind 'making the death of already disabled men inevitable'. Sidgwick instead considered 'making the death that is already inevitable more rapid and without increased pain'. The position he apparently asserted is nevertheless sufficiently clear. If death is already inevitable – for example, because the person in question is mortally wounded and no medical services would be available in time – then hastening his or her death without aggravating pain might be humane in certain circumstances. Doing so in the right circumstances would or should be indifferently permitted by humanity.

Such logic is unconvincing as a ground for seeking a release from the unqualified IHL prohibition against killing persons placed *hors de combat*.[118] Sidgwick's rejoinder, insofar as it can be understood as being directed at this prohibition, rather than (misguidedly) at the St. Petersburg Declaration, mirrors humanity's indifferent counter-liberty that is accounted for and extinguished by the rule in question. Hassan's killing was a clear breach of that prohibition.

8.4.3.4 Forcibly Preventing Civilians from Leaving Besieged Localities

In 1941, the German forces besieging Leningrad were ordered to prevent civilians from leaving the city by firing upon them.[119] Military Tribunal

[117] Sidgwick, *Elements of Politics*, p. 255 n.1. See also Taylor, *Nuremberg and Vietnam*, p. 36.
[118] Article 41, Additional Protocol I.
[119] 'Letter of Transmittal and, "Reichenau Order", of 10 October 1941, Distributed by XXVIII Army Corps of the 18th Army, Commanded by Defendant von Kuechler' in *Trials of War Criminals before the Nuremberg Military Tribunals under Control Council*

V, which tried Field Marshal Wilhelm von Leeb, noted in its judgment that the German artillery did fire upon civilian residents of Leningrad who were attempting to flee the siege.[120]

It was once considered lawful for the besieging party to deny exit to civilians trapped in the besieged locality.[121] Today, there is an unqualified IHL prohibition against starving civilians as a method of warfare.[122] A fortiori, it is unqualifiedly prohibited to prevent civilians from leaving besieged localities and receiving humanitarian relief.[123] Sean Watts explains:

> In light of the aforementioned prohibition on starvation of civilian populations, it seems clear that neither a besieging nor a besieged force may compel civilians to remain in a besieged area that lacks adequate food and water ... At a minimum, Parties engaged in siege are obliged to arrange for removal of starving civilian populations from besieged areas to the extent they are unable or unwilling to supply them with adequate food and water in the besieged area.[124]

This ban accounts for, and sets aside, any counter-liberty that may otherwise emanate from indifferent considerations. The rule precludes all indifference pleas that purport to except, justify or excuse specific

Law No. 10, 15 vols. (Washington, DC: United States Government Printing Office, 1951), vol. X, 1211, at 1212.

120 *High Command*, at 563.

121 Article 18, Lieber Code; Roxburgh (ed), *Oppenheim's International Law* (3rd edn), p. 219; *High Command*, at 563 (citing Charles Cheney Hyde, *International Law Chiefly as Interpreted and Applied by the United States*, 2nd rev. edn, 3 vols. (Boston: Little, Brown, 1945), vol. III, pp. 1802–03); US Department of the Army, *Law of Land Warfare*, p. 20.

122 Of interest here is this unqualified ban during siege. We are not concerned with Article 54(5) of Additional Protocol I, which exceptionally authorises scorching earth even if it also entails starving civilians where such a tactic is 'required by imperative military necessity'. Article 54(5), Additional Protocol I.

123 Article 70(1), Additional Protocol I. See also Charles A Allen, 'Civilian Starvation and Relief during Armed Conflict: The Modern Humanitarian Law' (1989) 19 *Georgia Journal of International and Comparative Law* 1; Sean Watts, 'Under Siege: International Humanitarian Law and Security Council Practice Concerning Urban Siege Operations' (2014) *Harvard Law School Brookings Project on Law and Security: Counterterrorism and Humanitarian Engagement Project*, at 70; UK Defence Ministry, *Joint Service Manual*, pp. 87–88, 220–21. But see Yoram Dinstein, 'The Right to Humanitarian Assistance' (2000) 53 *Naval War College Review* 77, at 84.

124 S Watts, 'Under Siege', at 16. See also Benvenisti, 'Human Dignity in Combat', at 101–02; Office of General Counsel, *Law of War Manual*, pp. 290–91; UN Security Council Resolution 2139 (2014), 22 February 2014, paras 4–6.

instances of forcibly preventing civilians from fleeing a besieged locality.[125]

Traditional justifications for this tactic would run as follows.[126] The purpose of a siege is to compel the surrender of an opponent holed up in a locality. Sieges involve, among other things, cutting off supplies and encouraging those trapped inside to exert pressure upon the adversary to surrender. Surrender would arguably be hastened if civilians were denied exit and made increasingly desperate.[127] Shooting fleeing civilians to force them back into the besieged locality may therefore be deemed consistent with military necessity for the besieging party.[128] This is admittedly a tactic that involves brutalising the locality's civilian residents. All things considered, however, forcibly denying civilians exit should be deemed no more brutal than allowing humanitarian relief and/or civilian flights, because the former means shortening the sieges whereas the latter means lengthening it.

Even if, *arguendo*, it were conceded that forcibly trapping civilians in a siege might be considered humane in the sense just described, and even if, *arguendo*, it were conceded that humanity might indifferently permit such conduct, pleas on this ground would still be inadmissible in support of specific instances where the tactic is used.

Furthermore, the act's alleged consistency with humanity is itself suspect. One may agree that shorter sieges would generally be more humane than longer ones, all else being equal.[129] Similarly, one may agree that sieges that do not involve the forcible denial of civilian flight or humanitarian relief (let us call such sieges 'open' sieges) would be considered more humane than those involving such denial ('sealed'

[125] Yoram Dinstein, 'Siege Warfare and the Starvation of Civilians' in Delissen and Tanja (eds), *Humanitarian Law of Armed Conflict* 145, p. 151: 'Compelling humanitarian considerations demands that, if civilians attempt to evacuate an invested town, they must not be precluded by the besieging force from crossing the lines'.

[126] Roxburgh (ed), *Oppenheim's International Law* (3rd edn), pp. 218–19; *High Command*, at 563 (citing CC Hyde, *International Law Chiefly as Interpreted and Applied by the United States*, pp. 1802–03); Greenspan, *Modern Law of Land Warfare*, pp. 350–51.

[127] This is a perception doubtless reinforced by the historical fact that the defenders of a besieged locality were held responsible for the plight of its residents. Matthew Waxman, 'Siegecraft and Surrender: The Law and Strategy of Cities as Targets' (1998) 39 *Virginia Journal of International Law* 353, at 363–64, 397–98.

[128] Dinstein, 'Siege Warfare and the Starvation of Civilians', at 146.

[129] Waxman describes how offers of surrender immunities and threats of post-assault sacking (in the event that the besieged declines that offer) were combined in medieval European siege warfare to great effect. Waxman, 'Siegecraft and Surrender', at 355–66.

sieges), all else being equal. From these stipulations, one may derive four types of sieges, each having one of the following characteristics: (a) short and sealed; (b) short and open; (c) long and sealed; and (d) long and open. Identifying these siege types enables us to group them into six sets of comparisons for the purpose of assessing their degrees of humanity. The six sets are:

- Comparison 1: Short and sealed vs. short and open;
- Comparison 2: Long and sealed vs. long and open;
- Comparison 3: Sealed and short vs. sealed and long;
- Comparison 4: Open and short vs. open and long;
- Comparison 5: Short and open vs. long and sealed; and
- Comparison 6: Short and sealed vs. long and open.

Holding the shortness of the two siege types equal (comparison 1) yields the result that one type that is open would be deemed more humane than the other that is sealed. Of the two siege types that are comparably long (comparison 2), it is clear that the type that is open would be more humane than the type that is sealed. If sealed (comparison 3), the short siege type would tend to generate greater humanity than the long type. For those inside a locality under open siege (comparison 4), it would be more humane if the siege lasted shorter rather than longer. These four comparisons merely reiterate and confirm our initial stipulations.

If we were to compare one siege type that is short and open with another siege type that is long and sealed (comparison 5), the former would clearly be more humane than the latter. When comparing a siege type that is short and sealed on the one hand, and a siege type that is long and open on the other (comparison 6), however, we may not so readily come to any conclusion as to which one would tend to be more humane than the other.

The traditional argument for forcibly preventing civilian flights and denying humanitarian relief revolves around a particular take on comparison 6. On this view, a siege type that is sealed yet short would yield greater net humanity than a siege type that is open yet long. The veracity of this claim rests on three assumptions. First, sealed sieges tend to be short.[130] Second, opening sieges typically lengthens them. Third,

[130] Mudge, 'Starvation as a Means of Warfare', at 266–68; Rosenblad, 'Starvation as a Method of Warfare', at 256.

shortening sieges would bring greater net humanity than reducing their brutality, all things considered. However, none of these assumptions is self-evidently true, or even intuitively sound. The greater net humanity claimed is undermined by the eminent possibility that sealed sieges can be long, open sieges can be short, and reducing brutality in a siege may very well bring greater net humanity than shortening it. Moreover, sealing or opening a siege is up to the besieging party[131] – also the party more likely to assert the lawfulness of sealed sieges – but shortening or lengthening a siege is not.[132]

8.4.3.5 Implementing von Moltke's 'Greatest Kindness'

Helmuth von Moltke's observation that '[t]he greatest kindness in war is to bring it to a speedy conclusion'[133] is rejected for the same reason. In an 1880 letter, he argued:

> It should be allowable with that view to employ all methods save those which are absolutely objectionable ('dazu müssen alle nicht geradezu verwerfliche Mittel freistehen'). I can by no means profess agreement with the Declaration of St. Petersburg when it asserts that 'the weakening of the military forces of the enemy' is the only lawful procedure in war. No, you must attack all the resources of the enemy's Government: its finances, its railways, its stores, and even its prestige. Thus energetically, and yet with a moderation previously unknown, was the late war against France conducted. The issue of the campaign was decided in two months, and the fighting did not become embittered till a revolutionary Government, unfortunately for the country, prolonged the war for four more months.[134]

In von Moltke's view, 'you *must* attack all the resources of the enemy's Government'. His real assertion would best be understood as 'you *must be permitted* to attack all the resources of the enemy's Government'.

Similar sentiments have been expressed elsewhere. Article 29 of the Lieber Code notes: 'The more vigorously wars are pursued, the better it is

[131] Article 70, Additional Protocol I. See also Watts's discussion of Security Council Resolution 2139. S Watts, 'Under Siege', at 20–22.

[132] As the Duke of Alva was to learn towards the end of his increasingly frustrated campaign in the Low Countries. Waxman, 'Siegecraft and Surrender', at 366–68.

[133] 'Letter from von Moltke to Bluntschli' in Thomas Erskine Holland, *Letters to 'The Times' upon War and Neutrality (1881–1920)*, 3rd edn (London: Longmans, Green and Co., 1921) 23, p. 25.

[134] Ibid.

for humanity. Sharp wars are brief'.[135] Garner quoted Paul von Hindenburg as saying:

> [o]ne cannot . . . make war in a sentimental fashion. The more pitiless the conduct of the war, the more humane it is in reality, for it will run its course all the sooner. The war which of all wars is and must be the most humane is that which leads to peace with as little delay as possible.[136]

Similarly, in Best's words: 'Short wars, [Julius von Hartmann, a Prussian-born general] said – it was a common refrain in those years – were the most humane; whatever apparent severity finished a war quickly might in the long run appear to be the superior humanity'.[137]

More recently, Jeremy Rabkin observed: 'Perhaps, for example, lives would be saved, overall, by pursuing a speedy victory, even if doing so risks more casualties in the short run. Strict adherence to rules, if it prolonged the conflict and substantially increased the casualty count – let alone if it inhibited a democracy's war effort enough to give victory to a brutal tyrant – might then be judged *less* humane'.[138]

According to the St. Petersburg Declaration, it is illegitimate to seek any objects in war that are more or other than the weakening of the military force of the enemy.[139] Von Moltke's 'greatest kindness' purports to show, first, that seeking these other objects is capable of being humane – or, at any rate, no less humane than limiting oneself to the St. Petersburg Declaration's admonitions. Second, in specific cases where seeking objects other than the weakening of the military force of the

[135] Article 29, Lieber Code. See also Brandt, 'Utilitarianism', at 160–61; Walzer, *Just and Unjust Wars*, pp. 263–68; Waxman, 'Siegecraft and Surrender', at 366.

[136] Garner, *International Law and the World War* (vol. II), pp. 281–82, esp. 281 n.4.

[137] Best, *Humanity in Warfare*, p. 146 (footnote omitted). See also ibid, p. 146 n.23: 'This maxim was no doubt popularized by its appearance in Article 29 of Lieber's Code . . . That this was believed only by the "less cultured and less educated military men" (as Gustave Moynier had alleged) was rather indignantly denied by Britain's leading military expert on the Geneva Conventions, Colonel W. G. Macpherson, 1910, p. 607: "It is an opinion held by some of the most humane and thoughtful officers in the armies of all nations"; also by the Kaiser, who apparently thought "methods of terrorism" ("alone capable of affecting a people as degenerate as the French") would get the war over in two months'.

[138] Jeremy Rabkin, 'The Strange Pretensions of Contemporary Humanitarian Law' in Christopher A Ford and Amichai Cohen (eds), *Rethinking the Law of Armed Conflict in an Age of Terrorism* (Lanham, Boulder, New York, Toronto and Plymouth: Lexington, 2012) 41, at 56–57.

[139] Preamble, St. Petersburg Declaration.

enemy is indeed humane in the sense just described, 'it should be allowable' to seek them.

Even if this were all true, implementing von Moltke's 'greatest kindness' does nothing to justify deviations from unqualified IHL rules. Moreover, the very claim underlying this argument – namely, that with respect to a choice between a war that is short yet brutal and a war that is long yet humane, it is the former that embodies greater kindness – is questionable. As is the case with sieges, the defensibility of von Moltke's claim rests on the truth of three assumptions. First, brutal wars tend to be short. Second, humane wars tend to be long. Third, shortening wars tends to bring greater net humanity than reducing brutality in them.[140] These assumptions are all eminently contestable. Brutalising wars may not shorten them. Nor is it necessarily true that humanising wars lengthens them. Reducing brutality in wars may very well bring greater net humanity than shortening them.

Moreover, while it is possible for one warring party to control the brutality or humanity of its own actions, it is not possible for that party alone to control the length of its wars. In addition, being subjected to brutality may not undermine one's will or ability to continue fighting; in fact, it may have the opposite effect on that person's morale. During World War II, for instance, the news of the Malmédy massacre[141] 'undoubtedly stiffened the will of the American combatants'.[142] According to Hugh M. Cole, a military historian, '[t]here were American commanders who orally expressed the opinion that all SS troops should be killed on sight and there is some indication that in isolated cases express orders for this were given'.[143]

8.5 Admitting Non-indifference Pleas

Our discussion has so far concerned itself with how IHL norm-creation accounts for contradictions between imperatives and counter-liberties. This does not show, in one way or another, whether IHL norm-creation accounts for genuine norm conflicts. What happens to non-indifferent considerations that generate counter-imperatives?

[140] Best, *Humanity in Warfare*, pp. 145–46.
[141] See also Chapter 3.
[142] Cole, *Battle of the Bulge*, p. 261.
[143] Ibid, p. 264 (footnote omitted).

The inevitable conflict thesis asserts that unqualified IHL rules exclude pleas emanating from humanitarian demands and condemnations. That is so, because the framers of unqualified IHL rules have accounted for all contrary considerations of humanity and decided to extinguish all of them. The joint satisfaction thesis finds this assertion unpersuasive. As will be seen below, it is not inconceivable that humanitarian considerations that generate imperatives may escape exclusion when IHL framers posit unqualified rules. Consequently, these considerations may function as residual lawfulness-modifiers over and above such rules.

8.5.1 *Counter*-Kriegsräson

Before proceeding further, however, we need to dispose of one theory that purports to present military necessity in a non-indifferent light.

Let us call this notion 'counter-*Kriegsräson*'. This is a variant of *Kriegsräson*, because it is about military necessity's residual effects in relation to positive IHL rules. This is a 'counter' doctrine, because the alleged residual effects are restrictive rather than permissive. Counter-*Kriegsräson* is predicated on two perceptions of normative military necessity. First, some aspects of military necessity escape exclusion through the process of IHL norm-creation and consequently act as free-floating lawfulness modifiers. In other words, positive IHL does *not* fully account for military necessity. Second, those aspects of military necessity that remain unaccounted for are *not* indifferent. In the juridical context, they function as additional layers of normative restraint over conduct that is otherwise in conformity with positive IHL.

8.5.1.1 Lack of Military Necessity as Conclusive Unlawfulness, All Things Considered

As noted earlier, *Kriegsräson* is unacceptable because the framers of unqualified IHL rules have already accounted for military necessity. The vast majority of authorities who readily espouse this line of reasoning inexplicably go on to accept that, over and above positive IHL rules, military necessity outlaws unnecessary acts. The *US Navy Commander's Handbook* states:

> [The goal of military necessity] is to limit suffering and destruction to that which is necessary to achieve a valid military objective. Thus it prohibits

> the use of any kind or degree of force not required for the partial or complete submission of the enemy with a minimum expenditure of time, life, and physical resources.[144]

This position, especially the idea expressed in the second sentence above, also finds support among numerous commentators.[145] Of those, Nils Melzer is perhaps the most vocal and articulate.[146] His views on the matter appear to have evolved primarily in connection with the so-called 'capture rather than kill' debate, a long-running IHL theme that has regained currency in recent years.

In 2008, Melzer asserted that 'the principle of military necessity reduces the sum total of lawful military action from that which positive IHL does not prohibit *in abstracto* to that which is actually required *in concreto*'.[147] The ICRC's 2009 *Interpretive Guidance* on the notion of direct participation in hostilities – of which Melzer was the principal author – registers a subtle yet significant modification to this formulation:

[144] US Department of the Navy et al., *Commander's Handbook*, p. 5-2. See also UK Defence Ministry, *Joint Service Manual*, p. 22: '[T]he use of force which is not necessary is unlawful'. This formulation is curious, however, and, in honesty, quite mysterious. The *UK Joint Service Manual* continues to state that unnecessary use of force is unlawful 'since it involves wanton killing or destruction'. It is far from clear whether unnecessary use of force always involves wanton killing or destruction. According to Nils Melzer, Colombia's Manual of Operational Law says the same thing. Nils Melzer, 'Keeping the Balance between Military Necessity and Humanity: A Response to Four Critiques of the ICRC's Interpretive Guidance on the Notion of Direct Participation in Hostilities' (2010) 42 *New York University Journal of International Law and Politics* 831, at 910.

[145] Schwarzenberger, *International Law as Applied by Courts and Tribunals* (vol. II), p. 135; Taylor, *Nuremberg and Vietnam*, p. 34; Borch, 'Targeting After Kosovo', at 66; Greenwood, 'Historical Development', pp. 36–37, 38; Meyrowitz, 'Principle of Superfluous Injury or Unnecessary Suffering', at 107; Shue, 'Civilian Protection and Force Protection', pp. 136–37; Venturini, 'Necessity in the Law of Armed Conflict and International Criminal Law', at 48–50; Corn et al., *Operational Approach*, pp. 115–17; O'Connell, 'Historical Development and Legal Basis', p. 37; Ohlin, 'Duty to Capture', at 1298–306; Yves Sandoz, 'Land Warfare' in Clapham and Gaeta (eds), *Oxford Handbook of International Law in Armed Conflict* 91, at 93; Lawrence Hill-Cawthorne, 'The Role of Necessity in International Humanitarian and Human Rights Law' (2014) 47 *Israel Law Review* 225, at 231; Yishai Beer, 'Humanity Considerations Cannot Reduce War's Hazards Alone: Revitalizing the Concept of Military Necessity' (2015) 26 *European Journal of International Law* 801; Henry, *Principe de nécessité militaire*, pp. 685–86.

[146] Nils Melzer, 'Targeted Killing or Less Harmful Means? – Israel's High Court Judgment on Targeted Killing and the Restrictive Function of Military Necessity' (2006) 9 *Year-Book of International Humanitarian Law* 87, at 108–13.

[147] Melzer, *Targeted Killing*, p. 286.

> *In conjunction*, the principles of military necessity *and of humanity* reduce the sum total of permissible military action from that which IHL does not expressly prohibit to that which is actually necessary for the accomplishment of a legitimate military purpose in the prevailing circumstances.[148]

Melzer further retreated from his initial position when he subsequently noted: 'In conjunction, the principles of military necessity and of humanity *could be said* to reduce the sum total of permissible military action'.[149]

As will be seen below, adding the principle of humanity to the mix broadens Melzer's argumentative basis. For the time being, however, let us concentrate on how he invokes the principle of military necessity. Melzer's case is that, even on its own, this latter principle does, or could be said to, reduce that sum total:

> a direct attack against an otherwise legitimate military target constitutes a violation of IHL if that attack is not required for the submission of the enemy with a minimum expenditure of time, life and physical resources ... [T]he various provisions of IHL which permit a particular conduct in armed conflict constitute the result of 'equations' which already include the 'necessity-factor.' Since it is precisely this necessity-factor which makes that conduct lawful despite its deviation from the more restrictive rules applicable in peace time, the loss or absence of this factor necessarily changes the equation to the effect that the said conduct becomes unlawful ... The restrictive aspect of military necessity has significant practical consequences because it requires at least a basic assessment of military necessity in each case, and not only where positive IHL expressly so demands. While positive prohibitions may restrict the extent to which military necessity can justify military action, the absence of a prohibition does not liberate parties to the conflict from the fundamental constraints imposed by the principle of military necessity.[150]

[148] International Committee of the Red Cross, *Interpretive Guidance on the Notion of Direct Participation in Hostilities under International Humanitarian Law* (Geneva: International Committee of the Red Cross, 2009), p. 79 (emphasis added; footnote omitted).

[149] Nils Melzer, 'Targeted Killings in Operational Law Perspective' in Terry D Gill and Dieter Fleck (eds), *The Handbook of the International Law of Military Operations* (Oxford: Oxford University Press, 2010) 277, p. 300 (emphasis added; footnote omitted). See also Nils Melzer, 'The ICRC's Clarification Process on the Notion of Direct Participation in Hostilities under International Humanitarian Law' in Christian Tomuschat (ed), *The Right to Life* (Leiden: Martinus Nijhoff, 2010) 151, p. 162; Nils Melzer, 'The Principle of Distinction between Civilians and Combatants' in Clapham and Gaeta (eds), *Oxford Handbook of International Law in Armed Conflict* 296, p. 330.

[150] Melzer, *Targeted Killing*, p. 287 (footnotes omitted).

Melzer refers to 'particular conduct' without further qualification, rather than particular conduct *that entails evil.* It would appear that he asks himself whether materially unnecessary per se means unlawful and *not* – to be abundantly clear – whether materially unnecessary *evil* means unlawful.

In its strictly material sense, military necessity separates that belligerent conduct which is conducive to the accomplishment of its objective from that which is not.[151] It is also true that the act's material necessity or non-necessity involves its 'basic assessment ... in each case'.[152] As demonstrated earlier, however, an act's lack of material military necessity does not per se mean illegitimacy;[153] nor does this lack alone offer IHL framers reason to restrict or prohibit the act.[154] Thus, the mystery still remains: How, in Melzer's view, does the proposition 'an act is *materially unnecessary* in view of its basic military necessity assessment' transform itself into the proposition 'an act is *unlawful* in view of its basic military necessity assessment'?

Melzer's arguments open three lines of inquiry. First, he asserts that positive IHL rules are merely necessity-based derogations in armed conflict from their more stringent counterparts in peace time. Second, Melzer puts forward a classic counter-*Kriegsräson*. Third, he defends Pictet's duty to 'capture rather than kill'.

8.5.1.2 Positive IHL Rules as Necessity-Based Derogations from Peacetime Rules

Melzer's passage quoted above speaks of the 'more restrictive rules applicable in peace time' from which 'this necessity-factor ... makes [belligerent] conduct lawful despite its deviation'.[155] In essence, he treats every belligerent act as a deviation from its peacetime counterpart, and therefore every positive IHL rule as a necessity-driven derogation clause on account of armed conflict from its 'more restrictive' counterpart applicable in times of peace. From the latter rule, only that deviant instance which proves militarily necessary would, on a case-by-case basis, be eligible for derogation.

This is a highly idiosyncratic construal of IHL. One would rather think that IHL constitutes a stand-alone – albeit admittedly non-exclusive –

151 See Chapter 2.
152 Melzer, *Targeted Killing*, p. 287. See also Chapter 2.
153 See Chapter 5.
154 See Chapter 4.
155 Melzer, *Targeted Killing*, p. 287.

normative framework applicable in armed conflict by which a given belligerent act's compliance *with its own rules* can be intelligibly assessed.

Even if an act lacking in material military necessity did expose itself to those more restrictive peacetime rules and, even if the rules did render such an act unlawful, it is these latter rules, *not* the absence of material military necessity, that would make it so. By Melzer's own admission, with this 'necessity-factor' now removed, the act would be assessed by reference to the more restrictive peacetime rules.[156] Puzzlingly, however, he continues to insist that 'a direct attack against an otherwise legitimate military target constitutes *a violation of IHL* if that attack is not required for the submission of the enemy with a minimum expenditure of time, life and physical resources'.[157] The position implied here is therefore *not* that of another, epistemologically distinct body of law (such as international human rights law) functioning as *lex specialis* relative to IHL. It is rather that conduct that is otherwise lawful according to positive IHL becomes unlawful *according to the same body of law*, all things considered, if the conduct is lacking in military necessity and thus becomes 'deviant from the more restrictive rules applicable in peace time'.[158]

It would appear that, even according to Melzer's theory, a 'loss or absence'[159] of material military necessity merely reverts the act in question to the more restrictive peacetime rules. This loss or absence itself seems incapable of constituting the restrictive or prohibitive norm needed to establish the act's unlawfulness.

8.5.1.3 Purported Non-exclusion of Elements of Military Necessity through IHL Norm-Creation

Melzer's inability to substantiate military necessity as a restrictive notion also invalidates his assertion that military necessity considerations somehow escape exclusion through IHL norm-creation. He posits:

> [C]ontrary to what powerful States and many authors appear to believe, the fact that IHL does not prohibit direct attacks against combatants does not give rise to a legal entitlement to kill combatants at any time and any place so long as they are not *hors de combat* within the meaning of Article 41(2) AP I [Additional Protocol I of 1977]. Strictly speaking, although the absence of such a prohibition is undisputedly intentional, it constitutes no

[156] Ibid.
[157] Ibid (emphasis added).
[158] Ibid.
[159] Ibid

> more than a strong presumption that, in a situation of armed conflict, it will generally be militarily necessary to kill, injure, or capture combatants of the opposing armed forces in order to bring about the submission of the adversary with a minimum expenditure of time, life and physical resources. It does not permit the senseless slaughter of combatants where there manifestly is no military necessity to do so, for example where a group of defenseless soldiers has not had the occasion to surrender, but could clearly be captured *without additional risk to the operating forces.*[160]

According to Melzer, the absence of an express IHL prohibition against direct attacks on eligible enemy combatants is 'no more than a strong presumption that . . . it will generally be militarily necessary to kill, injure, or capture' them in order to compel the adversary's submission efficiently.[161] In other words, the fact that IHL takes military necessity into consideration does not leave the belligerent at liberty to do what is, in fact, militarily unnecessary. Where rules are formulated without reference to military necessity, it merely means that whatever these rules authorise is deemed *generally* militarily necessary. In the event of a collision between an act being militarily *un*necessary, and it being otherwise lawful according to positive IHL rules, the former wrongs or vitiates the latter.[162] Where the military necessity for particular belligerent conduct is not, or no longer, present, the law, all things considered, prohibits it.[163] This is so, because the idea that a given act's lack of military necessity should be a reason for its prohibition has escaped exclusion through IHL norm-creation.

This line of reasoning is identical in structure, if not in direction, to that used in *Kriegsräson.*[164] Since military necessity is normatively indifferent, it does not escape exclusion when IHL framers posit unqualified rules. Even if some aspects of military necessity did escape exclusion (which they did not), the notion's normative indifference means that these aspects would contain nothing restrictive or prohibitive. An act's lack of material military necessity does not wrong or vitiate its lawfulness if it complies with positive IHL, just as an act's consistency with such necessity does not right or repair its unlawfulness if it flouts an unqualified IHL rule. We have no reason to accept *Kriegsräson* or counter-*Kriegsräson.*[165]

160 Ibid, at 288 (footnotes omitted; emphasis in original).
161 Ibid.
162 Ibid, at 289–90.
163 Ibid, at 297.
164 See above.
165 Dapo Akande, 'Clearing the Fog of War? The ICRC's Interpretive Guidance on Direct Participation in Hostilities' (2010) 59 *International and Comparative Law Quarterly* 180,

8.5.1.4 'Capture Rather than Kill'

Pictet famously observed: 'If we can put a soldier out of action by capturing him, we should not wound him; if we can obtain the same result by wounding him, we must not kill him. If there are two means to achieve the same military advantage, we must choose the one which causes the lesser evil'.[166] Could Melzer be trying to assert the existence of a similar duty? When a choice is possible between disabling eligible enemy combatants via two alternative means, one involving less evil than the other, is the belligerent duty-bound to choose the less evil alternative?

Elsewhere, I have argued that Melzer's least injurious means theory would fail as a species of counter-*Kriegsräson*.[167] That, it is submitted here, still remains the case as the foregoing discussion demonstrates. One major trouble is the fact that Melzer couches most of his arguments around what he sees as restrictive aspects of military necessity. This book shows that military necessity is the wrong heading under which to pursue the 'capture rather than kill' debate.

Once we look beneath the surface, it becomes apparent that the matter may be considered more meaningfully under the heading of humanity.[168] Melzer himself implies as much:

> In sum, while operating forces can hardly be required to take additional risks for themselves or the civilian population in order to capture an armed adversary alive, *it would defy basic notions of humanity* to kill an adversary or to refrain from giving him or her an opportunity to surrender where there manifestly is no necessity for the use of lethal force.[169]

As an element of humanity, there are at least four distinct possibilities. One concerns what Melzer calls 'the more restrictive rules applicable in

at 192; Schmitt, 'Military Necessity and Humanity', at 835; Schmitt, 'Interpretive Guidance', at 41–42.

166 Pictet, *Development and Principles*, pp. 75–76. See also ICRC, *Interpretive Guidance*, p. 82 n.221; Melzer, *Targeted Killing*, p. 289; Melzer, 'Targeted Killing or Less Harmful Means?', at 108–13. On the rejection of Pictet's assertion, see Frits Kalshoven, 'The Soldier and His Golf Clubs' in Kalshoven, *Collected Essays* 359, pp. 368–75; W Hays Parks, 'Part IX of the ICRC "Direct Participation in Hostilities" Study: No Mandate, No Expertise, and Legally Incorrect' (2009–2010) 42 *New York University Journal of International Law and Politics* 769, at 785–87, 799; Schmitt, 'Military Necessity and Humanity', at 835.

167 N Hayashi, 'Contextualizing Military Necessity', at 268–77.

168 Parks, 'No Mandate, No Expertise, and Legally Incorrect', at 785 (citing Pictet, *Humanitarian Law and the Protection of Victims*, p. 32).

169 ICRC, *Interpretive Guidance*, p. 82 (emphasis added). See also Melzer, 'ICRC's Clarification Process', p. 162.

peace time'.[170] *If* it were agreed that these rules do impose such a restraint during military operations – whatever positive IHL rules say about the conduct in question[171] – *then* 'capture rather than kill' might indeed come to bind belligerents.[172] The interplay between IHL and international human rights law in times of armed conflict, a debate with a long history that has become lively again recently,[173] may be relevant in this regard. Similarly, some general principles of public international law may impose restrictions on belligerent conduct independently of IHL.[174] Only one difficulty remains: It does *not* follow from this possibility that the duty in question would be a duty of IHL.

A second possibility is where it is shown that the peacetime restraint enters the *corpus juris* of positive IHL through connecting clauses such as the Martens Clause. Here too, we have already touched upon some of the problems associated with the clause's interpretation.[175] A third possibility exists if, or when, IHL framers posit a new rule imposing a duty upon belligerents to capture rather than kill enemy combatants.[176] Interestingly, Schmitt's main complaint about the judicial activism of international criminal tribunals in IHL development is not the law's new content per se, but judges 'supplant[ing] states in their role as arbiter of the [military necessity–humanity] balance'.[177] Conversely, adding a duty to capture rather than kill to positive IHL would not be so problematic as long as it was done by states themselves.

Fourth, it may be asked whether humanitarian considerations that are *not* normatively indifferent escape exclusion through IHL norm-creation and operate as extra determinants of a given act's lawfulness. What

170 Melzer, *Targeted Killing*, p. 287.

171 Whether it is or should be so agreed is an entirely different question.

172 *Public Committee against Torture in Israel et al. v The Government of et al.*, HCJ 769/02, *Judgment*, 11 December 2006, para. 40.

173 Louise Doswald-Beck, 'The Right to Life in Armed Conflict: Does International Humanitarian Law Provide All the Answers?' (2006) 88 *International Review of the Red Cross* 881; Doswald-Beck and Vité, 'International Humanitarian Law and Human Rights Law'; Françoise Hampson, 'Human Rights Law and International Law: Two Coins or Two Sides of the Same Coin?' (1992) 91 *Bulletin of Human Rights* 46; Melzer, 'Targeted Killings in Operational Law Perspective', pp. 298–99.

174 Melzer, 'Targeted Killings in Operational Law Perspective', p. 299.

175 See Chapter 7. With special reference to the clause and belligerent occupation, see Yutaka Arai-Takahashi, *The Law of Occupation: Continuity and Change of International Humanitarian Law, and Its Interaction with International Human Rights Law* (Leiden and Boston: Martinus Nijhoff, 2009), pp. 657–60, 666.

176 Jens David Ohlin and Larry May, *Necessity in International Law* (New York: Oxford University Press, 2016), pp. 225–30.

177 Schmitt, 'Military Necessity and Humanity', at 822.

Melzer calls 'basic notions of humanity' may very well belong there. Let us then turn to two variations of such considerations.

8.5.2 Humanitätsgebot?[178]

As noted in Chapter 7, humanitarian demands and condemnations are not normatively indifferent. It is over their treatment in the context of positive IHL that the joint satisfaction thesis departs most radically from the inevitable conflict thesis. The idea of joint satisfaction leaves open the possibility that non-indifferent considerations may escape exclusion when IHL framers posit rules, including, in particular, unqualified rules. It is possible that this process does not resolve such genuine norm conflicts as these rules may have with contrary imperatives.

Genuine norm conflicts are by no means unique to the international legal regulations of armed conflicts. On the contrary, all sorts of genuine norm conflicts are a fact of life in general. How these conflicts are dealt with varies from one body of positive legal rules to another. If we have reason to believe that norm conflicts remain unresolved, then we also have reason to accept the possibility that non-indifferent considerations[179] may operate as additional layers of lawfulness modification over and above positive law for particular acts.

This possibility echoes one tenet of inclusive legal positivism. A given legal system may, though need not, contain a Hartian rule of recognition that requires its would-be rules to conform to substantive moral or ethical norms. This school of thought itself appears ambivalent as to (a) whether a would-be rule's failure to do so would merely result in its invalidity; (b) whether the moral or ethical norm to which the would-be rule fails to conform would take its place as a valid rule on the matter;[180] or (c) whether the impugned rule would retain its validity but the moral

[178] Elsewhere, I have used various expressions, such as 'non-indifferent *Humanitätsräson*' (N Hayashi, 'Military Necessity as Normative Indifference', at 766) and 'affirmative *Humanitätsräson*' (N Hayashi, 'Basic Principles' in Rain Liivoja and Tim McCormack (eds), *Routledge Handbook of the Law of Armed Conflict* (London and New York: Routledge, 2016) 89), to convey the same idea.

[179] They include what public morals, religious beliefs, justice, fairness, chivalry, honour and the like demand or condemn. In connection with honour, for example, see Grotius, *De Jure Belli Ac Pacis Libri Tres* (vol. II), p. 716.

[180] Matthew H Kramer, *In Defense of Legal Positivism: Law without Trimmings* (Oxford: Oxford University Press, 1999); Matthew H Kramer, *Where Law and Morality Meet* (Oxford: Oxford University Press, 2004); WJ Waluchow, *Inclusive Legal Positivism* (Oxford: Clarendon Press, 1994).

or ethical norms would function as exceptions, justifications or excuses for individual cases of deviation therefrom.

How might this work in relation to positive IHL rules? In Jeff McMahan's view:

> When the morality of war requires what the law forbids, I believe that one must do what morality requires. And those who violate the law for moral reasons ought not, in general, to conceal the violation but ought instead to acknowledge what they have done and cite their moral justification for having done it. In this way, they demonstrate their respect for the law, thereby encouraging a general climate in which even morally motivated violations of the law are exceptional and undertaken only with reluctance. This is important precisely because it is so easy for people to persuade themselves that their own violations of the law are morally necessary.[181]

Since humanitarian imperatives are species of non-indifferent considerations, it is possible that compliance with their demands may be invoked as a ground for non-compliance with unqualified IHL rules. This points to the potential existence of a *Humanitätsgebot* doctrine (where humanity demands what positive IHL rules prohibit) and a counter-*Humanitätsgebot* doctrine (where humanity condemns what positive IHL rules authorise).

We will consider two representative examples of *Humanitätsgebot*:[182] repatriating or not repatriating POWs after the cessation of hostilities; and interning POWs on land or aboard vessels at sea.

181 McMahan, 'Morality of War and the Law of War', p. 39. McMahan's solution might be contrasted with John Finnis's. One interesting aspect of Finnis's natural law theory is its assertion that even some iniquitous rules of law may have to be obeyed if the legal system is itself legitimate on the whole. Finnis, *Natural Law and Natural Rights*, pp. 361–62, 365. Arguably, the iniquitousness of a legal rule as understood by Finnis may include not only the conduct it stipulates generally, but also certain specific instances where they become iniquitous by virtue of the particular circumstances surrounding them. Where a positive legal rule unqualifiedly forbids an act, and yet refraining from that act in a specific situation happens to be less humane than performing it, and where humanity demands its performance in that particular situation, Finnis would still argue that one should refrain from it.

182 Admittedly, there may be further examples that this chapter does not examine. Thus, in certain 'transformative' types of belligerent occupation, a potentially insoluble norm conflict may arise between Article 43 of the 1907 Hague Regulations and Article 64 of Geneva Convention IV requiring the Occupying Power to preserve the local law in force (such as sharia law), on the one hand, and certain human rights obligations by which the Occupying Power is bound, on the other. Gregory H Fox, *Humanitarian Occupation* (Cambridge: Cambridge University Press, 2008), pp. 233–72; Marko Milanović, 'Norm Conflicts, International Humanitarian Law, and Human Rights Law' in Ben-Naftali (ed), *International Humanitarian Law and International Human Rights*

8.5.2.1 Repatriating vs. Not Repatriating POWs after the Cessation of Hostilities

To Schapiro's dismay, the long history of not repatriating certain categories of POWs (such as deserters[183]) experienced an unfortunate turn at the 1899 Hague Peace Conference:

> At The Hague, in the laudable attempt to achieve the humane object of ensuring repatriation without the delay or hindrance occasioned by the necessity of a special agreement, the equally humane requirement that the unwilling prisoner should not be repatriated, at any rate without some guarantee for his safety where he had compromised himself in the eyes of his own state, was forgotten.[184]

Be that as it may, the practice of states declining to repatriate POWs against their will – or without some guarantee of their safety at any rate – continued well after World War I.[185] According to Schapiro, 'the fate of the prisoners of war whom he repatriated after hostilities was, on grounds of humanity, a responsibility of the repatriating belligerent'.[186] Some argued that Article 75 of the 1929 POW Convention[187] did not change the situation.[188]

Article 118 of Geneva Convention III stipulates that '[p]risoners of war shall be released and repatriated without delay after the cessation of active hostilities'.[189] The idea that this provision creates an unqualified obligation finds support in some scholarly writings[190] as well as its

Law 95, pp. 121–23; Philip Spoerri, 'The Law of Occupation' in Clapham and Gaeta (eds), *Oxford Handbook of International Law in Armed Conflict* 182, pp. 192–98. Others, including Dinstein, do not appear convinced by such a construal, if read in conjunction with the rules contained in Article 27 of Geneva Convention IV. Yoram Dinstein, *The International Law of Belligerent Occupation* (Cambridge: Cambridge University Press, 2009), p. 113.

183 On the notion of deserters, see also Sassoli, 'Status, Treatment and Repatriation of Deserters'.

184 Schapiro, 'Repatriation of Deserters', at 319.

185 Ibid, at 319–22.

186 Ibid, at 318.

187 Article 75, POW Convention (1929).

188 Gutteridge, 'Repatriation of Prisoners of War', at 209–10. For a brief discussion of the post-1929 state practice offering POWs an option of non-repatriation, see Jan P Charmatz and Harold M Wit, 'Repatriation of Prisoners of War and the 1949 Geneva Convention' (1953) 62 *Yale Law Journal* 391, at 401–02.

189 Article 118, Geneva Convention III.

190 Horst Fischer, 'Protection of Prisoners of War' in Fleck (ed), *Handbook of International Humanitarian Law* (2nd edn) 367, p. 416.

drafting history.[191] Austria proposed, and Israel supported, an amendment that envisaged exceptions to mandatory repatriation, inspired inter alia by the notion that '[p]risoners of war must have the option of not returning to their country if they so desire'.[192] The Soviet Union and the United States objected.[193] The Soviet delegate argued that such a provision 'could be used to the detriment of the prisoners themselves and of their country'.[194] He also asserted that the Detaining Power might exert undue pressure on POWs, hindering their ability to express themselves 'with complete freedom'.[195] The proposed amendment was defeated by a 'large majority'.[196]

This particular episode in the drafting process of Article 118 stands in contrast to that of Article 109 of the same Convention. The latter article provides that no sick or injured POW who is eligible for repatriation may be repatriated against his or her will during hostilities.[197] This prohibition, proposed by the ICRC and supported by Belgium, New Zealand, Italy, Switzerland and the Soviet Union, survived Canadian and British objections.[198] The Red Cross commentary insists that Article 109, despite

191 But see Sassoli, 'Status, Treatment and Repatriation of Deserters', at 31–32 (emphasis in original; footnotes omitted): 'Although the 1949 Diplomatic Conference almost unanimously rejected the Austrian proposals stating that prisoners of war shall be entitled to apply for their transfer to any other country which is ready to accept them or that at least they must have the option of not returning to their country if they so desire, this rejection is not to be construed as laying down the principle of forcible repatriation; it was meant to prevent prisoners of war from having the *right* to be sent at great expense "to the other side of the world" and to avoid introducing an escape clause which Detaining Power might use as a pretext to refrain from repatriating all prisoners of war (at the time, some two million World War II prisoners of war who had served in the forces of the Axis Powers were still detained in the Soviet Union)'.

192 Federal Political Department, *Final Record of the Diplomatic Conference* (vol. II-A), p. 462.

193 Ibid; Pictet (ed), *Commentary Geneva Convention III*, pp. 542–43.

194 Federal Political Department, *Final Record of the Diplomatic Conference* (vol. II-A), p. 324.

195 Ibid, p. 462.

196 Ibid.

197 Article 109, paragraph 3, Geneva Convention III: 'No sick or injured prisoner of war who is eligible for repatriation under the first paragraph of this Article, may be repatriated against his will during hostilities'.

198 Federal Political Department, *Final Record of the Diplomatic Conference* (vol. II-A), pp. 291, 373, 391; Federal Political Department, *Final Record of the Diplomatic Conference* (vol. II-B), pp. 312–14. The Swiss delegate pointedly stated that the provision 'not only affect[ed] prisoners of war as prisoners, but also as refugees' (Federal Political Department, *Final Record of the Diplomatic Conference* (vol. II-A), p. 397). The United Kingdom unsuccessfully argued that 'a country should be allowed to decide for itself

its text to the contrary, covers not only sick or wounded POWs but also able-bodied ones.[199]

A Detaining Power may find itself bound by Article 118 to repatriate POWs, on the one hand, and a humanitarian demand against their repatriation in certain cases, on the other. The entity entitled to the fulfilment of this seemingly unqualified duty of repatriation is the state on which the POWs depend. Those supporting the view that Article 118 obligates the Detaining Power to repatriate all of its POWs, by force if need be, 'considered that the duties which the Convention laid upon the Detaining Power were duties for which that Power was responsible towards the Power of origin of prisoners of war, but not towards the prisoners themselves'.[200]

Article 118 itself does not appear to entitle POWs to demand non-repatriation. Any humanitarian demands against their repatriation as might exist would be extrinsic to Article 118 itself.[201] It is the advent of international human rights law – together with international refugee law, and particularly its *non-refoulement* principle – that has strengthened the case for humanity demanding non-repatriation in appropriate circumstances.[202]

whether it will give refuge and asylum to a foreigner who has come to that country not by a voluntary act of his own; for instance, when a Detaining Power is satisfied that he has good grounds for staying, but there should not be an obligation on the Detaining Power to keep a prisoner of war who, as the Convention itself says, ought no longer to be a prisoner of war' (Federal Political Department, *Final Record of the Diplomatic Conference* (vol. II-B), p. 313).

199 Pictet (ed), *Commentary Geneva Convention III*, pp. 512–13.

200 Pictet (ed), *Commentary Geneva Convention III*, p. 544. According to Fischer, the Detaining Power's duty to repatriate POWs in its custody to the state of their destination may only be waived 'on a case-by-case basis taking into account the supervision by the ICRC', since ICRC delegates 'alone are in a position to determine whether prisoners of war in fact prefer to remain in the state of the detaining power, or in another state, rather than returning to their home country'. Fischer, 'Protection of Prisoners of War', at 416. Whereas the ICRC's humanitarian role is beyond reproach, it is doubtful whether its opinion on the POWs' preferences alone can relieve their Detaining Power of its duty to repatriate them to their state of destination.

201 Carl E Lundin, Jr, 'Repatriation of Prisoners of War: The Legal and Political Aspects' (1953) 39 *American Bar Association Journal* 559, at 563; Pitman B Potter, 'Repatriation of Prisoners of War' (1952) 46 *American Journal of International Law* 508, at 509.

202 Sassoli, 'Status, Treatment and Repatriation of Deserters', at 32, 34–35; Meron, 'Humanization', at 253–56. See also Françoise Hampson, 'The Scope of the Obligation Not to Return Fighters under the Law of Armed Conflict' in David James Cantor and Jean-François Durieux (eds), *Refuge from Inhumanity? War Refugees and International Humanitarian Law* (Leiden and Boston: Brill Nijhoff, 2014) 373.

There is a genuine norm conflict here.[203] On the one hand, the Detaining Power owes vis-à-vis the state of origin an unqualified obligation to repatriate POWs after the cessation of hostilities. On the other hand, the Detaining Power 'owes' vis-à-vis POWs held in its custody a humanitarian demand not to return persons to a place where they may be persecuted or tortured.

This dilemma arose in the aftermath of the Korean War.[204] Formally, Article 118 of Geneva Convention III was not binding upon the parties at that time. They nevertheless undertook to abide by the Geneva Conventions or, in any event, by the humanitarian principles underpinning them.[205] The rule contained in Article 118 became the subject of heated debate,[206] exacerbated by the ideological undercurrent of the Cold War.[207] Commentators offered increasingly complex and, at times farfetched, interpretations of Article 118 with a view to reconciling a positive IHL rule unqualifiedly obligating repatriation with humanity demanding non-repatriation.[208] The issue resurfaced during the Iran–Iraq War,[209] and again in the Gulf War.[210]

[203] Jaro Mayda, 'The Korean Repatriation Problem and International Law' (1953) 47 *American Journal of International Law* 414, at 435.

[204] Pictet (ed), *Commentary Geneva Convention III*, pp. 543–46.

[205] Lundin, 'Repatriation of Prisoners of War', at 560; Mayda, 'Korean Repatriation Problem', at 424–26; Potter, *supra* note 406, at 508 ('[T]he principles of . . . Article 118 may be regarded as repeating established law').

[206] United Nations General Assembly Resolution 610 (VII) (3 December 1952), para. 2.

[207] Charmatz and Wit, 'Repatriation of Prisoners of War and the 1949 Geneva Convention', at 393–94, 414; Lundin, 'Repatriation of Prisoners of War', at 561–63. On the difficulty associated with ascertaining the true intentions of POWs requesting – or not requesting – asylum, see RR Baxter, 'Asylum to Prisoners of War' (1953) 30 *British Yearbook of International Law* 489; Charmatz and Wit, 'Repatriation of Prisoners of War and the 1949 Geneva Convention', at 412–14; Yves Sandoz, 'The International Committee of the Red Cross as Guardian of International Humanitarian Law' (31 December 1998) (www.icrc.org/eng/resources/documents/misc/about-the-icrc-311298.htm).

[208] Pictet (ed), *Commentary Geneva Convention III*, pp. 546–50, esp. 548: 'While recognizing the possibility of recourse to general humanitarian rules, one should nevertheless make a rather strict appraisal of each case, since the Third Geneva Convention has certainly not established a system under which repatriation depends solely on the wishes of the prisoner of war concerned. Each case must therefore be dealt with individually, on its own merits. A decision against repatriation must be reserved for exceptional cases where the dangers involved for the person concerned seems manifestly unjust and grave'. See also Gutteridge, 'Repatriation of Prisoners of War', at 212, 216; Lundin, 'Repatriation of Prisoners of War', at 560–61; Schapiro, 'Repatriation of Deserters', at 323.

[209] John Quigley, 'Iran and Iraq and the Obligations to Release and Repatriate Prisoners of War after the Close of Hostilities' (1989–1990) 5 *American University Journal of International Law and Policy* 73, at 81–83.

[210] The ICRC reportedly took the view that 'no Iraqi prisoners of war will be repatriated against their will' and that 'all Iraqi prisoners of war who expressed an unwillingness to return to Iraq . . . should be considered as refugees'. Peter Rowe, 'Prisoners of War in the

The inevitable conflict thesis would have no choice but to insist that Article 118's adoption in 1949 compulsorily resolved this norm conflict by letting the duty of repatriation in all cases trump the humanitarian demand of non-repatriation in certain cases. It would follow that pleas drawn from the latter demand are inadmissible vis-à-vis Article 118.

Adherents of the inevitable conflict thesis might counter that techniques such as *lex specialis*[211] and *jus cogens*[212] would take care of the problem. The difficulty persists, however, since – according to their own thesis – it is unqualified rules of positive IHL themselves that account for military necessity and humanity, and it is this very fact that precludes military necessity and humanity pleas alike vis-à-vis such rules. Appealing to extra-IHL rules for explanations is therefore not an answer that the thesis's adherents can accept without contradicting themselves.

Gulf Area' in Peter Rowe (ed), *The Gulf War 1990–91 in International and English Law* (London: Routledge, 1993) 188, at 203 (footnote omitted) (citing *The Times* (5 March 1991) and International Committee of the Red Cross, ICRC Bulletin, no.184 (May 1991)). See also International Committee of the Red Cross, Annual Report (1991), p. 101 (referring to an ICRC memorandum presented to Iraqi and coalition authorities in which it was stipulated that 'no prisoner of war or civilian internee may be returned to his country of origin against his will'), 102 (reporting that those Iraqi citizens in Saudi camps who had refused repatriation were given refugee status by the Riyadh authorities). It is now the policy of the United Kingdom that 'prisoners of war should not be repatriated against their will'. UK Defence Ministry, *Joint Service Manual*, p. 205.

211 Repatriating or not repatriating POWs after the cessation of hostilities is possibly one area where international human rights law and/or international refugee law prohibiting repatriation in certain situations functions as the *lex specialis* relative to IHL obligating repatriation in all situations. Typically, it is IHL that is seen as *lex specialis* relative to international human rights law in situations of armed conflict. *Nuclear Weapons*, para. 25; Greenwood, '*Jus ad Bellum* and *Jus in Bello*', pp. 248, 252, 265. But see Arai-Takahashi, *Law of Occupation*, pp. 401–07, 414–25; Vera Gowlland-Debbas, 'The Right to Life and the Relationship between Human Rights and Humanitarian Law' in Tomuschat (ed), *Right to Life* 123, pp. 137–42; Christopher Greenwood, 'Scope of Application of Humanitarian Law' in Fleck (ed), *Handbook of International Humanitarian Law* (2nd edn) 45, pp. 74–75; Henckaerts and Doswald-Beck, *Customary International Humanitarian Law* (vol. I), pp. 299–305; Stephane Jaquemet, 'The Cross-Fertilization of International Humanitarian Law and International Refugee Law' (2001) 83 *International Review of the Red Cross* 651, at 663–64; Sassòli and Olsen, 'Relationship between International Humanitarian Law and Human Rights Law Where It Matters', at 600, 603–05; Vincent Chetail, 'Armed Conflict and Forced Migration: A Systematic Approach to International Humanitarian Law, Refugee Law, and International Human Rights Law' in Clapham and Gaeta (eds), *Oxford Handbook of International Law in Armed Conflict* 700, pp. 730–32.

212 For a discussion as to whether *non-refoulement* has attained the status of *jus cogens*, see Walter Kälin et al., 'Article 33, para. 1' in Andreas Zimmermann (ed), *The 1951 Convention Relating to the Status of Refugees and Its 1967 Protocol: A Commentary* (Oxford: Oxford University Press, 2011) 1327, pp. 1347–49.

They might also argue that the subsequent practice has effectively modified Article 118,[213] such that it now contains an implicit exceptional humanity clause. This argument may have the superficial appeal of describing how the law has 'caught up' with humanitarian imperatives regarding post-hostilities POW repatriation. Such a conclusion would not have assisted those during the Korean War who found themselves grappling with the norm conflict created with Article 118's adoption in 1949.

Humanitätsgebot, if it does exist, arguably offers a more cogent explanation. The mere fact that a positive IHL rule in the form of Article 118 unqualifiedly obligates post-hostilities POW repatriation may not have resolved potential norm conflicts with contrary non-indifferent considerations. It is not clear whether the *unqualifiedness* of Article 118 in relation to such considerations was, in 1949, or has since been, conclusive for positive IHL on the matter.[214] Perhaps, despite its categorical language, Article 118 cannot be said to have extinguished that element of humanity which demands non-repatriation under certain circumstances. Consequently, it is possible that pleas emanating from such demands are admissible vis-à-vis Article 118.

8.5.2.2 Interning POWs on Land vs. Interning Them aboard Vessels at Sea

Article 22 of Geneva Convention III unqualifiedly obligates the Detaining Power to intern its POWs on land.[215] No corresponding obligation was included in Article 9 of the 1929 POW Convention.[216] It was inserted in Article 20 of the Stockholm draft[217] and adopted at the 1949 Diplomatic Conference without discussion.

During the Falklands/Malvinas conflict, British forces held a large number of Argentine POWs aboard military vessels at sea. This, according to the United Kingdom, was done 'with the concurrence of the ICRC, because there was nowhere suitable to hold [POWs] on the

[213] Article 31(3)(b), Vienna Convention on the Law of Treaties.

[214] Office of General Counsel, *Law of War Manual*, p. 636 (footnote omitted): 'Thus, [Geneva Convention III] does not itself change accepted principles of international law under which asylum is applicable to POWs, and the Detaining Power may, but is not required to, grant asylum'.

[215] Article 22, Geneva Convention III. See also Pilloud, 'Protection of the Victims of Armed Conflict', p. 175.

[216] Article 9, POW Convention (1929).

[217] Article 20, Stockholm Draft.

Falkland Islands and the intention was to repatriate them as soon as possible'.[218] The *UK Joint Service Manual* asserts that '[t]emporary internment on board ship for the purpose of evacuation from the combat zone is permissible'.[219] On this view, IHL authorises POW internment aboard military vessels at sea if and to the extent demanded by humanity, notwithstanding a positive IHL rule that unqualifiedly obligates internment on land. Here, a genuine norm conflict pitches Article 22 against the humanitarian demand arising from the circumstances of the Falklands/Malvinas conflict that the Argentine POWs be interned aboard vessels at sea.

The inevitable conflict thesis would have to hold that positive IHL has conclusively resolved this norm conflict in favour of land-based POW internment. If the thesis were nevertheless to defend the lawfulness of sea-borne internment by reference to that law, it would have to do so with techniques other than an appeal to humanity demanding such an arrangement. *Humanitätsgebot* would suggest, first, that humanity demands POW internment in locations other than land under certain circumstances. Second, *Humanitätsgebot* would acknowledge the possibility that this humanitarian demand had escaped exclusion when Article 22 was adopted. Consequently, Article 22 might be susceptible to pleas emanating from that demand.

In substance, McCoubrey's appeal to impracticality as a justification for deviation from unqualified IHL rules is better understood as an appeal to *Humanitätsgebot*:

> Here the particular circumstances of conflict on and around South Atlantic islands rendered the primary aims of the Third Convention, humane conditions of internment and early repatriation, more readily achieved through a technical violation than through a strict 'black letter' compliance and no complaint was made in respect of the procedure adopted. This may be regarded as a form of 'necessity', albeit not strictly 'military', which dictated a variation in the detailed application of a 'humanitarian' provision without compromising the attainment of the fundamental objective.[220]

[218] UK Defence Ministry, *Joint Service Manual*, p. 158 n.123.

[219] Ibid, p. 158 (footnote omitted).

[220] McCoubrey, 'Modern Doctrine of Military Necessity', at 228. According to Charles Garraway, the United Kingdom, having consulted the matter with the ICRC, decided that the hostilities had already ceased and that the Argentine POWS were placed on the ship as the first step of their repatriation under Article 118, rather than detained within the meaning of Article 22. I am grateful to Garraway for his insight here.

In other words, IHL would exceptionally authorise deviations even from the prescriptions of its unqualified rules when humanity so demands.

8.5.3 *Counter*-Humanitätsgebot?

The same might be true of a counter-*Humanitätsgebot*. A positive IHL rule may authorise what humanity condemns. The manner in which this manifests itself may vary from one situation to another. It can also be subtle. Typically, the case involves a positive IHL rule declining or failing to obligate what humanity demands or, in any event, obligating less than what humanity demands. The rule thereby authorises what humanity condemns – i.e., choosing not to act as demanded by humanity. The question is whether there is any normative basis for supposing that this choice might wrong or vitiate its compliance with positive IHL.

Consider the case of a combatant assuming risk of self-endangerment with a view to sparing civilians.[221] It has been suggested that positive IHL obligates some risk-taking in this regard.[222] The kind and extent of this obligation in a given situation remain unclear.[223] Does humanity demand that a combatant assume greater risks of self-endangerment than positive IHL rules do? Would humanity condemn the combatant if he or she chose to risk only the obligatory minimum? Could that combatant have acted in breach of IHL, all things considered, whatever lower degree the law's positive rules might appear to obligate? Should

221 Walzer, *Arguing about War*; McMahan, *Killing in War*, pp. 198–202 (regarding extra risk-taking vis-à-vis child soldiers); Jean-Philippe Kot, 'Israeli Civilians v. Palestinian Combatants? Reading the Goldstone Report in Light of the Israeli Conception of the Principle of Distinction' (2011) 24 *Leiden Journal of International Law* 961.

222 APV Rogers, 'Conduct of Combat and Risks Run by the Civilian Population' (1982) 21 *Military Law and the Law of War Review* 293, at 310; William J Fenrick, 'Attacking the Enemy Civilian as a Punishable Offense' (1997) 7 *Duke Journal of Comparative and International Law* 539 (1997), at 548–49.

223 See Chapter 6; R George Wright, 'Noncombatant Immunity: A Case Study in the Relation between International Law and Morality' (1991) 67 *Notre Dame Law Review* 335, at 354–57; *Prosecutor v Dražen Erdemović*, Case No. IT-96-22-A, *Joint Separate Opinion of Judge McDonald and Judge Vohrah*, 7 October 1997, para. 84; ibid, *Separate and Dissenting Opinion of Judge Cassese*, paras 47, 50; Nobuo Hayashi, 'The Role of Judges in Identifying the Status of Combatants' (2006) 2 *Acta Societatis Martensis* 69; Steven P Lee, *Ethics and War: An Introduction* (Cambridge: Cambridge University Press, 2012), pp. 218–22; N Hayashi, 'Is the Yugoslav Tribunal Guilty of Hyper-Humanising International Humanitarian Law?'

counter-*Humanitätsgebot* exist, we might respond to the latter question in the affirmative.

Similarly, *if* humanity demanded 'capture rather than kill', and *if* the process of norm-creation through which 'kill rather than capture' had come to be seen as lawful under positive IHL did not fully account for that demand, *then* it might be argued that killing rather than capturing is unlawful.[224]

8.5.3.1 'Capture Rather than Kill' Redux: Stretching the Envelope of Positive Law

The current debate primarily revolves around whether today's IHL framework contains a duty to minimise harm inflicted on eligible enemy combatants. Melzer himself asserts that '*within the parameters* set by the more specific provisions of IHL governing the conduct of hostilities, *considerations of* military necessity and *humanity* should serve as guiding principles in determining the kind and degree of force which is permissible against legitimate military targets'.[225]

On 27 February 1991, towards the conclusion of hostilities in the Persian Gulf, a large number of Iraqi forces retreating from Kuwait along Highway 8 came under attack from the Coalition forces.[226] According to one account:

> The run down the highway showed more clearly than any other episode the weaknesses of Iraqi field forces and the onesidedness of the conflict. Through the afternoon and night of 27 February the tankers, Bradley gunners, and helicopter crews and artillerymen of the 1st and 4th Battalions, 64th Armor, fired at hundreds of vehicles trying to redeploy to meet the new American attack from the west, or simply to escape north across

[224] If morality requires capturing rather than killing the enemy combatant while the law permits killing the enemy combatants, then, according to McMahan, one ought simply to obey the requirement. McMahan, 'Morality of War and the Law of War', p. 37; ICRC, *Interpretive Guidance*, p. 82; Melzer, 'ICRC's Clarification Process', p. 162.

[225] Melzer, 'Keeping the Balance between Military Necessity and Humanity', at 904 (emphasis added; footnote omitted). See also ibid, at 907–08 (emphasis added): 'It appears justified ... to regard considerations of military necessity and of humanity, which are generally recognized as underlying and informing the entire normative framework of IHL, as guiding principles for the *interpretation* of the rights and duties of belligerents *within the parameters set by the more specific provisions of IHL* governing the conduct of hostilities'.

[226] This incident is not to be confused with a similar incident involving a much larger number of Iraqis which took place on 26 February 1991 on Highway 80 (also known as the 'Highway of Death').

> the Euphrates River valley and west on Highway 8. With no intelligence capability left to judge the size or location of the oncoming American armored wedges and attack helicopter swarms, as well as insufficient communications to coordinate a new defense, Iraqi units stumbled into disaster. Unsuspecting drivers of every type of vehicle, from tanks to artillery prime movers and even commandeered civilian autos, raced randomly across the desert or west on Highway 8 only to run into General McCaffrey's firestorm. Some drivers, seeing vehicles explode and burn, veered off the road in vain attempt to escape. Others stopped, dismounted, and walked toward the Americans with raised hands. When the division staff detected elements of the *Hammurabi Division* of the *Republican Guard* moving across the 24th's front, McCaffrey concentrated the fire of nine artillery battalions and an Apache battalion on the once elite enemy force. At dawn the next day, the twenty-eighth, hundreds of vehicles lay crumpled and smoking on Highway 8 and at scattered points across the desert.[227]

McCaffrey's purpose here may be described as 'disabling able-bodied, non-surrendering Iraqi combatants', and his conduct as 'applying overwhelming military force by the Coalition'.

Positive IHL rules unqualifiedly prohibit attacking persons *hors de combat*,[228] as well as employing methods of warfare of a nature to cause superfluous injury and unnecessary suffering.[229] Assuming that most of the Iraqi combatants were retreating rather than offering to surrender,[230] had they nevertheless placed themselves *hors de combat*, with the result that it would have been unlawful to attack them? Would the incident have amounted to using methods of warfare of a nature to cause superfluous injury and unnecessary suffering?

Ryan Goodman proposes an interpretation of *hors de combat* as well as superfluous injury and unnecessary suffering which, if correct, would render McCaffrey's actions arguably in breach of IHL.[231] First, building

227 Frank N Schubert and Theresa L Kraus (eds), *The Whirlwind War: The United States Army in Operations Desert Shield and Desert Storm* (Washington, DC: Center for Military History, United States Army, 1995), pp. 194–95.

228 Article 41, Additional Protocol I.

229 Article 35(2), Additional Protocol I.

230 We do not know exactly what happened to those who 'stopped, dismounted, and walked toward the Americans with raised hands'. For the sake of argumentative focus, let us exclude them from the scope of our discussion here. If (heavens forbid) these soldiers were attacked, that would clearly be an IHL breach.

231 Ryan Goodman, 'The Power to Kill or Capture Enemy Combatants' (2013) 24 *European Journal of International Law* 819.

on the Red Cross commentary[232] on Article 41(2)(a) of Additional Protocol I,[233] Goodman argues that 'combatants who no longer have the means to defend themselves – who are at the mercy of their adversary – are, indeed, covered by this more direct and, in some cases, more protective framework'.[234] Strictly speaking, neither one's actual capture or detention, nor a clear expression of his or her intention to surrender, would be a pre-requisite. Second, Goodman enlists the Red Cross commentary's observation that:

> An escape, or an attempt to escape, by a prisoner or any other person considered to be *hors de combat*, justifies the use of arms for the purpose of stopping him. However, once more, the use of force is only lawful to the extent that the circumstances require it. It is only permissible to kill a person who is escaping if there is no other way of preventing the escape in the immediate circumstances.[235]

Third, Goodman asserts that the prohibition against the use of means and methods of a nature to cause superfluous injury and unnecessary suffering means that such use 'may be unlawful if the magnitude of harm to enemy fighters far outweighs the military benefit'.[236] In his opinion, 'the specific rule on superfluous injury and unnecessary suffering includes a prohibition on unnecessary killing'.[237]

Critics respond that Goodman conflates the expression 'methods of warfare' (i.e., of a nature to cause superfluous injury or unnecessary

[232] Jean de Preux, 'Article 41 – Safeguard of an enemy *hors de combat*' in Sandoz et al. (eds), *Commentary on Additional Protocols* 479, p. 484: 'Some consider that having fallen into the power means having fallen into enemy hands, i.e., having been apprehended. This is virtually never the case when the attack is conducted by the airforce, which can certainly have enemy troops in its power without being able, or wishing, to take them into custody or accept a surrender (for example, in the case of an attack by helicopters). In other cases land forces might have the adversary at their mercy by means of overwhelmingly superior firing power to the point where they can force the adversary to cease combat . . . A defenceless adversary is *hors de combat* whether or not he has laid down arms'.

[233] The provision reads: 'A person is *hors de combat* if . . . he is in the power of an adverse Party'.

[234] Goodman, 'Power to Kill or Capture', at 836. See also Sergei A Egorov, 'International Legal Protections for Persons *Hors de Combat*' in Doria et al. (eds., *Legal Regime of the International Criminal Court* 561, p. 565: 'A defenceless adversary is *hors de combat* whether or not he has laid down his arms'.

[235] De Preux, 'Safeguard of an enemy *hors de combat*', p. 488; Goodman, 'Power to Kill or Capture', at 850.

[236] Goodman, 'Power to Kill or Capture', at 839–40.

[237] Ibid, at 840.

suffering) with the act of killing or capturing.[238] They also contend that the expression 'in the power' found in Article 41(2)(a) means capture or detention,[239] with the crucial question being:

> [W]hether an individual is unambiguously in the captor's control, such that he poses no risk to the captors or civilians (e.g., a risk of suicide bombing) and taking custody would be operationally feasible in the attendant circumstances. In other words, the *hors de combat* rule prohibits an attack that is nothing but an execution because the individual concerned has already been captured.[240]

It would also appear that there is a key difference between escaping or attempting to escape following capture or detention (i.e., already placed *hors de combat*) and evading initial capture or detention (i.e., not yet placed *hors de combat*).[241] The former places itself in a protective paradigm and triggers a requirement of minimum escalation of force.[242] The latter, in contrast, would remain part of hostilities where disablement sets the parameters. Clearly, the permissible choice among otherwise lawful methods of combat is capped at the point of superfluous injury or unnecessary suffering. Nevertheless, no formal hierarchy exists amongst various forms of disablement. Nor, as least as far as positive IHL rules are concerned, must these various forms be attempted in a particular order.

Of the Iraqi soldiers, A. V. P. Rogers states:

> There can be no question that the column was a legitimate target. It comprised enemy soldiers who had not surrendered. They represented a military threat to coalition operations . . . As for the question of bad faith, this is not established by examination of the facts. On 22 February 1991, President Bush presented Saddam Houssein with an ultimatum, which expired the following day. It required the Iraqis to commence their

238 Michael Schmitt, 'Wound, Capture, or Kill: A Reply to Ryan Goodman's "The Power to Kill or Capture Enemy Combatants"' (2013) 24 *European Journal of International Law* 855, at 856–57; Geoffrey S Corn, Laurie R Blank, Chris Jenks and Eric Talbot Jensen, 'Belligerent Targeting and the Invalidity of a Least Harmful Means Rule' (2013) 89 *International Law Studies* 536, at 593–96; Ohlin and May, *Necessity in International Law*, pp. 218–25.

239 Corn et al., 'Belligerent Targeting and the Invalidity of a Least Harmful Means Rule', at 586–88. But see Ryan Goodman, 'The Power to Kill or Capture Enemy Combatants: A Rejoinder to Michael N. Schmitt' (2013) 24 *European Journal of International Law* 863, at 864–65.

240 Schmitt, 'Wound, Capture, or Kill', at 860.

241 Ohlin and May, *Necessity in International Law*, pp. 213–18.

242 Pictet (ed), *Commentary Geneva Convention IV*, pp. 245–47. See also ibid, pp. 247–48, in connection with the suppression of a POW rebellion.

> withdrawal from Kuwait before expiry of the ultimatum and complete it within one week. In return, the allied undertook not to attack withdrawing troops so long as the withdrawal continued according to the ultimatum. Iraq did not accept these terms, so the conditions of the ultimatum lapsed and the ground attack started on 24 February. Even after that the allied announced that the retreating Iraqis would be safe so long as they abandoned their weapons and vehicles. Needless to say, those on the Basra road did not do so.[243]

Françoise Hampson, although apparently commenting on a subsequent, more controversial 'turkey shoot' incident in March 1991, observes:

> The military forces and equipment of the adversary are a legitimate target of attack until they surrender. There may have been a misunderstanding if the [retreating] Iraqis thought they would not be attacked, provided they did not attack the coalition forces, whereas what was required was the abandonment of all their equipment. Allowing the coalition forces the benefit of the doubt on that score, it would appear that the Iraqi forces could be attacked. The question then becomes whether they were subjected to 'unnecessary suffering or superfluous injury.' . . . If the devastation was wrought by general purpose bombs or the strafing of the columns of vehicles and forces, this would appear to be lawful unless it represented 'unnecessary suffering or superfluous injury.' The killings might seem both unnecessary and superfluous, but the prohibition concerns suffering or injury, rather than unnecessary or superfluous actions . . . This may suggest, particularly if military forces were unwilling to carry on attacking an unresisting adversary, the need for a new principle. It would be an extension of the existing rule. It would require that an attack should not proceed, even against a legitimate target and by means of a lawful weapon, where it is unnecessary or superfluous to the attainment of the war aim. The principal difficulty with such a rule would be in distinguishing between an unresisting enemy and one in tactical retreat. So long as the Iraqi government took no steps to obtain a ceasefire, its fighting forces were a legitimate target, even if they no longer offered an immediate threat to the coalition forces.[244]

243 Rogers, *Law on the Battlefield* (2nd edn), p. 31. See also Roy Gutman et al. (eds), *Crimes of War 2.0: What the Public Should Know*, rev. edn (New York: W.W. Norton & Company, 2007), p. 165; Dinstein, *Conduct of Hostilities* (2nd edn), pp. 102–03.

244 Françoise J Hampson, 'Means and Methods of Warfare in the Conflict in the Gulf' in Rowe (ed), *The Gulf War 1990–91* 89, p. 107. Footnote omitted. See also US Department of the Navy et al., *Commander's Handbook*, p. 5-3: military necessity does not prohibit the 'application of overwhelming force against enemy combatants, units and material consistent with the principles of distinction and proportionality'.

I do not believe that the Iraqi soldiers were placed *hors de combat* at the time of the incident. Nor were they subjected to methods of warfare of a nature to cause superfluous injury and unnecessary suffering. The mere fact that their disablement took the form of death and wounding rather than capture does not per se constitute a breach of positive IHL.

8.5.3.2 'Capture Rather than Kill' Redux: Ripping the Envelope of Positive Law

More fundamentally, counter-*Humanitätsgebot* would place humanity's imperatives over and above positive IHL itself. As noted by Emily Crawford, Pictet's admonition is more of a 'philosophy'[245] than an interpretive technique of existing IHL rules. Thus, even if killing the Iraqi combatants were in compliance with positive IHL rules, would it still be unlawful under IHL, all things considered, as long as they could have been disabled alive?

There is a hint of double effect in such an argument. First developed by Thomas Aquinas, double effect requires that the agent (1) exclusively intends to achieve good, and (2) intends to minimise the foreseeable evil that the good's pursuit may cause.[246] The standard IHL context in which double effect is discussed today is that of minimising collateral damage.[247] This narrow focus has been criticised.[248] In fact, there is no

[245] Emily Crawford, *Identifying the Enemy: Civilian Participation in Armed Conflict* (Oxford: Oxford University Press, 2015), p. 87.

[246] Thomas Aquinas, *Summa Theologiæ* (Basel: Michael Wenssler, 1485). See also Sidgwick, *Elements of Politics*, p. 254; Walzer, *Just and Unjust Wars*, p. 153; Mangan, 'Historical Analysis of the Principle of Double Effect', at 43; Keenan, 'Function of the Principle of Double Effect'; Alison McIntyre, 'Doing Away with Double Effect' (2001) 111 *Ethics* 219; McKeogh, *Morality of Killing in War*, pp. 64–65; Neuman, 'Force Protection and Cumulative Assessment'; TM Scanlon, *Moral Dimensions: Permissibility, Meaning, Blame* (Cambridge, MA: Harvard University Press, 2008); Ralph Wedgwood, 'Scanlon on Double Effect' (2011) 83 *Philosophy and Phenomenological Research* 464; Dean Cocking, 'Collateral Damage: Intending Evil and Doing Evil' in Lovell and Primoratz (eds), *Protecting Civilians during Violent Conflict* 53; Luban, 'Risk Taking and Force Protection'.

[247] Sidgwick, *Elements of Politics*, pp. 254–57; Neuman, 'Force Protection and Cumulative Assessment', at 104–05; Walzer, *Just and Unjust Wars*, pp. 155–56; Hampson, 'Means and Methods of Warfare', p. 106; Noam J Zohar, 'Double Effect and Double Intention: A Collectivist Perspective' (2007) 40 *Israel Law Review* 730; S Lee, *Ethics and War*, pp. 173–81; Bradley Gershel, 'Applying Double Effect in Armed Conflicts: A Crisis of Legitimacy' (2013) 27 *Emory International Law Review* 741.

[248] Elizabeth Anscombe, 'War and Murder' in Malham M Wakin (ed), *War, Morality, and the Military Profession* (Boulder: Westview Press, 1979) 285, pp. 294–96; van Baarda, 'Perspective from Military Ethics', at 32–35.

reason why double effect as a concept cannot also apply to the disablement of enemy soldiers. On this view, IHL would obligate the belligerent always to seek the least injurious form of disablement available. Thus, *if* double effect were what humanity demanded, and *if* counter-*Humanitätsgebot* existed, *then* killing rather than capturing in circumstances where both forms of disablement had been reasonably available might constitute a breach of IHL.[249]

8.6 Promoting Humanity Above and Beyond Positive IHL Obligations

At this point, both *Humanitätsgebot* and counter-*Humanitätsgebot* are simply hypotheses. In view of their potentially far-reaching ramifications, we should carefully scrutinise them.

The situation is quite different where positive IHL rules unqualifiedly obligate less than what humanity permits. In such cases, acting in accordance with humanity *ipso facto* fulfils – and goes beyond – IHL obligations.[250]

Take the regulation of non-international armed conflicts, for example. As noted earlier, the legislative history of common Article 3 reveals that the ICRC had initially endeavoured to render the four 1949 Geneva Conventions applicable in their entirety to all armed conflicts.[251] Against this background, states deemed it permitted by considerations of sovereign interests to limit the scope of these conventions to international armed conflicts. At the 1949 Diplomatic Conference, this norm contradiction resulted in common Article 3 capturing only the 'compulsory minimum' joint satisfaction between humanitarian demands and sovereign liberties.[252] It is clear, however, that positive IHL authorises

[249] The same might be said of non-lethal weapons. Thus, *if* double effect were what humanity demanded, and *if* counter-*Humanitätsgebot* existed, *then* choosing to use lethal weapons rather than non-lethal weapons where both types of weapons were available for the purposes of enemy disablement might constitute a breach of IHL. See Chapter 4.

[250] Bruno Zimmermann, 'Article 1 – General Principles and Scope of Application' in Sandoz et al. (eds), *Commentary on Additional Protocols* 33, p. 37. The kind of behaviour at issue closely echoes that which exhibits ethical qualities requisite for the broader, humanity-preserving conception of vocational competence as a soldier. See Chapter 3.

[251] See Chapter 7; Pictet (ed., *Commentary Geneva Convention III*, pp. 28–31.

[252] Pictet (ed), *Commentary Geneva Convention IV*, p. 37; see also *Nicaragua*, para. 114; Joyce AC Gutteridge, 'The Geneva Conventions of 1949' (1949) 26 *British Yearbook of International Law* 294, at 300.

bringing further humanity to non-international armed conflicts. Indeed, there is a standing 'invitation to exceed that minimum'[253] enshrined in common Article 3. States remain at liberty to act on this invitation, for instance, by concluding special agreements.[254] Although strictly as a matter of policy rather than law, several states, including Germany,[255] no longer distinguish between international and non-international armed conflicts when instructing their military personnel on IHL. William J. Fenrick notes:

> Although a technical interpretation of the law may result in the conclusion that the armed forces are engaged in a non-international armed conflict, it may be considered desirable to require those forces to comply with the higher standards of IHL/LOAC for international armed conflicts. Indeed, as many armed forces prefer to train to a 'One Book' standard and, where IHL/LOAC is concerned, that standard is the law applicable to international armed conflicts, it may not be difficult to require the armed forces to comply as a matter of policy with IHL/LOAC for international armed conflicts on all occasions when they are deployed on out-of-country operations.[256]

Today's positive IHL does not appear to obligate the belligerent to capture rather than kill an adversary where both forms of disablement are reasonably available. Plainly, however, the law permits the belligerent to do so.[257] Strictly as a matter of permissive further humanisation, this choice makes eminent sense.[258]

[253] Pictet (ed), *Commentary Geneva Convention IV*, p. 37.

[254] Article 3 common to Geneva Conventions I–IV: 'The Parties to the conflict should further endeavour to bring into force, by means of special agreement, all or part of the other provisions of the present Convention'. See also Article 19(1)–(2), Hague Cultural Property Convention.

[255] Wolff Heintschel von Heinegg, 'The German Manual' in Nobuo Hayashi (ed), *National Military Manuals on the Law of Armed Conflict* 2nd edn (Oslo: Torkel Opsahl Academic EPublisher, 2010) 109, p. 112.

[256] William J Fenrick, 'Reflections on the Canadian Experience with Law of Armed Conflict Manuals' in N. Hayashi (ed), *National Military Manuals* 97, p. 105. See also Dieter Fleck, 'The Law of Non-international Armed Conflicts' in Fleck (ed), *Handbook of International Humanitarian Law* (2nd edn) 605, pp. 629–30.

[257] Parks, 'No Mandate, No Expertise, and Legally Incorrect', at 809; Schmitt, 'Military Necessity and Humanity', at 861.

[258] Capturing an eligible enemy combatant would generally be deemed more humane than killing him or her.

8.7 Conclusion

The inevitable conflict thesis argues that every positive IHL rule contains the military necessity–humanity interplay. Neither is therefore admissible as pleas in defence of non-compliance with unqualified rules.

This chapter has demonstrated that the first claim is empirically false. Some rules exhibit the involvement of military necessity but not humanity in the process of their creation. Meanwhile, some other rules embody humanity's juxtaposition with considerations other than military necessity. Accepting this fact compels the inevitable conflict thesis to contradict itself, because it must then accept the possibility that military necessity and humanity pleas may in fact be admissible vis-à-vis at least some unqualified IHL rules.

The joint satisfaction thesis explains the mechanics of IHL norm-creation differently. Unqualified IHL obligations preclude military necessity pleas because the very fact of their adoption logically extinguishes all indifferent counter-liberties. Since military necessity considerations are normatively indifferent, none of the permissions they generate, and hence no plea emanating from them (e.g., *Kriegsräson*), may be invoked vis-à-vis unqualified IHL rules. The same goes for humanity's indifferent permissions and pleas supposedly built on them (e.g., *Humanitätsräson*).

Both the inevitable conflict and joint satisfaction theses reject counter-*Kriegsräson*. The latter thesis, however, counsels against dismissing too hastily the possibilities of what might be called *Humanitätsgebot* and counter-*Humanitätsgebot*. These possibilities arise from the fact that the process of IHL norm-creation may leave genuine norm conflicts unresolved.

The same may even be said of chivalry. Although it is difficult to decipher its content,[259] chivalry appears indifferent regarding certain kinds of belligerent conduct (e.g., ruses) and not indifferent regarding others (e.g., improper use of enemy uniforms). One may ask whether chivalry is admissible as a justification or excuse for deviation from positive IHL, or whether it functions as an additional layer of normative restraint thereon. As is the case with *Humanitätsräson*, both a

[259] Thomas C Wingfield, 'Chivalry in the Use of Force' (2001) 23 *University of Toledo Law Review* 111; Rain Liivoja, 'Chivalry without a Horse: Military Honour and the Modern Law of Armed Conflict' in Rain Liivoja and Andres Saumets (eds), *The Law of Armed Conflict: Historical and Contemporary Perspectives* (Tartu: Tartu University Press, 2012) 75.

Ritterlichkeitsräson[260] and a counter-*Ritterlichkeitsräson* are safely rejected. Their non-indifferent variants, i.e., a *Ritterlichkeitsgebot* and a counter-*Ritterlichkeitsgebot*, may be harder to dismiss.[261]

This chapter has shown the exclusionary effects that adopting unqualified IHL rules generates for indifferent considerations, as well as the possible absence of such effects for non-indifferent considerations. We have not said anything about situations where a positive IHL rule specifically envisages military necessity pleas. To what consequences does IHL norm-creation give rise where the framers have chosen to retain military necessity as valid exceptions from the principal prescriptions of positive IHL? How are we to interpret and apply such exceptions? In the next chapter, we will investigate the significance and content of express military necessity clauses.

260 That is, '*Ritterlichkeitsräson geht vor Kriegsmanier*' (necessities of chivalry override rules of war).

261 Rain Liivoja, 'Law and Honour: Normative Pluralism in the Regulation of Military Conduct' in Jan Klabbers and Touko Piiparinen (eds), *Normative Pluralism and International Law: Exploring Global Governance* (Cambridge: Cambridge University Press, 2013) 143; Gill, 'Chivalry', pp. 43–49.

9

Significance and Content of Juridical Military Necessity

In its juridical context, military necessity exempts measures from certain positive IHL rules that principally prescribe contrary behaviour. These measures are authorised to the extent that they are required for the attainment of military purposes and otherwise remain in conformity with positive IHL.[1] If not, or no longer, in fulfilment of these conditions, a measure ceases to be exempted and reverts to being governed by the principal prescriptions, which in turn render it unlawful. Juridical military necessity exempts eligible conduct from certain principal IHL obligations, whereas juridical military non-necessity returns ineligible conduct to them.

This chapter begins by distinguishing juridical military necessity as an exception from the state of necessity as a circumstance precluding wrongfulness. It then endeavours to elucidate the significance and content of juridical military necessity. This involves interpreting the principal IHL rules and their exceptional clauses to the particular set of facts at issue.

Juridical military necessity appears exclusively as an exception from those principal rules of positive IHL that envisage its admissibility explicitly and in advance. Express military necessity clauses indicate where normative military necessity has escaped exclusion through IHL norm-creation. As an exception, military necessity contains four discernible requirements. First, the measure must be taken primarily for some specific military purpose. Second, the measure must be required for the purpose's attainment. Third, the purpose must be in conformity with IHL. Fourth, the measure itself must otherwise be in conformity with that law.[2] Our discussion will reveal continuing disagreements in

[1] Robin Geiß, 'Military Necessity: A Fundamental "Principle" Fallen into Oblivion' in Hélène Ruiz Fabri et al. (eds), 2 *Select Proceedings of the European Society of International Law* (Oxford: Hart Publishing, 2010) 554, pp. 558–65.

[2] Asa Kasher and Amos Yadlin, 'Military Ethics of Fighting Terror: An Israeli Perspective' (2005) 4 *Journal of Military Ethics* 3, at 11–12.

some areas, in particular the criteria of proportionality for determining whether the measure taken was required for the attainment of the military purpose sought.

9.1 Juridical Military Necessity as an Exception

Exceptional military necessity has not yet been authoritatively defined. In this book I propose the following definition: Military necessity exempts a measure from certain specific rules of positive IHL that principally prescribe contrary action, to the extent that the measure is required for the attainment of a military purpose and otherwise in conformity with that law.

It is submitted that this definition embodies custom. As will be seen below, the definition's various aspects find support in major military manuals reflecting state practice and/or *opinio juris*,[3] and are confirmed by judicial decisions[4] as well as scholarly writings.[5]

3 US Department of the Navy et al., *Commander's Handbook*, p. 5-1; Canadian JAG, *Law of Armed Conflict*, pp. 2-1, 16-5; UK Defence Ministry, *Joint Service Manual*, pp. 21–23; Office of General Counsel, *Law of War Manual*, pp. 51–58. See also Henckaerts and Doswald-Beck, *Customary International Humanitarian Law* (vol. I), pp. 1002–10. Caution may be advisable, however, because it is arguable that not all military manuals necessarily enjoy the same probative value on the practice and/or *opinio juris* of the states that issue them. Nobuo Hayashi, 'Introduction' in N Hayashi (ed), *National Military Manuals* 17, pp. 33–34; Charles Garraway, 'Military Manuals, Operational Law and the Regulatory Framework of the Armed Forces' in N Hayashi (ed), *National Military Manuals* 45, pp. 50, 53; David Turns, 'Military Manuals and the Customary Law of Armed Conflict' in N Hayashi (ed), *National Military Manuals* 65.

4 See below.

5 Burleigh Cushing Rodick, *The Doctrine of Necessity in International Law* (New York: Columbia University Press, 1928), pp. 59–61; William Gerald Downey, Jr, 'The Law of War and Military Necessity' (1953) 47 *American Journal of International Law* 251, at 254; BVA Röling, 'The Law of War and the National Jurisdiction Since 1945', *Collected Courses of the Hague Academy of International Law* (Leiden and Boston: Martinus Nijhoff, 1960), vol. C, 323, pp. 382–87; Dunbar, 'Military Necessity in War Crimes Trials'; O'Brien, 'Meaning of Military Necessity'; Robert W Gehring, 'Loss of Civilian Protections under the Fourth Geneva Convention and Protocol I' (1980) 90 *Military Law Review* 49, at 54–58; Dinstein, 'Military Necessity' (1st edn); Greenwood, 'Historical Development', pp. 36–38; Yutaka Arai-Takahashi, 'Excessive Collateral Civilian Casualties and Military Necessity: Awkward Crossroads in International Humanitarian Law between State Responsibility and Individual Criminal Liability' in Freya Baetens and Christine Chinkin (eds), *Sovereignty, Statehood and State Responsibility: Essays in Honour of James Crawford* (Cambridge: Cambridge University Press, 2015) 325, p. 332.

9.2 Military Necessity as an Exception vs. State of Necessity as a Circumstance Precluding Wrongfulness

Before proceeding further, we need to clarify two key differences between military necessity as an exception, on the one hand, and the state of necessity as a circumstance precluding wrongfulness, on the other. The first difference concerns their status: exceptional military necessity forms part of what we call 'primary rules' of international law, whereas the state of necessity is a 'secondary rule'. The second difference involves the two concepts' distinct contents.

9.2.1 Primary and Secondary Rules

For some time, our standard discourse on the international law of state responsibility has separated primary rules from secondary rules.[6] To the former group belong those rules that determine the content of a substantive obligation and whose breach constitutes an internationally wrongful act. Exceptional clauses modify the content of the primary rules to which they are attached. It may therefore be said that juridical military necessity forms part of these rules and that acts in fulfilment of its requirements are not internationally wrongful.[7]

[6] Pierre-Marie Dupuy, 'The International Law of State Responsibility: Revolution or Evolution?' (1989) 11 *Michigan Journal of International Law* 105; Y Matsui, 'The Transformation of the Law of State Responsibility' in René Provost (ed), *State Responsibility in International Law* (Burlington: Ashgate, 2002) 3, pp. 3–4; James Crawford, *The International Law Commission's Articles on State Responsibility: Introduction, Text and Commentaries* (Cambridge: Cambridge University Press, 2002), pp. 14–16. It should be noted that legal philosophers often use the same pair of expressions to denote notions that are quite different. Kelsen, *General Theory of Law and State*, pp. 58–61, 143–44; Hart, *Concept of Law* (2nd edn), pp. 77–96.

[7] International Law Commission, 2 *Yearbook of the International Law Commission* Pt II (2001) 20, p. 84 (footnotes omitted): 'as embodied in article 25, the plea of necessity is not intended to cover conduct which is in principle regulated by the primary obligations. This has a particular importance in relation to the rules relating ... to the question of "military necessity" ... which is, in the first place, the underlying criterion for a series of substantive rules of the law of war and neutrality, as well as being included in terms in a number of treaty provisions in the field of international humanitarian law ... while considerations akin to those underlying article 25 may have a role, they are taken into account in the context of the formulation and interpretation of the primary obligations'. See also Robert D Sloane, 'On the Use and Abuse of Necessity in the Law of State Responsibility' (2012) 106 *American Journal of International Law* 447, at 497; Arai-Takahashi, 'Excessive Collateral Civilian Casualties and Military Necessity', pp. 336, 337–38.

To the group of secondary rules belong the conditions for the existence of an internationally wrongful act,[8] as well as the legal consequences that flow from it.[9] Justifications and excuses are examples of secondary rules. Circumstances precluding 'wrongfulness' – as opposed to, say, 'blameworthiness' – may be considered functionally analogous to justifications.[10] In the international law of state responsibility, necessity constitutes such a circumstance.[11]

In its earlier consideration of justificatory necessity, the ILC treated military necessity separately as an exception under IHL:

> The Commission finally came to consider the cases in which a State has invoked a situation of necessity to justify actions not in conformity with an international obligation under the law of war and, more particularly, has pleaded a situation coming within the scope of the special concept described as 'necessities of war'. There has been much discussion, mainly in the past, on the question whether or not 'necessity of war' or 'military necessity' can be invoked to justify conduct not in conformity with that required by obligations of the kind here considered. On this point a preliminary clarification is required. The principal role of 'military necessity' is not that of a circumstance exceptionally precluding the wrongfulness of an act which, in other circumstances, would not be in conformity with an obligation under international law ... [W]hat is involved is certainly not the effect of 'necessity' as a circumstance precluding the wrongfulness of conduct which the applicable rule does not prohibit, but rather the effect of 'non-necessity' as a circumstance precluding the lawfulness of conduct which that rule normally allows.[12]

The commission's allusion to non-necessity 'as a circumstance precluding the lawfulness of conduct which that rule normally allows' comes dangerously close to counter-*Kriegsräson*.[13]

Be that as it may, the ILC concluded that the state of necessity would be inadmissible as a justification for non-compliance with a provision of IHL conventions:

[8] Articles 1–15, Articles on State Responsibility.

[9] Ibid, Articles 28–41.

[10] But see Robert Rosenstock, 'Symposium: The ILC's State Responsibility Articles: The ILC and State Responsibility' (2002) 96 *American Journal of International Law* 792, p. 794; Desierto, *Necessity and National Emergency Clauses*, pp. 103–08.

[11] It is in this context that the *Coleman v Mexico* case is best understood. *Bond Coleman (U.S.A.) v United Mexican States*, United States and Mexico General Claims Commission, 3 October 1928, 4 *Reports of International Arbitral Awards* (2006) 365, pp. 367–68; Desierto, *Necessity and National Emergency Clauses*, p. 51 n.60.

[12] ILC, 2 *Yearbook of the International Law Commission* Pt II (1980) 13, pp. 45–46.

[13] See Chapter 8.

> The second category of obligations to which the Commission referred, with the same aim, was that of obligations established in the text of a treaty, where the treaty is one whose text indicates, explicitly or implicitly, that the treaty excludes the possibility of invoking a state of necessity as justification for conduct not in conformity with an obligation which it imposes on the contracting parties. This possibility is obviously excluded if the treaty explicitly says so, as in the case of certain humanitarian conventions applicable to armed conflicts. However, there are many cases in which the treaty is silent on the point. The Commission thinks it important to observe in this connection that silence on the part of the treaty should not be automatically construed as allowing the possibility of invoking the state of necessity. There are treaty obligations which were especially designed to be equally, or even particularly, applicable in abnormal situations of peril for the State having the obligation and for its essential interests, and yet the treaty contains no provision on the question now being discussed (this is true of other humanitarian conventions applicable to armed conflicts). In the view of the Commission, the bar to the invocability of the state of necessity then emerges implicitly, but with certainty, from the object and the purpose of the rule, and also in some cases from the circumstances in which it was formulated and adopted.[14]

According to the ILC, the inadmissibility of necessity as a circumstance precluding wrongfulness vis-à-vis positive IHL rules emanates from the very nature of the activities these rules are intended to regulate.[15] This solution, while not without merit, effectively precludes any room for *Humanitätsgebot*.[16] The commission observes that '[t]here are treaty obligations which were especially designed to be equally, or even particularly, applicable in abnormal situations of peril for the State having the obligation and for its essential interests, and yet the treaty contains no provision on the question now being discussed', adding: 'this is true of other humanitarian conventions applicable to armed conflicts'. Those 'abnormal situations of peril', however, are also situations where

[14] ILC, 1980 *Yearbook*, pp. 50–51. See also Article 25(2)(a), Articles on State Responsibility: 'In any case, necessity may not be invoked by a State as a ground for precluding wrongfulness if ... [t]he international obligation in question excludes the possibility of invoking necessity'.

[15] ILC, 2001 *Yearbook*, p. 84; David Kretzmer, 'The Advisory Opinion: The Light Treatment of International Humanitarian Law' (2005) 99 *American Journal of International Law* 88, at 99; Sarah Heathcote, 'Circumstances Precluding the Wrongfulness in the ILC Articles on State Responsibility: Necessity' in James Crawford et al. (eds), *The Law of International Responsibility* (Oxford: Oxford University Press, 2010) 491, p. 498; Venturini, 'Necessity in the Law of Armed Conflict and International Criminal Law', at 52.

[16] See Chapter 8.

humanitarian considerations become particularly acute. It is to these situations that IHL conventions are 'especially designed to be equally, or even particularly, applicable'. Consequently, 'the bar to the invocability' of all humanity pleas 'then emerges implicitly, but with certainty . . . from the circumstances in which [the rule] was formulated and adopted'.

9.2.2 Distinct Contents

In addition to their dissimilar status, military necessity and the state of necessity have distinct requirements. For example, according to Article 25(1)(a) of the Articles on State Responsibility, necessity may be invoked by a state only where the act in question 'is the only means available' to safeguard its imperilled interest.[17] The ILC's commentary states that '[t]he plea is excluded if there are other (otherwise) lawful means available, even if they may be more costly or less convenient'.[18] In addition, Article 25(2)(b) disqualifies a state from invoking necessity if it has contributed to the situation of necessity.

As will be shown below, exceptional military necessity does not contain these conditions. In order to be eligible for military necessity exceptions, the belligerent need *not* show that its conduct was a *conditio sine qua non* for the purpose's attainment. Nor is the belligerent's contribution to the creation of circumstances of exceptional military necessity a ground for its inadmissibility. The mere fact that the belligerent becomes involved in an armed conflict certainly does not disqualify it from relying on military necessity clauses. The same goes for such strategic, operational and tactical decisions, or such manners in which campaigns, manoeuvres and military operations unfold, as may place the belligerent in situations where acting in a certain way becomes militarily necessary.

Nor is it a prerequisite for exceptional military necessity that the conduct should also qualify as justificatory necessity.[19] Although, as a

17 ILC, 2001 *Yearbook*, p. 83.

18 Ibid.

19 Arai-Takahashi, 'Excessive Collateral Civilian Casualties and Military Necessity', pp. 337–38. But see International Humanitarian Law Research Initiative, *The Separation Barrier and International Humanitarian Law: Briefing Paper* (2004), p. 6: 'The second test [of military necessity] relates to the existence of a state of necessity that justifies the measures the occupying power intends to take. This state of necessity varies according to circumstances: it could be a clear danger facing the forces of occupation, it could emerge from the requirement of military operations, or it could be a present need of the occupation forces (like food, water, medical equipments, command posts, etc.). In any

matter of fact, certain conduct may satisfy both sets of requirements simultaneously, this does not mean that exceptional military necessity and the state of necessity are identical notions or that one entails the other.

9.3 Specific Requirements of Juridical Military Necessity

In its juridical context, military necessity exempts a measure from certain specific rules of positive IHL that principally prescribe contrary action, to the extent that the measure is required for the attainment of a military purpose and otherwise in conformity with that law. Defined thus, the notion may be broken into four requirements:[20]

1. That the measure was taken primarily for some specific military purpose.
2. That the measure was required for the attainment of the military purpose, it being understood that 'required' here means:
   a. That the measure was materially relevant to the military purpose's attainment;
   b. That, of those materially relevant and reasonably available measures, the one taken was the least evil; and
   c. That the evil that the measure would cause was not disproportionate to the gain that it would achieve.
3. That the military purpose for which the measure was taken was in conformity with IHL.
4. That the measure itself was otherwise in conformity with IHL.

These four requirements are cumulative. Should a given measure fail to satisfy any one or more of them, the measure would be 'militarily unnecessary' within the meaning of exceptional military necessity clauses.

Two notable consequences follow. First, failing to satisfy these requirements is distinct from being militarily unnecessary in its strictly material

case, the state of necessity refers only to situations that are *within* the occupied territory, and facing the occupying power in the course of occupation. The occupying power has the burden of demonstrating the existence of this state of necessity'. See also ibid pp. 8–9, 12–13.

20 Henry offers three somewhat analogous conditions. They are: 'situation de nécessité et urgence', 'aptitude de la mesure à atteindre l'objectif' and 'choix du moyen le moins dommageable'. Henry, *Principe de nécessité militaire*, pp. 582–604.

sense.[21] Whereas criterion (2)(a) is common to both material and juridical military necessity, the latter alone contains criteria (2)(b) and (2)(c).[22] Also, whereas juridical military necessity formally requires both the measure taken and the purpose sought to comply with IHL, compliance is, at best, merely an expedient desideratum for strictly material military necessity.[23] In other words, juridical military necessity is more restrictive in scope than material military necessity. It is therefore possible that a belligerent act is consistent with military necessity in its strictly material context and yet fails to qualify for the application of a military necessity clause. Thus, the particular route chosen by the Israel Defence Forces (IDF) Commander for the erection of a separation fence in some parts of the West Bank may have constituted a material military necessity, but it was found by the Israeli Supreme Court to be ineligible for a military necessity exception.

Second, an act being 'militarily unnecessary' in its juridical sense simply means that the exceptional clause ceases to apply to it.[24] The clause's inapplicability exposes the conduct to the IHL rule's principal content. It is the latter rule that renders the conduct unlawful. The conduct's unlawfulness emanates neither from its lack of judicial military necessity, nor from the now inoperative military necessity clause. For example, Article 53 of Geneva Convention IV principally prohibits the destruction by the Occupying Power of real or personal property in territories it occupies, 'except where such destruction is rendered absolutely necessary by military operations'.[25] Before the Eritrea-Ethiopia Claims Commission, Ethiopia declined to contend that the destruction of Tserona Town constituted a military necessity, or that the exceptional clause found in Article 53 of Geneva Convention IV applied to it. The commission proceeded to find Ethiopia responsible for the destruction, an act principally prohibited by Article 53 of Geneva Convention IV.[26]

[21] See Chapter 2.

[22] Conversely, material military necessity alone entails the comparison between the degrees to which two reasonably available courses of action would be conducive towards a common military goal under the prevailing circumstances. See ibid.

[23] See Chapters 2, 4 and 5.

[24] *Legal Consequences*, para. 135 (finding that the court was not convinced that 'the destructions carried out contrary to the prohibition in Article 53 of the Fourth Geneva Convention were rendered absolutely necessary by military operations').

[25] Article 53, Geneva Convention IV.

[26] *Ethiopia v Eritrea*, Eritrea-Ethiopia Claims Commission, *Partial Award Central Front – Eritrea's Claims 2, 4, 6, 7, 8, & 22*, 28 April 2004, paras 63, 71.

In addition to the four requirements listed above, military necessity involves questions about both the knowledge and the formal competence of the person invoking it. These questions will be considered later.

9.3.1 Measure Was Taken Primarily for Some Specific Military Purpose

This requirement is two-fold. First, it must be shown that there was, in fact, a specific purpose for which the measure was taken. Second, it must be shown that this purpose was primarily military in nature. It is not a requirement of juridical military necessity that the belligerent seek the submission of its enemy, despite occasional suggestions to the contrary.

9.3.1.1 Existence of a Specific Purpose

Military necessity exception is unavailable where the measure is taken for no purpose.[27] If, for example, an area was devastated purposelessly, it would lack any meaningful point of reference against which the devastation's necessity is to be assessed. '[N]ecessary ... for *what*?', one might ask in vain.[28] In the words of Myres S. McDougal and Florentino P. Feliciano,

> [a] particular combat operation, comprising the application of a certain amount of violence, can be appraised as necessary or unnecessary only in relation to the attainment of a specified objective. Obviously, further clarification of the principle of military necessity is, in corresponding part, contingent upon specification of legitimate belligerent objectives.[29]

Similarly, in *Hostage*, Military Tribunal V held:

> [Military necessity] does not permit the killing of innocent inhabitants for purposes of revenge or the satisfaction of a lust to kill. The destruction of property to be lawful must be imperatively demanded by the necessities of war. Destruction as an end in itself is a violation of international law ... [Military necessity] does not admit the wanton devastation of a district or the willful infliction of suffering upon its inhabitants for the sake of suffering alone.[30]

[27] See Chapter 2.
[28] McDougal and Feliciano, *Law and Minimum World Public Order*, p. 525 (emphasis in original).
[29] Ibid.
[30] *Hostage*, 757, pp. 1253–54. Albeit in the context of deportation/forcible transfer as a crime against humanity, one ICTY trial chamber ruled that military necessity does not justify evacuation for the sake of evacuation. *Krstić Trial Judgment*, paras 524–27.

9.3.1.2 Purpose's Primarily Military Nature

Even if a specific purpose is shown to have existed, it must additionally be shown that the purpose was primarily military in nature. Here, the expression 'military' may be understood as a quality characterising or purportedly characterising[31] sound strategic, operational or tactical thinking in the planning, preparation and execution of belligerent activities. It follows that military necessity is inadmissible in respect of measures taken for purposes that are *not* primarily military in the sense just described.[32]

In the event of an aerial bombardment, '[t]he officer in command of an attacking force must, before commencing a bombardment, except in cases of assault, do all in his power to warn the authorities'.[33] According to commentators, the officer in question would be exempt from his duty to warn the authorities should military necessity so require.[34] One primarily military purpose cited in this regard is the aversion of danger to the attacking aircraft.[35] Factors such as oversight on the part of the officer, and the absence of friendly local population likely to be affected by the bombardment, would not suffice.

No less pertinent for the requirement that the measure be taken for a primarily military purpose are situations of belligerent occupation. This is so because the occupier might present its geopolitical, demographic, ideological and/or economic ambitions as legitimate military concerns.[36]

Two Israeli cases may be illustrative of the intricacies involved. In *Elon Moreh*, the Supreme Court of Israel, sitting as the High Court of Justice, declared null and void an order issued by the IDF Commander for the Judaea and Samaria Region to requisition privately owned Palestinian

[31] 'Purportedly characterising' accounts for incompetence.

[32] Roxburgh (ed), *Oppenheim's International Law* (3rd edn), p. 213: '[i]n every case destruction ... must not be merely be the outcome of a spirit of plunder or revenge.'

[33] Article 26, Hague Regulations (1907).

[34] Stone, *Legal Controls of International Conflict*, pp. 622–23; Rogers, *Law on the Battlefield* (2nd edn), p. 88.

[35] Stone, *Legal Controls of International Conflict*, p. 622; Rogers, *Law on the Battlefield* (2nd edn), p. 88.

[36] *Yoav Hess et al. v The Commander of IDF Forces in the West Bank, GOC Central Command and the State of Israel*, HCJ 10356/20, and *The Hebron Municipality et al. v Major General Moshe Kaplinsky et al.*, HCJ 10497/20, *Judgment*, 4 March 2004, para. 12; *Beit Sourik Village Council v The Government of Israel and Commander of the IDF Forces in the West Bank*, HCJ 2056/04, *Judgment*, 30 June 2004, paras 26–27.

land for the establishment of a civilian settlement.[37] The court found that the settlement's establishment was a predominantly political decision in which military considerations would have been of secondary importance at best. The court determined that, in the final analysis, the establishment would not have been approved by the government but for the purposes of satisfying the desire of a religious interest group and acting on 'the Jewish people's right to settle in Judaea and Samaria'.[38]

At issue in *Elon Moreh* was whether the requisition order was in conformity with the customary IHL rules contained in Article 52 of the 1907 Hague Regulations. According to this article, '[r]equisitions in kind and services shall not be demanded from municipalities or inhabitants [of the territory under occupation] except for the needs of the army of occupation ... Such requisitions and services shall only be demanded on the authority of the commander in the locality occupied'.[39]

Traditionally, the Israeli Supreme Court has interpreted 'the needs of the army of occupation' broadly to encompass:

(i) All kinds of purposes demanded by the necessities of war;
(ii) Military movements, quartering and the construction of defence positions;
(iii) What is required to 'safeguard public order and security' within the meaning of Article 43 of the 1907 Hague Regulations; and
(iv) What the army needs in order to fulfil its task of defending the occupied area against hostile acts liable to originate from outside.[40]

In considering the matter at hand, the court directed its attention to the decisions of the Ministerial Defence Committee and the Cabinet, as well as the professional opinion provided to them by the then Chief of

[37] *Izat Muhamed Mustafa Dweikat et al. v The Government of Israel et al.*, HCJ 390/79, *Judgment*, 22 October 1979 (reprinted in (1980) 19 *International Legal Materials* 148) (hereinafter *Elon Moreh*).
[38] Ibid, at 170.
[39] Article 52, Hague Regulations (1907).
[40] *Elon Moreh*, at 168–69. See also *Hess et al.* and *Hebron Municipality et al.*, at para. 9. According to Stone, however, the expression 'needs of the army of occupation' is intended to be narrower in scope than the expression 'necessities of war'. Stone, *Legal Controls of International Conflict*, p. 708. See also Schwarzenberger, *International Law as Applied by Courts and Tribunals* (vol. II), pp. 245–46, 270–71; Pertile, 'Missed Opportunity?', at 135; David Kretzmer, 'The Supreme Court of Israel: Judicial Review during Armed Conflict' (2004) 47 *German Yearbook of International Law* 392, at 447; Kretzmer, 'Advisory Opinion', at 97; David Kretzmer, 'The Law of Belligerent Occupation in the Supreme Court of Israel' (2012) 94 *International Review of the Red Cross* 207, at 216–18.

Staff (C-o-S) according to which the requisition would indeed be consistent with military needs.[41]

The court held:

> [T]his professional view of the C-o-S would in itself not have led to the taking of the decision on the establishment of the Elon Moreh settlement, had there not been another reason, which was the driving force for the taking of said decision in the Ministerial Defence Committee and in the Cabinet plenum – namely, the powerful desire of the members of Gush Emunim to settle in the heart of Eretz-Israel, as close as possible to the town of Nablus … [B]oth the Ministerial Committee and the Cabinet majority were decisively influenced by reasons lying in a Zionist point of view of the settlement of the whole Land of Israel.[42]

The evidence showed that political bodies initiated the civilian settlement's establishment at the site; the IDF authorities did not initiate the settlement's establishment, as would be expected if the matter involved genuine military needs.[43] On the contrary, the C-o-S gave his approval only *post factum* to what was essentially a political programme.[44] In the court's view, this particular sequence of events did not attest to 'there having been from the outset a military necessity to take private land in order to establish the civilian settlement, within the bounds of Article 52 of the Hague Regulations'.[45] Justice M. Landau, writing for the unanimous court,[46] concluded:

> The political consideration was, therefore, the dominant factor in the Ministerial Defence Committee's decision to establish the settlement at that site, though I assume the Committee as well as the Cabinet majority were convinced that its establishment *also* (emphasis in the original – Trans.) fulfils military needs; and I accept the declaration of the C-o-S that he, for his part did not take into account political considerations, including the pressure of the Gush Emunim members, when he came to submit his professional opinion to the military level. But a secondary reason, such as the military reason in the decisions of the political level

[41] The C-o-S's 'central point', as described by the court, was that 'a settlement on that site serves as a stronghold protecting freedom of traffic on the nearby roads at the time of deployment of reserve forces on the eastern front in time of war'. *Elon Moreh*, at 155; see also ibid, at 153–54.

[42] Ibid, at 169.

[43] Ibid, at 171.

[44] Ibid, at 173.

[45] Ibid, at 175.

[46] Two justices concurred with Justice Landau. The other two justices also concurred but appended separate opinions of their own. Ibid, at 148.

> which initiated the settlement's establishment does not fulfil the precise strictures laid down by the Hague Regulations for preferring the military need to the individual's right to property. In other words: would the decision of the political level to establish the settlement at that site have been taken had it not been for the pressure of Gush Emunim and the political-ideological reasons which were before the political level? I have been convinced that had it not been for these reasons, the decision would not have been taken in the circumstances which prevailed at the time.[47]

The court declined to rule upon the truth of the claim that it was militarily necessary to establish a civilian settlement at the site in question.[48] On this matter the court deferred, as it had done so in previous cases,[49] to the C-o-S's professional opinion.[50] Through this deference, the court arguably acknowledged that the settlement *might* have actually fulfilled the military needs as suggested by the C-o-S if the requisition order had been upheld and the settlement established.

This arguable acknowledgement is significant. It would appear that the court was prepared to annul a predominantly political decision to requisition private land in occupied territory despite its potential fulfilment of genuine military needs. It would also appear that the lawfulness of the *Elon Moreh* requisition order depended on whether it had really been decided for the right purposes,[51] not whether it would have generated the right results.

In *Beit Sourik*, the Israeli Supreme Court had before it a petition against orders issued by the IDF Commander in the area of Judea and

47 Ibid. Justice Landau went on to (a) dispose of the problem associated with the plurality of purposes in decision-making by holding that a decision's lawfulness should be judged according to its dominant purpose, and to (b) defend the approach he had taken to purposes and motives whereby the two notions are treated as sharing a common area of meaning. Ibid, at 175 (citing SA de Smith, *Judicial Review of Administrative Action*, 3rd edn (London: Stevens and Sons, 1973). See also *Elon Moreh*, at 175–76.

48 The court did, however, note the existence of diametrically opposing views on this subject. *Elon Moreh*, at 154–56.

49 Kretzmer, 'Law of Belligerent Occupation', at 228.

50 *Elon Moreh*, at 152–56. The court, quoting a passage from its previous ruling (not yet published at the time), said (ibid, at 156): 'In a dispute of this sort on military-professional questions, in which the course [*sic*] has no fixed view of its own, we shall presume that the professional views expressed in the affidavit on behalf of the respondents, speaking in the name of those who are responsible for the preservation of security in the administered territories and within the Green Line, are the correct views. Very convincing evidence is needed to contradict this presumption'.

51 *Beit Sourik*, para. 27. See also *Zaharan Yunis Muhammad Mara'abe et al. v The Prime Minister of Israel et al.*, HCJ 7957/04, *Judgment*, 15 September 2005 (hereinafter *Alfei Menashe*), para. 98.

Samaria to seize land for the purpose of erecting a separation fence.[52] The petitioners were landowners and village councils affected by the orders. They alleged, among other things, the commander's lack of authority to issue the orders; the fence's political, non-military purpose; the lack of military necessity for the fence being erected along the planned route; defects in the procedure that rendered the land seizures illegal; and violations of the local inhabitants' fundamental rights.[53]

The court upheld the commander's authority to construct the fence.[54] It then proceeded with the examination of the fence's route chosen by the commander and its lawfulness under IHL.[55] The court looked, inter alia, to Articles 53 of Geneva Convention IV for this purpose, yet without considering whether the erection of the barrier constituted 'military operations' within the meaning of that article.[56] Marco Pertile suggests that it does not, on the ground that

> [t]he construction of the wall, as a complex project, planned over a span of years and substantially preventive in nature is quite different from the traditional concept of military operations. A flexible interpretation of the text of Article 53 [of Geneva Convention IV] would be necessary in order to include the wall amongst military operations. Such a solution however seems to be precluded by the wording of the Article which, after stressing the overall prohibition of the destruction of property, recognises the necessities of military operations in the form of a derogatory clause. As for all derogatory clauses strict interpretation is required.[57]

It may be asked whether the expression 'military operations', even if strictly interpreted, actually precludes a project such as the one in question here simply because it is complex, involves years of planning and pursues preventive purposes. Far from being 'quite different from the

[52] *Beit Sourik*, paras 1–6.
[53] Ibid, paras 10–11.
[54] Ibid. The court dismissed the petitioners' claim that the military commander decided to erect the fence on political, not military, considerations. It also dismissed alleged defects in the seizure proceedings and the exercise of the military commander's authority therein. Ibid, paras 26–32. See also *Alfei Menashe*, paras 15–23, 98–101.
[55] *Beit Sourik*, paras 33–35.
[56] Ibid, para. 35.
[57] Pertile, 'Missed Opportunity?', at 135–36. See also ibid, at 150–51; Alexander Orakhelashvili, 'Legal Consequences of the Construction of a Wall in the Occupied Palestinian Territory: Opinion and Reaction' (2006) 11 *Journal of Conflict & Security Law* 119, at 137: 'Military operations in the West Bank ceased a long time ago and the Wall itself is hardly meant to serve the needs of the Israeli army. Whatever the situation in the West Bank, it cannot currently be denoted as a state of war.'

traditional concept of military operations', as Pertile puts it, constructing defensive fortifications with these characteristics has been part and parcel of territorial warfare. The mere fact that such a project occurs on occupied territory does not alter its character as a military operation.

If it were true that the wall's erection did not constitute 'military operations' within the meaning of Article 53, however, then it would be arguable that the seizure orders of the IDF commander had not been issued 'primarily for some military purpose'.

9.3.1.3 Submission of the Enemy?

The military purpose sought need not be complete submission of the enemy.[58] While this formulation was found in some, typically older, military manuals,[59] it is not the case with most of the later ones[60] and commentaries.[61]

There is some authority for the view that military necessity may be admissible even for purposes that are purely defensive in nature or for the sanitary requirements of an occupation force. In *Hostage*, for instance, the US Military Tribunal acquitted Lothar Rendulic of wanton destruction of private and public property in Finnmark, Norway, a charge based on the rules contained in Article 23(g) of the 1907 Hague Regulations. The tribunal held: 'The destruction of public and private property by retreating military forces which would give aid and comfort to the enemy may constitute a situation coming within the exceptions contained in Article 23g [of the Hague Regulations]'.[62] At no point did the tribunal consider whether the destruction ought to have been

[58] Roxburgh (ed), *Oppenheim's International Law* (3rd edn), p. 212 (emphasis in original): 'All destruction of, and damage to, enemy property for the purpose of offence and defence is *necessary* destruction and damage, and therefore lawful, whether it be on the battlefield during battle, or in preparation for battle or siege'.

[59] Canadian JAG, *Law of Armed Conflict*, p. 2-1 (allowing complete submission only as 'the *primary aim* of armed conflict') (emphasis added); The War Office, *The Law of War on Land, Being Part III of the Manual of Military Law* (1958), p. 1; US Department of the Army, *Law of Land Warfare*, p. 4.

[60] De Mulinen, *Handbook on the Law of War*, pp. 82–83 ('overpowering of the enemy'); UK Defence Ministry, *Joint Service Manual*, p. 21 ('complete or partial submission of the enemy'); UK Defence Ministry, *Joint Services Manual Amendment 3*, p. 5; US Department of the Navy et al., *Commander's Handbook*, p. 5-2 ('partial or complete submission of the enemy'); Office of General Counsel, *Law of War Manual*, pp. 56–57.

[61] Schwarzenberger, *International Law as Applied by Courts and Tribunals* (vol. II), pp. 131–32; Rogers, *Law on the Battlefield* (2nd edn), p. 5; Solis, *Law of Armed Conflict*, p. 260; Greenwood, 'Historical Development', p. 36.

[62] *Hostage*, pp. 1296–97.

militarily necessary to defeat the advancing Soviet troops, let al.one the armed forces of the Soviet Union as a whole.[63]

In *Hardman*, the Great Britain–United States Arbitral Tribunal ruled that the measures taken by an occupation force for the maintenance of its sanitary conditions constituted military necessity. The tribunal stated:

> In the present case [involving an 1898 United States military campaign in Cuba], the necessity of war was the occupation of Siboney, and that occupation ... involved the necessity, according to the medical authorities ... of taking the said sanitary measures, i.e., the destruction of the houses and their contents. In other words, the presence of the United States troops at Siboney was a necessity of war and the destruction required for their safety was consequently a necessity of war.[64]

Similarly, Rogers observes:

> The reference to the complete submission of the enemy, written in light of the experience of total war in the Second World War, is probably now obsolete since war can have a limited purpose as in the termination of the occupation of the Falkland Islands in 1982 or of Kuwait in 1991.[65]

Admittedly, Rogers has made this observation specifically with the 1958 British manual[66] in mind. Nevertheless, his observation would also be valid vis-à-vis other manuals that refer to the complete submission of the enemy or adversary as an aspect of military necessity.

9.3.2 Measure Was Required for the Attainment of the Military Purpose

For military necessity pleas to be admissible, the measure taken must be 'required'[67] for the attainment of the military purpose. Assessing the

[63] McDougal and Feliciano, *Law and Minimum World Public Order*, pp. 74–75.

[64] *Hardman*, p. 26. See also Schwarzenberger, *International Law as Applied by Courts and Tribunals* (vol. II), pp. 131–32; McCoubrey, 'Modern Doctrine of Military Necessity', at 222–23.

[65] Rogers, *Law on the Battlefield* (2nd edn), p. 5.

[66] UK War Office, *Law of War on Land.*

[67] Various expressions, such as 'indispensable', 'need', 'requirement', 'necessary' and so on, have been used to denote essentially the same notion of 'required'. See, e.g., Article 14, Lieber Code ('indispensable'); de Mulinen, *Handbook on the Law of War*, p. 83 ('indispensable'); McDougal and Feliciano, *Law and Minimum World Public Order*, pp. 524, 527 ('necessary'); Downey, 'The Law of War and Military Necessity', at 254 ('need'); Gehring, 'Loss of Civilian Protections', at 55 ('requirement'); O'Brien, 'Meaning of Military Necessity', at 138 ('indispensable'); Dinstein, 'Military Necessity' (1st edn), p. 275 ('necessary').

admissibility of such pleas therefore involves evaluating the relationship between the measure taken on the one hand and the purpose it was meant to attain on the other.

Within the meaning of juridical military necessity, a measure cannot be considered required for a particular military purpose unless it satisfies all of the following criteria:

1. That the measure was materially relevant to the attainment of the military purpose;
2. That, of those materially relevant measures that were reasonably available, the one taken was the least evil; and
3. That the evil that the measure would cause was not disproportionate to the gain that it would achieve.[68]

Where a given measure fails to satisfy the three cumulative criteria, it is arguably better described as a military 'advantage' or 'convenience'[69] ineligible for exception than as a military 'necessity'. A situation may also arise where even the least evil of those reasonably available and materially relevant measures causes, or is expected to cause, disproportionate injury. Where this is the case, juridical military necessity may leave the belligerent with no alternative but to modify the military purpose or abandon its pursuit altogether.[70]

9.3.2.1 Measure's Material Relevance to the Military Purpose's Attainment

Military necessity is inadmissible where the measure would have no material bearing on the attainment of the stated military purpose.[71]

[68] David Kretzmer observes that this three-pronged test is 'accepted in some domestic systems as a general principle in international law' and 'adopted by international bodies'. Kretzmer, 'Judicial Review During Armed Conflict', at 450.

[69] *Von Lewinski (called Manstein)*, p. 522 ('Now first and obvious comment on the wording of [Article 23(g) of the 1907 Hague Regulations] is that the requirement is "necessity" and not "advantage"'); Melzer, *Targeted Killing*, pp. 291–92; O'Keefe, *Protection of Cultural Property*, pp. 74–75, 122–23; Solis, *Law of Armed Conflict*, p. 264 ('Sometimes, military necessity is invoked when military convenience is closer to truth'); Draper, 'Military Necessity and Humanitarian Imperatives', at 134 ('One thing seems to be clear. Military "necessity" is not synonymous with "military convenience"' (quoting *von Lewinski (called Manstein)*, p. 522)).

[70] Walzer makes a similar ethical argument regarding Hiroshima. Walzer, *Just and Unjust Wars*, pp. 263–68.

[71] *Hostage*, pp. 1253–54 ('There must be some reasonable connection between the destruction of property and the overcoming of the enemy forces'). See also Dinstein, 'Military Necessity' (1st edn), p. 275; McDougal and Feliciano, *Law and Minimum World Public Order*, pp. 524–25; Pertile, 'Missed Opportunity?', at 151.

In *Peleus*, Heinz Eck was brought before a British Military Court on charges of ordering the killing of survivors of a sunken Allied vessel in violation of the laws and usages of war. Eck argued that the elimination of the vessel's traces with a machine gun and hand grenades was operationally necessary to save his U-boat and its crew.

Relevant facts of the case are as follows.[72] On the South Atlantic Ocean, the U-boat commanded by Eck sank the *Peleus*, a Greek ship chartered by the British Ministry of War Transport. Those members of the thirty-five-strong *Peleus* crew who had survived the sinking reached two rafts and floating wreckage. The submarine surfaced, called over one of the survivors for interrogation, and left the scene of the sinking for about 1,000 metres. The submarine then returned, opened machine-gun fire and threw grenades on those in the water and on the rafts. The firing went on for about five hours at night, killing all but three (a fourth survivor died later).

Eck contended, inter alia, that:

- All possibility of saving the survivors' lives had lapsed;
- It was against the order of the German U-boat Command to take them on board his U-boat;
- He was in a vulnerable region of the Atlantic Ocean where many U-boats had been sunk;
- He considered the rafts to be a danger since they would indicate to aeroplanes the exact spot of the sinking and they could be equipped with signalling communication devices;
- No humans were seen on the rafts when he opened fire; and
- He thought the survivors had jumped out of the rafts.[73]

The judge advocate summarised the notion of operational necessity, as alleged by Eck, thus:

> The purpose of that firing was primarily the destruction of the wreckage in order that every trace of the sinking might be obliterated. [Eck] says he realized that a consequence of the carrying out of that order must have been the death of certain survivors, and that it was a decision that he

[72] John Cameron (ed), *Trial of Heinz Eck, August Hoffmann, Walter Weisspfennig, Hans Richard Lenz and Wolfgang Schwender (The* Peleus *Trial)* (London: William Hodge and Co., 1948), pp. 56–57; *Trial of Kapitänleutenant Heinz Eck and Four Others for the Killing of Members of the Crew of the Greek Steamship Peleus, Sunk on the High Seas*, United Nations War Crimes Commission, *Law Reports of Trials of War Criminals*, 15 vols. (London: His Majesty's Stationery Office, 1947), vol. I, 1 (hereinafter *Peleus*), pp. 1–21.

[73] *Peleus*, pp. 4–5.

> regretted: but he says . . . he was under an operational necessity to do what he did because he had as his first duty to ensure that the submarine was protected against attack by Allied aircraft. He says that the only way of doing that was to take every possible step on that night to destroy every trace of the sinking. If as a result of that survivors were killed it was unfortunate for them, but he was under the paramount necessity of protecting his boat and his crew.[74]

For our purposes, we might treat 'operational necessity' as an alleged variant of military necessity. McCoubrey observed:

> At the post-war trial before a British Military Tribunal of the U-Boat commander, Kapitanleutnant Eck, and others of the personnel of the submarine, an argument was advanced peripherally that the massacre might have been justified by the need to prevent the survivors revealing the location of the U-Boat, in effect a form of military necessity.[75]

Eck's argument was unsuccessful. The court found him guilty as charged and sentenced him to death by shooting.[76]

In his summary to the court, the judge advocate conceded that circumstances *could* arise in which a belligerent might be justified in killing an unarmed person for the purpose of saving his own life.[77] Be that as it may, the judge advocate asked the court:

> Do you or do you not think that the shooting of machine-guns at substantial pieces of wreckage and rafts would be an effective way of destroying every trace of this sinking? Do you or do you not think it fairly obvious that in any event a patch of oil would have been left after this steamship had sunk, which would have been an indication to any aircraft that was in the neighbourhood that a ship had recently been sunk, and that a submarine was probably in that area and it was well worth searching for it?[78]

74 Cameron (ed), *Trial of Heinz Eck*, pp. 126–27.

75 McCoubrey, 'Modern Doctrine of Military Necessity' at 225. It is acknowledged here, however, that views may differ as to whether *Peleus* really involves any issue of military necessity at all. Doubts emanate primarily from the fact that the underlying prohibition does not appear to admit military necessity exceptions.

76 Cameron (ed), *Trial of Heinz Eck*, p. 127; *Peleus*, pp. 20–21.

77 Cameron (ed), *Trial of Heinz Eck*, p. 127; *Peleus*, pp. 12, 15.

78 Cameron (ed), *Trial of Heinz Eck*, p. 127. In this connection, see also the *Llandovery Castle* case as reported by the United Nations War Crimes Commission. United Nations War Crimes Commission, *History of the United Nations War Crimes Commission and the Development of the Laws of War* (London: His Majesty's Stationery Office, 1948), pp. 48–49.

It is possible that the judge advocate was sceptical about the truthfulness of Eck's claim that Eck had ordered the shooting in order to preserve the U-boat and the lives of its crew.[79] But if the judge advocate was sceptical, it does not appear from the trial record that he invited the court specifically to entertain this matter.

Instead, the judge advocate took issue with the notion that shooting the floating rafts and wreckage would have actually resulted in every trace of the sinking being eliminated – and hence, supposedly, the location of the U-boat being concealed. He did so by suggesting that the shooting would not have erased the oil patches whose continued presence would lead to detection.[80]

A measure's relevance to its purpose also became an issue in *Beit Sourik*. The petitioners in that case submitted alternative routes for the fence.[81] Members of the non-governmental Council for Peace and Security, acting as *amici curiae*, provided expert opinions on security that differed in part from those of the respondents.[82] The Israeli Supreme Court ruled that Articles 23(g), 46 and 52 of the 1907 Hague Regulations, as well as Articles 27 and 53 of Geneva Convention IV, 'create a single tapestry of norms that recognizes both human rights and the needs of the local population as well [as] recognizing security needs from the perspective of the military commander'.[83] 'Between these conflicting norms', continued the court, 'a proper balance must be found'.[84]

The court held that such a balance would be found by reference to proportionality, a principle rooted not only in international law but also in Israeli administrative law.[85] The court divided proportionality into

[79] Cameron (ed), *Trial of Heinz Eck*, p. 127: 'Remember [Eck] cruised about the site of this sinking for five hours. He refrained from using the speed which was at his disposal of 18 knots to get away as quickly as he could from the site of the sinking. He preferred to go round shooting, as he says, at wreckage by means of machine-guns'.

[80] Eck admitted to his defence counsel that he could not possibly erase all traces of the sinking. But he 'only wanted to destroy the bigger pieces which were recognizable to aeroplanes'. Ibid, p. 52.

[81] *Beit Sourik*, para. 17.

[82] Ibid, paras 17, 47.

[83] Ibid, para. 35.

[84] Ibid.

[85] Ibid, paras 36–37. See also Kretzmer, 'Law of Belligerent Occupation', at 228–29 n.104 (citing Aharon Barak, *Proportionality: Constitutional Rights and Their Limitations* (Cambridge: Cambridge University Press, 2011)).

three subtests.[86] According to one subtest, referred to in the judgment as the 'appropriate means' or 'rational means' test, '[t]he means that the administrative body uses must be constructed to achieve the precise objective which the administrative body is trying to achieve. The means used by the administrative body must rationally lead to the realisation of the objective'.[87]

Using this test, the court reiterated its traditional deference to the professional opinion of the military commanders who had been in charge. The petitioners failed to persuade the court that it should prefer the position of the Council for Peace and Security when it differed from that of the commander.[88] Consequently, the court held that the commander's chosen route satisfied this test.[89]

9.3.2.2 Least Evil among Materially Relevant and Reasonably Available Measures

It is not necessary that the measure taken be the *only* reasonably available course of action for the attainment of a given military purpose. Such singular availability hardly ever occurs. There would almost always be two or more reasonably available courses of action that are materially relevant to the purpose.[90] It follows that in almost no case does a measure's 'requiredness' for a military purpose depend on whether the purpose would not have been attained but for the measure taken. Here, no question of counter-factual *conditio sine qua non* – which, by definition, cannot be proven[91] – need be considered.

Exceptional military necessity demands that, among all reasonably available and materially relevant measures vis-à-vis a given military purpose, the belligerent choose one that causes the least injury to objects

[86] The three subtests are: (a) the 'appropriate means' or 'rational means' test; (b) the 'least injurious means' test; and (c) the 'proportionate means' test (or proportionality 'in the narrow sense'). *Alfei Menashe*, para. 30.

[87] *Beit Sourik*, para. 41.

[88] Ibid, paras 46–47, 56–57, 66, 70, 75, 80.

[89] In the end, of the eight orders challenged by the petitioners, the court unanimously nullified five in their entirety and two in part. The court found that these orders failed to satisfy the third, 'proportionate means' test. In respect of the remaining order, the route had already been changed and the petitioners did not raise any argument during the proceedings. The court denied the petition in respect of this latter order, as the parties had not substantially disputed it. Ibid, paras 50, 80.

[90] Article 6(a)(ii), Hague Cultural Property Protocol II. See also below.

[91] See Chapter 2.

and interests otherwise protected by these rules.[92] In principle, military necessity is inadmissible where, in relation to the stated military purpose, at least one materially relevant yet less injurious measure was reasonably available to the belligerent other than the one taken.

This line of reasoning was proposed in *Peleus*, albeit indirectly. The judge advocate questioned the amount of cruelty involved in the killing of the survivors relative to the amount of cruelty involved in an alternative course of action that he implied had been reasonably available to Eck. The court was asked:

> Do you or do you not think that a submarine commander who was really and primarily concerned with saving his crew and his boat would have done as Kapitänleutnant Schnee, who was called for the Defence, said he would have done, namely, have removed himself and his boat at the highest possible speed at the earliest possible moment for the greatest possible distance?[93]

Implicit herein is the notion that, even if the shooting had eliminated all traces of the sinking, it would not have been operationally necessary to do so in order to save Eck's U-boat and its crew.[94] The judge advocate presented the court with the possibility that Eck would have achieved the same purpose by another means, namely by removing himself and his boat from the location of the sinking 'at the highest possible speed at the earliest possible moment for the greatest possible distance'.

The evidence showed that a man of comparable experience would have considered this alternative reasonably available to him had he found himself in a similar situation. The defence witness, Kapitänleutnant Schnee, was a member of the German U-boat Command who had sunk

[92] *Beni-Madan Rzini Case (Great Britain v Spain)*, Spanish Zone of Morocco Claims Commission, 29 December 1924, 2 *Annual Digest of Public International Law Cases Years 1923 to 1924* (1933) 168 ('It ought not to have been difficult for the military authorities, once they had seized the cattle, to separate the animals belonging to peaceful farmers from those owned by rebels. The slaughter of the animals was not justified by military necessity'); *Co-Prosecutors v Chea Nuon and Samphan Khieu*, Case No. 002/19-09-2007/ECCC/TC, *Case 002/01 Judgment*, 7 August 2014, para. 450; *Co-Prosecutors v Chea Nuon and Samphan Khieu*, Case No. 002/19-09-2007/ECCC/TC, *Case 002/02 Judgment*, 16 November 2018, para. 684; Gerhard Werle and Florian Jessberger, *Principles of International Criminal Law*, 3rd edn (Oxford: Oxford University Press, 2014), p. 474 ('if the military goal could be achieved through appropriation or similar means, destruction is not permitted as it is disproportionate').

[93] Cameron (ed), *Trial of Heinz Eck*, p. 127.

[94] That the actual elimination of all traces of the sinking would have saved Eck's boat and its crew does not appear to have been in issue.

about thirty Allied ships and received military decorations.[95] During cross-examination, Schnee said:

> What did you do after [sinking a ship]? – I have always tried to get away as quickly as possible out of the danger zone because it is well known that after the sinking of a ship the enemy is most alert to retaliate.
>
> Is that, in your opinion, the correct thing to do after you have sunk a ship? – That is according to my opinion the most important thing for my boat.
>
> ...
>
> What would you have done if you had been in Eck's position? – I would under all circumstances have tried my best to save life, as that is a measure which was taken by all U-boat Kommandanten; but when I am informed of this case, then I can only explain it as this, that Kapitänleutnant Eck through the terrific experience he had been through lost his nerve.
>
> Does that mean that you would not have done what Kapitänleutnant Eck did if you had kept your nerve? – I would not have done it.[96]

Had Eck chosen to act as Schnee said he would, it would not have been operationally necessary for Eck to order the killing of any unarmed person[97] – although, admittedly, the survivors on the rafts and wreckage would be left to their fate.[98]

The *Beit Sourik* case also featured this 'least injurious means' test. The Israeli Supreme Court defined it thus: '[T]he means used by the administrative body must injure the individual to the least extent possible. In the spectrum of means which can be used to achieve the objective, the least injurious means must be used.'[99]

One disputed segment of the fence's route surrounded the ridge of Jebel Muktam. The petitioners described the severe damage that would afflict the nearby villages, which already suffered from 75 percent unemployment. The fence along the chosen route was said to affect large areas of cultivated land as well as tens of thousands of olive and fruit

95 *Peleus*, p. 6.

96 Cameron (ed), *Trial of Heinz Eck*, pp. 69–70.

97 An unidentified reporter of the *Peleus* case noted that, 'on the facts of the case this behaviour [shooting at helpless survivors of a sunken ship] was not operationally necessary, i.e. the operational aim, the saving of ship and crew, could have been achieved more effectively without such acts of cruelty'. *Peleus*, p. 16.

98 The four men who survived Eck's machine gun fire and grenades spent the next twenty-five days drifting on the open sea. Cameron (ed), *Trial of Heinz Eck*, p. xxvi; *Peleus*, p. 3.

99 *Beit Sourik*, para. 41.

trees.[100] According to the affidavit provided by the Council for Peace and Security, no effective light weapon fire from Jebel Muktam was possible on any Israeli town or on Route 443 connecting Jerusalem to the centre of the country. It was argued that not every topographically controlling hill such as Jebel Muktam was required for the fence's defence. The council suggested that it would be easier to defend obstacles at a location three kilometres to the south of the current route. In the council's view, the local population would be dangerously and needlessly embittered by the inevitable construction of agricultural gates.[101] The petitioners presented two alternative routes.[102]

The commander responded that, topographically, the alternative routes were considerably inferior to his own. He stated that control of the Jebel Muktam hill overlooking the entire area was a matter of critical military importance; the fence would prevent the hill being taken and decrease the risk of attacks on Route 443.[103] The commander also differed from the petitioners on the scale of the injury.[104] It appears from the judgment that the commander had taken several concrete steps with a view to reducing the injury by creating agricultural gates, offering compensation, transferring rather than uprooting olive trees, considering the location of even unauthorised Palestinian buildings and locally correcting some portions of the route.[105]

The fact that the route suggested by the Council for Peace and Security was less injurious than the route chosen by the commander was not, however, in dispute. Once again, the court deferred to the commander's position that the alternative route would grant him less security than his proposed route would. The court ruled: 'By our very determination that we shall not intervene in that position, we have also determined that there is no alternate route that fulfills, to a similar extent, the security needs while causing lesser injury to the local inhabitants'.[106] The same was held to be the case for the other disputed segments of the commander's chosen route.[107]

[100] Ibid, para. 52.
[101] Ibid, paras 54–55.
[102] Ibid.
[103] Ibid, paras 51, 55.
[104] Ibid, para. 53.
[105] Ibid, para. 55.
[106] Ibid, para. 58.
[107] Ibid, paras 67, 70, 76, 80.

In fairness to the court, the comparison at issue was between alternatives that were reasonably available to the commander and materially relevant *to the same purpose*. It is only among these alternatives that the commander would be called upon to choose the least injurious. In the particular circumstances surrounding each disputed segment of the fence, the court did *not* agree that the commander's chosen route and the Council for Peace and Security's alternative route achieved the same degree of security.[108]

9.3.2.3 Proportionality between the Injury and the Gain

Military necessity is inadmissible where the harm resulting from the measure is disproportionate to the purpose's military value. This is so, even if the measure is the least injurious of all alternatives that are reasonably available and materially relevant to the purpose.

The precise relationship between military necessity and proportionality is not entirely clear. It appears uncontroversial that military necessity and proportionality are closely related concepts.[109] Beyond this, however, there is no consensus as to how proportionality operates within the notion of military necessity – or vice versa, for that matter. Some treat proportionality as an element of military necessity.[110] Others suggest that it is military necessity that constitutes an element of proportionality.[111]

108 Compare this ruling in *Beit Sourik* with the ruling in *Alfei Menashe* where the Israeli Supreme Court held that the least injurious means test had not been satisfied in respect of the fence surrounding the Alfei Menashe nucleus. *Alfei Menashe*, para. 114: 'It seems to us that the required effort has not been made, and the details of an alternative route have not been examined, in order to ensure security with a lesser injury to the residents of the villages. Respondents must reconsider the existing route.'

109 *Legal Consequences, Separate Opinion of Judge Kooijmans*, p. 219, para. 34; David Luban, 'Military Necessity and the Cultures of Military Law' (2013) 26 *Leiden Journal of International Law* 315, at 343–45; Henry, *Principe de nécessité militaire*, pp. 604–21.

110 McDougal and Feliciano, *Law and Minimum World Public Order*, p. 72; O'Brien, 'Meaning of Military Necessity', at 138, 148–49; IHLRI, *Separation Barrier*, p. 7; Elizabeth Samson, 'Necessity, Proportionality, and Distinction in Nontraditional Conflicts: The Unfortunate Case Study of the Goldstone Report' in Ford and Cohen (eds), *Rethinking of the Law of Armed Conflict* 195, p. 202; Arai-Takahashi, 'Excessive Collateral Civilian Casualties and Military Necessity', p. 332; *Prosecutor v Ljube Boškoski and Johan Tarčulovski*, Case No. IT-04-82-T, *Judgment*, 10 July 2008, para. 357.

111 Schmitt, 'Book Review', at 257 (reviewing Rogers, *Law on the Battlefield*); Rogers, *Law on the Battlefield* (2nd edn), p. 6 (referring to Schmitt's review of the first edition).

One difficulty is the fact that exceptional military necessity operates in the narrow confines of express IHL clauses, whereas proportionality is a highly open-textured concept that appears in various fields of international law and with scopes and variables that are not necessarily the same.[112] In *jus ad bellum* concerning the use of force in self-defence, for example, proportionality is typically determined on the basis of (i) the quantum of force used, in relation to (ii) the repulsion of the imminent or actual attack against which the right of self-defence is exercised.[113] Within *jus in bello* concerning the lawfulness of attacks on military objectives involving unintended civilian casualties, the most widely accepted pair of variables for comparison is between (i) 'incidental loss of civilian life, injury to civilians, damage to civilian objects, or a combination thereof', and (ii) the 'concrete and direct military advantage anticipated'.[114]

[112] Two disciplines of particular interest here are *jus ad bellum* and *jus in bello*. *Ethiopia v Eritrea*, Eritrea-Ethiopia Claims Commission, *Final Award on Ethiopia's Damages Claims*, 17 August 2009, para. 316; Mazzeschi, 'Book Review', at 1031–36; Andreas Zimmermann, '*Jus ad Bellum*, *Jus in Bello* and the Issue of Proportionality' (2007) 11 *Max Planck Yearbook of United Nations Law* 99; Christian J Tams and James G Devaney, 'Applying Necessity and Proportionality to Anti-Terrorist Self-Defence' (2012) 45 *Israel Law Review* 91; Enzo Cannizzaro, 'Proportionality in the Law of Armed Conflict' in Clapham and Gaeta (eds), *Oxford Handbook of International Law in Armed Conflict* 332; Michael Newton and Larry May, *Proportionality in International Law* (Oxford: Oxford University Press, 2014).

[113] Gardam, *Necessity, Proportionality and the Use of Force by States*, pp. 159–79; Giovanni Distefano, 'Use of Force' in Clapham and Gaeta (eds), *Oxford Handbook of International Law in Armed Conflict* 545, pp. 555–56; Office of General Counsel, *Law of War Manual*, p. 62; Theodora Chritodoulidou and Kalliopi Chainoglou, 'The Principle of Proportionality from a *Jus ad Bellum* Perspective' in Marc Weller (ed), *The Oxford Handbook of the Use of Force in International Law* (Oxford: Oxford University Press, 2015) 1187, pp. 1196–99.

[114] Articles 51(5)(b), 57(2)(b), Additional Protocol I. See also Ben Clarke, 'Contemporary Legal Doctrine on Proportionality in Armed Conflicts: A Select Review' (2012) 3 *Journal of International Humanitarian Legal Studies* 391; Ben Clarke, 'Proportionality in Armed Conflicts: A Principle in Need of Clarification?' (2012) 3 *Journal of International Humanitarian Legal Studies* 73; Corn et al., *Operational Approach*, pp. 123–25, 187–89; Jason Wright, '"Excessive" Ambiguity: Analysing and Refining the Proportionality Standard' (2012) 94 *International Review of the Red Cross* 819; Yoram Dinstein, 'The Principle of Proportionality' in Larsen et al. (eds), *Searching for a 'Principle of Humanity'* 72; Joshua Andresen, 'New Voices: Challenging the Perplexity over *Jus in Bello* Proportionality' (2014) 7 *European Journal of Legal Studies* 19; Jeremy Rabkin, 'Proportionality in Perspective: Historical Light on the Law of Armed Conflict' (2015) 16 *San Diego International Law Journal* 263.

As an element of exceptional military necessity,[115] proportionality weighs the injury the measure would cause to protected persons, objects and interests, against the value of the military purpose it would achieve. In *Beit Sourik*, considerations of proportionality in this sense proved decisive.[116] The Israeli Supreme Court called such considerations 'proportionality in the narrow sense'.[117] According to the court, 'the damage caused to the individual by the means used by the administrative body in order to achieve its objectives must be of proper proportion to the gain brought about by that means'.[118]

The court divided this narrow proportionality into two subgroups. One subgroup was to be applied with 'absolute values [by] directly comparing the advantage of the administrative act with the damage that results from it'.[119] The other, to be applied in a 'relative manner', was defined as follows:

> [T]he administrative act is tested vis-à-vis an alternate act, whose benefit will be somewhat smaller than that of the former one. The original administrative act is disproportionate in the narrow sense if a certain reduction in the advantage gained by the original act – by employing alternate means, for example – ensures a substantial reduction in the injury caused by the administrative act.[120]

It is this latter variant of proportionality, i.e., in the narrow sense applied in a relative manner, that the court used when considering the facts before it.

Proportionality was examined on a segment-by-segment basis.[121] For each disputed segment of the route, the court weighed the injury to the

[115] Kretzmer, 'Law of Belligerent Occupation', at 228–29. See also UN Crimes Commission, *History of the United Nations War Crimes Commission*, p. 488 (discussing the case involving 'a German officer who had completely destroyed a large Roman Catholic church when his unit left Horst-Melderslo in Holland. [Committee I] decided that, while military necessity may have existed for the destruction of the spire of the church to prevent its use as an allied observation tower, no necessity existed for the complete and utter destruction of the whole church').

[116] Kretzmer, 'Judicial Review during Armed Conflict', at 449 (referring to 'the big question'); Kretzmer, 'Law of Belligerent Occupation', at 229–30.

[117] *Beit Sourik*, para. 41.

[118] Ibid.

[119] Ibid.

[120] Ibid.

[121] Ibid, para. 49. The court, however, made observations about the overall injury to the local inhabitants affected by the entire length of the separation fence examined in the case. Ibid, paras 82–84.

local inhabitants[122] vis-à-vis the security benefit derived from the fence being erected along the route chosen by the commander.

As regards the Jebel Muktam segment of the fence, the court agreed that the alternative route presented by the Council for Peace and Security would substantially decrease the injury. The court so agreed, against the backdrop of the commander's opinion – which, as noted earlier, the court assumed to be correct – that he would have less security in the area as a result.[123] Effectively, the court ruled in favour of the decrease in the injury caused to the local inhabitants over the decrease in the degree of security accruing to the commander. In the court's view, 'the security advantage reaped from the route as determined by the military commander, in comparison to the ... route [proposed by the Council for Peace and Security], does not stand in any reasonable proportion to the injury to the local inhabitants caused by this route'.[124]

The court found that the commander's order to seize land for the construction of the separation fence in the Jebel Muktam area was disproportionate in its injurious effect on the local inhabitants relative to the security gain he sought by it.[125] The court made similar findings regarding the other disputed segments of the fence: The 'severe' injury that the commander's route caused to the local inhabitants was held to be more disproportionate to the level of security he sought than the injury caused by an alternative route – such as the one suggested by the Council for Peace and Security – would be to the somewhat lower level of security it would achieve.[126]

Consequently, the seizure orders concerning the fence's disputed segments were declared null and void.[127] The court considered the measure taken by the commander militarily *un*necessary within the meaning of relevant IHL clauses, because it accepted the possibility of at least one

[122] The court added to the injury side of the equation 'human rights and the necessity of ensuring the provision of the needs and welfare of the local inhabitants' and 'family honour and rights ... protected in the framework of the humanitarian provisions of the Hague Regulations and the Geneva Convention'. *Beit Sourik*, para. 59.

[123] In other words, the commander's route may very well have constituted a strictly material military necessity relative to the council's alternative route. See Chapter 2.

[124] *Beit Sourik*, para. 61.

[125] Ibid, paras 60–62.

[126] Ibid, paras 67, 70–71, 76, 80.

[127] Ibid, para. 86.

alternative measure whereby a minor modification to the original purpose would result in a significantly superior security–injury ratio.

The relative proportionality test affected the court's handling of the case in three important ways. Firstly, it reduced the difficulty of comparing two dissimilar variables. Had the court applied an absolute proportionality test, it would have had to compare the amount of injury caused to the local inhabitants with the degree of security gained through the commander's route. Thanks to the relative proportionality test, the court had two sets of comparison, each containing two variables to be weighed on the same measurement. These sets were:

1. A comparison between the amount of injury to the local inhabitants resulting from the route chosen by the commander, on the one hand, and the amount of injury to the local inhabitants resulting from an alternative route, such as the one suggested by the Council for Peace and Security, on the other; and
2. A comparison between the degree of security sought by the commander's route, on the one hand, and the degree of security sought by the alternative route, on the other.

Where the reduction in injury was greater than the reduction in security, the alternative route would be superior to the commander's chosen route in terms of their security–injury ratios. Also, according to the relative proportionality test, the existence of such an alternative route would mean that the route chosen by the commander was disproportionate in its injurious effects vis-à-vis its security goal.

Secondly, the application of the relative proportionality test underscored the fact that the measure and the purpose were, in fact, both capable of measurement. This was particularly significant for the purpose at issue in *Beit Sourik*, namely the degree of security anticipated from the construction of the fence. A military purpose of this nature is qualitatively different from a military purpose that would be either attained or unattained, but not amenable to partial attainment of different degrees. As a means of assessing military necessity, the relative proportionality test might not be suitable for situations such as the one in which Eck found himself where the belligerent's purpose could not be measured in graduated terms.

Lastly – and, perhaps, most controversially – the court applied the relative proportionality test in an attempt to avoid some hard questions. The court observed:

> Indeed, the real question in the 'relative' examination of the third proportionality subtest is *not* the choice between constructing a separation fence which brings security but injures the local inhabitants, or not constructing a separation fence, and not injuring the local inhabitants. The real question is whether the security benefit reaped by the acceptance of the military commander's position (that the separation fence should surround Jebel Muktam) is proportionate to the additional injury resulting from his position (with the fence separating local inhabitants from their lands).[128]

Whether this is really what the relative proportionality test says, however, is debatable. For this test, as it was defined by the court, opens a veritable Pandora's Box. The court's conclusion was that, compared to the alternatives suggested by the petitioners, the route chosen by the commander was disproportionately injurious. It was *not* the court's conclusion that those alternatives themselves were proportionately injurious.[129] Whether these alternatives were proportionately or disproportionately injurious would depend on the availability or otherwise of some further alternatives with a superior security–injury ratio. Such a relative proportionality analysis could go on *ad infinitum*.[130]

The question, then, is this: Could there be a stage at which the IDF Commander in the West Bank would cease to be capable of proposing any route within the occupied territory that was less disproportionately injurious than, for instance, some alternative route outside the territory? Would this not mean that the construction of a fence with an acceptable security–injury ratio might be beyond the commander's authority? Would this also not mean that the commander himself might at some point have to choose not to construct the separation

[128] Ibid, para. 61 (emphasis added).

[129] Nor, to be sure, was the court called upon to identify any particular route with an acceptable security–injury ratio. The court noted (ibid, para. 71): 'This is the military commander's affair'. Also of note is the court's statement (ibid, para. 80): 'we are of the opinion that the military commander must map out an alternate arrangement . . . Such alternate routes were presented before us. We shall not take any stand whatsoever regarding a particular alternate route. The military commander must determine an alternative which will provide a fitting, if not ideal, solution for the security considerations, and also allow proportionate access of Beit Daku villagers to their lands'.

[130] Thus, theoretically, petitions could keep coming before the Israeli Supreme Court every time the military commander decided on a new route which was less disproportionately injurious than the previous route. In *Alfei Menashe*, the court noted that there had already been seven petitions arising from the new route chosen by the military commander in light of the ruling in *Beit Sourik*. *Alfei Menashe*, para. 36.

fence at all and therefore not to injure the local inhabitants at all? That these questions *may* yield an affirmative answer is inherent in the relative proportionality test.

It is therefore *not* because the relative proportionality test did not raise these questions that the court managed to avoid them. The court managed to avoid them for two reasons. First, the court refused to question the commander's authority in principle to erect the fence on the territory he occupied.[131] By refusing to question the commander's authority, the court refused to contemplate the prospect that even the least disproportionately injurious measure at his disposal might be too disproportionately injurious. Second, the specific alternatives presented by the petitioners and the Council for Peace and Security were mostly situated in the territory he occupied.[132] It would have been interesting to see the court's reaction had some or all of the alternative routes proposed by the petitioners been located on the Israeli side of the Green Line.

These questions did not escape the attention of two international institutions. Several months before the *Beit Sourik* case the ICRC issued a press release in which it expressed an unusually blunt view of the matter.[133] The ICJ rendered an advisory opinion on the legal consequences of the construction of the wall within ten days of the Israeli Supreme Court's ruling.[134]

Neither the ICRC nor the ICJ denied Israel's right to take lawful measures to protect its population.[135] Nor is there any indication that,

[131] *Beit Sourik*, paras 10–11.

[132] *Beit Sourik* (maps attached to the judgment).

[133] International Committee of the Red Cross, *Press Release, Israel/Occupied and Autonomous Palestinian Territories: West Bank Barrier Causes Serious Humanitarian and Legal Problems*, 18 February 2004. Strictly speaking, the ICRC's observations do not constitute judicial findings of any sort. They are nevertheless significant for our discussion, in view of the organisation's general policy of discreetness and the special place that it has occupied in the development and implementation of IHL.

[134] *Legal Consequences*. In its Resolution ES-10/14 adopted on 12 December 2003, the UN General Assembly requested an advisory opinion from the ICJ on the following question: 'What are the legal consequences arising from the construction of the wall being built by Israel, the occupying Power, in the Occupied Palestinian Territory, including in and around East Jerusalem, as described in the report of the Secretary-General, considering the rules and principles of international law, including the Fourth Geneva Convention of 1949, and relevant Security Council and General Assembly resolutions?'

[135] The ICRC recognised 'Israel's right to take measures to ensure the security of its population. However, these measures must respect the relevant rules of [IHL]'. ICRC, *West Bank Barrier Causes Serious Humanitarian and Legal Problems*. Similarly, the ICJ

in their view, the construction of the barrier *as such* lacked any material bearing on Israel's efforts to combat terrorist attacks launched from the West Bank. Rather, the two institutions juxtaposed the injury done and rights denied to residents in the occupied territory with the measures taken by Israel in view of its rights and obligations under international law.

Unlike the Israeli Supreme Court, both the ICRC and the ICJ treated as one object the entire length of the barrier that diverted from the Green Line into the occupied territory. The ICRC declared that the barrier, 'insofar as its route deviates from the "Green Line" into occupied territory', is contrary to IHL.[136] To the ICRC,

> [t]he problems affecting the Palestinian population in their daily lives clearly demonstrate that [the barrier] runs counter to Israel's obligation under IHL to ensure the humane treatment and well-being of the civilian population living under its occupation. The measures taken by the Israeli authorities linked to the construction of the Barrier in occupied territory go *far beyond* what is permissible for an occupying power under IHL.[137]

The ICRC essentially found that Israel's actions were disproportionate to the injury caused. It called upon Israel 'not to plan, construct or maintain this Barrier within occupied territory'.[138]

The ICJ declined to consider Article 23(g) of the 1907 Hague Regulations,[139] but it took note of the military necessity exception under Article 53 of Geneva Convention IV. The court held that it was, 'on the material before it', not convinced that 'the destructions carried out contrary to the prohibition in Article 53 of the Fourth Geneva Convention were rendered absolutely necessary by military operations'.[140]

observed (*Legal Consequences*, para. 141): 'The fact remains that Israel has to face numerous indiscriminate and deadly acts of violence against its civilian population. It has the right, and indeed the duty, to respond in order to protect the life of its citizens. The measures taken are bound nonetheless to remain in conformity with applicable international law'.

136 ICRC, *West Bank Barrier Causes Serious Humanitarian and Legal Problems.*

137 Ibid (emphasis added).

138 Ibid.

139 *Legal Consequences*, para. 124. For views supporting the exclusion of Article 23(g) from the scope of analysis in the ICJ's advisory opinion, see Pertile, 'Missed Opportunity?', at 134–36; Orakhelashvili, 'Opinion and Reaction', at 123. For criticisms, see Kretzmer, 'The Advisory Opinion', at 95–96.

140 *Legal Consequences*, para. 135.

The freedom of movement, a human right under Article 12 of the 1966 International Covenant on Civil and Political Rights,[141] was also considered. The court, quoting with approval General Comment No. 27 of the Human Rights Committee,[142] observed that restrictions to this freedom must be directed towards the ends authorised, 'conform to the principle of proportionality' and 'be the least intrusive instrument amongst those which might achieve the desired result'.[143] Here, too, the court found, '[o]n the basis of the information available to it', that Israel's measures did not meet these conditions. Consequently,

> the Court, from the material available to it, is not convinced that the specific course Israel has chosen for the wall was necessary to attain its security objectives. The wall, along the route chosen, and its associated régime gravely infringe a number of rights of Palestinians residing in the territory occupied by Israel, and the infringements resulting from that route cannot be justified by military exigencies or by the requirements of national security or public order.[144]

The court concluded that Israel was obligated to cease the construction of the wall in the Occupied Palestinian Territory, including in and around East Jerusalem; to dismantle those parts of the wall therein that have already been built; and to repeal or render ineffective all related legislative and regulatory acts.[145] Israel was also found

[141] Ibid, para. 136. Article 12 of the International Covenant on Civil and Political Rights (19 December 1966, in force 23 March 1976, 999 UNTS 171) states, in part, as follows:

> 1. Everyone lawfully within the territory of a State shall, within that territory, have the right to liberty of movement and freedom to choose his residence.
>
> . . .
>
> 3. The above-mentioned rights shall not be subject to any restrictions except those which are provided by law, are necessary to protect national security, public order (*ordre public*), public health or morals or the rights and freedoms of others, and are consistent with the other rights recognized in the present Covenant.

Israel is a state party to the covenant. *Legal Consequences*, para. 103.

[142] Human Rights Committee, *General Comment No. 27: Freedom of Movement (Art. 12)*, 1 November 1999, para. 14: 'Article 12, paragraph 3, clearly indicates that it is not sufficient that the restrictions serve the permissible purposes; they must also be necessary to protect them. Restrictive measures must conform to the principle of proportionality; they must be appropriate to achieve their protective function; they must be the least intrusive instrument amongst those which might achieve the desired result; and they must be proportionate to the interest to be protected'.

[143] *Legal Consequences*, para. 136.

[144] Ibid, para. 137.

[145] Ibid, para. 151.

duty-bound to make reparations to the victims by way of restitution or compensation.[146]

When the ICJ ruled that the construction of the wall in occupied Palestine by Israel was unnecessary for its security objectives, it did so on the basis of the 'specific course Israel has chosen'.[147] Would this mean that the court might have arrived at a different conclusion had Israel chosen some other route? What if Israel had invited the court to consider the routes suggested by the petitioners in the *Beit Sourik* case – which, as noted earlier, still remained in the occupied territory for the most part? In other words, would the court have been prepared to consider the wall's relative proportionality?

The court might have been prepared to do so. Even if it had, however, it is doubtful whether the court's conclusion would have been different. After all, the court declared Israel's construction of the wall to be a breach of international law as long as it occurred in the Occupied Palestinian Territory.[148] It would appear that, in the view of the court, the injury done and rights denied to the local inhabitants were such that no route with an acceptable security–injury ratio would conceivably exist within the occupied territory.[149] The same could be said of the ICRC's view of the matter.

Israel chose to limit its involvement in the ICJ's advisory proceedings to jurisdictional issues.[150] As a result, at no point during the proceedings

[146] Ibid, paras 152–53.

[147] Ibid, para. 137.

[148] Ibid, para. 163(3)(A).

[149] For a different take of the ICJ's position on this matter, see Kretzmer, 'Judicial Review During Armed Conflict', at 100: 'The only possible explanation for the conclusion that the construction of the whole barrier contravenes international law in general, and international humanitarian law in particular, is that some principle forbids an occupying power from building such a barrier in occupied territory, even when this construction involves neither the attempted annexation of territory, nor a specific violation of international humanitarian law or international human rights law, such as the unlawful seizure or destruction of property, unjustified limitations on freedom of movement, or arbitrary interference with the right to privacy and family. Does such a principle exist?'

[150] *Written Statement of the Government of Israel on Jurisdiction and Propriety*, 30 January 2004. Israel stated (*Legal Consequences*, para. 55): 'According to Israel, if the Court decided to give the requested opinion, it would be forced to speculate about essential facts and make assumptions about arguments of law. More specifically, Israel has argued that the Court could not rule on the legal consequences of the construction of the wall without enquiring, first, into the nature and scope of the security threat to which the wall is intended to respond and the effectiveness of that response, and, second, into the impact of the construction for the Palestinians. This task, which would already be

did the court benefit from the kind of detailed submissions made by the IDF commander on his security considerations the Israeli Supreme Court had in *Beit Sourik*.[151] Instead, the ICJ found itself relying heavily on the reports and other materials submitted to it by the Secretary-General of the United Nations describing Israel's concerns and actions, as well as submissions made by other participants in the proceedings and information available in the public domain.[152]

The court determined that it still had sufficient information and evidence upon which to render an opinion.[153] Indeed, the court rendered its opinion on the basis of the material 'before it'[154] or 'available to it'.[155] Of such material, however, one cannot fail to notice the abundance of

difficult in a contentious case, would be further complicated in an advisory proceeding, particularly since Israel alone possesses much of the necessary information and has stated that it chooses not to address the merits'. The court noted however that 'Israel's Written Statement, although limited to issues of jurisdiction and judicial propriety, contained observations on other matters, including Israel's concerns in terms of security, and was accompanied by corresponding annexes'. Ibid, para. 57.

151 In this connection, see *Written Statement of the Government of Israel on Jurisdiction and Propriety*, 30 January 2004, at 107–10. Israel asserted that the court would lack sufficient information and evidence to perform '[a]ny assessment of the military necessity of the fence' including, in particular (ibid, at 108–09):

(a) an assessment of the security threat faced by Israel, which would in turn require an assessment of the nature and scale of terrorist attacks, the continuing nature of the threat, and the likely nature and scale of future attacks;
(b) an assessment of the effectiveness of the fence to address the security threat relative to other available means;
(c) an assessment of the motives behind the construction of the fence;
(d) an assessment of the routing of the fence, including an assessment of whether the routing was justified by military necessity so far as concerns individual sections of the fence;
(e) an assessment of the specific nature and extent of the construction, including an assessment of whether these aspects were justified by military necessity so far as concerns individual sections of the fence, to cover, for example, the issue of whether there was a justification on grounds of military necessity for those short sections of wall;
(f) an assessment of the specific nature of the threat to the Israeli population at different sections of the fence;
(g) in the light of the claim that the requirements of proportionality can better be met by different routing of the fence, an assessment of the relative threat arising as a result of such different routing and of whether the requirements of military necessity could thus be satisfied.

152 *Legal Consequences*, para. 57.

153 Ibid, para. 58.

154 Ibid, para. 135.

155 Ibid, para. 137.

information regarding the injury to the residents in the occupied territory, as opposed to the dearth of information regarding the security benefit sought by the occupying power. The advisory opinion was criticised by several ICJ judges[156] and others[157] for this reason.

Similarly, the ICRC stated that its conclusions were 'based on the ICRC's monitoring of the living conditions of the Palestinian population and on its analysis of the applicable IHL provisions'.[158] The extent to which the ICRC actually took into consideration the degree and nature of

[156] Ibid, *Declaration of Judge Buergenthal*, p. 244, para. 7 ('Instead, all we have from the Court is a description of the harm the wall is causing and a discussion of various provisions of international humanitarian law and human rights instruments followed by the conclusion that this law has been violated. Lacking is an examination of the facts that might show why the alleged defences of military exigencies, national security or public order are not applicable to the wall as a whole or to the individual segments of its route. The Court says that it "is not convinced" but it fails to demonstrate why it is not convinced, and that is why these conclusions are not convincing'); ibid, *Separate Opinion of Judge Owada*, p. 260, paras 22–23 ('What seems to be wanting, however, is the material explaining the Israeli side of the picture, especially in the context of why and how the construction of the wall as it is actually planned and implemented is necessary and appropriate . . . It seems clear to me that here [i.e., where the court has stated that it is not convinced that the course Israel has chosen is essential to maintaining national security] the Court is in effect admitting the fact that elaborate material on this point from the Israeli side is not available, rather than engaging in a rebuttal of the arguments of Israel on the basis of the material that might have been made available by Israel on this point'). But Judge Owada was prepared to accept that 'no justification based on the "military exigencies", even if fortified by substantiated facts, could conceivably constitute a valid basis for precluding the wrongfulness of the act on the basis of the stringent conditions of proportionality'. Ibid, para. 24. Judge Higgins observed that, the 'very partial' nature of the information directly provided by Israel notwithstanding, 'there is undoubtedly a significant negative impact upon portions of the population of the West Bank that cannot be excused on the grounds of military necessity allowed by those Conventions; and nor has Israel explained to the United Nations or to this Court why its legitimate security needs can be met only by the route selected'. Ibid, *Separate Opinion of Judge Higgins*, 207, para. 40. Judge Kooijmans expressed his preference for more references to terrorist acts in the opinion but agreed that the court dealt with Israel's positions sufficiently. In his view, the court did not put the wall to the proportionality test. Ibid, *Kooijmans Separate Opinion*, para. 13. Referring to the *Beit Sourik* case, Judge Kooijmans considered that the route chosen by Israel rendered the injury caused to the inhabitants 'manifestly disproportionate' to the interests that Israel sought to protect. Ibid, para. 34.

[157] *Alfei Menashe*, paras 62–65; Geoffrey R Watson, 'The "*Wall*" Decisions in Legal and Political Contexts' (2005) 99 *American Journal of International Law* 6, at 25; Kretzmer, 'Advisory Opinion', at 98–100; Ardi Imseis, 'Critical Reflections on the International Humanitarian Law Aspects of the ICJ *Wall* Advisory Opinion' (2005) 99 *American Journal of International Law* 102, at 110–14; Pertile, 'Missed Opportunity?', at 153.

[158] ICRC, *West Bank Barrier Causes Serious Humanitarian and Legal Problems*.

security sought by Israel through the construction of the barrier is not clear.

The Israeli Supreme Court, the ICJ and the ICRC all concluded that, at a minimum, military necessity was inadmissible in the particular instance of the wall being built along the route chosen by the IDF's regional commander in some part of the Greater Jerusalem area.[159] Yet this apparent consensus among the three institutions masks their profound disagreements about what proportionality entails within the context of exceptional military necessity. Their disagreement persists in:

1. The choice of variables – should proportionality be examined relatively between the rate of reduction in benefit and the rate of reduction in injury with respect to two alternative measures, or should it be examined absolutely between the benefit and injury with respect to one measure?
2. The scale of comparison – should proportionality be examined microscopically, involving only certain identifiable portions of the measure and their discrete benefit–injury ratios, or should it be examined macroscopically, involving the totality of the measure and its overall benefit–injury ratio?[160]
3. The choice, quality and quantity of relevant data necessary to make an informed assessment.

Admittedly, the scope and manner of scrutiny were framed, to some extent, not by the forum itself, but by the particulars of the issue that was brought before it. Nevertheless, the controversy arising from Israel's conduct reveals that IHL rules remain highly indeterminate in this area.

[159] For similarities between the ICJ and the Israeli Supreme Court, see Watson, 'The "Wall" Decisions in Legal and Political Contexts', at 22.

[160] *Alfei Menashe*, para. 58: 'The ICJ held that the building of the wall, and the regime accompanying it, are contrary to international law (paragraph 142). In contrast, the Supreme Court in *The Beit Sourik Case* held that it is not to be sweepingly said that any route of the fence is a breach of international law. According to the approach of the Supreme Court, each segment of the route should be examined to clarify whether it impinges upon the rights of the Palestinian residents, and whether the impingement is proportional. It was according to this approach, that the fence segments discussed in *The Beit Sourik Case* were examined. Regarding some segments of the fence, it was held that their construction does not violate international law. Regarding other segments of the fence, it was held that their construction does violate international law'. See also ibid, paras 66, 70.

9.3.2.4 Note on Urgency

According to several commentators, it is not sufficient that the measure is required for the attainment of its military purpose. In their view, it must be required *urgently*.[161] Analogous terms are also used in several treaty provisions.[162]

It is possible that urgency is an aspect of military necessity. If it is, however, then urgency or a lack thereof appears to be already implied in the notion of the measure being 'required' or 'not required' for the attainment of its purpose. The range of reasonably available and materially relevant alternatives, as well as the degree of thoroughness with which the belligerent would be expected to assess them, would in general increase or decrease with the amount of time he or she had before making a decision. The less urgent an action was in view of a particular purpose, the more carefully the belligerent would be expected to choose it and hence the more effectively he or she would be expected to minimise its injurious effect.

Thus, where the purpose was not urgent for the belligerent at the time, it would be appropriate for the trier of fact to assess critically the availability of relevant alternatives and their respective degrees of injuriousness. For example, what would have happened if Lothar Rendulic had genuinely felt the Russian attack less imminent? Such a feeling might not have stopped Rendulic from considering the devastation of Finnmark as a plausible precautionary measure. Nevertheless, he would have considered it – or, in any event, he would have been expected to consider it – against a wider range of reasonably available and materially relevant alternatives. And this wider range of options might very well have included at least one that would be less injurious than devastating Finnmark.

Where the purpose was urgent, the trier of fact might grant that the measure taken by the belligerent – though perhaps not as carefully chosen or harmless as it would otherwise have been – was really the best anyone in his or her position could do at the time.

[161] Downey, 'The Law of War and Military Necessity', at 254–56 ('urgent need admitting of no delay'); McDougal and Feliciano, *Law and Minimum World Public Order*, p. 72 ('prompt realization'); O'Brien, 'Meaning of Military Necessity', at 138–41 ('immediately indispensable').

[162] Articles 33 ('urgent military necessity'), 34 ('urgent necessity'), Geneva Convention I; Article 28 ('urgent military necessity'), Geneva Convention II.

9.3.2.5 Note on Degrees

In certain treaty provisions, exceptional military necessity appears with qualifying adverbs or adjectives such as 'imperative(ly)',[163] 'absolute(ly)'[164] and 'unavoidable'.[165] In other provisions, the notion appears with no such adverbs or adjectives.[166] This textual variation has led some commentators to suggest that there is a hierarchy of military necessity.[167] Others have expressed their doubts.[168]

[163] Article 23(g) ('imperatively demanded by the necessities of war'), Hague Regulations (1907); Article 8 ('imperative military necessities'), Geneva Convention I; Article 8 ('imperative military necessities'), Geneva Convention II; Article 126 ('imperative military necessity'), Geneva Convention III; Articles 49 ('imperative military reasons'), 143 ('imperative military necessity'), Geneva Convention IV; Article 4(2) ('military necessity imperatively requires'), Hague Cultural Property Convention; Articles 54(5), 62(1), 67(4), 71(3) ('imperative military necessity'), Additional Protocol I; Article 17(1) ('imperative military reasons'), Additional Protocol II; Articles 8(2)(b)(xiii) ('imperatively demanded by the necessities of war'), 8(2)(e)(xii) ('imperatively demanded by the necessities of war'), 8(2)(e)(xii) ('imperatively demanded by the necessities of the conflict'), Rome Statute; Article 6 ('imperative military necessity'), Hague Cultural Property Protocol II.

[164] Article 54 ('absolute necessity'), Hague Regulations (1907); Article 53 ('absolutely necessary by military operations'), Geneva Convention IV.

[165] Article 11(2) ('unavoidable military necessity'), Hague Cultural Property Convention.

[166] Article 6(b), Nuremberg Charter; Article 50, Geneva Convention I; Article 51, Geneva Convention II; Article 147, Geneva Convention IV; Articles 2(d), 3(b), ICTY Statute; Article 8(2)(a)(iv), Rome Statute.

[167] Schwarzenberger, *International Law as Applied by Courts and Tribunals* (vol. II), pp. 134–35 (referring to the Nuremberg Charter as adopting a 'more lenient' test for military necessity than the 'imperatively demanded' military necessity under the 1907 Hague Regulations); E Rauch, 'Le Concept de Nécessité Militaire Dans le Droit de la Guerre' (1980) 19 *Revue de droit pénal militaire et de droit de la guerre* 209, at 216–18 (distinguishing among *nécessité militaire 'simple'*, *nécessité militaire 'inéclutable, la plus grave ou urgente'*, *nécessité militaire 'absolute'*, and *nécessité militaire 'impérieuse'*); Sylvie-S Junod, 'Article 17 – Prohibition of Forced Movement of Civilians' in Sandoz et al. (eds), *Commentary on Additional Protocols* 1471, pp. 1472–73; Andreas Zimmermann, 'Prohibited Destruction' in Triffterer (ed), *Commentary on the Rome Statute* 395, p. 400; Roger O'Keefe, 'Protection of Cultural Property' in Fleck (ed), *Handbook of International Humanitarian Law* (3rd edn) 425, p. 440. Pertile states (Pertile, 'Missed Opportunity?', at 136): 'Necessity being qualified by Article 53 [of Geneva Convention IV] as "absolute", one may moreover think that a generic military advantage would not be sufficient'. See also ibid, at 151–52.

[168] McCoubrey, 'Modern Doctrine of Military Necessity', at 224 ('The practical distinction between "military necessity" and "imperative military necessity" is far from clear, but the details of "Nuremberg" jurisprudence does not appear to support the contention of a loosening of a critical standard'), 234 ('The precise significance of the addition of the term "imperative" is less than wholly clear'). See also Rogers, *Law on the Battlefield* (2nd

Indeed, there might be something counterintuitive about scaling different degrees of military necessity – such as, for example, from 'mere' military necessity to 'unavoidable' military necessity and then to 'imperative' military necessity. It would be particularly so, if military necessity were understood to denote an action without which the belligerent could not hope to achieve his or her professed purpose in the first place.

It would be less odd, however, should one accept the three aforementioned criteria for the measures to be considered 'required' for the purpose. Where the expression 'military necessity' is modified by a restrictive adjective, it *could* mean, e.g., that the interests protected are considered so important the belligerent ought to:

1. Search more extensively for measures other than the one being contemplated that may be reasonably available and materially relevant to the purpose;
2. Evaluate more vigorously the relative injuriousness between all reasonably available and materially relevant measures identified; and/or
3. Set a more stringent standard of acceptable benefit–injury ratio for the measure being considered.[169]

In other words, it is not inconceivable that a given measure passes an 'ordinary' military necessity threshold and yet fails to pass a 'higher' military necessity threshold.

edn), p. 145 (regarding 'imperative' military necessity versus 'unavoidable' military necessity), 152 (quoting Carcione's dismissive account of the different shades of military necessity implied in the conventional régime of cultural property protection). Dinstein observes (Dinstein, *Conduct of Hostilities* (2nd edn), pp. 7–8 (footnote omitted): 'Each of these adverbs or adjectives is devised to stress that military necessity has to be mulled over attentively and not acted upon flippantly. But this is true of all [law of international armed conflict] strictures'. See also ibid, p. 177; de Mulinen, *Handbook on the Law of War*, p. 83; Hand Boddens Hosang, 'Article 8(2)(b)(xiii) – Destroying or Seizing the Enemy's Property' in Roy S Lee (ed), *The International Criminal Court: Elements of Crimes and Rules of Procedure and Evidence* (Ardsley: Transnational Publishers, 2001) 171; Eve La Haye, 'Displacing Civilians' in R Lee (ed), *International Criminal Court* 215, p. 216; Melzer, *Targeted Killing*, pp. 295–96; O'Keefe, *Protection of Cultural Property*, pp. 123, 157–59; Rogers, *Law on the Battlefield* (2nd edn), pp. 145, 152; Venturini, 'Necessity in the Law of Armed Conflict and International Criminal Law', at 53; Dinstein, 'Military Necessity' (2nd edn 2009), para. 13; Lindsay Moir, 'Conduct of Hostilities – War Crimes' in Doria et al. (eds), *Legal Regime of the International Criminal Court* 487, p. 524; Lindsay Moir, 'Displacement of Civilians as a War Crime Other than a Violation of Common Article 3 in Internal Armed Conflicts' in Doria et al. (eds), *Legal Regime of the International Criminal Court* 639, p. 641; Werle and Jessberger, *Principles of International Criminal Law*, p. 472.

[169] Pertile appears to make similar suggestions. Pertile, 'Missed Opportunity?', at 151–52.

Article 6(a) of Hague Cultural Property Protocol II is arguably a case in point. Article 6(a) restricts the 'imperative military necessity' exception available under Article 4(2) of the 1954 Hague Cultural Property Convention further to acts of hostility against cultural property where:

1. That cultural property has, by its function, been made into a military objective; and
2. There is no feasible alternative available to obtain a similar military advantage to that offered by directing an act of hostility against that objective.[170]

9.3.3 *Military Purpose for Which the Measure Taken Was in Conformity with IHL*

Military necessity pleas are inadmissible where the purpose for which the measure was taken was itself contrary to IHL. This is so, even if the belligerent chooses among the relevant and available measures the one that is the least evil and whose injurious effect is not disproportionate to the gain.

In *Beit Sourik*, the Israeli Supreme Court noted the IDF commander's affidavit that 'the fence is intended to prevent the unchecked passage of inhabitants of the area into Israel and their infiltration into Israeli towns located in the area'.[171] The latter part of this statement clearly refers to the settlements on the West Bank. If it were true that these settlements have been established in breach of Article 49 of Geneva Convention IV, would it not follow that 'measures taken to protect the residents of such settlements from terror attacks are in themselves illegal'?[172]

Some appear to respond to this question in the affirmative. In his declaration attached to the ICJ's *Legal Consequence*, Judge Buergenthal noted that the existence of the Israeli settlements in the West Bank

170 Article 6(a), Hague Cultural Property Protocol II. See also ibid, Articles 10, 13 (regarding the granting and lifting of enhanced protection); O'Keefe, *Protection of Cultural Property*, pp. 252–56, 271–74; Jean-Marie Henckaerts, 'New Rules for the Protection of Cultural Property in Armed Conflict: The Significance of the Second Protocol to the 1954 Hague Convention for the Protection of Cultural Property in the Event of Armed Conflict' in María Teresa Dutli, *Protection of Cultural Property in the Event of Armed Conflict: Report on the Meeting of Experts (Geneva, 5–6 October 2000)* (Geneva: International Committee of the Red Cross, 2002) 27, pp. 35–46.

171 *Beit Sourik*, para. 29. See also Kretzmer, 'Judicial Review during Armed Conflict', at 445.

172 Kretzmer, 'Judicial Review during Armed Conflict', at 446. See also Kretzmer, 'Advisory Opinion', at 93.

'violates Article 49, paragraph 6 [of Geneva Convention IV]. *It follows* that the segments of the wall being built by Israel to protect the settlements are *ipso facto* in violation of international humanitarian law.'[173] Ardi Imseis likewise argues that 'military necessity can operate only to protect the security interests of the occupying power's military forces, and then only within the occupied territory. An attempt to extend the concept of military necessity to protect the interests of Israeli colonies and their civilian inhabitants would offend this general principle'.[174]

A common Latin maxim – *ex injuria jus non oritur* – springs to mind.[175] Others disagree, however. In David Kretzmer's view,

> a theory that posits that the fact that civilians are living in an illegal settlement should prevent a party to the conflict from taking any measures to protect them would seem to contradict fundamental notions of international humanitarian law. After all, the measures may be needed to protect civilians (rather than the settlements in which they live) against a serious violation of [IHL].[176]

Kretzmer goes on to state that

> [i]f one takes Imseis' view, one is led to the conclusion that the Israeli forces are prevented from lifting a finger to defend civilians in the settlements. This would seem to be an unacceptable conclusion, especially if one accepts (as Imseis does) that there has not been a close to military operations in the occupied territories.[177]

It is proposed here that a useful distinction might be drawn between (i) the availability of an exceptional relief from a contrary obligation, on the one hand, and (ii) the exercise of a general right, on the other. While Imseis is very clear about the former, his position on the latter may not be as categorical as Kretzmer describes. Once this distinction has been drawn, the differences between Imseis and Kretzmer may begin to seem somewhat less stark than meets the eye.

For the sake of argument, let us agree that the Israeli settlements in occupied Palestine are in breach of Article 49 of Geneva Convention IV. What follows this is that, insofar as the wall is erected to perpetuate

[173] *Legal Consequences Buergenthal Declaration*, para. 9 (emphasis added). See also Imseis, 'Critical Reflections', at 112; Orakhelashvili, 'Opinion and Reaction', at 138.
[174] Imseis, 'Critical Reflections', at 112 (footnote omitted).
[175] *Legal Consequences, Separate Opinion of Judge Elaraby*, p. 246, para. 3.1; Imseis, 'Critical Reflections', at 112.
[176] Kretzmer, 'Advisory Opinion', at 93 (footnotes omitted).
[177] Ibid, at 93 n.41.

unlawfulness by securing these settlements, neither the wall nor the adoption of various measures needed for its erection is eligible for the exceptional military necessity clauses attached to the relevant provisions of the 1907 Hague Regulations and/or Geneva Convention IV. It follows further that the principal rule contained in these provisions remains applicable to the matters at hand. In other words, the unlawfulness of the purpose sought by the wall's erection disqualifies it from exceptional military necessity.

What does *not* necessarily follow is the suggestion that the settlements' unlawfulness exposes their civilian residents to the kind of attacks and harm against which civilians are ordinarily protected.[178] It is entirely possible that the residents of an unlawful settlement have the right to defend themselves in the event of unlawful attacks on them, and/or that Israel has the right to send IDF troops with a view to protecting their immediate safety against such attacks. The wall may disqualify itself as a lawful measure because it breaches Article 49's principal prohibition, but this disqualification is surely without prejudice to measures that may be lawful based on separate foundations. On this view, it is, as Kretzmer argues, indeed 'not self-evident that the fact that the settlements were established in violation of international law means that *any* measures to protect civilians in those settlements are necessarily illegal'.[179]

But then, Imseis's position – with which Kretzmer contrasts his – does not seem so sweeping either. Imseis essentially holds that Israel may not plead exceptional military necessity for the construction of the wall because its purpose is unlawful. Nowhere does he appear to suggest that IHL prevents 'the Israeli forces . . . from lifting a finger to defend civilians in the settlements'.[180] Nor is this necessarily a conclusion to which 'one is led' if one agrees with Imseis.

In October 2015, a growing number of incidents occurred in Israel and Occupied Palestinian Territories, including the city of Hebron in the West Bank, where armed Palestinian individuals attacked Israeli settlers and were killed as a result.[181] I suggest that the issue be best looked at

[178] It may be said that some, if not all, of the civilian residents participate directly in hostilities from time to time, and that they are liable to hostile acts for the duration of their direct participation therein. This, however, is a separate issue altogether.
[179] Ibid (emphasis in original).
[180] Ibid, at 93 n.41.
[181] 'Israeli-Palestinian Violence: Knife Attackers Shot Dead', BBC News, 17 October 2015.

from the angle of individual self-defence for the Israelis, and questions be asked as to whether the responses were necessary and proportionate.

9.3.4 *Measure Itself Was Otherwise in Conformity with IHL*

Juridical military necessity does not exempt measures from the prescription of unqualified IHL rules.[182] The unqualified prohibition against the killing of POWs and enemies who have surrendered at discretion[183] is a case in point. If the circumstances surrounding the captor are such that it becomes no longer feasible to keep his POW in custody – e.g., encirclement by enemy formations, shortage of food rations – and if the captor kills the POW as a result, then he or she is not entitled to plead military necessity.[184] The US Military Commission in Augsberg, Germany, convicted Gunther Thiele and Georg Steinert of killing an American POW notwithstanding their military necessity pleas.[185]

In *Hostage*, Walter Kuntze was charged with the killing of unarmed civilians in occupied Greece and Yugoslavia. He asserted that, with ground troops in short supply, intimidating the population was militarily necessary in order to maintain order and security. This assertion was rejected.[186]

The fact that military necessity is inadmissible for measures in violation of unqualified IHL rules could be seen as a choice between all-or-nothing alternatives. Where the belligerent must choose between measures which are relevant to his or her lawful purpose yet involve unlawful acts, on the one hand, and measures which amount to abandoning that purpose yet involve no unlawful act, on the other, juridical military necessity would demand that the belligerent choose the latter. Extreme as it might appear, an analogous view was offered in *Rauter*:

182 See Chapters 7 and 8. See also *Krupp*, p. 1347; *in re Wintgen*, Special Criminal Court, Amsterdam, 11 February 1949; Special Court of Cassation, 6 July 1949, 16 *Annual Digest and Reports of Public International Law Cases Year 1949* (1955) 484.

183 Article 23(c), Hague Regulations (1907); Article 6(b), Nuremberg Charter; Article 130, Geneva Convention III; Articles 8(2)(a)(i), 8(2)(b)(vi), Rome Statute.

184 Article 41(3), Additional Protocol I.

185 *Trial of Gunther Thiele and Georg Steinert*, United Nations War Crimes Commission, *Law Reports of Trials of War Criminals*, 15 vols. (London: His Majesty's Stationery Office, 1948), vol. III, 56, p. 58. See also Howard S Levie, *Terrorism in War – The Law of War Crimes* (Dobbs Ferry: Oceana Publications, 1993), p. 501 (quoting observations about *United States of America v Ludwig Klüttgen*, Case No. 12-1502 (1947)).

186 *Hostage*, p. 1281.

> The circumstance that, if [the laws of war] are observed, a territory cannot be held under occupation, gives the Occupant no right to commit acts which are unequivocally prohibited by the law of nations; the proper alternative is for him to evacuate the whole or part of the occupied territory.[187]

In 1949, von Manstein was brought before the British Military Court at Hamburg on charges including the devastation of occupied Ukraine and the deportation of local inhabitants during World War II.[188] The defence apparently alleged that the devastation had been rendered unavoidable by the military exigencies of the situation[189] and that, once it had been so rendered, 'the deportation followed of necessity'.[190] The judge advocate advised the court that '[d]eportation of the population from their homes is upon a different footing. Article 23(g) [of the 1907 Hague Regulations] has no application to this, and if it is to be defended at all, it must be upon some ground other than military necessity'.[191] While the judge advocate might have thought that the prohibition against deportation admitted certain exceptions,[192] he clearly did not think that military necessity was one of them. As noted earlier,[193] Article 49 of Geneva Convention IV does allow military necessity exceptions from the prohibition against deportation.

In a somewhat similar development, the 1935 Roerich Pact on the protection of artistic and scientific institutions and historic monuments protects eligible property without reference to military necessity

187 *Rauter*, p. 543.
188 *Von Lewinski (called Manstein)*, pp. 509–10.
189 Ibid, p. 521.
190 Ibid, p. 523.
191 Ibid.
192 According to the judge advocate, 'any suggestion that the deportation was upon humanitarian grounds was expressly repudiated'. Ibid. But the fact that he made this observation does not necessarily mean that he regarded evacuation on humanitarian grounds as a lawful exception from the prohibition against deportation. In this connection, see Roxburgh (ed), *Oppenheim's International Law* (3rd edn), p. 216 (footnote omitted): 'whenever a belligerent resorts to general devastation, he ought, if possible, to make some provision for the unfortunate peaceful population of the devastated tract of territory. It would be more humane to take them away into captivity rather than let them perish on the spot. The practice, resorted to during the South African War, of housing the victims of devastation in concentration camps, must be approved. The purpose of war may even oblige a belligerent to confine a population forcibly in concentration camps.'
193 See Chapter 7.

exceptions.[194] Its successor, the 1954 Hague Cultural Property Convention, makes allowances for such exceptions.[195] Roger O'Keefe quotes the UNESCO expert committee as saying that 'the law regulating the protection of cultural property in the course of hostilities had always been qualified by reference to military necessity [and declaring] the need to preserve this qualification'.[196]

Military necessity may be inadmissible even where it is prima facie admissible. One rule may expressly authorise exceptions on account of military necessity, but another (typically subsequent) rule may restrict or extinguish such exceptions. Article 53 of Geneva Convention IV prohibits the belligerent from destroying real or personal property in the territory he or she occupies 'except where such destruction is rendered absolutely necessary by military operations'.[197] It is generally agreed that the types of military operations envisaged in this exceptional clause include the so-called 'scorched earth' policy by an occupying force in retreat.[198] By virtue of Article 54(2) of Additional Protocol I,[199] however, such a force is no longer eligible for this exception in respect of objects indispensable to the survival of the civilian population.[200]

The same is arguably true of demolishing or using cultural property covered both under Article 4(1) of the 1954 Hague Cultural Property Convention and under Article 53 of Additional Protocol I. Whereas the former is subject to the imperative military necessity exception

[194] Articles 1, 5, Treaty on the Protection of Artistic and Scientific Institutions and Historic Monuments, 15 April 1935, in force 26 August 1935.

[195] Article 4(2), Hague Cultural Property Convention.

[196] O'Keefe, *Protection of Cultural Property*, p. 122.

[197] Article 53, Geneva Convention IV.

[198] Pictet (ed), *Commentary Geneva Convention IV*, p. 302.

[199] Article 54(2), Additional Protocol I: 'It is prohibited to attack, destroy, remove or render useless objects indispensable to the survival of the civilian population, such as foodstuffs, agricultural areas for the production of foodstuffs, crops, livestock, drinking water installations and supplies and irrigation works, for the specific purpose of denying them for their sustenance value to the civilian population or to the adverse Party, whatever the motive, whether in order to starve out civilians, to cause them to move away, or for any other motive'.

[200] If militarily necessary, a party to the conflict may still destroy objects indispensable to the survival of the civilian population which are located in its own territory. Article 54 (5), Additional Protocol I; Pilloud and Pictet, 'Protection of Objects Indispensable to the Survival of the Civilian Population', p. 659. According to the ICRC's *Customary Law Study*, the rule contained in Article 54 embraces custom. Henckaerts and Doswald-Beck, *Customary International Humanitarian Law* (vol. I), pp. 189–93. But see Article 8(2)(b)(xxv), Rome Statute.

found in the convention's Article 4(2), the latter is not subject to any such exception.[201]

9.4 Miscellaneous Observations

The foregoing elucidates what juridical military necessity contains. In addition to its content, however, the notion involves factors such as requisite knowledge and formal competence.

9.4.1 Knowledge

Exceptional military necessity pleas based solely on hindsight are inadmissible. They must be assessed in light of the particular purpose the belligerent had in mind when he or she took the measure. The mere fact that a measure taken initially for some non-military purpose happens to fulfil a military one afterwards does not, retrospectively, turn it into military necessity. A given measure's reasonable availability to the belligerent, its material relevance to his or her stated military purpose, and the scope and nature of its evil should also be assessed on the basis of that belligerent's contemporaneous and bona fide knowledge.[202]

9.4.1.1 Knowledge of Purpose

As noted earlier, in *Elon Moreh*, the Israeli Supreme Court did not dispute the C-o-S's strictly professional opinion that the settlement, if established, would fulfil military purposes. Nor did the court question that he had advised the Ministerial Defence Committee of his opinion. Yet, the court nullified the requisition order on the ground that its underlying decision had been made primarily for political purposes and only secondarily for military purposes. It would appear, then, that the

[201] O'Keefe, *Protection of Cultural Property*, pp. 217, 251.

[202] *Affaire des bien britannique au Maroc espagnol (Spain v United Kingdom)*, 1 May 1925, 2 *Reports of International Arbitral Awards* (2006) 615, p. 645 ('*Cela admis, il faut se souvenir, d'autre part, que le règlement auquel la clause susmentionnée se rattache fait une place très grande aux nécessités militaires. L'appréciation de ces nécessités doit être laissée dans une large mesure aux personnes mêmes qui sont appelées à agir dans des situations difficiles, ainsi qu'à leurs chefs militaires*'); *von Lewinski (called Manstein)*, p. 522; Melzer, *Targeted Killing*, pp. 296–97; Brian J Bill, 'The Rendulic "Rule": Military Necessity, Commander's Knowledge, and Methods of Warfare' (2009) 12 *Yearbook of International Humanitarian Law* 119, at 125 (quoting *Hostage*, pp. 1295–97); Dinstein, 'Military Necessity' (2nd edn 2009), para. 28; Office of General Counsel, *Law of War Manual*, p. 57.

requisition would have been upheld only if it had been decided primarily for military purposes. This would entail the showing, at a minimum, that such purposes actually existed and were known to those who made the decision.

Justice Landau's observations in *Beit-El*[203] are instructive here. In what appears to be a separate opinion, Justice Landau expressed his presumption that, on establishing the civilian settlement at Beit El, the military authorities 'first gave thought and military planning to the act of settlement'.[204] Indeed, it is on this basis that Justice Landau distinguished the *Beit-El* case from the *Elon Moreh* case: '[t]his time [i.e., in the *Eron Moreh* case] it was not demonstrated … that in the establishment of the civilian settlement the act of settlement was preceded by the military authorities' thought and *military planning* (emphasis in the original – Trans.), as we noted in the Beit-El case'.[205]

In *Hostage*, the US Military Tribunal acquitted Rendulic of wanton destruction in Finnmark, Norway. Rendulic contended that he devastated the area as a precautionary measure against an anticipated attack by his superior Russian pursuers. A question arose as to whether the devastation was justified by military necessity.[206] The tribunal held:

> We are not called upon to determine whether urgent military necessity for the devastation and destruction in the province of Finmark actually existed. We are concerned with the question whether the defendant at the time of its occurrence acted within the limits of honest judgement on the basis of the conditions prevailing at the time. The course of a military operation by the enemy is loaded with uncertainties, such as the numerical strength of the enemy, the quality of his equipment, his fighting spirit, the efficiency and daring of his commanders, and the uncertainty of his intentions. These things when considered with his own military situation provided the facts or want thereof which furnished the basis for the

203 *Ayub et al. v Minister of Defence*, HCJ 606/78, *Judgment*, 15 March 1979, in Meir Shamgar (ed), *Military Government in the Territories Administered by Israel 1967–1980: The Legal Aspects*, 2 vols. (Jerusalem: Hebrew University Press, 1982), vol. I, p. 382.

204 Ibid, p. 386.

205 *Elon Moreh*, at 173–74. For an account of the political background to the difference between *Beit-El* and *Elon Moreh*, see David Kretzmer, *The Occupation of Justice: The Supreme Court of Israel and the Occupied Territories* (Albany: State University of New York Press, 2002), pp. 88–89.

206 It is arguable that, at the relevant moment, the Finnmark region resembled territory under belligerent occupation. The rule considered in the case, however, was Article 23(g) of the Hague Regulations concerning armed hostilities, rather than Articles 46–56 of the same Regulations concerning the treatment of property in occupied territory.

> defendant's decision to carry out the 'scorched earth' policy in Finmark as a precautionary measure against an attack by superior forces. It is our considered opinion that the conditions, as they appeared to the defendant at the time were sufficient upon which he could honestly conclude that urgent military necessity warranted the decision made. This being true, the defendant may have erred in the exercise of his judgement but he was guilty of no criminal act.[207]

The evidence adduced at trial showed that military necessity did not, in fact, exist. The tribunal ruled however that Rendulic's genuinely perceived danger of an enemy attack, under the circumstances prevailing at the time, should not be second-guessed simply because the full facts as they had become subsequently available contradicted or otherwise undermined his original perception about the danger.[208] This ruling would be sensible

[207] *Hostage*, p. 1297. See also *High Command*, at 541: 'Defendants in this case were in many instances in retreat under arduous conditions wherein their commands were in serious danger of being cut off. Under such circumstances, a commander must necessarily make quick decisions to meet the particular situation of his command. A great deal of latitude must be accorded to him under such circumstances. What constitutes devastation beyond military necessity in these situations requires detailed proof of an operational and tactical nature.' Accordingly, in *High Command*, two accused were acquitted of property destruction in occupied territory. Ibid, at 609 (judgment as to defendant Hans Reinhardt), 628 (judgment as to defendant Karl Hollidt).

[208] *Hostage*, p. 1296: 'There is evidence in the record that there was no military necessity for this destruction and devastation. An examination of the facts in retrospect can well sustain this conclusion. But we are obliged to judge the situation as it appeared to the defendant at the time. If the facts were such as would justify the action by the exercise of judgement, after giving consideration to all the factors and existing possibilities, even though the conclusion reached may have been faulty, it cannot be said to be criminal. After giving careful consideration to all the evidence on the subject, we are convinced that the defendant cannot be held criminally responsible although when viewed in retrospect, the danger did not actually exist.' See also *von Lewinski (called Manstein)*, p. 522. In his summary to the British Military Court at Hamburg, the judge advocate reiterated the principles of no second-guessing and *in dubio pro reo*:

> In coming to a conclusion on this question as to whether the destruction caused by the accused was excusable upon this ground [of military necessity], it is essential that you should view the situation through the eyes of the accused and look at it at the time when the events were actually occurring. It would not be just or proper to test the matter in the light of subsequent events, or to substitute an atmosphere of calm deliberation for one of urgency and anxiety. You must judge the question from this standpoint: whether the accused having regard to the position in which he was and the conditions prevailing at the time acted under the honest conviction that what he was doing was legally justifiable. If, in regard to

only if it were significant that Rendulic knew what the military purpose of the devastation was. If this were the case, however, the reverse would also be the case. Where the evidence makes it clear that the belligerent did not act in pursuit of a genuinely perceived military purpose, he or she would not be entitled to claim otherwise on account of hindsight. As noted earlier, *Elon Moreh* supports the view that the mere potentiality of right results does not necessarily imply the existence of right purposes.

9.4.1.2 Knowledge of Pertinence, Injuriousness and Proportionality

Whether a given measure was 'required' for the attainment of its stated military purpose is also a matter that should be assessed on the basis of the belligerent's contemporaneous and bona fide knowledge. If, in view of the information available at the time, the belligerent honestly believed that the measure taken was required for the attainment of his or her purpose, the belligerent's belief should not be second-guessed on account of subsequent events.

Emphasis on the belligerent's contemporaneous and bona fide knowledge about the measure's requiredness is particularly important in active combat. Its exigencies may leave the belligerent with no option but to articulate a military purpose, identify a range of available and relevant measures, evaluate their relative injuriousness, and assess their proportionality – all in an extremely short period of time, on the basis of fragmented, incomplete and often contradictory information, and under highly stressful circumstances.

Conversely, the belligerent would not be entitled to take advantage of the hindsight and claim that the measure was required where the evidence makes it clear that he or she acted without such knowledge. One may refer to the ruling of an ICTY trial chamber in *Galić* – albeit in an admittedly different context of proportionality in attacks.[209] The chamber held:

> any particular instance of seizure or destruction, you are left in doubt upon the matter, then the accused is entitled to have that doubt resolved in his favour.

There is a clear link between the contemporaneous knowledge requirement of military necessity as an exception, on the one hand, and mistake of fact as a negation of the mental element required by a crime, on the other. This link, however, is a matter that goes beyond the scope of this chapter.

209 Harvard Program on Humanitarian Policy and Conflict Research, *Commentary on Air and Missile Warfare Manual*, pp. 91–92; Christine Byron, 'International Humanitarian

> In determining whether an attack was proportionate it is necessary to examine whether a reasonably well-informed person in the circumstances of the actual perpetrator, making reasonable use of the information available to him or her, could have expected excessive civilian casualties to result from the attack.[210]

One incident considered by the chamber involved two shells landing and exploding amid an impromptu football match held in a residential area of Sarajevo. All players were off-duty combatants, surrounded by approximately 200 civilian and combatant spectators. According to one military report, the explosions killed six combatants and five civilians, and wounded fifty-five combatants and thirty-two civilians.[211] These numbers are classic examples of hindsight. Unless one was somewhat arbitrarily to assign different values to different types of human life, it would be difficult if not impossible to say definitively whether the attack was proportionate or disproportionate. The trial chamber's majority declared the attack unlawful, but *not* on the basis of the eventual casualty figures. Rather, it did so on the basis of the consequences that the attack 'would clearly be expected' to generate:

> Although the number of soldiers present at the game was significant, an attack on a crowd of approximately 200 people, including numerous children, would clearly be expected to cause incidental loss of life and injuries to civilians excessive in relation to the direct and concrete military advantage anticipated.[212]

It would appear that, in the majority's view, the arguably proportionate casualty figures do not retroactively alter the clear expectations that an attack such as the one in question would cause disproportionate civilian casualties.[213]

Law and Bombing Campaigns: Legitimate Military Objective and Excessive Collateral Damage' (2010) 13 *Yearbook of International Humanitarian Law* 175, at 192; Yutaka Arai-Takahashi, 'A Battle over Elasticity – Interpreting the Concept of "Concrete and Direct Military Advantage Anticipated" under International Humanitarian Law' in Yves Haeck et al. (eds), *The Realisation of Human Rights: When Theory Meets Practice: Studies in Honour of Leo Zwaak* (Antwerp: Intersentia, 2014) 351, p. 352.

210 *Galić Trial Judgment*, para. 58 (footnotes omitted).

211 Ibid, paras 386–87.

212 Ibid, para. 387.

213 Judge Nieto Navia dissented. *Galić Trial Judgment, Separate and Partially Dissenting Opinion of Judge Nieto-Navia*, paras 63–65, esp. para. 65: 'In light of the preceding evidence regarding [defending forces'] presence in and near the site of the incident, I conclude that the Prosecution has not established beyond a reasonable doubt that the

9.4.2 *Competence*

Under certain circumstances, a person's reliance on military necessity may become invalid by virtue of his or her status alone. For example, only the commanders of forces in the field are authorised to make use of the buildings, material and stores of fixed medical establishments in case of urgent military necessity.[214] Similarly, where fighting occurs on a warship, its sick bays and their equipment may be used for other purposes only if considered militarily necessary by the commander into whose power they have fallen.[215]

Within the context of cultural property, potential abuses of military necessity exceptions became the subject of particular concern.[216] This concern resulted in the adoption of Article 11(2) of the 1954 Hague Cultural Property Convention, which designates an officer competent to establish military necessity.[217] In respect of cultural property 'specially protected' under Article 9 of the convention, only an officer commanding a force the equivalent of a division in size or larger may establish 'unavoidable military necessity' whereby the property's immunity is withdrawn.[218]

Article 4(2) of the convention also permits the belligerent to waive his obligations under Article 4(1) if 'military necessity imperatively requires such a waiver'.[219] The convention itself contains no restriction as to who is authorised to invoke Article 4(2). According to Article 6(c) of Hague Cultural Property Protocol II, only an officer commanding a force the equivalent of a battalion in size or larger, or a force smaller in size where circumstances do not permit otherwise, may invoke Article 4(2).[220] As regards the lifting of cultural property's enhanced protection under Article 10 of the protocol, an attack may be ordered only 'at the highest operational level of command'.[221]

two shells that exploded on 1 June 1993 in Dobrinja were fired deliberately or indiscriminately by the [attacking forces] at civilians.'

214 Article 33, Geneva Convention I.

215 Article 28, Geneva Convention II.

216 Toman, *Commentary on the Hague Cultural Property Convention*, pp. 79, 146–47.

217 Article 11(2), Hague Cultural Property Convention. See also O'Keefe, *Protection of Cultural Property*, pp. 159–60.

218 Article 4(1), Hague Cultural Property Convention.

219 Ibid, Article 4(2).

220 Article 6(c), Hague Cultural Property Protocol II.

221 Ibid, Article 13(2)(c)(i).

It has been suggested that IDF commanders lack the power to seize property in occupied Palestine because Israel '[does] not have such power at all'.[222] This view emanates from the argument that Article 23(g) of the 1907 Hague Regulations – which, if applicable, would have vested the commander with such power – does not apply to situations of belligerent occupation.[223] The issue raised in this argument is whether the law applies to the IDF commanders to begin with, rather than whether the applicable law properly authorises them.

9.5 Conclusion

This chapter has shown how juridical military necessity appears as exceptional clauses attached to specific IHL rules that principally prescribe contrary action.

We began by noting that military necessity as an exception under IHL is distinct in status and content from necessity as a circumstance precluding wrongfulness under the international law of state responsibility. Our discussion also identified and substantiated four cumulative requirements of exceptional military necessity. In order to be eligible, the measure must be taken primarily for the attainment of some specific military purpose; it must be required for the purpose's attainment; the purpose must be in conformity with IHL; and the measure itself must otherwise be in conformity with that law.

When a measure can be deemed 'required' for a purpose's attainment is an area that is in need of further clarification. Beyond the fact that some reasonable ratio ought to be struck between the harm occasioned by the measure and the gain sought by it, much remains unsettled. There are also issues associated with the application of military necessity clauses, such as the requisite kind and scope of knowledge and the competence of the person relying on the notion.

This leaves us with one major form of juridical military necessity yet to be examined. Several property and displacement-related war crimes contain an element according to which the underlying act, such as destruction and forcible transfer, must be shown to lack military

222 Orakhelashvili, 'Opinion and Reaction', at 137.

223 Ibid. But see *Hostage*, pp. 1296–97, where the tribunal found Rendulic not guilty of wanton destruction in Finnmark by applying Article 23(g) of the 1907 Hague Regulations.

necessity.[224] The same is true of their corresponding crimes against humanity. In Chapter 10, we will explore the sizable case law developed by the ICTY and the MICT, as well as the ICC's nascent jurisprudence, to see how these jurisdictions have grappled with the complex factual and legal issues that surround this element.

224 *In re Esau*, Special Criminal Court, 's-Hertogenbosch, 27 April 1948; Special Court of Cassation, 21 February 1949, 16 *Annual Digest and Reports of Public International Law Cases Year 1949* (1955) 482.

10

Military Necessity and Elements of Crimes

Chapters 8 and 9 dealt with how juridical military necessity manifests itself through exclusion and as exceptional clauses, respectively. In this chapter, we will study juridical military necessity's third form, i.e., as a negative element of several war crimes and crimes against humanity.

The fact that military necessity in this context appears as a negative element of specific criminal acts – rather than as a justificatory or excusory plea – should not be surprising. First, this is a direct result of the general inadmissibility of military necessity pleas under positive IHL.[1] As will be seen below, substantive IHL rules form the basis on which all war crimes and some crimes against humanity are built. Where a given IHL prohibition is unqualified, there is no reason why the *actus reus* of its corresponding war crime or crime against humanity should admit military necessity as an exception. Nor, for that matter, should the crime be susceptible to military necessity pleas as a justification or excuse.

Second, the reverse is also true. We have seen that a number of IHL rules expressly permit deviations from their principal prescriptions on account of military necessity. If penal provisions were to criminalise these rules' breaches, their *actus reus* would also reflect the availability of such deviations. This is particularly the case for offences involving property destruction[2] and forcible population displacement. The onus rests with the prosecution to show the absence of military necessity in order to prove that these crimes have been committed in the first place.[3]

[1] See Chapter 8.

[2] And, albeit to a significantly lesser extent, property misappropriation including pillage. Where appropriate, this chapter will also make occasional references to these offences.

[3] *Prosecutor v Jadranko Prlić et al.*, Case No. IT-04-74-A, *Judgment*, 29 November 2017, para. 411.

The foregoing observations are broadly consistent with the material available in ICL.[4] Of such material, however, that produced by today's three major international criminal jurisdictions – i.e., the ICTY, the MICT and the ICC – is the most comprehensive, systematic and detailed. Our discussion will therefore focus primarily on them.

This chapter proceeds as follows. We will begin by reviewing how the ICTY and the MICT have identified and articulated military necessity as a negative element of offences involving property destruction and forcible population displacement. We will then assess the quality of judicial reasoning and application of the law to the facts in the two entities' voluminous cases. Three themes will receive our critical attention: (i) property destruction in the context of combat; (ii) property destruction outside of combat; and (iii) deportation and forcible transfer. Although its quality on military necessity exceptions varies, the ICTY and MICT case law, seen as a whole, is consistent with the four requirements identified in Chapter 9.

The chapter will then move on to the ICC. Its statutory treatment of military necessity exceptions largely mirrors ICTY and MICT judgments, as well as corresponding IHL rules, on the matter. The ICC finds itself at an earlier stage of jurisprudential development. Its pronouncements to date are more limited in content and sophistication as a result. One potential source of contention concerns some of the grounds for excluding individual criminal responsibility under Article 31 of the Rome Statute. These grounds are vulnerable to abuse as backdoors through which defendants may attempt to introduce military necessity pleas as a justification or excuse for their crimes.

10.1 International Criminal Tribunal for the Former Yugoslavia and the International Residual Mechanism for Criminal Tribunals

As of 30 June 2019, neither the ICTY nor the MICT has authoritatively defined juridical military necessity. Nor have they discussed the requirements of military necessity as an element of crimes at any length. Yet these bodies' various chambers have not shied away from making factual determinations about the existence or absence of military necessity in the context of specific incidents.

[4] See, in particular, the various post-World War II criminal trials referred to in Chapter 9 and elsewhere in this book.

These factual determinations appear in connection with two crime categories. The first is large-scale property destruction, of which the absence of military necessity constitutes an element. Forcible displacement of persons is the other. Since temporary evacuation is not unlawful if, inter alia, 'imperative military reasons' so demand, it must be shown that the victim's displacement was either permanent or, though temporary, not demanded by imperative military reasons.

10.1.1 Absence of Military Necessity as an Element of Large-Scale Property Destruction

The ICTY Statute empowers the tribunal to prosecute large-scale property destruction under three headings. They are:

1. Article 2(d), a grave breach of the 1949 Geneva Conventions;
2. Article 3(b), a violation of the laws or customs of war; and
3. Article 5(h), a crime against humanity.

10.1.1.1 Article 2(d), ICTY Statute

Causing 'extensive destruction and appropriation of property, not justified by military necessity and carried out unlawfully and wantonly' constitutes a grave breach of Geneva Conventions I, II and IV.[5] This grave breach is incorporated into Article 2(d) of the ICTY Statute.[6] The tribunal has considered Article 2(d) charges in six cases.[7]

[5] Article 50, Geneva Convention I; Article 51, Geneva Convention II; Article 147, Geneva Convention IV.

[6] Article 2(d), ICTY Statute.

[7] *Prosecutor v Radoslav Brđanin*, Case No. IT-99-36-T, *Sixth Amended Indictment*, 9 December 2003, count 10 ('[u]nlawful and wanton extensive destruction and appropriation of property, not justified by military necessity'); *Prosecutor v Tihomir Blaškić*, Case No. IT-95-14, *Second Amended Indictment*, 25 April 1997, count 11 ('extensive destruction of property'); *Prosecutor v Dario Kordić and Mario Čerkez*, Case No. IT-95-14/2, *Amended Indictment*, 30 September 1998, counts 37, 40 ('extensive destruction of property'); *Prosecutor v Mladen Naletilić (a/k/a 'Tuta') and Vinko Martinović (a/k/a 'Štela')*, Case No. IT-98-34-PT, *Second Amended Indictment*, 28 September 2001, count 19 ('extensive destruction of property'); *Prosecutor v Ivica Rajić a/k/a Viktor Andrić*, Case No. IT-95-12-PT, *Amended Indictment*, 13 January 2004, count 9 ('extensive destruction not justified by military necessity and carried out unlawfully and wantonly'); *Prosecutor v Jadranko Prlić et al.*, Case No. IT-04-74-T, *Second Amended Indictment*, 11 June 2008, counts 19 ('extensive destruction of property, not justified by military necessity and carried out unlawfully and wantonly'), 22 ('appropriation of property, not justified by military necessity and carried out unlawfully and wantonly').

Several tribunal decisions identify two types of property under Article 2(d).[8] The first type includes civilian hospitals, medical aircraft and ambulances that are said to be 'generally protected' by the Geneva Conventions.[9] Such property is protected against destruction or appropriation irrespective of its location. The intended juxtaposition appears to be between 'general' in the sense that protection is not territorially conditional, on the one hand, and 'limited' in the sense that protection is territorially conditional, on the other.

Some ICTY trial chambers apparently concluded that military necessity exceptions do not apply to the prohibition against the destruction of property under general protection. According to the *Tuta and Štela* Trial Chamber,

> two types of property are protected under the grave breach regime: (i) property, regardless of whether or not it is in occupied territory, that carries general protection under the Geneva Conventions of 1949, such as civilian hospitals, medical aircraft and ambulances [irrespective of any military need to destroy them]; and (ii) property protected under Article 53 of the Geneva Convention IV, which is real or personal property situated in occupied territory *when the destruction was not absolutely necessary by military operations* ... The Chamber considers that a crime under Article 2(d) of the Statute has been committed when: ... (iii) the extensive destruction regards property carrying general protection under the Geneva Conventions of 1949, or; the extensive destruction *not absolutely necessary by military operations* regards property situated in occupied territory.[10]

It is debatable whether this conclusion finds support in the plain language of either Article 2(d) of the ICTY Statute, or in the relevant provisions of Geneva Conventions I, II and IV that underpin it. The provisions cited by these chambers[11] protect the property in question

[8] *Kordić and Čerkez Trial Judgment*, para. 341; *Prosecutor v Mladen Naletilić (a/k/a 'Tuta') and Vinko Martinović (a/k/a 'Štela')*, Case No. IT-98-34-T, *Judgment*, 31 March 2003, para. 575; *Prosecutor v Radoslav Brđanin*, Case No. IT-99-36-T, *Judgment*, 1 September 2004, para. 586; *Prlić et al Trial Judgment* (vol. I), 122. See also Guénaël Mettraux, *International Crimes and the Ad Hoc Tribunals* (Oxford: Oxford University Press, 2005), p. 78.

[9] *Kordić and Čerkez Trial Judgment*, para. 336; *Tuta and Štela Trial Judgment*, para. 575; *Brđanin Trial Judgment*, para. 586 n.1490; *Prlić et al. Trial Judgment*, para. 125.

[10] *Tuta and Štela Trial Judgment*, paras 575, 577 (footnotes omitted; emphasis added). See also *Brđanin Trial Judgment*, paras 586, 588.

[11] *Tuta and Štela Trial Judgment*, para. 575 n.1436 (citing Chapters III, V and VI, Geneva Convention I, Articles 22–35 and 38–40, Geneva Convention II; and Article 18, Geneva Convention IV); *Brđanin Trial Judgment*, para. 586 n.1490 (citing Articles 19–23, 33–34

from *attacks* regardless of military necessity. This does not necessarily mean, however, that these provisions also protect the property – and, in particular, immobile property such as buildings – from *destruction* regardless of military necessity. The Red Cross commentary on Geneva Convention I observes:

> The provision [prohibiting intentional destruction of material and stores defined in Article 33, Geneva Convention I] covers the material of both mobile units and fixed establishments. It also refers to stores of material, but only to those belonging to fixed establishments, as the nature of mobile units excludes their having stores in the real sense. *The stipulation does not, however, cover the actual buildings, which may in certain extreme cases have to be destroyed for tactical reasons.*[12]

As will be shown, the destruction of property need not constitute an attack against that property, or vice versa.

Real and personal property in occupied territory forms the second type of property falling within the scope of Article 2(d) of the ICTY Statute.[13] All of the Article 2(d) charges filed have involved the destruction and/or appropriation of real and personal property located in what the prosecution alleged was occupied territory. Yet, it has become increasingly difficult for the prosecution to prove the existence of belligerent occupation.[14] This difficulty – together with considerations of judicial economy and a perceived lack of difference between the culpability of an accused convicted under Article 2(d) and under Article 3(b) – appears to have led to a decrease in the number of Article 2(d) charges.

10.1.1.2 Article 3(b), ICTY Statute

Article 3(b) provides for the prosecution of 'wanton destruction of cities, towns or villages, or devastation not justified by military necessity', a

and 35–37, Geneva Convention I; Articles 38–39, Geneva Convention II; Articles 18, 21 and 22, Geneva Convention IV).

12 Pictet (ed), *Commentary Geneva Convention I*, p. 276 (emphasis added). See also Pictet (ed), *Commentary Geneva Convention IV*, p. 601 ('[T]he destruction and appropriation mentioned here are dependent on the necessities of war').

13 *Prosecutor v Ivica Rajić a/k/a Viktor Andrić*, Case No. IT-95-12-R61, *Review of the Indictment pursuant to Rule 61 of the Rules of Procedure and Evidence*, 13 September 1996, para. 42; *Blaškić Trial Judgment*, paras 148–50; *Kordić and Čerkez Trial Judgment*, paras 337–41; *Tuta and Štela Trial Judgment*, para. 575; *Brđanin Trial Judgment*, paras 586, 588.

14 *Kordić and Čerkez Trial Judgment*, para. 808; *Tuta and Štela Trial Judgment*, paras 586–88; *Brđanin Trial Judgment*, paras 637–39. But see *Prlić et al. Trial Judgment* (vol. III), paras 577–89; *Prlić et al. Appeal Judgment*, paras 316–45, esp. 343.

violation of the laws or customs of war.[15] Several cases have been brought under this article.[16]

It is sometimes suggested that 'wanton destruction of cities, towns or villages' and 'devastation not justified by military necessity' are distinct offences.[17] On this view, the former offence would not admit military necessity exceptions. The drafting history of Article 6(b) of the Nuremberg Charter (from which Article 3(b) of the ICTY Statute is drawn verbatim) appears to indicate that the two notions could indeed be considered distinct. The charter's 11 July 1945 draft contained the

15 Article 3(b), ICTY Statute.

16 *Prosecutor v Naser Orić*, Case No. IT-03-68-PT, *Third Amended Indictment*, 30 June 2005, counts 3, 5 ('wanton destruction of cities, towns or villages, not justified by military necessity'); *Prosecutor v Pavle Strugar*, Case No. IT-01-42-PT, *Third Amended Indictment*, 10 December 2003, count 4 ('devastation not justified by military necessity'); *Brđanin Sixth Amended Indictment*, count 11 ('[w]anton destruction of cities, towns or villages, or devastation not justified by military necessity'); *Prosecutor v Milan Babić*, Case No. IT-03-72, *Indictment*, 6 November 2003, count 4 ('wanton destruction of villages, or devastation not justified by military necessity'); *Prosecutor v Enver Hadžihasanović and Amir Kubura*, Case No. IT-01-47-PT, *Third Amended Indictment*, 26 September 2003, count 5 ('wanton destruction of cities, towns or villages, not justified by military necessity'); *Prosecutor v Miodrag Jokić*, Case No. IT-01-42, *Second Amended Indictment*, 26 August 2003, count 4 ('devastation not justified by military necessity'); *Prosecutor v Milan Martić*, Case No. IT-95-11-PT, *Second Amended Indictment*, 14 July 2003, count 12 ('wanton destruction of villages, or devastation not justified by military necessity'); *Tuta and Štela Second Amended Indictment*, count 20 ('wanton destruction not justified by military necessity'); *Rajić Amended Indictment*, count 10 ('wanton destruction of a city or devastation not justified by military necessity'); *Kordić and Čerkez Amended Indictment*, count 41 ('wanton destruction not justified by military necessity'); *Blaškić Second Amended Indictment*, counts 2, 12 ('devastation not justified by military necessity'); *Prosecutor v Ljube Boškoski and Johan Tarčulovski*, Case No. IT-04-82-PT, *Amended Indictment*, 2 November 2005, count 2 ('wanton destruction of cities, towns or villages'); *Prosecutor v Vojislav Šešelj*, Case no. IT-03-67, *Third Amended Indictment*, 7 December 2007, count 12 ('wanton destruction of villages, or devastation not justified by military necessity'); *Prosecutor v Ante Gotovina et al.*, Case No. IT-06-90-T, *Amended Joinder Indictment*, 12 March 2008, count 5 ('wanton destruction of cities, towns or villages, or devastation not justified by military necessity'); *Prlić et al. Second Amended Indictment*, count 20 ('wanton destruction of cities, towns or villages, or devastation not justified by military necessity').

17 *Prosecutor v Enver Hadžihasanović and Amir Kubura*, Case No. IT-01-47-AR73.3, *Joint Defence Interlocutory Appeal of Trial Chamber Decision on Enver Hadžihasanović and Amir Kubura's Rule 98bis Motions for Acquittal*, 2 November 2004, para. 26; *Martić Trial Judgment*, para. 89; *Boškoski and Tarčulovski Trial Judgment*, para. 350; Mettraux, *International Crimes and the Ad Hoc Tribunals*, pp. 92–93.

expression 'wanton destruction of towns and villages'.[18] This formulation remained essentially unchanged throughout the negotiations.[19] In the US revision submitted on 31 July, the expression 'wanton destruction of cities, towns or villages; devastation not justified by military necessity' first appeared.[20] The record of the 2 August discussion does not reveal any information about this last-minute addition.[21] Nor is it clear how, after 2 August, the semicolon was replaced by the combination of a comma and the word 'or'. The charter was adopted six days later, on 8 August 1945.

It is submitted here that, even if the two notions were to be considered distinct, they only criminalise property destruction that is not justified by military necessity. Acts constituting 'wanton destruction of cities, towns or villages' have consistently been interpreted to be those not justified by military necessity. The International Military Tribunal (IMT) found that '[c]ities and towns and villages were wantonly destroyed without military justification or necessity'.[22] Article II(1)(b) of Control Council Law No. 10 lists 'wanton destruction of cities, towns or villages, or devastation not justified by military necessity' as a war crime. Neither the indictments nor the judgments in *High Command* and *Hostage* divided Article II(1)(b) into subgroups.

Only a limited number of ICTY decisions treat Article 3(b) as containing two distinct offences. In *Hadžihasanović and Kubura*, the appeals chamber discussed 'the wanton destruction of cities, towns or villages' as one offence articulated in Article 3(b) of the statute, and 'devastation not justified by military necessity' as another.[23] Even there, however, the chamber did not cite any authority in support of this distinction. On the contrary, it noted that 'wanton destruction of cities, towns or villages not justified by military necessity' was a customary prohibition.[24] According to the *Strugar Trial Judgment*, 'Article 3(b) codifies two

[18] Robert H Jackson, *Report of Robert H. Jackson United States Representative to the International Conference on Military Trials* (Washington, DC: Department of State, 1949), p. 197.

[19] Ibid, pp. 205, 293, 327, 351, 359, 373–74, 390, 392–93.

[20] Ibid, p. 395.

[21] Ibid, pp. 399–419.

[22] *Göring et al.*, p. 228.

[23] *Prosecutor v Enver Hadžihasanović and Amir Kubura*, Case No. IT-01-47-AR73.3, *Decision on Joint Defence Interlocutory Appeal of Trial Chamber Decision on Rule 98bis Motions for Acquittal*, 11 March 2005, para. 29.

[24] Ibid, para. 30.

crimes: "wanton destruction of cities, towns or villages, or devastation not justified by military necessity"'.[25] And yet, later in the same judgment, the trial chamber defined the elements of the crime of 'wanton destruction not justified by military necessity'.[26] Perhaps the expressions 'wanton'[27] and 'not justified by military necessity' are functionally synonymous. Be that as it may, it appears uncontroversial in contemporary IHL and ICL that large-scale, militarily unnecessary property destruction is generally prohibited, and that a violation of this prohibition constitutes a war crime.[28]

10.1.1.3 Article 5(h), ICTY Statute

Article 5(h) of the ICTY Statute specifies 'persecutions on religious, political and racial grounds' as a crime against humanity.[29] According to the tribunal's jurisprudence, property destruction may amount to persecutions under certain circumstances.[30] The tribunal has charged

[25] *Prosecutor v Pavle Strugar*, Case No. IT-01-42-T, *Judgment*, 31 January 2005, para. 291.

[26] Ibid, para. 292.

[27] The French term used is *sans motif* – i.e., 'without good reason'. See also UN Crimes Commission, *History of the United Nations War Crimes Commission*, pp. 34, 37–38 (American observations on charges of inhuman or atrocious conduct); O'Keefe, *Protection of Cultural Property*, pp. 26, 32.

[28] Article 23(g), Hague Regulations (1907); Article 6(b), Nuremberg Charter; Article II(1)(b), Control Council Law No. 10; Article 50, Geneva Convention I; Article 51, Geneva Convention II; Articles 53, 147, Geneva Convention IV; Articles 8(2)(b)(xiii), 8(2)(e)(xii), Rome Statute. See also *Martić Trial Judgment*, para. 91; *Boškoski and Tarčulovski Trial Judgment*, para. 350; *Prlić et al. Trial Judgment* (vol. I), paras 165–66; *Prosecutor v Zdravko Tolimir*, Case No. IT-05-88/2-T, *Judgment*, 12 December 2012, para. 858; *Prosecutor v Vujadin Popović et al.*, Case No. IT-05-88-T, *Judgment*, 10 June 2010, para. 985.

[29] Article 5(h), ICTY Statute.

[30] *Prosecutor v Momčilo Krajišnik*, Case No. IT-00-39-T, *Judgment*, 27 September 2006, paras 773–79, 782–83; *Prosecutor v Vidoje Blagojević and Dragan Jokić*, Case No. IT-02-60-T, *Judgment*, 17 January 2005, para. 594; *Kordić and Čerkez Appeal Judgment*, para. 108; *Prosecutor v Milomir Stakić*, Case No. IT-97-24-T, *Judgment*, 31 July 2003, para. 764, 768; *Prosecutor v Tihomir Blaškić*, Case No. IT-95-14-A, *Judgment*, 27 July 2004, para. 149; *Tuta and Štela Trial Judgment*, para. 704; *Prosecutor v Biljana Plavšić*, Case No. IT-00-39&40/1-S, *Sentencing Judgment*, 27 February 2003, para. 15; *Prosecutor v Miroslav Kvočka et al.*, Case No. IT-98-30/1-T, *Judgment*, 2 November 2002, para. 186; *Kordić and Čerkez Trial Judgment*, paras 202, 205, 207; *Blaškić Trial Judgment*, paras 227–28, 234; *Brđanin Trial Judgment*, paras 1021–24; *Prosecutor v Miroslav Deronjić*, Case No. IT-02-61-S, *Sentencing Judgment*, 30 March 2004, para. 123; *Prosecutor v Milan Babić*, Case No. IT-03-72-S, *Sentencing Judgment*, 29 June 2004, paras 14–17, 30–31; *Martić Trial Judgment*, para. 119; *Popović et al. Trial Judgment*, paras 982–87; *Prosecutor v Vlastimir Đorđević*, Case No. IT-05-87/1-T, *Judgment*, 23 February 2011, paras 1770–73; *Gotovina et al. Trial Judgment*, paras

property destruction as an underlying act of persecutions in relation to numerous cases.[31]

1825–30; *Tolimir Trial Judgment*, para. 859; *Prosecutor v Mićo Stanišić and Stojan Župljanin*, Case No. IT-08-91-T, *Judgment*, 3 vols., 27 March 2013, vol. I, para. 86; *Prosecutor v Radovan Karadžić*, Case No. IT-95-5/18-T, *Judgment*, 24 March 2016, paras 530–34; *Prosecutor v Ratko Mladić*, Case No. IT-09-92-T, *Judgment*, 22 November 2017, para. 3258 (see also ibid, para. 3250, for plunder).

31 *Prosecutor v Vidoje Blagojević and Dragan Jokić*, Case No. IT-02-60-T, *Fourth Amended Joinder Indictment*, 14 May 2004, count 5 ('persecutions on political, racial and religious grounds [by way of] destruction of personal property and effects'); *Brđanin Sixth Amended Indictment*, count 3 ('persecutions [by way of] destruction [of property]'); *Babić Indictment*, count 1 ('persecutions on political, racial and religious grounds [by way of] deliberate destruction of homes, other public and private property'); *Prosecutor v Miroslav Deronjić*, Case No. IT-02-61-PT, *Second Amended Indictment*, 29 September 2003, paras 36–37 ('persecutions [by way of] destruction of property'); *Martić Second Amended Indictment*, count 1 ('persecutions on political, racial and religious grounds [by way of] deliberate destruction of homes, other public and private property'); *Prosecutor v Milomir Stakić*, Case No. IT-97-24-PT, *Fourth Amended Indictment*, 10 April 2002, count 6 ('persecutions [by way of] destruction [of residential and commercial properties]'); *Prosecutor v Momčilo Krajišnik and Biljana Plavšić*, Case No. IT-00-39 & 40-PT, *Amended Consolidated Indictment*, 7 May 2002, count 3 ('persecutions on political, racial and religious grounds [by way of] intentional and wanton destruction of private property including houses and business premises and public property'); *Tuta and Štela Second Amended Indictment*, count 1; *Prosecutor v Radislav Krstić*, Case No. IT-98-33, *Amended Indictment*, 27 October 1999, count 6 ('persecutions on political, racial and religious grounds [by way of] destruction of personal property'); *Prosecutor v Blagoje Simić et al.*, Case No. IT-95-9, *Fifth Amended Indictment*, 30 May 2002, count 1 ('persecutions on political, racial and religious grounds [by way of] wanton and extensive destruction [of property]'); *Kordić and Čerkez Amended Indictment*, counts 1, 2 ('persecutions on political, racial or religious grounds [by way of] wanton and extensive destruction [of property]'); *Blaškić Second Amended Indictment*, count 1 ('persecutions on political, racial or religious grounds [by way of] destruction [of property]'); *Gotovina et al. Amended Joinder Indictment*, count 1 ('persecutions on political, racial and religious grounds [by way of] destruction and burning'); *Šešelj Third Amended Indictment*, count 1 ('persecutions . . . committed on political, racial and religious grounds [by way of] deliberate destruction of homes, other public and private property, cultural institutions, historic monuments and sacred sites'); *Prosecutor v Vlastimir Đorđević*, Case No. IT-05-87/1-PT, *Fourth Amended Indictment*, 2 June 2008, count 5 ('persecutions on political, racial and religious grounds [by way of] wanton destruction'); *Prosecutor v Radovan Karadžić*, Case No. IT-95-5/18-PT, *Third Amended Indictment*, 27 February 2009, count 3 ('persecutions [by way of] wanton destruction'); *Prosecutor v Zdravko Tolimir*, Case No. IT-05-88/2-PT, *Third Amended Indictment*, 4 November 2009, count 6 ('persecutions on political, racial and religious grounds [by way of] the destruction of personal property and effects'); *Prosecutor v Mićo Stanišić and Stojan Župljanin*, Case No. IT-08-91-PT,

While some ICTY judgments clearly indicate the absence of military necessity as an element of persecutions by way of property destruction,[32] others do not.[33] This discrepancy is unfortunate. The destruction of property justified by military necessity constitutes neither a grave breach of the Geneva Conventions nor a violation of the laws and customs of war. Yet this discrepancy might be taken to leave open the possibility that even militarily necessary – and, therefore, IHL-compliant – property destruction could constitute persecutions. As much was suggested, worryingly and without any additional authority, by the *Kvočka et al.* Appeals Chamber.[34]

Second Amended Consolidated Indictment, 10 September 2009, count 1 ('persecutions on political, racial and religious grounds [by way of] wanton destruction'); *Prosecutor v Vujadin Popović et al.*, Case No. IT-05-88-T, *Indictment*, 4 August 2006, count 6 ('persecutions on political, racial and religious grounds [by way of] destruction of personal property'); *Tolimir Trial Judgment*, paras 870–78; *Mićo Stanišić and Župljanin Trial Judgment* (vol. I), paras 86–90; *Prlić et al. Trial Judgment* (vol. III), paras 1694–713, 1725–29, 1737–41; *Prosecutor v Ratko Mladić*, Case No. IT-09-92-PT, *Fourth Amended Indictment*, 16 December 2001, count 3 ('persecutions on political, racial and religious grounds [by way of] the wanton destruction of private property including homes and businesses and public property, including cultural monuments and sacred sites').

32 *Blaškić Trial Judgment*, para. 234; *Blaškić Appeal Judgment*, paras 146, 149; *Blagojević and Jokić Trial Judgment*, para. 593; *Krajišnik Trial Judgment*, para. 776; *Gotovina et al. Trial Judgment*, para. 1827; *Popović et al. Trial Judgment*, paras 984–86; *Karadžić Trial Judgment*, para. 532; *Prlić et al. Appeal Judgment*, para. 423; *Mladić Trial Judgment*, paras 3256–57.

33 *Kordić and Čerkez Trial Judgment*, para. 205; *Kordić and Čerkez Appeal Judgment*, paras 108–09; *Tuta and Štela Trial Judgment*, paras 238, 704, 706; *Plavšić Sentencing Judgment*, para. 15; *Stakić Trial Judgment*, para. 763.

34 *Kvočka et al. Appeal Judgment*, para. 321 ('The Appeals Chamber recalls incidentally that acts underlying persecution under Article 5(h) of the Statute need not be considered a crime in international law.'). This *obiter* has since been treated as settled in the ICTY and ICTR case law. See *Prosecutor v Radoslav Brđanin*, Case No. IT-99-36-A, *Judgment*, 3 April 2007, para. 296; *Ferdinand Nahimana et al. v Prosecutor*, Case No. ICTR-99-52-A, *Judgment*, 28 November 2007, para. 985; *Popović et al. Appeal Judgment*, para. 738; *Prlić et al. Appeal Judgment, Dissenting Opinion of Judge Fausto Pocar*, para. 23. On the danger of recharacterising IHL-compliant conduct as a crime against humanity, see Payam Akhavan, 'Reconciling Crimes against Humanity with the Laws of War: Human Rights, Armed Conflict, and the Limits of Progressive Jurisprudence' (2008) 6 *Journal of International Criminal Justice* 6; Werle and Jessberger, *Principles of International Criminal Law*, p. 259; N Hayashi, 'Is the Yugoslav Tribunal Guilty of Hyper-Humanising International Humanitarian Law?'. But see José Doria, 'Whether Crimes against Humanity Are Backdoor War Crimes' in Doria et al. (eds), *Legal Regime of the International Criminal Court* 645, pp. 656–60.

10.1.2 Instances of Militarily Unnecessary Property Destruction

In *Kordić and Čerkez*, several trial-level findings of militarily unnecessary property destruction were overturned on appeal.[35] The appeals chamber found that no evidence had been adduced on the scale and manner of the destruction or on the absence of military necessity for it.[36] With respect to Nadioci, the chamber held:

> It is not sufficient for the Prosecution to prove that destruction occurred. It also has to prove when and how the destruction occurred. It has to establish that the destruction was not justified by military necessity, which cannot be presumed and especially in the context of the Indictment in which the Prosecution pleaded that fighting continued until May 1994. The Appeals Chamber considers that in the absence of further evidence as to how the destruction occurred, no reasonable trier of fact could find that wanton destruction not justified by military necessity . . . is established.[37]

The fact that the timing of the property destruction in Nadioci had not been proven meant that it might have occurred *during* the fighting. This, combined with the lack of evidence regarding how Nadioci's property was destroyed, arguably gave rise to the reasonable doubt that it was destroyed *by* the fighting.[38]

Underneath the appeals chamber's ruling lies a complex relationship between property destruction and active combat. Where property is destroyed amid active combat, what significance does the fighting have on such destruction's military necessity? Conversely, where property is destroyed outside the context of combat, is such destruction perforce militarily unnecessary?

10.1.3 Property Destruction in the Context of Combat

There are four major factors to consider when assessing the military necessity of property destruction in combat. First, as a threshold matter,

[35] *Kordić and Čerkez Trial Judgment*, paras 572, 625–49, 665, 806–07 (regarding Merdani, Nadioci, Pirići, Rotilj, Stari Vitez and Vitez); *Kordić and Čerkez Appeal Judgment*, paras 429, 465–66, 495, 503, 547 (regarding Merdani, Nadioci, Pirići, Rotilj and Stari Vitez).

[36] *Kordić and Čerkez Appeal Judgment*, para. 495.

[37] Ibid. See also *Martić Trial Judgment*, para. 93; *Prlić et al. Trial Judgment* (vol. I), para. 170. Since the absence of military necessity for property destruction cannot be presumed, the onus rests with the prosecution to show this absence. *Prosecutor v Naser Orić*, Case No. IT-03-68-T, *Judgment*, 30 June 2006, para. 586 (quoting *Kordić and Čerkez Appeal Judgment*, para. 495). Showing the absence of military necessity entails, in turn, proving that at least one of its requirements was unfulfilled.

[38] *Mićo Stanišić and Župljanin Trial Judgment* (vol. I), para. 334.

one may look to the lawfulness or otherwise of the military activities that underlie the destruction. Should property be destroyed as part of an assault on a locality that contains no military objective to begin with, then the property's destruction would *ipso facto* be militarily unnecessary.

Second, we need to unpack the subtle way in which attacking and destroying interact with each other. Failing to appreciate this interplay is responsible for some of the confusions in the ICTY's case law regarding military necessity. Third, these confusions are exacerbated by the fact that the tribunal has described military necessity by reference to military objectives.

Fourth, the most intricate area of military necessity assessment involves the destruction of civilian objects during hostilities that does not take the form of an attack. Establishing an object's civilian status does not per se warrant the conclusion that its destruction is militarily unnecessary. The assessor must additionally consider the four requirements of juridical military necessity.[39] This stands in contrast to the fact that an object's civilian status does make its deliberate attack *ipso facto* unlawful.

10.1.3.1 Lawfulness of the Underlying Military Activities

The *Blaškić* Trial Chamber held that the property destruction in Ahmići, Šantići, Pirići and Nadioci, as well as in Vitez and Stari Vitez, was militarily unnecessary because the underlying offensives on these localities were without military justification.[40] In so holding, the chamber effectively set forth two propositions: (1) as a matter of fact, there was nothing in these localities that justified the offensives and (2) as a matter of law, where an offensive is launched on a locality without military justification, military necessity is inadmissible in respect of property destruction occurring during the course of that offensive.

The *Blaškić* Appeals Chamber rejected the first proposition. It found that there was, in fact, some military justification for the offensives on the localities concerned, and consequently, that they were not per se unlawful.[41] This finding left the second proposition of the trial chamber unaddressed by the appeals chamber. It is submitted here that the second

[39] See Chapter 9.

[40] *Blaškić Trial Judgment*, paras 402–10, 507–12.

[41] *Blaškić Appeal Judgment*, paras 235, 331–35, 437–38, 444 (regarding Ahmići, Nadioci, Pirići, Šantići, Stari Vitez and Vitez).

proposition is correct as a matter of law, insofar as the property destruction forms part of the underlying military activities.[42] As noted earlier, military necessity does not exempt measures based on purposes that are contrary to IHL.[43] It would seem logical – indeed, truistic – to say that if an offensive is unlawfully launched on a locality, and if the offensive involves the destruction of property therein, this destruction is devoid of military necessity. It does not follow *a contrario*, however, that the lawfulness of an offensive on a locality renders all accompanying property destruction militarily necessary. Plainly, the underlying offensive's lawfulness is *not* determinative of the destruction's military necessity.[44]

What, then, *is* determinative? Articulating informed responses to this question involves:

1. Distinguishing between attacking and destroying a piece of property;
2. Distinguishing between military necessity and military objective, two similar-sounding yet very dissimilar concepts in positive IHL; and
3. Distinguishing between the destruction of property which also constitutes an attack against that property, on the one hand, and the destruction of property which does not, on the other.

10.1.3.2 Attack vs. Destruction

Article 49(1) of Additional Protocol I defines 'attacks' as 'acts of violence against the adversary, whether in offence or in defence'.[45] There is no formal definition of 'destruction' under IHL. Nevertheless, attack and destruction are clearly interrelated notions. In active combat, the destruction of property typically takes the form of an attack against that property, or an attack against some other objective in its vicinity. Similarly,

[42] Examples of unjustified offensives include attacks launched on localities that are in fact undefended or non-defended, and those launched on special zones such as demilitarised zones.

[43] See Chapter 9.

[44] The *Blaškić* Appeals Chamber stated that it 'does not therefore consider that the attack of 16 April 1993 on Vitez and Stari Vitez was unlawful *per se*, but agrees with the Trial Chamber only to the extent that crimes were committed in the course of the attack'. *Blaškić Appeal Judgment*, paras 438, 444.

[45] Article 49(1), Additional Protocol I. See Frits Kalshoven and Liesbeth Zegveld, *Constraints on the Waging of War*, 2nd edn (Geneva: International Committee of the Red Cross, 2001), p. 97 ('"acts of violence" means acts of warfare involving the use of violent means: the term covers the rifle shot and the exploding bombs, not the act of taking someone prisoner (even though the latter may also involve the use of force)'); Rogers, *Law on the Battlefield* (2nd edn), pp. 27–29.

when particular property becomes the object of an attack, this attack often results in the property being totally or partially destroyed.

Not every successful attack necessarily entails the destruction of its objective, however. During the 1999 Kosovo crisis, NATO attacked some of Serbia's electrical power switch stations. According to news reports, NATO released small filaments of graphite over these facilities.[46] This material caused large-scale short circuits; yet, other than burnt fuses, it left no material damage to the power switch stations.[47] Likewise, in 2003, the US Air Force reportedly deployed an electromagnetic pulse (EMP) as a weapon in its attack against Iraq's satellite television network.[48] Its programmes were disrupted for several hours after the EMP temporarily disabled the broadcaster's equipment.[49]

If one were to insist that all attacks constitute destructions and vice versa, one would need to argue that NATO actually attacked the electrical power switch stations' fuses (rather than the stations themselves) and that the US Air Force actually attacked the television network's circuitry (rather than the network itself). This, it is suggested here, would not accord with how the two notions are ordinarily understood and used.

Nor, even if the belligerent launches an attack with a view to destroying an objective, does the attack necessarily cause the objective's destruction or damage. For instance, the ordnance may simply fail to detonate; the target may move sufficiently away from the area of impact to escape or withstand the blast; an undersupplied mortar battery may exhaust its limited rounds without hitting the target.[50] If an attack is launched against an objective, and if the objective survives the attack, this does not mean that no attack has taken place at all.[51]

46 '"Soft Bombs" Hit Hard', BBC News, 3 May 1999. See also Rogers, *Law on the Battlefield* (2nd edn), pp. 27–9.

47 Ibid.

48 Joel Roberts, 'U.S. Drops "E-Bomb" On Iraqi TV', CBS, 25 March 2003.

49 Ibid.

50 Terry D Gill, 'International Humanitarian Law Applied to Cyberwarfare: Precautions, Proportionality and the Notion of "Attack" under the Humanitarian Law of Armed Conflict' in Nicholas Tsagourias and Russell Buchan (eds), *Research Handbook on International Law and Cyberspace* (Cheltenham and Northampton: Edward Elgar, 2015) 366, pp. 374–75.

51 Article 8(2)(b)(ii), Rome Statute (designating as a war crime the act of '[i]ntentionally directing attacks against civilian objects, that is, objects which are not military objectives'). This war crime does not require that the attacks result in the objects being destroyed or damaged. The same can arguably be said of the elements of launching attacks in the knowledge that it will cause disproportionate collateral damage, a war crime stipulated under Article 8(2)(b)(iv) of the Rome Statute. See also Judith Gardam, 'Crimes

Conversely, under certain circumstances, property may be destroyed without being attacked.[52] During World War II, Japan demolished houses in order to create firebreaks in parts of its large cities (e.g., Nagoya) in anticipation of Allied aerial bombardments.[53] Even if Article 49(1) of Additional Protocol I had applied to these demolitions, they clearly would not have constituted 'acts of violence against' the United States.

In September 1944, the port city of Brest in Bretagne, France, experienced fierce urban combat between German and Allied forces.[54] According to one account,

> [t]he battle for Brest entered its final but most painful stage. The 2d and 8th Division [of the US Army] became involved in street fighting against [German] troops who seemed to contest every street, every building, every square. Machine gun and antitank fire from well-concealed positions made advances along the thoroughfares suicidal, and attackers had to move from house to house by blasting holes in the building walls, clearing the adjacent houses, and repeating the process to the end of the street.[55]

Allied combat engineers played a vital role in this process. They facilitated the advance of their infantry colleagues by partially or totally destroying local civilian buildings. Another account illustrates:

Involving Disproportionate Means and Methods of Warfare under the Statute of the International Criminal Court' in Doria et al. (eds), *Legal Regime of the International Criminal Court* 537, p. 546. As a matter of evidence, however, the prosecution may find it difficult to prove that an attack was deliberately directed against a particular objective except by showing that the objective was in fact destroyed or damaged as a result. At the ICTY, the *Galić* Trial Chamber ruled that the war crime of unlawful attacks on civilian persons requires the showing that the attacks *caused* death or serious injury. *Galić Trial Judgment*, paras 42–44, 56, 62. See also *Dragomir Milošević Trial Judgment*, para. 942.

52 Roger O'Keefe, 'Protection of Cultural Property' in Clapham and Gaeta (eds), *Oxford Handbook of International Law in Armed Conflict* 492, p. 501: 'As for the qualified prohibition on wilful destruction of or damage to cultural property other than by way of attacks, imperative military necessity may justify demolitions in order to impede the progress of enemy columns, to clear a line of fire or to deny cover to enemy fighters, although the extent of the destruction or damage in the event of will need to be calibrated to the degree of military necessity'.

53 Civil Defense Office, National Security Resources Board, Executive Office of the President, *Fire Effects of Bombing Attacks* (1950), pp. 18–19. See also John Antal, *City Fights: Selected Histories of Urban Combat from World War II to Vietnam* (New York: Presidio Press, 2003), p. 394 (regarding American army units during World War II using demolition charges to create a firebreak between Manila's north port area and residential districts).

54 Martin Blumenson, *The European Theater of Operations: Breakout and Pursuit* (Washington, DC: Center for Military History, United States Army, 1961), p. 646.

55 Ibid.

> [d]uring the bitter house-to-house street fighting that followed, the 2d Engineer Combat Battalion made its most valuable contribution. The engineers became adept at blowing holes in the walls of houses at points where the entering infantrymen would not have to expose themselves to enemy fire in the streets. On the eastern side, away from the enemy, the engineers blew holes through inner walls to enable the troops to pass safely from building to building and in ceilings to allow the infantry to pass from floor to floor when the Germans defended stairways. The engineers also developed several methods of quickly overcoming obstacles in the way of the advancing troops. The engineers . . . learned to fill craters and ditches quickly by blowing debris into them from the walls of adjacent buildings.[56]

Here, too, it would have been odd to characterise the actions of Allied engineers as 'attacks' against their adversary. Also, according to the *UK Joint Service Manual*, '[i]t may be permissible to destroy a house in order to clear a field of fire'[57] in non-international armed conflicts. Calling the destruction of such a house an 'attack' would appear counterintuitive, as the act of violence is not truly directed 'against the adversary'.

For the same reason, genuinely unintended destructions of civilian objects commonly known as 'collateral damage' would not constitute 'attacks' against such objects. Where an attack results in collateral damage, it means, by definition, that the act of violence is properly directed against some military objective, i.e., 'the adversary',[58] and *not* against the civilian objects that the act incidentally destroys or damages.[59]

56 Alfred M Beck et al., *The Technical Services: The Corps of Engineers: The War against Germany* (Washington, DC: Center for Military History, United States Army, 1985), pp. 384–85.

57 UK Defence Ministry, *Joint Service Manual*, p. 393.

58 Article 49(1), Additional Protocol I.

59 This raises a separate problem as to whether one can really speak of a deliberate 'attack' against civilians or civilian objects. After all, attacking a civilian person or object does not necessarily mean committing an act of violence against the adversary. Yet, Article 51(2) of Additional Protocol I clearly protects civilian persons from being made 'the object of attack'. Similarly, the protocol's Article 52(1) prohibits the belligerents from making civilian objects 'the object of attack'. Whether an attack *qua* IHL notion may encompass acts other than those stipulated in Article 49(1) of Additional Protocol I is a matter that goes beyond the scope of this book. Suffice it to note here that the ICRC has taken this issue into account when formulating the requisite threshold of harm as part of its interpretive guidance on the notion of direct participation in hostilities. ICRC, *Interpretive Guidance*, pp. 47 ('In order to reach the required threshold of harm, a specific act must be likely to adversely affect the military operations or military capacity of a party to an armed conflict or, alternatively, to inflict death, injury, or destruction on persons or objects protected against direct attack'), 49 ('In IHL, attacks are defined as "acts of

10.1.3.3 Military Necessity vs. Military Objective

The idea that destroying property and attacking property are two conceptually distinct acts also finds support in the dissimilar grounds on which their propriety depends. Property destruction is militarily necessary within the meaning of express military necessity clauses only if it is required for the attainment of a military purpose and otherwise in conformity with IHL.[60] Formulated thus, juridical military necessity pertains to the *measure* taken; that is, the very act of destruction. Compare this with the notion of a military objective that pertains to the *property* itself. The lawfulness of an attack against property depends primarily on whether the property constitutes a military objective. Under Article 52(2) of Additional Protocol I, property constitutes military objectives, only if (i) 'by their nature, location, purpose or use [they] make an effective contribution to military action'[61] and only if (ii) their 'total or partial destruction, capture or neutralization, in the circumstances ruling at the time, offers a definite military advantage'.[62] Where property constitutes a military objective, it is liable to attacks; where it does not, it constitutes a civilian object and is therefore immune from attacks.[63]

In other words, military necessity justifies the property's destruction, whereas the property's status as a military objective justifies attacks being directed against it. The acts of destroying property and attacking property are conceptually distinct from each other, because the notions of military necessity and military objectives are conceptually distinct from each other.[64] The *Strugar* Trial Chamber therefore arguably erred when it stated that 'military necessity may be usefully defined for present purposes with reference to the widely acknowledged definition of military objectives in Article 52 of Additional Protocol I'.[65] The same may be said of the *Strugar* Appeals Chamber:

violence against the adversary, whether in offence or in defence". The phrase "against the adversary" does not specify the target, but the belligerent nexus of an attack, so that even acts of violence directed specifically against civilians or civilian objects may amount to direct participation in hostilities' (footnotes omitted)).

60 See Chapter 9.

61 Article 52(2), Additional Protocol I.

62 Ibid.

63 Ibid, Article 52(1).

64 O'Keefe, 'Protection of Cultural Property' (*Handbook of International Humanitarian Law*), p. 440.

65 *Strugar Trial Judgment*, para. 295. See also *Kordić and Čerkez Appeal Judgment*, paras 465–66, 503; *Boškoski and Tarčulovski Trial Judgment*, para. 353; *Brđanin Appeal Judgment*, para. 337; *Prlić et al. Trial Judgment* (vol. I), para. 123; *Karadžić Trial*

> The Appeals Chamber also agrees that military necessity is not an element of the crime of destruction of, or damage to cultural property ... While the latter's requirement that the cultural property must not have been used for military purposes may be an element indicating that *an object does not make an effective contribution to military action in the sense of Article 52(2) of Additional Protocol I*, it does not cover the other aspect of military necessity, *namely the definite military advantage that must be offered by the destruction of a military objective.*[66]

The chamber is clearly of the view that military necessity is to be understood by reference to the two-prong definition of military objectives found in Article 52(2) of Additional Protocol I.[67]

This is an error, notwithstanding two familiar perceptions to the contrary.[68] First, it is true that most instances of property destruction in combat would also be instances of property attack, and vice versa. It is also true that today's IHL limits lawful attacks to those directed at military objectives. This merely amounts to upholding the somewhat obvious truth that, in principle, destroying a military objective by way of an attack is *ipso facto* militarily necessary.[69] It does not follow *a contrario* that destroying a civilian object by means other than an attack is perforce militarily unnecessary.[70]

Judgment, para. 533; William Fenrick, 'Specific Methods of Warfare' in Elizabeth Wilmshurst and Susan Breau (eds), *Perspectives on the ICRC Study on Customary International Humanitarian Law* (Cambridge: Cambridge University Press, 2007) 238, p. 244.

66 *Prosecutor v Pavle Strugar*, Case No. IT-01-42-A, *Judgment*, 17 July 2008, para. 330 (emphasis added).

67 Article 52(2), Additional Protocol I. See also Kriangsak Kittichaisaree, *International Criminal Law* (Oxford: Oxford University Press, 2001), p. 274 n.68: 'This was the subject of the decision of the Anglo-American Arbitral Tribunal in the *Hardman Claim* in 1913. It was held that the act constituted "military necessity". (McCoubrey, *International Humanitarian Law*, 201). It is submitted, however, that the defence accepted in that case would better be characterised as "necessity". It was not "military necessity" as the act did not target military objectives in order to secure military victory over the enemy.' Here, the confusion appears to be three-fold. First, as noted in Chapter 9, the matter at issue in *Hardman* was exceptional military necessity, not justificatory necessity. Second, it is not a requirement of military necessity that the measure in question 'target military objectives'. Third, military necessity does not require military victory over the enemy to be the purpose of the measure taken.

68 *Prlić et al. Appeal Judgment, Dissenting Opinion of Judge Fausto Pocar*, para. 8.

69 *Prlić et al. Appeal Judgment*, para. 411; O'Keefe, *Protection of Cultural Property*, p. 128. This is not the case, however, where the attack in question may also be expected to cause incidental loss of civilian life, injury to civilians, damage to civilian objects, or a combination thereof, which would be excessive in relation to the concrete and direct military advantage anticipated. See below.

70 See below.

Second, Hague Cultural Property Protocol II effectively restricts the loss of cultural property's protection not just against destruction, but also against military use and acts of hostility, to situations where it constitutes a military objective 'by its function'[71] or – in the case of enhanced protection – 'by its use'.[72] As O'Keefe observes:

> In addition, parties to a conflict to which the Second Protocol applies owe certain special obligations towards cultural property placed under Chapter 2's select regime of 'enhanced' protection. They are prohibited from attacking such property unless by its use, and use alone, it becomes a military objective and the attack is the only feasible means of terminating such use. *All acts of hostility against cultural property under enhanced protection other than attacks, such as its demolition even for military ends, are absolutely forbidden.*[73]

This, while undoubtedly significant for cultural property, is simply an extra layer of protection introduced under Hague Cultural Property Protocol II by which its states parties are bound. It does not change the fact that, as concepts, military necessity and military objectives are distinct from each other.

In *Kordić and Čerkez*, the appeals chamber held that no evidence allowed 'conclusions as to whether the shelling of Merdani was or was not justified by military necessity'.[74] In so holding, the chamber appears to have concluded that the relevant question for determining the military necessity or otherwise of the property destruction in Merdani was whether the *shelling of that locality* was or was not justified by military necessity. The chamber's approach here is problematic in two respects.

To begin with, the shelling of a locality is not amenable to being militarily necessary or unnecessary within the context of positive IHL. Rather, it is amenable to being lawful or unlawful, depending, inter alia, on whether the locality contains any military objective or objectives, and whether the shelling targets such an objective or objectives.[75]

71 Article 6(a)(i), Hague Cultural Property Protocol II.

72 Ibid, Article 13(1)(b).

73 O'Keefe, 'Protection of Cultural Property' (*Oxford Handbook of International Law in Armed Conflict*), p. 504 (emphasis added). See also O'Keefe, *Protection of Cultural Property*, pp. 255, 331–32.

74 *Kordić and Čerkez Appeal Judgment*, para. 429.

75 Should the attacker indiscriminately treat the locality itself as his or her target, however, it would be unlawful to launch an attack on it even if it did contain military objectives. Article 51(5)(a), Additional Protocol I; *Gotovina et al. Trial Judgment*, paras 1893, 1911,

Moreover, as noted earlier, whereas combat-related property destruction is *ipso facto* militarily unnecessary where the underlying offensive is unlawful, the offensive's lawfulness is not determinative of the destruction's military necessity. In other words, the shelling of military objectives in Merdani may have been lawful, but not all property destruction that took place during this offensive may have been militarily necessary. Nor, despite the position taken by the *Blaškić* and *Kordić and Čerkez* Trial Chambers to the contrary, does military necessity justify targeting civilian objects.[76]

10.1.3.4 Destruction of Property Constituting a Military Objective

Where property constitutes a military objective, the property's status as a military objective justifies attacks being directed against it. The property's status as a military objective also means that, if an attack against the property results in its destruction, then this destruction is militarily necessary. Since attacking a military objective is lawful and the objective's resulting destruction is militarily necessary, destroying a military objective, even without attacking it, would a fortiori be lawful and militarily necessary.[77] Thus, for instance, destroying enemy tanks, aircraft and other equipment that had already been captured would be consistent with military necessity.[78] Some ICTY trial chambers declined to find the destruction of houses to be lacking in military necessity on the ground that they may have constituted military objectives at the time of their destruction.[79]

1923, 1935, 1943; N Hayashi, 'Is the Yugoslav Tribunal Guilty of Hyper-Humanising International Humanitarian Law?'.

[76] *Kordić and Čerkez Trial Judgment*, para. 328; *Blaškić Trial Judgment*, para. 180. This error was acknowledged in *Galić* and other subsequent decisions. *Galić Trial Judgment*, para. 44; *Blaškić Appeal Judgment*, para. 109; *Prosecutor v Dario Kordić and Mario Čerkez*, Case No. IT-95-14/2-A, *Corrigendum to Judgment of 17 December 2004*, 24 January 2005, para. 54; *Strugar Trial Judgment*, para. 278; *Dragomir Milošević Trial Judgment*, para. 944; *Galić Appeal Judgment*, paras 130, 190; *Strugar Appeal Judgment*, para. 275; *Mladić Trial Judgment*, para. 3257; *Prosecutor v Vojislav Šešelj*, Case No. MICT-16-99-A, *Judgment*, 11 April 2018, para. 49. See also Shane Darcy, *Judges, Law and War: The Judicial Development of International Humanitarian Law* (Cambridge: Cambridge University Press, 2014), pp. 143–44.

[77] *Katanga and Chui Confirmation Decision*, para. 312.

[78] Ibid, para. 318.

[79] *Prlić et al. Trial Judgment* (vol. III), paras 1525, 1558, 1563.

If an attack against a military objective is itself in breach of IHL for some reason, however, its resulting destruction is no longer militarily necessary.[80] Such is the case, for instance, where the attack may be expected to cause excessive collateral damage.[81] The *Prlić et al.* Trial Chamber found that the Old Bridge of Mostar constituted a military objective at the relevant time.[82] Nevertheless, the bridge's destruction was unlawful because the 'damage to the civilian population' in the form of the humanitarian supplies cut as a result and very significant psychological impacts on Mostar's Muslim population was 'disproportionate to the concrete and direct military advantage expected by the destruction of the Old Bridge'.[83]

This ruling was reserved on appeal. In the words of the *Prlić et al.* Appeals Chamber's majority: 'Since the Trial Chamber found that the Old Bridge was a military target at the time of the attack, and, thus, its destruction offered a definite military advantage, the Appeals Chamber, Judge Pocar dissenting, finds that it cannot be considered, in and of itself, as wanton destruction not justified by military necessity.'[84] In his dissenting opinion, Judge Pocar noted that 'a disproportionate attack is *per se* unlawful and therefore cannot be justified by military necessity'.[85] His observation is correct, insofar as the attack's unlawfulness precludes the destruction's military necessity.

[80] See Chapter 9.

[81] See below. See also *Prosecutor v Vojislav Šešelj*, Case No. IT-03-67-T, *Judgment*, 31 March 2016, para. 204(a) n. 172 ('in order to find that destruction was committed as a war crime, not justified by military necessity, the majority first had to be in a position to assess the proportionality of such destruction'). The trial chamber found that the evidence was inconclusive, however. See also ibid, para. 204(a) n. 175 ('the JNA . . . attacked the city of Moster and . . . shelled the city indiscriminately with mortars for 30 hours. The majority can therefore reasonably infer that a significant amount of property was destroyed'). Here, too, the trial chamber concluded that it 'does not have sufficient evidence to find beyond all reasonable doubt that this destruction was not justified by military necessity' (ibid).

[82] *Prlić et al. Trial Judgment* (vol. III), para. 1582.

[83] Ibid, paras 1583–84, 1587. But see *Prosecutor v Jadranko Prlić et al.*, Case No. IT-04-74-T, *Judgment*, 6 vols., 29 May 2013, vol. VI, *Separate and Partially Dissenting Opinion of Presiding Judge Jean-Claude Antonetti*, pp. 318–25, esp. 325 ('to my mind, the Old Bridge was a legitimate military objective whose destruction gave the HVO a definite military advantage by cutting off communications and the supply of food. I fail to see how the principle of proportionality could be applicable in this case. If the Old Bridge was a military objective, it quite simply had to be destroyed. In any event, there is no such thing as proportionate destruction').

[84] *Prlić et al. Appeal Judgment*, para. 411 (footnotes omitted).

[85] *Prlić et al. Appeal Judgment, Dissenting Opinion of Judge Fausto Pocar*, para. 9.

Destroying a military objective, even without attacking it, would likewise be militarily unnecessary if its purposes was contrary to IHL. One example involves the destruction of property in order to adversely distinguish its owners on account of his or her religion.[86]

10.1.3.5 Destruction of Property Constituting a Civilian Object

A civilian object is per se immune from attacks. An attack against such an object is unlawful, be it deliberate or indiscriminate. If an attack is deliberately launched against a civilian object, and if the attack destroys that object and/or another civilian object or objects, then juridical military necessity does not exempt their destruction.[87] This is so, because the destruction in question does not satisfy the requirement that the measure be in conformity with IHL.[88] Similarly, if an attack is launched indiscriminately, and if the attack destroys a civilian object, then this destruction remains without military necessity.[89]

The *Strugar* Trial Chamber found that there was no military objective in the Old Town of Dubrovnik when it came under attack by the Yugoslav People's Army (JNA).[90] The JNA's shelling of the Old Town resulted in its partial destruction. The chamber rightly concluded that the shelling was deliberate or indiscriminate[91] and that the destruction of the Old Town was therefore not justified by military necessity.[92] As noted earlier, however, it did so by equating the notion of military necessity with the notion of military objectives.[93] The correct reasoning would have been as follows:

[86] See below.

[87] *Kordić and Čerkez Appeal Judgment*, paras 419, 426, 477, 485, 526.

[88] See Chapter 9.

[89] *Brđanin Trial Judgment*, para. 626 (footnotes omitted): 'In some villages, attacks were preceded by an ultimatum: for example in the Hambarine area in late May 1992, an ultimatum was given for the surrender of a particular individual [Aziz Ališković, a checkpoint commander]. Following the expiration of the ultimatum, the Bosnian Muslim village of Hambarine was shelled by Bosnian Serb forces for the entire day. Houses were targeted indiscriminately. Tanks passed through the village and shelled the houses causing civilian casualties. Houses were looted and set on fire.' See also *Dragomir Milošević Appeal Judgement*, 12 November 2009, para. 53; *Šešelj Appeal Judgment*, para. 49.

[90] *Strugar Trial Judgment*, paras 193–94, 214, 284.

[91] Ibid, paras 214, 285–88, 329.

[92] Ibid, paras 328, 330.

[93] Ibid, para. 295.

1. Attacks launched deliberately or indiscriminately against civilian objects are unlawful;
2. Military necessity does not exempt property destruction involving unlawful measures;
3. The destruction of property in the Old Town took the form of unlawful shelling of civilian objects; and, therefore,
4. The property destruction in the Old Town was not justified by military necessity.

It may happen that civilian objects are destroyed as part of collateral damage. Suppose that Property A is a civilian object destroyed as a result of an attack specifically directed against Combatant B, an able-bodied, non-surrendering enemy combatant and therefore a military objective. Property A's destruction forms part of incidental civilian casualties and damage. Suppose further that such casualties and damage are expected to be proportionate to the concrete and direct military advantage anticipated by Combatant B's disablement. Property A's destruction will then be militarily necessary, because the measure taken is required for the attainment of a military purpose and otherwise in conformity with IHL.[94] In this scenario, the attack against Combatant B constitutes the measure taken, while his disablement constitutes the military purpose. The measure's conformity with IHL emanates from two facts. First, Combatant B is a military objective. Second, *ex hypothesi*, the attack against him is not expected to cause incidental loss of civilian life, injury to civilians, damage to civilian objects or a combination thereof, which are excessive in relation to the concrete and direct military advantage anticipated.[95]

If, however, Property A's destruction is incidental yet expected to be *dis*proportionate to the concrete and direct military advantage anticipated, it becomes unlawful and, accordingly, without military necessity. The measure taken runs counter to IHL, since disproportionate attacks are prohibited under Article 51(5)(b) of Additional Protocol I.[96] Nor,

[94] *Prosecutor v Enver Hadžihasanović and Amir Kubura*, Case No. IT-01-47-T, *Judgment*, 15 March 2006, para. 45: 'The protection offered by Article 3(b) of the Statute is, however, limited by the exception of military necessity. The Chamber finds that collateral damage to civilian property may be justified by military necessity and may be an exception to the principles of protection of civilian property.' See also *Katanga and Chui Confirmation Decision*, para. 313.

[95] Article 51(5)(b), Additional Protocol I.

[96] *Blaškić Trial Judgment*, para. 510: 'Consequently, it was impossible to ascertain any strategic or military reasons for the 16 April 1993 attack on Vitez and Stari Vitez. In the event that there had been, the devastation visited upon the town was out of all

within the meaning of juridical military necessity, is the attack against Combatant B 'required' for the concrete and direct military advantage anticipated insofar as the measure's injurious effect is disproportionate in relation to its stated purpose.[97]

The *Martić* Trial Chamber observed:

> The Trial Chamber recalls the evidence that there was intensive shelling in Škabrnja on the morning of the attack. Moreover, there is evidence that fire was opened on private houses by JNA tanks and using hand-held rocket launchers. The Trial Chamber recalls the evidence that members of Croatian forces were in some of the houses in Škabrnja. In the Trial Chamber's opinion, this gives rise to reasonable doubt as to whether the destruction resulting from these actions was carried out for the purposes of military necessity. The elements of wanton destruction of villages or devastation not justified by military necessity (Count 12) have therefore not been met.[98]

It might be said that some of the houses in Škabrnja were incidentally destroyed when JNA tanks engaged members of Croatian forces inside them. As far as these houses are concerned, the relevant consideration would be whether their destruction was excessive in relation to the objective of disabling the Croatian fighters. If the destruction was proportionate, it was militarily necessary; if not, it was militarily unnecessary.

Accordingly, where the destruction of a civilian object takes the form of an unlawful attack, the attack's unlawfulness conclusively indicates the absence of military necessity for the object's destruction. Arguably, this is what the *Hadžihasanović and Kubura* Appeals Chamber meant when it held that 'the conventional prohibition on attacks on civilian objects ... has attained the status of customary international law and that this covers "wanton destruction of cities, towns or villages not justified by military necessity"'.[99] The attack is unlawful if:

proportion with military necessity.' See also *Kordić and Čerkez Trial Judgment*, para. 734 (footnotes omitted): 'On 8 September 1993 the HVO launched a successful attack on the village of Grbavica, a hillside feature to the west of Vitez and close to the Britbat camp at Bila. This feature had been used by the ABiH as a position for the purposes of sniping and, according to the evidence of Britbat officers who saw the attack, it was a legitimate military target. However, according to the same witnesses, the attack was accompanied by unnecessary destruction. For instance, Brigadier Duncan said that the objective was secured by an excessive use of force against the local population, causing massive destruction of property beyond any military necessity'.

97 *Prlić et al. Appeal Judgment, Dissenting Opinion of Judge Fausto Pocar*, para. 9.

98 *Martić Trial Judgment*, para. 394.

99 *Hadžihasanović and Kubura Interlocutory Appeal Decision*, para. 30.

1. It is deliberately directed against the civilian object concerned, or against another civilian object or objects;
2. It is indiscriminate;[100] or
3. It is directed against a military objective but may be expected to cause disproportionate collateral damage.

If a civilian object is destroyed as a result of such an attack, then it means that the object's destruction lacks military necessity.

As noted earlier, however, there are situations during active combat in which a belligerent destroys a civilian object without attacking that object or any other object. Where this occurs, the object's destruction is militarily necessary if it satisfies all the requirements of juridical military necessity.[101] If the destruction fails to satisfy one or more of the requirements, then it is without military necessity.

The *Orić* Trial Chamber held that property was destroyed without military necessity in Brađevina.[102] The chamber held that, 'at the time of the attack, the property destroyed in Brađevina was neither of a military nature, nor was it used in a manner such as to make an effective contribution to the military actions of the Bosnian Serbs'[103] and that, '[c]onsequently, the destruction of property in Brađevina was not required for the attainment of a military objective'.[104]

With the first ruling, the trial chamber determined in effect that the haystacks, sheds, houses, stables and livestock destroyed in Brađevina constituted civilian objects. If, as civilian objects, they were destroyed by deliberate, indiscriminate or disproportionate attacks, then this would *ipso facto* mean that their destruction was militarily unnecessary. The chamber described the circumstances of property destruction in Brađevina thus:

> The attack on Brađevina was launched from the direction of Kaludra. The attackers entered Brađevina from its lower part, and surrounded it. They met with no resistance. The attack came in two waves, the first by fighters

[100] *Prlić et al. Trial Judgment* (vol. III), paras 1568–70.
[101] See Chapter 9. That is, unless the object in question constitutes cultural property and enjoys enhanced protection under Hague Cultural Property Protocol II.
[102] *Orić Trial Judgment*, para. 618.
[103] Ibid. See also ibid, paras 607, 618, 632, 675 (holding, inter alia, that the property destroyed in Ježestica and Ratkovići was 'neither of a military nature, nor . . . used in a manner such as to make an effective contribution to the military actions of the Bosnian Serbs').
[104] Ibid, para. 618.

> approaching the houses of Brađevina firing upon the prone position, and the second by fighters following behind. Witnesses heard detonations and saw burning of haystacks and sheds. In the course of the attack, Bosnian Muslim fighters torched houses after taking out goods. Bosnian Muslim civilians joined fighters in torching stables and burning livestock in the meadows between Brađevina and Magudovići. Eventually, all the buildings of Brađevina, except those used for storing grain and food, were set on fire. Bosnian Muslim civilians remained in the area after the attack, searching for food and other goods.[105]

In view of these circumstances, it would not have been unreasonable for the trial chamber to conclude that the objects destroyed not only constituted civilian objects but were, in fact, attacked *as such* – i.e., deliberately.

The trial chamber did not do so. In fact, nowhere in the judgment is there any specific finding that, as civilian objects, the property destroyed in Brađevina was destroyed by attacks, let alone by unlawful ones. Rather, it appears that, having determined the objects' civilian status, the trial chamber simply concluded – 'consequently' is the expression used – that their destruction is incapable of satisfying any military purpose. The way in which the chamber discussed the events in Brađevina leaves open the possibility that some civilian property was destroyed by acts not constituting attacks. Where such a possibility exists, whether the destruction of the property in question was or was not required for the attainment of a military purpose is a matter that must be considered on a case-by-case basis.

Similarly, the *Boškoski and Tarćulovski* Trial Chamber considered most of the houses set alight in the village of Ljuboten civilian objects, and yet it declined to treat them as having been destroyed in deliberate attacks.[106] Rather, the chamber found itself asking whether these houses were used for any military purposes. Then, as regards those houses without such purpose, the chamber proceeded to find that their destruction was all without military necessity.

The *Mladić* Trial Chamber was even more blunt. It found that all acts of destruction charged 'concerned private properties, sacred sites, and cultural monuments, none of which qualified as military objects whose destruction would make an effective contribution to military action or whose destruction would offer a definite military advantage. *The Trial*

[105] Ibid, para. 613 (footnotes omitted).
[106] *Boškoski and Tarčulovski Trial Judgment*, paras 359–80.

Chamber is therefore satisfied that the destruction identified in all incidents was not justified by military necessity.'[107]

Neither *Orić*, *Boškoski and Tarćulovski* nor *Mladić* contained charges of unlawful attacks on civilian objects. This remains so, although the *Orić Third Amended Indictment* uses the expression 'attack' to describe the events in Brađevina.[108] Also, the *Boškoski and Tarćulovski Amended Indictment* specifically characterises the properties in Ljuboten as 'wantonly damaged ... in this attack'.[109] We may never know the reasons behind these prosecutorial decisions. At any rate, it is possible that charges selected may have effectively tied the chambers' hands, forcing them to approach the matter in a somewhat roundabout way.

In *Kordić and Čerkez*, the appeals chamber upheld the trial chamber's ruling that the property destruction in Novi Travnik was not justified by military necessity:

> [A]part from the buildings destroyed or damaged due to the fighting along the separation line between the two forces, a number of buildings with no military interest belonging to civilian Muslims were destroyed in the part of the old town called Bare (the lower part, Ratanjska, at the entry of Novi Travnik). The nearest military objective was approximately 200–300 metres from there and other destroyed Muslim buildings were 700–800 metres from the front line ... The Appeals Chamber is of the view that, although part of the HVO attack on Novi Travnik might have pursued a legitimate military purpose, a reasonable trier of fact could have, on the basis of the evidence in question, come to the conclusion beyond reasonable doubt that wilful and large scale destruction of Muslim properties not justified by military necessity also occurred in its course.[110]

It was found that there was a considerable distance between the properties destroyed, on the one hand, and the nearest military objective ('approximately 200–300 metres') and the front line ('700–800 metres'), on the other.[111] This distance would effectively eliminate the possibility that the destruction of Muslim buildings was incidental to attacks directed against military objectives nearby. The distance would also make it unlikely that stray shells and the like launched across the front line

107 *Mladić Trial Judgment*, para. 3409 (emphasis added).

108 *Orić Third Amended Indictment*, paras 30, 35.

109 *Boškoski and Tarčulovski Amended Indictment*, para. 24.

110 The acronym 'HVO' refers to *Hrvasko Vijeće Obrane*, or 'Croatian Defence Council'. The HVO was the army of the Bosnian Croats. *Kordić and Čerkez Appeal Judgment*, para. 391.

111 Ibid.

accidentally destroyed the properties. It would follow that they were destroyed either by deliberate or indiscriminate attacks, or by acts not constituting attacks.

The appeals chamber also found that the Muslim buildings had 'no military interest'.[112] This might mean that the properties destroyed constituted civilian objects. If they constituted civilian objects, and if their destruction was the result of deliberate or indiscriminate attacks, then the attacks would be unlawful and the destruction would be without military necessity. If, however, the proprieties were destroyed by acts other than attacks, then the mere fact that they constituted civilian objects would not conclusively demonstrate the absence of military necessity for their destruction.

Alternatively, 'no military interest' might mean not only the properties' status as civilian objects but also the lack of military purpose served by their destruction. Provided this is the meaning that the appeals chamber had in mind, the destruction in question would fail to satisfy the requirement of juridical military necessity that the measure be taken for some specific military purpose[113] and would, accordingly, remain militarily unnecessary.

10.1.3.6 Property Destruction in the Context of Combat: A Summary

When assessing the juridical military necessity of combat-related property destruction, the trier of fact would consider the following questions.

- Was there any military justification for the combat activities of which the property destruction formed part? Absent any military justification, the trier of fact would find that the property destruction was militarily unnecessary. If at least some military justification existed,[114] then the trier would turn his or her attention to the property itself.
- Where there was some military justification for the underlying combat activities, did the individual property destroyed constitute a military

[112] Ibid.

[113] See Chapter 9.

[114] Launching an offensive on a locality would be militarily justified if, for example, the locality contained military objectives. A strategically important locality may contain exclusively civilian objects, but that does not mean that no offensive may be lawfully launched on it. Such an offensive would be lawful if it is met with no resistance and no attack is directed against any object. If an object is destroyed during such an offensive, its military necessity would depend on whether the destruction satisfied all the requirements of military necessity.

objective? If it did, its destruction, whether caused by an attack or not, was militarily necessary.[115] If it constituted a civilian object, then the trier of fact would examine the particular circumstances of its destruction.

- Was the property at issue, a civilian object, made the object of a deliberate attack, destroyed as a result of a deliberate attack against another civilian object, or destroyed by an indiscriminate attack? An affirmative answer would yield the finding that the destruction was without military necessity; a negative answer would bring the trier of fact to the next question.
- Was the civilian object destroyed as a result of an attack directed against a military objective? If so, were the incidental civilian casualties and damage expected – of which the object's destruction formed part – in proportion to the concrete and direct military advantage anticipated? The lack of proportion between the injury and advantage would mean that the destruction at issue was militarily unnecessary, whereas the existence of proportion would indicate the destruction's military necessity.
- Lastly, where the civilian object was destroyed by an act not constituting an attack, did the destruction satisfy the requirements of military necessity?

Table 1 represents the relevant considerations for the juridical military necessity of property destruction where the underlying combat activities are held to have some military justification.

In order for the prosecution to show beyond a reasonable doubt that the destruction of particular property in combat was without military necessity, it must prove:

(I) That the underlying combat activities (such as an offensive on a locality), of which the property's destruction formed part, lacked any military justification; or

(II) That, although some military justification (such as the strategic importance of the locality or the presence of military objectives

[115] That is, unless the measure itself (e.g., by dint of the excessive collateral damage that the attack against the property *qua* military objective may be expected to cause) or its purpose (e.g., by dint of racial discrimination for which the property is chosen for destruction) was otherwise in breach of IHL. See also Articles 6(a)(i), 13(1)(b), Hague Cultural Property Protocol II.

Table 1 *Military Necessity Status of Property Destruction in Combat*

		The property destroyed was . . .	
		. . . a military objective	. . . a civilian object
The property was destroyed . . .	. . . as a result of a deliberate attack against it.	Lawful per se and therefore militarily necessary.*	Unlawful per se and therefore militarily unnecessary.
	. . . as a result of a deliberate attack against a(nother) civilian object.	Unlawful per se and therefore militarily unnecessary.	Unlawful per se and therefore militarily unnecessary.
	. . . as a result of an indiscriminate attack.	Unlawful per se and therefore militarily unnecessary.	Unlawful per se and therefore militarily unnecessary.
	. . . as a result of an attack against a (nother) military objective.	Lawful per se and therefore militarily necessary.*	If not part of proportionate civilian casualties and/or damage, then unlawful and therefore militarily unnecessary. If part of proportionate civilian casualties and/or damage, then lawful and therefore militarily necessary.
	. . . not as a result of an attack.	Lawful per se and therefore militarily necessary.*	Depends on whether the act of destruction was: (a) required for the attainment of (b) a military purpose, and (c) otherwise in conformity with IHL.

* That is, unless the destruction or its purpose was otherwise in breach of IHL.

therein) existed for the underlying combat activities, and although the property destroyed was a military objective:

(1) Its destruction was otherwise in breach of IHL; or

(2) The purpose of its destruction was in breach of IHL; or

(III) That, although some military justification existed for the underlying combat activities:

(1) The property destroyed was a civilian object; and

(2) The property was destroyed by:

(i) An attack:

- directed deliberately against it or against another civilian object;
- directed indiscriminately; or
- directed against a military objective yet disproportionate in its harmful effect on civilian persons and/or objects; or

(ii) An act, not constituting an attack, such that the property's destruction failed to satisfy at least one requirement of juridical military necessity.

The extent to which the prosecution can discharge its onus successfully depends on the quantity and quality of the evidence adduced. The prosecution's ability in this regard may be limited by the realities of active combat that make it difficult, if not impossible, to obtain the relevant evidence.

The April 1993 destruction of Muslim houses in Vitez and Stari Vitez is a case in point. The *Kordić and Čerkez* Trial Chamber found that the destruction was without military necessity.[116] This finding was, however, overturned on appeal:

> The Appeals Chamber takes into account the testimony of Col. Watters according to which most of the destruction during the April attacks was in the Muslim area of the town of Vitez, but has already held that the scale of such destruction is unknown. Exh. Z2715 does not specify when eighty houses were destroyed in the town of Vitez; part of these houses were obviously destroyed as a result of the 18 April truck bomb, which the Trial Chamber did not link with either of the Accused. Moreover, there were military objectives in Vitez/Stari Vitez, including the headquarters of the Muslim TO and the private houses from where combatants, (including members of the ABiH, the TO and every person taking a direct part in hostilities), were resisting. In the absence of evidence as to the scale of the destruction and as to the lack of military justification, the Appeals

[116] *Kordić and Čerkez Trial Judgment*, para. 808.

> Chamber finds that no reasonable Trial Chamber could have concluded that destruction not justified by military necessity occurred in Vitez/Stari Vitez in April 1993.[117]

It appears that the insufficiency of evidence with respect to Vitez and Stari Vitez left, inter alia, the following three reasonable doubts unresolved. First, the presence of military objectives in Vitez and Stari Vitez could have militarily justified the underlying combat activities taking place in these localities. Second, at the time of their destruction, some Muslim houses might have constituted military objectives themselves and neither their destruction itself nor the purpose of their destruction might have been in breach of IHL. Third, even if the houses destroyed in Vitez and Stari Vitez were all civilian objects, it was not shown that they were destroyed by deliberate, indiscriminate, or disproportionate attacks, or by acts such that their destruction failed to satisfy one or more requirements of military necessity.[118]

10.1.4 Property Destruction outside the Context of Combat

In *Tuta and Štela*, the prosecution restricted the scope of its property destruction charges to events that occurred after the attacks.[119] The post-World War II United Nations War Crimes Commission took a similar approach.[120]

The absence of combat activities is relevant when determining the juridical military necessity of property destruction. The absence of

117 The acronym 'TO' refers to *teritoriajalna odbrana*, or 'territorial defence', a militia organisation originating from the defence structure of the former Social Federal Republic of Yugoslavia. The acronym 'ABiH' refers to *Armija Bosne i Hercegovine*, or 'Army of Bosnia and Herzegovina'. *Kordić and Čerkez Appeal Judgment*, paras 465–66.

118 Ibid. See also *Hadžihasanović and Kubura Trial Judgment*, paras 1794, 1797, 1799, 1806–07, 1830, 1832 (regarding Guča Gora, Maline, Šušanj, Ovnak, Brajkovići and Grahovčići).

119 *Tuta and Štela Second Amended Indictment*, paras 55–56, 58 ('[f]ollowing the capture' of villages).

120 UN Crimes Commission, *History of the United Nations War Crimes Commission*, p. 488: 'Committee I [of the Commission] often had to decide whether a given set of facts arising from the destruction of personal property, public property, or local monuments was a war crime, or whether such destruction was justified on the basis of military necessity in time of war. For example, the Committee refused to list for war crimes those Germans responsible for the demolition of a French lighthouse at Pas-de-Calais in September, 1944 (Commission No. 3603). Generally, the test applied was whether military operations were in progress, or were imminent'.

combat, however, does not per se indicate the absence of military necessity. As noted earlier, in *Hardman*, an occupation force's destruction of a house and its contents for the maintenance of sanitary conditions among its members was held to constitute military necessity. The destruction in question did not occur in the context of active combat.[121] Indeed, where an ICTY chamber found property destruction militarily unnecessary on the basis of little or no fighting, it typically did also so on the ground that the destruction was ethnically driven.[122] In many cases, property destruction occurred in localities inhabited predominantly by members of a targeted ethnicity.[123] In other localities, only the property belonging to members of a targeted ethnicity or ethnicities was destroyed.[124]

121 *Hardman*, p. 26.

122 *Kordić and Čerkez Appeal Judgment*, paras 484–85, 583–86 (holding that damage done in Šantići and Ahmići was restricted to Muslim houses; that a reasonable trier of fact could have found that it was 'of such a nature that it could not have been caused by the fighting' and 'thus not justified by military necessity'; and that a reasonable trier of fact could have found that property destruction in Han Ploča Grahovci in Kiseljak was not justified by military necessity '[s]ince only Muslim houses were destroyed, and the destruction occurred when there was not much fighting'); *Blaškić Trial Judgment*, paras 543–44, 549–50, 556–57, 559 (regarding Donja Večeriska, Gačice, and Grbavica); *Tuta and Štela Trial Judgment*, paras 583, 585 (regarding Sovići and Doljani). The *Blagojević and Jokić* Trial Chamber found that the destruction of personal property taken from Bosnian Muslim detainees was not justified by military necessity. *Blagojević and Jokić Trial Judgment*, para. 615.

123 *Blaškić Trial Judgment*, paras 565, 569, 579, 595–96 (regarding Lončari and Očehnići in Busovača, and Behrići and Gomionica in Kiseljak); *Brđanin Trial Judgment*, paras 600, 608–34 (regarding Bosanska Krupa; Bosanski Novi; Blagaj Rijeka in Bosanski Novi; Donji Agići in Bosanski Novi; Bosanski Petrovac; Čelinac; Bašići in Čelinac; Ključ; Kotor Varoš; Stari Grad in Prijedo; Biščani, Kozaruša, Kamičani, Kevljani, Rakovčani, Čarakovo and Rizvanovići in Prijedor; Hambarine in Prijedor; Kozarac in Prijedor; Briševo in Prijedor; Mahala in Sanski Most; Begići in Sanski Most; and Šipovo); *Kordić and Čerkez Trial Judgment*, paras 740, 807 (regarding Stupni Do); *Mićo Stanišić and Župljanin Trial Judgment* (vol. I), para. 264 (regarding Doganovci).

124 *Blaškić Trial Judgment*, paras 418, 510, 544, 598, 600, 605, 608, 613–14, 616, 619, 620, 622 (regarding Ahmići, Šantići, Pirići, Nadioci, Vitez, Stari Vitez, Donja Večeriska, Gromiljak in Kiseljak, Polje Višnijica, Višnijica in Kiseljak, Svinjarevo in Kiseljak, Grahovci, Han Ploča, and Tulica); *Blaškić Appeal Judgment*, para. 444 (regarding Vitez and Stari Vitez); *Kordić and Čerkez Trial Judgment*, paras 635, 643, 807(i), 645, 659–60, 677, 805, 807(iv) (regarding Ahmići, Vitez, Donja Večeriska, Očehnići in Busovača, and Gačice); *Kordić and Čerkez Appeal Judgment*, paras 484–85, 534, 558, 562, 563–64, 583–86 (regarding Šantići in Ahmići, Očehnići, Gomionica, Višnjica, Polje Višnjica, and Han Ploča-Grahovci in Kiseljak); *Tuta and Štela Trial Judgment*, paras 582–85 (regarding Sovići and Doljani); *Brđanin Trial Judgment*, para. 1022 ('Unlike non-Serb property, Bosnian Serb property was systematically left intact and only sporadically

It is submitted here that ethnically driven property destruction is *ipso facto* devoid of military necessity both within and outside the context of combat.[125] Any decision to destroy property based on its owner's ethnicity would fail to satisfy the requirement of juridical military necessity that the measure's purpose be in conformity with IHL.[126] There are two reasons for this failure. First, ethnicity-based selectiveness in the treatment of property would amount to adverse distinction. IHL prohibits adverse distinction in its application based on race, colour, sex, language, religion or belief, political or other opinion, national or social origin, wealth, birth or other status, or on any other similar criteria.[127] Whatever disagreement there might be about the definition of ethnicity, it would undoubtedly fall within one or more of these criteria. Second, where property is selectively destroyed with a view to adversely distinguishing its owners on the basis of their ethnicity,[128] and where other relevant facts are present,[129] the conduct may also constitute persecutions, a crime against humanity.

The *Hadžihasanović and Kubura*, *Orić* and *Prlić et al. Trial Judgments* are exceptional in the treatment of property destruction outside the context of combat. Regarding Vareš, the *Hadžihasanović and Kubura* Trial Chamber noted that the indictment had alleged militarily unnecessary destruction of dwellings, buildings and civilian personal property belonging to Bosnian Croats and Bosnian Serbs.[130] The chamber found

damaged'); *Martić Trial Judgment*, paras 258, 381, 383 (regarding Saborsko); *Prlić et al. Trial Judgment* (vol. III), paras 1523–24, 1535–43, 1546–49, 1551–52, 1554–57, 1559–62, 1564–66, 1571–74, 1575–78, 1588–91, 1593–94, 1596–99 (regarding Prozor; Duša, Hrasnica, Ždrimci, and Uzričje; Sovići and Doljani; Borojevići and Stolac; Bivolje Brdo; Stupni Do; Parcani; Skrobućani, Lug and Podaniš); *Mićo Stanišić and Župljanin Trial Judgment* (vol. I), paras 264, 282, 347, 491, 700, 812, 880, 982, 1041, 1119, 1190, 1248, 1286, 1356, 1498, 1688 (regarding Donji Vakuf, Prusac, Šeherdžik, Sokolina, Ključ, Kotor Varoš, Prijedor, Sanski Most, Taslić, Bileća, Bosanski Šamac, Brčko, Doboj, Gacko, Ilijaš, Pale, Vlasenica, Zvornik).

125 *Brđanin Appeal Judgment*, paras 339–41; *Prlić et al. Trial Judgment* (vol. III), para. 1579–80.

126 See Chapter 9.

127 Henckaerts and Doswald-Beck, *Customary International Humanitarian Law* (vol. I), p. 308.

128 The prohibition against adverse distinction under IHL is equivalent to the principle of non-discrimination under international human rights law. Ibid, p. 309. See also *Mladić Trial Judgment*, para. 3259.

129 Such as, for example, where the property was destroyed within the context of a widespread or systematic attack against a civilian population.

130 *Hadžihasanović and Kubura Trial Judgment*, para. 1833.

that such destruction did indeed occur following the cessation of armed hostilities in Vareš.[131] In so doing, however, the chamber made no determination as to the ethnicity of the owners of the property destroyed. Rather, according to the judgment, the Bosnian Muslim perpetrators destroyed the doors and windows of the houses in Vareš for the 'sole purpose' of committing plunder.[132] To the extent that this was in fact what the perpetrators intended, it was indeed militarily unnecessary because the purpose pursued was neither primarily military in nature nor in conformity with IHL.

The *Orić* Trial Chamber noted that the villages in which post-combat property destruction occurred were inhabited exclusively or almost exclusively by Bosnian Serbs.[133] This ethnic component of the destruction, however, does not appear to have had any impact on the chamber's ruling that the destruction was militarily unnecessary. The judgment indicates that the chamber viewed the absence of combat to mean the absence of military necessity:

> after the fighting has ceased, destruction can in principle no longer be justified by claiming 'military necessity'. A different situation arises if a military attack is launched against a settlement from which previously, due to its location and its armed inhabitants, a serious danger emanated for the inhabitants of a neighbouring village who are now seeking to remove this danger through military action. It may be that, after such a settlement has been taken, destruction of houses occurs in order to prevent the inhabitants, including combatants, [from returning and resuming attacks] … [E]xcept for the rare occasions in which such preventive destruction could arguably fall within the scope of 'military necessity', the principle must be upheld that the destruction of civil settlements, as a rule, is punishable as a war crime.[134]

The chamber's decision, it is submitted here, is at variance with the law. No authority or rationale exists for the view that, in the event of post-combat property destruction, military necessity is admissible only for one military purpose – i.e., to prevent members of the adversary party from re-occupying their combat positions. The two cases cited in the judgment fail to provide valid support, for the following reasons.

[131] Ibid, para. 1846.
[132] Ibid, paras 1844–46.
[133] *Orić Trial Judgment*, paras 593–94, 621, 660 (regarding Gornji Ratkovići and Ježestica).
[134] Ibid, para. 588 (footnotes omitted). See also ibid, paras 607, 632–33, 674–75 (regarding Gornji Ratkovići and Ježestica). See also *Tuta and Štela Trial Judgment*, para. 589; *Martić Trial Judgment*, para. 93; *Mladić Trial Judgment*, para. 3257.

The judgment refers to *Peleus* in support of the proposition that 'after the fighting has ceased, destruction can in principle no longer be justified by claiming "military necessity"'.[135] At issue in *Peleus*, however, was *not* whether military necessity pleas should be admissible once the fighting had ceased. As noted earlier,[136] the judge advocate in that case had conceded that circumstances *could* arise in which a belligerent in Eck's position might be justified in killing an unarmed person for the purpose of saving his own life. At no point did the judge advocate limit the scope of his concession to situations where active combat was in progress. Rather, he questioned whether the measure taken by Eck had any material relevance to his stated purpose and, even if it did, whether it was the least injurious of those means that were materially relevant to the purpose and reasonably available to him.

The *Orić Trial Judgment* also relies on the ruling by the IMT against Alfred Jodl for the view that 'the principle must be upheld that the destruction of civil settlements, as a rule, is punishable as a war crime'.[137] In so doing, the judgment notes that '[a] policy of "scorched earth", *i.e.*, the destruction of any facilities that might be useful to the enemy while withdrawing from an area, was not recognised at the Nuremberg Tribunal to be justified by military necessity'.[138]

This reliance is unhelpful, because the IMT offered virtually no reason when it made the relevant ruling. One cannot establish, for instance, whether the tribunal considered (i) that scorching earth *as such* could never be militarily necessary, or (ii) that the evidence rendered Jodl's specific order concerning northern Norway militarily unnecessary. The first interpretation, while possible, is unlikely. It appears to have been uncontroversial during World War II that scorching occupied territory was considered lawful if required by military necessity.[139] The second interpretation is more likely, although it

[135] *Orić Trial Judgment*, para. 588 (footnote omitted).

[136] See Chapter 9.

[137] *Orić Trial Judgment*, para. 588.

[138] Ibid, p. 207 n.1581. The relevant passage of the International Military Tribunal ruling reads as follows (*Göring et al.*, p. 324): 'By teletype of 28 October 1944, Jodl ordered the evacuation of all persons in northern Norway and the burning of their houses so they could not help the Russians. Jodl says he was against this, but Hitler ordered it and it was not fully carried out. A document of the Norwegian Government says such an evacuation did take place in northern Norway and 30,000 houses were damaged'.

[139] See Chapter 9. By virtue of Article 54 of Additional Protocol I, scorching earth no longer admits military necessity exceptions where it involves a party to the conflict destroying

suffers from the complete absence of any analysis in the IMT's ruling. Compare this with the US Military Tribunal in *Hostage*. As noted earlier, this latter tribunal actually did offer legal and factual reasons for acquitting Rendulic of devastating the Finnmark area, a measure carried out on Jodl's orders.[140]

The *Prlić et al.* Trial Chamber found that the destruction of houses in Parcani by members of HVO special units in retaliation for the villagers hiding in the woods and refusing to surrender their weapons was not justified by military necessity.[141]

10.1.5 Absence of Military Necessity as an Element of Forcible Displacement

Article 49 of Geneva Convention IV prohibits deportation and transfer of protected persons from occupied territory, except in situations of temporary evacuation where 'the security of the population or imperative military reasons so demand'.[142] According to the ICRC, imperative military reasons exist 'when the presence of protected persons in an area hampers military operations'.[143] Permanent transfer of protected persons for any reason, as well as their temporary evacuation not demanded by their security or for imperative military reasons, constitutes a grave breach of the convention.[144] This grave breach is incorporated into Article 2(g) of the ICTY Statute.[145] The ICTY has considered Article 2(g) charges against several defendants.[146]

'objects indispensable to the survival of the civilian population' not located in its own territory.

140 This is not to say that the *Hostage* ruling on this matter is without criticism. See, e.g., Best, *War and Law since 1945*, pp. 328–30.

141 *Prlić et al. Trial Judgment* (vol. III), paras 1526–28.

142 Article 49, Geneva Convention IV.

143 Pictet (ed), *Commentary Geneva Convention IV*, p. 280. The commentary continues (ibid): '[e]vacuation is only permitted in such cases, however, when overriding military considerations make it imperative; if it is not imperative, evacuation ceases to be legitimate'. See also Kretzmer, 'Advisory Opinion', at 93–94 n.43; Chapter 9.

144 Article 147, Geneva Convention IV.

145 Article 2(g), ICTY Statute.

146 *Prosecutor v Blagoje Simić et al.*, Case No. IT-95-9-T, *Judgment*, 17 October 2003, paras 120, 1117, 1121, 1125; *Tuta and Štela Trial Judgment*, paras 569–71, 763, 767; *Prosecutor v Stevan Todorović*, Case No. IT-95-9/1-S, *Sentencing Judgment*, 31 July 2001, para. 8; *Prlić et al. Trial Judgment* (vol. I), para. 132.

Deportation is also a crime against humanity eligible for prosecution under Article 5(d) of the ICTY Statute. Whether deportation requires the victim to have crossed at least one international border remains a matter of dispute.[147] Owing in part to this unsettledness, the prosecution has developed a practice whereby one charge under Article 5(d) would frequently be accompanied by another, 'back-up' charge of inhumane acts under Article 5(i) – also a crime against humanity – perpetrated through forcible transfer within the territory of one state. Charges of deportation and/or forcible transfer have been ruled upon in multiple trials.[148]

[147] This particular issue need not detain us here. Suffice it to note the contrast between the growing majority of ICTY decisions upholding the existence of a cross-border element and a minority of decisions rejecting its existence. Those decisions upholding the requirement include: *Tuta and Štela Trial Judgment*, para. 670; *Prosecutor v. Milorad Krnojelac*, Case No. IT-97-25-T, *Judgment*, 15 March 2002, para. 474; *Krstić Trial Judgment*, para. 521; *Brđanin Trial Judgment*, para. 542; *Simić et al. Trial Judgment*, paras 123, 129; *Prosecutor v Slobodan Milošević*, Case No. IT-02-54-T, *Decision on Motion for Judgment of Acquittal*, 16 June 2004, para. 68. Those decisions rejecting the requirement include: *Prosecutor v Dragan Nikolić*, Case No. IT-94-2-R61, *Review of Indictment Pursuant to Rule 61 of the Rules of Procedure and Evidence*, 20 October 1995, para. 23; *Stakić Trial Judgment*, paras 671–84. The *Stakić Appeal Judgment* holds that deportation must involve expulsion across a *de jure* border to another country or across a *de facto* border of occupied territory. *Prosecutor v Milomir Stakić*, Case No. IT-97-24-A, *Judgment*, 22 March 2006, paras 278, 289–303, 308 (but see partly dissenting opinion of Judge Shahabuddeen, paras 19–76). As far as the ICTY jurisprudence is concerned, the *Stakić Appeal Judgment* has put the matter to rest. See *Prosecutor v Blagoje Simić*, Case No. IT-95-9-A, *Judgment*, 28 November 2006, paras 172–75; *Prosecutor v Milan Milutinović et al.*, Case No. IT-05-87-T, *Judgment*, 4 vols., 26 February 2009, vol. I, paras 165, 169; *Krajišnik Trial Judgment*, para. 723; *Prosecutor v Mladen Naletilić (a/k/a 'Tuta') and Vinko Martinović (a/k/a 'Štela')*, Case No. IT-98-34-A, *Judgment*, 3 May 2006, paras 152, 212–13 (separate and partly dissenting opinion of Judge Schomburg); *Martić Trial Judgment*, paras 107, 110; *Prosecutor v Vlastimir Đorđević*, Case No. IT-05-87/1-A, *Judgment*, 27 January 2014, paras 532–42; *Prlić et al. Trial Judgment* (vol. I), paras 47, 55–56; *Mladić Trial Judgment*, para. 3118.

[148] *Brđanin Trial Judgment*, paras 539–70; *Milutinović et al. Trial Judgment* (vol. I), paras 163–72; *Šainović et al. Appeal Judgment*, paras 286–527; *Blagojević and Jokić Trial Judgment*, paras 629–30; *Prosecutor v Momčilo Perišić*, Case No. IT-04-81-T, *Judgment*, 6 September 2011, paras 113–16; *Martić Trial Judgment*, paras 105–11; *Đorđević Trial Judgment*, paras 1603–14; *Gotovina et al. Trial Judgment*, paras 1737–41; *Tolimir Trial Judgment*, paras 793–803; *Mićo Stanišić and Župljanin Trial Judgment* (vol. I), paras 60–65; *Prosecutor v Jovica Stanišić and Franko Simatović*, Case No. IT-03-69-T, *Judgment*, 30 May 2013, paras 991–95; *Prlić et al. Trial Judgment* (vol. I), para. 47; *Karadžić Trial Judgment*, paras 487–95; *Šešelj Appeal Judgment*, para. 150; *Mladić Trial Judgment*, paras 3117–19.

Lastly, under Article 5(h) of the ICTY Statute, persecutions may be committed by way of deportation and/or forcible transfer.[149] This form of persecution has been adjudicated in many trials.[150]

The crimes against humanity of deportation, inhumane acts by way of forcible transfer and persecutions by way of deportation/forcible transfer all contain the element that the victim was forcibly displaced 'without grounds permitted under international law'.[151] Such grounds include 'imperative military reasons' within the meaning of Article 49 of Geneva Convention IV and Article 17(1) of Additional Protocol II.[152]

149 *Krnojelac Trial Judgment*, paras 433–34; *Prosecutor v Milorad Krnojelac*, Case No. IT-97-25-A, *Judgment*, 17 September 2003, para. 222; *Tuta and Štela Trial Judgment*, paras 671–72; *Simić et al. Trial Judgment*, para. 48; *Blagojević and Jokić Trial Judgment*, paras 629–31; *Martić Trial Judgment*, para. 119; *Popović et al. Trial Judgment*, para. 989; *Đorđević Trial Judgment*, paras 1763–64; *Gotovina et al. Trial Judgment*, paras 1738, 1740; *Perišić Trial Judgment*, para. 120; *Tolimir Trial Judgment*, paras 851, 860; *Mićo Stanišić and Župljanin Trial Judgment* (vol. I), paras 81–82; *Mladić Trial Judgment*, para. 3236.

150 *Milutinović et al. Trial Judgment* (vol. II), paras 1207–12; *Martić Trial Judgment*, para. 432; *Krajišnik Trial Judgment*, paras 748–49, 807–09, 1182; *Blagojević and Jokić Trial Judgment*, paras 616–18, 621; *Brđanin Trial Judgment*, paras 556, 1025–28, 1082, 1088, 1152; *Babić Sentencing Judgment*, paras 11, 15; *Deronjić Sentencing Judgment*, paras 29, 99–101, 120; *Prosecutor v Momir Nikolić*, Case No. IT-02-60/1-S, *Sentencing Judgment*, 2 December 2003, paras 12, 40–42; *Prosecutor v Ivica Rajić a/k/a Viktor Andrić*, Case No. IT-95-12-S, *Sentencing Judgment*, 8 May 2006; *Simić et al. Trial Judgment*, paras 1034–50, 1115, 1119, 1123; *Stakić Trial Judgment*, paras 881–82; *Tuta and Štela Trial Judgment*, paras 669–72, 711, 763, 767; *Plavšić Sentencing Judgment*, paras 5, 15; *Krnojelac Trial Judgment*, paras 472–85, 534; *Krstić Trial Judgment*, paras 537, 676, 727; *Todorović Sentencing Judgment*, para. 45; *Kordić and Čerkez Trial Judgment*, 305; *Blaškić Trial Judgment*, p. 267 (disposition); *Popović et al. Trial Judgment*, para. 901; *Đorđević Trial Judgment*, paras 1774–78; *Gotovina et al. Trial Judgment*, paras 1804, 1812–13; *Perišić Trial Judgment*, paras 743–46; *Tolimir Trial Judgment*, paras 879–81; *Jovica Stanišić and Simatović Trial Judgment*, paras 1242–43; *Karadžić Trial Judgment*, paras 515–16; *Šešelj Appeal Judgment*, para. 163; *Mladić Trial Judgment*, para. 3236.

151 *Stakić Trial Judgment*, para. 672; *Stakić Appeal Judgment*, para. 278; *Prosecutor v Momčilo Krajišnik*, Case No. IT-00-39-A, *Judgment*, 17 March 2009, paras 304, 307–08; *Simić et al. Trial Judgment*, para. 125; *Tuta and Štela Trial Judgment*, para. 521; *Krnojelac Trial Judgment*, para. 475; *Krnojelac Appeal Judgment*, para. 222; *Blagojević and Jokić Trial Judgment*, paras 595, 597; *Blaškić Trial Judgment*, para. 234; *Blaškić Appeal Judgment*, paras 150–53; *Martić Trial Judgment*, paras 107, 109; *Milutinović et al. Trial Judgment* (vol. I), para. 166; *Đorđević Trial Judgment*, para. 1607; *Tolimir Trial Judgment*, paras 798–99; *Prlić et al. Trial Judgment* (vol. I), para. 52; *Mićo Stanišić and Župljanin Trial Judgment* (vol. I), para. 61; *Jovica Stanišić and Simatović Trial Judgment*, para. 994; *Mladić Trial Judgment*, para. 3120.

152 *Brđanin Trial Judgment*, para. 556; *Milutinović et al. Trial Judgment* (vol. I), para. 166; *Mladić Trial Judgment*, para. 3120; Article 49, Geneva Convention IV; Article 17(1), Additional Protocol II.

The tribunal has not dealt extensively with 'grounds permitted under international law' or 'imperative military reasons' in this context.[153] Only in some cases, such as *Tuta and Štela*, *Brđanin*, *Đorđević* and *Tolimir*, was the description of victims leaving or being transferred followed by some general finding that their departure was 'unlawful'[154] or that it was not demanded by imperative military reasons.[155] No further insight was offered. In *Martić*, the trial chamber acknowledged that the absence of 'grounds permitted under international law' and 'imperative military reasons' was an element of deportation,[156] yet it did not engage in any factual discussion on this matter.[157] In a somewhat more elaborate manner, the *Krstić* Trial Chamber found that

> [i]n this case no military threat was present following the taking of Srebrenica. The atmosphere of terror in which the evacuation was conducted proves, conversely, that the transfer was carried out in furtherance of a well organised policy whose purpose was to expel the Bosnian Muslim population from the enclave. The evacuation was itself the goal and neither the protection of the civilians nor imperative military necessity justified the action.[158]

The same may be said of *Mladić*, although its trial judgment does discuss the absence of security considerations for the persons involved – another ground under international law that would have permitted their temporary displacement – in greater detail.[159]

This relative brevity[160] stands in contrast to the considerable factual detail in which the tribunal has examined the military necessity of property destruction.

[153] *Blagojević and Jokić Trial Judgment*, para. 618; *Đorđević Trial Judgment*, paras 1618–79; *Mićo Stanišić and Župljanin Trial Judgment* (vol. I), paras 221, 281, 346, 490, 699, 810, 879, 934, 981, 1040, 1189, 1247, 1285, 1355, 1413, 1497, 1552, 1686; *Krajišnik Appeal Judgment*, paras 308, 314.

[154] *Tuta and Štela Trial Judgment*, paras 542, 544, 551, 563 (regarding Mostar generally, and Mostar on 9 May 1993, 12–14 June 1993, and 29 September 1993).

[155] Ibid, para. 526 (regarding Sovići and Doljani); *Brđanin Trial Judgment*, para. 556 (1 September 2004) (in general, except Čelinac); *Đorđević Trial Judgment*, paras 1691–92; *Tolimir Trial Judgment*, paras 812, 828.

[156] *Martić Trial Judgment*, para. 107; *Karadžić Trial Judgment*, paras 488, 492.

[157] *Martić Trial Judgment*, paras 426–32. See also *Krajišnik Trial Judgment*, paras 727–32.

[158] *Krstić Trial Judgment*, para. 527.

[159] *Mladić Trial Judgment*, para. 3164.

[160] *Krajišnik Appeal Judgment*, para. 308 (emphasis added): 'While the Trial Chamber did not explicitly find that the forcible displacements in the case at hand are "without grounds permitted under international law", the Appeals Chamber is not satisfied that *this defect* of the Trial Chamber invalidates the verdict'. See also ibid, para. 314.

10.2 International Criminal Court

Within the context of positive IHL, military necessity has no role outside express exceptional clauses. It exempts deviations from the prescription of a rule only if the rule itself provides for military necessity exceptions. In this respect, the Rome Statute raises some awkward questions concerning the potential use before ICC proceedings of military necessity not only as an exception but also as one of the 'grounds for excluding criminal responsibility'.[161]

10.2.1 Article 8 and Elements of Crimes: Military Necessity as an Exception

The ICC has jurisdiction over crimes specified in Articles 5–8*bis* of the Rome Statute.[162] They are defined in the Elements of Crimes document, an instrument by which the court is to guide itself when considering cases before it.[163] Four war crimes under Article 8 expressly admit exceptions on account of military necessity.[164] The absence of military necessity is an element of each of these crimes. They are:

1. Extensive destruction and appropriation of property, a grave breach of the Geneva Conventions;[165]
2. Destruction or seizure of the enemy's property, a serious violation of the laws and customs of war in international armed conflict;[166]
3. Ordering the displacement of the civilian population for reasons related to the conflict, a serious violation of the laws and customs of war in non-international armed conflict;[167] and

161 Article 31(1), Rome Statute. See also Olásolo, *Unlawful Attacks in Combat Situations*, p. 238.

162 Articles 5–8*bis*, Rome Statute.

163 Ibid, Articles 9(1), 21(1)(a).

164 There are also offences which implicitly admit exceptions on account of military necessity. See below. These offences typically involve deportation or transfer of persons.

165 Article 8(2)(a)(iv), Rome Statute. One element of this war crime is that '[t]he destruction or appropriation was not justified by military necessity'. Elements of Crimes, ICC-PIOS-LT-03-002/15_Eng, pp. 20-21.

166 Article 8(2)(b)(xiii), Rome Statute. One element of this crime is that '[t]he destruction or seizure was not justified by military necessity'. Elements of Crimes, pp. 30–31.

167 Article 8(2)(e)(viii), Rome Statute. One element of this crime is that '[s]uch order was not justified by the security of the civilians involved or by military necessity'. Elements of Crimes, p. 46.

4. Destruction or seizure of the property of an adversary, a serious violation of the laws and customs of war in non-international armed conflict.[168]

The absence of military necessity also appears as part of an element of pillage,[169] a serious violation of the laws and customs of war in international and non-international armed conflicts alike.[170] In a somewhat mysterious ruling, however, the *Bemba* Trial Chamber held that 'the reference to "military necessity" in footnote 62 of the Elements of Crimes does not provide for an exception to the absolute prohibition on pillaging, but rather ... clarifies that the concept of military necessity is incompatible with a requirement that the perpetrator intended the appropriation for private or personal use'.[171]

For the most part, the corresponding IHL rules expressly provide for military necessity exceptions.[172] When a substantive rule envisages an exception, and when the rule's violation constitutes a crime, it is only logical that the absence of circumstances satisfying the exception's requirements is itself an element of that crime.[173]

Where the absence of military necessity is an element of a war crime, the onus rests with the prosecution to show this absence.[174] Showing the

[168] Article 8(2)(e)(xii), Rome Statute. One element of this crime is that 'the destruction or seizure was not justified by military necessity'. Elements of Crimes, p. 48.

[169] The second element of the crime of pillage is that 'the perpetrator intended to deprive the owner of the property and to appropriate it for private or personal use'. Elements of Crimes, pp. 31–32. An explanatory footnote is appended to this element (ibid; emphasis added): 'As indicated by the use of the term "private or personal use", *appropriations justified by military necessity cannot constitute the crime of pillaging*'. In earlier drafts of the elements of this war crime, the absence of military necessity appeared as an independent element. Dörmann, *Elements of War Crimes*, pp. 272–73.

[170] Articles 8(2)(b)(xvi), 8(2)(e)(v), Rome Statute.

[171] *Prosecutor v Jean-Pierre Bemba Gombo*, Case No. ICC-01/05-01/08, *Judgment Pursuant to Article 74 of the Statute*, 21 March 2016, paras 123–24 (footnote omitted).

[172] As regards extensive destruction and appropriation of property, a grave breach of the Geneva Conventions, see Article 50, Geneva Convention I; Article 51, Geneva Convention II; Article 147, Geneva Convention IV. As regards destruction or seizure of the property of the enemy or adversary, see Article 23(g), Hague Regulations (1907). As regards ordering the displacement of the civilian population, see Article 17(1), Additional Protocol II. The sole exception in this regard is pillage. Dörmann, *Elements of War Crimes*, pp. 272–73. See also *Krajišnik Trial Judgment*, para. 769; *Mladić Trial Judgment*, paras 3250, 3395.

[173] Cryer et al. (eds), *Introduction to International Criminal Law and Procedure* (2nd edn), p. 423.

[174] *Brđanin Appeal Judgment*, para. 337; *Kordić and Čerkez Appeal Judgment*, para. 495; *Milutinović et al. Trial Judgment* (vol. I), para. 208; *Karadžić Trial Judgment*, para. 533.

absence of military necessity entails, in turn, proving that at least one of its requirements was unfulfilled.[175] The prosecution's failure to do so means that it has not proved the crime's occurrence. When an accused is charged with a war crime of which the absence of military necessity is an element, and when he pleads military necessity, he challenges the notion that the crime occurred at all. Strictly speaking, therefore, pleading military necessity in this context does not constitute a 'defence'.[176]

Conversely, in no other crimes enumerated under the Rome Statute does military necessity expressly appear as an exception. Nor does the absence of military necessity appear implicitly as one of their elements. This is in line with the fact that the underlying positive IHL rules contain no military necessity exceptions.

There are, however, several offences in the Rome Statute which would admit, albeit implicitly, exceptions on account of military necessity. One is the crime of unlawful deportation or transfer, a grave breach of the Geneva Conventions listed under Article 8(2)(a)(vii) of the Rome Statute.[177] This grave breach emanates from Article 147 of Geneva Convention IV, which in turn is based on the convention's Articles 45 and 49. Article 49 exceptionally permits temporary evacuations of an area in occupied territory if, inter alia, 'imperative military reasons so demand'.[178] Temporary evacuations demanded by such reasons are not 'unlawful' within the meaning of Article 8(2)(a)(vii) of the Rome Statute.[179] Similarly, the offence of deportation or transfer, a crime against humanity under Article 7(1)(d), contains as one of its elements the requirement that the victim was forcibly displaced 'without grounds permitted under international law'.[180] As noted earlier, the ICTY and

175 Article 67(1)(i), Rome Statute (protecting the accused against having any reversal of the burden of proof imposed on him). It is unclear, however, whether the prosecution would be required to allege specifically and in advance which requirement or requirements of military necessity remained unfulfilled.

176 This is so although, in an adversarial setting, the accused would most likely plead military necessity as part of his 'defence' case and this plea would be colloquially referred to as a 'defence'. George P Fletcher, *Basic Concepts of Criminal Law* (New York and Oxford: Oxford University Press, 1998), pp. 93–110.

177 Article 8(2)(a)(vii), Rome Statute.

178 Article 49, Geneva Convention IV.

179 Dörmann, *Elements of War Crimes*, p. 106: 'Arts. 45 and 49 [of Geneva Convention IV] set forth the conditions for unlawfulness.'

180 Elements of Crimes, p. 10.

the MICT have interpreted these grounds to include 'imperative military reasons' demanding temporary evacuation of an area in occupied territory. Lastly, offences within the jurisdiction of the ICC – including those of which the absence of military necessity is an explicit or implicit element – may amount to persecutions under Article 7(1)(h) of the statute.[181]

As of 30 June 2019, the ICC has issued arrest warrants or laid charges against the following individuals for some of the crimes in question:

1. Ahmad Muhammad Harun ('Ahmad Harun'),[182] Ali Muhammad Al Abd-Al-Rahman ('Ali Kushayb'),[183] Germain Katanga,[184] Mathieu Ngudjolo Chui,[185] Callixte Mbarushimana,[186] Sylvestre Mudacumura,[187] Abdel Raheem Muhammad Hussein,[188] Bosco Ntaganda,[189] Patrice-Edouard Ngaïssona[190] and Alfred Yekatom[191] for property destruction (Article 8(2)(b)(xiii) or Article 8(2)(e)(xii)).

[181] Ibid, p. 14.

[182] *Prosecutor v Ahmad Muhammad Harun ('Ahmad Harun') and Ali Muhammad Al Abd-Ali-Rahman ('Ali Kushayb')*, Case No. ICC-02/05-01/07, *Warrant of Arrest for Ahmad Harun*, 27 April 2007, counts 8, 19, 38, 50.

[183] *Prosecutor v Ahmad Muhammad Harun ('Ahmad Harun') and Ali Muhammad Al Abd-Ali-Rahman ('Ali Kushayb')*, Case No. ICC-02/05-01/07, *Warrant of Arrest for Ali Kushayb*, 27 April 2007, counts 8, 19, 38, 50.

[184] *Prosecutor v Germain Katanga and Mathieu Ngudjolo Chui*, Case No. ICC-01/04-01/07, *Amended Document Containing the Charges Pursuant to Article 61(3)(a) of the Statute*, 26 June 2008, count 13.

[185] *Katanga and Chui Amended Document Containing the Charges*, count 13.

[186] *Prosecutor v Callixte Mbarushimana*, Case No. ICC-01/04-01/10, *Document de notification des charges présenté par l'Accusation en application de l'article 61-3 du Statut de Rome*, 15 July 2011, count 1.

[187] *Prosecutor v Sylvestre Mudacumura*, Case No. ICC-01/04-01/12, *Decision on the Prosecutor's Application under Article 58*, 13 July 2012, count 11.

[188] *Prosecutor v Abdel Raheem Muhammad Hussein*, Case No. ICC-02/05-01/12, *Warrant of Arrest for Abdel Raheem Muhammad Hussein*, 1 March 2012, p. 8.

[189] *Prosecutor v Bosco Ntaganda*, Case No. ICC-01/04-02/06, *Document Containing the Charges*, 10 January 2014, count 18.

[190] *Prosecutor v Patrice-Edouard Ngaïssona*, Case No. ICC-01/04-02/18, *Public Redacted Version of 'Warrant of Arrest for Patrice-Edouard Ngaïssona'*, 13 December 2018, p. 37.

[191] *Prosecutor v Alfred Yekatom*, Case No. ICC-01/14-01/18, *Public Redacted Version of 'Warrant of Arrest for Alfred Yekatom', ICC-01/14-01/18-1-US-Exp, 11 November 2018*, 17 November 2018, p. 21.

2. Kushayb,[192] Jean-Pierre Bemba Gombo,[193] Harun,[194] Katanga,[195] Joseph Kony,[196] Raska Lukwiya,[197] Chui,[198] Okot Odhiambo,[199] Dominic Ongwen,[200] Vincent Otti[201] and Omar Hassan Ahmad Al Bashir ('Omar Al Bashir'),[202] Bahar Idriss Abu Garda,[203] Abdallah Banda Abakaer Nourain,[204] Saleh Mohammed Jerbo Jamus,[205] Mbarushimana,[206]

[192] *Kushayb Arrest Warrant*, counts 18, 36, 49.

[193] *Prosecutor v Jean-Pierre Bemba Gombo*, Case No. ICC-01/05-01/08, *Amended Document Containing the Charges Filed on 30 March 2009*, 30 March 2009, count 8.

[194] *Harun Arrest Warrant*, counts 18, 36, 37, 49.

[195] *Katanga and Chui Amended Charges Document*, count 12.

[196] *Prosecutor v Joseph Kony*, Case No. ICC-02/04-01/05, *Warrant of Arrest for Joseph Kony Issued on 8 July 2005 as Amended on 27 September 2005*, 27 September 2005, counts 9, 15, 19, 26, 33.

[197] *Prosecutor v Raska Lukwiya*, Case No. ICC-02/04, *Warrant of Arrest for Raska Lukwiya*, 8 July 2005, count 9. On 11 July 2007, the pre-trial chamber terminated proceedings against Lukwiya. *Prosecutor v Joseph Kony et al.*, Case No. ICC-02/04-01/05, *Decision to Terminate the Proceedings against Raska Lukwiya*, 11 July 2007.

[198] *Katanga and Chui Amended Charges Document*, count 12.

[199] *Prosecutor v Okot Odhiambo*, Case No. ICC-02/04, *Warrant of Arrest for Okot Odhiambo*, 8 July 2005, counts 15, 19. On 10 September 2015, the pre-trial chamber terminated proceedings against Odhiambo. *Prosecutor v Jospeh Kony et al.*, Case No. ICC-02/04-01/05, *Decision Terminating Proceedings Against Okot Odhiambo*, 10 September 2015.

[200] *Prosecutor v Dominic Ongwen*, Case No. ICC-02/04, *Warrant of Arrest for Dominic Ongwen*, 8 July 2005, count 33.

[201] *Prosecutor v Vincent Otti*, Case No. ICC-02/04, *Warrant of Arrest for Vincent Otti*, 8 July 2005, counts 9, 15, 19, 26, 33.

[202] *Prosecutor v Omar Hassan Ahmad Al Bashir*, Case No. ICC-02/05-01/09, *Warrant of Arrest for Omar Hassan Ahmad Al Bashir*, 4 March 2009, p. 7.

[203] *Prosecutor v Bahar Idriss Abu Garda*, Case No ICC-02/05-02/09, *Document Containing the Charges Submitted Pursuant to Article 61(3) of the Statute*, 24 September 2009, count 3.

[204] *Prosecutor v Abdallah Banda Abakaer Nourain and Saleh Mohammed Jerbo Mamus*, Case No. ICC-02/05-03/09, *Summons to Appear for Abdallah Banda Abakaer Nourain*, 27 August 2009, paras 15, 19.

[205] *Prosecutor v Abdallah Banda Abakaer Nourain and Saleh Mohammed Jerbo Jamus*, Case No. ICC-02/05-03/09, *Summons to Appear for Saleh Mohammed Jerbo Jamus*, 27 August 2009, paras 15, 19. On 4 October 2013, the trial chamber terminated proceedings against Jerbo. *Prosecutor v Abdallah Banda Abakaer Nourain and Saleh Mohammed Jerbo Jamus*, Case No. ICC-02/05-03/09, *Public Redacted Decision Terminating Proceedings Against Mr. Jerbo*, 4 October 2013.

[206] *Mbarushimana Charges Document*, count 12.

Mudacumura,[207] Hussein,[208] Ntaganda[209] and Ngaïssona[210] for pillaging (Article 8(2)(b)(xvi)) or Article 8(2)(e)(v)).

3. Hussein,[211] Ntaganda,[212] Ngaïssona[213] and Yekatom[214] for forcible transfer (Article 8(2)(e)(viii)).
4. Harun,[215] Kushayb,[216] Omar Al Bashir,[217] Ntaganda,[218] William Samoei Ruto,[219] Henry Kiprono Kosgey,[220] Joshua Arap Sang,[221] Francis Kirimi Muthaura,[222] Uhuru Muigai Kenyatta,[223] Mohammed Hussein Ali,[224] Ngaïssona[225] and Yekatom[226] for deportation or forcible transfer (Article 7(1)(d)).
5. Harun,[227] Kushayb,[228] Hussein,[229] Ntaganda[230] and Ngaïssona[231] for persecution by way of pillaging (Article 7(1)(h)).

207 *Mudacumura Arrest Warrant Decision*, count 12.

208 *Hussein Arrest Warrant*, p. 8.

209 *Ntaganda Charges Document*, count 11.

210 *Ngaïssona Arrest Warrant*, p. 37.

211 *Hussein Arrest Warrant*, pp. 8–9.

212 *Ntaganda Charges Document*, count 13.

213 *Ngaïssona Arrest Warrant*, p. 37.

214 *Prosecutor v Alfred Yekatom*, Case No. ICC-01/14-01/18, *Public Redacted Version of 'Warrant of Arrest for Alfred Yekatom', ICC-01/14-01/18-1-US-Exp, 11 November 2018*, 17 November 2018, p. 21.

215 *Harun Arrest Warrant*, counts 9, 20, 51.

216 *Kushayb Arrest Warrant*, counts 9, 20, 51.

217 *Al Bashir Arrest Warrant*, p. 7.

218 *Ntaganda Charges Document*, count 12.

219 *Prosecutor v William Samoei Ruto et al.*, Case No. ICC-01/09-01/11, *Document Containing Charges*, 15 August 2011, count 3. On 6 April 2016, the trial chamber decided to terminate the case against Ruto.

220 *Ruto et al. Charges Document*, count 3.

221 Ibid, count 4. On 6 April 2016, the trial chamber decided to terminate the case against Sang.

222 *Prosecutor v Francis Kirimi Muthaura et al.*, Case No. ICC-01/09-02/11, *Decision on the Prosecutor's Application for Summonses to Appear for Francis Kirimi Muthaura, Uhuru Muigai Kenyatta and Mohammed Hussein Ali*, 8 March 2011, count 2.

223 Ibid. On 13 March 2015, the trial chamber terminated proceedings against Kenyatta. *Prosecutor v Uhuru Muigai Kenyatta*, Case No. ICC-01/09-02/11, *Decision on the Withdrawal of Charges against Mr Kenyatta*, 13 March 2015.

224 *Muthaura et al. Summonses Decision*, count 2.

225 *Ngaïssona Arrest Warrant*, p. 37.

226 *Yekatom Arrest Warrant*, p. 21.

227 *Harun Arrest Warrant*, counts 10, 21, 39.

228 *Kushayb Arrest Warrant*, counts 10, 21, 39.

229 *Hussein Arrest Warrant*, pp. 6–7.

230 *Ntaganda Charges Document*, count 10.

231 *Ngaïssona Arrest Warrant*, p. 37.

6. Harun,[232] Kushayb,[233] Hussein,[234] Ntaganda,[235] Ruto,[236] Kosgey,[237] Sang,[238] Ngaïssona[239] and Yekatom[240] for persecution by way of property destruction (Article 7(1)(h)).
7. Harun,[241] Kushayb,[242] Hussein,[243] Ntaganda,[244] Ruto,[245] Kosgey,[246] Sang,[247] Muthaura,[248] Kenyatta,[249] Ali,[250] Ngaïssona[251] and Yekatom[252] for persecution by way of deportation or forcible transfer (Article 7(1)(h)).

10.2.2 Rulings to Date

Some of these cases have reached confirmation,[253] trial[254] and appellate[255] stages. Confirmation decisions are often quite superficial in their

[232] *Harun Arrest Warrant*, counts 1, 10, 21, 39.
[233] *Kushayb Arrest Warrant*, counts 1, 10, 21, 39.
[234] *Hussein Arrest Warrant*, pp. 6–7.
[235] *Ntaganda Charges Document*, count 10.
[236] *Ruto et al. Charges Document*, count 5.
[237] Ibid.
[238] Ibid, count 6.
[239] *Ngaïssona Arrest Warrant*, p. 37.
[240] *Yekatom Arrest Warrant*, p. 21.
[241] *Harun Arrest Warrant*, counts 1, 10, 39.
[242] *Kushayb Arrest Warrant*, counts 1, 10, 39.
[243] *Hussein Arrest Warrant*, pp. 6–7.
[244] *Ntaganda Charges Document*, count 10.
[245] *Ruto et al. Charges Document*, count 5.
[246] Ibid.
[247] Ibid, count 6.
[248] *Muthaura et al. Summonses Decision*, count 5.
[249] Ibid.
[250] Ibid.
[251] *Ngaïssona Arrest Warrant*, p. 37.
[252] *Yekatom Arrest Warrant*, p. 21.
[253] *Prosecutor v Jean-Pierre Bemba Gombo*, Case No. ICC-01/05-01/08, *Decision Pursuant to Article 61(7)(a) of the Rome Statute on the Charges of the Prosecutor against Jean-Pierre Bemba Gombo*, 15 June 2009; *Prosecutor v Bahar Idriss Abu Garda*, Case No. ICC-02/05-02/09, *Decision on the Confirmation of Charges*, 8 February 2010; *Prosecutor v Abdallah Banda Abakaer Nourain and Saleh Mohammed Jerbo Jamus*, Case No. ICC-02/05-03/09, *Corrigendum of the 'Decision on the Confirmation of Charges'*, 7 March 2011; *Prosecutor v Callixte Mbarushimana*, Case No. ICC-01/04-01/10, *Decision on the Confirmation of Charges*, 16 December 2011; *Ntaganda Confirmation Decision*; *Prosecutor v Dominic Ongwen*, Case No. ICC-02/04-01/05, *Decision on the Confirmation of Charges against Dominic Ongwen*, 23 March 2016.
[254] *Prosecutor v Mathieu Ngudjolo Chui*, Case No. ICC-01/04-02/12, *Judgment Pursuant to Article 74 of the Statute*, 18 December 2012; *Prosecutor v Germain Katanga*, Case No. ICC-01/04-01/07, *Judgment Pursuant to Article 74 of the Statute*, 7 March 2014; *Bemba Trial Judgment*.
[255] *Prosecutor v Jean-Pierre Bemba Gombo*, Case No. ICC-01/05-01/08 A, *Judgment on the Appeal of Mr Jean-Pierre Bemba Gombo against Trial Chamber III's 'Judgment Pursuant to Article 74 of the Statute'*, 8 June 2018.

legal and factual discussions. For example, the *Bemba Confirmation Decision* states, without further elaboration, that the property 'deprivation was not justified by military necessity'.[256] The *Ntaganda Confirmation Decision* finds that the forcible transfer charged was without military necessity because 'there is no indication of . . . any reason linked to the conduct of military operations'.[257] The same decision also notes that the property destructions were militarily unnecessary because there is no evidence that the party involved 'made a distinction between military objectives and civilian objects while shelling the densely populated villages'[258] and that the perpetrators 'destroyed and burned the villages after the departure of the adverse party'.[259]

One element of property destruction as a war crime under the Rome Statute is that the property enjoyed IHL protection at the time.[260] In its *Katanga and Chui Confirmation Decision*, the pre-trial chamber noted that this excludes (a) military objectives destroyed during an attack[261] and (b) civilian objects destroyed as part of a proportional attack against a military objective.[262] The chamber also held that this offence does not cover military objectives that are destroyed before or after falling into the hands of the attacking party and to the extent militarily necessary.[263] When finding specific destructions to be devoid of military necessity,

[256] *Bemba Confirmation Decision*, para. 322. See also *Bemba Trial Judgment*, paras 643–45 (focusing primarily on the personal or private use for which the property was appropriated).

[257] *Ntaganda Confirmation Decision*, para. 68. See also *Prosecutor v William Samoei Ruto et al.*, Case No. ICC-01/09-01/11, *Decision on the Confirmation of Charges Pursuant to Article 61(7)(a) and (b) of the Rome Statute*, 23 January 2012, para. 268 ('the PNU supporters were forcibly displaced without grounds permitted under international law from the areas where they were lawfully present'); *Prosecutor v Francis Kirimi Muthaura et al.*, Case No. ICC-01/09-02/11, *Decision on the Confirmation of Charges Pursuant to Article 61(7)(a) and (b) of the Rome Statute*, 23 January 2012, para. 253 ('the established facts do not reveal any grounds permitting the displacement under international law').

[258] *Ntaganda Confirmation Decision*, para. 72.

[259] Ibid, para. 73.

[260] Elements of Crimes, pp. 26, 44.

[261] *Katanga and Chui Confirmation Decision*, para. 312. See also *Mbarushimana Confirmation Decision*, para. 172.

[262] *Katanga and Chui Confirmation Decision*, para. 313. See also *Mbarushimana Confirmation Decision*, para. 172.

[263] *Katanga and Chui Confirmation Decision*, para. 318 (quoting Hassang, 'Destroying or Seizing the Enemy's Property'). See also *Mbarushimana Confirmation Decision*, para. 172.

however, the decision merely states that the property destroyed did not constitute military objectives.[264]

Much the same was reiterated in the *Katanga Trial Judgment*.[265] Three novel features may nevertheless be noted. First, the trial chamber looked to Article 14 of the 1863 Lieber Code for the definition of military necessity.[266] The definition given in that article[267] is not itself problematic, though somewhat antiquated and perhaps not entirely up to date if read together with the code's Article 15 that goes on to discuss the notion in greater detail.[268] When adjusted for modern IHL rules, Article 14 largely corresponds to the definition of juridical military necessity proposed in Chapter 9. Second, the trial chamber interpreted the expression 'imperatively demanded' found in Article 8(2)(e)(xii) of the Rome Statute to mean that the perpetrator ought to have 'no other option' but to destroy the property in order to be eligible for military necessity.[269] Here, too, although a *sine qua non* causation is not a requirement of juridical military necessity,[270] a more stringent construction of its degrees is arguably consistent with the addition of qualifying adjectives and adverbs such as 'imperative' and 'imperatively.'[271]

Third, according to the *Katanga Trial Judgment*, whether the destruction of property fell within military necessity is a case-by-case assessment to be carried out 'by considering, for example, whether the destroyed

264 *Katanga and Chui Confirmation Decision*, para. 324. See also *Mbarushimana Confirmation Decision*, paras 175, 196, 208, 225.

265 *Katanga Trial Judgment*, paras 889–95.

266 Ibid, para. 894 (citing *Kordić and Čerkez Appeal Judgment*, para. 686).

267 Article 14, Lieber Code: 'Military necessity, as understood by modern civilized nations, consists in the necessity of those measures which are indispensable for securing the ends of the war, and which are lawful according to the modern law and usages of war'.

268 Ibid, Article 15 (emphasis in original): 'Military necessity admits of all direct destruction of life or limb of *armed* enemies, and of other persons whose destruction is incidentally *unavoidable* in the armed contests of the war; it allows of the capturing of every armed enemy, and every enemy of importance to the captor; it allows of all destruction of property, and obstruction of the ways and channels of traffic, travel, or communication, and of all withholding of sustenance or means of life from the enemy; of the appropriation of whatever an enemy's country affords necessary for the subsistence and safety of the army, and of such deception as does not involve the breaking of good faith either positively pledged, regarding agreements entered into during the war, or supposed by the modern law of war to exist. Men who take up arms against one another in public war do not cease on this account to be moral beings, responsible to one another and to God.'

269 *Katanga Trial Judgment*, para. 894.

270 See Chapter 9.

271 Ibid.

property was defended or whether specific property was destroyed'.[272] For this proposition, the judgment cites paragraphs 534[273] and 586[274] of the *Kordić and Čerkez Appeal Judgment*. The *Katanga* Trial Chamber apparently understood these paragraphs to mean that there is no military necessity where 'the destroyed property was defended' and where 'specific property was destroyed'. This interpretation is deeply problematic. Plainly, neither factor is relevant when determining the existence or absence of juridical military necessity. As discussed earlier, it may become militarily necessary to destroy civilian objects, whether defended or not, in some circumstances. Nor is the fact that specific property was destroyed while the remainder was not per se indicative of military necessity's absence. What the relevant passages of the *Kordić and Čerkez Appeal Judgment* reveal is rather that all the property destroyed was civilian in character at the time and that it was destroyed based solely on the ethnic identity of its owner.

[272] *Katanga Trial Judgment*, para. 894.

[273] The paragraph reads (footnote omitted): 'Paragraph 659 [of the *Kordić and Čerkez Trial Judgment*] describing the events at Očehnići reads as follows:

> The village of Očehnići is to the south of Busovača. According to the Prosecution, it was subject to HVO attack in April 1993. The prosecution evidence was as follows. In the afternoon of 16 April 1993 masked HVO soldiers attacked the village by firing incendiary bullets into the houses. Within half an hour all the Muslim houses were burning. The villagers were unarmed and did not put up any resistance. One resident heard, at second-hand, that Paško Ljubičić was the leader of the unit that had attacked the village and that he had been ordered to do so by Brigadier Duško Grubešić, commander of the Zrinski Brigade, to 'cleanse' Muslims from the area. The damage to Očehnići is clearly shown on the video recording taken during a helicopter flight over the area in May 1996 and played to the court during the trial. Around 20 men from Lončari were detained and taken to Kaonik on 16 April 1993. Upon arrival they were lined up and their valuables were stolen by HVO soldiers.

In the Appeals Chamber's view, a reasonable trier of fact could have concluded that the wilful destruction of all Muslim houses in Očehnići was of a large scale and not justified by military necessity since the villagers were unarmed and did not put up any resistance. Therefore, Kordić's argument that the Trial Chamber erred in finding that wanton destruction was committed in Očehnići in April 1993 fails. The Appeals Chamber upholds the Trial Chamber's finding that the crime was established.'

[274] The paragraph reads: 'The Appeals Chamber considers that a reasonable trier of fact could have found that the destruction was wilful and not justified by military necessity since only Muslim houses were destroyed, and the destruction occurred when there was not much fighting. The Appeals Chamber therefore upholds the Trial Chamber's finding that wanton destruction not justified by military necessity, Count 38 (Kordić), was established.'

The *Katanga* Trial Chamber considered the following pieces of property destroyed in Bogoro on 24 February 2003:

- Houses, especially thatched houses and those with roofing sheets owned and occupied by Bogoro's predominantly Hema population;[275]
- The *manyata* (small houses occupied by adversaries);[276] and
- Buildings in Diguna Mission, including the CECA 20 church.[277]

Of these objects, the chamber apparently found all but the *manyata* to have been destroyed without military necessity. Oddly, besides determining that the *manyata* arguably constituted military objectives[278] and implicitly that the others did not, the chamber did not even apply the two bases of assessment that it had derived from the *Kordić and Čerkez Appeal Judgment*. This lack of reasoning is unilluminating. The facts as described in the judgment show that only the *manyata*, Hema property and religious buildings not used for military purposes were destroyed in Bogoro that day. It would not have been too difficult to apply the proper criteria when finding the latter two types of destructions lacking in military necessity.

As for the war crime of pillage, the *Katanga* Trial Chamber found that the property was stolen for personal gain and therefore devoid of military necessity.[279]

10.2.3 Article 31: Military Necessity as a Justification/Excuse?

The potential use of military necessity as a justification or excuse affects war crimes which do not provide for military necessity exceptions and, accordingly, of which the absence of military necessity is not an element. A person charged with one of these war crimes who pleads military necessity does not seek to negate any of its elements. Rather, that person seeks to deny wrongdoing (hence justified) or blameworthiness (hence excused) in the event that the prosecution proves every element of the offence. The defendant's reliance on military necessity in this fashion would constitute a 'defence' properly so called.

[275] *Katanga Trial Judgment*, paras 917–18.
[276] Ibid, para. 921.
[277] Ibid, para. 922.
[278] Ibid, paras 921, 924, 946.
[279] Ibid, paras 906, 951. See also *Bemba Trial Judgement*, paras 122–25.

The proposition that military necessity should be admitted as a genuine defence is highly controversial. As noted earlier, unqualified rules of positive IHL already account for military necessity. Admitting military necessity as a genuine defence would amount to admitting it *de novo* for deviations from these rules.[280] The entire *corpus juris* of IHL would risk being unduly volatile and subservient to the exigencies of war.

Article 31(1) of the Rome Statute envisages several 'grounds for excluding criminal responsibility'.[281] According to one ground,

> a person shall not be criminally responsible if, at the time of that person's conduct ... (c) [t]he person acts reasonably to defend himself or herself or another person or, in the case of war crimes, property which is essential for the survival of the person or another person or property which is essential for accomplishing a military mission, against an imminent and unlawful use of force in a manner proportionate to the degree of danger to the person or the other person or property protected. The fact that the person was involved in a defensive operation conducted by forces shall not in itself constitute a ground for excluding criminal responsibility under this subparagraph.[282]

Note here that a person shall not be criminally responsible for war crimes if he acts 'reasonably to defend ... property which is essential for accomplishing a military mission, against an imminent and unlawful use of force in a manner proportionate to the degree of danger to the ... property protected'.[283]

Could this clause be construed in substance as introducing a military necessity-like justification or excuse for war crimes? It appears from the drafting history that military necessity was treated at first as a potentially

[280] See Chapter 9.

[281] It is not clear whether a 'ground for excluding criminal responsibility' within the meaning of Article 31 constitutes a justification or excuse, or both. Kittichaisaree, *International Criminal Law*, p. 269; Antonio Cassese, 'Justifications and Excuses in International Criminal Law' in Antonio Cassese et al. (eds), *The Rome Statute of the International Criminal Law: A Commentary*, 2 vols. (Oxford: Oxford University Press, 2002), vol. I, 951, pp. 954–55; E van Sliedregt, *The Criminal Responsibility of Individuals for Violations of International Humanitarian Law* (The Hague: TMC Asser Press, 2003), p. 258; Albin Eser, 'Article 31' in Triffterer (ed), *Commentary on the Rome Statute* 863, pp. 871–72; Geert-Jan Alexander Knoops, 'The Diverging Position of Criminal Law Defences before the ICTY and the ICC: Contemporary Developments' in Doria et al. (eds), *Legal Regime of the International Criminal Court* 779, p. 779.

[282] Article 31(1)(c), Rome Statute.

[283] Ibid.

separate ground for excluding criminal responsibility.[284] During the final negotiations of the statute, the expression 'in the case of war crimes, property which is essential for accomplishing a military mission' was added to what is now Article 31(1)(c).[285]

Several commentators have expressed their concern that this ground might be construed as though it were military necessity. E. van Sliedregt, for example, notes that the lack of clarity in the wording of Article 31(1)(c) 'might be interpreted as allowing for a plea of military necessity. The clause "property which is essential for accomplishing a military mission" might be taken to constitute a blank and open-ended allowance for a plea of military necessity, which would, however, be a violation of the laws of war'.[286]

It seems undeniable that there is such a risk. It is submitted here, however, that the clause's inclusion in Article 31(1)(c) would have more limited practical ramifications than it might appear.

The way in which the clause is formulated indicates that its admissibility is subject to the satisfaction of several requirements. They are:

1. That the act was taken to defend property;
2. That the act was reasonable;
3. That the property was essential for accomplishing a military mission;
4. That the act was taken against force;
5. That the force was imminent;
6. That the force was unlawful; and

[284] Preparatory Committee, *Report of the Preparatory Committee on the Establishment of an International Criminal Court, Vol. II (Compilation of Proposals)*, U.N.Doc. A/51/22 (1996) in M Cherif Bassiouni (ed), *The Statute of the International Criminal Court: A Documentary History* (Ardsley: Transnational Publishers, 1999) 441, p. 495. See also Preparatory Committee, *Addendum, Report of the Preparatory Committee on the Establishment of an International Criminal Court*, A/CONF.183/2/Add.1 (14 April 1998), p. 59 n.39: 'It was questioned whether such grounds as military necessity could be dealt with in connection with the definition of war crimes.'

[285] Eser, 'Article 31', p. 548; van Sliedregt, *Criminal Responsibility of Individuals*, p. 258.

[286] Van Sliedregt, *Criminal Responsibility of Individuals*, p. 259. See also Geert-Jan G.J. Knoops, *Defenses in Contemporary International Criminal Law* (Leiden: Martinus Nijhoff, 2001), pp. 89–91 (quoting Nico Keijzer, 'Réponse à la Question 2' (2000) 33 *Revue belge de droit international* 440, at 443); Keijzer, 'Réponse à la Question 2', at 444–45; Catherine Denis and Miguel Romero, 'Synthèse des débats de l'atelier du 12 juillet 2000' (2000) 33 *Revue belge de droit international* 463, at 480; Eric David, 'Self-Defence and State of Necessity in the Statute of the ICC' in Doria et al. (eds), *Legal Regime of the International Criminal Court* 757, pp. 769–70; Knoops, 'Diverging Position of Criminal Law Defences', pp. 786–88.

7. That the act was taken in a manner proportionate to the degree of danger to the property protected.

10.2.3.1 Narrower in Content than Military Necessity as an Exception

The requirement that the act be taken with a view to defending certain property is foreign to the traditional understanding of military necessity. As noted earlier, military necessity as an exception encompasses a far wider range of purposes – from the maintenance of the belligerent's sanitary condition to the military defeat of its enemy.[287] Typically, the purposes concerned are abstract (e.g., the attainment of a degree of security for the occupation force), rather than material (e.g., the protection of an object), in character. It is, among other things, this broad and abstract scope of permissible purposes that makes the potential introduction of military necessity as a genuine defence so contentious. If, as is the case with the exclusionary ground under Article 31(1)(c), the very notion of military necessity had been restricted to measures taken in defence of property, virtually none of the successful military necessity pleas in the history of IHL would have been successful.

Nor, for the exclusionary ground to be admissible under Article 31(1)(c), is it sufficient that the act be taken to defend *any* property. Rather, the property must be essential for accomplishing a military mission. Whatever it may mean for particular property to be 'essential for accomplishing a military mission',[288] it seems highly likely that such property also constitutes a military objective. As a military objective, the property is liable to all lawful attacks and acts of destruction, and its destruction would *ipso facto* be militarily necessary.[289] Conversely, only rarely would property 'essential for accomplishing a military mission' retain its status as a civilian object. Where particular property does constitute a civilian object, it is immune from deliberate, indiscriminate or disproportionate attacks.

Unlike the ground under Article 31(1)(c), exceptional military necessity does not require that the measure be taken in response to force.

[287] See Chapter 9.

[288] The looseness of this expression, as well as the difficulty that may arise in connection with its interpretation, has been noted elsewhere. Eser, 'Article 31', p. 549; Antonio Cassese, 'The Statute of the International Criminal Court: Some Preliminary Reflections' (1999) 10 *European Journal of International Law* 144, at 155.

[289] That is, unless the destruction or its purpose was otherwise in breach of IHL.

A person is not eligible for the exclusionary ground under Article 31(1)(c) if the force against which he or she acts to defend the property is itself lawful. Since, as noted above, the type of property at issue here is nearly always a military objective, the person in question will be eligible only (a) in a limited set of circumstances where military objectives enjoy IHL protection against attacks or acts of destruction, or (b) in the unlikely event that the property defended is essential for a military mission and yet enjoys immunity as a civilian object.[290]

The remaining requirements of Article 31(1)(c) are substantively similar, if not identical, to those of military necessity as an exception. Thus, the clause requires that the act be 'reasonable' for the property's defence.[291] This would resemble the requirement of juridical military necessity that the measure be 'materially relevant' to and the 'least injurious' for the attainment of a military purpose.[292] There is some authority for the view that the 'reasonable act' test is an objective one.[293] If true, this test would arguably be more stringent than the belligerent's contemporaneous and bona fide knowledge, i.e., subjective awareness, of the various requirements of exceptional military necessity discussed earlier.[294]

The clause also requires that the act be taken against an 'imminent' use of force.[295] This requirement would be akin to the notion of 'urgency' implied in military necessity. Finally, the clause requires that the act be 'proportionate' to the degree of danger to the property defended.[296] It would appear that the relevant ratio here is one between the danger to the property averted by the defensive act, on the one hand, and the harm caused by the same act, on the other.[297] Such a ratio would be analogous to the benefit–injury ratio used for the proportionality requirement of military necessity.

In view of the foregoing, the clause would not affect war crimes that already provide for military necessity exceptions. In other words, if all of

[290] Gabor Rona, 'Réponses à la Question 2' (2000) 33 *Revue belge de droit international* 446, at 449–50.
[291] Article 31(1)(c), Rome Statute.
[292] See Chapter 9.
[293] Van Sliedregt, *Criminal Responsibility of Individuals*, pp. 260–61.
[294] See Chapter 9. The Rome Statute treats mistake of fact separately. Article 32(1), Rome Statute.
[295] Article 31(1)(c), Rome Statute.
[296] Ibid.
[297] Rona, 'Réponses à la Question 2', at 450.

the conditions in fulfilment of Article 31(1)(c) exist, then it is likely that they also satisfy all the requirements of juridical military necessity. Conversely, where the acts are not such as fulfil all of the latter, then they are unlikely to qualify for Article 31(1)(c).

10.2.3.2 Broader Availability to Offences Not Subject to Military Necessity Exceptions

To the extent that Article 31(1)(c) might affect those crimes which envisage no military necessity exceptions, its scope is so restrictive that it would justify or excuse a far narrower range of measures than military necessity, if introduced as a genuine defence, would. The fact remains however that, no matter how restrictive in scope, this exclusionary ground is a qualitatively new defence to war crimes hitherto unknown in IHL. In Antonio Cassese's words:

> [V]ia international criminal law a norm of international humanitarian law has been created whereby a serviceman many now lawfully commit an international crime for the purpose of defending any 'property essential for accomplishing a military mission' against an imminent and unlawful use of force. So far such unlawful use of force against the 'property' at issue has not entitled the military to commit war crimes. They could only react by using lawful means or methods of combat or, *ex post facto*, by resorting to lawful reprisals against enemy combatants.[298]

To be sure, by virtue of Article 21 of the Rome Statute, IHL does appear as part of the law that the ICC is bound to apply.[299] The statute contains no interpretive device whereby IHL mandatorily trumps its statutory provisions such as Article 31(1)(c).[300] It would be incumbent upon the court itself to keep this clause in check by using its Article 31(2) powers wisely.[301]

Lastly, Article 31(3) provides for exclusionary grounds not enumerated under Article 31(1) where such grounds are derived from applicable

[298] Cassese, 'Statute of the International Criminal Court', at 154–55. See also Antonio Cassese et al. (rev.), *Cassese's International Criminal Law*, 3rd edn (Oxford: Oxford University Press, 2013), p. 213.

[299] Article 21, Rome Statute: 'The Court shall apply ... (b) [i]n the second place, where appropriate, applicable treaties and the principles and rules of international law, including the established principles of the international law of armed conflict'.

[300] This problem would remain notwithstanding Article 21(3).

[301] Article 31(2), Rome Statute: 'The Court shall determine the applicability of the grounds for excluding criminal responsibility provided for in this Statute to the case before it.'

law as set forth in Article 21.[302] Whether military necessity could constitute such a ground would depend on how the court interprets the 'applicable treaties and the principles and rules of international law, including the established principles of the international law of armed conflict'. Our discussion on the nature and scope of juridical military necessity exclusively as an exception makes it abundantly clear that no treaty, principle or rule of international law admits military necessity pleas as a genuine defence.[303] Nor, in all likelihood, would the court recognise military necessity as an unenumerated exclusionary ground under Article 31(3).

10.3 Conclusion

This chapter has revealed the intricacies of military necessity as a negative element of several war crimes and crimes against humanity. In particular, it has shown where the trier of law and fact must tread carefully when adjudicating military necessity claims.

On the whole, the ICTY and MICT jurisprudence on exceptional military necessity offers an encouraging prospect for its effective interpretation even in highly complex circumstances such as those involving combat-related property destructions. The two bodies' chambers have by and large captured relevant aspects of exceptional military necessity, evaluated evidence in accordance with its requirements, and come to sensible factual conclusions. Inevitably, some decisions come across as more attuned to military necessity's nuances than others. Several potential pitfalls may be noted. The first two concern how the conceptual distinctions between attacks and destructions, and between military necessity and military objective, may be overlooked. Despite their significant overlap and interplay, the two sets of notions have their unique spheres of meanings and legal foundations. Occasional oversights in this regard have resulted in several instances of inadequate reasoning and questionable findings where combat-related destructions of civilian objects did not take the form of attacks against them.

[302] Article 31(3), Rome Statute.

[303] Denis and Romero, 'Synthèse des débas', at 480. But see William A Schabas, *An Introduction to the International Criminal Court*, 4th edn (Cambridge: Cambridge University Press, 2011), pp. 238–39; Gerhard Werle, 'General Principles of International Criminal Law' in Antonio Cassese (ed), *The Oxford Companion to International Criminal Justice* (Oxford: Oxford University Press, 2009) 54, p. 58.

Two other situations that also envisage military necessity exceptions – i.e., property destruction outside of combat and forcible population displacement – have received a limited amount of judicial attention by the ICTY or the MICT. There, too, most chambers have reached appropriate conclusions. With the notable exception of *Orić*, those judgments dealing with property destruction outside of combat base their findings on pertinent factors besides the absence of fighting at the time. As regards forcible population displacements, the two bodies' rulings on the absence of grounds permitted under international law are primarily made as a matter of form rather than substance.

The ICC's case law on military necessity exceptions is still at an early stage of development. Unsurprisingly, the various pre-trial chambers' military necessity findings in their confirmation decisions have so far been tentative and perfunctory. Neither *Bemba*, *Ntaganda* nor *Katanga and Chui* has added much material that is new in this respect. On the contrary, the *Katanga Trial Judgment* exhibits the same inadequacy that afflicts some of its ICTY and MICT counterparts – namely, a failure to entertain the possibility that the destruction of civilian objects may in certain circumstances be militarily necessary. The fact that most of the ICC cases considered in this book involve non-international armed conflicts and omit charges of unlawful attacks on civilian objects as a result, may mean that militarily unnecessary destructions are in effect used as substitute offences. This remains a conjecture at present, however.

Whether the ICC's current and future trials will hear sustained claims of exceptional military necessity remains to be seen. The same uncertainty surrounds Article 31 of the Rome Statute. Although, on its own, this article's reference to the defence of property may have relatively modest practical ramifications on the applicable law, there is a real danger that it will undermine the clarity and precision with which the ICC builds its case law on exceptional military necessity proper. In addition, Article 31's residual clause can be seen – though erroneously – as inviting military necessity pleas as a justification or excuse. The court has all the more reason to adjudicate its upcoming cases with care.

PART V

Conclusion

11

Conclusion

Military necessity is indifferently permissive. It is so, regardless of the context – be it material, normative or juridical – in which the notion appears. Materially, military necessity signifies the degree to which a specific belligerent act is conducive towards the attainment of its military purpose under a given set of circumstances. Conversely, material non-necessity signifies the degree to which it is not so conducive. Normatively, the notion prompts the framers of IHL rules to leave the belligerent at liberty not only to pursue military necessities and avoid non-necessities, but also to forgo necessities and encumber itself with non-necessities. It follows that military necessity never conflicts with what humanity demands or condemns. Juridically, military necessity serves as an exceptional ground for deviation from principal IHL rules, but only where the rules themselves envisage it expressly and in advance. If not, or no longer, militarily necessary, the deviant act reverts to being a non-exempted instance now bound and rendered unlawful by the principal rule.

We can now appreciate in greater detail what it really means to say that IHL accounts for military necessity, as well as the normative consequences to which the answer to this question gives rise.

11.1 Accounting for Military Necessity

To agree or disagree that a specific act is militarily necessary is, first and foremost, to assess how fit it is as a means with which the belligerent seeks to accomplish a specific goal. IHL accounts for military necessity when the law's framers decide what to do about a given kind of belligerent act, in view of its capacity or tendency to constitute a material necessity or non-necessity. The belligerent always has the option to act as directed by humanity, thereby jointly satisfying both military necessity and humanitarian considerations. This means that the framers are to decide whether to obligate such behaviour and, if so, whether to obligate it unqualifiedly, principally, indeterminately or exceptionally.

11.1.1 *Material Military Necessity as Fitness of Means and Vocational Competence*

Material military necessity evaluates the cogency between the means taken or considered and the ends sought under the circumstances prevailing or anticipated at the time. It is also a relational concept. The military necessity of a particular course of action is a function of alternative courses of action, other military ends and different circumstances. A given act can therefore be a military necessity compared to some alternatives, yet a non-necessity compared to some other alternatives. With a sufficient amount of information, the material military necessity of this or that act can be reasonably assessed. It does not follow, however, that all similarly competent assessors in possession of the same information necessarily arrive at the same conclusion. Nor can the military necessity assessment of particular action be meaningfully generalised or seen outside of its factual context.

Material military necessity focuses on fighting militarily well *qua* soldier, rather than behaving ethically well *qua* person. While the question of fighting well may acquire an ethical dimension, this possibility does not negate the idea that it is conceptually separable from behaving well. Furthermore, whether only a soldier's ethically competent behaviour should count as his or her truly militarily competent behaviour depends on why we are asking the question. In this strictly material context, we are concerned with that narrow part of fighting's vocational competence which does not involve ethics.

11.1.2 *Military Necessity as Normative Indifference*

The framers of IHL rules have no reason to obligate acts deemed militarily necessary, or to prohibit those deemed militarily unnecessary.

The illegitimacy of a military purpose taints the legitimacy of any measure taken in order to fulfil it. Such a measure is illegitimate, whether it is materially necessary or not. Where the purpose sought is legitimate, however, the measure taken is not necessarily legitimate. The latter's legitimacy must be assessed by reference to its evil or non-evil, as well as its military necessity or non-necessity. Accordingly, should an act be considered evil and devoid of military necessity, it would be deemed illegitimate and appropriate for restriction or prohibition. For instance, it is illegitimate to cause superfluous injury or unnecessary suffering because the evil (i.e., injury or suffering) is lacking in military necessity (i.e., superfluous or unnecessary). Where an act is seen as evil yet militarily necessary – war's necessary evil, in other words – whether it becomes legitimate or illegitimate would depend on how IHL framers weighed (i) the general value harmed by the act's evil vis-à-vis (ii) its legitimate military purpose. In other words, should the act in question be evil, its legitimacy would depend, at least in part, on its military necessity status. Even then, however, the lack of military necessity is not what delegitimises an evil act. Rather, it is the act's evil, now laid bare because it is militarily unnecessary, that delegitimises it.

The situation is quite different for an act that entails no evil. Plainly, whether an un-evil act is militarily necessary or unnecessary is immaterial to its legitimacy. It would be perfectly legitimate to perform, or to refrain from performing, an act that entailed no evil and accorded with military necessity. The same would be true of an act that was neither evil nor militarily necessary.

Military necessity's normative indifference refutes the inevitable conflict thesis according to which military necessity and humanity are fundamentally irreconcilable with each other. First, this theory erroneously asserts that what is militarily necessary is always inhumane, and what is humane is always militarily unnecessary. Second, the inevitable conflict thesis mistakenly holds that both considerations of military necessity and those of humanity generate imperatives. On this view, military necessity would demand that the belligerent always perform necessary acts and avoid unnecessary ones; similarly, humanitarian considerations would demand all humane acts and condemn all inhumane acts. Third, the inevitable conflict thesis incorrectly suggests that every positive IHL rule embodies a dialectic compromise between the diametrically opposed imperatives of military necessity and humanity.

The joint satisfaction thesis shows that, since military necessity is normatively indifferent, it is never truly in conflict with humanity. To begin with, belligerent conduct is often both humane and consistent with military necessity, or both inhumane and contrary to military necessity. Nor does military necessity generate imperatives. While humanity does frequently demand humane action and condemn inhumane action, it sometimes merely praises the former and tolerates the latter.

Besides, there are numerous situations where humanity demands militarily necessary conduct, and where humanity condemns militarily unnecessary conduct. IHL framers account for these situations when they posit unqualified obligations to act in a manner that jointly satisfies military necessity and humanity. This remains true, despite the fact that *third* considerations, especially sovereign interests, limit the number of positive IHL rules that contain such obligations.

Furthermore, joint satisfaction is possible even when humanity condemns what military necessity permits, or when humanity demands what military necessity merely tolerates. Where this occurs, what the belligerent experiences is a norm contradiction ('You may decline to do *X*' vs. 'You must do *X*'), rather than a norm conflict ('You must not do *Y*' vs. 'You must do *Y*'). The belligerent therefore satisfies both military necessity and humanity by acting as directed by humanity. A wide variety of positive IHL rules indicate instances where their framers made the pursuit of joint satisfaction:

- *Unqualifiedly* obligatory, thereby eliminating all of the belligerent's indifferent liberties arising from military necessity to act otherwise;
- *Principally* obligatory, thereby limiting contrary liberties to situations where they in fact prove militarily necessary;
- *Indeterminately* obligatory, thereby authorising the non-pursuit of joint satisfaction to the extent indifferently permitted by military necessity and obligating pursuit to the extent demanded by humanity, but without determining the point at which the former gives way to the latter;
- *Exceptionally* obligatory, while conferring a broad discretion upon the belligerent to act otherwise; or
- *Entirely* discretionary, thereby declining or failing to obligate the pursuit of joint satisfaction at all.

11.2 Normative Consequences

Three major normative consequences arise from IHL accounting for military necessity.

First, having accounted for military necessity, IHL precludes all pleas derived from it except where their admissibility is envisaged expressly and in advance. Second, as an exception attached to specific IHL rules, military necessity authorises deviant behaviour from the rules' principal prescriptions to the extent it is required for the attainment of a primarily military purpose, provided that both the behaviour and purpose otherwise remain in conformity with the law. Third, where violations of these qualified rules constitute war crimes and/or crimes against humanity, the absence of military necessity appears as one of their elements.

11.2.1 Exclusionary and Non-exclusionary Effects

Where military necessity and humanity are at stake, accounting for them can mean two things. It can mean that IHL framers posit rules obligating the pursuit of jointly satisfactory behaviour unqualifiedly, principally, indeterminately or exceptionally. Alternatively, it can mean that IHL framers decline or fail to posit such rules. Unqualified IHL obligations do not admit military necessity pleas because these obligations have *ipso facto* accounted for, and extinguished, all divergent indifferent considerations.

Accordingly, despite *Kriegsräson*'s insistence to the contrary, the military necessity of a belligerent act does not repair its unlawfulness otherwise established by unqualified IHL rules. The law's framers may have weighty reasons to consider authorising material military necessities. Such reasons have all been set aside, however, where positive IHL unqualifiedly prohibits certain behaviour. Offenders may not rely on military necessity in defence of their deviations.

Nor, for that matter, is the lack of an act's military necessity sufficient to impair its conformity with positive IHL rules and render it unlawful as a result. Counter-*Kriegsräson* presents us with two problems. On the one hand, it relies on the very construal of IHL norm-creation with which it faults *Kriegsräson*. Counter-*Kriegsräson* fails to explain why those aspects of normative military necessity that would validate *Kriegsräson* should be considered accounted for and extinguished, whereas those that would validate counter-*Kriegsräson* should not. On the other hand, counter-*Kriegsräson* requires military non-necessity to possess a normative property that is restrictive or prohibitive. However, nowhere does the theory in fact locate the origin of such a property. Counter-*Kriegsräson* misattributes this property to military necessity, although certain non-indifferent aspects of humanity and/or some other IHL precepts such as chivalry would more likely be its sources. Here, too, the prohibition against causing superfluous injury or unnecessary suffering is a case in point. Military necessity does not condemn superfluous or unnecessary action. Rather, it is humanity that condemns injury and suffering. Superfluousness and non-necessity simply lay humanity's condemnation of injury and suffering bare.

Whether the humanity of a belligerent act repairs its illegality established by unqualified IHL rules depends, in part, on whether the underlying considerations are normatively indifferent. If they are, then the act's humanity does not repair its illegality. *Humanitätsräson* is untenable because it amounts to applying *Kriegsräson*'s flawed reasoning to humanity – namely, that necessities of humanity override rules of war. If the underlying considerations are not indifferent, however, we have reason to wonder whether we should seriously consider the possibility of the act's illegality being repaired. *Humanitätsgebot* hypothesises this latter possibility.

Whether the inhumanity of a belligerent act invalidates its compliance with positive IHL also depends partly on whether the underlying considerations are normatively indifferent. If indifferent, then the act's inhumanity does not vitiate its lawfulness; to hold otherwise would be tantamount to acknowledging counter-*Humanitätsräson*. If the underlying considerations are not indifferent, perhaps counter-*Humanitätsgebot* should not be dismissed too hastily.

11.2.2 Juridical Military Necessity as an Exception

IHL admits military necessity pleas only where its rules envisage their admissibility expressly and in advance through exceptional clauses. These clauses also mark instances where IHL framers have specifically chosen to let military necessity considerations escape exclusion through the law-making process.

As an exception, juridical military necessity modifies the content of the principal rule to which it is attached. Where a positive IHL rule stipulates that the belligerent may not do *Z* unless it is required by military necessity, those specific cases of *Z* that fulfil the requirements of juridical military necessity are exempted from the rule's principal prohibition and become lawful. If not, or no longer, in fulfilment, these cases revert to being governed by the prohibition of which they now constitute non-exempted instances and become unlawful.

Interpreting military necessity clauses yields the following results. These clauses authorise conduct in deviation from the principal prescriptions of those IHL rules to which they are attached, insofar as that conduct is required for the attainment of a military purpose and otherwise in conformity with the law. The conduct in question must satisfy four cumulative requirements. First, it must be taken primarily for some specific military purpose. Second, the act must be 'required' for the purpose's attainment. In order to be considered 'required', the act must (a) be materially relevant to the purpose; (b) constitute the least evil among those options that are materially relevant and reasonably available; and (c) remain within an acceptable injury–benefit ratio. Third, the purpose sought must be in conformity with IHL. Fourth, the act itself must otherwise be in conformity with that law.

These requirements also show that military necessity in its juridical context is narrower in scope than military necessity in its material context. Conduct that is materially necessary yet not in fulfilment of the four requirements may be branded mere military advantage or convenience ineligible for military necessity exception.

11.2.3 Military Non-necessity as an Element of War Crimes and Crimes against Humanity

Where a substantive rule envisages an exception, and the rule's violation constitutes a punishable offence, the absence of circumstances satisfying the exception's requirements is itself an element of that offence. Several property and displacement-related war crimes and crimes against humanity are derived from substantive IHL rules to which military necessity clauses are attached. It follows that each of these crimes contains an element according to which the act must have been committed without military necessity. Since the absence of military necessity is an element to be proven, its onus rests with the prosecution.

Numerous ICTY and MICT judgments consider allegations of militarily unnecessary property destruction and, on the whole, they do so quite competently. A key distinction has emerged between property destroyed during combat and property destroyed outside of combat. Some rulings unhelpfully conflate the act of destroying property with that of attacking property, and military necessity with military objective. By and large, however, the judges have identified appropriate factors for consideration – such as the property's status as a civilian object, and the possibility that a civilian object may be destroyed without being attacked – and come to reasonable conclusions as to whether a given instance of property destruction had been militarily necessary or unnecessary. Outside of combat, many decisions correctly regard ethnically driven property destruction as lacking in military necessity and therefore unlawful. The two jurisdictions' treatment of exceptional military necessity with respect to forcible displacements is less elaborate.

The ICC, in contrast, is still at a relatively early stage of its jurisprudential development. Its rulings on military necessity as an element of crimes remain superficial and perfunctory.

Juridical military necessity has no role to play where the underlying IHL rules are unqualified and their violations constitute war crimes, or both war crimes and crimes against humanity as the cases may be. The prosecution need not prove that the act in question was militarily unnecessary. Nor would the defence help itself by pleading military necessity vis-à-vis such charges. Troublingly, Article 31(1)(c) of the Rome Statute excludes individual criminal responsibility on account of acts performed in defence of property that is 'essential for accomplishing a military mission'. On the one hand, the provision is so narrow that it is unlikely to broaden the scope of the military necessity exception that already appears as a negative element of some Rome Statute offences. On the other hand, Article 31(1)(c) introduces a hitherto unknown defence that risks being seen as inviting military necessity pleas vis-à-vis the remaining Rome Statute offences as well.

11.3 Summary

This book's principal findings are summarised in Table 2.

11.4 Implications beyond the Immediate Scope of This Book

IHL is not an isolated discipline. It adjoins and overlaps various fields of public international law, including, in particular, *jus ad bellum*, IHRL and ICL. Scholars have scrutinised the relationship between IHL, on the one hand, and each of these other fields, on the other, in detail.

This book has shown that military necessity itself engages elements of *jus ad bellum*, IHRL and ICL.

11.4.1 In Relation to Jus ad Bellum

Whether *jus ad bellum* and *jus in bello* exist separately is a question that has animated numerous commentators.[1] At one end stand those in favour of maintaining the two disciplines' traditional separation.[2] Those at the other end question its veracity or wisdom.[3] There are also

[1] Weiler and Abby Deshman, 'Far Be It from Thee'; Milanović, 'Non-response'; Gill, 'Role of *Ius ad Bellum* in Targeting', p. 101.

[2] Moussa, 'Reaffirming the Separation'; Moussa, 'Nuclear Weapons and the Separation of *Jus ad Bellum* and *Jus in Bello*'; Kolb and R Hyde, *International Law of Armed Conflict*, pp. 21–27; Roberts, 'Principle under Pressure'; Roberts, 'Principle of Equal Application'; Sloane, 'Cost of Conflation'; Blank, 'Lawfare and the Mixing of Proportionalities'.

[3] McMahan, *Killing in War*; Coates, 'Way to Limit War?'; Kutz, 'Fearful Symmetry'; McMahan, 'Morality of War and the Law of War', p. 44; Giladi, 'Reflections'.

Table 2 *Military Necessity Assessment in Context*

Context	Principal assessors	What military necessity means	Act assessed	Nature of assessment	Typical question asked	Criteria
Material	Those concerned with effective fighting, e.g.: • Commanders • Planners • Historians	Military necessity: • Degrees of conduciveness to military purpose's achievement Military non-necessity: • Degrees to which such conduciveness is absent	Specific acts	Evaluative	Does [did, would, etc.] this or that act help the belligerent achieve military success and avoid failure?	• Purpose • Act • Circumstances
Normative • IHL 'accounting for' military necessity occurs here	Those concerned with articulating legal standards of belligerent behaviour, e.g.: • State representatives • Military manual writers • Legal scholars	Military necessity: • Indifferently permissive reason to leave belligerent at liberty to do what is materially necessary and avoid what is unnecessary Military non-necessity: • Indifferently permissive reason to leave belligerent at liberty to forgo what is materially necessary and encumber itself with what is unnecessary	Kinds of acts	Stipulative	Should IHL obligate, permit, restrict or prohibit this or that kind of act, given its capacity or tendency to be militarily necessary or unnecessary?	N/A

Table 2 (*cont.*)

Context	Principal assessors	What military necessity means	Act assessed	Nature of assessment	Typical question asked	Criteria
Juridical • Normative consequences appear here	Those concerned with IHL compliance, e.g.: • IHL duty-holders • Critics and observers • Fact-finders • Prosecutors • Defence counsel • Judges	Military necessity: • Exceptional ground for deviation from principal IHL rules where admissibility is envisaged expressly and in advance • No such ground elsewhere Military non-necessity: • No independent ground for act's unlawfulness if it is otherwise in compliance with positive IHL • Element of several war crimes and crimes against humanity	Specific acts	Interpretive	Did this or that act fulfil requirements of exceptional military necessity clauses envisaged under IHL?	• Primarily military purpose • 'Required' for purpose's achievement o Pertinence o Least evil o Proportionality • Purpose's conformity with IHL • Act's conformity with IHL

disagreements as to whether, once armed force has been resorted to, *jus ad bellum* continues to apply alongside *jus in bello*.[4]

Our discussion of military necessity involves *jus ad bellum* on three distinct occasions. First, *jus ad bellum*'s contentious interplay with *jus in bello* forms part of the general framework within which we examine military necessity's normativity. As seen in Chapter 4, espousing thoroughgoing utilitarianism amounts to abandoning the *jus ad bellum–jus in bello* distinction. This is the case, insofar as that version of utilitarianism renders *any* belligerent conduct that is materially necessary for victory in a just war *ipso facto* legitimate and, conversely, *any* belligerent conduct that is materially unnecessary *ipso facto* illegitimate.

Second, Chapter 8 recasts *jus ad bellum* as an impermissible extension of *Kriegsräson* and as a potential source of genuine norm conflict. The idea that self-preservation as *Kriegsräson*'s more radical variety does not entitle belligerents to act in breach of unqualified IHL rules is uncontroversial. In *Nuclear Weapons*, however, the ICJ conceded its inability definitively to determine whether the threat or use of nuclear weapons would be lawful or unlawful in extreme self-defence.[5] If it were lawful according to *jus ad bellum*, then these weapons' threat or use could be frustrated by certain unqualified IHL prohibitions, such as those against launching an indiscriminate attack on cities.[6] This book leaves open the possibility that IHL framers do not resolve genuine norm conflicts

[4] Nobuo Hayashi, 'Using Force by Means of Nuclear Weapons and Requirements of Necessity and Proportionality *Ad Bellum*' in Nystuen et al. (eds), *Nuclear Weapons* 15. Some argue that *jus ad bellum* and *jus in bello* do not share an overlapping scope of application *ratione temporis*. Norman G Printer, Jr, 'The Use of Force against Non-state Actors under International Law: An Analysis of the US Predator Strike in Yemen' (2003) 8 *UCLA Journal of International Law and Foreign Affairs* 331, at 343; David Rodin, *War and Self-Defense* (Oxford: Oxford University Press, 2003), p. 112; Yaël Ronen, 'Israel, Hizbollah, and the Second Lebanon War' (2006) 9 *Yearbook of International Humanitarian Law* 362, at 362; Yoram Dinstein, *War, Aggression and Self-Defence*, 5th edn (Cambridge: Cambridge University Press, 2011), p. 262. Others insist that *jus ad bellum* applies not only as a matter of armed force's initial use, but also as a matter of its continuity. Judith Gail Gardam, 'Proportionality and Force in International Law' (1993) 87 *American Journal of International Law* 391, at 404; Gardam, 'Necessity and Proportionality', pp. 277 n.9, 280–81; Gardam, *Necessity, Proportionality and the Use of Force by States*, pp. 167–68; Tarcisio Gazzini, *The Changing Rules on the Use of Force in International Law* (Manchester: Manchester University Press, 2005), pp. 143, 146–47; Gill, 'Role of *Ius ad Bellum* in Targeting'.

[5] *Nuclear Weapons*, paras 96–97, 105(2)(E).

[6] Jeutner, *Irresolvable Norm Conflicts in International Law*, pp. 10–11, 27–30, 34–37.

between unqualified rules they posit, on the one hand, and independently valid rules that belong to another, unintegrated field of public international law, on the other.

Finally, Chapter 9 identifies proportionality as an element of one of juridical military necessity's four requirements. We contrast how that proportionality is assessed, with the proportionality principle typically associated with the use of force in self-defence under *jus ad bellum*.

11.4.2 In Relation to International Human Rights Law

The relationship between IHL and IHRL has long been the subject of extensive commentary and debate.[7] *Nuclear Weapons* – in which the court famously stated that what constitutes an arbitrary deprivation of one's life, a fundamental human right, 'falls to be determined by the applicable *lex specialis*, namely, the law applicable in armed conflict'[8] – ushered in an era of renewed interest in the two disciplines' interplay. Rival accounts have since been given of the proper levels at which IHL and IHRL would interact with each other,[9] as well as the precise manners in which IHL and IHRL rules in conflict should be resolved.[10] Critics note that meta-rules such as *lex specialis* are neither uniformly

[7] UN General Assembly Resolution 2444 (XXIII), 19 December 1968; UN General Assembly Resolution 2597 (XXIV), 16 December 1969; UN General Assembly Resolution 2675 (XXV), 9 December 1970; Francoise Hampson, 'Human Rights and Humanitarian Law in Internal Conflicts' in Meyer (ed), *Armed Conflict and the New Law* 53, p. 55; Centre for Human Rights, *Bulletin of Human Rights 91/1 I. Human Rights and Humanitarian Law II. Human Rights and Refugee Law* (New York: United Nations, 1992).

[8] *Nuclear Weapons*, para. 25.

[9] Those authorities for whom priorities are set between the two disciplines arguably include *Legal Consequences*, para. 106; Michael J Dennis, 'Application of Human Rights Treaties Extraterritorially in Times of Armed Conflict and Military Operations' (2005) 99 *American Journal of International Law* 119; Hampson, 'Relationship between International Humanitarian Law and Human Rights Law'; Hathaway et al., 'Which Law Governs during Armed Conflict?'. Those for whom priorities are set between specific IHL and IHRL rules, rather than between the two disciplines, include Koutroulis, 'Application of International Humanitarian Law and International Human Rights Law'; Marco Sassòli, 'The Role of Human Rights and International Humanitarian Law in New Types of Armed Conflict' in Ben-Naftali (ed), *International Humanitarian Law and International Human Rights Law* 34; Inter-American Commission on Human Rights, *Report on Terrorism and Human Rights* (2002), para. 141; International Committee of the Red Cross, *31st Conference of the Red Cross and Red Crescent: International Humanitarian Law and the Challenges of Contemporary Armed Conflicts* (2011), at 17.

[10] Sadat-Akavi, *Methods of Resolving Conflicts between Treaties*, pp. 213–32; Graf-Brugère, '*Lex Favorabilis*?'.

understood[11] nor really helpful when resolving norm conflicts.[12] Detention, hostilities and belligerent occupation are among those areas where today's complex IHL–IHRL interaction is most acutely felt.

At first sight, military necessity might appear to have little to do with human rights. Nevertheless, this book highlights two specific ways in which human rights enter our military necessity discussion. In one, we juxtapose a given act's military necessity or non-necessity vis-à-vis the evil or non-evil the same act may entail. The legitimacy of a necessary evil depends on the relative weight of its necessity and the harm it is likely to occasion. Unnecessary evil is evil *simpliciter*, and evil *simpliciter* is invariably illegitimate. The legitimacy of a belligerent act that is un-evil is less obvious. Chapter 4 reflects critically on the popular notion that the mere lack of material necessity is sufficient to delegitimise even an un-evil act. For the purposes of IHL norm-creation, disutilities in war are not per se illegitimate. Counter-*Kriegsräson* is problematic for this reason. Its adherents err where they assume that positive IHL rules are but necessity-based derogations from more restrictive IHRL rules applicable in peace time. Even if such an assumption were correct, however, an act's lack of necessity would place it outside the ambit of IHL and render it unlawful according to IHRL instead.

The second way through which IHRL comes into play is our treatment of humanitarian considerations in IHL norm-creation. Chapter 8 rejects *Humanitätsräson*, a position whereby humanity's mere indifferent permission restores the lawfulness of an act otherwise in breach of unqualified IHL rules. Nor is counter-*Humanitätsräson* tenable, insofar as it brands as unlawful a mere failure to do what humanity indifferently

11 Christopher J Borgen, 'Resolving Treaty Conflicts' (2005) 37 *The George Washington International Law Review* 573; Schabas, '*Lex Specialis*? Belt and Suspenders?'; Lubell, 'Parallel Application of International Humanitarian Law and International Human Rights Law'; Sassòli and Olsen, 'Relationship between International Humanitarian Law and Human Rights Law Where It Matters'; Orna Ben-Naftali, 'Introduction: International Humanitarian Law and International Human Rights Law – *Pas de Deux*' in Ben-Naftali (ed), *International Humanitarian Law and International Human Rights Law* 3; Yuval Shany, 'Human Rights and Humanitarian Law as Competing Legal Paradigms for Fighting Terror' in Ben-Naftali (ed), *International Humanitarian Law and International Human Rights Law* 13.

12 Lindroos, 'Addressing Norm Conflicts in a Fragmented Legal Order'; Milanović, 'Norm Conflict Perspective'; Marko Milanović, *Extraterritorial Application of Human Rights Treaties: Law, Principles, and Policy* (Oxford: Oxford University Press, 2011), pp. 249–52; Prud'homme, '*Lex Specialis*'; Watkin, 'Use of Force during Occupation'; N Hayashi, 'Do the Good Intention of European Human Rights Law Really Pave the Road to IHL Hell?'.

permits even where that failure otherwise complies with positive IHL rules.

Rights and obligations that are already valid under IHRL raise different matters. They come closer to *Humanitätsgebot* and counter-*Humanitätsgebot*, respectively. The process of norm-creation that has posited unqualified IHL rules may not fully account for humanity's contrary demands or condemnations. Accordingly, it cannot be excluded that acting consistently with humanitarian imperatives may repair its deviation from such rules. Article 118 of Geneva Convention III appears to bind a detaining power in an unqualified obligation to repatriate its POWs. Yet, it might not be a breach of IHL, all things considered, should a detaining power decline to repatriate some of its POWs on account of their safety concerns. Here, the advent of IHRL – together with international refugee law, including, in particular, its *non-refoulement* principle – has strengthened the case for humanity demanding non-repatriation in appropriate circumstances. Another example involves the IHRL prohibition against the use of excessive force. Should counter-*Humanitätsgebot* be true, killing rather than capturing one's adversary might be deemed an IHL breach where both actions were feasible. This would be so, insofar as it is arguable that positive IHL does not yet unqualifiedly obligate the belligerent to employ the least injurious form of disablement.

11.4.3 In Relation to International Criminal Law

Some commentators complain that international criminal courts and tribunals have unduly recalibrated the delicate balance between military necessity and humanity in the latter's favour and that, in so doing, these courts and tribunals have 'supplanted' state prerogatives in IHL development.[13] For many others, the IHL–ICL interplay is more complex than IHL setting forth substantive standards of belligerent behaviour and ICL enforcing them.[14] I have also noted that ICL judges must interpret IHL

[13] Schmitt, 'Military Necessity and Humanity', at 816–22; Shane R Reeves and Jeffrey S Thurnher, 'Are We Reaching a Tipping Point? How Contemporary Challenges Are Affecting the Military Necessity–Humanity Balance' (2014) *Harvard National Security Journal Features* 1. But see N Hayashi, 'Is the Yugoslav Tribunal Guilty of Hyper-Humanising International Humanitarian Law?'; N Hayashi, 'Performance of International Criminal Courts and Tribunals'.

[14] Yves Sandoz, 'The Dynamic But Complex Relationship between International Penal Law and Humanitarian Law' in Doria et al. (eds), *Legal Regime of the International Criminal*

with care, lest they alienate otherwise reasonable and law-abiding combatants or, conversely, undermine the confidence of those who depend critically on the law's protection.[15] This, as has been pointed out in literature, is easier said than done.[16]

Military necessity is one point where the two bodies of international law meet. Chapters 9 and 10 of this book show their encounter to be a generally coherent one. To begin with, in positive IHL, military necessity appears exclusively as an exceptional clause attached to certain principal rules. Military necessity also appears, explicitly or implicitly, as a negative element of war crimes and crimes against humanity that are derived from these rules. Moreover, when interpreting this element, the ICTY and the MICT have often found military non-necessity where the facts on the ground indeed fail to fulfil the requirements of military necessity exceptions under positive IHL.

Military necessity's main ICL challenges are two-fold. First, ICL adjudicators may sow confusion into the notion by conflating it with similar-sounding IHL concepts that are in fact distinct (e.g., military objectives), or by failing to consider pertinent facts (e.g., destroying objects without attacking them). Second, Article 31 of the Rome Statute raises troublesome prospects whereby military necessity may be seen as a justification or excuse for breaches of unqualified IHL rules.

11.5 Military Necessity: A New Theory

The precise content of military necessity, humanity, chivalry and the like will doubtless continue to stir debate. This book nevertheless shows that

Court 1049; Sivakumaran, *Law of Non-international Armed Conflict*, pp. 77–83; Carsten Stahn, 'Between Constructive Engagement, Collusion and Critical Distance: The ICRC and the Development of International Criminal Law' (2016) 15 *Chinese Journal of International Law* 139, at 164–65.

15 N Hayashi, 'Role of Judges'.

16 Darcy, 'Bridging the Gaps'; Laurie R Blank, 'Operational Law Experts Roundtable on the *Gotovina* Judgment: Military Operations, Battlefield Reality and the Judgment's Impact on Effective Implementation and Enforcement of International Humanitarian Law', *Public Law & Legal Theory Research Paper Series Research Paper No. 12-186* (2012); Walter B Huffman, 'Margin of Error: Potential Pitfalls of the Ruling in *The Prosecutor v. Ante Gotovina*' (2012) 211 *Military Law Review* 1; Rogier Bartels, 'Discrepancies between International Humanitarian Law on the Battlefield and in the Courtroom: The Challenges of Applying International Humanitarian Law during International Crimes Trials' in Matthee et al. (eds), *Armed Conflict and International Law* 339, p. 341; Gary D Solis, 'The *Gotovina* Acquittal: A Sound Appellate Course Correction' (2013) 215 *Military Law Review* 78.

their functions relative to IHL can be illuminated. The normative characteristics of these notions shape the dynamics of their interplay in the context of IHL norm-creation, as well as the consequences of such interplay vis-à-vis positive IHL rules.

More specifically, this book demonstrates that military necessity is indifferently permissive, regardless of the context in which it appears. This not only reaffirms the fallacy of *Kriegsräson* but also invalidates the idea that belligerent conduct otherwise consistent with positive IHL becomes unlawful solely by virtue of its military non-necessity. Moreover, this book confirms the inadmissibility of military necessity pleas vis-à-vis unqualified IHL obligations. It does so, however, without excluding the possibility that non-indifferent aspects of humanity and chivalry may escape exclusion through the process of IHL norm-creation and operate as additional layers of lawfulness determination over positive rules.

Here emerges a new theory of military necessity, as well as what it means to say that IHL accounts for it.

SELECT BIBLIOGRAPHY

Adler, Gerald J., 'Targets in War: Legal Considerations' (1970–71) 8 *Houston Law Review*, pp. 1–46

af Jochnik, Chris and Roger Normand, 'The Legitimation of Violence: A Critical History of the Laws of War' (1994) 35 *Harvard International Law Journal*, pp. 49–95

Akande, Dapo, 'Clearing the Fog of War? The ICRC's Interpretive Guidance on Direct Participation in Hostilities' (2010) 59 *International and Comparative Law Quarterly*, pp. 180–92

Akhavan, Payam, 'Reconciling Crimes against Humanity with the Laws of War: Human Rights, Armed Conflict, and the Limits of Progressive Jurisprudence' (2008) 6 *Journal of International Criminal Justice*, pp. 21–37

Ambrose, Stephen E., *D-Day, June 6, 1944: The Climactic Battle of World War II* (New York, London, Toronto and Sydney: Simon & Schuster, 1994)

Arai-Takahashi, Yutaka, 'Excessive Collateral Civilian Casualties and Military Necessity: Awkward Crossroads in International Humanitarian Law between State Responsibility and Individual Criminal Liability', in Freya Baetens and Christine Chinkin (eds.), *Sovereignty, Statehood and State Responsibility: Essays in Honour of James Crawford* (Cambridge: Cambridge University Press, 2015), pp. 325–39

Bartels, Rogier, 'Dealing with the Principle of Proportionality in Armed Conflict in Retrospect: The Application of the Principle in International Criminal Trials' (2013) 46 *Israel Law Review*, pp. 271–315

Baxter, R. R., 'Asylum to Prisoners of War' (1953) 30 *British Yearbook of International Law*, pp. 489–98

Beer, Yishai, 'Humanity Considerations Cannot Reduce War's Hazards Alone: Revitalizing the Concept of Military Necessity' (2015) 26 *European Journal of International Law*, pp. 801–28

Benvenisti, Eyal, 'Human Dignity in Combat: The Duty to Spare Enemy Civilians' (2006) 39 *Israel Law Review*, pp. 81–109

Best, Geoffrey, *Humanity in Warfare: The Modern History of the International Law of Armed Conflicts* (New York: Columbia University Press, 1983)

'The Restraint of War in Historical and Philosophical Perspective', in Astrid J. M. Delissen and Gerard J. Tanja (eds.), *Humanitarian Law of Armed*

Conflict; Challenges Ahead, Essays in Honour of Frits Kalshoven (Dordrecht: Martinus Nijhoff, 1991), pp. 3–26

War and Law Since 1945 (Oxford: Clarendon Press, 1994)

Bill, Brian J., 'The Rendulic "Rule": Military Necessity, Commander's Knowledge, and Methods of Warfare' (2009) 12 *Yearbook of International Humanitarian Law*, pp. 119–55

Blank, Laurie, 'A New Twist on an Old Story: Lawfare and the Mixing of Proportionalities' (2010–11) 43 *Case Western Reserve Journal of International Law*, pp. 707–38

Blank, Laurie and Gregory P. Noone, *International Law and Armed Conflict: Fundamental Principles and Contemporary Challenges in the Law of War* (New York: Wolters Kluwer Law & Business, 2013)

Blix, Hans, 'Means and Methods of Combat', in Henri Dunant Institute and UNESCO (eds.), *International Dimensions of Humanitarian Law* (Geneva, Paris and Dordrecht: Henri Dunant Institute, UNESCO and Martinus Nijhoff, 1988), pp. 135–51

Blum, Gabriella, 'The Laws of War and the "Lesser Evil"' (2010) 35 *Yale Journal of International Law*, pp. 1–69

Blumenson, Martin, *Kasserine Pass: Rommel's Bloody, Climactic Battle for Tunisia* (Boston: Houghton Mifflin Company, 1967)

The Mediterranean Theater of Operations: Salerno to Cassino (Washington, D.C.: Center of Military History, United States Army, 1969)

Boothby, William H., *The Law of Targeting* (Oxford: Oxford University Press, 2012)

Weapons and the Law of Armed Conflict (Oxford: Oxford University Press, 2009)

Brandt, R. B., 'Utilitarianism and the Rules of War' (1972) 1 *Philosophy and Public Affairs*, pp. 145–65

Brigety, Reuben E., II, 'Moral Ambiguities in the Bombing of Monte Cassino' (2005) 4 *Journal of Military Ethics*, pp. 139–41

Camins, Emily, 'The Past as Prologue: The Development of the "Direct Participation" Exception to Civilian Immunity' (2008) 90 *International Review of the Red Cross*, pp. 853–81

Carnahan, Burrus M., 'Lincoln, Lieber and the Laws of War: The Origins and Limits of the Principle of Military Necessity' (1998) 92 *American Journal of International Law*, pp. 213–31

Carnegie Endowment for International Peace, *The Proceedings of the Hague Peace Conferences Translation of the Official Texts: The Conference of 1899* (New York: Oxford University Press, 1920)

The Proceedings of the Hague Peace Conferences Translation of the Official Texts: The Conference of 1907, 3 vols. (New York: Oxford University Press, 1921)

Cassese, Antonio, 'The Martens Clause: Half a Loaf or Simply Pie in the Sky?' (2000) 11 *European Journal of International Law*, pp. 187–216

Che Guevara, Ernesto, *Guerrilla Warfare*, J. P. Morray (trans.) (New York: Vintage Books, 1961)

Churchill, Winston S., *The Second World War*, 6 vols. (Boston: Houghton Mifflin Company, 1951–53)

Cole, Hugh M., *The Ardennes: Battle of the Bulge* (Washington, D.C.: Chief of Military History, Department of the Army, 1965)

Coleman, Stephen, 'Discrimination and Non-lethal Weapons: Issues for the Future Military', in David W. Lovell and Igor Primoratz (eds.), *Protecting Civilians during Violent Conflict: Theoretical and Practical Issues for the 21st Century* (Surrey: Ashgate, 2012), pp. 215–29

Collier, Richard, *The War in the Desert* (Alexandria: Time-Life Books, 1977)

Corn, Geoffrey S. and Lieutenant Colonel Gary P. Corn, 'The Law of Operational Targeting: Viewing the LOAC through an Operational Lens' (2012) 47 *Texas International Law Journal*, pp. 337–98

et al., 'Belligerent Targeting and the Invalidity of a Least Harmful Means Rule' (2013) 89 *International Law Studies*, pp. 536–626

Cornish, Paul, 'Clausewitz and the Ethics of Armed Force' (2003) 2 *Journal of Military Ethics*, pp. 213–26

Crawford, Emily, *Identifying the Enemy: Civilian Participation in Armed Conflict* (Oxford: Oxford University Press, 2015)

The Treatment of Combatants and Insurgents under the Law of Armed Conflict (Oxford: Oxford University Press, 2010)

David, Eric, *Principes de Droit de conflits armés*, 3rd ed. (Bruxelles: Bruylant, 2002)

Davidson, Donald, *Essays on Actions and Events*, 2nd ed. (Oxford: Oxford University Press, 2001)

Davis, Paul K., *Aggregation, Disaggregation, and the 3:1 Rule in Ground Combat* (Santa Monica: RAND, 1995)

Dehn, John C., 'Permissible Perfidy? Analysing the Colombian Hostage Rescue, the Capture of Rebel Leaders and the World's Reaction' (2008) 6 *Journal of International Criminal Justice*, pp. 627–53

Deptula, David A., *Effects-Based Operations: Change in the Nature of Warfare* (Arlington: Aerospace Education Foundation, 2001)

Desierto, Diane A., *Necessity and National Emergency Clauses: Sovereignty in Modern Treaty Interpretation* (Leiden and Boston: Martinus Nijhoff Publishers, 2012)

de Lee, Nigel, 'Moral Ambiguities in the Bombing of Monte Cassino' (2005) 4 *Journal of Military Ethics*, pp. 129–38

de Mulinen, Frédéric, *Handbook on the Law of War for Armed Forces* (Geneva: International Committee of the Red Cross, 1987)

Dill, Janina and Henry Shue, 'Limiting the Killing in War: Military Necessity and the St. Petersburg Assumption' (2013) 26 *Ethics & International Affairs*, pp. 311–33

Dinstein, Yoram, 'Military Necessity', *Max Planck Encyclopedia of Public International Law* (Oxford: Oxford University Press, 2015)

'Siege Warfare and the Starvation of Civilians', in Astrid Delissen and Gerard Tanja (eds.), *Humanitarian Law of Armed Conflict*, pp. 145–52

The Conduct of Hostilities under the Law of International Armed Conflict, 3rd ed. (Cambridge: Cambridge University Press, 2016)

Dixon, Norman F., *On the Psychology of Military Incompetence* (London: Jonathan Cape, 1976)

Dörmann, Knut, et al. (eds.), *Commentary on the First Geneva Convention* (Cambridge: Cambridge University Press, 2016)

Commentary on the Second Geneva Convention (Cambridge: Cambridge University Press, 2017)

Elements of War Crimes under the Rome Statute of the International Criminal Court: Sources and Commentary (Cambridge: Cambridge University Press, 2003)

Doswald-Beck, Louise (ed.), *San Remo Manual on International Law Applicable to Armed Conflicts at Sea* (Cambridge: Cambridge University Press, 1995)

Downey, William Gerald, Jr., 'The Law of War and Military Necessity' (1953) 47 *American Journal of International Law*, pp. 251–62

Draper, G. I. A. D., 'Military Necessity and Humanitarian Imperatives' (1973) 12 *Military Law and Law of War Review*, pp. 129–42

Ducheine, Paul A. L., et al. (eds.), *Targeting: The Challenges of Modern Warfare* (The Hague: T. M. C. Asser Press, 2016)

Duffy, Helen, *The 'War on Terror' and the Framework of International Law*, 2nd ed. (Cambridge: Cambridge University Press, 2015)

Dunbar, N. C. H., 'Military Necessity in War Crimes Trials' (1952) 29 *British Yearbook of International Law*, pp. 442–52

'The Significance of Military Necessity in the Law of War' (1955) 67 *Juridical Review*, pp. 201–12

Duncan, James C., Lieutenant Colonel, 'A Primer on the Employment of Non-lethal Weapons' (1998) 45 *Naval Law Review*, pp. 1–55

Federal Political Department, *Final Record of the Diplomatic Conference of Geneva of 1949*, 3 vols. (Berne: Federal Political Department, 1949)

Official Records of the Diplomatic Conference on the Reaffirmation and Development of International Humanitarian Law Applicable in Armed Conflicts, 17 vols. (Berne: Federal Political Department, 1978)

Fenrick, W. J., 'Targeting and Proportionality during the NATO Bombing Campaign against Yugoslavia' (2001) 12 *European Journal of International Law*, pp. 489–502

Finnis, John, *Natural Law and Natural Rights* (Oxford: Clarendon Press, 1980)

Fleck, Dieter (ed.), *The Handbook of International Humanitarian Law*, 3rd ed. (Oxford: Oxford University Press, 2013)

French, Shannon E., 'Sergeant Davis's Stern Charge: The Obligation of Officers to Preserve the Humanity of Their Troops' (2009) 8 *Journal of Military Ethics*, pp. 116–26

Fuller, Lon L., *The Morality of Law*, rev. ed. (New Haven: Yale University Press, 1969)

Galula, David, *Counterinsurgency Warfare: Theory and Practice* (Westport and London: Praeger Security International, 1964)

Gardam, Judith, *Necessity, Proportionality and the Use of Force by States* (Cambridge: Cambridge University Press, 2004)

Garner, James Wilford, *International Law and the World War*, 2 vols. (London: Longmans, Green and Co., 1920)

Geiß, Robin, 'Military Necessity: A Fundamental "Principle" Fallen into Oblivion', in Hélène Ruiz Fabri et al. (eds.), *Select Proceedings of the European Society of International Law* (Oxford: Hart Publishing, 2010), pp. 554–68

Gershel, Bradley, 'Applying Double Effect in Armed Conflicts: A Crisis of Legitimacy' (2013) 27 *Emory International Law Review*, pp. 741–54

Giladi, Rotem M., 'Reflections on Proportionality, Military Necessity and the Clausewitzian War' (2012) 45 *Israel Law Review*, pp. 323–40

Gill, Terry, 'Chivalry: A Principle of the Law of Armed Conflict?', in Mariëlle Matthee et al. (eds.), *Armed Conflict and International Law: In Search of the Human Face Liber Amicorum in Memory of Avril McDonald* (The Hague: T. M. C. Asser Press, 2013), pp. 33–51

'Some Considerations Concerning the Role of *Ius ad Bellum* in Targeting', in Paul A. L. Ducheine et al. (eds.), *Targeting: The Challenges of Modern Warfare* (The Hague: T. M. C. Asser Press, 2016), pp. 101–19

Goodman, Ryan, 'The Power to Kill or Capture Enemy Combatants' (2013) 24 *European Journal of International Law*, pp. 819–53

Green, Leslie C., *The Contemporary Law of Armed Conflict*, 3rd ed. (Manchester: Manchester University Press, 2008)

Greenwood, Christopher, 'Historical Development and Legal Basis', in Dieter Fleck (ed.), *The Handbook of International Humanitarian Law*, 2nd ed. (Oxford: Oxford University Press, 2008), pp. 1–43

'The Law of Weaponry at the Start of the New Millennium', in Christopher Greenwood, *Essays on War in International Law* (London: Cameron May, 2006), pp. 223–73

Gutteridge, J. A. C., 'The Repatriation of Prisoners of War' (1953) 2 *International and Comparative Law Quarterly*, pp. 207216

Hampson, Françoise J., 'The Relationship between International Humanitarian Law and Human Rights Law from the Perspective of a Human Rights Treaty Body' (2008) 90 *International Review of the Red Cross*, pp. 549–72

'The Scope of the Obligation Not to Return Fighters under the Law of Armed Conflict', in David James Cantor and Jean-François Durieux (eds.), *Refuge from Inhumanity? War Refugees and International Humanitarian Law* (Leiden and Boston: Brill Nijhoff, 2014), pp. 373–85

Hart, H. L. A., *'Essays in Jurisprudence and Philosophy* (Oxford: Oxford University Press, 1983)

'Positivism and the Separation of Law and Morals' (1958) 71 *Harvard Law Review*, pp. 593–629

The Concept of Law, 2nd ed. (Oxford: Clarendon Press, 1994)

Hart, H. L. A. and Tony Honoré, *Causation in the Law*, 2nd ed. (Oxford: Clarendon Press, 1985)

Hayashi, Mika Nishimura, 'The Martens Clause and Military Necessity', in Howard M. Hensel (ed.), *The Legitimate Use of Military Force: The Just War Tradition and the Customary Law of Armed Conflict* (Hampshire and Burlington: Ashgate, 2008), pp. 135–59

Hayashi, Nobuo, 'Contextualizing Military Necessity' (2013) 27 *Emory International Law Review*, pp. 189–287

'Military Necessity as Normative Indifference' (2013) 44 *Georgetown Journal of International Law*, pp. 675–82

'Requirements of Military Necessity in International Humanitarian Law and International Criminal Law' (2010) 28 *Boston University International Law Journal*, pp. 39–140

Henckaerts, Jean-Marie and Louise Doswald-Beck, *Customary International Humanitarian Law*, 2 vols. (Cambridge: Cambridge University Press, 2005)

Henry, Etienne, *Le Principe de nécessité militaire: Histoire et actualité d'une norme fondamentale du droit international humanitaire* (Paris: Pedone, 2016)

Hogg, Ian V., *Barrage: The Guns in Action* (New York: Ballantine Books, 1970)

Hohfeld, Wesley Newcomb, 'Fundamental Legal Concepts as Applied in Judicial Reasoning' (1919) 26 *Yale Law Journal*, pp. 710–70

Honoré, Tony, 'The Basic Norm of a Society', in Stanley L. Paulson and Bonnie Litschewski Paulson (eds.), *Normativity and Norms: Critical Perspectives on Kelsenian Themes* (Oxford: Clarendon Press,1998), pp. 89–112

Howard, Michael (ed.), *Restraints on War: Studies in the Limitation of Armed Conflict* (Oxford: Oxford University Press, 1979)

Hull, Isabel V., '"Military Necessity" and the Laws of War in Imperial Germany', in Stathis N. Kalyvas et al. (eds.), *Order, Conflict, and Violence* (Cambridge: Cambridge University Press, 2008), pp. 352–77

Imseis, Ardi, 'Critical Reflections on the International Humanitarian Law Aspects of the ICJ *Wall* Advisory Opinion' (2005) 99 *American Journal of International Law*, pp. 102–18

International Committee of the Red Cross, *Interpretive Guidance on the Notion of Direct Participation in Hostilities under International Humanitarian Law* (Geneva: International Committee of the Red Cross, 2009)

Joint Chiefs of Staff, *Joint Operation (Joint Publication 3-0)* (2008)

Jeutner, Valentin, *Irresolvable Norm Conflicts in International Law: The Concept of a Legal Dilemma* (Oxford: Oxford University Press, 2017)

Kalshoven, Frits, 'Grotius' *Jus in Bello*, with Special Reference to Ruses of War and Perfidy', in *Frits Kalshoven, Reflections on the Law of War: Collected Essays* (Leiden and Boston: Martinus Nijhoff, 2007), pp. 327–38

'Reprisals and the Protection of Civilians: Two Recent Decisions of the Yugoslavia Tribunal', in Lal Chand Vohrah et al. (eds.), *Man's Inhumanity to Man: Essays on International Law in Honour of Antonio Cassese* (The Hague: Kluwer Law International, 2003), pp. 481–509

Keegan, John, *The Face of Battle: A Story of Agincourt, Waterloo and the Somme* (London: Jonathan Cape, 1976)

Keenan, James F., 'The Function of the Principle of Double Effect' (1993) 54 *Theological Studies*, pp. 294–315

Keijzer, Nico, 'Réponses à la Question 2' (2000) 33 *Revue belge de droit international*, pp. 440–45

Kelsen, Hans, *General Theory of Law and State*, Anders Wedberg (trans.) (Cambridge MA: Harvard University Press, 1949)

Pure Theory of Law, Max Knight (trans.) (Berkeley and Los Angeles: University of California Press, 1967)

Kleemeier, Ulrike, 'Moral Forces in War', in Hew Strachan and Andreas Herberg-Rothe (eds.), *Clausewitz in the Twenty-First Century* (Oxford: Oxford University Press, 2007), pp. 107–21

Kleffner, Jann K., 'Friend or Foe? On the Protective Reach of the Law of Armed Conflict: A Note on the SCSL Trial Chamber's Judgment in the Case of *Prosecutor v. Sesay, Kallon and Gbao*', in Mariëlle Matthee et al. (eds.), Armed Conflict and International Law: In Search of the Human Face Liber Amicorum in Memory of Avril McDonald (The Hague: T. M. C. Asser Press, 2013), pp. 285–302

Kolb, Robert, 'La nécessité militaire dans le droit des conflits armés: essai de clarification conceptuelle', in Sociéte française pour le droit international, *Colloque de Grenoble, La nécessité en droit international* (Paris: Pedone, 2007), pp. 151–86

'The Main Epochs of Modern International Humanitarian Law Since 1864 and Their Related Dominant Legal Constructions', in Kjetil Mujezinović Larsen et al. (eds.), *Searching for a 'Principle of Humanity' in International Humanitarian Law* (Cambridge: Cambridge University Press, 2013), pp. 23–71

Kolb, Robert and Richard Hyde, *An Introduction to the International Law of Armed Conflict* (Oxford and Portland: Hart Publishing, 2008)

Koskenniemi, Martti, 'Faith, Identity, and the Killing of the Innocent: International Lawyers and Nuclear Weapons' (1997) 10 *Leiden Journal of International Law*, pp. 137–62

Kramer, Matthew H., et al., *A Debate over Rights: Philosophical Enquiries* (Oxford: Oxford University Press, 1998)

'Rights without Trimmings', in Matthew H. Kramer et al., *A Debate over Rights: Philosophical Enquiries* (Oxford: Oxford University Press, 1998), pp. 7–91

Kretzmer, David, 'The Law of Belligerent Occupation in the Supreme Court of Israel' (2012) 94 *International Review of the Red Cross*, pp. 207–36

Larsen, Kjetil Mujezinović, et al. (eds.), *Searching for a 'Principle of Humanity' in International Humanitarian Law* (Cambridge: Cambridge University Press, 2013)

Lauterpacht, Hersch, 'The Problem of the Revision of the Law of War' (1952) 29 *British Yearbook of International Law*, pp. 360–82

Lawrence, T. E., *Seven Pillars of Wisdom* (London: Jonathan Cape, 1935)

Liivoja, Rain, 'Chivalry without a Horse: Military Honour and the Modern Law of Armed Conflict', in Rain Liivoja and Andres Saumets (eds.), *The Law of Armed Conflict: Historical and Contemporary Perspectives* (Tartu: Tartu University Press, 2012), pp. 75–100

Lindroos, Anja, 'Addressing Norm Conflicts in a Fragmented Legal Order: The Doctrine of *Lex Specialis*' (2005) 74 *Nordic Journal of International Law*, pp. 27–66

Lonsdale, David J., 'A View from Realism', in David Whetham (ed.), *Ethics, Law and Military Operations* (Basingstoke: Palgrave Macmillan, 2011), pp. 29–43

Luban, David, 'Military Necessity and the Cultures of Military Law' (2013) 26 *Leiden Journal of International Law*, pp. 315–49

'Risk Taking and Force Protection', in Yitzhak Benbaji and Naomi Sussmann (eds.), *Reading Walzer* (London and New York: Routledge, 2014), pp. 277–301

MacDonald, Charles B., *The European Theater of Operations: The Siegfried Line Campaign* (Washington, D.C.: Center of Military History, United States Army, 1963)

Mangan, Joseph T., 'An Historical Analysis of the Principle of Double Effect' (1949) 10 *Theological Studies*, pp. 41–61

Margulies, Peter, 'Valor's Vices: Against a State Duty to Risk Forces in Armed Conflict' (2012) 37 *Vermont Law Review*, pp. 271–307

May, Larry, *War Crimes and Just War* (New York: Cambridge University Press, 2007)

Mayda, Jaro, 'The Korean Repatriation Problem and International Law' (1953) 47 *American Journal of International Law*, pp. 414–38

McCoubrey, Hilaire, 'The Nature of the Modern Doctrine of Military Necessity' (1991) 30 *Revue de droit militaire et de droit de la guerre*, pp. 215–52

McDougal, Myres S. and Florentino P. Feliciano, *Law and Minimum World Public Order: The Legal Regulation of International Coercion* (New Haven: Yale University Press, 1961)

McKeogh, Colm, *Innocent Civilians: The Morality of Killing in War* (London: Palgrave Macmillan, 2002)

McMahan, Jeff, *Killing in War* (Oxford: Oxford University Press, 2009)

'The Morality of War and the Law of War', in David Rodin and Henry Shue (eds.), *Just and Unjust Warriors: The Moral and Legal Status of Soldiers* (Oxford: Oxford University Press, 2008), pp. 19–43

Melzer, Nils, 'Keeping the Balance between Military Necessity and Humanity: A Response to Four Critiques of the ICRC's Interpretive Guidance on the Notion of Direct Participation in Hostilities' (2010) 42 *New York University Journal of International Law and Politics*, pp. 831–916

Targeted Killing in International Law (Oxford: Oxford University Press, 2008)

'Targeted Killing or Less Harmful Means? Israel's High Court Judgment on Targeted Killing and the Restrictive Function of Military Necessity' (2006) 9 *Yearbook of International Humanitarian Law*, pp. 87–113

Meron, Theodor, 'The Humanization of Humanitarian Law' (2000) 94 *American Journal of International Law*, pp. 239–78

'The Martens Clause, Principles of Humanity, and Dictates of Public Conscience' (2000) 94 *American Journal of International Law*, pp. 78–89

Meyrowitz, Henri, 'The Principle of Superfluous Injury or Unnecessary Suffering: From the Declaration of St. Petersburg of 1868 to Additional Protocol I of 1977' (1994) 34 *International Review of the Red Cross*, pp. 98–112

Milanović, Marko, *Extraterritorial Application of Human Rights Treaties: Law, Principles, and Policy* (Oxford: Oxford University Press, 2011)

Mill, J. S., *On Liberty and Considerations on Representative Government* (Oxford: Basil Blackwell, 1948)

Miyazaki, Shigeki, 'The Martens Clause and International Humanitarian Law', in Christophe Swinarski (ed.), *Studies and Essays on International Humanitarian Law and Red Cross Principles in Honour of Jean Pictet* (Geneva and The Hague: International Committee of the Red Cross and Martinus Nijhoff, 1984), pp. 432–44

Moussa, Jasmine, 'Can *Jus ad Bellum* Override *Jus in Bello?* Reaffirming the Separation of the Two Bodies of Law' (2008) 90 *International Review of the Red Cross*, pp. 963–90

Munzer, Stephen, 'Validity and Legal Conflicts' (1973) 82 *Yale Law Review*, pp. 1140–74

Nagl, John A., *Counterinsurgency Lessons from Malaya and Vietnam: Learning to East Soup with a Knife* (Westport and London: Praeger Publications, 2002)

Neuman, Noam, 'Applying the Rule of Proportionality: Force Protection and Cumulative Assessment in International Law and Morality' (2004) 7 *Yearbook of International Humanitarian Law*, pp. 79–112

Newton, Michael A., 'Reconsidering Reprisals' (2009–10) 20 *Duke Journal of Comparative and International Law*, pp. 361–88

Nicholson, Joanna, *Fighting and Victimhood in International Criminal Law* (Oxford: Routledge, 2018)

Nozik, Robert, *Anarchy, State, and Utopia* (New York: Basic Books, 1974)

O'Brien, William V., 'The Meaning of "Military Necessity" in International Law' (1957) 1 *World Polity*, pp. 109–76

O'Connell, Robert L., *Of Arms and Men: A History of War, Weapons, and Aggression* (New York and Oxford: Oxford University Press, 1989)

Office of General Counsel, Department of Defense, *Department of Defense Law of War Manual* (2015)

Office of the Judge Advocate General, Canadian Forces, *Law of Armed Conflict at the Operational and Tactical Levels* (2000)

Office of US Chief of Counsel for Prosecution of Axis Criminality, *Nazi Conspiracy and Aggression*, 8 vols. (Washington, D.C.: United States Government Printing Office, 1946)

O'Keefe, Roger, *The Protection of Cultural Property in Armed Conflict* (Cambridge: Cambridge University Press, 2006)

Okimoto, Keiichiro, *The Distinction and Relationship between Jus ad Bellum and Jus in Bello* (Oxford and Portland: Hart Publishing, 2011)

Olásolo, Héctor, *Unlawful Attacks in Combat Situations: From the ICTY's Case Law to the Rome Statute* (Leiden: Martinus Nijhoff, 2008)

Ohlin, Jens D., 'The Duty to Capture' (2013) 97 *Minnesota Law Review*, pp. 1268–342

Ohlin, Jens D. and Larry May, *Necessity in International Law* (New York: Oxford University Press, 2016)

Orend, Brian, *The Morality of War* (Toronto: Broadview Press, 2006)

Parks, W. Hays, 'Conventional Weapons and Weapon Reviews' (2005) 8 *Yearbook of International Humanitarian Law*, pp. 55–142

Pauwelyn, Joost, *Conflict of Norms in Public International Law: How WTO Law Relates to Other Rules of International Law* (Cambridge: Cambridge University Press, 2003)

Pertile, Marco, 'Legal Consequences of the Construction of a Wall in the Occupied Palestinian Territory: A Missed Opportunity for International Humanitarian Law?' (2004) 14 *Italian Yearbook of International Law*, pp. 121–61

Phillipson, Coleman, *International Law and the Great War* (London: T. Fisher Unwin, 1915)

Pictet, Jean S., *Development and Principles of International Humanitarian Law* (Dordrecht, Boston and Manchester: Martinus Nijhoff, 1985)

Pictet, Jean S. (ed.), *Commentary I Geneva Convention for the Amelioration of the Condition of Wounded and Sick in Armed Forces in the Field* (Geneva: International Committee of the Red Cross, 1952)

Commentary II Geneva Convention for the Amelioration of the Condition of Wounded, Sick and Shipwrecked Members of Armed Forces at Sea (Geneva: International Committee of the Red Cross, 1960)

Commentary III Geneva Convention Relative to the Treatment of Prisoners of War (Geneva: International Committee of the Red Cross, 1960)

Commentary IV Geneva Convention Relative to the Protection of Civilian Persons in Time of War (Geneva: International Committee of the Red Cross, 1958)

Provost, René, *International Human Rights and Humanitarian Law* (Cambridge: Cambridge University Press, 2002)

Rabkin, Jeremy, 'Proportionality in Perspective: Historical Light on the Law of Armed Conflict' (2015) 16 *San Diego International Law Journal*, pp. 263–340

Rasiah, Nathan, 'The Court-Martial of Corporal Payne and Others and the Future Landscape of International Criminal Justice' (2009) 7 *Journal of International Criminal Justice*, pp. 177–99

Raz, Joseph, *Practical Reason and Norms* (Oxford: Oxford University Press, 1999)

'Kelsen's Theory of the Basic Norm', in Stanley L. Paulson and Bonnie Litschewski Paulson (eds.), *Normativity and Norms: Critical Perspectives on Kelsenian Themes* (Oxford: Clarendon Press,1998), pp. 47–67

The Authority of Law, 2nd ed. (Oxford: Clarendon Press, 2009)

Reeves, Shane R. and Jeffrey S. Thurnher, 'Are We Reaching a Tipping Point? How Contemporary Challenges Are Affecting the Military Necessity-Humanity Balance' (2014) *Harvard National Security Journal Features*, pp. 1–12

Reynolds, Michael, 'Massacre at Malmédy during the Battle of the Bulge', *World War II Magazine* (February 2003), p. 43

Richards, Frank, *Old Soldiers Never Die* (New York: Berkeley Publishing Corporation, 1966)

Roberts, Adam, 'The Equal Application of the Laws of War: A Principle under Pressure' (2008) 90 *International Review of the Red Cross*, pp. 931–62

Robertson, Geoffrey, *Crimes against Humanity: The Struggle for Global Justice*, 3rd ed. (London: Penguin Books, 2006)

Rogers, A. P. V., *Law on the Battlefield*, 2nd ed. (Huntington: Juris Publishing, 2004)

'What Is a Legitimate Military Target?', in Richard Burchill et al. (eds.), *International Conflict and Security Law: Essays in Memory of Hilaire McCoubrey* (Cambridge: Cambridge University Press, 2005), pp. 160–84

'Zero-Casualty Warfare' (2000) 82 *International Review of the Red Cross*, pp. 165–81

Rowe, Peter, 'Members of the Armed Forces and Human Rights Law', in Andrew Clapham and Paola Gaeta (eds.), *The Oxford Handbook of International Law in Armed Conflict* (Oxford: Oxford University Press, 2014), pp. 521–42

'The Obligation of a State under International Law to Protect Members of Its Own Armed Forces during Armed Conflict or Occupation' (2006) 9 *Yearbook of International Humanitarian Law*, pp. 3–24

Salter, Michael, 'Reinterpreting Competing Interpretations of the Scope and Potential of the Martens Clause' (2012) 17 *Journal of Conflict & Security Law*, pp. 403–37

Sandoz, Yves, et al. (eds.), *Commentary on the Additional Protocols of 8 June 1977 to the Geneva Conventions of 12 August 1949* (Geneva: International Committee of the Red Cross and Martinus Nijhoff, 1987)

Schabas, William A., *Genocide in International Law: The Crime of Crimes*, 2nd ed. (Cambridge: Cambridge University Press, 2009)

Schapiro, L. B., 'Repatriation of Deserters' (1952) 29 *British Yearbook of International Law*, pp. 310–24

Scheipers, Sibylle (ed.), *Prisoners in War* (Oxford: Oxford University Press, 2010)

Schmitt, Michael N., 'Discriminate Warfare: The Military Necessity-Humanity Dialectic of International Humanitarian Law', in David W. Lovell and Igor Primoratz (eds.), *Protecting Civilians during Violent Conflict* (London: Routledge, 2012), pp. 85-102

'Effects-Based Operations and the Law of Aerial Warfare' (2006) 5 *Washington University Global Studies Law Review*, pp. 265–93

'Military Necessity and Humanity in International Humanitarian Law: Preserving the Delicate Balance' (2010) 50 *Virginia Journal of International Law*, pp. 795–839

'The Interpretive Guidance on the Notion of Direct Participation in Hostilities: A Critical Analysis' (2010) 1 *Harvard National Security Journal*, pp. 5–44

'Wound, Capture, or Kill: A Reply to Ryan Goodman's "The Power to Kill or Capture Enemy Combatants"' (2013) 24 *European Journal of International Law*, pp. 855–61

Schwarzenberger, Georg, *International Law as Applied by International Courts and Tribunals: The Law of Armed Conflict*, 4 vols. (London: Stevenson and Sons, 1968), vol. II

Schwelb, Egon, 'Crimes against Humanity' (1946) 23 *British Yearbook of International Law*, pp. 178–81

Shue, Henry, 'Civilian Protection and Force Protection', in David Whetham (ed.), *Ethics, Law and Military Operations* (Basingstoke: Palgrave Macmillan, 2011), pp. 135–47

Sidgwick, Henry, *The Elements of Politics* (London and New York: Macmillan and Co., 1891)

Simmonds, N. E., *Central Issues in Jurisprudence: Justice, Law and Rights*, 2nd ed. (London: Sweet & Maxwell, 2002)

Sivakumaran, Sandesh, *The Law of Non-international Armed Conflict* (Oxford: Oxford University Press, 2012)

Sloane, Robert D., 'Puzzles of Proportion and the "Reasonable Military Commander": Reflections on the Law, Ethics, and Geopolitics of Proportionality' (2015) 6 *Harvard National Security Journal*, pp. 299–343

Solf, Waldemar A., 'Protection of Civilians against the Effects of Hostilities under Customary International Law and Protocol I' (1986) 1 *American University Journal of International Law and Policy*, pp. 117–35

Solis, Gary D., 'The *Gotovina* Acquittal: A Sound Appellate Course Correction' (2013) 215 *Military Law Review*, pp. 78–107

The Law of Armed Conflict: International Humanitarian Law in War (Cambridge: Cambridge University Press, 2010)

Steinhoff, Uwe, 'Moral Ambiguities in the Bombing of Monte Cassino' (2005) 4 *Journal of Military Ethics*, pp. 142–43

Stevens, G. R., *Fourth Indian Division* (Toronto: McLaren and Son, 1950)

Stone, Julius, *Legal Controls of International Conflict: A Treatise on the Dynamics of Disputes- and War-Law* (London: Stevens and Sons, 1954)

Taylor, Telford, *Nuremberg and Vietnam: An American Tragedy* (Chicago: Quadrangle Books, 1970)

Thomson, Judith Jarvis, *Normativity* (Peru: Open Court Publishing Company, 2008)

Trevelyan, Raleigh, *The Fortress: A Dairy of Anzio & After* (Glasgow: Collins, 1956)

UK Ministry of Defence, *JSP 383 The Joint Service Manual of the Law of Armed Conflict* (2004)

United Nations War Crimes Commission, *Law Reports of Trials of War Criminals*, 15 vols. (London: His Majesty's Stationery Office, 1949)

US Air Force, *US Air Force Doctrine: Doctrine Annex 3-60 – Targeting* (2019)

US Army and Marine Corps, *Counterinsurgency Field Manual* (2007)

US Department of the Army, *The Law of Land Warfare* (1956)

US Department of the Navy et al., *The Commander's Handbook on the Law of Naval Operations* (2007)

van Baarda, Th. A., 'Moral Ambiguities Underlying the Laws of Armed Conflict: A Perspective from Military Ethics' (2008) 11 *Yearbook of International Humanitarian Law*, pp. 3–49

van Creveld, Martin, *The Changing Face of War: Lessons of Combat, from the Marne to Iraq* (New York: Presidio Press, 2006)

The Transformation of War (New York: The Free Press, 1991)

Venturini, Gabriella, 'Necessity in the Law of Armed Conflict and International Criminal Law' (2010) 41 *Netherlands Yearbook of International Law*, pp. 45–78

Verri, Pietro, *Dictionary of the International Law of Armed Conflict* (Geneva: International Committee of the Red Cross, 1992)

von Bernstorff, Jochen, 'Martens Clause', *Max Planck Encyclopedia of Public International Law* (Oxford: Oxfrord University Press, 2009)

von Clausewitz, Carl, *On War*, Michael Howard and Peter Paret (eds. and trans.) (Princeton: Princeton University Press, 1976)

von Wright, Georg Henrik, 'Deontic Logic' (1951) 60 *Mind*, pp. 1–15

'Ought to Be – Ought to Do', in Georg Meggle (ed.), *Actions, Norms, Values: Discussions with Georg Henrik von Wright* (Berlin and New York: Walter de Gruyter, 1999), pp. 3–10

'Value, Norm, and Action in My Philosophical Writings', in George Meggle (ed.), *Actions, Norms, Values* (Berlin and New York: Walter de Gruyter, 1999), pp. 11–33

Vranes, Erich, 'The Definition of "Norm Conflict" in International Law and Legal Theory' (2006) 17 *European Journal of International Law*, pp. 395–418

Waluchow, W. J., 'The Many Faces of Legal Positivism' (1998) 48 *University of Toronto Law Journal*, pp. 387–449

Walzer, Michael, *Arguing about War* (New Haven: Yale University Press, 2004)

Just and Unjust Wars: A Moral Argument with Historical Illustrations, 4th ed. (New York: Basic Books, 2006)

Watkin, Kenneth, 'Assessing Proportionality: Moral Complexity and Legal Rules' (2005) 8 *Yearbook of International Humanitarian Law*, p. 3–53

Watts, Sean, 'Law-of-War Perfidy' (2014) 219 *Military Law Review*, pp. 106–75

'Under Siege: International Humanitarian Law and Security Council Practice Concerning Urban Siege Operations' (2014) *Harvard Law School Brookings Project on Law and Security: Counterterrorism and Humanitarian Engagement Project*

Waxman, Matthew, 'Siegecraft and Surrender: The Law and Strategy of Cities as Targets' (1998) 39 *Virginia Journal of International Law*, pp. 353–423

Zimmermann, Andreas, 'Jus ad Bellum, Jus in Bello and the Issue of Proportionality' (2007) 11 *Max Planck Yearbook of United Nations Law*, pp. 99–141

INDEX